P9-DVI-216

Robert M. La Follette

THE MACMILLAN COMPANY
NEW YORK · CHICAGO
DALLAS · ATLANTA · SAN FRANCISCO

THE MACMILLAN COMPANY
OF CANADA, LIMITED
TORONTO

ROBERT M. LA FOLLETTE

Photograph taken at Madison, Wisconsin, in 1922, by Fred L. Holmes.

Robert M. La Follette

JUNE 14, 1855—JUNE 18, 1925

CHAPTERS I-XXVI BY

BELLE CASE LA FOLLETTE

AND

CHAPTERS XXVII-LXXII BY

FOLA LA FOLLETTE

In Two Volumes

Volume I

THE MACMILLAN COMPANY *New York* · 1953

COPYRIGHT, 1953, by Fola La Follette

All rights reserved—no part of this book may be reproduced in any form without permission in writing from the publisher, except by a reviewer who wishes to quote brief passages in connection with a review written for inclusion in magazine or newspaper.

History

First Printing

Printed in the United States of America E

70835

DEC 15 1953

664
LI6
LI6
v.1

Permission to quote copyrighted material is acknowledged to publishers and authors as follows: The Bobbs-Merrill Company, Inc.—*War Memoirs,* by Robert Lansing, copyright 1935, The Bobbs-Merrill Company, Inc., used by special permission of the publishers; *My Memoir,* by Edith Bolling Wilson, copyright 1939, The Bobbs-Merrill Company, Inc., used by special permission of the publishers; Doubleday, Doran & Company, Inc.—*Woodrow Wilson Life and Letters,* by Ray Stannard Baker, 8 Vols. copyright 1927-1939, Ray Stannard Baker; *Taft and Roosevelt,* by Archie Butt, copyright 1930, Doubleday, Doran & Company, Inc.; Doubleday, Page & Company—*The Life and Letters of Walter H. Page,* by Burton J. Hendrick, copyright 1921, 1922, 1925, Doubleday, Page & Company, by permission of Arthur W. Page; Harcourt, Brace & Company, Inc.—*The Autobiography of Lincoln Steffens,* by Lincoln Steffens, copyright 1931, Harcourt, Brace & Company, Inc.; *The Letters of Lincoln Steffens,* copyright 1938, Harcourt, Brace & Company, Inc., by permission of publishers and Ella Winter; Houghton Mifflin Company—*Woodrow Wilson,* by William Allen White, copyright 1924, William Allen White; *The Intimate Papers of Colonel House,* by Charles Seymour, Vols. II and IV, copyright 1926, 1928, Houghton Mifflin Company; *Beveridge and the Progressive Era,* by Claude G. Bowers, copyright 1932, Claude G. Bowers; The Macmillan Company—*Ground Under Our Feet,* by Richard T. Ely, copyright 1938, Richard T. Ely, used by permission of Margaret Hale Ely; *These Things Are Mine,* by George Middleton, copyright 1947, George Middleton; Julian Messner, Inc.—*So Far So Good,* by Charles Hanson Towne, copyright 1945, Charles Hanson Towne; G. P. Putnam's Sons—*"You Takes Your Choice,"* by Clinton W. Gilbert, copyright 1924, Clinton W. Gilbert; Charles Scribner's Sons—*Selections from the Correspondence of Theodore Roosevelt and Henry Cabot Lodge,* copyright 1925, Charles Scribner's Sons; University of Colorado—*Papers of Edward P. Costigan Relating to the Progressive Movement in Colorado 1902–1917, edited by Colin B. Goodykoontz,* copyright 1941, University of Colorado.

53-13106
1-21-54

*To The People of Wisconsin
Who Made His Work Possible*

Preface

Robert Marion La Follette was born in 1855 in a log cabin at Primrose, Wisconsin. His heritage was French Huguenot and Scotch-Irish. Both his greatgrandfathers were American Revolutionary soldiers. Close association in his youth with sturdy, pioneering folk who had diversified cultural backgrounds gave him an enduring faith in the plain people. This faith was the compelling force throughout his many years of public service.

This biography begins in a midwestern pioneer community. It tells the story of American progressive democracy as it found expression in the life and leadership of one man during an important period of our history. As a boy on the farm he felt the Granger movement "swirling" about him. This revolt of the farmers made a lasting impression. While a student at the University of Wisconsin he was profoundly influenced by a great teacher, President John Bascom, who imbued him with a deep sense of the obligations of citizenship.

After being graduated in 1879, he studied law and was admitted to the Dane County Bar seven months later. When he became a candidate for district attorney in 1880 he met opposition from the powerful local boss of his own party. He conducted a horse-and-buggy campaign and won election to his first public office by taking the issue directly to the voters. Although the means of transportation changed, his method remained the same throughout his entire life.

Two years later he again defied the political machine and was elected to the House of Representatives as the youngest Member. He soon won a place in the front ranks of the Republican Party. After serving three terms under Presidents Cleveland and Harrison he was defeated in the Democratic landslide of 1890 and returned to the practice of law in Madison.

In 1897 he started his long educational campaign in Wisconsin for a direct primary election law, railroad regulation, tax reforms, conservation of natural resources and other measures which were subsequently enacted during the three turbulent terms he served as governor from

vii

1900 to 1905. An effective technic in securing these reforms was his then revolutionary nonpartisan reading of the roll call votes on important legislation. In framing laws he sought the assistance of experts and established a cooperation between university and State which contributed to making Wisconsin a laboratory for progressive legislation in other States.

In 1906 he began his twenty years service in the United States Senate under five Presidents, Theodore Roosevelt, Taft, Wilson, Harding, and Coolidge. Elected as a Republican, he steadily pursued an independent policy on legislation. When he began his first speech in the Senate four months after he was sworn in, Republican "Old Guard" Senators left the Chamber. He paused to warn them that "seats now temporarily vacant may be permanently vacated." During the summer he discussed the legislation of the session and read the roll call votes of both Republican and Democratic Senators to his large Chautauqua audiences in many States. The press soon began to note the effect of his roll call on the Senate. Year after year he carried on this educational campaign.

He founded *La Follette's Magazine* in 1909. Among its contributors were leading Progressives. Their articles, his editorials, and a roll call column on the votes of Senators and Representatives helped in contests where either progressive Republicans or progressive Democrats were candidates against reactionaries. Many Old Guard Senators were defeated or resigned. The 1910 elections registered the rising tide of the progressive movement. When the new Congress met in 1911 a little band of progressive Senators held the balance of power on many issues. This was reflected in national legislation.

As the recognized leader of the progressive Republicans in Congress he was endorsed for the 1912 Presidential nomination by many leading Progressives throughout the country. Subsequently Theodore Roosevelt became a candidate for the nomination, and many transferred their support to him. Several chapters of this biography deal in detail with the controversial and complex events of the 1912 campaign which resulted in the nomination of Taft and the election of Wilson.

For the first time La Follette was a minority Senator. He staunchly supported many of Wilson's domestic policies and some of his foreign policies which were bitterly attacked by prominent Republican Senators. But in 1917 he led the filibuster against the President's Armed Ship bill and voted against the entry of the United States into World War I. He was denounced and burned in effigy.

On September 20, 1917, he made an extemporaneous speech at St.

Paul, Minnesota, which was inaccurately quoted and grossly misrepresented in press reports from coast to coast. Some Senators and many prominent men and women demanded his expulsion from the Senate for disloyalty. Resolutions and petitions from Wisconsin and other States calling for his expulsion were received in the Senate day after day. For more than a year the Committee on Privileges and Elections had under consideration a resolution from the Minnesota Commission of Public Safety charging that he had made a disloyal and seditious address and petitioning that the Senate expel him. In January 1919 a majority of his colleagues finally voted to dismiss the resolution.

The attacks excluded him from the Chautauqua Circuits and other public platforms. *La Follette's Magazine* and his Senate speeches were his only means of correcting the persistent misrepresentation of his position on war legislation and foreign policy. Following the Armistice the intensity of feeling against him gradually diminished.

The Senate atmosphere became more cordial after the 1918 elections which resulted in a close margin of 49 Republicans to 47 Democrats. Early in 1919 he led a successful filibuster to protect the naval coal and oil reserves. He declined a third party nomination as a Presidential candidate in 1920 and steadily sought to build up the progressive forces in Congress. In 1922 he was reelected to the·Senate by the largest majority that had ever been given to any candidate in Wisconsin. As leader of a little band of progressive Senators, who again held the balance of power under a Republican Administration, he continued to ignore party lines in his legislative work. Convinced there was corruption in high places, he introduced the resolution in 1922 which initiated the investigation of Teapot Dome and other naval oil leases and led to the exposure of fraud and conspiracy in the Harding Administration.

On July 4, 1924, he was nominated as an independent Presidential candidate by the delegates to the Conference for Progressive Political Action. Subsequently Senator Burton K. Wheeler was chosen as the Vice Presidential candidate. In his speaking campaign La Follette again took the issues to the people. With a meager campaign fund and scant organization he obtained nearly 5,000,000 votes, the largest popular vote ever given to an independent movement at its first appearance in a national campaign. He died on June 18, 1925.

Throughout his life his wife Belle Case La Follette was intimately associated with his work. The portion of his biography which she wrote covers the period from his birth to 1910. Her record of his life from the time he was a freshman at the university in 1875 is inevitably both biography and autobiography, for they met as classmates when she was 16 and he was 21. A close companionship led to an engagement at the end of their junior year.

After their marriage she studied law and was the first woman to be graduated from the University of Wisconsin Law School. Although she never appeared in court, she prepared briefs for his law firm and followed his legal and legislative work with professional understanding. While he was a Member of the House she took care of his correspondence, attended the important debates, and traveled with him on his speaking campaigns. During these early years and his three terms as governor there were few important conferences in which she did not participate—probably none that he did not share with her. He himself described her as the "sane, far-sighted counselor of the little group of Progressives throughout all of the Wisconsin campaigns" and as "my wisest and best counselor." When he went to Washington as Senator, she continued to participate in the more intimate conferences and shared every important aspect of his work, including the editing of a department in *La Follette's Magazine.*

After his death she received many requests and petitions to become a candidate to fill his unexpired term. It was generally conceded that her election was assured. This would have made her the first woman to be elected to the United States Senate.

In a carefully considered letter dated July 28, 1925, she gave her reasons for declining to run: "For many years I have shared with Mr. La Follette the rewards and hardships of public life. My faith in the righteousness of his chosen work has been, like his, unshakable; but I know from long experience the exacting demands, the ceaseless strain of public service. At no time in my life would I ever have chosen a public career for myself. It would be against nature for me to undertake the responsibilities of political leadership. . . . In the messages and in the tributes to Mr. La Follette which have come to me and to my children from all over the world, there has been one common, comforting and encouraging note of assurance that the spirit of Mr. La Follette's work shall go on. To this end I hope to contribute my share in the future, as in the past." A part of her contribution became the writing of his biography. In her letter she said: "I undertake the work humbly but gladly. In so far as is in my power I shall make the record true and complete. To this undertaking and to the continuance of *La Follette's*

Magazine I shall dedicate my time and strength confident that it offers me the largest field of usefulness."

She did part of her work on the biography in Madison, where her son Philip lived. Part of it was written in Washington, where she made her home with her son Robert after his election to fill his father's unexpired term. When in Washington she sent copies of the chapters to Philip for his suggestion and recollections. On August 18, 1931, her sudden and unexpected death in Washington put an end to her work. An unfinished page of her manuscript was found in her typewriter.

Two years before my mother died I had promised to help her on the final editing of the biography. After her death I undertook the editing of her manuscript. My editorial work was chiefly condensation, although quotations were incorporated from a number of important letters found later. In some chapters I also incorporated additional material gleaned from documentary sources and from participants or observers of the scenes she had recounted. But in no instance has my mother's essential interpretation of events and people been changed. Copies of her manuscript, exactly as they were found after her death, are with the La Follette Papers.

My part of this biography covers the period from the end of my mother's manuscript to my father's death. For the research, interpretation, and writing of this period I assume entire responsibility. I have sought to follow my mother's desire to "make the record true and complete." Although aware that complete objectivity is an unattainable ideal, I have endeavored to approach it to the degree humanly possible. I have constantly sought to be guided by it in my method of research, in my writing, and in the selection of material which publication limitations dictate. I have striven to avoid the perpetuation of the contemporary misinterpretations of facts and motives which inevitably occur among the participants in the field of political and economic conflicts, where action must sometimes be hastily taken upon incomplete or inaccurate information. Conflicting contemporary reports of events relating to my father's life and work have been compared with available manuscript sources. When possible, contradictory accounts have been submitted to the participants who were still living. Men and women who had worked with my father, including some who had at times bitterly denounced him, generously gave me repeated interviews. They often amplified my records of the interviews dealing with controversial events which were submitted for correction. In addition to the recorded interviews many informal talks with men and women who knew my father were helpful.

The correspondence and records of talks with John J. Hannan, my father's intimate friend and his confidential secretary for fifteen years, fill two loose leaf books. The recorded interviews with my brother Robert M. La Follette, Jr., who was my father's secretary from 1917 to 1925, fill another book, although this represents only a small part of his contribution to the biography which he read and discussed with me chapter by chapter during the years I was working on it.

One of the basic sources for this biography is the large collection of La Follette Papers. My father was a hoarder of correspondence and documents. His lifelong interest in history led him to stress the importance of preserving written records. Against the frequent protests of secretaries he kept files which have been invaluable in writing this biography. Among these are the correspondence files of the 1912 La Follette Presidential campaign headquarters in Washington which are estimated to contain at least 25,000 letters. Through the years of moving back and forth from Wisconsin to Washington some letters were lost. But few, if any, were ever discarded with his consent.

He once wrote me: "I cannot destroy letters that are a part of someone I love." Among his papers can be found even the post cards from his young children which he received while away from home on his long speaking trips. His almost daily longhand letters to his wife when they were separated tell the story of his life and work as intimately and vividly as a diary. When in Washington he sometimes wrote from his Senate desk, frequently noting incidents which occurred on the floor but will not be found in the official *Congressional Record*. Often at night after a hard day's work in the Senate he would write a six or eight page letter giving a graphic account of the proceedings or recording informal conferences with some of his colleagues. It was his lifelong custom when he came home from his office to share with his wife and children the important or amusing aspects of the day's work. Absent sons or daughters received frequent letters which kept them in touch with the family circle. They treasured his letters as he did theirs.

His wife wrote the dedication for this biography of Robert M. La Follette. His daughter joins her in dedicating it "To the people of Wisconsin who made his work possible."

FOLA LA FOLLETTE

Washington, D.C.
September 1, 1953

Acknowledgments

For permission to quote from unpublished letters and private papers I am indebted to: Beulah Amidon; Roger Babson; Ray Stannard Baker; William Beard and Miriam Beard Vagts; Justice Louis D. Brandeis and Mrs. Brandeis; Senator Joseph L. Bristow; Professor John R. Commons; Irvin Cobb; John O. Crane and Frances Crane; William M. Cruikshank; Dr. Worth B. Daniels; Frances O. Dolliver; Margaret H. Ely; Elizabeth Glendower Evans; Mrs. Gilson Gardner; William Hard; Professor A. R. Hohlfeld; J. A. H. Hopkins; Mrs. William Kent; Rollin Kirby; Suzanne La Follette; Colonel Charles A. Lindbergh; Mrs. Basil M. Manly; Gordon Moses; Mrs. Fremont Older; Professor Max C. Otto; Robert F. Paine; Mrs. Amos R. E. Pinchot; John P. Robertson; Mrs. Gilbert E. Roe; Ruth Bryan Rhode; Charles E. Scripps; Rudolph Spreckels; William Lindsay White; Ella Winter; also to Jay N. Darling and John M. Baer for permission to publish their cartoons; and to Fred L. Holmes for the hitherto unpublished photograph reproduced in the frontispiece, which was taken by him in 1922. My gratitude includes all those mentioned in the bibliography who gave me personal interviews and many others who patiently answered my inquiries in letters.

For reading the manuscript of this biography, or portions of it, and giving constructive criticism I am deeply indebted to Ray Stannard Baker; Professor Charles A. Beard and Mary R. Beard; Professor Edwin Borchard; Alice Goldmark Brandeis; Dr. Helene Hooker; Dr. Horace M. Kallen; Edna Kenton; Philip F. La Follette and Isabel Bacon La Follette; Mary La Follette; Jeanne de Lanux; Professor Max C. Otto and Rhoda Otto; Alice Raphael; Ralph Curtis Ringwalt; John Ernest Roe and Eleanor Roe; Mrs. Gilbert E. Roe; Major General Walter K. Wilson; Dr. Louise Merwin Young. I am especially grateful to Professor Allan Nevins for his characteristic generous understanding and for his helpful suggestions after reading the entire manuscript.

My appreciation is expressed here for the continuous interest in this book of two friends of my parents. In addition to help on other aspects of the biography, Justice Louis D. Brandeis and Mrs. Brandeis made two financial contributions, one being in commemoration of their golden wedding anniversary. At a later time, when continuance of the work seemed in jeopardy, Professor Charles A. Beard and Mary R. Beard read many completed chapters of the manuscript and a detailed summary of the remaining chapters. A fund which they raised tided me over until the publisher made completion of the biography possible. My grateful acknowledgment is made to them and to the others who contributed.

I wish to record here my deep appreciation for the assistance of my friend Emma Wold from 1938 to 1944. Her previous interest in my father's work and her experience in legislative research made her cooperation exceptionally valuable. The continuous contribution Mrs. Gilbert E. Roe made to the preparation of this biography is similar to that which her husband made to the work he shared with my father during his lifetime. It is impossible to express in words my gratitude to my husband, George Middleton, for his assistance on many toilsome, elusive aspects of research, for his repeated reading of the manuscript, and for his constant encouragement throughout the years of my work.

During the years of research on this biography, so many members of the staff of the Library of Congress have helped to lighten my task that it is impossible to mention them all individually. Only a word of special appreciation can be expressed here to the Acting Librarian Verner W. Clapp; to David C. Mearns, Chief of the Manuscripts Division; to Katharine E. Brand for valuable assistance in relation to the recent collections, and to all members of the staff of this division where so much of my work has been done.

For permission to consult collections of manuscripts outside the Library of Congress I am indebted to Mrs. Harvey Clapp, Mrs. William Kent, and Joseph P. Tumulty; also to W. T. Rawleigh for generously making correspondence from his files available. For helpful materials from other sources my thanks are due to Professor Howard K. Beale, Dr. Kenneth Hechler, Dr. Helene Hooker, and Dr. Kenneth C. MacKay. To Marie Tremaine I am indebted for her wise counsel; to Adelaide T. Oberholtzer for typing the manuscript. My grateful acknowledgment is made to Milton Halsey Thomas, of Columbia University, for the index.

F. L.

Contents

Volume I

Volume II

Illustrations

Volume I

Robert M. La Follette 1922   Frontispiece

Pages 26–27

Drawing of the log cabin where Bob was born
"My name is Bob La Follette"
Bob's sister Josephine
Bob's mother, Mary Ferguson La Follette
Belle, wearing the checked woolen dress spun, woven, and made
   by her grandmother Lucetta Moore Case
Belle in 1879
Bob as district attorney of Dane County
Belle in Washington during Bob's last term in the House

Pages 122–123

Bob speaking at a Wisconsin county fair, 1897
Bob in 1904, during his second term as governor of Wisconsin
Maple Bluff Farm
Bob plowed a straight furrow and plowed deep
Bob speaking in Los Angeles, 1907

Volume II

Pages 834–835

The La Follette family in 1910
Belle in 1922
Bob in Jo Davidson's studio, Paris, 1923
Bob and his son Bob, Jr., Washington, D.C., 1924
Bob and his son Phil, St. Louis, October, 1924

Pages 1154–1155

Gilbert E. Roe and Bob, Jr., New York, 1924
Presidential campaign, 1924: "Fighting Bob," arriving in Chicago
Bob arriving in Madison, November 2, 1924
Bob speaking from the steps of the Wisconsin State Capitol, November 2, 1924
Statue of Robert M. La Follette by Jo Davidson, unveiled in the National Capitol, 1929

Cartoons and Facsimiles

Volume I

Volume II

Robert M. La Follette

CHAPTER I

Primrose, Wisconsin:
The Cradle of His Faith

Robert Marion La Follette was best known as "Bob" La Follette. He liked best to be called Bob, and I shall speak of him as Bob in this biography. The home where he was born on June 14, 1855, was a double log house built by his father near a spring not far from the road. The cabin was in the township of Primrose, Dane County, Wisconsin. A large boulder with a bronze tablet now marks the place. The surrounding country is one of high hills and low valleys, mostly prairie land with some timber near the springs and brooks. Here Bob played in childhood and later enjoyed spending his spare hours reading, thinking, and giving play to his imagination. Some of his letters to me before we were married were written "By the Big Spring."

There was an "upstairs" to the log house. The two rooms below had the necessary furniture common to the homes of early settlers: the usual plain dishes, chairs, tables, and bedsteads with feather beds, as well as a good supply of quilts, woolen blankets, and coverlets. Some of these coverlets were woven by his great aunt and are still in family use. There was a chimney with a large fireplace, but the cooking was done on a kitchen stove with elevated oven. One feature, not so common at that time, was a bookcase with a few books which Bob's father treasured.

The house was always in order and scrupulously clean. The little mother was a woman of forethought, industrious, capable, generous, and hospitable, yet careful and saving. She was an excellent cook and skilled with her needle. Like Bob, she was fastidious about her person. Her dresses, though few and simple, were well made and

1

becoming. The daily cold sponge bath was, even in log-cabin days, a ritual which she continued to the end of her life. Bob's mother, Mary Ferguson, had what her Scotch-Irish ancestors would have called the growing hand; seeds and slips came to life and flourished for her. In summer there were flowers in her garden, and she always found time to tend the plants which blossomed in her house throughout the long Wisconsin winters. To the end of her life, Bob and his sister Josephine shared this interest with their mother.

The father was an intelligent, determined man and a "good provider"; he disliked debt and was prudent in money matters—a man of integrity, high purpose, and strong will. His interest and ambition centered on making the four hundred acres he had acquired afford the advantages of a good home for his family, an education and a competency for his children.

When Bob was born, Dr. J. M. Kelly was in attendance. He was the widely-known country doctor from the village of Mount Vernon, four miles distant, where there was a store, a mill, and a post office. Mary Ann Chandler, a friend and neighbor, wife of Moses Chandler, whose farm was some three miles away, took care of the mother. Many years later, when Bob was speaking in Iowa, Moses Chandler, then over eighty, said to him after the meeting, "I have come forty miles to hear you, and my good wife told me before I left home to remind you that she put the first little shirt on your back." One month before Bob's birth, his mother had done a like service for Mrs. Dick Chandler when her son Warren was born. Such were the accepted obligations of pioneer conditions. Neighbors planned as a matter of course to help each other out in sickness. Mary La Follette did her full share. She was a wonderful nurse, and much sought after whenever there was illness.

Josiah La Follette and Mary Ferguson, Bob's father and mother, had been sweethearts in Indiana when quite young. He had wanted to marry before she thought they were ready. Their engagement was broken, and he went back to his boyhood home in Kentucky. In 1840 she married Alexander Buchanan, who died within the year.

Communication was slow, but when Josiah, in Mount Sterling, Kentucky, finally chanced to learn of this he threw down his ax, quit the work he had in hand, and started back to Indiana, declaring he was going to marry Mary Ferguson. Five years after the death of her first husband, she and Josiah La Follette were married. For four years they lived on the Buchanan farm, where their first two sons, William and Marion, were born. Josephine, their third child, was born in Wisconsin. She was two years older than Bob. In childhood they were almost inseparable and always at heart very close. Bob was his mother's fifth child. Ellen, her first-born, the posthumous child of her previous marriage, was fourteen years older. An attractive girl of good mind and sweet disposition, she was greatly beloved by each member of the family.

Josiah and Mary Ferguson La Follette, with three children, settled in Primrose, Wisconsin, in 1850. They came from Indiana with their household goods in two covered wagons and a covered buggy. Within five years Josiah and his brothers—William, Warren, Elhanan, Robert, and Harvey—bought and preempted more than a thousand acres of land in and about Primrose.

The La Follette brothers were tall, handsome men, Bob's father being six feet two and three-quarter inches. He had a high forehead, luminous dark eyes, and thick wavy hair, with heavy beard and eyebrows. For a man of his height his hands and feet were small and slender. His wife, Mary, was only four feet ten. She was remembered by those who knew her as a very pretty young woman with clear, fair skin, light gold-brown hair, and blue eyes. She was of the sturdy type, though her arms were long and her hands slender. Sitting up—she always sat up very straight—she gave the impression of being much taller than she was. Physically, Bob resembled his mother more than his father, although he had a long stride, like a tall man, with a grace and rhythm all his own.

The Ferguson family came to North Carolina from the north of Ireland, probably Ulster. They were the type of Protestants who would now be known as "fundamentalists." John Ferguson, Bob's great-grandfather, who lived to be ninety-four, is believed to be the first of the family to come to America. He was a Revolutionary soldier who came to Indiana from North Carolina, settled in Union County, and later moved to Boone County. His son, Bob's grandfather, was also named John Ferguson. With his wife, Mary Green, a native of Maryland, he left North Carolina and settled in Indiana in 1809. On their farm near Liberty, Bob's mother, Mary Ferguson, was born on November 22, 1817.

This sturdy Irish grandfather, who died at the age of eighty-five, had an enduring influence on his grandson. When Bob was about three, his mother took him from Wisconsin to Indiana to visit her father. One of his earliest recollections was of how his Grandfather Ferguson took him on his knee and explained very solemnly what an awful thing it was to tell a lie. The Fergusons were honest, thrifty, churchgoing people, most of them Democrats in politics. They were long-lived, independent, forthright, and endowed with the power of vivid and sometimes biting speech. They worked hard and took life rather seriously, but had exceptionally keen humor and ready wit.

On his father's side, Bob's ancestors were French Huguenots. Joseph La Follette, his great-grandfather, came to New Jersey with his parents and two brothers from the valley of the Loire in France, where the father had been engaged in the manufacture of silk. There is a tradition that during the provincial wars at the close of the twelfth century, an ancestor, because of his headlong bravery, was surnamed "Le Follet"—the reckless. This was retained as the family cognomen until the brothers, because of admiration for General La Fayette, under whom they are said to have served at Yorktown, changed it from the masculine form of Le Follet to the feminine La Follette in conformity with that of La Fayette. It is a fact that the family Bible of Joseph La Follette shows the births of the first four children recorded under the name Le Follet and those born later as La Follette.

Joseph La Follette, Bob's great-grandfather, was a Revolutionary soldier[1] who served under Casimir Pulaski as head wagoner. He is also said to have participated with his brothers in the battle of Brandywine, where he was wounded. The La Follette pioneers were a venturesome, strong-willed race of men and women, with deep family attachment which led them to keep together in their migrations to new lands. After the Revolution Joseph and his second wife, Phoebe Gobel, whom he had married in 1771, moved from New Jersey to join his brothers in Virginia. Later they took the typical pioneer route over the mountains to Hardin County, Kentucky, where he and his brothers bought land and made homes. Bob's paternal grandfather, Jesse La Follette, was born in 1781, and at the age of twenty-seven married a sister of his oldest brother Usual's wife. On July 4, 1817, Bob's father, Josiah, was born in a Kentucky log cabin built on the land Jesse La Follette had bought which adjoined the farm of Thomas Lincoln, father of the President. The court records show that Thomas Lincoln and Jesse La Follette were contemporaries and neighbors.[2] There is a well-founded family tradition that some of the La Follette children and Abraham Lincoln were playmates; there is also good reason for believing the anecdote that when one of Thomas Lincoln's Hardin County neighbors called on Abraham Lincoln at the White House the President asked after "Uncle Jesse La Follette" and said he remembered playing in Uncle Jesse's barn.

Ten years after the Lincolns had gone, the La Follette family, desiring to raise their children in a free State, began migrating from Kentucky. Bob's grandfather Jesse, in 1828, took up a farm in Putnam County, Indiana, near that of his eldest brother, Usual, who had arrived two years earlier. When the family made this journey, Josiah was eleven. The move from Kentucky was like some primitive caravan of early people: the children walking part of the time, helping drive the cattle and sheep; the men bringing up the horses or tending the wagons with the women and small children; Joseph, Bob's Revolutionary great-grandfather, riding horseback all the way from Kentucky. He spent the rest of his days in Indiana with his oldest son, dying at the recorded age of eighty-eight. But the tradition is that he was more than a hundred. He is said to have enjoyed perfect health throughout his life. Coming home one noon, he was asked to sit down and rest until dinner was ready. When called a few minutes later, he was found dead. In the family cemetery, on the old homestead, Joseph La Follette and seventy-five of his descendants are buried.

Bob and I had similar backgrounds, for, although my family came from the East to Ohio, they were early settlers in Wisconsin. Always my thought harks back to the pioneers—their character and influence were so fundamental to our lives and our understanding of each other. I well remember, when a child of ten, my grandmother Case telling me that when she was ten the family had come by ox team over unbroken roads from Vermont to Ohio; and how, soon after they had settled in their primitive home, her mother had died in childbirth, leaving my grandmother, the eldest, to care for the household and younger children. "I had no chance for an education," my grandmother said.

Even as a child I wondered what there was that my grandmother did not know. She knew the Bible and had absorbed not only the spiritual lessons, but its choice English. She was in close touch with nature; she could name the constellations and tell time by the stars. She could make beautiful vegetable dyes and knew the medicinal use of herbs. She was a wonderful nurse in sickness. There is hardly a principle in the most up-to-date authorities on the care of infants that was not among my grandmother's maxims. She wove and spun. Better than anything I have ever worn, I remember a checked woolen dress and a Balmoral skirt she made me. They wore so long I could not forget them.

She dipped the candles, gathered the sap, and made maple syrup. She hived the swarming bees. She made butter and cheese and dried fruits. She always had such good things to eat; and she had time to read, to knit, and to sew—to sew carpet rags. I well remember looking up from the stint that she had given me and asking, "Grandma, don't you hate to sew short rags that take such a long time to do, and make such a small ball when you get them done?" And of her looking at me over her glasses and saying, "No, child, I don't hate to do anything that needs to be done."

Bob's father had been very enthusiastic about coming to Wisconsin. He said he expected to live among these hills to an age equal to his grandfather's. But eight months after Bob's birth he died of an illness then diagnosed as a complication of pneumonia and diabetes. Dr. William Fox, uncle of Dr. Philip Fox, our family physician and lifelong friend, was called in consultation.

Josiah La Follette knew he must die. He said he had no fear of death but dreaded to be forgotten. This thought, often repeated by his mother, made a deep impression on Bob. He thought of his father by day and dreamed of him at night. His father held somewhat liberal religious views and had never joined any church. When Bob came to realize that the strict orthodox doctrine which pervaded the family atmosphere during part of his earlier years would condemn his father to eternal punishment, his spirit revolted at the thought. The desire was strong for a Hereafter where he might know his father. He resented any religious teaching that closed the gates of Heaven to so just and upright a man as he knew his father to be. All that took place at the time of his father's death and illness was, I believe, more vivid to Bob's imagination than if he had been old enough to remember what happened.

The funeral services for Josiah La Follette were very simple—

just a prayer by his neighbor and good friend Deacon David Thomas, and some hymns. They were too far away to get a minister. When the little brother Marion died, he had been buried on a hillside of the farm in sight of the house. The mother wanted the child buried with his father. The boy's coffin was taken from the grave, which had been carefully boarded up, and brought to the house and opened. The child's face was perfect as if asleep. While they were looking, it fell to ashes. Father and son were taken to the Postville cemetery on Green's prairie and placed together in one grave.

I have heard Bob say he often pictured the sad home journey his mother made on that cold, dreary winter day. She often recounted her suffering to her children; for, though a woman of courage and fortitude, she expressed her emotion freely and vividly in words. A boyhood friend, who was their nearest neighbor, remembers his mother saying that little Bob would often ask: "Mrs. Osmundsen, won't you come to see my mother? She is so very lonesome."

In 1894, after his mother's death, it was decided to move the father's remains to Madison for burial beside her. Bob consulted his friend, Dr. Cornelius Harper, as to the necessary preparations and with his brother William drove to Postville on this mission. When the gravedigger got down to where the coffin had been, they found it had disappeared; but the outlines could be traced in the surrounding clay. Bob himself carefully removed the relics of his father's skeleton. Dr. Harper, who assisted at the reburial in Madison, says that before the coffin was finally closed Bob studied the relics carefully. He commented on the prominent forehead, the small hands and feet. They talked for more than an hour. Bob asked many questions and seemed intent on reproducing in imagination the form of his father as he looked in life.

Josiah La Follette had come to Primrose with $100 in money, two or three horses, and a cow. Among a few of the treasured books he brought were the *Lives of the Presidents of the United States* by Robert W. Lincoln and *A Practical System of Modern Geography; or A View of the Present State of the World. Simplified and Adapted to the Capacity of Youth.*[3] The geography he had used when he had taught night school in Kentucky. In the course of the probate and settlement of his estate, his land was valued at $4,000 and personal property at over $600. He had a span of horses, a yoke of oxen, four cows, four heifers, and other young livestock. There were five hundred bushels of grain, but no so-called farm machinery. At that time grain was cut with a cradle, grass cut with a scythe, and crops were generally cultivated and garnered by hand. The inventory states that the family had a barrel of pork and 128 pounds of ham, showing how pioneers provided themselves with meat for the winter. There were twenty-two milk crocks, a churn, and butter firkin, indicating that butter was made not only for immediate family use, but packed to supply extra needs.

Although essentially a farmer, Josiah La Follette was also a good practical carpenter. He had a complete chest of tools. This interested me because Bob had an inherent love of tools and was very handy in their use. I recall on one of his visits to my home, my mother said something about wishing she had another window in the kitchen. He told her he could do that job and, much to my amazement, went about it with all the dexterity of a professional carpenter. I had never even heard it mentioned that he had this kind of skill.

At the time of his death, Josiah had the lumber and other materials ready for a new frame house, which he himself expected to build. His brother, William, undertook the building of the new home, but as an economy measure he insisted on modifying Josiah's design and eliminating one room. It was the first frame house in Primrose. When completed, it was a story-and-a-half upright with a wing. There were three rooms downstairs: kitchen, living room with large fireplace, and bedroom; upstairs were two rooms, the large one partitioned off with curtains to meet the needs of the family. Near the house an orchard was planted. No apples ever tasted to Bob like the "bellflowers" of this orchard.

Less than two years after he had settled in Primrose, Josiah La Follette was elected town clerk. The records show that he received all of the thirty-six votes cast at the election. At a number of elections, years after, his son Bob received the unanimous vote of the town of Primrose. Josiah was reelected clerk in 1853; a year later he was elected assessor, and in 1855 he was made town chairman but died before he had served a year. It is told that while attending the session of the county board, in the old state capitol, Josiah La Follette was impressed with the advantages of more lights; so when he came home one night and found his wife with only one candle he said, "Mary, this won't do." With what was considered unheard-of extravagance at the time, he lit three more home-dipped tallow candles.

As soon as Bob was old enough to understand, his mother impressed upon him that he must never do anything to dishonor his father's name and must be like him in character and devotion to what was right. This conception of his father's integrity was planted deep in Bob's nature by his mother and the friends and neighbors from whom he was always seeking to learn more of his father.

Being ardent abolitionists, the La Follette brothers who came to Wisconsin were among the first to join the Republican Party. William La Follette, after reading in the weekly paper that on May 22 Preston Brooks of South Carolina had assaulted Senator Charles Sumner, mounted his horse and rode to his brother Harvey La Follette's home to ask if they had decided on a name for their son who had been born on March 14, 1856. When told the child had not yet been named, Uncle William said, "Then I think you should name him Charles Sumner." So Bob's favorite cousin was named Charles Sumner La Follette.

When Bob was three years old, his half-sister, Ellen Buchanan, married Dean Eastman, a good-looking, upstanding, hard-working young man from Maine. Dean taught school, played the fiddle at country dances, and led the singing at church services. Mother La Follette took Dean to her heart, as she did all her "in-laws." She relinquished her dower right in the Buchanan estate to provide a good home for her daughter and son-in-law, who with their large family were an intimate part of Bob's life.

Bob's boyhood impressions of Primrose had a deep and abiding influence on his character and career. So enduring were his memories of neighbors, incidents, and early experiences that through his vivid scription they became a part of our family traditions. Bob would n tell his children how he had ridden horseback Sunday morn- to the home of his father's friend, Deacon David Thomas, to him a shave, and Bob said "he had a beard like wire, so it was easy job." David Ash, born in 1792, was a near neighbor and a arkable man who Bob said "must have been a soldier, for he ed to make a soldier out of me. He would come to our house hen I was about four years old and after my night clothes were on, he would give me his cane and put me through the military maneuvers in front of the fire-place."

Bob's childhood had its hardships, but all in all his first seven years were happy and normal. The thought of his father, and his desire not to be forgotten, were always a part of the little lad's consciousness. But he worshiped his mother, and never questioned the depth and warmth of her love. I have heard him say that when she punished him, he never resented it; his feeling was to throw his arms about her and beg forgiveness. She could not resist this sort of appeal. So long as she lived there was this perfect bond of mutual understanding between them.

Between Bob and his sister Josephine, whom he liked best to call "Jo," there was also lifelong mutual companionship and devotion. In a letter to her in 1901, he wrote: "From my very earliest recollections of childhood you were the other half. I can recall no pleasure of those dear old days without the memory of a black-eyed sweet-faced little girl in it all. Then as we grew older the companionship grew, if possible, closer. You knew all my hopes, ambitions, disappointments, and discouragements and shared in them all."

Bob accompanied his mother on all occasions. With her he attended church services, held at homes and schoolhouses, or went to quilting bees and other neighborhood doings. When the roads were bad, his mother would go on horseback, taking the two youngest children, who rode in front of her, "spending the day" in the good old pioneer way of visiting. When Bob was between three and four, there was an entertainment in the newly-built schoolhouse; it was on this occasion he made his first speech in public. He was so short that he could not be seen standing in front of the teacher's desk. Someone lifted him up on it and he recited:

> "You'd not expect one of my age
> To speak in public on the stage."

He went to school quite early to keep his sister Jo company. T both wore copper-toed boots. They had about a mile to walk. W the snow was deep or the weather bad, their good neighbor Jayne, who had a large family, would fetch them. The year Civil War broke out, their teacher, William Moon, was among first to enlist and among the first to be killed. Bob's impressions the war were intense and lasting. When the story of the early battle came, he went off by himself and cried bitterly, he hardly knew why.

He reverenced all the war heroes who had saved the Union, and worshiped Lincoln and Grant. He was a boy of ten when Lincoln was assassinated. He was out in the road when a neighbor brought the word. Bob ran as fast as he could to tell his mother. They all wept. The depth of the sorrow and solemnity of the mourning for the martyred President were distinct memories never to be forgotten.

Incidents of Bob's childhood days were often recalled to him during his speaking tours. Once, when he was governor, speaking in North Dakota, an old man came up to shake hands and asked Bob if he remembered when he gave him a quarter. Like a flash the picture came to his mind. He was five years old; he and Jo were coming home from the Rock Hill school. In the road he found a pocketbook which he took home to his mother. The next morning, on their way to school, they suddenly came upon a man with a beard who asked, "Did either of you children find a pocketbook?" Bob was startled, fearing he had done something wrong, but was much relieved when the good man said: "I think this is the little boy who found it; I just got it from your mother, and here is a quarter for you." It was Bob's first money, a precious keepsake. He had a hole bored in the coin and wore it around his neck on a ribbon. Forty years later he recognized the North Dakota farmer, with whom he was shaking hands, as Olaf Osmondsen, the man with the beard, whose gift of twenty-five cents had been such a wonderful event in his young life.

Scandinavians were among the earliest settlers in Primrose. Some Norwegians were already established on their homesteads when Josiah La Follette and his brothers arrived. Christian Hendrickson, the first Norwegian settler in the township, came in 1846. In the early fifties there was a large increase in the number of Norwegian immigrants. Eli Pederson, who was to sponsor Bob for the nomination of district attorney, had known and worked for Bob's father. He settled in Primrose the year Bob was born. Intelligent, industrious, homemaking, and public-spirited, the Scandinavian element readily assimilated with their Yankee neighbors. From earliest childhood Bob had Norwegian playmates. He picked up some Norwegian and could give the ordinary salutations and engage in a little commonplace conversation. These close early childhood associations established a mutual understanding and confidence between him and his Norwegian neighbors which strengthened his following with that element of our population as his political leadership was extended.

Always he recognized the value to our national life of the immigrants who left their homeland in the hope of larger opportunity in the new country. He understood and valued their cultural heritages. In childhood and youth he lived among sturdy, courageous pioneer men and women who came from Europe and from our own Southern and Eastern states bringing their different religious faiths, racial traditions, and ways of life. Cooperation and tolerance were necessities of that westward-moving frontier on which his family and many of his neighbors had lived for three generations.

Out of this background and his firsthand experience among these folk, where intelligence was constantly tested more by deed than by word, grew the abiding convictions of his own life. Here were forged that coordinated idealism and realism which made his later work effective and significant.

The village of Primrose, Wisconsin, was the cradle of his enduring faith in democracy.

CHAPTER II

"My Name Is Bob La Follette"

In 1862, when Bob was seven, his mother married Deacon John Z. Saxton, of Argyle, Wisconsin, who was twenty-six years her senior. Generally known as "Uncle John," he was looked upon as a leading citizen. For some thirty years he had lived in Lafayette County, had been town chairman, leading merchant, and postmaster of Argyle, and had at one time also kept a hotel. Although a rival store had been recently started, Uncle John had a good country trade and was considered prosperous—even wealthy for those days.

I never heard Bob say how he felt when his mother married John Saxton. But he would have gone to the stake for her, and this loyalty may have kept him from ever expressing his own feeling. Such an experience, at best, is usually a hard ordeal for children. He had never known his father, but his devotion to his memory was almost morbid. Even in childhood the fortitude, which carried him undaunted through so many bitter conflicts in afterlife, doubtless helped him bear this first great trial of his childhood. He insisted on keeping his own name. When he started school at Argyle, he went up to a group of boys who were playing together and said: "My name is Bob La Follette, what is yours?" If ever strangers called him "Saxton," he would correct them: "My name is La Follette."

Although Saxton was a severe disciplinarian, Bob never spoke of his stepfather with anything but respect. Sometimes, however, he would tell humorous stories and mimic the conversations in the store between the customers and the very deaf old man who found it hard to understand what they wanted.

Bob said his stepfather taught him good behavior; never to leave a door open, to close it and do it quietly; good table manners; the

right form of address, "sir" and "ma'am," and at all times polite-
ness and courtesy. The deacon belonged to the school that believed
"Spare the rod and spoil the child." Although Bob was sometimes
whipped so hard that his mother had to intervene, the stepfather
appears to have recognized the boy's unusual gifts, for he would
say to his wife: "Mary, he will either turn out to be a very wonderful man or a very bad one. I haven't made up my mind which."

He evidently encouraged his stepson's ambition, for Bob remembered that when he said to his stepfather that he wanted to be a
statesman, "he told me I had better study law; so I planned it all in
the back of my head to study law and be a statesman before I knew
what it meant." Once, when Bob was even younger, someone told
him that his mouth was too small for a "statesman" and that "smart
men had big mouths." He answered, "I will stretch it." Picking up
a large pair of shears, he proceeded to stretch it to the utmost.

Saxton was an ardent Baptist, a deacon, and a leader in the
church. He had a good home, lived well, entertained the minister,
and was active in the social life of the church and community. Bob's
mother had been brought up from childhood as a strict Baptist. All
her life she found great comfort in her religion. She looked up to the
deacon as a church leader and as an exemplary businessman of
superior knowledge and experience. She was ambitious for her children, anxious that they should have opportunities for education
which she never had. Since Saxton and his first wife had been generous to their adopted children, Bob's mother anticipated he would
provide liberally for his stepchildren, guiding them and giving them
advantages they might not otherwise have.

But she was disappointed in her expectation that he intended to
provide a home for them. Had he really been as well off as she
thought, he might have appeared in a better light; but he was
seventy, his powers were waning, and his business going downhill.
Bob's mother seemed not to know these facts. She had been self-
reliant, and by good management had kept the 440-acre farm intact
and made it support herself and her children, whose guardian she
was. But after her marriage she yielded complete control of her
affairs to Saxton, following his directions in everything relating to
the La Follette estate.

Almost immediately after their marriage, Saxton began keeping
in his own handwriting an itemized account of all expenditures for

the children, including their mending, washing, and trifling items like three cents for elastic or ten cents for spending money. Within a week of their wedding they went to Madison, saw Judge Thomas Hood, and filed a lengthy estate report covering the previous two years and claiming $238.86 for her as guardian. This included repairs to the house following a fire, taxes, and board for the children. Two weeks later another petition was filed to appropriate $150 of the estate for farm fences and repairs.

By 1863 Saxton was planning to have some of the estate sold, and in July, 1864, Bob's mother asked the court's authority to sell part of the land to provide for the children's maintenance and education. Judge Hood authorized the sale of 120 acres, but because of the war it was not effected until two years later, when it brought $800. Judge Bryant, who had succeeded Hood, allowed the sale, but made it plain he would not approve any further inroads on the estate, for it was evident the farm could support the children. This was their first introduction to General George E. Bryant, who became Bob's intimate friend and political godfather.

The children fared well at Argyle, however, in having a good school and good teachers. Daniel Mills, although he had an almost maniacal temper, was a thoroughgoing, old-fashioned schoolmaster. He used the rod at times until he drew blood, and Bob came in for his share of hard lickings. He often told of Mills' violent outbreaks. One day the teacher appeared in a fine pair of specially made boots which cost some $8. They soon began to "draw" because of the heat. The scholars could see the rising storm of fury on his face. Finally he took out his knife and slashed the boots in shreds from toe to instep. His pupils dared not look up from their books, much less laugh.

In one of his blind rages Mills seized Bob by the scruff of the neck, shaking him and hurling him again and again toward the floor. As he was very agile, Bob would light on his feet each time, and the jouncing had no effect except to increase the teacher's ire. But when the blows became too hard, Bob feigned being driven out of his senses so well that his teacher grew alarmed and sent him home. He confided the trick to his mother, who, of course, never gave him away. In spite of Mills' cruel punishment, Bob appreciated his ability as a teacher. Mills, in turn, was interested in Bob's dramatic talent and drilled him in the art of "speaking pieces."

In 1864 an excellent teacher, Frank Higgins, came from Pennsylvania to Argyle and started a private "select school," as it was called at the time. The terms were six weeks, for which he charged fifty cents per pupil. When he taught at the public school, he was paid $25 a month and boarded himself. When Bob attended his school, there were no grades, and Higgins taught everything from ABC's to algebra. At times he had over a hundred pupils. For some thirty years he taught in southern Wisconsin. When he was eighty-nine, some five hundred of his former pupils met in his honor in 1928 at Darlington, Wisconsin. As governor, Bob arranged to have his old schoolmaster appointed to a clerkship in the capitol.

Frank Higgins remembers Bob as a small, strong, chubby boy who often sat in deep thought, which greatly impressed the teacher. He also recognized in him, at that early day, "a natural-born orator." Bob's chums would get him to stand on a drygoods box in his stepfather's store and make speeches to them.

Bob had a fine group of boy friends at Argyle. Among his special chums were Charlie Pullen and Perry Wilder, who in after years were active and effective political supporters. They were both three years older than Bob; although he was small for his age, his playmates were usually older. The Civil War was on. His brother William left home, and although under age enlisted without his mother's consent. The young boys of Argyle organized a military company. They had gay uniforms: brown pants, with red trimmings, red shirts, and blue Zouave caps. The boy company had a band. Charlie Pullen was the drummer, Bob La Follette fifer.

One morning on their way to Sunday school, when the ice was breaking in the Pecatonica River, Bob, Charlie, Perry, and other boys pried a large cake loose, got on it, and were carried several miles down the river before they could land. They had a good scare and missed Sunday school. Bob said his stepfather made it as hot for him when he got home as it had been cold on the ice raft. I have heard him tell of another chastisement when the boys were giving a show in the barn. Bob had painted the entire body of one of them with indigo and was exhibiting him in a cage as a "wild man." They were charging a small admission, but this was ignored by his stepfather, who broke up the show with a rawhide. I always wondered how Bob could make light of these whippings, as he afterward did. One reason probably was that his stepfather never had any hold on his affections. Once, when Saxton unjustly charged him with telling a lie, he was enraged and there was a scene. But when whipped for boyish pranks, it seemed to have no effect. However, what roused his indignation and caused him to suffer agony was his stepfather's preachment, day in and day out, of the doctrine of eternal punishment for all who died and were not baptized. The implication that his own father was burning in everlasting hell-fires created a passionate resentment and anguish which the young boy fought out alone in long, wakeful hours of the night.

In 1866 the family moved to Fayette, a small town not far from Argyle, where the deacon opened a store. There Bob attended a private school conducted in a church by Mr. and Mrs. John B. Parkinson. Afterward Parkinson was for many years professor at the University of Wisconsin, where he and his wife were beloved by the students. Both Bob and I were in his classes. Later he was a candidate for Congress on the Democratic ticket against Bob.

After an unsuccessful year at Fayette, the stepfather decided to return to Argyle. But he could no longer make a success of storekeeping, and a year or so later the family went back to the La Follette farm in Primrose. Bob was determined, however, to continue his schooling at Argyle. He had learned to cut hair and shave, just as he had acquired many other manual skills, without anybody's knowing when or how. When he proposed to the proprietor of the hotel in Argyle that he set up a barber's chair, Hawley hesitated; but his wife, whose heart Bob had won, said "Yes." She and Bob improvised a barber's chair that would slide into the closet under the stairs. As a barber, he built up a good business and earned so much money that he entered into the "wild life" of the small town. One Saturday night his teacher discovered he was drunk and advised him to go home and think it over. He mounted his horse and headed for Primrose. Before he reached home, he was sober. He was humiliated, and resolved it should never happen again. For many years he never touched liquor.

When Bob went home to Primrose "to think it over" and repent his dissipation, his brother Will, who had been running the farm since his return from the war, announced he was going West. Suddenly Bob realized his responsibility as head of the family, for his stepfather was now quite feeble. He gave up going back to Argyle and helped with the farm work in earnest. His brother stayed until fall and sold the crops, but for the next two years Bob, with part-time help of a hired man, worked the farm.

Keeping in mind his fixed purpose to go on with his education later, he attended a few winter terms of the Primrose district school. One was taught by Carrie Baker, an excellent teacher whom the family all loved. She boarded with Bob's mother at the farm. Later, when Bob was about fifteen, she wrote to his sister Jo, "He is a boy whose future I shall look forward to with great interest."[1] Another district teacher, whom he found helpful, was James Smith. Smith enjoyed Bob's ready wit, appreciated his dramatic gifts, aided his study of literature, and first introduced him to Shakespeare. Bob also remembered Helen Root as a good teacher; he was not enrolled in her school but went almost every day to get the needed help in the higher branches he was studying by himself in preparing for the university. Except for a term at an excellent Baptist seminary in Evansville, conducted by the Reverend Mr. Bradley and his wife, this was the extent of his schooling until he was eighteen.

While at Evansville, Bob and his sister boarded with "Aunt Nancy Smith," who formerly lived in Argyle. He had his picture taken with a group of boys who also boarded there. Tom Dryden, now seventy-eight, is the only one who survives at this writing. He says, "It seems but yesterday we were a jolly bunch of boys and 'Little Bob' was the moving spirit." Dryden recalls that in their games Bob was "quick as a cat and as agile."

After Bob took charge of the farm, he entered heartily into the life of Primrose and the neighboring village of Mount Vernon. He organized a band similar to that in Argyle. Dean Eastman, his brother-in-law, played good old-fashioned music, and there were many neighborhood dances. No one appreciated the joke better than Bob when, years later, an old neighbor told a newspaper reporter seeking an interview that "Bob La Follette was popular with the home folks, all right, but he always wanted to be floor manager at the dances and usually made out to have his way." He was a good dancer, and at any time in his life he could dance a merry jig.

Bob was also a fine wrestler as a boy, strong, skilled, and gritty. His habitual mobility and freedom of gesture doubtless did more to keep his body fit and youthful than gymnastics, although in later years he usually took a few special exercises each day. He liked boxing, and taught each of our children something of the art. He was much pleased when our little girl Fola came to the defense of a small boy who had been assailed by a larger one. Taken by surprise, the bully called out, "Say, who learned you to hit?" Fola, triumphant, called back, "My dad."

Spelling bees, school exhibitions, and, of course, school picnics were important features in the social life of Primrose, as elsewhere in the country, when Bob and I were young. He did not excel as a speller, but he always had a "star" part on these occasions, for he was in great demand as a speaker and actor. Sometimes he recited "The Polish Boy." It was his first declamation when a freshman at the university, as I well remember. Often he would stage a play; once it was a David and Absalom scene, with his brother William in the coffin as the dead Absalom. Bob sometimes enacted a German barber singing a German dialect song as he shaved away, which made a great hit. The Good Templars movement was strong in the early seventies. He and his sister Jo joined. They took their pledges seriously and enjoyed the social diversion of the lodge meetings. When Jo applied for a school, he went with her to present her claims and qualifications to the school board. She got her contract.

While attending district school, he was hurt and for a time unable to walk without crutches. But he built a sled of boards and iron barrel hoops and trained his dog to draw him to school through the snow. His schoolfellows built a house for the dog and helped him from the school to his sled.

Bob's liking for animals was part of his being. He had many animal pets, and an exceptional aptitude for training them. As a child, he had a dog named Caesar which was allowed to sleep in front of his door at night. A dappled-gray mare, whose dam and grandam he had claimed as his own, was foaled in 1870. He named her Gypsy, and taught her all kinds of tricks, to kneel, lie down, and roll over. He pretended illness, staying home from church on enough Sunday mornings to train Gypsy to go up and down stairs. As soon as the deacon and his dutiful family had left, he would spring from bed and fetch the colt into the house for her lesson. When the stepfather returned, Bob would still be in bed but "feeling a little better," about ready to get up and enjoy the rest of the Sunday holiday. Gypsy would follow him anywhere and come from anywhere when he whistled. He broke her to the saddle gaits he liked and to trot in harness. She was fast and had good endurance. He would drive her from his home in Madison to mine in Baraboo, a good forty miles, in five hours. For the work of the farm, a part of it anyway, he had a much-valued yoke of oxen. He prized a family cow and could tell her good points as well as he could those of a horse. Except when in Washington, we always had milk from our own cows to supply our family need.

In November, 1872, John Saxton died after a prolonged illness requiring constant attention, which Bob's mother dutifully gave. When his eyes failed, Jo, of whom he was very fond, read to him, mostly from the Bible and the *Christian Standard*. During the four and a half years he lived at Primrose, he had not been able to do much work. But he often rode about the countryside, or drove an old, white-faced sorrel mare hitched to a small high buggy. In his tall silk hat, wide-winged collar, and old-style cut of clothes, he made a picturesque figure.

CHAPTER III

"Mamma Laughed When
I Proposed to Her"

Bob was in his eighteenth year when his stepfather died. For two years he had been working the Primrose farm, taking a man's responsibility, and was no longer a green boy. Most of the produce was marketed in Madison, twenty-four miles distant. It was a day's drive with a team of horses and a load over dirt roads and long, steep hills. Farmers would start from home the day before market day in order to reach the Gorham House, a few miles out of town, toward evening; there they would spend the night and be up early next morning to dispose of their grain and produce, returning home the same day. Many years later in the Senate, when arguing for his resolution to investigate the monopolistic control of the elevator and grain business of the country, Bob recalled and contrasted his own experience as a young farmer in selling grain at Madison to the highest bidder "in a real competitive market."[1]

Often when we were passing the old Gorham House, better known as the Spring Hotel, Bob would recall in his humorous, dramatic way how he had slept there and awakened in the morning with high hopes to the adventure of the day. The money he was to get for the load of grain, butter, eggs, or poultry was a very important matter to him and the family at home. More often than not the prices were ridiculously low and disappointing. However, in the home-coming there was good cheer and hope for better luck next time.

It was always amusing to hear Bob and his law partner, Gilbert Roe, also a Dane County boy, compare their boyhood experiences in selling their farm products to Madison housewives. One day, many years later, when Bob, Jr., and Phil were selling cherries from the orchard on our farm, the leading Madison grocer did not offer what they thought a fair price. So they decided to market the fruit by a back-door house-to-house canvass of the most prosperous residential street. When they came home late in the afternoon with an empty wagon and a fat pocketbook, their father complimented the boys on their initiative. He remarked that their luck was better than his when, long ago, he had driven twenty-four miles from Primrose and tried to sell his butter and eggs at these same back doors. No one had bought. Some farmer had covered the ground just ahead of him. It was a long drive home with an empty purse and his unsold butter and eggs.

There was no work on the farm that he could not do and do well. He plowed a straight furrow and plowed deep. He handled a scythe with an ease and rhythm delightful to watch. He knew how the crops should be planted, the stock cared for; how the haying, harvesting, and all the things that are a part of the day's work on the farm should be done. He could do these things himself and direct others to do them. He never looked upon his early responsibility as a hardship. He always appreciated what the work and obligations of the farm had done for him—the training of judgment, the power to think and act on his own. Bob was by nature many-sided and unusually gifted. To whatever walk in life he had been born, he would have carved out a notable career. Nevertheless, it has always been plain to me that his early experience and environment had much to do with shaping his life work.

At eighteen he had thought much and read some. Newspapers were becoming more numerous and books cheaper. It was a period of practical awakening on economic questions. He read Henry George's *Our Land and Land Policy*, published in 1871, which embodied many ideas later set forth in *Progress and Poverty*. The dog-eared pamphlet was lent to him by a rather unusual man named Dixon, a blacksmith who was a thinker and reader, and who had taken an interest in Bob.

In the early seventies Bob felt the Granger movement swirling about him, the effect of which always stayed with him. He said it was the first powerful revolt in Wisconsin against the rise of monopolies, the arrogance of railroads, and the waste and robbery of public lands: "Those old hard-headed pioneers from New England and from northern Europe who thought as they plowed, went far toward roughing out the doctrine in regard to railroad control which the country has since adopted."[2] In his public speaking he often traced the genesis of the progressive movement back to the rise of the Patrons of Husbandry.

At eighteen Bob had met his full share of the experiences, trials, and adventures of youth and childhood. Endowed with a deeply affectionate, highly imaginative, sensitive nature, he was capable of suffering much; but he had an inherent joy and faith in life, a cheerfulness, wit, and humor that nothing could down. Never once in all the years we traveled the road together, did I hear him question that life was worth living or that any good effort was worth whatever it cost.

Bob early showed the gift of leadership and developed unusual talents for it. His dramatic ability, his power to move an audience, though it had only been tested at school exhibitions, had interested his teachers and left a lasting impression on those who heard and saw him. It was an innate gift of which he himself must have been conscious. From earliest childhood he had loved and understood people, valuing each human being as an individual. These were the elements of his leadership which, combined with rare strength of mind and character, bespoke the life of action and usefulness which he lived.

After his stepfather's death he worked the farm another year. Then it was rented to his brother-in-law, Dean Eastman. Bob was ambitious and determined to have a college education. At commencement time, 1873, he went to Madison to find out what preparation he must have to enter the state university. It was then he heard the great address of the Wisconsin Chief Justice Edward G. Ryan, who had written the epoch-making decision sustaining the Granger law, which helped to lay the foundation for judicial action upon corporation control. This address had an enduring influence on Bob, who always vividly remembered Justice Ryan's "bowed figure, his fine, almost feminine features, his wavy auburn hair, and the luminous impressive eyes which glowed as the old man talked there in the Assembly Chamber to the graduating students." His voice shook with emotion, and his prophetic words, which Bob never forgot, "conveyed powerfully the feeling of many thoughtful men of that time." These are the "prophetic words" which profoundly impressed the youth from the farm at Primrose: "There is looming up a new and dark power. I cannot dwell upon the signs and shocking omens of its advent. The accumulation of individual wealth seems to be greater than it ever has been since the downfall of the Roman Empire. The enterprises of the country are aggregating vast corporate combinations of unexampled capital, boldly marching, not for economic conquests only, but for political power. . . . Already, here at home, one great corporation has trifled with the sovereign power, and insulted the state. There is grave fear that it, and its great rival, have confederated to make partition of the state and share it as spoils. . . . The question will arise, and arise in your day, though perhaps not fully in mine, 'Which shall rule—wealth or man; which shall lead—money or intellect; who shall fill public stations—educated and patriotic free men, or the feudal serfs of corporate capital?' "[3]

In this era of telephones, daily papers, airplanes, movies, radios, with their accompanying diversions and amusements, it is hard to understand how seriously the Granger movement took hold of the farmers and stirred them to action. It has always seemed to me that the experience of the Granger movement, and listening to Ryan's great address predicting that "the question will arise in your day," did more than even Bob himself realized to shape his political career. In his early manhood the conviction was thus deeply implanted, to become the very fiber of his political thought, that our government was being subverted from its true purpose by the great corporate interests and that the people were thereby being robbed of their birthright. I do not mean that he was then and there overwhelmed with a sense of responsibility to right the pending evil; but I am sure his mind was made up that when the time came he would do his part to preserve the fundamental principle of justice and equality, which, as he understood it, was guaranteed in the Declaration of Independence and the Constitution.

Throughout the years of his life he used Chief Justice Ryan's denunciation and warning with telling effect on the stump, the Chautauqua platform, and the floor of the United States Senate. I, too, made it the text of many talks; our children, and the men and women of their generation, are using it. "Which shall rule—wealth or man?" was a fitting slogan of the Progressives in the 1928 campaign in Wisconsin. So long does it take! But as Bob always pointed out, the struggle is never ending. The mistake most of us make is in thinking that the conflict can be settled either one way or the other by an election. So many times I have heard him repeat to his audiences—I hear him now—"Eternal vigilance is the price of democracy!"

In November, 1873, Bob went to Madison to get an education. It was characteristic of him to move from Primrose with his mother and sister instead of coming alone to attend school. They rented a small place with a barn and pasture on the outskirts of the city. He drove the twenty-four miles from Primrose in a spring wagon leading the family cow. In order that the cow might follow willingly, he put the calf in the back of the wagon box.

He immediately entered the Wisconsin Academy, an ungraded school attended largely by boys and girls from the country who were allowed to take whatever studies they chose. The principal, H. P. Harrington, was assisted by his sister.

Carl Grimstad tells me of an early interest in Bob before he first met him at the academy. In 1870 Carl's brother, Ole, a Civil War veteran, had been appointed census enumerator. Carl stayed at his brother's home to help with the chores while Ole was out taking the census. When his brother returned from his trips, he would relate his experiences. One evening he told of being at the farm of a widow named La Follette, whose son Robert was about the same age as Carl. Ole said Robert had been able to give all the information the census required. Ole thought this remarkable because he frequently found older people could not answer these questions satisfactorily. This set Carl thinking, for he knew he couldn't answer all the questions; that boy with the odd name La Follette must be smart. When Carl entered the Wisconsin Academy, he was thrilled during the first roll call to hear the name Robert La Follette. So there was the boy who could answer all those questions; Carl was surprised and disappointed to find how small Bob was. He had thought the boy who could answer all those questions must be a big strapper.

But Carl says he soon found that what Bob lacked in stature he made up in native ability: "He was popular with the boys and with the girls also. It was plain even then that he was a natural born leader of men and could hold his own under all circumstances." Both came from nearby farms and were interested in the same things. They formed a lasting friendship. Loren Ketchum, a son of their

Primrose neighbor, was also attending this school, and the three brought their dinner pails. At noon they visited, discussing school, religion, politics. Sometimes Carl and Bob would meet at the library of the capitol, read for a while, and then stroll about looking at the oil portraits of Wisconsin's great men.

Christopher Gorham, also a fellow student at the academy, remembers Bob as a slim, wiry youth with thick brown hair. He recalls they were once selected to defend the protective tariff in the school debating society; but neither knew what a protective tariff meant. Not wishing to confess their ignorance to Professor Harrington, Bob, being more of a "ladies' man" than Gorham, was selected as spokesman to ask Miss Harrington; but she merely referred them back to her brother. Years later, when Bob was making tariff speeches in Congress, Gorham wondered if he remembered the tariff incident at the academy. Gorham says that though Bob was a good debater, there were others just as good: "But we had no one who could compare with him as a declaimer—he was the feature of every program."

Like almost every student of his time trying to earn his way through school, Bob spent one vacation selling books. It may not have been a great financial success, but it was good practical experience. With the books he sold a hand mirror, and always had it ready so that when "the lady of the house" opened the door she could see her face reflected and would naturally be more gracious to the book agent.

The following year he registered as a sub-freshman at the university. He also attended, part of the year, what was known as Professor George's school. This unusual school relied on the students' own interest for their progress. Later, when a sophomore at the university, Bob taught some classes at the George school. It was there also that he first met Robert G. Siebecker, who was teaching German, having attended as a student the year before. Siebecker's father was one of the revolutionary emigrants who had come to Wisconsin from Germany in 1848 and settled on a farm in Sauk County. The family spoke German in the home, and Siebecker's only training in English had been in the district school. Later he married Bob's sister Jo and was his law partner until appointed Judge of the Circuit Bench. It was a treat to hear "Robert" and "Bob," as we designated them, tell of their coming to town to attend

Drawing of the log cabin where Bob was born

My name is Bob La Follette

Bob's sister Josephine

Bob's mother, Mary Ferguson La Follette
In time of trouble we leaned on her.

Belle in 1870
We all wore trains at graduation.

Belle, wearing the checked woolen dress spun, woven,
and made by her grandmother Lucetta Moore Case

Bob as district attorney of Dane County

Belle in Washington during Bob's last term in the House

school: Bob leading his cow, Robert walking from the railroad station to his room, shouldering his small trunk to save the cost of cartage.

In the academic year of 1875, Bob entered the university as a freshman in general science. I was in the modern classical course, but owing to gaps in the high-school curriculum I had many required studies to make up; so he and I were in the first-year German class taught by Miss S. A. Carver. She once sharply reprimanded a group of boys who were laughing and creating a disturbance. Bob was sitting in their midst, his face quite sober; but when I became better acquainted with him I suspected he was the prime cause of the mischief.

The family had moved to a house nearer the university, where Bob's mother and sister undertook to cook for a club of some twenty boys who furnished the food and paid for preparing it. However, the work proved hard with too little profit. So, to help out with the expenses they took a few roomers and boarders. Jeff Simpson and Sam Harper, who afterward became Bob's most intimate friend and political associate, were members of this club.

Bob was interested in the university's military training, but could afford only one suit. As the uniform in those days was blue, he got a blue suit of the right shade which he wore for all purposes. When he was made an officer, a new problem was presented which he ingeniously solved. He had his sister Jo make eyelets on the shoulders of the coat so that they didn't show, and hooks on the shoulder straps; by this simple device he could, at need, put on and take off the insignia of his rank.

The winter of his freshman year he was obliged to earn money to keep things going. Poorly prepared as he was in the required studies, he arranged to teach a country school in the town of Burke and do his university work nights. But he continued to live at home, riding his horse Gypsy five miles to and from school each morning and evening. He also cared for his horse and cow, sawed wood, and otherwise carried the responsibility of the "man of the house." The Burke school was a stiff job, for he had taken it after another teacher had failed because of the belligerent students. Bob had one tussle with a big boy who was the ringleader. He settled who was boss of the school somewhat after the method of his old schoolmaster Mills of Argyle, I fear. But there was no more trouble, for he was an excellent teacher and had an inherent power of control that seldom required force.

In our day the literary societies were a very important part of university life, since a majority of the students were members. Class loyalty and loyalty to these organizations were both strong. There was keen rivalry to get the most promising new students. During week ends the libraries were filled with students preparing for programs which included debates, orations, essays, and declamations. Regular meetings were held on Friday nights in rooms reserved in the university buildings. But there were also frequent public meetings, sometimes held in the Assembly Chamber of the capitol, which were well attended by townspeople and students. Joint debates were the great scholastic events of the time, and to be chosen to represent one's literary society was a foremost distinction. Bob joined Athenae, the oldest of the societies, organized in 1850, but did not seek a place on "joint debate," for he realized this would exact too much time. Otherwise, he entered into the activities of Athenae with enthusiasm, taking a hand in the occasional stormy all-night sessions.

Very soon his college chums began coming to him for help in the delivery of their declamations and orations. He not only knew the art of interpreting thought himself, but was wonderfully successful in helping others. For many years after graduation he would spend hours coaching the university contestants, even when the pressure of his own work was intense. His experience in the Athenae Society undoubtedly developed confidence and made him aware of his own special gifts. His sister Jo remembers perfectly that in 1876, when Bob was a freshman, they walked out to the cemetery for the Memorial Day exercises and heard an impressive address by Colonel William F. Vilas. On their way home the dust was flying and fine carriages were passing. Bob stopped suddenly, took her by the arm, looked into her face, and said earnestly, "Jo, I can do that—some day they will be coming out to hear me speak." The first time his voice was heard in the capitol was on the twenty-sixth Athenaen anniversary, when he paid a brief tribute to Dr. I. A. Lapham, Wisconsin's distinguished scientist, who had recently died.

The university had recently joined the Inter-State Collegiate Association, comprising ten thousand students in fifty colleges of the six Western States, Ohio, Indiana, Illinois, Iowa, Missouri, and Wisconsin. In the spring of our freshman year, a mass meeting was called to elect representatives for the home oratorical contest. It was discovered that the secret societies had made up a slate which they had put over, leaving the great body of students unrepresented. This was the climax to prolonged fraternity manipulation in dominating college politics by electing their men to all the important posts. There was good ground for fearing that the literary societies were being undermined by the secret fraternities. Bob had spoken against this flagrant abuse of power at the mass meeting. He was indignant and his fighting spirit was aroused. That night he went to work to overturn the machine rule of the secret societies, organizing a room-to-room canvass of the non-fraternity students, who were then in an overwhelming majority. He got some two hundred students to sign a protest against the action taken at the mass meeting, with a demand for reconsideration. At a second mass meeting the secret-society slate was repudiated and the "antis" had everything their own way.[4]

I took no part in the anti-secret-society proceedings and little understood what it was all about. But I remember the excitement and the milling about of the students on the campus. Most of the girls from Ladies Hall, where I lived, who attended the mass meeting were "pro-frat" and very much disgusted when the "antis" won out.

Lulu Daniels (Lucy Daniels Thompson), one of our classmates, who was then an ardent fraternity partisan, wrote that "feeling ran high," and they "looked upon him as an outsider and a demagogical disturber of the peace." But subsequently she got a different view of him: "My roommate and I were finishing lessons late one spring evening when we were summoned downstairs to find there this same 'Bob' La Follette, come to bring us word of the expulsion from the University that afternoon of one of our closest friends, a girl from our class whom we greatly admired and loved, and who was guilty of nothing more serious than a trifling infraction of the rules in connection with her attendance at a fraternity dance the night before. The news had reached him that evening through some faculty 'leak,' ahead of the official announcement, and he had come to us at once, too full of indignation and a burning sense of the injustice of this extreme penalty to wait until morning, even, to ask our aid in uniting the class in common protest. . . .

"What thrilled us . . . was the glimpse we got of his inner nature —the quick sympathy and understanding, the revolt against injustice . . . the utter absence of anything like resentment of our earlier opposition, with instead, perfect confidence in our friendship and loyalty and a certainty that we were as ready as he to take a stand against injustice."[5]

Bob entered his sophomore year as a special student. The family had moved to a rambling old house on Frances Street, with quite a piece of ground running to the lake. Later, whenever he was in this neighborhood, he would remind us that he had once pastured his cow on some of the finest residential property in Madison, and call our attention to the fortune he could have made had he then bought the place.

During the vacation of his freshman year Bob had bought the *University Press*. He had to borrow the money, and he always had a kindly feeling for J. C. Gregory, an eminent lawyer and much-esteemed citizen of Madison, who lent him $400 on his note. Although Bob undertook the enterprise alone, he was soon able to sell a half-interest. The *Chicago Inter-Ocean* described the *University Press* of this time as "one of the liveliest and sprightliest of the college papers that comes to our table." It was published semi-monthly, financed entirely by subscriptions—of which there were about a thousand—and by advertisements, the number depending on skill and diligence in solicitation. The advertisements were often paid in merchandise, and it was a problem to dispose of it profitably. Bob went about his new undertaking with zeal, working day and night, writing editorials, gathering college news, sometimes setting type and soliciting advertising himself. The *Press* paid well, averaging some $700 a year, which afforded relief from financial pressure. He liked the work, and this experience created a longing to own a paper that was not satisfied until he started *La Follette's Magazine* some thirty years later.

In the spring of our sophomore year the Laurean Literary Society planned an entertainment to raise money for their library fund. The principal feature was a play, *Ici On Parle Français*, which portrays the troubles into which Mr. Spriggins, who kept a lodginghouse, got himself and his family by putting out a sign that

French was spoken within. Bob's impersonation of Mr. Spriggins and his frantic efforts to speak French were fine comedy. Just how Bob managed to prepare his lessons and carry on all his outside activities, I do not know; but he was able to enter his junior year as a regular student in the scientific course.

That spring he was active in amateur readings and dramatics. He appeared as the "villain" in a play at the Burrows Opera House entitled *Waves.* Major Charles G. Mayers, an Englishman who had written a number of poems, was the author. He read aloud his poems with an English enunciation which Bob listened to with a delight that doubtless helped his own clear diction. Bob never slurred a word and seldom mispronounced one; his ear was accurate, but when in doubt he always consulted a dictionary; and he also kept a thesaurus handy.

College rhetoricals in our junior and senior years consisted of orations which we prepared with some care, as they materially affected our standings. John M. Olin, our young instructor, was very strict. When I attempted to deliver my first oration, I failed to remember a word or so, gave up, and went to my seat, overwhelmed with a sense of disgrace. I thought him very hardhearted when he told me that to get any credit for my rhetorical work that year I must write a new oration and recite it perfectly.

Naturally, I was impressed with the different way Bob La Follette met a similar experience. Short and slight, there was nothing striking in his appearance as, head slightly bent, he walked up the aisle with long strides until he stood upon the rostrum and faced the audience. Then his fine brow, keen eyes, mobile face, and that something we called magnetism arrested and held the attention. His natural ease and grace, the moving quality of his voice, fine enunciation, and dramatic gesture bespoke the orator.

"The Tramp" was his theme. We were following with intense interest the speaker's portrayal of a tramp's vagabond life when suddenly, in the midst of an impassioned sentence and fitting gesture that brought the orator in side view of the audience, he "forgot." The prompter, as usually happens, had lost the place and took no end of time to find it. Bob, without the slightest change of countenance, held his arm upraised, body outstretched from toe to fingertip, until he got the cue; then, apparently unconscious of any break, unmindful that his audience was convulsed with laughter, he went on and finished in splendid form. Olin had been compelled to laugh with the rest of us; but when he made his customary criticism he sarcastically congratulated La Follette on his "cheek." When Bob told me afterward that he had been deeply humiliated by the incident and by Olin's reference to his "cheek," I could hardly take him seriously. I admired the cool self-mastery with which he had recovered his ground and effectively closed his oration.

The "Junior Ex" (exhibition) was held once a year in the Assembly Chamber at the capitol. The program was presented by representatives from the literary societies. It was not competitive; nevertheless, we thought it quite an event. There was always a good audience of students and townspeople. In 1878 Bob represented Athenae. I represented Laurea. "The Stage" was the subject of Bob's oration. In looking over the local papers of that time, I found that the *Madison Democrat* reported he placed the drama "as an art above painting and sculpture" in power and influence; and, by historical illustrations, showed the drama to be a medium of "often arousing people to the appreciation of their political state of affairs," causing them to find a remedy. The *Democrat* also spoke of his holding his audience because of his grace and because "it was evident that he believed what he said."[6]

Bob reported the Junior Exhibition for the *University Press,* omitting any notice of his own oration but praising the rest of us highly. Of my part in the program he wrote: "The audience were on the *qui vive* as the president announced the next orator's subject—'Children's Playthings'—and Miss Case, of the Laurean Society, took the stage. She fully sustained her reputation as a writer of uncommon merit. Gracefully, and in a clear ringing voice heard easily in every part of the Assembly Chamber, she pronounced an oration that for force and originality of thought and finish of composition was probably not equalled during the evening. She clearly showed how all the best natural impulses are cramped and stifled at the very beginning of life by substituting silly artificial baubles as children's playthings, for real animated living things; that, born cowards, we learn courage only by practical proofs; and the only reason why the modern young lady faints at a mouse or flies from a cow is that positive proof of their harmlessness is wanting; that, if children had living objects with which to amuse themselves and were not forced to supply with a strained imagination the animation that companionship craves, the mind would grow and develop together into a perfect unit and the other faculties would not be dwarfed by, and subject to, a wild imagination—an imagination that is the source of much injurious reading, that leads to the formation of erroneous, hurtful ideas of the world and results in the whole manhood and womanhood being spent in considering misspent childhood."[7]

After the Junior Exhibition Professor S. H. Carpenter, a rare teacher of literature, told me my talent for writing was worth cultivating. Olin also said he believed I might achieve a place as a contributor to current literature. I did not take these suggestions seriously then, as I would if I were beginning life over again. But now I realize that even the occasional writing and speaking had more value for me in afterlife than anything else at the university. To learn to speak and write easily, as a matter of course, whatever we have to say, should be one of the first objects of educational training. When our daughter Fola was in the university, the daily theme she was required to write impressed me as a wonderful advance in the method of teaching English.

At the close of our junior year, Bob and I were engaged. He would tell the children that "Mamma laughed when I proposed to her," and I would say if that was so it was Papa's fault, he had been so disposed to make me laugh when I was in his company how could I be sure he was not joking. And it was true, our relationship had been free from sentiment, so lighthearted and joyous that I preferred to keep it on that basis—at least until we finished college. But he had his own way, as he usually did; so before we parted for the summer vacation it was settled that we were to travel the road together.

CHAPTER IV

"Iago" Helps Bob Win a Degree

The outstanding event of Bob's senior year, as well as of his college course, was winning the Inter-State Oratorical Contest in May, 1879. I remember when he first read his "Iago" to me. We walked out along University Drive and sat down on a knoll under a big tree. He took the manuscript from his pocket and read reflectively, without emphasis, as though to himself. I had no knowledge by which to judge his conception of the character of Iago, but I knew how he had read and studied, how carefully every word had been chosen, every phrase considered. Before the home contest he had worked out the delivery as definitely as the thought and composition—the three standards by which the orations were judged. This does not mean that his gestures were mechanical, for he studied to make them interpretative, just as he always tried to have the right word. As an artist, he had analyzed the character of Iago; the inspiration came from within.

I have often thought of the joy it must have given Bob to write the Iago oration. His disposition was to perfect and polish whatever he wrote, and he was always reluctant to let a manuscript leave his hands. After satisfying himself that the oration was as good as he could make it, he conferred with everyone he believed might give helpful criticism. He consulted with his fellow students and with Judge A. B. Braley, a Shakespearean scholar, whose library he had used. He rehearsed with Professor David Frankenburger, head of the rhetoric department after Olin resigned to practice law. He also sought Olin's criticism.

The home contest was held in the state capitol on April 25. Bob was deeply gratified at being awarded first place. The state contest, which he had to win for the university as well as for himself, was held at Beloit a week later; a few girls, mostly classmates, were among the crowd of students who went. There was a "special train" —a coach and engine, as I recall. The day was lovely. We were much excited. The engineer and conductor must have shared our enthusiasm. We were permitted to ride in the cab, two at a time, between stations. It was a real adventure. I was sorry not to cross the state line, for at that time I had never been out of Wisconsin.

The church where the contest was held was long, narrow, and not well lighted. The character of Iago seemed more sinister, the effect of the oration more somber than at Madison. There could be no doubt about the result. He had the audience from the start. After the judges finally announced their verdict, the university boys took him on their shoulders from the church to the train, cheering and singing all the way home. It was late when we arrived at Madison, but there was a crowd of students with a band. The winner of the state contest was carried from the station to his small house on Gilman Street. There the climax of the day of triumph awaited him—the happiness and pride of his spirited little mother.

The Inter-State Contest followed at Iowa City, Iowa, on May 7, 1879. Bob arrived the day before with his friend Arthur Puls, Wisconsin delegate to the Inter-State Association. It had been arranged that Bob should stay with the president of Iowa University, and Puls with one of the professors; but he managed to have Puls go to the president's house, while he slipped away and kept to himself until time to appear on the platform the next night. The rumor got about that he was ill and might not be able to take part in the contest. Puls paid little attention to the story. He knew Bob sometimes had indigestion, but suspected he was planning a good stage entrance. It is true that when Bob appeared on the platform, the audience was so relieved he was there that he received an ovation. I do not remember ever having heard of this incident until it came to me through Dr. Puls. My own deduction is that he wanted to be by himself for a final rehearsal to make every detail as nearly perfect as he could. Dr. Puls says when he finished everyone knew he had won. Half a century later, Puls remembers how Bob held the audience spellbound. The Reverend F. L. Kenyon, of Iowa City, commented on the contest shortly afterward: "He who by the verdict of all took the first prize was the most natural in action and therefore the most effective. His words fitted his thought and his thought filled his words. . . . The truth concerning Iago was so in his mind that he was able to present to the hearer the truth and the image in such a way as to make them appear living realities."[1]

Bob had reached the goal he had set. He was modest about it, but rejoiced in the achievement and got his share of pleasure from the ceremonies and recognition that went with such a college victory. The next day, when his train reached Beloit, a crowd of citizens and students from the college welcomed him at the station. They took him from the train to the campus for a jubilation and later gave him a reception. The *Beloit Free Press* reported, "He received the profuse congratulations of his admirers as one who fully appreciated them, yet would not be unduly 'puffed up' thereby."[2] The Beloit celebration delayed Bob's return home for a day, but a large crowd with a brass band met his train at Madison. There was a long line of march, with many carriages and hundreds walking from the station to the university campus, where a great throng gathered to hear the various speeches. Our classmate, Harry Martin, presented Bob with a handsome copy of Shakespeare on behalf of the Athenae Oratorical Society.

At the evening celebration the Assembly Chamber filled early, and soon there was no standing room left. Colonel E. W. Keyes, one of the university regents, famous boss, and later Bob's bitter political enemy, presided. Professor Frankenburger, for whom Bob had a deep affection, spoke of the untiring work done by La Follette, who was modest but "had lots of thunder and lightning in him." Two eminent lawyers, George B. Smith and Colonel William F. Vilas, expressed appreciation for what the victory meant to the state and university. When the program ended, there was a call for "Iago," and Bob delivered the oration.

Winning the Inter-State Oratorical Contest doubtless helped him get his diploma. His standings in some studies and the general average of his marks were low. When the matter came up in faculty meeting, everyone conceded that La Follette had not loafed and that his time had been worthily spent. I have been told that Professor Frankenburger made a strong argument in his favor and that President Bascom cast the deciding vote for his graduation.

Bob had come to the university poorly prepared, and had earned his way through college. Then, too, he was inclined to follow his bent. If this had not been so, he would have had better marks as a student. But he would not miss a good lecture, an important court trial, or participation in extracurricular activities for the sake of his lessons the next day. He would even take the time and spend the money to go to Milwaukee or Chicago to hear a great actor, though he ran the risk of being conditioned in an examination.

Bob's course was not, however, governed by any abstract theory. He always had a profound regard for scholarship and more faith in the conventional system of education than I had. While we were still at the university, even with my limited grasp of what constituted "education," I was impressed by Bob's better knowledge of some subjects we were both studying, and his ability to apply what he knew. Most of my time was spent striving to get my lessons, and I probably had higher marks than he, in mechanics, for example, but his understanding of the principles and application of the screw and lever was practical; mine was confined to what the book said. His wider interests and more intense desire to participate in the events of life as they came along led him to seize opportunities which I missed altogether.

Among the able teachers on the faculty when we were at the university, I was particularly fortunate in coming under the influence of Dr. John B. Feuling, who taught German and French. He suggested that when we left school we should spend a few minutes a day rereading, without the use of a dictionary, the French and German we had studied. I followed the suggestion, and to Dr. Feuling I owe many years of recreation in reading German and, to a less extent, French literature. Professor William F. Allen was my favorite teacher. He was sympathetic and gentle and had a delightful appreciation of humor. From his lectures on the growth of institutions, I got my first glimpse of the relation of history to life—that it was something more than a chronological record of wars and dates.

Dr. John Bascom was the great outstanding teacher of the University of Wisconsin for the thirteen years he served as president. Bob himself said Dr. Bascom's "addresses to the students on Sunday afternoons, together with his work in the classroom were among the most important influences in my early life."[3] The university then had less than four hundred students. It was therefore possible for a man of Dr. Bascom's intellectual and moral power to impress himself on the student body in a way difficult to understand now that the university counts its students by the thousands. His manner of lecturing was formal but earnest and clear, with an occasional touch of rare humor. At times he was truly eloquent, and always impressive and moving. He "met the seniors daily throughout the year, in classes which covered the whole range of philosophy, and this meant the range of the students' serious thinking. For with him Philosophy meant not so much an inquiry into the ultimate nature of reality as a discussion of the rational side of human life. . . . Its questions were discussed from the personal and social sides."[4]

Dr. Bascom held the strict attention of his classes without any apparent effort. His examinations were especially fair. He never asked "catch" questions, his purpose being to ascertain whether his students had grasped the principles which had been thoroughly explained and emphasized. He stressed the spiritual side of life but was ever mindful of its inseparable relationship to the everyday world. Progressive in spirit, uncompromising with what he believed to be wrong, Dr. Bascom urged us to think and reason for ourselves and to translate our convictions into action. Especially did he emphasize the obligations of citizenship. Again and again he would tell us what we owed the State and impress upon us our duty to serve the State in return. Here, as in other phases of our university course, my understanding of what President Bascom was trying to implant seems to have been rather vague and general; while to Bob it was concrete truth, the living gospel, whose application was as plain as a pikestaff. In my student days I stood somewhat in awe of Dr. Bascom. Bob loved, honored, and understood him as well then as in later life. He enjoyed and made a good record in the branches which Dr. Bascom taught.

There is more reason for the mutual friendship that existed between President Bascom and Bob throughout the years than may appear on the surface. Of strikingly different mold and method, they had in common the spirit of the reformer, the same faith in what they believed a righteous cause; they had a like intensity of nature, will power, and determination to achieve practical results; both had self-mastery and an inner calm that nothing could disturb. I vividly recall that at one time, when Bob was governor, President Bascom came purposely to give him the encouragement and advice he knew so well how to render. After the first affectionate greetings, the two men spoke not at all of lesser matters. For a long time they sat together in the library talking earnestly of what was at stake in the pending political struggle, President Bascom stressing the momentous importance of the ethical victory, whatever else the outcome.

More than anyone I ever met, President Bascom impressed me as being innately sincere and conscientious, always striving to guide his action by the light of reason. He led an upright, abundant, yet restrained and disciplined, religious life. He tried to inculcate a love of nature and the beautiful in the hearts of his pupils, and he taught us true respect for labor. He found joy and recreation in working with his hands, and always cultivated his own garden. In his book *Things Learned by Living,* he expressed his philosophy when he wrote that "the world seems to me to be the very garden of God, resting under the first warm spring days of his love, and our prayer becomes that we all may thrive in this vital sunshine."[5]

Although President Bascom was awe-inspiring to some of us in the classroom, we all appreciated his social charm. His son and daughter, George and Jean Bascom, were members of our class, and for that reason we were more intimately acquainted with their ideal family life. In his home President Bascom would at times unbend and be quite playful and humorous. With his wife he was especially affectionate. They were true comrades.

Bob and I felt there never was another such strong bond of friendship among the members of a graduating class as that of 1879. Fifty years afterward, I feel that these college friendships, even though we may lose track of each other, wield an influence like that of our teachers, which enriches all the years of our lives. Bob's unusually extended personal acquaintance with the students during and after his own college days was a source of strong political support, as well as a personal joy and inspiration.

The intimate friendship with some of our classmates became an important factor in the work of later years. Harry Martin, of Darlington, who served in the state senate while Bob was governor and for some years thereafter, was a stanch, able co-worker and leader whose services cannot be overestimated in the Wisconsin progressive fight. Dr. Charles R. Van Hise, for fifteen years president of the university, was a member of the class of 1879. Dr. and Mrs. Van Hise were "Charles and Alice" to us and we were "Bob and

Belle" to them. The cordial relationship of the university and the State, their interdependence and helpfulness, were in part founded on the close ties and understanding of Van Hise and La Follette in college days. Lulu Daniels, another classmate, was professor of history at the University of West Virginia when she married J. David Thompson. They came to Washington when he became a member of the staff of the Library of Congress. With her rare qualities of mind and heart, she became an essential part of our family life at the Capital—equally helpful as counselor and friend to Bob and to me.

In our time the commencement-day program consisted of essays and orations by members of the graduating class. Our average class standing over the four years determined whether we were to have a place on the program. Sixteen of the class of thirty-five took part in the commencement exercises on June 18, 1879. It was a beautiful, bright, cool June day. Commencement exercises began at nine. Long before, people were coming in throngs through the park, up the walks into the corridors of the capitol to await the opening of the Assembly Chamber. As soon as the doors were opened, all seats were filled, many were standing as far outside as they could hear, while hundreds went away disappointed.

At that time what was known as the Lewis Prize was awarded the one whose essay or oration was marked highest by the judges. Bob's standings were too low for him to compete; and for the same reason other members of the class who were considered our best speakers were not on the program. I had chosen the subject "Learning to See." The inspiration for my theme was a few weeks of "laboratory" work under Dr. E. A. Birge, then a brilliant young instructor of zoology. He had assembled a few corals, sea urchins, starfish, and the like. As he handed us the specimens to observe and describe he said, "Tell me what you see." This was a new educational experiment for me, and I was amazed to discover how little I knew of the art of seeing.

I prepared my oration with genuine enthusiasm. Bob studied it carefully; he did not suggest any changes in thought, but he touched up the language and gave the oration rhythm and ring, as he knew how to do. Then he began drilling me in its delivery and kept me at it until he had done all he could for me. I think he expected me to win the Lewis Prize. I had little confidence in winning but was greatly pleased when it was awarded me. Though my father almost never left the work of the farm, he and Mother, who had made so many sacrifices to keep me in school in spite of the hard times, had come to see me graduate. I remember seeing their faces while I was speaking. I was happy most of all for their sakes to hear the applause that followed the judges' decision.

Before graduation from the university, Bob and I had a long talk as to the profession he might best choose and most enjoy as his life work. Besides the law, the stage had a strong appeal for him. Because of his interest in literature and teaching, we also considered a university instructorship, which would lead to a professorship, as a congenial and attractive career. After talking it all over seriously, we agreed that the most practical and ideal plan was the law for a profession and at some time a farm for a home.

CHAPTER V

Bob's First Horse-and-Buggy Campaigns

Two weeks after graduation Bob made a Fourth of July speech at Sun Prairie. "Home and the State" was the subject. It was a popular theme, suited to almost any time or place; he often spoke along the same line on later occasions. Though he had this address printed, I am unable to find a copy. I know he spoke earnestly of the interdependence of the home and the State. His feeling for their inseparable relationship never changed. A boyhood friend who was present says: "I well remember just how fine he looked on that occasion, as he stepped out confidently upon the platform erected under the shade of the native trees, on the south side of the old mill pond, dressed in Prince Albert coat, white vest, white tie and everything strictly up to date, and he certainly looked fit for the task in hand; of course his audience, made up of his old friends and neighbors, was with him heart and soul from the first word to the finish; and while I have heard many Fourth of July orations since that time, I verily believe I never heard one equal to it, or in any way approaching it in eloquence. . . . After that address I think every one present would have been willing to vote for Bob for any office within the gift of the people, including the presidency."[1]

While studying for his bar examination, Bob gave occasional readings in private homes and in neighboring towns for school or church benefits. He found great delight in listening to dialect, for his musical ear would catch the slightest burr, and he could always detect nationality in speech. He especially enjoyed the Scotch dialect and loved Burns. While in college, he spent many evenings listening to his neighbor, John Anderson, a Scotch carpenter, read his

42

favorite poet, "Bobbie" Burns. Whenever Bob read aloud from the Scotch poet, he always told us how much his friendship with John Anderson had meant.

On the bookshelves above my desk is his treasured set of *100 Choice Selections*. They belong, perhaps, to the days when "reading" was more in the nature of "elocution." But though dramatic, Bob was not "elocutionary"; his interpretation was always from *within*. In the table of contents of each volume there is a pencil mark before those most in demand. Among many others I note "Cuddle Doon," "Sheridan's Ride," "Mark Twain's First Interview with Artemus Ward" (and many others from Twain), "The First Banjo," "Thanatopsis," "Leedle Jawcob Strauss," "Curfew Must Not Ring To-Night," "Darius Green and His Flying-Machine." When we were laughing over D'rius' answer to the question, "How do yeou like flyin'?" "Wal, I like flyin' well enough, but the' ain't sich a thunderin' sight o' fun in't when ye come to light," how little we thought then that Darius' dream of a flying machine would be realized in our day, and that the problem of "lightin'" would be the very one the modern aviator would be up against.

Among his notes made long ago with a blue pencil on a yellow slip of paper, I find: "The truly great reader, like the truly great actor, is more than a mere interpreter of the author. At most, long and short—all of the speeches of the prominent character of the play furnish but a mere outline of the personality of the character. . . . The great reader, with a truly creative mind and wealth of feeling, fills out this mere outline into a full-orbed man or woman."[2] It was from this viewpoint that Bob interpreted Shakespeare or any great masterpiece of literature. He was the artist, re-creating the conception of the author.

Although Bob had won the intercollegiate prize for oratory on his analysis of Iago, he rarely gave a reading of *Othello*. He sometimes chose *King Lear, Macbeth, Richard the Third, The Taming of the Shrew,* or *The Merchant of Venice,* but *Hamlet* was closest to his heart. Though he never committed *Hamlet* entirely to memory, its language and thought were a part of his life. He read from Edwin Booth's *Prompt Book of Hamlet*, edited by William Winter. I remember when he found a paper-covered copy in a bookshop in Washington. It was good print, convenient size, and he had it bound in black morocco. Although he had many other editions, this was the one he took on his travels and kept where he could lay his hands on it day or night.

Soon after our graduation Lawrence Barrett played in Madison and, having read the Iago oration, asked Bob to make for him a similar study of Hamlet. Bob gladly agreed. After much research and thought, that afforded delightful recreation in a life of intense strain, he finally completed, to his satisfaction, his lecture on Hamlet—twenty years later!

When Bob visited us during the summer vacation after graduation, he won the hearts of all my family, including aunts, uncles, and grandparents. We had a picnic for him at Devil's Lake and spent a day at the Dells of the Wisconsin River; it was quite an event for farmers to leave their work in harvest-time and give a whole day to pleasure. In all the years afterward, when we were to come to the old home, my mother would write, "Be sure that Bob brings something to read." At the Christmas holiday season on those long winter evenings, the day's work done, our relatives and friends gathered to hear him. We would not let him stop. For refreshments mother had a large dish of popcorn ready and father brought up apples from the cellar. It was late for country people when the party broke up. When he interpreted *Hamlet*, my father would follow him, forgetful of everything else; he would grow pale with emotion and his fine face would reveal the understanding of a mind profoundly in touch with nature. Bob was always conscious of this native power of the plain people to grasp thought. It never occurred to him to speak "down" to his audiences or to consider any theme beyond their reach. He talked straight to them on the basis of mutual native intelligence and mother wit. In my judgment no one will ever fully understand his power over people who does not take into account his dramatic instinct, which enabled him to enter into the lives of his fellow men and stir them to action.

Bob was admitted to the bar on February 5, 1880, seven months after graduation from the university. In the meantime he had attended one term of law school and had been working in the law office of R. M. Bashford, a lawyer of high standing, who later became a Wisconsin Supreme Court Justice. Seven months of study were meager preparation for a bar examination even when the requirements were on the basis of only two years of law school. But for several years he had attended court whenever important cases were being tried. His retentive memory and alert mind enabled him to make good use of what he gained by listening to the leading lawyers. It was excellent training both for a bar examination and for subsequent law practice. Although in his *Autobiography* he referred lightly to his first cases, he prepared and tried each one with the same personal interest and zest that characterized all his later work. His first case, the defense of a tramp, the *State* vs. *Rogers,* was tried in the municipal court before Judge Braley, whose Shakespearean library Bob had used when preparing his Iago oration.

Four tramps had entered a schoolhouse to spend the night. A small posse was organized to arrest them and drive them from the neighborhood. In the encounter a shot was fired which slightly wounded the constable. The tramps escaped, but two days later one of them, named Rogers, was arrested and charged with shooting with intent to kill. The tramp secured the firm for which Bob was working to defend him. Although not yet admitted to the bar, he was practically put in charge of the case. He immediately saw Rogers at the county jail and became convinced that the tramp was innocent of the crime. When captured, Rogers had a small revolver carrying the smallest cartridge manufactured. Bob questioned the physician who had dressed the constable's wound, and Dr. Ward said it must have been made by a larger bullet. The following night Bob cautiously confided to his diary, "I really think I can make a strong case for Rogers; unless the prosecution have proof of which we have no intimation."[3]

There was a large crowd in the courtroom when the case came up the next day, November 17, 1879. The trial consumed the entire day. Bob worked his defense out step by step and, although the prosecution brought in testimony which surprised him, he met it better than he would have thought he could. Under his searching cross-examination several prosecution witnesses, who had been present at the shooting, admitted they could not definitely identify the defendant although they believed he had fired the shot. The district attorney briefly reviewed the testimony, and Bob made his first plea to a jury. Within an hour they returned a verdict of "not guilty." That night Bob noted in his "Private Journal and Night Thoughts": "I do not know how long I spoke I lost the time and all else save the testimony & the truth in it. . . . Though not unmindful of the words of honest praise bestowed on my effort by both the Judge and lawyers present, the words of gratefulness given me by my first client was more than all else & his great joy at the verdict of not guilty returned in an hour by the jury paid me better than would a heavy fee."[4]

But all approval was not equally welcomed even at the age of twenty-four. A few days later Bob made a notation in this same private diary which shows he had already clearly defined certain principles that guided his later work: "I have been many times complimented for getting him [Rogers] acquitted by Dr. Baker Col Keyes & others but I do not like the way they bestow their praise. They seem to consider that I did a smart thing—that I was sharp in the management of the matter and keen in the argument —but they don't seem to think that I did it all because I thought he was innocent—that I was simply fighting a fight for the truth—that his vindication was a *truth*. That is the way I like to think of it & the way I did think of it else I should not have tried so earnestly to win. This must be my rule in all my work & will give me the approval of my conscience & my little girl [Belle]."[5]

The *Madison Democrat*, in a report of the trial which was to be widely circulated later, stated that Bob's "argument to the jury was effective and eloquent and called forth the greatest praise from the bench and the bar."[6] His defense of the tramp and his method of handling a few other cases were important factors a year later in his campaign for district attorney. The Democratic opponent was R. M. Bashford, who, when Bob was working in his office, had put him in charge of the tramp case. A Democratic campaign circular was issued stating that La Follette had no experience as a lawyer. Whereupon a committee of Republican lawyers, among the most distinguished at the bar, prepared a statement quoting the *Madison Democrat* and citing an eminent legal authority who said that in a criminal case of legal importance "Mr. La Follette made his defense with marked ability and displayed a familiarity with criminal law which surprised him."[7]

The district attorneyship attracted Bob because he could go into practice immediately and also earn a salary. He knew criminal-trial work would appeal to him, and at that time he was especially interested "in being a lawyer—a good lawyer."[8]

Wisconsin was then a boss-ridden, corporation-controlled State.

It was a bold thing for a young man to become a candidate for district attorney of Dane County, as Bob had, without the consent of the Republican boss Colonel E. W. Keyes, then postmaster of Madison. Keyes called him into his office and told him that he was wasting his time and money, that the next district attorney had already been slated, and that his name wasn't La Follette. "Boss Keyes did not know it," Bob said, "but opposition of that sort was the best service he could have rendered me. It stirred all the fight I had in me."[9]

His indignation aroused, he went to work as though his life depended on winning the office. His method was the simple one he adhered to through the years. He went directly to the voters. With his gray mare Gypsy and a buggy loaned by his friend and supporter Ben Miner, he canvassed Dane County. It was harvest-time, and he went into the fields and talked with the farmers face to face. Visiting with them in the evenings at their homes, he would spend the night and get a good start next morning. His opponents called him the "night rider." The friends he made would tell him which neighbors he should see. He covered the ground thoroughly, keeping a memorandum of everyone he met, particularly those who expressed interest. The chief objection he met was, "Ain't you over-young?" Even then he had an issue; the retiring district attorney had been inefficient and had employed a great deal of help, which increased the taxpayers' burden; Bob promised he would do all the work himself.

It was before the days of primaries; at the caucuses delegates were chosen to the county convention which decided the nominations on the county ticket. There were five candidates, and it was the voters in the section about Primrose, his birthplace and boyhood home, who decided the contest. Eli Pederson, prosperous farmer and local political leader, who had known Bob's father, was their spokesman. At a critical moment between ballots, Pederson's moving speech claiming Bob as "our boy" resulted in his nomination for district attorney.

Although the district was normally Republican, he had a hard fight to be elected, for Boss Keyes preferred the Democratic candidate to this young Republican rebel who had defied his dictatorship. Again Bob personally canvassed the county and organized his friends to work for him. He and some of his university friends, including Sam Harper, spoke in the 1880 campaign; the younger men did teamwork with the older, more experienced speakers. Bob won by ninety-three votes. The first newspaper account of a political speech by him was probably the *Wisconsin State Journal*'s report of a meeting at Paoli which noted that he spoke "briefly but eloquently" and "closed with a glowing appeal to old soldiers and young men to reclaim the country from threatened rebel domination, and not to allow the fruits of the war to go unplucked."[10]

The first case Bob tried as district attorney had a painful moment which he often described amusingly. He had made very thorough preparation, but when the case was called and he answered "Ready," the judge asked if the accused had been "arraigned." Bob had only a vague idea as to the legal meaning of "arraigned." To hesitate or admit ignorance of this elementary step in criminal procedure would be fatal. He boldly replied that he would examine the papers prepared for the case by his predecessor to see what the record showed. As he thumbed them rapidly, his good friend F. J. Lamb, one of the oldest attorneys at the bar, took a seat at the table, and Bob, still noisily turning the papers, whispered to him, "For Heaven's sake, tell me what it means to 'arraign' a prisoner!" Lamb, realizing the situation, replied without attracting attention, "Ask the prisoner to stand up and say whether he is guilty or not guilty of the charge." Bob, laying down his bundle of papers, gravely announced that the record did not show whether the accused had been "arraigned" but that there might be no question he would "arraign" him. He then went through the customary procedure without hesitation.

He carried out his pledge to the Dane County voters to do the work himself. Nights and Sundays found him at his office "digging, digging."[11] He keenly enjoyed preparing the cases and presenting them in perfect order to the court. When a crime was committed, he always tried to be the first on the ground to interview all the witnesses and see the surroundings. He believed, "It is the facts that settle cases; the law is always the same."[12] An eminent member of the bar thus describes his method as a prosecuting officer: "La Follette mastered every conceivable detail of a case. . . . He tried his case like a trip hammer. There was no groping about; fact followed fact in quick succession, creating to the jury the picture which the young district attorney himself had framed in his mind."

He had a keen detective sense, was resourceful and knew when to employ strategy. One case admirably illustrates his skill and intuition. A series of burglaries had been committed in Madison. Among other things a blue suit had been taken from a boarding-house, some neckties from a clothing store, some tools from a black-smith shop, and a café had been burglarized. Two men who gave their names as Edwards and Simmons were finally trapped in an old deserted house on Lake Mendota known as the "Castle." One of them wore the blue coat and vest, the other the trousers of the missing suit. They had on stolen neckties. These were relatively lesser crimes. However, Bob was convinced they were hardened criminals and went about finding proof that they had robbed the café safe. The tools taken from the blacksmith shop were finally found hidden in the "Castle" with the belongings of the two thieves —among them a sledge, a punch, and a drill. The locksmith Bob took with him to examine the safe after the burglary thought a larger drill had been used than the one found; but Bob observed that the difference in size of the opening was due to the wobbling of the drill, that the punch had an irregular end, and that an indentation in the brass lock exactly fitted the irregular punch. These and other discoveries made fine circumstantial evidence against the prisoners.

On the day of the trial, Bob noticed in the back of the courtroom two strange women who were evidently much concerned over the case. One was holding a baby. Intuitively he sensed that an attempt would be made to establish an alibi. Sure enough, one of the prisoners testified that on the night of the crime he had been in Baraboo and that he remembered the exact time of his visit because his sister's baby was born that night, June 16. Mrs. Merritt, the woman with the baby, proved to be the prisoner's sister and confirmed his alibi. Unless the testimony could be overthrown by rebuttal, the case was lost. Bob used every possible device to delay the trial until the hour of adjournment arrived. The judge was obviously exasperated. Older lawyers sent notes warning Bob to stop if he wished to continue practicing law before that court. Finally the judge censured him sharply for wasting time. He bore the chastisement meekly.

The moment court adjourned, he sent the sheriff to Baraboo, instructing him to be at his office early next morning with the baby's father and the nurse who had assisted at the birth. This necessitated a forty-mile horse-and-buggy drive and a return on the four o'clock morning train. Bob slept in his office awaiting the sheriff. When court opened, he had the husband and nurse seated behind the door where they could not be seen.

When the trial was resumed, the counsel for the defense was smiling and confident of a speedy acquittal. "How much time is wanted for argument?" asked the judge. Against the protest of opposing counsel and the court, Bob insisted he had witnesses in rebuttal. In a ringing voice he called "Soloman Merritt." At this name the prisoner, suddenly losing his cool self-assurance, slunk into his chair while the two women rushed for the door. "Stop them," the district attorney ordered. The silence was intense as Bob drew from the husband the fact, confirmed by the nurse, that the baby had been born on May 10, instead of June 16, as testified the previous day; he also brought out the prisoner's real name and bad record. The testimony of her husband established the wife's perjury beyond doubt. The case was submitted to the jury without argument, and the two men were sent to the penitentiary. One of them said after the trial: "That damned little cuss seemed to know every single step I took and everything I did. When he opened the case to the jury he actually told some things I had forgotten."

Bob had an instinct for cross-examination of witnesses. What I consider one of his most notable addresses was made before the graduating class of Howard University Law School in 1886. The address in its entirety indicates how much thought he had given to his profession, though at that time he had only practiced law five years. Of cross-examination he said:

"To be able always to conduct a cross-examination with advantage is indeed a rare power. It is difficult to define. It is that 'other intuition,' which makes you know the witness when he has answered the first question as though he were a part of you; it enables you to determine the workings of his mind; to anticipate his thoughts; to know when he is about to hurt you with invented testimony; to know how to lead him along, step by step, just up to that critical point—deceiving him into the belief that he is deceiving you—getting all that is helpful to your cause out of him, and then dismissing him just short of where he had aimed to strike the fatal blow. This is genius and is, in part at least, the gift of nature. It can never be acquired in its fullest perfection."[13]

Bob's dramatic gift was helpful both in his criminal cases and in general law practice. I have heard him say that he could assume the posture and expression of a witness and tell whether he was lying or not. But he never relied in advance on his dramatic intuition. At times, in anticipation of a trial, a speech in Congress, or a political campaign, I felt he was overzealous, too cautious, in making his preparation. His standard was perfection; he wanted to be sure his proof was invulnerable. Every speech was important to him: it had its moment of dread before he began, its inspirational thrill when he had won the audience, and its satisfaction when his hearers expressed their approval afterward. Although overapprehensive in the preparatory stage of any work, once engaged in the fray he was alert, aggressive, confident, courteous, ready to meet emergencies and surprises with a spontaneous skill and swift decision that made him a dreaded adversary. He seldom failed to make the most of every opportunity to convince a jury or audience. That he was often at his best when speaking spontaneously all who ever observed him well knew.

In reply to a letter giving an account of the trial of a criminal case by our son Phil, who was then district attorney of Dane County, Bob wrote on April 30, 1925: "In my trial work, I used to have a logical skeleton of the argument framed by the time the case was ready to submit, with the language of special features of the argument and climaxes well thought out at least in advance of delivery. But of course each one must work out his own system. However, I have no sympathy with, nor confidence in, the fellow who pretends that he gets the best results on the inspiration of the moment. He may have a flash of mental ecstasy while under the intellectual stress of speaking, but he is more likely to have a brain fluke—with a mediocre result."[14]

Bob's successful trial of criminal cases soon brought him a great deal of civil practice—more than he could handle. Convinced that he and his brother-in-law, Robert Siebecker, would do well in partnership, the firm La Follette and Siebecker was established in the fall of 1881. It was a daring venture for the two young men, "Bob" and "Robert," to start out alone in their profession without any financial backing. I have heard Robert say he had doubts and fears; but Bob was confident they would be much more independent and successful by themselves. He was right: with his success in the trial of criminal cases the civil practice grew so rapidly that when he left the district attorneyship La Follette and Siebecker had more civil cases on the circuit-court calendar than any firm in Madison. Bob's inclination and gifts were more especially for trial work, Robert's for preparing briefs and making legal argument. Robert would sometimes say that Bob knew better off hand what the law of a case would be than most lawyers after they had looked it up. But Bob's intuitive sense of legal principles never led him to rely on "guessing the law." Bob's high ideals of the authority and essential purpose of the law and the courts always remained the same. He recognized the need of reforms to meet changing conditions; but in all his efforts toward securing greater social justice he always sought to preserve legal principles and the courts.

While Bob was making such rapid and brilliant headway in his profession, I was teaching school. I had loved school. Though each day I walked a mile to and from school, I had attended for twelve successive years without being late or missing a day except for one brief illness of measles. I never missed a class nor was I late while in the university. The day I went to Beloit to hear Bob give "Iago," I had to skip out before a class was finished to catch a train. This compromise cost me quite a struggle. I wasn't sure I could conscientiously say I had not missed a class.

During the first year I taught, I was assistant principal of the Spring Green High School. The principal, Mr. Delamatyr, an old experienced teacher, was a Civil War veteran. He exercised an easy, natural control over the school. There were apparently no rules. Great freedom and much give-and-take existed between teachers and scholars, but never a suggestion of disorder or disrespect. Once, when I asked the principal the secret of his management, he laughingly replied, "I put them on their honor and then watch 'em." The students, though poorly graded—ahead in some things, behind in others—were there because they were eager for an education. They were paying tuition, more often than not with money they had earned themselves. Some were older than I; some were district schoolteachers. I had to work hard to keep in advance of them in the branches I taught. It was interesting and stimulating. There was growth in teaching such a school. Bob once visited me at Spring Green. I do not remember it, but was told not long ago there is a tradition that Bob La Follette and Belle Case ran a race "right in the village street." It is not recorded who won, but I was a good runner for a girl. When I was nine years old, there was only one boy in school who could run faster than I could.

The next year I taught seventh grade in the Baraboo school, where the pupils' ages ranged from twelve to fourteen. Some of them, especially the boys, were bored, attending only because their parents insisted. I was not altogether successful in solving the problem of arousing their interest. For one thing, I had to keep them all headed for the same goal—passing their examinations for the next grade. And I did not appreciate the importance of encouraging the natural bent of a pupil when I had the chance to do so; I put all the emphasis on having a good lesson.

John Ringling, a tall, heavy, dark-eyed boy, was one of my pupils. Good-natured, full of fun but not unruly, he had little taste for lessons or books. When it came to "composition," I was wise enough to ask the class to write of things they knew about. But when John Ringling read a long account—interrupted with giggles from the school—of the side shows he and other boys had been giving every night, instead of praising what was John's first attempt at self-expression, I lectured him and drew the moral that if John would put his mind on his lessons as he did on side shows, he might yet become a scholar. Fortunately, the scolding had no effect. Soon after, he and his older brothers started a small circus in which they themselves took the leading parts as musicians, tumblers, clowns, ringmaster, and animal trainer. Such was the beginning of "Ringling's World-Renowned Circus."

On December 31, 1881, Bob and I were married at my home in Baraboo. The ceremony was performed by a Unitarian minister; the word "obey" was omitted. My grandfather had recently died, but our wedding would have been simple under any circumstances—just Bob's folks and mine.

On the day of our marriage, he was in court trying an important case. The story, often told by a friend, was that, noticing a memorandum on the table in front of Bob which read, "Five p.m. Go to Baraboo," he asked what it meant. Bob replied: "Yes, I am going to

Baraboo tonight to be married. I mustn't forget that." It is true that he left his work and came back to it without interruption. Following our wedding, we took the train to Madison and went to his home on West Wilson Street, where we were to live for nineteen years. To buy this home, the old farm in Primrose had been sold. I know it cost him a struggle to part with the farm, but he consoled himself with the thought that he would buy it back some day. The Madison home, which he and his mother and sister bought, had large grounds; the main part of the house had been a dignified old residence whose good architecture, high ceilings, French windows, and marble mantels we did not at that time appreciate. Jo had married Robert Siebecker, and although our two families and Bob's mother occupied the house together it was so large we had to close some of the rooms. Later we made it over into two separate homes.

At that time the salary of the Dane County district attorney was $800 a year. To me, who had always lived on a farm, this seemed a magnificent sum with which to start housekeeping. I soon learned the difference between the cost of living in town, where everything is bought, and on the farm, where there is usually something to sell. One of our first extravagances was to buy some books. Besides several editions of Shakespeare, Bob had a small collection of poetry, novels, histories, and speeches. He had given me a set of Goethe and Schiller. We bought Walter Scott, Washington Irving, George Eliot, Fenimore Cooper, and a few others, which, with our *Encyclopaedia Britannica* acquired later, just filled a bookcase we ordered specially made for our "library."

Bob felt the need of more thorough preparation in elementary law, and the first year we were married he and I spent many evenings reading Blackstone, Kent's *Commentaries*, and other elementary lawbooks. When some troublesome questions arose in his cases, we would go to the office, look up the law, and discuss it together. Thus I became interested in reading law and found it a keenly enjoyable intellectual training, quite different from any other studying I had ever done.

When our first baby, Fola, was born, I was profoundly happy. During the first year of infancy her care absorbed my thought and time. I experienced wonderful contentment and restfulness of spirit, although I had never been troubled over problems of a career. I believe the supreme experience in life is motherhood; yet I am sure there is no inherent conflict in a mother's taking good care of her children, developing her talents, and continuing to work along lines adapted to motherhood and homemaking.

Bob was the first to suggest that I take the University of Wisconsin law course. It did not require much urging to convince me I could do so without neglecting my child and other home duties. The course was then two years. I entered in 1883 and was graduated in 1885, being the first woman to graduate from the University of Wisconsin Law School.

Living in Madison brought us in close touch again with some of our dearest university friends. We were also especially fortunate in our next-door neighbors, the Burdicks. Elisha Burdick was a large real-estate owner who had come to Madison from New York State in the early days. Unusual in mind and character, when occasion demanded he had a power of varied and vigorous speech which Bob used to say he had never heard equaled. His wife, Maria Edmond Burdick, had come from New York City as a lovely bride of eighteen. Intelligent, gracious, and kind, she always upheld the tradition of the old Livingston family to which she belonged. She enjoyed having Bob read at their home; and he delighted in the gaiety and discerning wit of this interesting and original family. A daughter, Mary Burdick, relates that when Fola was a little girl her father sent her to invite the Burdicks to some function at our home. When asked who should come, she answered, "Oh, Papa said to invite *all* the Burdicks because they don't stand around in corners and say nothing." A strong bond existed between the families.

When we could afford it, we built a partnership barn with the Siebeckers across the street. Over one of the box stalls was written "Nut Brown Maid." This was Gypsy's chestnut colt which my father had raised for us. Sam Harper named her. She lived to be thirty years old and was the family pet all our children learned to ride and drive. Naturally, Bob wished to raise a colt from Maid. Each year he sent her to be bred. I sometimes said his political opponents would be discouraged if they knew his determination to perpetuate the line of horses he had owned and loved from boyhood. Maid was eighteen years old before she foaled, and then her colt was a weakling with an undershot jaw. The veterinarian said the colt could not live, but Bob would not give up; he worked with the veterinarian night and day to save her. "Maidie," as we nick-named her, grew up to be a beautiful combination driving and saddle mare.

Although we had ample grounds and were happy at the Wilson Street house, we never thought of it as our lifetime home. We had agreed that when we could afford it we would have a farm. It was not Bob's intention to give up his profession or his part in politics, but he wanted the farm life for himself and his family. In this we were in accord, as we were in most things. It was probably quite natural that, having much the same background and having gone through college together, we should have a similar attitude toward life. We seldom seriously differed, and I think I can honestly say we never quarreled. At times one or the other or both may have been deeply hurt, as happens in making life's adjustments; but we did not nurse the sense of wrong, nor did we discuss it. We treated it as we would physical pain—a cut or burn which it was useless to think much about and which would heal in time. We were ourselves good comrades and we were comrades with our children. In his home Bob was habitually cheerful; his wit and humor gladdened our lives in a way only those who knew him well can understand. For the most part he was able to bear his disappointments with light heart and jest. Only a few times did he ever yield to depression. And those were dark days.

Bob was renominated for district attorney by acclamation at the Republican convention in 1882. So generally had he won the ap-proval of the people that even Boss Keyes did not attempt to oppose his renomination. As district attorney Bob's time and thought had been occupied exclusively with his legal work. His only encounters with the political ring came through attempts to influence the prose-cution of cases. These pressures were manifested in subtle ways: witnesses faded out of reach of the sheriff's office, juries disagreed, or Bob was indirectly warned to drop cases.

When the chairman of the Republican State Central Committee, who had been gambling and drinking in a Madison hotel, was robbed, he tried to prevent prosecution of the case lest it give publicity to his disreputable conduct. Bob told him the case would be tried regard-less of reputations, and he subpoenaed the chairman as a witness. At another time, while Bob was ill in bed, word came that because

Boss Keyes was using his influence the judge was about to dismiss a case that should be tried. Against the doctor's advice Bob insisted upon being carried into the courtroom to protest the action of the judge. The case was put over and the defendant subsequently found guilty.

Dane County went Democratic in 1882. Bob was the only Republican candidate elected. He ran 2,000 votes ahead of his ticket and won by 118 votes over his Democratic opponent, A. E. Hayes. The second term made the same exacting demands on his time and had the same absorbing interest for him.

On May 30, 1884, Bob delivered the Memorial Day address at Madison's beautiful cemetery, under the auspices of the C. C. Washburn Grand Army Post. Many of his audience were Civil War veterans, and I believe this address materially helped his nomination and election to Congress in 1884. Our beloved friend General George E. Bryant introduced him. After Bob began, it seemed to me no one moved until he had finished. No one was more spellbound than I. The cadence of his voice, the rhythm of his words carried me along, quite unconscious of who was speaking.

I see him now in his youth, against the background of trees and sky—at one with his audience, in perfect accord with the spirit of the day.

CHAPTER VI

The Youngest Member of Congress

Sam Harper's suggestion that Bob run for Congress was at first rather casual, but soon they were giving it serious thought. The fact that Bob had run 2,000 ahead of his ticket in his reelection to the district attorneyship had made his candidacy possible. But in those days, and through the years, for that matter, we never took an important step without careful consideration.

General Bryant, who had been an intimate friend of General Grant's, was an indispensable factor in Bob's election to Congress. Though Bryant came from a fine old New England family and was a native of Vermont, he had a large following among the old soldiers throughout the Third Congressional District, many of them having served in his Wisconsin regiment. Through his own experience on his well-managed farm, he understood the farmers' point of view. He was a good lawyer, who had for years been county judge, and knew the people. He had advised Bob's mother on the administration of their estate. While a student at the university, Bob had frequently consulted this wise, lovable man, and a strong bond had grown up between them. Years later, during his last illness, the "general," as we affectionately called him, wrote Bob that next to his wife and his two boys, "I loved you and Sam Harper better than any one else in the world."

My instinctive love of home and dread of change led me, in a mild way, to take the negative side of the argument. Bob was on the road to success in his profession; Madison offered every advantage of a permanent home for ourselves and the children we wanted. Why sacrifice such a prospect for the uncertainty of a public career with its inevitable change in our mode of living? I was not insistent; I recognized his unusual gifts and wanted him to follow his bent. It

was not long before I was happy and content in the thought of his
going to Congress.

Bob canvassed Dane County as he had before. He went directly
to the people, but now he was widely known and had many friends.
Sam spent thirty days making a similar horse-and-buggy campaign
in his home county of Grant. General Bryant worked untiringly in
his own effective way.

Soon the pattern of Bob's first campaign for district attorney was
repeated. But instead of Boss Keyes himself, it was his lieutenant,
Philip Spooner, brother of John C. Spooner, afterward United States
Senator, who stopped Bob on the street and told him he could not go
to Congress. It was unheard of, he said, to nominate a Congressional
candidate from the capital-city district without consulting Keyes
and his friends.

One unusual incident is pleasant to remember. Senator Spooner's
father was a learned lawyer and courteous gentleman who lived in
our neighborhood. Meeting Bob on the street one day, he gave him
his hand, saying he intended to vote for him, as he thought Bob
would make a worthy representative. Bob was deeply touched by
this impartial expression of confidence.

From start to finish the fight for the nomination was bitter. Boss
Keyes and his allies, the Federal office holders, were working day
and night to beat Bob. He and his friends were equally determined
and busy. Both sides were surprised at the numbers who came to the
caucuses. On the very night Bob got the final returns, showing he
had won Dane County, he received a telegram from Sam saying he
had also carried Grant County. After the votes were counted at
one of the caucuses, Boss Keyes looked over the crowd and remarked stoically, "It's the young fellows that did it." The Congressional convention met on September 9 at Dodgeville. H. C. Adams,
a well-known dairy farmer, made the nominating speech, seconded
by Sam Harper. Bob was nominated on the first ballot. His acceptance speech was brief and conventional. On his return to Madison
he was given an enthusiastic reception at the Republican wigwam.
Governor Rusk predicted, in his characteristic fashion: "The hero
of Dodgeville was destined to be a great man . . . to go to Washington
where I have been and he'll have to follow my tracks. He'll probably
go further than I have gone. He'll probably yet be President of the
United States."

Bob started a vigorous speaking campaign for election. He paid
the conventional tributes to the Republican Party, arraigned Democratic free-trade policy, and upheld the protective tariff because it
benefited the workingman. But he had been out only a short time
when illness compelled him to come home and go to bed. His friends
ran headquarters and carried on the speaking campaign. The Democratic candidate was Burr W. Jones, a man of fine character and
a lawyer of high standing. He had made a good record during his
two years in Congress and had an excellent chance of reelection.
The Keyes forces were pitted against Bob, and he was, therefore,
well satisfied when he won by the small margin of a 491 plurality.

Throughout the nomination campaign the *Madison Democrat*,
alarmed by his big vote two years earlier, had fought him. In the
election campaign it went even further, reporting that "for dema-
goguery and falsehood" his Dodgeville acceptance speech "was a
great success. . . . It opened with a wholesale charge that every
man who ever voted the democratic ticket—living or dead—was
both a thief and a traitor."[1] The absurdity of such a statement
should have been its own answer, since Bob, with the Keyes forces
against him, was depending on Democratic support in Dane County
for his election. But the boldness and persistent reiteration of the
falsehood had some effect, for I remember that we received many
serious inquiries about it in spite of specific denials by those who
had heard the speech.

It was my first experience with newspaper vilification.

Bob was elected to Congress in November, 1884. Though his
term of office and salary began on March 4, 1885, he was not due to
take his seat until the following December. However, he made good
use of the year's interim by starting at once to equip himself in a
practical way. In January, following his election, he went to Washington and stayed until after President Cleveland was inaugurated
on March 4. Bob was twenty-nine and had never been east of
Chicago. The journey was always a vivid memory. He went by way
of Harper's Ferry and saw the battlefields and the prison where
John Brown had been confined. His first view of the Capitol stirred
him deeply, evoking thoughts of Jefferson, Hamilton, Clay, and
Lincoln. Among the impressions he never forgot were a day spent
at Mount Vernon and his visit to Lincoln Park before breakfast on
the first morning in Washington. There he stood, with head bared,

before the statue of Lincoln holding in one hand the Proclamation of Emancipation, the other extended over the head of a kneeling Negro from whose wrists the shackles had fallen. He attended the sessions of Congress with the same regularity and interest as though already a Member. Listening to the discussion of important questions led him to read political history, the great speeches, and Elliott's debates, for he was eager to master the fundamental principles and understand the underlying causes of current issues.

I remember how vividly he related his impressions when he came home. For the first time I began to realize what a change it was to be—what a break in the current of our quiet home life. It was even greater than I anticipated. During the many years we were in Washington, our experiences varied, but one feeling was always the same—that of being unsettled. Washington is a beautiful city, the official life interesting and colorful. Officially we met many delightful people and made some close friends; but however pleasantly we were situated, however long we occupied a house, it was never *home*. While in Washington we were thinking of returning home; when at home we knew we must soon return to Washington.

At the time that Bob was elected to Congress, it was the practice of railroad companies to give public officials passes, which they and their families used without question or scruple. When Bob received the usual favors, we conferred with General Bryant, Sam Harper, and others. Bob argued that he should be under no obligation to railroad companies which were likely to be the subject of legislation. Finally it was agreed that, since the question was not then a public issue, it would avail nothing to return the passes and become involved in a futile controversy. They were, therefore, delivered in a sealed envelope to Sam Harper's keeping, and Bob paid his railroad transportation. Doubtless his attitude was a reflection of the Granger movement and the deep impression which Chief Justice Ryan's warning had made.

When we left for Washington, my plans were tentative. Our little daughter, Fola, was to stay with my mother until, as I thought, we could adjust ourselves to the new environment and find the right place to live. We wanted to be near the Capitol, and we found a private house in southeastern Washington. Like many houses at that time, the only heat was a Latrobe heater. When a cold wave struck Washington, it was impossible to keep warm. In all our hard Wisconsin winters, we had never suffered so much from the cold indoors. We moved to 18 Grant Place, N.W., where we had a grate fire and were comfortable in a "back parlor" with "use of the front parlor." Hotels were popular for Congressmen who could afford it. There were few apartment houses. For the Congressman wholly dependent on his salary, the boardinghouse seemed the only choice. We could not afford to keep our room throughout the year, so we were obliged to change many times. There were always some interesting people wherever we lived, although the social life was too much influenced by women without any special occupation, whose thoughts were centered on society, dress, cards, and gossip.

The opening of Congress always has a thrill for the public. The wife of a new Member watches with quickening pulse as the Congressmen assemble on the floor. The appearance of the Speaker at his desk, the calling of the House to order, the prayer of the chaplain, the taking of the oath, the allotment of seats, were all matters of absorbing interest to me when the Forty-ninth Congress convened.

Bob had described to us in his vivid way Speaker Carlisle of Kentucky, Reed of Maine, McKinley, and other interesting personalities, but Speaker Carlisle was even more impressive than I had anticipated. As seen from the galleries, presiding over the House, he seemed created for the part. His perfect poise, judicial manner, even voice, sound reasoning, and impartial ruling invested the office with power and importance that stay with me to this day. It was at one of Mrs. Carlisle's receptions that I first met the Speaker and was much disappointed at the near view of his face. He had the distinguished bearing and courtly manners I had expected, but his eyes were cold, the expression hard, almost repellent.

At that time and until recent years, Members of the House drew their seats by lot. Bob's choice came late, but he was fortunate in getting a seat next to Ben Butterworth of Ohio and not far from Tom Reed. Tom Reed was a commanding figure, but, unlike Carlisle, his personality made a more favorable impression near at hand. When observed from the galleries, his imposing stature, serious countenance, high-pitched voice, brevity of statement, and cutting wit revealed the masterful leader that he was, but did not suggest his genial, social qualities. Nearby, however, his large black eyes lighted up when he smiled; his humor was kindly; his attitude that of a friendly philosopher who enjoyed the company of his fellow men. Nothing suggested the "czar." He was cordial, democratic, and magnetic. The report by Reed in favor of woman suffrage was in great demand throughout the years the subject was under discussion. It was the argument of a statesman and carried weight. Mrs. Reed was attractive and pleasing, but somewhat reserved. She never became as popular as Mrs. Carlisle, who seemed born for the part she played in the social life of Washington.

When the Forty-ninth Congress convened, Joe Cannon had already served six terms. He was not then known as "Uncle Joe," but he had already won the reputation of being a good fighter and a rough-and-ready debater. I was always glad when he got into the fray, because I felt sure "our side" would have the best of it.

McKinley's personality was much the same whether studied from the galleries or at close range. He was a fine speaker, earnest, often eloquent. His voice had a moving quality always to be remembered. He inspired the admiration of spectators and the affectionate regard of his associates. He had an innate dignity and at the same time a warm, sympathetic nature. Bob was very fond of him. Mrs. McKinley was an invalid, and her countenance had a worn look, but it was evident she had been a beautiful girl. Major McKinley was devoted to her. When away, he sent her a message each day. Once, in reply to the question of a friend as to what he could find to say, I heard her answer, "He can say he loves me."

The senior Senator from Wisconsin at this time was Philetus Sawyer, a multimillionaire lumberman, who was later to subject Bob to a painful ordeal which had a profound influence on his life and proved to be a turning point in his career. Sawyer, born in Vermont in 1816, was a "self-made man" with a shrewd, active mind. His schooling was meager but he had native ability. "He had tramped the forests, cruised timber, slept in the snow, built saw mills" and made several million dollars.[2] Politics was to him, as to many men of his time and type, an instrument for promoting the enterprises with which he and his friends were identified. Bob always thought that Sawyer's methods did not violate his own conscience, and that when necessary he bought men as he had saw logs or an interest in a railroad. His generous contributions and particular abilities made him a dominant figure both in the state and national Republican organizations. He was closely associated with

Henry C. Payne, Boss Keyes, and John C. Spooner, the junior
Senator from Wisconsin. Sawyer had served ten years in the House
and had been elected to the Senate in 1881. He was a loyal Republican, according to his lights, and a power in Wisconsin politics
until his death in 1900.

Soon after we came to Washington, Sawyer had shown Bob the
courtesy of taking him to call on President Cleveland and members
of the Cabinet. As they drove about in Sawyer's carriage, he talked
to Bob "in a kindly, fatherly manner—very matter-of-fact," looking at him "from time to time with a shrewd squint in his eye."
Introducing Bob as "Follette," a young man who "we think . . . is
going to amount to something," he said: "I'd like him to get all
that is coming to him in his district. I hope you will treat him right
when he has any business in your department."[3] As they drove away
from their last call, Sawyer asked if there was any special committee
on which Bob would like to serve.

He asked for Public Lands, innocently explaining that he would
like to tackle the legal questions involved in the land-grant for-
feitures then pending. When Sawyer benignly said he would see
Speaker Carlisle about it and it would be all right, Bob was duly
grateful. But he had evidently been too frank. When the committees
were announced, it was another Wisconsin Congressman, Isaac
Stephenson, a wealthy lumberman, who had been placed on Public
Lands. Bob was safely assigned to Indian Affairs.

Although disappointed, he promptly invested quite a little money
in secondhand books about the Indians, had treaties and public
documents sent to his rooms, and devoted himself to the study of
Indian Affairs. He was appointed a subcommittee of one to consider
a bill introduced by Congressman Richard Guenther of Oshkosh,
who was also from Sawyer's home town, to sell the pine timber from
the Menominee Indian Reservation in Wisconsin. Study of the bill
convinced Bob that it offered unlimited opportunity to steal timber
from the Indians. He consulted with J. D. C. Atkins, Commissioner
of Indian Affairs, who said, "I think this a little the worst Indian
bill I ever saw." Soon after, Guenther asked Bob why he didn't
"report that bill out." Bob told him it was a bad bill and he would
report it adversely. Guenther advised against his doing so, explaining that he had introduced it at the request of Sawyer, who had
himself introduced the same bill in the Senate; Sawyer wanted it

favorably reported and on the calendar when his Senate bill reached the House. When Bob insisted he would not report the bill favorably, that ended it and the bill died in committee. Sawyer never spoke to him about it. The Indian bill was Bob's first experience with such pressures, but it was not his last.

Bob was the youngest member of the Forty-ninth Congress, and that fact is always a subject of comment. A press clipping entitled "La Follette and La Follette" went the rounds of the newspapers soon after we arrived in Washington. It seemed to me that everyone I met asked if I was a lawyer and a member of the firm. Newspaper correspondents are inclined to poke fun at the new Congressman and to convey the impression that, however great he is at home, he amounts to little in Washington. A wise woman in whose home we boarded in those early days was nearer the truth when she said, "A Congressman is always somebody in particular—and so is his wife."

Naturally, all my impressions were vivid. The Washington social season opens with the New Year's reception at the White House, which is the most picturesque official function in Washington social life. Rose Elizabeth Cleveland, sister of the President, was the White House hostess until he married. She was unassuming but gentle, and especially kind to the public. I remember the long lines of people who waited to call at her weekly afternoon reception. She was, perhaps, the last "first lady" to keep open house. Mrs. Cleveland, with her youth and beauty, was naturally idolized. Bob and I both thought the dignity with which this young girl, just out of college, bore herself and remained unspoiled by adulation was quite wonderful. Bob's first casual impression of the President at the inauguration had been unfavorable, but he later came to have great admiration for Cleveland's courage and integrity.

I was fortunate in my first impression of the social side of Washington. Through Mrs. Hazelton, a beautiful woman of lovely character, the wife of a former Wisconsin Congressman, I met, in a more intimate way, many of the prominent women of the official group. Without any introduction, the new Congressman's wife has the official privilege of making the first call on the lady of the White House, on the wives or social representatives of all members of the diplomatic corps, the Supreme Court, the Cabinet, and also the wives of those Senators and Representatives who have served

longer than her husband. At that time these calls were in the nature
of an official obligation. I proceeded to do this social "stunt" reli-
giously. It sounds like a large undertaking, but "calling" in Washington was then, and is still, more or less a well-systematized
institution. Days and hours were definite; I met the same persons
day after day; and within a week I was astonished to find how
many I knew, how well acquainted I felt, and how easy it all was.
Fortunately, I did not take it too seriously. I soon realized that
most of these acquaintances were "for the time being." In Washington "good morning" and "goodbye" were said with equal ease,
whether for the day, the season, or forever. Woe to the woman in
official life who takes it for granted she will stay permanently. In
making my first calls, I met the wife of a prominent Congressman
who told me she was looking for a more suitable place to live next
year when her husband "was sure to be elected to the Senate." He
was not elected either to the Senate or to the House.

Although I realized there was a great waste of time in the social
whirl of Washington, I enjoyed it and found it an excellent experience in many ways. I have always cared to meet people, even casually, and I believe it a mistake for anyone in public life to ignore
the value of its social side. Social functions and usages that include
the entire official group are necessarily democratic in spirit. They
should be distinguished from the insidious phase of Washington
society, which is the undoing of many a well-intentioned Member
of Congress whose position on public questions is influenced by the
flattery and attention of the inner circle, to which he and his family
like to feel they belong.

Bob objected to all formal social functions, but he would go
when I asked him, and he seemed to be having the best time in the
world, though he would never admit it. He could not understand
why a dinner invitation was so important that it must be answered
long in advance. In later years I declined everything that had to be
decided far ahead. No one enjoyed better than he an informal company, especially in his own home. When he was present, I was sure
our guests would have a good time. He genuinely appreciated a
social gathering where there was good music, reading, worth-while
conversation, and discussion.

Throughout those early years we were mindful that the old-line
politicians were busy back home laying plans to defeat Bob at the

next election. He therefore began at once to organize his district and keep in touch with his constituents. He had forms printed with spaces for names and addresses of twenty-five "active Republicans" and fifteen "fair-minded Democrats." These he sent to friends to be filled out in all townships of the district. Later he had poll lists marked with politics and occupation. When a speech on a leading issue was made, he would send it to each person on the township lists and sometimes to the poll lists. Although speeches reprinted from the *Congressional Record* are frankable, copies of the speeches must be paid for by the Congressman who orders them. It was quite a heavy expense, but it kept the constituents informed and created good will. A Congressman in those days, unless he was chairman of a committee, had neither office nor clerk assigned him. The bags of speeches were sent to our room where I addressed them. I personally sent out public documents and the quota of garden seeds Congressmen then had for distribution. In covering the list so many times, I became familiar with the names and addresses, so that when I accompanied Bob on his campaigns through his Congressional district I was able, sometimes, to jog even his excellent memory with a hint as to "who was who."

Congress ordinarily meets at noon. Bob spent the greater part of his morning hours at the Departments looking after matters requiring personal attention. I helped out with the routine Departmental correspondence. When constituents visited Washington, I took pleasure in piloting them through the Capitol, the Smithsonian Institution, the Art Gallery, and elsewhere. Pennsylvania Avenue was then the principal shopping street. At holiday time Bob and I would gaze at the window displays, and he would try to find out what piece of jewelry I would like for Christmas. He could never understand why I didn't care for rings and jewels. The city today has extended far out into what was then the country; electric lines take the place of horse cars and herdics; automobiles have supplanted horses and carriages—much speedier but far less picturesque. From the window where I write, I look out on Rock Creek Park. I recall that when the bill was passed for the purchase of the park everyone asked: "Where in the world is it? How will any one ever be able to get to it?" Now the principal residential section adjoins this beautiful tract of wooded land. The Washington of today, with all its changes, is always associated in my mind with the Washington of long ago.

We never missed a good play, and the great actors of that time became a part of our existence—Booth, Barrett, Modjeska, Salvini, Ada Rehan, Sarah Bernhardt, Fanny Davenport, and Mantell. After the assassination of Lincoln, Edwin Booth never came to Washington. But whenever he played in Baltimore, though it meant severe economies afterward, Bob and I would go to see him every night during his entire engagement there.

We attended the light operas of Gilbert and Sullivan and others. We heard *The Flying Dutchman, Lucia di Lammermoor,* and other operas sung by the Chicago Grand Opera Company. We never forgot the impression. Our Washington experience outside Congress was like a continuation school for us. We had been out of the university only five years; we had seen very little of the world; we were impressionable and blessed with enthusiasm and joy in life.

The first speech Bob made in Congress was on March 25, 1886, in memory of Joseph Rankin, a member of the House from Wisconsin. He carefully worked out what he was to say, memorized and rehearsed it. Though not striving for perfection, as in "Iago," he prepared in somewhat the same spirit, and the address bears the imprint of the college orator. When he rehearsed, the speech had seemed to me quite perfect. But when he delivered it in the House, there were only a few members present and few people in the galleries. The effect of his formal oration in the large chamber with many empty seats was not so moving as I had anticipated.

On April 22, 1886, when the Rivers and Harbors bill was under consideration, he made what is called his "maiden speech." It was not a set speech, but an extemporaneous attack on the bill during debate under limitation of the ten-minute rule. He spoke vigorously, convincingly, and to the point. As the gavel fell to indicate that his time was up, Joe Cannon of Illinois and others yielded him their time, and Bob went on to show that the bill flagrantly ignored the engineers' estimates and recommendations. "No individual, no corporate interests," Bob said, "could stand such management for a day." In concluding he stated the principle which, throughout his public service, guided his action regarding Federal expenditures: "Is there any very good reason why the public interests should not be managed upon business principles? . . . Not one dollar of this money belongs to any State, any district, any locality. It all belongs to the United States, and whatever is appropriated with any other view is a misappropriation of public funds. . . . Let the committee report a bill for the improvement of only such rivers and harbors as the interest of national commerce demands."[4]

There was applause when he finished. He had held the close attention of the House—in itself an achievement. The speech was given unusual space in the newspapers; he received clippings and letters from all parts of the country—some from professors at the University of Wisconsin—approving his stand. The bill passed. That was forty-three years ago. Conditions may have improved somewhat, but the rivers and harbors bills are not yet shaped according to the statesmanlike principles Bob then advocated.

Six weeks later, on May 31, 1886, Bob delivered to the graduating class at the Howard University Law School the address to which I have already referred. Memory of the audience of Negroes, who filled the church, and the effect of his closing words have always stayed with me. Frederick Douglass, the noted orator of his race, was there, and was very appreciative of Bob's address. It was then only twenty-three years after the Emancipation Proclamation, and the racial question was much more in evidence in Washington than now.

On June 2 Bob delivered a speech in the House in favor of a bill to tax oleomargarine, an imitation of butter which was undermining the dairy industry. The packing interests under the leadership of Henry C. Payne were lobbying against the bill. During the debate the prohibitory tax on oleomargarine had been assailed as unconstitutional, and this attack had been feebly met. Bob argued that there was the same constitutional right to use the internal-revenue taxing power for the general welfare as there was to levy taxes upon imports to that end. I well remember how pleased he was when, after long search and the assistance of Ainsworth R. Spofford, then Librarian of Congress, he found the letter written by John Quincy Adams which, going back to the reasoning of the framers of the Constitution, furnished the highest possible authority on this point. Members who had previously doubted the constitutionality of the tax were now convinced, and they voted for the bill, which passed by a larger majority than had been anticipated. Bob was much congratulated. In a way an important constitutional controversy had been settled, not only for this particular measure, but for future legislation.

Congress did not adjourn until August. Toward the close of the session Sam Harper had come on to Washington. He accompanied us home by way of New York City and up the Hudson by boat. We spent a glorious day at Niagara Falls. I can close my eyes now and recall its impression and hear the sound.

It was wonderful to be home again. After the long strain of the first session, a respite from politics would have been welcome, but never were we allowed to forget that the campaign for renomination and election was at hand. While Bob was a Member of the House, about the same thing happened every two years. There would be opposing candidates in the several counties of his district. Then, when enough caucuses and county conventions had been heard from to demonstrate that Bob would certainly be nominated by a good majority, announcements would appear that the opposing candidates would support him. These were not sham battles. The same forces that first fought his nomination would have beaten him each time if they could. The persistent efforts to oust him troubled me much more than Bob, who accepted the hostility of the Keyes machine as a part of the game. His keen political insight and balanced judgment forestalled needless worry. Each time he tackled the work of carrying caucuses and conventions with the same zeal and enthusiasm that characterized his work in Congress.

If I was sometimes unduly anxious over the opposition, I was made commensurately happy by approval and recognition of his services. The Congressional convention renominated him on September 15, 1886, without a dissenting vote. I naturally thought the *Dodgeville Chronicle* quite right when it said, "This is a proud distinction, but one which Mr. La Follette has fairly earned by his eminent ability, the untiring industry and unswerving integrity and faithfulness with which he discharged the arduous duties of the position during the session of Congress recently closed."[5]

It happened that, even at this early period, I began to get in touch with the people and to acquire a practical understanding of politics. When we were conferring on his campaign for the election, General Bryant said: "Bob, you better take Belle along; the good people of the district like to see a Congressman accompanied by his wife." Bob often praised my political judgment, but whatever special value it had was due to direct contact and experience.

No one enjoyed hearing him speak more than I; but best of all I liked to listen to him and watch him on the stump. In the Congressional debates he had been alert and resourceful, but he had not given play to the spontaneous wit which was an essential part of his nature. When I once said to an intimate friend in his presence that none of the reputed humorists of the House were his equal, Bob remarked that it was dangerous for a man to get the reputation of being a wit; nothing he could say would ever be taken seriously. Not that he was influenced by any such fear; in fact, he never seemed conscious of his own gift. But when he was preparing a formal speech, it never occurred to him to introduce a joke, anecdote, or funny story.

Even when he was full of his subject, he always felt it necessary to shape his material into a formal speech before starting out on any campaign. Although he did not actually read the manuscript, at the first few meetings he followed the written text closely. Very soon, however, he would get into a heart-to-heart way of talking to his audience. Then he would be moved by much the same spirit as when in the company of family and friends. Although speaking with compelling earnestness, even his most serious thought would be relieved by spontaneous wit and humorous anecdotes which drove his arguments home. His audience would listen for hours without ever seeming to weary. Sometimes, when they were laughing so hard that they hung onto each other, he would suddenly turn their thoughts to a dramatic event or make an appeal to their imaginations, and you could hear a pin drop.

Campaigns were not speeded up in the eighties. The speaking was usually opened in a larger city by a political leader of the party—the governor or United States Senator—who made the keynote speech. The candidate was not expected to make more than one or occasionally two speeches a day. Before we had automobiles, it would sometimes take a day to get from one meeting to the next. The train service was slow, the connections roundabout. Often we would ride in the caboose of a freight train to make our destination.

There were always people to talk with on the trains, and the long stops of the freight train would be spent visiting with those who gathered at the station. I don't remember that they ever asked for a speech, but they liked to get personally acquainted with their Congressman. He was always genuinely interested and would think of just the right thing to say. They would soon be calling him "Bob"; when we said goodbye it was like parting with old friends. Nevertheless, the continuous meeting of people made a long day. I was glad when we had to "take a livery" and make places not on the railroad. Then Bob and I would have a cozy, refreshing drive through the country, always so beautiful in the fall.

There was not much outdoor campaigning at that time. Though he often spoke at picnics, fairs, and Fourth of July celebrations, political meetings were usually held at night in halls that had been closed for weeks. Whatever the hour when he finished, the crowd would stop, shake hands, and have a word with him; some always followed him to the hotel and would have kept him up all night. I had to be the ogre and insist on his getting sleep. His habit of talking too long grew out of his own desire to cover the ground thoroughly and the insistence of his audiences that he go on. When I thought it was getting late, I would signal to him to stop. He would sometimes give me away: "There's my wife shaking her head and looking daggers at me. She thinks I'm talking too long." The crowd would laugh and urge him to go ahead. Once a man sitting next to me said: "Are you his wife? I thought when I saw you shaking your head you didn't like what he was saying and was sure you must be a *Democrat*."

In later years Bob, Jr., who became his father's right-hand man in the work of political organization and accompanied him on campaigns, would often slip notes into his hand while he was talking, begging him to shorten his speech and save his strength. Sometimes these pleas were heeded, but more often not. When Bob, Jr., began his political campaign for the Senate in the special election called in 1925 to fill his father's unexpired term, his experience in public speaking had been very limited. He thought it well to start out in the old Third Congressional District where the people had known his father as a young man and would be kindly disposed toward his young son. Grant County, Sam Harper's old home county, was friendly territory, but Lancaster, the county seat, where he found himself billed the first week, was a stalwart stronghold. He was surprised to see a fine audience awaiting him, and felt he must do his best. He spoke for an hour and a quarter. As the crowd came up to shake hands, he noticed a grizzled old man down the line who was eyeing him closely and who, when he reached for Bob's hand, held on to it, looked him up and down critically, and said, "Well, young feller, I guess you'll do; but you ain't as good as your Pa and never will be." To which Bob, Jr., replied, "My friend, I know that better than any other man in the world." His critic went on to say: "For one thing, you don't talk *long* enough. Why, I remember once, when your Pa was running for Congress, I came across him on the corner over there and I says to him, 'Bob, what you doin' here?' and he says to me, 'I was to speak here, but no one has put up the bills,' and I says, 'Bob, you just go over to the hotel and wait and we'll get a crowd for you'; and I took my horse and buggy and got two or three other fellows in town to take theirs and we each took a different road out of here and we stopped at every farm and told the boys Bob La Follette was in town, to hurry up and hear him speak. By four o'clock this whole bloomin' square was packed and Bob began to speak, and he kept on speaking until after dark. Why, he talked so long every darn' cow in this part of the country was bellerin' to be milked; but the crowd just kept hollerin' for Bob to go on."

CHAPTER VII

A Place in the Front Ranks

Bob was reelected in November, 1886, for his second term by a majority of 3,510, running about 537 votes ahead of his ticket in his Congressional district. The figures did not disclose how many "fair-minded" Democrats had voted for him and thus offset the considerable boss-ruled element that always knifed him at the polls.

I had made up my mind never to go to Washington again without our little daughter. We planned also to have Bob's mother accompany us for the short session which convened on December 6, 1886, and adjourned on March 3, 1887. She was interested in the Congressional debates and thoroughly enjoyed every aspect of Washington. We settled at 812 Twelfth Street, N.W., at the Strathmore Arms, a popular boardinghouse kept by Mary Lockwood, who was a suffragist, and active in the D.A.R. She organized a literary club and instituted activities to make the social life of her house more worth while.

Early in his second term Bob spoke in favor of what became known as the Transportation Act of 1887, which created an Interstate Commerce Commission for the regulation of railroads. He was, even then, for more radical legislation than the Transportation Act, which he considered an evolution of the Granger movement. But he supported it enthusiastically because he believed it sound in principle and a good beginning. His early impressions of the Wisconsin struggle for railroad regulation and his interest in the 1887 legislation kept him constantly alive to this important issue so that he found himself prepared to deal with it when he became governor. Years later, when he went to the Senate, the Hepburn railroad bill was pending, and the amendments he offered were thus based on twenty years of study and work.

For nearly four decades he fought to have the regulation of railroads based on the fundamental principles which he stated in the closing sentence of the speech he made in the House on January 20, 1887, when he was thirty-two: ". . . I believe the time will surely come, and I hope it is not far off, when railways will be limited to their legitimate sphere as common carriers; when they will conduct their business upon the same principles of impartiality toward persons, places, and things as govern the United States mail service; when they will have but one standard of regulating rates, the cost of transportation; when they will seek but one object, perfect service to the public and fair profits upon the great capital actually invested."[1] The speech is a close-knit argument very interesting to read now in view of the long struggle and the still unsettled state of the conflict. In simple language it defines the law for common carriers: to "provide efficient service . . . be fair and impartial," make "just and reasonable" charges and "treat all alike. Discriminations and favoritisms are forbidden." As an example of the violation of these principles, he cited an instance of the Standard Oil Company having received ten million dollars in rebates in sixteen months and stated that its wealth represented rewards obtained by railroad favoritism. "No one on this floor can defend such acts as these," he said. "Any measure which deals temperately and fairly with the great interests involved, but at the same time brings the railways back and confines them with strong hand to their legitimate business as common carriers, restoring to the public its own again, would be little less than a second bill of rights."[2] Years later Bob said that of all the speeches he made in the House, this one "gives me to-day the greatest satisfaction."[3]

The most casual survey of his record for control of the railroads as a member of the House, as governor, and as Senator, some forty years in time, reveals the underlying motive of all his public service. His purpose was ever to resist the encroachment of the few upon the rights of the many and so to preserve the fundamental principle of government for and by the people. Once convinced of the necessity of a reform, he could not be driven from his course; he adhered to it with patience and determination, no matter how powerful the opposition.

Very few of the constructive achievements of his long public service gave Bob more enduring satisfaction than the establishment of the United States Agricultural Experiment Stations under the law passed, during the same session, on February 25, 1887. In speaking for the measure, he said, "It annexes an experimental farm to every man's land, places him next door to a chemical laboratory, makes him neighbor to and sharer in all technical skill and scientific information touching the business in which he is engaged."[4] As so frequently in his legislative work, however, the speech was only a small part of his contribution to enactment of the law. At the old Ebbitt House in Washington, he conferred with President Chamberlin of the University of Wisconsin, President George W. Atherton of Pennsylvania State College, and President James K. Patterson of Kentucky State Agricultural and Mechanical College, who were trying to secure the appropriation for the experiment stations. Although the legislative situation was critical because it was near the end of the session, Bob worked out a successful method of procedure. After the bill passed, President Patterson said: "We must thank ... Mr. La Follette, for putting the bill through, for without his help we should have failed for this session, at least. His success seems to be in making friends with all whom he meets and organizing them so they will pull together."

Bob grasped the significance of scientific agriculture early and throughout his life cooperated in strengthening the department at the University of Wisconsin, which is noted the world over for agricultural research as well as for the teaching of scientific and practical farming. In 1878, while Bob and I were still attending the university, the first student graduated from the Department of Agriculture, created under the Morrill Act of 1862. When the diploma was awarded, the audience laughed audibly, though good-humoredly—so strange was the idea fifty years ago that an institution of learning could have aught to do with farming!

Bob became a national figure in the Republican Party during the tariff debate which held the center of the stage in the Fiftieth and Fifty-first Congresses. In the preceding Congress the Democrats had offered the Morrison bill for a horizontal reduction of tariff rates. It had failed to pass in the House because of the protectionists in the Democratic Party. In the Fiftieth Congress Roger Q. Mills of Texas, who had charge of the tariff bill, opened the discussion and, according to custom, would have closed the debate. But when Tom Reed made the closing argument for the Republican opposition, on May 19, 1888, Speaker Carlisle himself took the floor and delivered the final speech in its defense. Bob thought Carlisle's speech was dangerous for the Republicans. He went first to Reed and then to McKinley suggesting that someone should answer it. Each replied in a jocular way, "Bob, you answer it." A bit nettled, he said to McKinley: "Well, if no one else will answer it, then I will try to. At least I will see if it can be answered."

I had been in the gallery listening to the greater part of the debate. When Reed finished, I felt the Republicans had much the best of the argument. After hearing Carlisle, I was as disturbed as Bob. We talked it over very earnestly that evening, and for some days could not get away from the subject. We knew that in Wisconsin and the Midwest Carlisle's speech could do great harm as a campaign document unless answered. We realized it was a bold venture for a young Member, with limited experience, to undertake to answer the distinguished Speaker. It required courage and it meant work.

Carlisle's argument was for a tariff for revenue only. He had painted in glowing terms the prosperity in manufacturing under the tariff Acts of 1846 and 1857 and had cited as proof what appeared to be a convincing array of statistical data. Bob was satisfied Carlisle's facts and deductions were subject to historical challenge; but to prove this sophistry called for hard digging; the work must be done speedily, for debate would not last much longer. From the time Bob was nominated for Congress, he had read a great deal on the tariff but had never made the thorough preparation he thought necessary for a speech. Almost a dray load of *Congressional Records* and books were brought to our rooms. He put in two weeks of intensive research preparing a logical argument. The oratorical effect of Carlisle's speech had been extraordinary; but it yielded to attack like the proverbial straw man.

When Bob finally took the floor, on July 14, 1888, the tariff bill was being debated under the five-minute rule for amendments. A Member could not speak longer than five minutes nor more than once on any amendment he submitted unless other Members asked to have the time extended and leave was granted. When Bob started, there was confusion on the floor, and as the gavel fell at the end of the first five minutes he had only begun to get the attention of the House. However, a colleague asked for a five-minute extension of time, which was granted. The interest kept growing. Reed was writing at his desk when Bob started, but very soon he was listening. When the gavel fell again, both Butterworth and Reed were asking that the time of "the gentleman from Wisconsin" be extended. Unanimous consent was given. The argument of the youngest Member of the House was made especially dramatic and effective by the circumstances and the occasion. When he finished, there was long-continued applause on the Republican side and, from the gallery, I noted that almost every Member on the floor filed up the aisle to congratulate him. The speech had given him a place in the front ranks of his party.

His reply to Carlisle undoubtedly won him appointment on the powerful Ways and Means Committee of the Fifty-first Congress— the "Reed Congress," as it has become known in history. Reed and McKinley were rival candidates for the Speakership. It was in this contest that Bob first met Theodore Roosevelt, then United States Civil Service Commissioner. Roosevelt was enthusiastic for Reed. He and Bob often conferred together about the Members they had seen, comparing notes on which would support, which oppose Reed. Bob liked Roosevelt, and they became well acquainted. Although Bob felt a peculiar admiration and affection for McKinley, he supported Reed because he thought Reed better equipped for the struggle which they all knew must follow over the counting of a quorum.

The Republicans were in power. They had elected Benjamin Harrison President in 1888; they had retained control of the Senate, and secured a majority of four in the House. The Republican Party was, therefore, charged with the responsibility of putting through a legislative program. The House must have a quorum to transact business. But their small majority of four did not ensure a dependable Republican quorum. In so large a legislative body there are always some unavoidably absent. The Democrats, by remaining in their seats and refusing to answer when their names were called, could break a quorum and prevent legislation at will. In preceding Congresses both Democrats and Republicans had successfully used this method to filibuster against the majority. No former Speaker had ever asserted the constitutional right to count, as present and making a quorum, Members sitting in their seats but not voting.

Several weeks passed before Speaker Reed took this revolutionary step. Although I spent much of my time in the gallery, I missed this stirring event—the most dramatic that occurred during the six years Bob was in the House—in fact, one of the most notable in the history of parliamentary proceedings. No notice was given when it was to occur. Members, though ready for it, were taken by surprise when the clash actually came. On January 29, 1888, the roll call on a contested election case showed less than a quorum, although, counting those in their seats not voting, many more than a majority were present. The point of no quorum was made and a tense hush fell upon the House. Reed's face was set and grim. Bob found himself holding fast to his desk as "Reed raised his gavel, and with the mallet end in his hand, deliberately pointed out and called the names of members present and not voting, and directed the clerk to so record them. Then he proclaimed a quorum present, announced the vote, and declared the result," calmly stating that the action he had taken was necessary and constitutional.[5] Bob said that never in a legislative body did he witness anything like the intensity of emotion and excitement which attended this proceeding. An angry roar went up; there were cries of "Czar," "Tyrant." Both sides rushed forward, Democrats to assail, Republicans to defend the Speaker. Reed's superb self-control and magnetic power quelled the mob spirit.

Bob was naturally pleased when Speaker Reed notified him he was to have a place on the Ways and Means Committee. It was an unusual distinction for a young man to be on the foremost committee of the House with its notable membership. From the time the committee was organized until the McKinley tariff bill was reported out, he worked late into the night all days of the week. Open committee hearings were held which lasted several weeks. No one was excluded, but those who appeared were mostly manufacturers, importers, and other interested parties; their facts and figures were accepted as reliable. At that time Bob did not seriously question this unscientific method of securing information as a basis for tariff rates.

The objects of the measure were declared to be protection of home products and industry, free trade in things not produced in the United States, and taxation of luxuries. All schedules were revised on the theory long advocated by the Republican Party,

which Bob also accepted at this time, that it made little difference
how high the duties were because competition between domestic
manufacturers within the tariff wall would ensure to the consumer
the lowest prices commensurate with American wages for American
workmen. Although trusts and combinations were then looming on
the horizon, it was believed the threatened monopoly of big business
would be overcome by legislation. A bill declaring trusts and combinations in restraint of trade and production unlawful had been
introduced by Senator John Sherman of Ohio. It became a law
three months before the McKinley tariff was adopted. The country
then had great faith in the Sherman Anti-Trust Act, and Bob never
ceased to believe it could be enforced.

McKinley assigned the different tariff schedules to subcommit-
tees. When they had completed their work, they reported back to
him. Bob and other Members spent night after night with Mc-
Kinley at his rooms in the Ebbitt Hotel, going over, comparing,
and arranging schedules. As Bob was eager to know as much as
possible about the bill, he gladly volunteered to do all he could
toward putting it into final shape.

For the first time in tariff history the bill included a thoroughgoing schedule of protective duties on competing farm products, of
which Bob, as I remember, was given charge. He always thought
of economic problems in their concrete relation to human experience, and his imagination invested abstract figures with power to
stir an audience. Anyone who cares to know how he succeeded in
interesting all kinds of audiences in questions involving statistics
should read his speech of May 10, 1890, on the McKinley tariff.
His major premise was that labor in every field of industry, on the
farm no less than in the factory, was the great issue at stake—that
the protective tariff preserved for the people of this country the
superior advantages of a diversified, independent development
which free trade would destroy; an old theory, but vividly applied
and sustained by compelling argument. I remember how effective
he was when speaking of the difference in conditions at home and
abroad.[6]

It is nearly forty years since this speech was made. Bob's views
underwent material change with the evolution of economic conditions, and yet today it is to me interesting reading. He was in fine
voice, entirely at home with his subject. His delivery had a freedom

and sweep that held the close attention of the House and galleries throughout his address. Bob's tariff speech received wide newspaper notice. The Chicago *Daily Inter-Ocean* commented that he had "by his speech, won a place for himself in the front ranks, not only of tariff debaters, but of the students of economic questions in Congress."[7]

After Bob made his tariff speech, we went to Old Point Comfort, Virginia, for a week; a little thing to recall in the pages of a book, but a rare memory to me, as I know it was to him; a few lovely days in the warm sun, on the beach with nothing to do except stroll and hunt for moonstones and shells. He knew how to relax and throw off care, but it was very seldom he would stop work for play. I doubt if there were a half-dozen times in all the years of politics when he enjoyed a vacation like the one at Old Point Comfort.

During both sessions of the Fifty-first Congress we were happily situated at 52 B Street, N.E., where the Senate Office Building now stands, facing Capitol Park. This view of the park is always associated in my mind with Fola, as I could see her from my desk at the window, roller skating. I had tried sending her to kindergarten, but it did not seem to agree with her, so I began teaching her myself. After lessons were over, the park was her playground.

The more familiar Bob became with the inside working of Congress, the more clearly he saw the encroachment of private interests upon public rights. In his first term he had discovered and thwarted an attempt to steal the timber of the Menominee Indian Reservation in Wisconsin. His service on the Indian Committee brought another revelation to him during his second term which was more far-reaching in consequences. While listening in committee to the reading of a bill to open for settlement 11,000,000 acres of the Sioux Indian Reservation in Dakota, he was struck by a provision to ratify an agreement, made by the Chicago, Milwaukee, and St. Paul and the North Western railroads with the Indians, for a right of way through the reservation. Each road, in addition to the right of way, was to have 160 acres every ten miles for "station privileges." He told the committee that it looked to him like a "town-site job" and asked to have the paragraphs laid over, not heeding the warn-

ing of a committee member who whispered: "Bob, you don't want
to interfere with that provision. *Those are your home corporations.*"[8]

Shortly after the committee adjourned, Sawyer sent word that he
would like to see Bob in the cloakroom. After some casual conversation the Senator remarked that when the Sioux Indian bill came
up in committee, he wished Bob would look after the provisions "for
our folks up in Wisconsin." Bob replied the bill had already come
up and he was opposed to the "town-site" scheme; he believed the
railroads should have the land necessary for right of way, yards,
depots, and shops, but thought it would be unjust to the Indians
and the public to give them land for speculative purposes. Sawyer
showed no ill temper, but said he would see him again about it.

As soon as a train could bring him from Milwaukee, Henry C.
Payne, lobbyist for the St. Paul road and the packing interests,
arrived on the scene. Payne and Sawyer came to see Bob night after
night for a week or more trying to persuade him to quit his fight on
the Sioux Indian bill. But he put through his amendment. It gave
the railroads the lands necessary for transportation, prohibited the
use or sale of any of it for town-site or speculative purposes, and
provided that the railroads should forfeit their lands to the government unless the roads were constructed and in operation within
three years. During the controversy Congressman Nils P. Haugen
of Wisconsin told Bob he had run across Payne in the Ebbitt Hotel.
Payne had said that La Follette was a crank, and that if he thought
he could buck a railroad with five thousand miles of line which
gridironed his district he would find out his mistake. "We'll take
care of him when the time comes," said Payne.

Bob and Haugen had previously had an encounter with Sawyer
on the Nicaraguan Canal bill in the session preceding the Presidential campaign of 1888. They were both actively opposing the
measure. Sawyer invited Bob to his committee room to meet Colonel
William W. Dudley of Indiana, old-school politician, famous for
his letter to his henchmen instructing them how to round up the
voters of the Hoosier State in "blocks of five" on election day.
Dudley argued the necessity of passing the Nicaraguan bill, before
the close of the session, on the ground that the interested parties
would contribute $100,000 to the Republican campaign fund. Bob,
who had observed that a prominent Democrat was also lobbying
for the bill, asked Dudley how much the Democrats were going to

get. Dudley frankly replied they were to receive a like amount. When Bob jokingly inquired if these contributions would not offset each other, Dudley answered that the Republicans had more sense than the Democrats in spending their campaign funds, explaining that a plan was afoot by which the Republicans hoped to carry Delaware, and that this fund, or part of it, was to be used to buy up a tract of swampland in Delaware, "and parcel it out among the laboring men so as to qualify them as voters."[9] The Nicaraguan bill did not pass at this session. But with some amendment it did pass in 1889.

Later, when a ship-subsidy bill was pending in the Fifty-first Congress, Bob denounced it as a flagrant effort of private interests to dig into the public treasury. It was generally supported by Republicans and opposed by Democrats. He made a canvass of his Republican friends trying to get enough of them to join the Democrats and defeat the bill. Among others he talked with Myron Mc-Cord, a Republican Member from Wisconsin who was serving his first term. McCord voted against the bill, and it was defeated by five votes. As often happens when the Clerk recapitulates the roll call on a close vote, "there was great bustling about by the leading supporters of the measure, seeking out members who might be induced to change their votes."

When Bob saw a group of Members coming out of the cloak-room, urging, almost pushing McCord down the aisle and heard him call out "Mr. Speaker," he knew McCord was about to change his vote. Bob slipped through the crowd, seized hold of McCord, and kept him going until he had him back in the cloakroom. McCord was not resentful, and when Bob asked what it meant, he said: "I've got to change my vote. Sawyer has just sent a page over here and insists on my voting for the bill. I've got to do it. He has loaned me money; he has a mortgage on everything I possess." Persuading McCord to take his hat and coat and get out of reach, Bob returned to the floor. As he was passing up the center aisle, Sawyer, white with rage, came at him: "Young man, young man, what are you doing? You are a bolter. The Republican platform promises this legislation. You are a bolter, sir; you are a bolter." Bob was furious and told Sawyer he had no business on the House floor, violating the rules, trying to influence legislation; and finally warned him, "You get out of here, or I will call the Speaker's attention to you." Sawyer knew he meant it, and immediately left the floor. A few days later, when they chanced to meet, Sawyer stopped him and said: "I am sorry for what I said the other night. You were right and I was wrong. You have a perfect right to vote as you please."[10]

Sawyer had boldly fought this skirmish on the floor of the House. But Bob learned how legislation in the public interest could also be quietly and subtly killed in committee by the pressure of special interests. This does not mean that individual Members of Congress were personally dishonest. They were silenced by fear of vengeance from the powerful corporations without, perhaps, sensing the cost to the public. During the time he was in the House, Bob saw these evils singly, but did not then realize that a great system of "community of interests" was getting control of political parties, government, and courts.

Although he had openly clashed with Sawyer and Henry Payne, he did not, during his six years in the House, have any break with Senator John C. Spooner of Wisconsin, who was serving his first term in the Senate. Spooner was an able man, an orator, and brilliant debater. Before his election to the Senate, he had been general counsel for the Chicago, St. Paul, Minneapolis and Omaha Railway system and their lobbyist when the state legislature was in session. He was the ally of Payne and Sawyer, and their spokesman; but he disliked personally to be in the political fray and kept aloof except when actually forced to take part.

Bob's relations with Members of the House generally, and with the Wisconsin delegation especially, were cordial and friendly. For Lucian B. Caswell, much older in years and service, he had real affection. He was also very fond of Isaac Stephenson, a pioneer lumberman whose wealth rivaled that of Sawyer. Stephenson had a philosophical wisdom, a quaint sense of humor, and his stories of pioneer experiences were classic. Mrs. Stephenson was handsome, had unusual character, heart, and intellect. I was especially fond of her. Two Wisconsin Members elected to the Fiftieth Congress were more nearly Bob's age, and especially congenial. Nils P. Haugen was a man of intellect, courage, education, and integrity. He and Bob had much the same outlook on politics, and soon came to have absolute faith in each other. Charles B. Clark, although a wealthy manufacturer, understood public questions from the stand-

point of the plain people whom he loved and who loved him. He
and Bob had much the same democratic spirit and were close
friends. Unfortunately, he died in 1891. I have always thought that
if he had lived, he would have been on the progressive side in the
long conflict against reactionary forces in Wisconsin. Mrs. Clark,
Mrs. Haugen, and I saw much of each other in a neighborly spirit;
our children were playfellows.

It is my impression much more emphasis was then placed on
state and sectional lines than in later years. Whether one came from
Massachusetts or California, Wisconsin or Mississippi, from the
East, West, North, or South, ranked next to the weather as a subject
of conversation in Washington. The women of the Wisconsin group
were all friendly. None were prominent socially, other than the
Senators' hostesses. Mrs. Spooner, a very pleasing hostess, had wit
and magnetism. There was freshness in her cordial greeting and
sparkle in her conversation. She had a beautiful voice and would
sometimes sit down at the piano and sing for her guests. As Mrs.
Sawyer was an invalid, a daughter, Mrs. White, did the honors of
the mansion Senator Sawyer built on Connecticut Avenue, then a
fashionable residential street. Mrs. White was reputed to be intellectual. She was always beautifully dressed, but impressed the
average caller as cold and formal. Doubtless she was admired by
the inner circle of Washington society. The refreshments served
were elaborate and generous. In this respect the hospitality was
similar to that found at the home of Leland Stanford, a wealthy
Senator from California. Mrs. Stanford was a large, plain, richly
dressed woman. Her receptions were always crowded, and people
of whom you never would have believed it vied with each other in
being served. Mrs. Hearst's afternoons were in marked contrast.
She was also the wife of a California Senator with millions to spend.
But her collections of rare pictures and beautiful rugs made a visit
to her house a real privilege. And she herself, traveled and cultured,
left the impression of simplicity, poise, and charm.

When the Department of Agriculture was created, President
Harrison appointed as Secretary, General Jerry Rusk of Wisconsin,
who, prior to his appointment, had served seven years as governor
of the State. In the seventies he had represented his Congressional
district three terms in the House. He had received limited education
in his youth, but had great native ability and a fine Civil War

record. Mrs. Rusk, quiet and dignified, was ever gracious and kind.
Mary Rusk, the daughter, who always assisted her mother on social
occasions, had a pleasing personality, was wise politically and help-
ful to her father. She had been a friend of ours at the university.
It was at a New Year's reception at the Rusks that I first met
Theodore Roosevelt. He and Henry Cabot Lodge were making the
round of Cabinet calls. I was assisting in the dining room. The fact
that Roosevelt, Lodge, and Bob had been working together to elect
Reed Speaker of the House was the subject of lively conversation.
Roosevelt was talking with his usual vigor and emphatic gestures.
It chanced that when I offered him a cup of coffee, his hand struck
the cup, and the black coffee spilled over the front of the white
dress I wore. He was terribly distressed; he feared I was burned,
and my dress ruined. I assured him the coffee was not hot, and the
dress of no consequence. He sent flowers the next day with a
charming note. Many times when we met in afteryears he would
refer to the episode and make a good story of it. I remember that
he once said, "I blush when I wake up in the dark and think about
spilling that coffee over Mrs. La Follette's dress."

Bob was intensely interested in the Wisconsin campaign of 1888,
which in some respects resembled the old Granger fight, since it
united the farmers and in a measure wiped out party lines. The
packing interests, under the able leadership of Henry C. Payne,
had aggressively lobbied state legislatures and Congress against
oleomargarine legislation. This active invasion of the dairy-products
market had aroused the farmers. They walked to the caucuses and
conventions with cornstalks over their shoulders, making an organized fight to nominate and elect as governor William Dempster
Hoard, owner and publisher of the leading dairy paper of Wisconsin. Hoard had no political experience, but was well known in the
State. He had a Lincoln-like face, picturesque personality, and
earnestly believed in government for and by the people. Horace
Taylor, always known as "Hod" Taylor, was the candidate of the
Republican machine. He was also widely known; was good-humored,
likable, and a canny politician. He owned and edited the *Wisconsin State Journal*. Bob greatly admired Hoard and strongly
sympathized with the idea back of his candidacy. He loaned his
poll lists to be used in sending out campaign literature; General

Bryant, "Cully" Adams, and many of Bob's close friends were active workers for Hoard. We felt it a signal victory when Hoard was nominated and elected governor.

In the spring of 1890 the Wisconsin state delegation was invited to meet Henry C. Payne, chairman of the State Central Committee, at Senator Sawyer's Washington residence. The women of the delegation were included in the invitation for Sunday dinner. We were asked to come early. While the women were shown about the big house, the men went into the library, where Payne made a bitter speech sharply arraigning Governor Hoard for having put through the Bennett compulsory-education law, intimating it had been done underhandedly and secretly. Payne urged the delegation to denounce the law and protest against Hoard's being a candidate for reelection. There was a dead silence when he finished. Bob waited for older men to speak, but when no one did so he took the initiative and said he would not join in any such declaration. Congressman Caswell from Fort Atkinson, Governor Hoard's home town, took the same position. It was finally decided that unless the delegation were unanimous, none of them would act. That put a quietus on Payne's proposition, but it did not prevent his continuing to work against Hoard and Bob underground.

The McKinley tariff bill passed the House on October 1, which left less than a month for a state speaking campaign. Bob had been unanimously nominated at the Congressional convention in August while attending to his work in Congress. Allen R. Bushnell, a lawyer, appointed a United States district attorney by President Cleveland, was his Democratic opponent.

After making a few speeches at various points in his district, Bob's own election seemed so certain that he responded to the urgent request of the State Central Committee to go into other parts of the State. It was important to have a Republican legislature, as it would elect the United States Senator, and Spooner was a candidate for reelection. Bob also went over into Iowa to speak for David B. Henderson. They had seats near each other in the House and had become warm friends. My own recollections of the campaign are confirmed by the newspaper reports of the time. Wherever he went, there were the same crowds overflowing the halls, the same enthusiasm; and however long he spoke his audience would insist he go on. All the surface manifestations indicated a tremendous Republican victory.

Speaker Thomas B. Reed spoke in Madison on October 29. He was accompanied on the train by Henry Payne, Secretary Rusk, L. B. Caswell, Horace A. Rublee, editor of the *Milwaukee Sentinel,* and others. With the Republican University Club and a committee consisting of H. W. Chynoweth, Charles M. Dow, and General Bryant, Bob met Reed at the station. When they entered the train to greet the guest, Reed towered above Bob as he took his hand and asked heartily, "How are you, Robert, my boy." A reporter noted that Bob "fairly hugged the speaker; or came as near to hugging him as short arms could to surrounding a man whose girth is simply enormous." Reed was escorted to the capitol, where Bob introduced him to the largest audience that had ever gathered in the Assembly Chamber, as a man who once belonged to the State of Maine but now belonged to the whole country. About midway in his address Reed commented on Bob's work in Congress, describing him as "one of the ablest members" of the Ways and Means Committee, and predicting that "If the Republicans of this district do their duty" he "has a great career before him, and you and your state may well be proud of him." For "fully a minute Reed was unable to proceed because of the cheers of the audience."[11]

Bob closed the campaign on Monday, November 3, at the Assembly Chamber. For dramatic effect and lasting impression on an audience, this speech in the crowded chamber, where even the window casements were occupied, was one of the most notable he ever made. Throughout the years since, I have met people who recall it vividly. Those who heard him describe Reed's counting of the quorum seem to feel they had been present when the historic incident took place.

Walter Owen, Wisconsin Supreme Court Justice, in recalling that he first heard Bob at this meeting, says, "I knew there was such a Congressman as La Follette and that he had a great reputation as a speaker, so a number of us students at the University went to hear him in the Assembly Chamber. That speech completely got me. I had never heard one like it before and probably none since. It made me a La Follette man from that time on."

After supper, on the evening of election day, Bob sat thrumming his guitar, whistling an accompaniment. I remember that I remarked that I did not believe his opponent Bushnell was whistling. When

Bob went uptown later to get the returns, I thought it only a question of how large a majority. I couldn't believe him when he came home about eleven o'clock and called upstairs in a matter-of-fact way, "Well, Belle, Bushnell is elected to Congress from the Third District, and I am elected to practice law."

CHAPTER VIII

A Bribe to Influence the Court

There was nothing personal in Bob's defeat; he had run 700 votes ahead of his ticket in spite of the organized opposition of Republican machine leaders. His friends believed almost any political honor in the gift of the State might come to him in time. In the 1890 election the whole country underwent sweeping changes. Hard times and the McKinley tariff probably had an influence on the general result. In Wisconsin, however, the Democratic landslide was attributed chiefly to the Bennett law, which provided that parents must send children under their control, between the ages of seven and fourteen, to a public or private school for not less than twelve weeks each year. The law defined "school" as one that taught reading, writing, arithmetic, and United States history in the English language. The large Lutheran and Roman Catholic elements in Wisconsin believed the Bennett law was a blow at their parochial-school systems. Disapproval was chiefly expressed by many staying away from the polls. The stay-at-home vote in Dane County alone would have elected Bob. A Democratic state ticket and legislature were elected by a surprising majority. Congressman Haugen was the only Republican Representative in the State to pull through, although his previous majority of 10,000 was cut to 2,500.

When Bob first told me he was defeated, I thought he was joking. But finally realizing what had happened, I thought "Republicans ungrateful," and was indignant that his six years of devoted service had not been rewarded. Naturally I expected him to be a good sport and meet the inevitable result gracefully, yet I was amazed at the way he accepted defeat. There was no break in his habitual good cheer, not a word of complaint, nor one moment wasted in regret. I learned then that he valued life too much to let the ordinary

chances of politics spoil it for him. It is not possible to explain
what comfort it gave me to realize that our everyday happiness
rested on this sure foundation. There were only a few times in the
long years of struggle when extraordinary circumstances disturbed this inner peace.

I had supposed Washington life had no lure for me. During the
short session that winter I would laugh when reminded that our
official existence ended on the fourth of March, though at heart
I was not altogether happy about it. Bob went directly home after
adjournment; but I had to stay on in Washington as Fola was ill
with measles. On my return to Madison, our house seemed desolate.
The hall was filled with bags of public documents which must be
addressed and sent to constituents. I had a funereal feeling about
the task. When we were changing every year from Madison to
Washington, I had not minded that the house was meagerly
furnished, rugs worn, and many things needed repairs, but it was
different now we had come home to stay. We were poor and in debt;
Bob's income was uncertain. We had the problem of a Dakota ranch
to wrestle with.

We had expected the ranch would be a good investment but it had
proved a costly experiment. When Congress had adjourned in March,
1887, Bob was able to enjoy his first leisure in years. On a visit
to South Dakota, where his half-sister, Ellen, lived, we became
interested in the purchase of the ranch. South Dakota was then the
El Dorado of low-priced land, and at that time the breeding of
Percheron horses was a highly successful business in Wisconsin.
We were enthusiastic about the venture and bought a beautiful
stretch of a thousand acres of benchland on the Missouri River about
fifteen miles south of Chamberlain. It had rich black soil, a hundred
feet deep, and thirty acres of timber. We had a fine time driving
about Sauk County selecting the young mares with which to stock
the place. Gypsy went to the ranch to spend her last days. Several
years of drought made it necessary to buy feed for the horses. For
eleven years we carried the heavy burden, but finally had to sell just
when the price of both land and horses was at lowest ebb.

However large Bob's income—and at times, according to our
simple standard of living, he earned a good deal of money lecturing,
writing, and in law practice—all he could spare went into the cause
for which he was working. He had confidence in his earning power,

however, and though our home was mortgaged and we had debts we never lacked the essential comforts of life. My ambition and interest were centered in the home; it did not occur to me to join him in the practice of law. Fola was happy to be settled, and relieved to be assured, in answer to her anxious inquiry, that lawyers did not have to be elected to practice law. I made up my mind we would have more children and raise the family we had always planned. Any thought Bob had of returning to the public service was vague and remote. I do not recall that a future political career was even mentioned. He intended as a citizen to contribute his share toward making government serve the public interest; but otherwise he purposed to devote himself to his law practice.

Bob went back to his profession confident that he could soon build up a good practice. The law firm was La Follette, Harper, Roe, and Zimmerman. Sam Harper, Bob's closest personal friend and political adviser; Gilbert E. Roe, a well-known lawyer in New York City; and Albert Zimmerman, subsequently a Wisconsin circuit judge, were younger men to whom Bob was already much attached. Between sessions of Congress, he had participated in the trial of a few cases for the love of it and to help out. He had taken no share in the profits.

Wisconsin Supreme Court Justice Burr W. Jones attributed Bob's success as a lawyer to his indefatigable preparation of his cases. He was, Jones said, always bringing in surprising new material, new witnesses, unexpected evidence. He knew how to appeal to the average man; he had been poor himself and worked hard with his hands, knew men and how to move them. Members of the bar sometimes thought he took liberties with the jury; he would go over and stand close, occasionally even putting his hand on a juryman's knee, to which the lawyers would "object."

The last jury trial in which Bob took part was the State of Wisconsin against Charles Nolan for the murder of Thomas Good. He was employed to assist in the trial at the request of M. S. Dudgeon, the Dane County district attorney. The murder was committed in a lonely spot in the eastern part of Madison, where the two men had a short time before cooked a stew over an open fire and eaten it together. Nolan was a hard character; Good was a hunchback. The circumstances created much interest, and the fact that Bob had charge of the prosecution drew crowds far beyond the capacity of the courtroom. The waiting line at times extended a long way out on the sidewalks. The trial occupied a week. A sensational feature of the testimony for the State was the introduction of the contents of the murdered man's stomach. As soon as Bob examined the case, he was impressed with the importance of this evidence in definitely fixing the time of Good's death as within the period the circumstantial evidence showed the two men had been together. He had the embalmed body disinterred, the stomach removed, and the food preserved. This was done four months before the trial, but it was kept a secret and was a complete surprise to the defense.

The *Wisconsin State Journal* commented on Bob's final argument to the jury: ". . . Three full hours he held the great audience —the greatest ever assembled in the Dane County court house— held it as a hypnotist holds his subject. Pleading, accusing, reasoning, and humor followed one on the other with ceaseless changings. . . . Nolan's plans had been laid at the outset for the murder . . . , and, basing his lines on this assumption, [he] constructed one of the most masterly arguments heard in the northwest during a decade."[1]

Nolan was convicted and sentenced to state prison for life. On his way to Waupun he told the official in charge, "La Follette knew more than I did myself."

Bob was a strong believer in the jury system. He always assumed members of a jury were honest, quite capable of following logical argument and understanding any clearly presented evidence. He never appealed to religious, class, race, or political prejudices.

Gilbert E. Roe, for ten years Bob's closest associate in the practice of law, said that during this decade he never knew a jury to bring in a verdict against him: "He had an intuitive knowledge of the principles of equity and justice and an almost uncanny appreciation of the relative value of evidentiary facts. These gifts, coupled with a thoroughness of preparation which I have never seen equalled by any other lawyer, made him, when he entered the court room to try a case, a most dangerous antagonist, and a wise and safe counselor in his office when he advised a client respecting his rights. . . .

"Unlike, however, many lawyers who prepare their cases with great thoroughness, he was never disconcerted by any sudden and unexpected development in a trial . . . I have often been with him in the trial of a case when I knew that something unexpected had happened which came to him as a complete surprise and, perhaps, disarranged his whole plan of trial, but never by his manner or by the tone of his voice was the court or jury led to suspect that he was disconcerted by what had occurred."[2]

He recalls that on one occasion when a case against a town was being tried for damages resulting from a defective highway, a question of fact arose "between witnesses for the plaintiff and defendant as to the exact character and location of the defect. Senator William F. Vilas represented the defendant town. He was a master of trial work as he was of the principles of law. When court adjourned for the day, things looked dark for the plaintiff, and everyone on our side of the table except Mr. La Follette, clearly showed distress. He apparently was quite content with the course of events, joking with opposing counsel and witnesses on both sides, as we gathered up our papers to leave the courtroom. No sooner were we alone, however, than Mr. La Follette's whole manner changed. He became the officer in command at a critical point in the battle. He gave his orders in short, sharp sentences. The place of the accident was some fifteen miles or more away. A well-known engineer and surveyor was called up, his services engaged for an all night's job, with the necessary helpers. A team and light wagon were engaged and the necessary tools, instruments, and lantern for night work secured. Automobiles had not then come into use. We repaired immediately to the scene of the accident, surveyed and plotted the highway at the place in dispute in the most careful manner, returned to the office of the engineer and surveyor about daylight, and when court convened at nine the next morning, we walked into court with a model of the highway at the place of the accident, which demonstrated the correctness of the testimony of witnesses for the plaintiff and the fallacy of the defendant's testimony, and the case was won."[3]

Bob's work as a lawyer had, Roe believed, a significant relation to his public career: "The patient, careful and exhaustive study, which as Governor and United States Senator he gave to every question upon which he was called to act, was merely applying the same methods which as a lawyer he used in preparing a case for trial. . . . It was, however, his labors as a lawyer which fitted him for his great service in the larger field of statesmanship. In this field his cause was Equal Rights v. Special Privilege, his clients, the plaintiffs, were the common people of the country."[4]

When Bob was defeated for Congress and "elected to practice law," his first examination of the firm's accounts convinced him there was not enough business for five lawyers. He thought it would be necessary to withdraw and practice alone. But three months after his return, there was enough work for all, and the partnership was continued. It was plain that he would soon have a leading place at the Madison bar, which then ranked among the greatest in Wisconsin's history. There was no cause for financial worry. He enjoyed the law and had a distinguished career ahead of him. We were both truly content. This was the situation when one day in response to a request from Senator Sawyer, Bob went to Milwaukee to meet him. Twenty years later he said, "Nothing else ever came into my life that exerted such a powerful influence upon me as that affair."[5]

The background of Bob's crucial meeting with Senator Sawyer was a time-honored political graft in Wisconsin. It had long been the practice for state treasurers to take interest on state funds; they deposited the public money in favored banks and shared the income as agreed upon. The new Democratic administration immediately started proceedings for restitution to the State of the money thus appropriated during the preceding twenty years. Legal action was brought against the treasurers and their bondsmen. These were pioneer cases in the enforcement of proper trusteeship of state funds, and excited great interest. Sawyer had been the principal bondsman for some of the treasurers, his liability amounting to some $300,000. It was known that the cases would be fearlessly prosecuted by the able, brilliant attorney general, James L. O'Connor. The treasury cases were to be tried in the Circuit Court of Dane County before Judge Robert G. Siebecker, Bob's brother-in-law. Shortly before they were to come on for argument, Bob received the following letter from Sawyer:

Dictated. Oshkosh, Wisconsin,
September 14, 1891.

Hon. Robert M. La Follette,
Madison, Wisconsin.

My Dear La Follette:
I will be in Milwaukee, at the state fair, on Thursday. I have some matters of importance that I would like to consult you about, that escaped my

mind yesterday. If convenient can you be in Milwaukee on that day and meet me at the Plankinton House at 11 o'clock A.M.? If not on that day, what day would suit your convenience this week? Please answer by telegraph. All you need to say, if you can meet me that day is merely telegraph me "yes." If not simply mention day you can meet me.

Yours truly,
PHILETUS SAWYER[6]

Sawyer's allusion to talking with Bob on the previous day referred to a chance meeting which had occurred at Neenah, Wisconsin, when they both attended the funeral of former Congressman Clark. On receiving Sawyer's letter, Bob, as usual, consulted with Sam Harper. They both decided the proposed interview related to politics and that the brief answer was requested as a precaution against newspaper publicity. Bob wired "Yes." The fact that the top of the single sheet of paper on which the letter was typed had been torn off did not impress Bob at the time. But after his interview with Sawyer, he investigated and discovered the letter had been typed on the office stationery of the former treasurer, Harshaw, who was among those being sued.

On Thursday, September 17, Bob went to the Plankinton House in Milwaukee, where he found Sawyer waiting for him. The Senator said he had been unable to get a room as the hotel was crowded, and they went up to the parlors on the second floor. After some preliminary conversation, he said he wanted to talk to Bob about Siebecker and the treasury cases; he explained that he had come alone, that no one knew he was to meet Bob. Then, with pocketbook in one hand and a roll of bills in the other, he offered Bob a sum of money in cash, not as a retainer to try the case in court as a lawyer, but as an advance payment to be followed by more when Siebecker decided the cases "right."

For a second Bob was speechless, then he answered: "Senator Sawyer, you can't know what you are saying to me. If you struck me in the face you could not insult me as you insult me now." Sawyer said, "Wait—hold on!" Bob replied: "No, you don't want to employ me as an attorney. You want to hire me to talk to the Judge about your case off the Bench." Seeing his anger, Sawyer sought to right the situation by asking how much Bob would "take as a retainer." Bob replied, "You haven't enough money to employ me as an attorney in your case, after what you have said to me."

Bob's first emotion was elemental—a surge of indignation at a personal insult that reflected on his honor. For an instant he was dazed and felt he could not keep his hands off Sawyer's throat. The interview ended, he rushed from the hotel and walked and walked.[7]

As I opened the door for him on his return home that evening, there was something in his face that made me ask, "What has happened?" He did not answer but remained silent until we sat down to supper. Then he said: "Belle, something *has* happened. Our life will never be the same." And it never was the same after that.

To a few close friends he immediately disclosed what had happened and told them he believed it his duty, as a member of the bar and an officer of the court, to inform Judge Siebecker. Some urged against this, pointing out Sawyer's great power, insisting it would avail nothing and only destroy Bob's usefulness. I well remember the anxiety of those conferences and how glad I was when it was suggested that the matter be submitted to Judge Bunn, the Federal judge of the Western District of Wisconsin, who was held in highest esteem by everyone who knew him. I am sure Bob's mind was made up and that nothing would have prevented his placing the matter before Judge Siebecker; but it was great support to have Judge Bunn, after listening to his statement of the Sawyer interview, respond: "You must tell Judge Siebecker. You cannot permit him to sit in the case without telling him all about it. I doubt very much whether he will feel that he can try the cases. That is for him to decide—but you must tell him."[8]

That same day Bob told Siebecker, who at once decided that the attempt to corrupt the court made it impossible for him to sit as judge in the cases. He called the attorneys on both sides together and told them only the bare fact that he was obliged to withdraw from the cases and would call in any other judge in the State on whom they agreed. He carefully refrained from giving out any information or taking any action that might prejudice the trial of the cases.

Judge Siebecker's announcement caused great surprise and consternation. It was followed by sensational stories in the leading newspapers of Wisconsin. On Sunday, October 23, 1891, the *Chicago Times* blazoned the charge that an attempt had been made to influence the court and a penitentiary offense committed. The headlines read:

BRIBERY THEIR GAME

PERSONS INTERESTED IN THE WISCONSIN STATE TREASURY

SUITS ATTEMPT DESPERATE MEANS

AN EFFORT MADE TO "INFLUENCE" JUDGE SIEBECKER . . .

HE REFUSES TO AT PRESENT MAKE PUBLIC THE DETAILS. . . .

STARTLING DISCLOSURES EXPECTED.[9]

The morning after the publication of the story, former State Treasurer Harshaw came to Bob's office and asked, "Bob, will you meet Sawyer at the Grand Pacific Hotel in Chicago tonight?" Bob answered, "No, I will never meet Sawyer or have any communication with him as long as I live."[10] It was evident that Sawyer was then in Milwaukee awaiting Harshaw's return, prepared to go to Chicago. When Harshaw returned and reported that Bob refused to meet him, Sawyer that same night gave the *Milwaukee Sentinel* an interview. In advance of any public charge of guilt, he protested his innocence.

For up to the time Sawyer's interview appeared in the newspaper, no public charge had yet been made connecting him with Judge Siebecker's retirement from the treasury cases. In his statement, printed in the *Milwaukee Sentinel* on Tuesday, October 27, 1891, Sawyer gave an inaccurate version of the interview, implying an "improper interpretation" had been put upon the conversation. He asserted it had never entered his mind "to influence the action of the court," and that it was impossible for him to think that his "conversation with Mr. La Follette" was "the basis of Judge Siebecker's refusal to sit in the case." The publication of Sawyer's statement, wholly misrepresenting the facts, made it necessary for Bob to make public the truth regarding the interview. He wrote a signed statement on Wednesday, October 28, giving a long, detailed account of what actually took place. It was published in the *Milwaukee Sentinel* on the following day. He did not point out the weakness and inconsistency of Sawyer's statement; nor did he note that Sawyer could not, as he claimed, have been ignorant of the fact that Bob and Siebecker were brothers-in-law, as there had been wide public discussion of their relationship when Siebecker was appointed circuit judge. It was characteristic of Bob to state with utmost care, as though he had been on the witness stand in court, only the facts required to make a public record of the exact truth.

It is hard today to conceive the consequences of Bob's statement. Probably nine-tenths of the people of Wisconsin did not doubt its truth. But at that time party fealty and fear of the powerful party organization were so strong that had Bob accepted Sawyer's bribe, been prosecuted and convicted of it, he could hardly have been more completely ostracized. Some of those who had been very close to him were alienated because they believed that regardless of Sawyer's conduct, Bob should have kept silent to protect the Republican Party. Even his intimate friends, who approved his course, were unable to see how he could ever rise above the political ruin this conflict with Sawyer had brought upon him. Dear old General Bryant, sitting in our home one evening with Bob, Sam Harper, and me, gave way to his grief. He spoke of his love for Bob being that of a father, and of the hope he had cherished for his future public career; he said he knew the power of the hostility which had been aroused, and that it would follow Bob to his grave.

The Republican press almost universally condemned his action, charging him with ulterior motives and even questioning the truth of his statement. Prepared as he was to meet criticism, no one could have anticipated the violence of the storm that broke upon him. A part of the Democratic press also joined the chorus of denunciation. About a month after the Sawyer encounter, thousands of copies of what was evidently an advance Democratic campaign document were circulated in Wisconsin. These leaflets printed Sawyer's first statement and La Follette's reply. The *Madison Democrat* charged in an editorial that this document emanated from La Follette or his friends.[11] Bob publicly declared, "No friend of mine, with my knowledge or consent . . . has caused them to be printed or circulated."[12] These documents may have aided in getting the facts to the people of the State, but it hurt him to the quick that anyone should believe he was using such indirect methods.

Whatever happened, he did not complain, but he was determined not to be crushed and that the outside world should not know what he suffered. Fortunately he had all the work he could do, and devoted himself to it. In his office, in the courtroom, wherever he might be in the public eye, he gave no sign of the struggle within. But in his home and with his intimate friends he made no attempt to appear the same. I feared he might not recover his buoyant spirit, wit, and humor again. I cared nothing for the incident it-

self except as it affected him. My only anxiety was for him. His
life was threatened; though I tried not to worry needlessly, I knew
he was followed, and sensed the sullen hatred and real danger which
menaced him. Sam Harper made his home at our house almost
entirely, accompanying Bob to and from his office and guarding
against his being alone. I hardly see how I could have come through
that crisis without Sam's help.

It was a hard fight. In the private room at his office and in the
little study at home throughout the long hours of the night, Bob
thought over many things that had occurred during his service in
the House. His encounters with Sawyer, Payne, and Colonel Dudley
now came back to him with new meaning. Instinctively he had
revolted against certain manifest evils which he had seen singly as
unethical acts of individuals. But Sawyer's offer of a bribe to influence the court had been a terrible shock that opened his eyes.
He began to see really for the first time the meaning and menace
of that community of political and economic influences which had
been manifested in the Menominee timber steal, the Sioux Indian
land-grant bill, the Nicaraguan Canal bill, the ship-subsidy, oleomargarine, and railroad bills.

It took Bob time to recover from the Sawyer experience and
think his way through. But out of the ordeal came understanding,
and out of understanding came resolution. Once the crisis was over
and he clearly understood the work that needed to be done, he
did not hesitate to undertake it. He did not underestimate the power
of the opposition. He had been made to feel its full force. He knew
Sawyer and his associates were allied with the railroads, the press,
and the leading politicians of every community. He knew the
struggle would be a long one, and that he must encounter repeated
defeat, but he was determined that the power of this corrupt influence should be broken in Wisconsin.

It was in this faith that he assumed leadership of the long political struggle which followed.

CHAPTER IX

"A Victory by a Fighting Minority"

Although Bob had no money, no organization, no newspaper support, he profoundly understood the mind and heart of the plain men and women of Wisconsin with whom he had always been identified. He knew they would be moved to action when they understood what was happening to their government. The fight had to be made, and he never shirked a responsibility. Bob's political work was grounded in his belief that "all great movements in society and government, . . . are the result of growth," and "that it is our duty to do, day by day, with all our might, as best we can for the good of our country the task which lies nearest at hand."[1]

On the surface there was not much evidence of an awakened public conscience and few signs of an uprising among the citizens. But there were certain inarticulate and unorganized forces upon which to build. Although there had been little public expression of indignation over Sawyer's attempt to bribe the court, the fact had shocked many people and made them ready to join a new movement. Bob believed the electorate to be sound and he knew the corrupt influence of political bosses in combination with the corporate interests was bipartisan.

Boss Keyes' defeat for election as Dane County municipal judge in 1890 had foretold the passing of the old order. The breakdown of rigid party lines after the Civil War made the new movement possible. In this election Keyes, a Republican, had carried the city of Madison, normally Democratic, while his opponent, Anthony Donovan, a Democrat, had received enough votes in the normally Republican country towns of Dane County to elect him judge. Anthony Donavan was a blacksmith with a taste for books, who had studied law by himself and later graduated from the university law

school. He and Bob frequently exchanged books and had long been
friends. Keyes attributed his defeat to Bob's support of Donovan.
It was a good piece of work. Bob took special satisfaction in it, for
Keyes was not only closely associated with Payne, Sawyer, and
Spooner, but, as chairman of the executive committee of the Board
of Regents, he had been absolute dictator of university affairs over
a long period. Keyes had made life difficult for President Bascom,
who was strongly supported by the student body.

The election of Governor Hoard, although the issue had not been
openly made, had also been a protest against boss rule, the packing-
interest lobby, and corporation control of legislation. During Hoard's
administration Henry C. Payne had been so offensively active in
opposing the Dairy and Food Commission bill that Governor Hoard
personally told him in plain English to quit interfering or he would
send a message to the legislature stating that the Republican chairman of the State Central Committee was acting as the paid lobbyist
of the Armour Packing Company. Payne quit open opposition to the
commission, but there is proof he worked undercover to defeat
Hoard's reelection. The governor's many friends among the farmers
resented Payne's disloyalty to the Republican nominee. This dissatis-
faction within the Republican Party was a good cause for revolt
against the old political-machine dictatorship.

The Granger movement had also done important educational work
on some problems which were again becoming issues. It had popu-
larized the doctrine that railroads were public highways, subject to
the law of common carriers; that rates should be reasonable; that
discriminations were unfair and unlawful; that free passes were an
evil and should be prohibited. The pass scandal had become serious
in Wisconsin. Public officials and their families had annual passes
as a matter of course. During legislative sessions much of the legislators' time was consumed in securing free transportation for the
folks back home and in looking after these same folks when they
visited the capitol because they could get a free ride. Sometimes the
conductor would go through a train and hardly pick up a fare. The
railroad lobbyists who distributed these favors held powerful sway
over legislators and legislation.

When Bob had come home from Congress in the spring of 1891,
Assemblyman Albert R. Hall was waging a hard fight to abolish railroad passes. It was natural that Bob and Sam Harper should be profoundly interested in the anti-pass legislation. They spent much time

working with Hall, who was often at our home when in Madison. The three men became close personal friends and allies in this and other reform fights. Hall was a remarkable man, with qualities of true statesmanship; able, fearless, incorruptible. When not occupied with public affairs, he lived rather an isolated life on his large, successful stock farm near the town of Knapp, Wisconsin. He had formerly been speaker of the Minnesota assembly. His experience there had made him a fine parliamentarian, and he became a powerful factor in the Wisconsin progressive movement. In writing of him Bob said: "I never knew a better man. Plain, modest, without guile, patient, lovable, tender-hearted, his whole life was so simple, so unselfish, so humble that he was sometimes underrated. He feared nothing except to do wrong."[2] The value of his service cannot be overestimated.

Looking back, it is hard to understand how Hall, the author of the anti-pass legislation, could have been scoffed at as a demagogue and a crank, when he should have been honored for his devotion to public welfare. Probably nine-tenths of the plain citizens of Wisconsin felt as my father did. I remember when it was suggested that he ask for a pass, he said if he had time for a railroad junket he would take money out of his own pocket to pay for it. But my father took no part in politics other than to vote the Republican ticket on election day. The public opinion he represented did not reach the legislature or find its way into the newspapers. Fortunately, this sort of sentiment did exist, ready to be utilized in a reform movement.

Bob knew that if he was to prove effective in the fight against the corrupt machine he must seize every opportunity to make it clear he had not been politically annihilated by Sawyer, the most powerful boss in the State. The Republican National Convention, which met at Minneapolis on June 7, 1892, offered such an opportunity. He did not seek election as a delegate but went with Sam Harper as a spectator. The Sawyer matter had been given wide publicity. As the election of Wisconsin delegates was dictated by the machine, they were all bitterly hostile to Bob. At the convention he anticipated a similar animosity among prominent Republican leaders. He met coldness and rebuke from men who had been warm friends in the House and was treated in the main as a political outcast. But some greeted him cordially, among others, Governor McKinley, who gave him a warm handshake and an understanding look.

Bob had used his influence to secure McKinley as National Day

speaker for July 29, 1892, at the Monona Lake Assembly, a well-
known Chautauqua at Madison. It was generally understood he
would be Wisconsin's choice for the Republican Presidential nomination in 1896. Bob knew Payne, Sawyer, Keyes, and Spooner would
work for a delegation pledged to Tom Reed. Although he admired
and liked Reed, he had a closer personal attachment to McKinley,
whom he believed more sympathetic to the plain people. Even little
things count in politics. At least we weighed everything, big and
little. We counseled with our friends about entertaining McKinley.
We didn't want him to be our guest if, because of the Sawyer affair,
it would cause trouble for him. General Bryant said people would
expect us to entertain him, and if we didn't it would hurt, as people
would say McKinley had gone back on Bob.

He arrived the day before his address and spent the night at our
house. We had an informal lunch for him the next day with a few
intimate friends. McKinley drew a large crowd and made a fine
speech, which added to his popularity among people. Bob introduced
him, and that evening attended a dinner given to a distinguished
company in honor of McKinley at the home of General and Mrs.
Lucius Fairchild, who were politically conservative and socially
prominent. A reception followed in the Madison Club rooms, and
McKinley left for Chicago and Nebraska.

Only those who had lived through the period following the break
with Sawyer could realize the real aid and comfort McKinley's visit
was to Bob. To meet his friend again on the old basis of good fellowship and understanding, and to be so cordially greeted, by the
Chautauqua audience and elsewhere, lightened the load he had been
carrying and inspired him with new confidence.

A few weeks after McKinley's visit, the Republican State Convention met, on August 18, 1892, and selected John C. Spooner as candidate for governor. All the nominations were dictated by Sawyer,
Payne, Spooner, and the reactionary leaders. But Payne withdrew
as chairman of the State Central Committee because of the hostility
his treatment of Hoard had aroused. H. C. Thom, a leader of the
Hoard followers, was made chairman in the interest of "party harmony."

When Bob saw that he was not to be invited to participate in the
campaign as in previous years, he thought it indicated an attempt

to read him out of the party. He did not propose to "recognize the authority of any man or any set of men to decide"[3] his party status, and he wrote to Thom offering his services. Thom called on him and explained frankly that, because of the bitter feeling of Sawyer's friends, it was believed he had better not go on the stump lest his appearance on the platform lead to violence. Bob told Thom that if the State Central Committee preferred not to sponsor his meetings, he would arrange his own. Thom then decided it would be better for him to speak under the auspices of the committee. It was so arranged; but Bob made out his own speaking schedule. Everywhere he met with a most cordial reception. Although towns were placarded with flaming red posters, probably of Democratic origin, setting forth questions which audiences were urged to ask him on the Sawyer matter, not once did the anticipated interruption or disturbance occur.

Theodore Roosevelt came to Madison to address the Wisconsin State Historical Society on January 24, 1893. He was then United States Civil Service Commissioner. During his two days' visit he was much entertained. On the first evening we gave a reception for him at our home. It was in the nature of open house and was largely attended. Politicians, reformers, scholars, big-game hunters, and people generally were much interested in meeting him. He was "delighted" to meet them. In introducing the callers, Bob gave the cue as to who they were, and Roosevelt came back with just the right response. The occasion was a success, as were all the social events of his visit. I think he had come in advance intending to do some work on his speech, but he was absorbed in having a good time and his address gave the impression of lack of preparation.

In spite of the demands on him, he made a party call and afterward wrote a cordial note saying he had enjoyed every moment of his stay and the reception at our house most of all. Roosevelt had the advantages of family, wealth, and culture. He was observant of social usages, yet seemed always informal and free of restraint— equally at home with people in all walks of life. He genuinely liked people. His dynamic personality, abounding enthusiasm, varied interests, were great assets to popularity. In these earlier years Bob entertained a genuine feeling of regard and good fellowship for

Roosevelt; but it was never in the nature of close personal friendship and understanding, such as he felt for McKinley.

Although much absorbed in his law practice, Bob was determined to start in the 1894 campaign the fight for reform of Wisconsin political conditions. We discussed again and again all phases of the problem with our close friends. It was necessary to find a strong candidate for governor who would command respect and guarantee the movement was launched in good faith. Had Bob believed himself the strongest candidate, he would have made the race; but he knew that, so soon after the Sawyer encounter, the contest would inevitably be centered about that incident instead of the real issue— the overthrow of the political machine.

When Bob suggested that Congressman Nils P. Haugen might consent to lead the revolt, everyone agreed his candidacy would be a master stroke. Haugen had been a member of the state legislature and a state officer. He had served nine years in the House of Representatives with distinction. His integrity, ability, courage, and fitness were beyond question. Haugen was the best type of American public servant; at the same time he made a strong appeal to the liberty-loving Scandinavian element of Wisconsin. Bob asked Haugen to stop off at Madison on his way to Washington in November, 1893. At this first conference Haugen saw and stated very clearly the heavy odds against a protest movement in its first open fight with the long-entrenched, powerful political machine. He agreed, however, that Bob should write to representative Wisconsin men, asking their opinion as to the support Haugen would receive if he became a candidate. Later Haugen and Bob met in Chicago to consider some 1,200 answers to these letters. The enthusiasm and promised support showed that a good fight could be made, and that, under the circumstances, he was the strongest candidate.

It was at our home, in the spring of 1894, that Haugen definitely decided to enter the race. Besides Haugen, Bob, and myself there were present at the final conference General Bryant, Sam Harper, and Herbert Chynoweth. The convention was to meet in Milwaukee on July 25. Bob, who had agreed to conduct Haugen's campaign, established headquarters in his law offices. He worked night and day dictating letters, holding conferences, and organizing groups of workers in different parts of the State.

Our house was also given over to campaign work. My heart was set on Haugen being governor. It seemed to me the people of Wisconsin must seize this wonderful opportunity to nominate a candidate of such superior character and ability tested by years of public service. I worked hard writing letters and getting out literature, confident the voters would come to the caucuses and vote for Haugen delegates.

Under the old system of nominating candidates by the caucus-delegate method, there was no discussion of issues or candidates in a speaking campaign. It was a question of getting a majority of the voters at the precinct caucuses to elect delegates to county conventions, where, in turn, a majority determined who should go to the state convention. Each precinct and each county decided its own time of holding its caucuses and convention. As a rule the caucus was a perfunctory affair, its action being determined by a few local leaders.

When a real fight was on, however, like the Haugen contest, the caucus became the storm center, and getting the voters to attend required thorough organization. Some had a special gift for doing this. I remember to this day with a thrill of gratitude Albert Stondahl, a fine-looking young man of the Norse type; he said very little, but when he went into a township he made a house-to-house canvass and made sure every Haugen voter was at the caucus. It was only this kind of zeal, especially on the part of the young men, that might carry Dane County, which, next to Milwaukee, was the largest in the State. Unless Bob could go to the state convention with Dane County back of him, the Haugen campaign would collapse. It may seem strange, but as I look back no other political contest in which I was interested seems to me to have been quite so desperate as the fight for these delegates. Madison and Stoughton caucuses were the first held in Dane County. It was a gloomy time at our headquarters when we learned every precinct in the two cities had been lost. I could hardly believe Bob meant what he said when, apparently undismayed, he told his disheartened followers we could, must, and would yet carry Dane. Then and there he began a survey of the situation in the country townships, calling on each man present to tell what he knew of the work to be done, securing promises they would all be about it early that morning and wouldn't quit until the last caucus was held.

However, when our little intimate group gathered later at our home, Bob was very serious and admitted he knew we were hard hit, but insisted that if we kept our nerves steady we still had a good chance to carry Dane County. It was like him to be cool in an emergency and not lose his head either in defeat or in victory. Our courage was renewed; our efforts redoubled. We carried the country towns as overwhelmingly as our enemies had carried the cities. The Dane County Convention adopted strong resolutions endorsing Haugen for governor; Bob was chosen to head the delegation to the state convention. Soon after, the other counties of Bob's former Congressional district were carried for Haugen.

The day before the state convention, a Milwaukee reporter noted that "Bob La Follette struck the Pfister [Hotel] like a young cyclone today and if he has only done half what rumor credits him with, must be about as pleasant company for the bosses as a wildcat would be at a picnic. He is working tooth and nail for Haugen, and has alarmed the bosses so that every henchman in the employ of both Spooner and Sawyer has jumped into the fight intent on downing La Follette first, and looking for candidates afterwards. Promises, money and whiskey are all in the scale against the doughty little champion from Dane, and although he will probably be beaten, he has the sympathy of a large number of delegates who dare not declare themselves in his favor.

"The fight has waxed so hot that Boss Sawyer has become afraid that his lieutenants might lose the battle, and he came in on the morning train to personally direct the battle." The reporter commented: "The reason why the Sawyer men fight La Follette is obvious. He refused a bribe and is therefore considered a dangerous lunatic by the sawdust contingent."[4]

When the convention met on July 25 ten candidates for governor were placed in nomination. On the first formal ballot the four highest candidates stood: Upham, 85½; Haugen, 75; Scofield, 74½; Taylor, 46. Bob wired me from Milwaukee that day, "We are giving them a pretty fight adjourned this morning."[5] Upham, Scofield, and Taylor represented the machine element in their various sections of the State; when it became necessary, they of course united to defeat the insurgents. Upham and Haugen continued to gain until the morning of the next day, when the candidates representing the machine element united and Upham was nominated on the sixth formal ballot, receiving 216 votes to Haugen's 99.[6]

After the convention Bob was detained in Milwaukee by legal business. Eager for inside news, I was mystified by the triumphant way our returning delegates discussed the convention results. The Haugen forces had stood together bravely; after his defeat they had continued to vote as a unit and succeeded in nominating some candidates for state offices. At first I could not realize it meant a victory by a fighting minority who had launched a movement they were sure would grow in power and achieve its purpose. The only attempt to reform the platform was the anti-pass resolution offered by A. R. Hall. Haugen accepted the result in fine spirit. He was very generous toward Bob and all who had asked him to lead the new movement. He laughed at my distress over his defeat, and gave me a set of after-dinner coffee cups as a souvenir of my part in the campaign.

During the campaign Bob had demonstrated his skill in organization. In leading the revolt against the old political machine, he had especially captured the imagination of young men. In holding his forces together after defeat, he had awakened the admiration of independent-thinking voters. He knew a good beginning had been made by the Haugen campaign. But to advance the cause steadily Bob realized he must systematically devote time to it. He must also earn the money to care for his family and meet the additional expenses of his political undertakings. For these reasons he decided to leave the law firm and engage in practice by himself. There was no change in the close personal friendship of the firm members; Sam Harper and his brother formed a new firm, Harper and Harper; Roe and Zimmerman became an independent firm. But Roe devoted much of his time to helping Bob prepare and try cases. Bob was thus free to give a few weeks each year to campaigning the State.

Bob's mother died on April 21, 1894. The funeral services were simple. He read a poem and, in accordance with what we felt would be Mother's wishes, we secured a former Baptist pastor, of whom she had thought highly, to preach the sermon. It was severely orthodox. Her death had come suddenly, following what we believed a light attack of pneumonia. Although she was seventy-six, she was of sturdy constitution; her faculties alert; her spirit unbroken. All winter she had attended a physical-culture class, greatly enjoying the exercises, which she practiced with delightful absence of self-consciousness. Bob's emotional nature was intense and all family ties were sacred. He had always worshiped his mother; they had been inseparable. It seemed as though he had never thought she might die, and was wholly unprepared for her passing. Only once thereafter, when our son, Bob, Jr., was dangerously ill for many months during the war, did I ever know him to be so overwhelmed and helpless.

Bob's mother was one of Nature's noblewomen. Her parents had come from North Carolina and settled in Indiana in an early day; although highly intelligent, she had almost no schooling. The tradition is that Bob's father taught her to write; but she never referred to the fact. In youth her reading had been confined chiefly to the Bible, which she continued to read daily throughout her life. Naturally, she loved to hear Bob read aloud; to that extent she became acquainted with good literature other than the Bible. She read the papers and was interested in politics, especially where he was concerned. I quite envied her the wit and sarcasm with which, in the privacy of our home, she would label and refute his opponents. She did not always speak grammatically, but she never lacked for words. Her enunciation was distinct and her speaking voice pleasing. She loved music and, even in later years, sang hymns in a strong, rich soprano voice.

From his mother Bob got his indomitable spirit and courage. She would fret and scold about little things—if the soup was too salty, or not salty enough; if the housework was not done as it should be—although she would keep dinner hot in the oven for hours awaiting his coming and make no complaint. But whenever real trouble came, she rose to the emergency with consummate poise and strength. In time of trial, quite unconsciously we leaned on her and were sustained by her wisdom and example. His mother was very dear to me, and I missed her greatly. My own feeling helped me realize Bob's sense of loneliness and irreparable loss. He kept hard at work, as always, and time healed, as it must if we are to go on living, the intense and passionate phase of his suffering; but Bob's memory of his mother was always singularly fervent.

Our second child was born on February 6, 1895. Bob had longed for a son, and I rejoiced that his wish was fulfilled. We decided without hesitation that his name would be Robert Marion, Jr. On

May 8, 1897, we were blessed with a second son. He was named Philip Fox, after our beloved family physician, Dr. Philip Fox. Our home was made complete by a fourth child, a daughter, born on August 16, 1899; we named her Mary, after her two grandmothers. We were happy and fortunate in our four children. Except for illness, not one of them ever caused us serious anxiety. However fierce the political struggle in which Bob might be engaged, his supreme interest centered in his family; his children were an unfailing source of joy and comfort to him. Without effort he made himself a part of their life. It was his nature to express freely his sympathy, understanding, and love. The children had his confidence. He had theirs. They were present at the councils of the grownups if they cared to be, and those who participated for the first time would be surprised to find them listening to the most solemn and confidential political matters.

Sometimes I questioned the wisdom of letting them become engrossed in subjects so remote from the thought of other children their age, but Bob was never troubled by any such doubts. He pointed out that they were normal and healthy, full of fun, carefree and as fond of play as anybody's children. Thus they grew up as familiar with politics as children raised on the farm are with its day's work; and in that same spirit of practical knowledge and experience they were ready, when it came their turn, to put their hands to the plow and go straight ahead to the end of the furrow. Bob appreciated the support his family gave him. He idolized his children and they idolized him. When he would put his arm about me and say, as he often did, "Mamma, aren't our children wonderful?" I might smile at his enthusiasm, but I shared it; my heart was full and nothing was wanting to make our life complete.

With four children instead of one, I could not have continued to give as much time to the work Bob was doing if Fola, the eldest, had not been such a help to me. My conscience always troubles me when I recall how much responsibility I let her carry. She had her father's natural leadership and control. She joined in their play, and they had the best time in the world with "Sister"; but they never questioned her authority. She was their comrade, and at the same time their oracle. When Mary was born and Bobbie was told he had a baby sister, he expressed his joy: "A sister. Why, she'll be like Fola!"

For some ten years I was deeply interested in the Emily Bishop League, a physical-culture organization started in Madison in 1893, of which I was president. I drifted into the work, but it had a wholesome effect on all my life thereafter. My friend Dr. Almah Frisby was preceptress at Ladies Hall, where a large number of university girls resided. She asked me to suggest someone who could speak on the subject of health and dress. I recommended Emily M. Bishop, co-principal of the School of Expression at the New York Chautauqua, whom we had met in Washington. She was a lecturer of note and author of many books in relation to her work, but was, above all, a born teacher. There are few friends to whose influence I owe so much. I was interested in the educational philosophy of William James, C. Hanford Henderson, and G. Stanley Hall; Mrs. Bishop applied the educational principles they laid down to everyday living; the mutual interdependence of mind and body was the keystone of her philosophy and teaching. Mrs. Bishop came to Madison a second year, and so many women were interested in her work that an informal school was organized. Gwyneth King, her assistant at Chautauqua, taught the league for two years; then I undertook the beginners' classes and gave informal talks.

Gilbert E. Roe, Bob's associate in law practice, married Gwyneth King in 1889, and they went to New York, where he established himself in his profession. The ties of friendship between our two families have, if possible, grown stronger with the years. When Fola went to New York to make the stage her profession, she made her home, until she married George Middleton, with Mrs. Bishop, who was "Aunt Emily" to all our children and to the Roe children as well.

Thus are the precious human ties interwoven and the currents of life separated and united again.

In November, 1894, William H. Upham, who had defeated Haugen for the nomination, was elected governor over his Democratic opponent George W. Peck, who was seeking a third term, by a majority of 53,869. Although the two Peck administrations had produced scandals and an unsatisfactory legislative record, the vigorous prosecution of the treasury cases had returned over half a million dollars. The quarter of a million still to be retrieved became a foremost campaign issue. Democrats warned that Republicans would never collect the remaining obligations. As soon as the Republicans came to power, the legislature passed bills relieving the former treasurers and their bondsmen from further payments. Governor Upham, who had been the candidate of the Sawyer-Payne-Pfister forces, signed the bills and thus prevented the State from receiving the remainder of the money won by the prosecution of the treasury cases. A dominant factor in putting through this legislation was Charles Pfister of Milwaukee, who, through his fortune, was closely associated with Henry Payne in public utilities and other business enterprises. There was a judgment of over $100,000 against the estate Pfister had inherited from his father, who had been one of the bondsmen. From this time on, Charles Pfister was counted as one of the big Republican bosses of Wisconsin.

The same legislature as a matter of course defeated Hall's antipass bill, but he was not disheartened. Hall, Bob, and Sam Harper promptly worked out a plan for a statewide unofficial referendum. Ballots were sent out shortly before the spring elections to as many town clerks as possible, who were asked to secure for their townships an expression of public sentiment on railroad passes and regulation. In this educational campaign Hall spent for postage and printing something like $2,000 of his own money.[7] Out of 51,000 votes, only 600 were cast against the proposed reform. At the next state convention Hall made good use of this referendum.

In the winter of 1896, after an unusually long, hard term of court, Bob was seriously ill. Our good Dr. Fox, who had more influence over Bob than anyone else, insisted he go South, and arranged to go with him. The day before they left, William Osborn, a cousin of McKinley, called at our home. Presenting a letter from McKinley, he stated his mission was to ask Bob if he would support McKinley as against Reed for President. Bob replied that he was confident the people of Wisconsin were for McKinley; although he himself was obliged to go away for his health, his friends would help in every way they could to carry Wisconsin. Bob called Sam Harper and others into conference and they agreed to start organization work at once.

While in the South, Bob was elected as a delegate to the Republican National Convention. Delegates were then elected by the caucus-and-convention method, each Congressional district choosing two delegates. Boss Keyes was a candidate against him, but Bob carried all the counties except one and was nominated by acclama-

tion at the Congressional-district convention. When the state convention met in Milwaukee, the delegates at large were instructed for
McKinley. The Sawyer-Payne-Spooner forces favored Reed, but at
the local caucuses and conventions most of the delegates had been
instructed for McKinley. At the St. Louis convention the Wisconsin
delegation obeyed instructions and cast its solid vote for McKinley.

At every national convention each state delegation selects its chairman, its representative on the various committees, and names its
member of the national committee. Bob was surprised to learn he
was to be on the Resolutions Committee. It was an unexpected honor.
Nevertheless, he protested the election of Sawyer for chairman and
Payne for national committeeman. Five votes were cast against
Sawyer, eight against Payne. Former Governor Hoard, one of the
four delegates at large, spoke against Payne. Although Payne had
enough votes to elect him national committeeman, his friends wished
to make it unanimous. While the matter was pending, Bob received
word that Mark Hanna wished to see him at the McKinley headquarters.

Hanna was very cordial, and told Bob he knew McKinley would
like to see Payne on the national committee, and he hoped that in
the interest of harmony the Wisconsin delegation would stand together for the election of Payne. Bob replied that in behalf of the
new movement in Wisconsin the issue must be raised against the old
organization. For that reason the protest against Payne must be
made. Mark Hanna's manner changed abruptly and the interview
ended.

In the balloting for the Vice Presidential nomination, Henry Clay
Evans, of Chattanooga, Tennessee, was running second. He was a
former Wisconsin man who had enlisted in the Civil War with a
Wisconsin regiment. Most of the Wisconsin delegation were supporting him. At the last moment the Tennessee delegation asked Bob,
who had served with him in Congress, to second Evans' nomination.
He stood up on a chair and shouted for recognition. A call went up
for him to go to the platform. He had hardly spoken a sentence
when he had the close attention of the vast audience. E. D. Coe,
later a bitter political enemy, reported to his paper that the speech
"seconding the nomination of Mr. Evans was the greatest oratorical
success of all the nominating speeches, excepting Chancy [*sic*] M.

Dapew's [*sic*], and it was delivered on the briefest notice to a tired-out audience."[8]

Sam Harper returned from St. Louis much elated over Bob's part in the convention. When Sam said this had made him an entirely different man in the eyes of the nation, I laughingly replied I was glad he looked the same to me. But Sam was in earnest and tried to make me understand that a Presidential convention was a great national stage with delegates and spectators from every State; that all the leading newspapers had representatives there; that Bob had made a "great hit" in defending the next President from unjust attack; and that he had "electrified" the vast assemblage with a short speech nominating a candidate for Vice President. Sam explained how this would strengthen his leadership in Wisconsin. Bob was silent and thoughtful while Sam was talking. Finally he said: "Sawyer is not going to last many years; I ought to be a candidate in his life-time and try out before the people of Wisconsin the issue that has been raised by the trouble between us. I don't want it said that I waited until he was dead before I dared to hazard the contest."*

* Sawyer died in March, 1900.

CHAPTER X

The County-Fair Crusade

Bob was determined to have a candidate for governor to oppose the old machine. Our forces must be held together, the movement kept alive and militant. There was no telling how long it would take, but he was confident we would eventually win. If a candidate could be found who would arouse less personal antagonism than himself, he was ready to support him; but if no other available man was willing he would be the candidate. The matter was seriously discussed and the field thoroughly canvassed. Leaders were generally willing to back him, but no one else wanted to face the defeat awaiting the man who dared oppose the powerful machine. Bob therefore announced he was a candidate—an anti-machine candidate.

At first the Sawyer-Payne-Pfister tactics were to ridicule his candidacy. But they soon saw the headway he was making and marshaled all their forces—money, newspapers, officeholders, and henchmen—in a bitter fight. Governor Upham had done their bidding in signing the bills which released the former treasurers and their bondsmen from paying what they owed the State. This had, however, made him unpopular and unavailable as a candidate for renomination. At a conference held during the St. Louis Convention, the same bondsmen and political bosses had told Upham he must get out of the way; they had decided Major Edward Scofield should be the next governor. Major Upham did as he was told.

When the state convention met at Milwaukee on August 5, 1896, Bob's friends believed he had at least twelve more votes than were necessary to nominate. These delegates were pledged and instructed to vote for him on the first formal balloting. Former Governor Hoard made a dramatic and eloquent nominating speech. A great demonstration followed. But before the nomination was made, an adjourn-

116

ment was taken. The Sawyer-Payne-Pfister forces worked fast during the interval.

The six candidates for governor all had headquarters at the Hotel Pfister. Shortly after ten o'clock, Captain John T. Rice, leader of a delegation from Rock County, came and told Bob, in the presence of General Bryant, Sam Harper, and others, that he had been taken into a private room and offered $700 if the seven delegates of his assembly district were transferred to Scofield. Before midnight other delegates reported attempts to buy their votes for Scofield. The statements of twenty men were taken down. There was no way of telling how many delegates yielded to temptation, since those who took the money did not report to La Follette Headquarters.

After midnight Pfister came and told Bob they had him licked; they had taken away enough delegates to defeat him, but they didn't want to hurt the party or have any scandal; if Bob would behave they would take care of him. Bob told Pfister he was able to take care of himself, and would smash their rotten machine. The next day Scofield was nominated.

The work of the bosses had been coarse and rank. Bob's loyal delegates knew what had defeated them. Indignant and excited, they marched back to headquarters in a body to demand that Bob run as an independent candidate. One young fellow—it was his first convention—broke down and sobbed like a child. Bob promised that defeat would only drive him on, and repeated to them the lines from one of Henley's poems which came to him. The words had meaning for the listening men—changed the anger of frustration to renewed courage. Speaking out of the burning faith that was in him, Bob said that men who win final victories are only stimulated to better fighting by defeat. The people had been betrayed by those they trusted to serve them. If anyone was forced to leave the Republican Party, it should be the corrupt bosses. He would never abandon the fight to make government represent the people.

Although their candidate for governor was defeated, the progressive forces had won an encouraging victory. By skillful parliamentary tactics A. R. Hall finally got his anti-pass resolution before the convention. Hall's resolution passed and became part of the Republican platform.[1] Bob made some twenty-five speeches in the 1896 election campaign. Relying on memory. I should say he altogether ignored Scofield's candidacy. The national issues in this McKinley Presidential campaign were sound money and the protective tariff. Because of his strong personal friendship for McKinley and his familiarity with the tariff, Bob entered into the campaign with enthusiasm. The night before election, he closed his tour at Milwaukee, making his first political speech in that city. It was published in full in the *Milwaukee Sentinel*, which reported: "He interpolated the dry, hard facts of financial history with pathos and humor, and carried his audience with unflagging interest. . . . When he finally sat down the great audience rose up and gave three rousing cheers for the speaker."[2]

After McKinley's election Wisconsin and national-machine politicians joined in a great drive to have Henry Payne appointed Postmaster General. At the same time friends of former Governor Hoard in Wisconsin and over the country were urging his appointment as Secretary of Agriculture. In behalf of Hoard, Bob wrote to McKinley and, at the invitation of the President-elect, went to see him at his home in Canton, Ohio, early in February, 1897. When Bob arrived, about ten in the morning, McKinley told his secretary he would see no one else until five that afternoon. They drove about the town, went over and visited his mother, "a beautiful old lady, to whom he was devoted." I recall Bob's telling us that when he congratulated her on her son's achievement, she replied he had always tried to do what was right and so had his brother Abner, who was "just as able and conscientious as William."[3]

Bob had luncheon with McKinley at his home and they discussed Cabinet appointments. McKinley said that Hoard had strong endorsement from nearly every State; that he had met Hoard, and regarded him as a strong character, a genial and companionable man; and that he had confidence in his administrative ability. But on the other hand the appointment of Henry Payne as Postmaster General had been urged by every member of the national committee, every Republican Senator and Congressman who had visited him at Canton. McKinley said he believed no other man had ever been so strongly endorsed by prominent and influential politicians. Bob protested his appointment, told Payne's history in Wisconsin politics, explained the interests he represented, and recalled his lobbying activities in Washington, especially while the oleomargarine bill was pending. When it was about time to go, McKinley said, "Bob, I may not be able to appoint Hoard, but I will say to you that Henry Payne shall not be a member of my cabinet."

Months later, when Bob called upon McKinley at the White House after his inauguration, the President told him of the final effort to secure Payne's appointment. Just before McKinley's decision Mark Hanna had come to him and said, "You may wipe out every obligation that you feel toward me, and I'll ask no further favors of you, if you'll only put Henry Payne in the cabinet." McKinley answered, "Mark, I would do anything in the world I could for you, but I cannot put a man in my cabinet who is known as a lobbyist."[4]

"The evil work" of that 1896 convention night forced Bob to do some hard thinking. Determined to overthrow the corrupt interests that had betrayed representative government by the brazen purchase of instructed delegates, he tried to find a practical way for the voters to enforce their wishes. His attack on the problem foreshadowed the method he used repeatedly throughout his long public service. To meet the specific abuse encountered through direct experience and observation, he worked out a concrete legislative plan: the direct nomination of candidates by the voters. Once the program was clearly formulated, he started in on an educational campaign to win the understanding and support of the people.

The Constitution had provided for the election, but not for the nomination, of public officials. The complicated caucus-and-convention system had been evolved to allow voters to nominate as well as elect their representatives. But this intricate succession of town, county, district, state, and national meetings to elect delegates to other meetings offered opportunity for manipulation at each stage. It discouraged the plain citizen, and control inevitably fell into the hands of professional politicians representing special interests.

Bob's plan was that throughout the State voters should *nominate* all candidates by secret ballot on a given day at regular polling places under the same legal safeguards that were provided on election day. When he and Sam Harper discussed this reform with me, I was thrilled by the improved political conditions it promised. Of course, the direct primary has not been a cure-all for political evils, but it was a great advance toward a truer democracy. Perhaps only those who have experienced the change can realize how much more secure the voter is in choosing candidates under the primary election. Look-

ing back, it seems strange that this reform which Bob brought about
in Wisconsin was denounced throughout the State and the Nation
as a "menace" and the "populistic scheme of a hare-brained demagogue."

When Bob was invited by President William R. Harper to deliver
the annual Washington's Birthday address at the University of
Chicago in 1897, he decided to make direct primary elections his
theme. His speech was entitled, "The Menace of the Machine." The
style bears the imprint of careful preparation and some of the sentences recall the "Iago" of college days. The annual address had
become a university feature; McKinley had spoken in 1895, Roosevelt in 1896.

The distinguished audience assembled at Kent Theater to hear
Bob with the customary ceremony; the faculty in cap and gown
followed by the student body and invited guests. They listened with
close attention as he analyzed and contrasted the necessary work of
legitimate political organization with the corrupt activities of the
political machine. The speech was widely reported and at first received favorable comment in the press. Soon, however, certain newspapers, realizing the practical implications of his primary-election
plan, began to make sharp attacks, charging that Bob himself was a
machine politician.

While preparing his address Bob, Sam Harper, and others had, as
a test of its workability, outlined a law embodying the primary-
election reform he first proposed at Chicago. Soon after, such a bill
was introduced in the Wisconsin legislature by Assemblyman William T. Lewis. There was no hope of securing legislation that session,
but this made the primary election a concrete political issue. Bob
realized there was a long struggle ahead and that he must get the
support of the people. He asked the Wisconsin weekly newspapers
if they would furnish their readers with supplements containing his
Chicago address. In this way some four hundred thousand copies of
of "The Menace of the Machine," together with copies of the primary-election bill, were distributed over the State. The supplement
also contained a scholarly address by Charles Noble Gregory on the
English Corrupt Practices Act.

On the following Fourth of July, Bob was invited to speak at
Mineral Point. On his way he was surprised to receive a telegram
from President McKinley tendering him the appointment of Comp-

troller of the Currency. This position paid a salary of $6,000 and had been held by able lawyers. Any appointive office, however, which removed him from the Wisconsin battleground had no appeal for him. Without hesitation he declined this appointment, just as he had a Federal judgeship in Indian Territory soon after his defeat for Congress. It caused much newspaper comment and demonstrated his sincerity regarding the new movement.

His refusal of a $6,000 job probably made a more profound impression on Wisconsin citizens than happenings of much greater importance. Such is often the case. The offer was variously interpreted. According to usage, the state patronage was controlled by John C. Spooner, who had been elected United States Senator by the 1897 legislature. Some astute observers inferred the offer had been made to get Bob out of the way. When Bob went to Washington in July with Sam Harper and Grant Thomas, he wrote me that they "went up to the Senate where we all called on Spooner. In everybody's presence I thanked him for 'the part he had in sending me the message respecting the comptrollership of Treasury.' He mumbled something about 'being glad' but did not clearly say just what his 'part' had been." Later in the day, when he saw the President at the White House, McKinley said the comptrollership had not been tendered at anyone's suggestion but because he wanted Bob "in his administration."[5]

During the summer and fall of 1897, Bob made a series of county-fair speeches which stirred the State and began to break down strict party lines. At Mineral Point, in his Fourth of July address entitled "Dangers Threatening Representative Government," he began applying to specific Wisconsin situations the general principles he had discussed in "The Menace of the Machine."

He attacked the Scofield administration for deliberately violating platform pledges. Analyzing the previous session of the legislature, he described the defeat of Hall's anti-pass resolution and told how Davidson's bills requiring the corporations to pay their just share of the taxes had been killed. From the legislative records he made it plain that special interests ruled both parties and that Republicans and Democrats must share the responsibility for failure to enact laws to serve the people. Public servants should, he insisted, represent the public interest—not special interests. As an effective instrument to break the old bipartisan machine rule, he urged passage of a primary-election law. At the Tower Hill Chautauqua, where he gave practically this same address, I well remember the enthusiasm of the audience and the hearty approval of Jenkin Lloyd Jones, of the Chicago Lincoln Memorial Church, who presided. He was ever one of Bob's most loyal friends and supporters.

By the time Bob spoke at the state fair in Milwaukee on September 24, people were excited over the crusade he was making. The *Milwaukee Sentinel* and the *Milwaukee Journal* printed his speech in full, so that it was widely read throughout the State. As the effect and significance were felt, newspapers took sides. Opposition and support were manifested along bipartisan lines. A leading Democrat, T. J. Cunningham, promised the support of his newspaper if La Follette stood for election on the platform outlined in his Milwaukee speech.[6] The county-fair managers were criticized for asking him to speak, but they paid no heed to critics. He drew large crowds and had many more invitations than he could fill.

An attempt to break up Bob's meeting at Oshkosh, Senator Sawyer's home town, provoked state-wide attention. He was speaking from a farm wagon, which often proved a convenient platform at county fairs. The wagon had been placed in front of the audience which filled the grandstand. He had hardly begun when the bell in the judges' stand signaled for the horse races to start. Boys commenced shouting in all parts of the grandstand, "Score cards for sale." Five or six horses were heading for a start down the track. It was plain he must act quickly or lose the day. He directed that his wagon platform be drawn across the track, and, turning to the judges' stand, he announced he was speaking on invitation of the association, had been given a certain length of time, and would not budge until he had finished. He threatened, if again interrupted, to occupy the rest of the afternoon to the exclusion of the horse races. The five thousand people in the grandstand stood up and cheered approval. He was not again interrupted.

A Democrat, B. J. Daly, who heard this Oshkosh speech, remembers how these county-fair meetings broke down party lines, set men thinking, and converted them into those "fair-minded Democrats" who helped make Wisconsin a progressive laboratory for the Nation. "That was the first time," Daly says, "I had ever heard a

Wisconsin, 1897
Bob's county-fair speeches begin a long fight for progressive legislation.

Bob in 1904, during his second term as governor of Wisconsin

Maple Bluff Farm

There was no work on the farm that Bob could not do, and do well. He plowed a straight furrow and plowed deep.

Los Angeles, 1907
Bob reads the roll call on the Senate in 17 States.

was made editor. The name of the paper was changed to the *State,* and a platform of principles became a conspicuous feature of the make-up. I recall how Bob prized the *State.* The paper grew and gained enough influence throughout Wisconsin to alarm the bosses, who sought to have the Post Office Department at Washington deny it second-class mail privilege. Satisfied that Keyes had instigated this move, Bob wrote to the Department asking for a thorough investigation, which was made by post-office inspectors. That ended the attempt to take away the second-class privilege.

Bob's persistent work for reform legislation was making him more widely known. On March 12, 1898, he was invited to speak on primary elections before the Good Government Club of the University of Michigan at Ann Arbor.* This lecture covered much the same ground as his Chicago address, but the style was less studied, the content more profound. It justly ranks among his finest speeches.

On his return to Madison, he found Sam Harper critically ill with pneumonia. Bob scarcely left his bedside. I was at Sam's home most of the time. Everywhere his hosts of friends were anxiously awaiting the verdict. He died on March 19, 1898. The members of his family who survived him were his mother, a wonderful woman, three brothers, and four sisters, all men and women of unusual character. The bond between our two families has been close through all the years. From the day of their first meeting, when Bob was a freshman at the university, until the day of Sam's death they had been inseparable in mind and heart. The sympathy between them was closer than any ties of kinship.

Throughout his county-fair campaigns Bob had assailed the Scofield administration for its favoritism to corporations. By using his influence to defeat the anti-pass legislation, Governor Scofield had violated the platform pledge of the convention which nominated him. When he moved from his home at Oconto to the Executive Residence at Madison, he made the mistake of shipping his household goods and other belongings, including his cow, under a free express frank. Although there was no law forbidding it, this dramatized the pass issue. Cartoonists, newspapers, humorists, and

---

* This address was subsequently printed in pamphlet form, with an introduction by Bob, and distributed to aid in securing support for primary-election law in Wisconsin.

speakers made the most of the gentle Jersey's free ride. "Scofield's cow" soon became his political white elephant.

Machine leaders counseled that another man be substituted, but Scofield refused to be sidetracked and announced his candidacy in April. He was strong with the railroads, he was an old soldier, and the custom of a second term was generally accepted. The chances were all against defeating him for the nomination. Some Progressives urged that a protest be made without putting up a candidate to be shot to pieces. Many of Bob's friends feared if he was defeated a second time, it would destroy faith in both the reform movement and his leadership. But he contended, as always, that failure to be nominated could not destroy any man whose candidacy was based upon important principles, and that the movement would disintegrate unless an active campaign was kept up against corporation-machine rule. As in 1896, he offered to support any recognized Progressive who would run against Scofield, but insisted that an out-and-out fight must be made.

For months he had continuously overworked; Sam Harper's death had been a hard blow; it cost him an effort to enter the conflict this time as a candidate. He would have preferred to back another, but no one else was available. By what was then an unusual procedure in Wisconsin politics, he formally announced his candidacy on July 15. He issued an address to the people which was virtually a platform. Briefly summarized, it promised to keep platform pledges and declared for the following legislation: (1) making untaxed property pay its share of the burden of government, (2) effectually prohibiting corrupt practices in campaigns and elections, (3) securing all possible relief from combinations and trusts that destroy competition and restrain trade, (4) prohibiting use of passes and franks by public officials, (5) abolition of the caucus-and-convention system and enactment of a direct primary election to nominate candidates. Hundreds of thousands of copies of this platform address were mailed, together with a letter asking for support. A pamphlet followed soon, giving a sketch of Bob's life, excerpts from his speeches, and newspaper comments on his record.

Effective in this and later campaigns was the Republican Club of Milwaukee County, organized in the spring of 1898 by Bob's boyhood friend Charles Pullen, a prominent Milwaukee banker. This club sponsored and distributed 75,000 copies of another pamphlet, signed by Pullen, entitled "Governor Scofield's Record as Shown by His Official Acts." It was probably the most scathing arraignment of a public official ever published in Wisconsin up to that time.

Scofield was defended by Senator Spooner in a carefully prepared two-column interview.[11] After giving out this vindication, Spooner, as was his habit, left the State. By temperament he shrank from the actual combat of politics, but he had a strong hold on Wisconsin quite independently of the old political machine with which he cooperated as inconspicuously as possible. He was twelve years older than Bob and had graduated from the university in 1864. The fact that he had served with a Wisconsin regiment in the war appealed to old soldiers. His exceptional ability as a lawyer had been generously rewarded by a large public-service corporation practice. Beginning as secretary for Governor Fairchild, his political affiliations in the State had always been with the Payne, Sawyer, Keyes forces. From 1885 to 1891, while Bob was a member of the House, Spooner, then the junior United States Senator, had been closely associated with Aldrich, Allison, and Platt as their authority on constitutional questions. Defeated in the Wisconsin Democratic landslide of 1891, he was made the Republican nominee for governor in 1892, but was again defeated by a Democrat. However, the Wisconsin legislature had reelected him to the Senate for the term beginning March 4, 1897. From this time on his growing national prestige was steadily, though subtly, directed against the progressive movement in Wisconsin.

In spite of Spooner's vindication of Scofield, the 1898 convention would have nominated Bob on the first ballot had money not again been used to buy delegates. Isaac Stephenson, who was then supporting Scofield and who was a power in the old political machine, often said that "the total amount of money required to handle delegates the night before the balloting began was $8,300."[12] Scofield was nominated.[13] But the platform was practically dictated by the Progressives. The Scofield forces attempted to rush through nominations before adoption of a platform. But General Bryant protested, "Before I vote for a candidate for governor I want to know what platform he stands on." His brief, effective speech forced an adjournment. Gilbert Roe, who had done valiant service throughout the campaign, carried on the fight for a progressive platform in the

Resolutions Committee. The people of the State were now so wrought up over the issues discussed in the county-fair and campaign speeches that the Scofield supporters were forced to adopt most of the program Bob had pledged when he announced his candidacy.

After the convention was over, Bob and some of the delegates took the night train home. As he left Judge Albert H. Long at the Madison station, Bob said: "Well, Albert, we lost the day. But we made a fight that was worth the making. There is another day coming and I shall expect to see you there again."

A little over a year later, on October 16, 1899, McKinley spoke from the capitol steps at Madison, where he was introduced by Governor Scofield. The President came to Madison from Galena. He was accompanied by a large party, including five of his Cabinet —Gage, Long, Wilson, Root, and Griggs. Bob went as far as Mount Horeb to meet the train. He gave his card to the proper official with greetings to the President but received no answer. I believed, and Bob thought it quite possible, McKinley did not get the word that he was on the train. Bob, Jr., then aged four and a half, a blue-eyed boy with golden curls, rather wise for his years, accompanied his father with the expectation that he was to meet the President. After they came home, Bob told me that Bobbie had asked no explanation of why they had not spoken to McKinley. "He understood without asking," his father said.

CHAPTER XI

The Road Ahead Seemed Smooth
and Certain

Bob took no part in the 1898 election campaign. While trying a lawsuit, he was taken seriously ill and was obliged to cancel all his speaking dates. The greater part of the next six months he spent in bed and convalescence. As soon as he was able to travel, Dr. Fox insisted on a warmer climate and offered to accompany him. Bob would not go without me, so it was arranged that Bob, Jr., and Phil should stay with my mother, and Fola with her Aunt Jo.

We spent some weeks at San Diego, then a city of less than twenty thousand. From there we often went to La Jolla for the day, where we were fascinated by the isolated rocky coast and pounding waves. Except for the home of Ellen Scripps, there were only a few haphazard cottages on the long wide slope from Mount Soledad to the sea. The California trip restored his health, and, as always after recovery from serious illness, he promised to be more careful in the future. During the ensuing year he gave most of his time to his law practice, but it was evident that he was the coming man politically and would be the next governor. Various factors contributed to the nomination being practically conceded to him. An aroused public opinion had finally forced Governor Scofield and a reactionary legislature to enact an anti-pass law. After years of heroic effort, A. R. Hall had won an outstanding victory. The effect on Wisconsin political conditions was significant because the political bosses were now deprived of this insidious source of power. Furthermore, the enactment of some mild taxation measures had inspired confidence and created a widespread demand for a governor who would put through the primary election and other progressive reforms.

Ill feeling among some of the old-line Republican leaders over the election of Joseph V. Quarles as United States Senator by the 1899 legislature contributed to the nomination being conceded to Bob. Congressman J. W. Babcock and Isaac Stephenson, both ambitious for the office, felt they had been badly treated by Sawyer, Spooner, and Payne, who had supported Quarles. To get even, Babcock now proposed to join the progressive movement which looked so much like a winning cause. In January, 1900, Bob told Babcock's emissary, Henry Casson: "Well, you know what I am fighting for in this state. You know that I am standing for certain issues, and am welcoming all the help that I can get."[1]

A close friend of Babcock's, Emanuel L. Philipp, afterward governor, then a Milwaukee corporation man, also professed to believe there were abuses which should be reformed. At the request of these two men, Bob agreed, if Governor Hoard was present, to state his position on railroad taxation directly to Marvin Hughitt, president of the Chicago and North Western Railroad. The meeting was arranged at Hughitt's Chicago office, where, in the presence of Hoard and Babcock, Bob frankly said he would recommend and approve "a bill taxing railroad companies upon the value of their property, just as other taxpayers of Wisconsin are assessed and taxed upon their property." Hughitt answered that this was "perfectly satisfactory to the Northwestern," and the interview ended. Bob never met him again, but believed Babcock and Philipp had volunteered support and arranged the interview because it was plain he would be elected and they hoped to maintain friendly relations with the new administration. The railroads could have been under no illusion, however, as to Bob's taxation program, for he also stated it clearly in a letter to Thomas Gill, general attorney for the Wisconsin Central.[2]

The support of politicians of the Babcock-Philipp type later proved definitely harmful because it put us off our guard in campaigning for a really progressive legislature. At the time it was recognized as temporary and of doubtful value while it lasted. But Isaac Stephenson's support was believed to be on a different basis, even though he had undoubtedly broken with his old political associates because they had not supported him for Senator. However, once having made the break, we regarded him as a genuine convert to the progressive movement, for he had real native strength of character. Born in New Brunswick in 1829, he had risen from poverty and had a sincere respect for the individual rights of the plain people. As a pioneer lumberman he had himself made a large fortune and believed every man should have his chance. He often declared he didn't want anybody to pay any part of his taxes. A warm personal attachment had existed between Bob and "Uncle Ike" during their years in the House of Representatives. I was also fond of him. Although somewhat vain of his success and susceptible to flattery, he had a picturesque, interesting personality, was a keen observer, and narrated his unique experiences with quaint humor and philosophy. He had the gaming spirit; liked horse-racing and wanted his yacht to pass everything on the Great Lakes. This trait characterized his enjoyment of politics. He backed the progressive movement with zest and gave generously of his money in support of it.

The Progressives had lost out in three successive campaigns. But the political situation had altered. This change was largely due, I believe, to the cumulative effect of the previous years of work: to speaking campaigns, especially at county fairs, to wide distribution of literature relating to the issues, to newspaper discussion. Bob had been twice defeated for the nomination for governor. But now Wisconsin was so permeated with La Follette sentiment that he was certain, if a candidate, to be elected in spite of the old machine.

On May 15, 1900, Bob announced his candidacy. In striking contrast to previous years, many newspapers now declared that since the principles he advocated had been incorporated in the last platform, he should be given the credit and the responsibility of enacting the reform program.[3] Years of educational campaigning had aroused the electorate. The usual tactics of the old-line politicians seemed no longer effective. As in 1896 and 1898 they again raised the cry that if elected, La Follette would use his prestige as governor to "sacrifice Spooner" and secure his own election to the Senate. To answer these persistent rumors, Bob issued a statement on May 30 that he would be neutral on the Senatorship, and intended so to conduct the affairs of the State as to entitle him to reelection as governor.[4] An announcement by Governor Scofield that La Follette's election would be disastrous to the harmony and permanent interest of the party in Wisconsin also proved ineffective. His home county of Oconto was carried for La Follette the next day. The opposition was disheartened. One after another, the candidates withdrew. Long before the convention it was practically certain Bob would be nominated without contest.

To the amazement of everyone, Spooner, on July 5, gave out a formal statement that he had "unalterably determined not to be a candidate for reelection" at the expiration of his term in 1903.[5] Since he later became a candidate, this statement is a noteworthy bit of Wisconsin history. Although obviously intended to imply that his decision was motivated solely by duty to his family and had no relation to recent political events, it was generally interpreted that he preferred to retire with honors rather than struggle against the new forces represented by Bob's successful candidacy. His withdrawal silenced the "sacrifice Spooner" cry and left the old machine helpless and leaderless at the state convention contest a month later. As the spokesman of an apparently united Republican Party, General Earl M. Rogers, with three other candidates, who had also previously withdrawn, visited Bob the morning of the convention to say: "Mr. La Follette, we call for the purpose of striking our colors and surrendering to you. From this time forward we are all of us for Bob La Follette."[6]

The convention was held August 8, at the Exposition Building in Milwaukee. The great audience was a moving sight. There were no contests over delegates; it was known who would be nominated and what platform would be adopted. In spite of the "harmony," which was designated a "love feast," a spirit of responsibility and earnestness, rather than jubilation, pervaded the atmosphere. General Bryant nominated Bob in a short, eloquent address. The platform embodied the fundamental state issues, endorsed the national Republican platform, and expressed regret for Spooner's determination to retire. It was adopted by acclamation. Isaac Stephenson, A. R. Hall, J. W. Babcock, Nils P. Haugen, and Judge Albert H. Long constituted the notification committee. "As La Follette entered the hall on the arm of the 'tall sycamore from Marinette' [Isaac Stephenson] the ovation given him was perhaps then unparalleled in the history of state conventions of Wisconsin."[7]

His acceptance speech expressed a firm purpose to carry out the platform pledges.[8] Unbounded enthusiasm characterized the congratulations that closed the day. Bob, Jr., who had attentively followed the formal proceedings, edged his way through the throng to make sure his father was not being hurt by the demonstrations. Farther back on the platform, Fola, Bob's sister Jo, and I shared in the felicitations. Jo's memory naturally reverted to childhood days and to the happiness it would have given the little pioneer mother to have been with us.

On the morning of the convention, Zona Gale, world-famous author, then a reporter on the *Milwaukee Journal*, interviewed me at the Hotel Pfister. To the question how a woman could be a power politically and more especially as the wife of a governor, she has me say, "We aren't there yet," and then she adds I cautiously suggested, "I should like to see women appointed to the University regents." Little did we think that Zona herself would later become an outstanding regent of the University of Wisconsin. When asked if I believed women ready to have a voice in matters of state, she reports I laughingly replied, "Yes I think the women are. But I think . . . the state is not. That is the trouble." As to how my position in Madison would be affected by the change, I said, "Everything would be the same as it is now, excepting that the wife of the governor has an added social duty. I know the house would always be open—and though there would be only the plainest hospitality, it would be for everyone."[9]

Theodore Roosevelt, candidate for Vice President, opened the Presidential campaign on September 10, 1900, at a big Republican rally in La Crosse. From the surrounding farms people streamed in by team for forty-eight hours. Regular trains added extra coaches and special trains were crowded with visitors. Bob rode with Roosevelt in the first carriage of the procession which wound through the gayly decorated city to the accompaniment of bands and enthusiastic cheers "given for 'Teddy' [and] for 'Bob' La Follette."[10] At the evening meeting, where Roosevelt was given an ovation, there were calls for Bob, but he did not speak.

In 1900, as in 1896, Bob campaigned for President McKinley, giving a week to the national campaign outside Wisconsin. His opening speech was delivered at Schlitz Park, Milwaukee, on September 19. He devoted most of his time to national issues, but in discussing state affairs he covered the primary-election issue at length and made a telling summary of the other pledges.[11] The next evening at Fond du Lac the crowd was said to be the largest ever known there. At Primrose he spoke in a tent put up near his birth-place. It seemed as though all the men, women, and children from the surrounding townships were there. Eli Pederson, who had been influential in Bob's nomination for district attorney, was master of ceremonies. At Necedah, Congressman Babcock's home, great pains had been taken to decorate a high balcony of the hotel where Bob was to speak. But it was too far from the crowd, and he insisted on using a wagon box for his platform, much to the delight of the farmers who had come long distances to hear him.

As the campaign advanced, requests for him to speak poured in from all parts of the State. General Bryant, chairman of the State Central Committee, conferred with him about getting an engine and special car for the last three weeks of the campaign. Bob felt sure that with these easier traveling conditions he could make eight or ten speeches a day. But he cautioned General Bryant that the railroad companies must be paid regular rates, so as not to incur any obligations, and insisted there must be a written memorandum signed by the general and the railroad company. There were no established rates for such service, but General Bryant made a contract with the Wisconsin Central Railway by which the Repub-lican State Central Committee paid $40 a day to each company over whose road the special train ran for any portion of the day; it cost $40 or $80 or $120, according to the day's schedule. The special train was made up of a Pullman, a combination baggage car and coach. The supplies and wages of cook and porter were also paid by the State Central Committee.

We left Milwaukee in the comfortable special car on October 14. From then till election, November 6, Bob spoke ten or fifteen times a day, excepting Sundays. Before the era of automobiles, this was a new record in Wisconsin campaigning. It was dramatic and excited great interest. Meetings at smaller towns and stations, where he spoke from the car platform, were stirring. Farmers quit work, driving long distances to hear him. Factories, mines, and schools were closed for the occasion. Arches were built, music pro-vided, flowers strewn. A Young Ladies' La Follette Club was a striking campaign feature before women had the vote.

Two days before election, Robert F. Howard, the genial life-long newspaperman who represented the *Milwaukee Sentinel* during the entire campaign, wrote a summary of the special car trip. Illustrated with a photograph of the special and a map showing where Bob had spoken, it reported he had traveled 6,433 miles, making 208 speeches in 61 counties, talking to nearly 200,000 people. This record had never before been approached in Wisconsin.[12]

Bob was elected governor on November 6, 1900, by the then unprecedented plurality of 102,745 votes. Mindful of the great responsibility and hard work ahead, but believing the way cleared for the enactment of the bitterly contested platform principles, I was filled with a deep sense of satisfaction and contentment. Perhaps at no time in all our years of political experience did a long, hard fight seem so surely won, and the road ahead so smooth and certain.

CHAPTER XII

"No Bread Is Often Better Than
Half a Loaf"

After election, for a few days' respite from politics, Bob and I went to French Lick Springs, where he and Dr. Fox had spent some time on their return from Florida. The November weather was lovely; each day we enjoyed never-to-be-forgotten horseback rides among the beech-wooded hills of southern Indiana. We returned much refreshed—he, to get ready for his new responsibilities and to discontinue his law practice; I, to make plans for moving to the Executive Residence, or Governor's Mansion, as it was more often called, whose spacious grounds sloped down to Lake Mendota.

The residence was fully furnished and a going concern, vacated by Governor Scofield at the close of his term. The State provided heat, light, and janitor service. There was also a man to take care of the stable. We needed only to rent our house furnished, take our books and personal belongings, our horses and cow to the other side of town, and be settled in our new abode.

There were, however, other aspects of the change which seemed to me quite momentous—even more so than when Bob was elected to Congress. Our way of living had always been simple. We usually had one maid, but if, as sometimes happened, none was to be had, I could do my own work and was glad that health and strength permitted. Our social contacts were chiefly with our university, neighborhood, and political friends. Bob liked to bring someone home with him when he came to his meals, and I always planned for an extra plate. We were both inherently hospitable, and there were many gatherings of friends at our home; but we took very little part in the formal social functions of Madison.

The home provided by the State of Wisconsin for its chief executive is a plain, well proportioned house of native stone, with wide porches, long, deep windows, and high ceilings. There is a center hall between the drawing room and library, which are spacious rooms. It has the historic charm of having for a time been the home of Ole Bull, the world-famous violinist. In 1870 he married the young daughter of J. C. Thorpe, a Wisconsin millionaire lumberman, whose home was then the Executive Residence. It was a great event when he gave a concert in Madison. I remember the joy I experienced when, as a freshman at the university, I first heard him play.

While we occupied the house, I made few changes other than for more hygienic housekeeping. I was delighted to find a good hardwood floor in the drawing room under a gorgeous motheaten carpet, and I substituted hardwood floors for carpets in other rooms. In one chamber there was a massive bed and dresser which had been brought from Norway by Ole Bull. The children never forgave me for taking down from the library an Oriental "cozy corner" lighted with a red lantern, whose highly colored tapestry hangings supported with long bright spears suggested a fortune-telling gypsy tent.

Bob appropriated for his study a summer house on the grounds which was said to have been built for Ole Bull. There was an ugly barn and a heavy open carriage which the children christened "The Ark." Maid, our family horse, and Max, loaned us by a friend, were our carriage team. Besides, we had Nancy, a gaited Kentucky saddler which Bob rode, and Rowdy, a Welsh pony for the children.

Though our plan of living changed considerably, the children enjoyed the greatest possible freedom, and after school the grounds echoed with Indian war cries and other games. Bob often brought friends and callers home for lunch or dinner; at times we would invite a dozen or more people to meet an out-of-town guest. We entertained, of course, with due formality when occasion required. I was fortunate in finding two experienced women who relieved me of the entire care of running the household.

Bob was inaugurated governor on January 7, 1901, and three days later delivered his message to the legislature in person, which was an innovation. The occasion was impressive. The senate and assembly met in joint session. The state officers and members of the Supreme Court were present. The galleries and floor were crowded.

The audience was expectant. He had prepared his message with great care and was profoundly in earnest; yet he spoke with a natural ease as though talking to each individual in the audience personally.

At forty-five, though his life had been one of hard work, responsibility, and strain, with more than his share of illness, he nevertheless looked young for his age. When speaking, his fine head, strong features, mobile countenance, lithe body, gave his audience the impression of abounding vitality and power. He always fascinated me, as though I were listening to him for the first time; yet I was ever critical, making mental note of how he might improve his speeches. Sometimes I was so eager to point out where he might do better that I forgot to express my appreciation of how well he had done. He always listened patiently, knowing my wifely anxiety that he should attain a perfect standard every time. When he finished his address to the legislature, there was not one flaw to my way of thinking.

Up to the time the legislature met, he was confident they would enact the laws for which the people of the State had declared. It was therefore a great shock, two days after his inauguration, to read in the newspapers the startling announcement that the "Stalwart" Republicans, as this reactionary element of the party now for the first time called themselves, controlled the senate and proposed to fight the administration measures.[1]

When one reviews the bitter party conflict that began immediately after inauguration, it is not easy to understand why Bob had failed to see the impending storm. But so inherent was his faith in the power of public opinion that he still believed a majority of the senate would vote right when they heard from their constituents. Bob and I never quite agreed as to how much the back-home influence could be depended upon. When I would suggest that he overestimated the interest of the rank and file, he would always say "if they understood" they would make themselves heard. Time, for the most part, justified his confidence; but, oh, more often than not, it took long years of abiding faith and patient waiting!

A severe test of this faith came during the first legislative session. Two important measures, in accord with platform pledges, were introduced soon after his inauguration. On January 28, 1901, a carefully drafted primary-election bill, which was practically the Wisconsin primary as it now stands, was sponsored in the senate by a strong Progressive, George P. Miller; in the assembly by E. Ray Stevens, later Wisconsin Supreme Court Justice, whom Bob considered one of the ablest men in public life in Wisconsin. Three days later two bills prepared by the Tax Commission were introduced in each house. One, known as the license-fee bill, continued the existing method of taxing the railroads but increased the percentage to be paid on gross earnings; if enacted it would add $600,000 a year to the taxes they paid. The ad valorem bill, which Bob had advocated throughout his campaign and in his message, taxed the railroads on their physical valuation; it would increase their annual taxes a little over $1,000,000.

As soon as these measures were introduced, the big corporation interests and political bosses joined forces to defeat them. The railroads were more directly interested in preventing increased taxation, the bosses in holding on to the caucus and convention system of nominating candidates. But they worked together as always; for they were mutually dependent and inseparable parts of the political machine. Knowing well they could not win by direct attack on the measures which had finally, through years of campaign discussion, become platform pledges, they sought to crush the reform movement by destroying confidence in the leader.

It was a heavy blow when we learned, not long after Bob's inauguration, that the powerful Milwaukee multimillionaire boss, Charles Pfister, and his associates had bought the most influential newspaper in Wisconsin.[2] Established in 1837, the *Milwaukee Sentinel*, under the able leadership of Horace Rublee, had built up a large following who accepted it as final authority on questions of public interest. Continuing his policy of exposing political corruption, the *Sentinel* had attacked Pfister and Payne for their activities in securing a Milwaukee city administration which practically gave away franchise rights valued at millions. Pfister brought libel suits. When the managers notified him they would proceed to trial and justify the charges, he and his associates bought a controlling interest at double the par value of the stock and made Lansing Warren editor. Previous experience on the *Chicago Inter-Ocean*, when Charles T. Yerkes, of franchise notoriety, dictated that newspaper's policy, had admirably prepared Warren for his new post.

One of the first things he did was to call on Bob at the executive office, brazenly announcing Pfister had directed him to say "that the paper prefers to support your administration and will do so provided you change your attitude on the subject of primary elections and railroad taxation. If the *Sentinel* opposes your administration, you will be defeated and retired to private life. You are a young man. You are popular with the people. With the support of the *Sentinel* you can have a successful career. . . . If you let up the legislature will be taken care of." When Bob declared he intended to go on fighting for the issues upon which he had been elected governor, Warren threatened, "If that is your answer, the *Sentinel* will begin skinning you to-morrow."

Bob replied, "You may be able to prevent passage of this legislation, and you may defeat me, but I will use all the power the people have given me to fulfill every pledge in the platform. And you may carry that to Mr. Pfister as my answer."[3]

Warren bowed himself out of the office, and from that moment the war began. The campaign of personal attack on Bob was carried to every corner of the State. With this powerful newspaper support the lobby at the Capitol grew more brazen. It became generally understood that a legislator "could better his financial condition." In "a poker game with a lobbyist, the member was sure to win." Railroad mileage could be procured free and railroad lands purchased cheaply if a member was "right." Where money could not turn the trick, threats of ruin by advancing freight rates changed some votes.[4]

About two months after the legislature had been in session, another attempt was made to force a compromise. Late one night Emanuel L. Philipp, then president of the Union Refrigerator Transit Company, and subsequently governor of Wisconsin for three terms, came to the executive office. Moving his chair up close to Bob's he said: "Well, now look here. This railroad taxation matter—wouldn't you be willing to let that go if you could get your primary bill through?"

When Bob answered, "No, these pledges are straight promises," Philipp argued, "But if you can get this primary election bill through you will have done a great thing. And I will pass it for you, if you will let up on railroad taxation."

"Just how will you pass it?" Bob asked.

"How will I pass it?" Philipp repeated. "How will I pass it? Why, I'll take those fellows over to a room in the Park Hotel, close the door and stand them up against the wall. And I'll say to them, 'You vote for the primary election bill!' And they'll vote for it, because I own them, they're mine!'"[5]

Nobody knows whether Philipp could have made good if his offer had been accepted. It was Bob's last interview with Philipp.

At home, among ourselves, we thought and spoke of little except politics. We soon began to realize the fight to hold our ground was every hour becoming harder. Bob worked night and day making every legitimate effort to bring public sentiment to bear on legislators who showed signs of weakening. At the end of each day I awaited his return from the Capitol with mingled hope and dread. Would he have good news or bad to report about this senator and that assemblyman whom we had counted on absolutely; for one by one they were being picked off until our majority was getting dangerously close.

Although anxious and under tremendous strain, he kept his poise. In all his political contests, while he fought unsparingly what he felt were false principles and wrong policies, he never resorted to personal abuse of his opponents. He also made it an inviolable rule not to notice personal attacks; not because he did not feel like striking back, nor that he did not know how. He was not meek, and had a gift for quick answer and apt retort. But he believed that personal controversy was a trick to divert public attention from the real issues.

Although personalities were rigorously excluded from his public discussions, the intimate table conversation of Bob and Jerre Murphy, his secretary, would have made brilliant reading. Their play of wit was akin to that of Bob and Sam Harper, with this difference—Sam was ever inclined to be kindly and tolerant even toward his enemies, while Jerre's shafts were merciless and deadly. In appearance Jerre always reminded me of pictures of Edgar Allan Poe; he was of poetic temperament with a tinge of melancholy, had fine literary taste and a passion for collecting rare books and Oriental rugs. He had made an enviable reputation as an editor and paragrapher. His intellectual acumen, satire, and keen political judgment were feared by our opponents. They seized every opportunity to hit at him in their effort to undermine Bob's hold on the people of the State. Yet even in those days of disappointment and disillusion there was still much laughter about the family board; but it lacked mirth and gaiety.

Large crowds attended the hearings on the Stevens primary bill which began on February 12. When it finally came up in the assembly on March 19, action was blocked during an entire night session of "wild carousals and debauchery" such as had never been seen in a Wisconsin legislative hall even in frontier days.[6] One of the committee rooms had been "made a kind of liquor supply house. . . . The federal office holders' lobby remained on deck all night, and finally some of their members became so obnoxious in their efforts against the bill that . . . all persons who had no right to the floor [were ordered] to the lobby." An observer noted that at six o'clock in the morning the assembly floor "was a sight to behold. Just in front of the first tier of desks was an empty bottle marked 'Hunter's Rye.' . . . In short, witnesses of the all-night session declare that the opponents of the primary election bill on that memorable night did not attack the measure upon its merits, but strove to accomplish its defeat by use of money and drink."[7] When it finally passed the assembly on March 22, by 51 to 48 after an extraordinary struggle, our satisfaction in the hard-won victory was tempered by the bitter fight we knew would later be made in the senate.

The opposition succeeded in postponing any action on taxation until the lobby had enough votes to kill both bills drawn by the Tax Commission. But while they were using these abortive tactics to block railroad taxation, the legislature suddenly played into Bob's hand by passing a bill to tax dogs, only a week after the assembly had defeated the license-fee bill which would have made the railroads pay $600,000 more to the State. He immediately seized upon this ironic contrast to dramatize to the people the influences dominating their representatives at the Capitol.

On the morning of May 2, before the bill he had advocated, increasing railroad taxes $1,000,000, was to come up, he sent a terse message to the legislature vetoing the dog-tax bill. He drove the issue home in a way the farmers would not forget when he pointed out that upon the farm "the watch dog and shepherd are as much a necessity as the other domestic animals which they protect and guard." Reviewing the long struggle to equalize taxation, the message cited the people's grievances and urged passage of the pending tax bill.[8] However, the assembly ignored the message and, as soon as it was read, defeated by a vote of 51 to 45 the ad valorem bill which Bob had advocated. That same day, in the senate, platform pledges were brazenly broken; both taxation bills were withdrawn and killed without debate. But the press reported the veto message simultaneously with the defeat of the tax bills. It dramatized the abstract principles and made the issue a living force in the everyday thought of the people.

During the final months of the session the legislature also played politics with the primary bill. Both United States Senators worked against it. At Washington, Quarles tried unsuccessfully to squeeze a formal protest from the Wisconsin Congressional delegation.[9] Several Federal appointees, owing their positions to Spooner, spent most of their time at the Madison capitol directing the opposition. At a critical time, when it seemed the bill might pass the senate, Spooner himself came to Madison and "met certain State Senators." After the conference some switched and became "outspoken opponents."[10] By these tactics and cruder undercover pressure, the Stevens primary bill was finally defeated. Then a farcical substitute measure known as the Hagemeister bill was passed. This was an ingenious device designed to discredit the primary-election principle. It limited the direct vote to nomination of county officers and delegates, but retained the old convention system for nominating all important candidates.

In a message which stirred the State, Bob vetoed the bill, denouncing it as "a mockery of platform pledges."[11] Since *"no bread is often better than half a loaf"* in legislation, he thought it more realistic to admit temporary defeat and "come right back at the next session" to "fight for a thoroughgoing law." Believing that anything worth fighting for involved a principle, he insisted "on *going far enough to establish that principle* and to give it a fair trial." He wished to go "forward a step at a time, but it must be a *full step.*"[12] Difference as to the length of "a full step" later proved a fundamental source of his conflict with Theodore Roosevelt.

His veto denounced in strong words the methods used to defeat the Stevens primary bill: "An array of federal office-holders, joining with certain corporation agents and the representatives of the machine in the regular legislative lobby, moved upon the capitol, took possession of its corridors, intruded into the legislative halls, followed members to their hotels, tempted many with alluring forms of vice, and in some instances brought them to the capitol in a state of intoxication to vote against the bill."[13]

Bob was censured in a senate resolution adopted, after fierce debate, by a vote of eighteen to eight. Charging he had transcended "all bounds of official propriety and constitutional right," it protested "against the aspersions cast upon our official acts, upon our personal motives, and upon our private characters by the Governor."[14] But this censure proved a boomerang, for it gave wide publicity to his veto message.[15]

After the longest session then on record in Wisconsin, the legislature adjourned on May 15, 1901, without passing any of the promised laws. Bob took this failure seriously. His defeat for Congress had been a mere incident in the game. Loss of the campaigns for the governorship he had accepted philosophically, counting as victory the growing number of adherents to the reforms he advocated. But the 1901 failure, he felt, was radically different. When elected governor he had been buoyantly confident his legislative program would be adopted. With all the long process of hardening, he was not prepared for this defeat. Especially hard to bear had been the falling away of trusted adherents. But he knew how to value the support of those who remained steadfast. His faith in the ultimate judgment of the people was unshaken.

CHAPTER XIII

"With Individuals I Have No Quarrel"

A few weeks after this harassing session of the legislature adjourned, Dr. Bascom, who had been president of the university when we were students, came to Madison to deliver the Phi Beta Kappa address on June 6, 1901. It was heartening to have a visit with him, for his counsel and support meant a great deal to us. Bob always treasured the words Dr. Bascom said to him as they talked together in the library of the Executive Residence: "Robert, you will doubtless make mistakes of judgment as governor, but never mind the political mistakes so long as you make no ethical mistakes."[1]

In an informal speech to the students and faculty on June 5, Dr. Bascom referred to Bob's work: "In proportion as the students of a state university in active life help the people of the state to better social conditions, to better government, they will have justified the trust the state has placed in their hands. . . . If I am correct as to the fundamental purpose of Governor La Follette, and I think I am not mistaken, you young men and young women, students in the University, may well regard Governor La Follette's sturdy fight in behalf of the people against powerful and not too scrupulous opposition, as a guide to the action which, if pursued, will repay the state for the great gifts she has bestowed upon you. What purpose can be more fundamental than that our government may truly be 'of the people, by the people, and for the people.'"[2]

At a banquet given in Dr. Bascom's honor two days later, Bob spoke. In paying tribute to the former president, he accurately expressed the enduring influence this great teacher had on his own

145

life: "Whoever shall set bounds, or fix limitations upon your noble work, let him look beyond executive orders and the presidential office. Let him look beyond the covers of any book and the walls of any classroom. He will readily determine that everywhere, underlying all work, and all life in the institution, pervading its whole atmosphere, entering into the daily thought and being of each student, was the mysterious power with which you laid hold of youth, grounded and established principles admitting of no compromise with error and evil, builded character of adamant, yet preserved individuality—in short, made well-rounded, full-orbed men and women, and finally gave them back to the state with a quality of citizenship which will run through all the generations to come."[3]

At commencement the university gave Bob the honorary degree of Doctor of Laws. In addressing the alumni banquet, on June 19, he spoke on "The State," taking as his text a recent declaration of Dr. Bascom's and developing his theme that "the state was not created for the University; the University exists for the state."

The week following commencement, Bob was very ill. He suffered intense pain; the source of his illness was obscure, and caused grave anxiety. Although confined to the house, he would not give up. He insisted on keeping in touch with his office and the political situation. Never did he relinquish the intention, if he lived, to keep on fighting until what he had started to do was achieved. For several months Bob continued to lose weight and was depressed in spirit. Never during our twenty years of married life had he failed, no matter how ill, to relieve the strain with his habitual wit and cheer. I do not remember ever having felt so helpless.

But early in October he was finally able to go to Dr. Fox's farm near Madison for convalescence. No one ever had quite the power over Bob that he had. He knew when and how to tell him the time had come to get out from under the strain so that Bob would heed the warning. Under the influence of good company and the quiet, wholesome outdoor life, he gained rapidly and was soon riding horseback every day. While we were at the farm, Dr. Fox first introduced us to Herminie Templeton Kavanagh's *Darby O'Gill and the Good People*, who became members of our family through Bob's frequent reading aloud of these captivating folk tales. From the time they first met, when Bob was a student in the university, Dr. Fox was the beloved family physician; he was in attendance at the birth of each of our four children. Our second son was named for him. Always Dr. Fox and Bob were the closest friends and perfectly happy in each other's company. On his ninetieth birthday, March 27, 1930, the only message I could send him was that, as always, I longed for words to tell him what his life had meant to Bob and me and our children.

Opposition to Bob's renomination looked formidable at the beginning of 1902. Early in January President Roosevelt had "dealt the progressive cause a body blow" by appointing as Postmaster General, Henry C. Payne, who "was to Wisconsin what Mark Hanna —with whom he was intimately associated—was to the country."[4] Under any conditions Payne would have used all his influence to defeat Bob. But it made a great difference whether he did this as a private citizen, politician and lobbyist, or from the vantage ground of the Roosevelt Cabinet.

During the summer that Bob was so ill, the Stalwarts had been organizing their campaign to defeat him. A year after he had been unanimously nominated governor at Milwaukee, stalwart politicians from over the State had met in that same city, on August 7, 1901, to prevent his renomination and put an end to the reform movement.[5] Ten days later a manifesto was issued by the self-styled "Republican League of Wisconsin" inviting Republicans to enroll and welcoming them to the expensive new quarters on the eleventh floor of the Herman Building in Milwaukee. It was signed by 18 senators and 41 assemblymen. With the exception of two assemblymen, captured after the legislature adjourned, these 59 men had voted against the party platform pledges of 1900.

In his small but influential newspaper, the *Jefferson County Union*, Governor Hoard told Wisconsin voters the corporations had banded together to prevent tax legislation and that inside the "Eleventh-Story League" could be found "every paid lobbyist in the state leagued together to keep up this sort of infamy, and every man Jack of them cursing La Follette."[6]

Bob's long illness had been a handicap. There was a debt left over from the last campaign, whereas the opposition coffers were overflowing. However, the *Milwaukee Free Press*, first issued on June 18, 1901, was a great source of strength and encouragement to the Progressives. Isaac Stephenson was the chief financial backer. The editor, H. P. Myrick, who had been on the *Sentinel* before it was bought by Pfister, was a writer of good political judgment, loyal to the standards of Horace Rublee. I vividly remember the satisfaction and enthusiasm Bob felt over what the founding of the new paper meant to the cause.

The importance of the *Free Press* was soon evident in its early exposure of Eleventh-Story-League activities. Seven months later it dealt the first smashing blow to the powerful opposition when it featured a six-column news article which created a sensation throughout Wisconsin.[7] It had become obvious to us that the Eleventh-Story League had obtained control of a considerable portion of the state press. Friendly newspapers had suddenly switched; the same editorials and press comments attacking the administration appeared simultaneously in various papers. When we discussed the situation, Bob insisted that if the facts could be proved the fight would be over. I remember how gratified he was when John J. Hannan, who made the investigation for the *Free Press*, obtained affidavits which irrefutably proved the league was engaged in the wholesale purchase of editorial opinion of some three hundred Wisconsin local newspapers. When this venal betrayal became known, people throughout the State were shocked and angry. Their resentment was even greater than Bob had anticipated. Neither side then fully realized the vital effect these disclosures would have on the election.

The real opening of Bob's campaign for a second term began unexpectedly with a speech he made on March 19, 1902, at the round-up of the Farmers' Institutes at Oconomowoc. On short notice he accepted an invitation to substitute for Governor Hoard, who was ill. His speech recalled the struggle to establish Agricultural Experiment stations while he was in Congress and outlined the amazing changes these had wrought in the agricultural life of Wisconsin in less than two decades. In concluding, he briefly discussed primary elections and taxation, pointing out "that the burdens borne by real property" were "nearly twice as great as those of certain corporations." To the farmers, who were the largest real property owners, he stressed the importance of equalizing these burdens, predicting that although the last legislature had violated its duty, "equal and just taxation must come." The farm men and women, many of whom had driven long distances to hear him, responded enthusiastically.[8]

For months stalwart agencies had spread propaganda that La Follette, if reelected governor with a legislature to carry out his reforms, would "sacrifice" Spooner. It was charged that the real purpose of the primary law was "to place the election of a successor to Spooner in the hands of Governor La Follette."[9] This stalwart red herring was greatly aided when a Madison paper quoted President Roosevelt's emphatic admonition to a prominent Wisconsin citizen: "That man Spooner is my right hand man and if you people of Wisconsin do not return him to the senate when his term expires next winter it will be infamous, infamous!"[10] This was widely commented on in the state press.[11]

The constant misrepresentation of issues in the *Sentinel* and the local newspapers recently acquired by the Eleventh-Story League could not be counteracted by the comparatively limited circulation of the *Free Press*, although it was doing good work. Bob's health did not permit of a long preconvention campaign. Yet if he was to win, he must reach the voters with specific proofs as to the nature and cause of the bitter warfare against him. A notable campaign document, the *Voters' Hand-Book*, was prepared to meet this need. It was published by the *Free Press*, which thus assumed liability for its accuracy and truth.

Later our headquarters issued an eight-page supplement entitled *The Battle Only Half Over*, which warned the voters to "Look Out For the Legislature." The *Sentinel* printed a facsimile, declared it "one of the most revolutionary documents ever distributed in Wisconsin," and denounced it as "sublimated populism and calculated to array class against class."[12] The particularly "inflammatory" paragraph which was described as an "attack on Spooner" warned candidates for the United States Senatorship that advocates of primary elections and equal taxation would *"endure no further opposition to the platform pledges of the republican party,* by federal officials, in open violation of civil service rules and all decent party obligations, without such a protest as shall command the attention of the President, the party and the country."[13]

When the proof of the *Voters' Hand-Book*—a paper-covered pocket-size document of 144 closely printed pages—was ready for the printer and plans made for its distribution in every precinct, Bob was satisfied and confident of the result. He was in a mood to entrust the details of the preconvention campaign to others and devote himself to building up his health.

We took a plain little cottage at Colladay's Farm, Lake Kegonsa, several miles from a railroad station, yet near enough for him to ride horseback or drive in to his office when necessary. The Siebeckers rented an adjoining cottage, and we renewed the happy relation of living next door to each other. One day, through a letter of introduction from Henry Cochems, of whom Bob was very fond, the director of a physical-culture institute came to see us. He proposed to make Bob a well man with a special system of exercise. Soon all of us were devoting a number of hours each day to physical training. Bob, Jr., Phil, and even little Mary, together with the Siebecker children, became ardent gymnasts rivaling each other in games and stunts. Bob, throwing off all care, joined in their sports with the single-minded zest that characterized his pursuit of any object which had once awakened his interest. During our summer at Lake Kegonsa, Bob did not, however, devote all his time to recreation. He presided at the Memorial Day services in Madison, addressed the League of Municipalities at Grand Rapids,* and spoke at a huge Fourth of July celebration on top of Blue Mound, near Primrose.[14]

The 1902 Republican State Convention had been called to meet at Madison on July 16 by the progressive-controlled State Central Committee. The Stalwarts raised a storm of protest against violating the precedent of seven consecutive conventions previously held in Milwaukee. But Bob and his advisers had decided that removal from the neighborhood of Eleventh-Story-League intrigues more than compensated for any possible ill feeling.

The Dane County caucuses set the pace and early scored a sweeping victory for Bob, although Boss Keyes and other old-time antagonists did their best to carry the county for the stalwart candidate, state Senator John M. Whitehead. Throughout the State the Stalwarts made a hard fight. But 45 counties elected solid delegations for La Follette; 13 had solid delegations for Whitehead; 12 elected divided delegations. Although Bob had three times as many delegates as Whitehead, about half the counties passed some kind of resolution endorsing Spooner's reelection.

When the convention met, a great audience packed the university gymnasium. Some spectators even occupied the beams which span the great hall. The weather was sweltering; yet throughout the two

* Later renamed Wisconsin Rapids.

days the auditorium was filled with representative people from over the State, intensely interested in the dramatic struggle which was attracting national attention.

The *Milwaukee Sentinel* had transferred headquarters to Madison, bringing practically the entire editorial staff, special writers, photographers, and uniformed messenger boys. Pfister himself was present, and the usually quiet town was wakened at five in the morning by the "newsies" selling his paper. In front of *Sentinel* headquarters a twenty-five-piece band gave evening concerts and a staff of his employees sent kites above the capitol advertising the paper. The Eleventh-Story League forces operated from various hotels and office buildings rented at Madison.

But neither noise, money, nor the Spooner issue prevented the progressive forces winning two important victories on the first day. Telegraph wires ticked astonishing news across the country. Although the President had, only the previous day, again publicly urged the Senator's reelection,[15] the convention passed a resolution making party support of Spooner, should he reconsider "his announced determination" to retire, conditional upon his support of the Wisconsin Republican platform. Also, in spite of the opposing influence of two United States Senators and the powerful Postmaster General, the majority report on the primary election plank was passed that day by 768 votes to 279 for the minority report. After this test of strength the Stalwarts gave up the fight. The convention adopted the previous Republican platform, demanded that "all candidates for Senate and Assembly at the coming election be called upon by the voters to give assurance of their support" of platform pledges, and censured those who had "obstructed the earlier fulfillment of these party obligations."[16]

On the second day of the convention, a great demonstration followed Herbert W. Chynoweth's nominating speech for Bob, which was an eloquent argument based on the facts. It seemed to me then, as it does now, that if all other records were wiped out this address would leave a vivid picture of Bob's life and purpose to the time of his second nomination for governor. When the roll was called, it stood 790 for La Follette, 266 for Whitehead.

An unprecedented ovation greeted Bob when he entered the hall, and he had difficulty in calming the excited crowd. But the audience listened in rapt attention after he started, and the whole speech was singularly impressive. He warned that the fight was not completely won; the same forces which had been our undoing in the last legislature must be met when the next legislature convened. It was vital to elect only men who would publicly pledge support of the promised legislation. "Let all else of this contest be forgotten. . . . I do not treasure one personal injury or lodge in memory one personal insult. With individuals I have no quarrel and will have none. The span of my life is too short for that."[17]

When he finished, he seized a moment in the midst of the tumultuous applause to greet me and the children. As we clasped hands, I suddenly realized how differently I felt than at the close of the 1900 convention. He had won a more significant and striking victory in his second nomination. His leadership and the principles for which he had long contended were more firmly established. My joy and satisfaction were no less sincere and profound now than then; but I better understood the nature of the struggle. Never again could I take for granted that the fight was won and the war over.

CHAPTER XIV

University and State

The Democratic State Convention met in Milwaukee on September 3, 1902, and nominated for governor David S. Rose, mayor of that city. As a delegate to the Democratic National Convention two years before, he had told the Wisconsin delegation that "standing up and dying for principle was all rot." During his administration as mayor, valuable railway franchises had been secured by the Payne-Pfister interests. In a scathing editorial former Governor Hoard stated, "Rose is the creature and obedient tool of the grasping corporations to-day as mayor, and they know on which side their bread is buttered."[1] Although in previous years the party had supported equalization of taxation and primary elections, the convention now adopted a platform clearly showing the bipartisan alliance between reactionary Democrats and stalwart Republicans. On the convention floor it was charged that this platform which declared primary elections "un-American and un-democratic" had been framed at the "dictation of the corporations." William Jennings Bryan promptly denounced the platform in his paper the *Commoner*.[2] Later he told Bob that he had not come into Wisconsin to make a political speech, either in the 1902 or in the 1904 campaigns, because he wanted the Democrats of the State to help the progressive movement. Some leading Wisconsin Democrats came out openly for Bob; others indicated their feeling about Rose and his platform by refusing to help elect him.

Bob began his campaign with a three-hour speech at the West Side Turner Hall in Milwaukee on September 30. He referred briefly to national issues. Although still favoring a protective tariff, he warned that by secret agreement producers of like articles were combining to destroy free competition which was a necessary complement to a protective tariff. Expressing agreement with Theodore Roosevelt's recent public assertions that the great monopolies constituted the foremost national issue, he urged support of the President "in his efforts to curb these trusts by the enforcement of the laws now on the statute books." Perhaps never before in any one address had he presented so comprehensive a treatise on taxation and primary-election reforms. He did not mention the Democratic candidate for governor. For three weeks Mayor Rose had been conducting a campaign of personal vilification against Bob. As the campaign proceeded and Rose became more virulent, if possible, the public was more and more interested and amused that Bob ignored him. Not once during the entire contest did he mention Rose's name or otherwise refer to him.

Bob made fifty-five speeches as widely distributed over the State as train schedules and driving overland permitted. Former Governor Hoard said Bob had "stirred the state from center to circumference as no other man ever stirred it."[3] Even the hostile *Milwaukee Sentinel* reports of his meetings show they were effective and picturesque. After his first formal speech, as was his custom, he talked in more familiar fashion. He discussed the issues earnestly, but took the crowds into his confidence, addressing them as homefolks and always making a stirring appeal for reelecting candidates with good legislative records. The contest became more and more intense because the same legislature which would enact the reform program would also elect a United States Senator.

Spooner made his first speech to a great audience in Milwaukee on October 13, under the auspices of the National Republican Committee. Postmaster General Henry Payne, Charles Pfister, Boss Keyes, and many other distinguished Wisconsin Stalwarts were on the platform. In the midst of Spooner's address someone called out, "What is the matter with La Follette?" "If my friend had waited a few minutes," the Senator replied, "I would have told him to vote for the whole ticket from Governor La Follette down."[4] This was generally interpreted as an instruction to scratch La Follette's name and vote for the Republican state ticket *below* the governorship.

Bob, in his Milwaukee speech, had referred to Spooner's "constructive statesmanship" and commended his public service in the national field. As the audience was starting to leave the hall after Bob's speech at Appleton on Saturday, October 25, a defeated stalwart candidate asked the direct question, "Are you in favor of the unconditional reelection of Senator Spooner to the United States senate?"[5]

A hush fell upon the crowd. Without hesitation Bob replied: "I will answer you this way, sir; I am for the success . . . and for the principles of the Republican party, and the day and the hour that Senator Spooner raises his voice for the principles of the Republican party as laid down in the state platform, I will raise my voice for his reelection to the United States senate. Because I then can do so in conformity with the platform of my party."

The audience "fairly went wild with enthusiasm over the governor's answer to this question. . . . Spontaneous cheers shook the building as he concluded. Men jumped on chairs and waved their hats and many, not waiting to go up the stairs to the platform, climbed up over the reporters' tables. . . . Aside from the governor there was one in the meeting who displayed no emotion. Mrs. La Follette sat to the rear of the platform. The quick flash of her penetrating eye . . . showed that she realized the importance of the question and her gaze was fixed upon the governor, who stood calmly at the speaker's table. Her eyes rested upon the governor until he finished the answer and then when the great burst of approval came from the throats of the audience the glance of pride in him as she looked at the surging, cheering crowd was certainly excusable."[6]

It is true. I was glad to have him publicly reaffirm his position and proud that the audience responded as it did. I agreed with him that it was better to suffer defeat if need be than to swerve in the slightest degree from the platform declaration relating to Spooner. Indeed, I never understood how his friends expected him to answer the question otherwise. My own judgment is that this incident did not materially affect the election, for the stalwart Republicans and their Democratic allies were determined in any event to vote for Rose. Yet some of Bob's best, most loyal advisers believed he had made a fatal mistake and despaired of his election. In fact, General Bryant closed up the La Follette headquarters in Milwaukee that same Saturday night, saying to John Hannan, "It's all over; Bob's licked." Bob called a meeting in Madison on Sunday, and the Milwaukee headquarters opened again on Monday morning.

A week after the Appleton meeting he made his closing speech to a huge audience at the Exposition Building in Milwaukee, where he received what was said to be the greatest welcome ever given to a political candidate in the State. A prominent Democrat, Herman Reel, who introduced him, predicted, "You cannot beat Bob La Follette with a man whose whole political creed may be summed up in one phrase, 'This dying for principle is all rot.'"[7] On Tuesday, November 4, 1902, Wisconsin reelected Bob by a plurality of 47,599 votes, giving him the second largest off-year majority any governor of the State had so far received.

Shortly before the 1903 legislature convened, Spooner renounced his intention to retire and publicly stated he now thought it his "duty" to accept if chosen.[8] He was elected on January 28 by a joint session of the legislature to succeed himself. The choice unquestionably expressed Wisconsin sentiment, for he received the unanimous Republican vote. Since many of these legislators were Progressives, this was later admitted to be evidence "that La Follette had not lifted a finger to oppose" him.[9] Throughout the session, however, Spooner's influence with the legislature was to be used against the long-contested primary-election and taxation measures.

The choice of Irvine L. Lenroot as speaker of the assembly seemed to indicate we had enough votes to pass the primary-election and taxation bills in the assembly. He was an able young lawyer, with political acumen, who had won a foremost place in the 1901 legislature. In our councils, as I remember, we relied upon him to point out obstacles and state objections rather than initiate new proposals. However, once enlisted in a cause, he was a fearless champion, a sagacious and effective lieutenant. He was a ready debater, with a special gift in drafting legislation, and had a strong influence on the most important statutes of Wisconsin enacted from 1901 to 1905. From their first meeting the young man gained Bob's confidence and affection. Although A. R. Hall, the pioneer crusader against railroad domination, had not been a candidate because of failing health, two new members of the assembly, Herman L. Ekern and James A. Frear, immediately showed exceptional leadership.

We knew the Progressives had a good working majority in the assembly, and expected the senate would be favorable but close. However, some new senators, although elected on the strength of signed statements to support platform pledges, yielded to pressure and eventually joined the Stalwarts. The result was that with the help of reactionary Democrats they could count on 17 of the total of 33 senators to vote against measures opposed by the railroads.

Bob had again delivered his message in person, the reading taking three hours. He had prepared the part dealing with primary elections and taxation "as though on trial for his life," for he feared if the legislature again failed to pass these measures the people might lose faith in ever being able to get results. Professor John R. Commons, already a widely known economist and authority on taxation, happened to be in Madison at this time, and Bob seized the opportunity to consult with him. This was the beginning of their long friendship and association.

More than half the message presented statistics comparing Wisconsin railroad-made rates with commission-regulated rates in Iowa and Illinois. These tables, prepared with the able help of Halford Erickson, Commissioner of Labor and Industrial Statistics, demonstrated that 151 Wisconsin towns were paying an average of 39.9 per cent more than the towns at similar distances from their markets in the two neighboring States.

The issue was not new, for A. R. Hall had long denounced unfair rates. But Bob's vivid way of presenting the figures proving that Wisconsin people in specific localities were paying more to ship the same product the same distance brought the facts home and stirred a popular protest. Newspapers called him a "visionary," a "demagogue," and a "hare-brained theorist," but invective did not answer the factual proof of exorbitant freight rates charged in the very locality where the paper was published.

During the 1903 session Bob stirred up the voters in the home districts by bombarding the legislature at strategic intervals with special messages. They came so frequently that the Stalwarts ironically suggested a card system be installed to classify them. In the preelection campaign he had already started his educational propaganda for rate regulation by warning the people that the railroads were threatening to make the public pay every cent of increased taxation by a corresponding increase in rates. His first message at the beginning of the session stressed rate regulation for tactical reasons. From experience with the previous legislature he knew that he could hardly expect, at the first tryout, to pass a bill creating a commission. But he hoped to make the fight for it so hot that the railroads would let the primary and taxation bills pass in order to stave off a law for rate regulation.

Following his plan to keep the rate issue in the foreground, he later sent a message calling attention to a recent Minnesota investigation and recommending a law to investigate the railroad companies' books to discover whether in Wisconsin they were accurately reporting gross earnings and paying taxes thereon.[10] Although he could not then present legal evidence to prove that the railroads were violating the law by granting rebates to favored shippers, he was absolutely sure of the fact. The railroads dared not openly oppose a bill providing for an investigation, and it soon passed both houses. The report, made a year later, had an important effect on the political situation.

As Bob predicted in his first message, the railroads and other corporation interests marshaled all their power against the bill to regulate rates. While the battle was on in the assembly, he worked with Erickson day and night, under intense strain, preparing a special message which he read to the legislature on April 28, the day before the final public hearings on the bill. The railroads charged that he had selected for comparisons in his first message stations where conditions were exceptional.

In his special message he listed every station in Wisconsin on the two principal railroads of the State, comparing rates between them and their markets with corresponding stations in Iowa and Illinois. The facts covered practically the entire State and could not be controverted. The message with tables made a book of 181 pages.

The final hearings on the rate-regulation bill brought shippers and manufacturers to Madison the next day in even greater throngs than Bob had predicted. Intense excitement pervaded the capitol; the corridors were filled with milling men. The hotels were "crowded to overflowing, the parlors and hallways" were filled with cots, and sleeping room of any kind was "at a premium."[11] At a mass meeting in the senate chamber, the shippers and manufacturers, their pockets lined with rebates, adopted resolutions denouncing the governor's special message and denying his "charges and insinuations" that they were receiving rebates or special favors from the railroads.[12] These resolutions and protests, signed by a formidable array of names of important industrial concerns, were printed and placed on the legislators' desks preceding the vote on the bill.[13] Members were deluged with telegrams from big factory owners in their districts. Spooner's arrival at Madison on the same day[14] may have been coincidence, but his presence could not fail to strengthen the stalwart forces.

During the bitter debate Speaker Lenroot left the chair to make a dramatic and brilliant argument for the bill from the floor, but it was finally defeated a half-hour after midnight of May 1. The Stalwarts celebrated this triumph after the manner of their 1901 legislative victories. But Bob promptly sent another message which had a sobering effect and gave the railroad lobby a real scare. He asked, on May 8, for enactment of a law to prevent railroads from *increasing their existing rates*.

A bill to this effect passed the assembly four days later. It came up in the senate at practically the same time as the railroad-taxation bill. Bob's strategy won. As he had foreseen, the people had been so stirred that the senate did not dare defeat both bills. The long-contested ad valorem railway-taxation measure was passed, but the bill to prohibit increasing existing rates was killed.

Early in the session a measure which was practically the Stevens primary bill passed the assembly but was held up in the senate for over six weeks. During this interval stalwart leaders appealed to Washington for help. A messenger was sent to explain. Spooner, Quarles, Babcock, and other members of the Wisconsin delegation held repeated conferences. Spooner, who shrank from open political conflicts, insisted as a condition to his cooperation that "the primary election bill with a referendum clause was to be passed by the state senate." Then it "was agreed that the two United States senators," Spooner and Quarles, and the congressmen opposed to La Follette would actively campaign to defeat "the bill when it was presented to the people for their endorsement by popular vote."[15] Responding to the stalwart S O S call, Congressman Babcock appeared upon the Wisconsin scene and "proceeded to get busy."[16] With "his efficient lieutenant, E. L. Phillip doing the field work and button-holing senators," Babcock "kept pretty close to his room" at the hotel where he saw "local statesmen" and "brought some of the wavering brethren into line."[17]

While this tug of war was on, Bob said to an inquiring reporter at the executive office: "If they want to kill all the platform measures in the senate, it is up to them! . . . We can stand it if they can. The people will take the hide of every Stalwart senator who comes up for re-election next year."[18]

At a time when the primary bill appeared to be indefinitely dead-locked in conference and the Stalwarts were predicting no important legislation would pass, Roosevelt, accompanied by Secretary Loeb, John Burroughs, and Senator Quarles, stopped off at Madison. On this Western tour his schedule, as communicated to Bob on the telephone by Secretary Loeb, allowed Madison only two hours which were fully occupied with speechmaking and permitted no time for social entertainment. On April 3 the President was met at the station by the usual committee and the governor, who rode in the carriage with him to the capitol. There he addressed a joint session of the legislature and then spoke from the capitol steps, where he was introduced by Bob, to the large crowd. The President made no reference to politics in either of his Madison speeches, although a word on the primary bill and the fulfillment of platform pledges would have had great influence at this time. However, the Wisconsin Progressives well knew that after the appointment of Henry Payne to the Cabinet they could not expect help from the Roosevelt Administration.

Until three days before final adjournment of the legislature on May 23, the Stalwarts fought the primary bill. Then they finally allowed it to pass the senate with a "referendum clause," as de-manded by Spooner, which left the caucus-and-convention system in effect for almost two years and gave them a chance to defeat it at the polls.[19] Three days after the legislature adjourned, it was announced that every township would be organized against La Fol-lette by Congressman Babcock, who had been the stalwart com-mander-in-chief at Madison during the 1903 legislative session.

The 1903 legislative session, like that of 1901, was a period of hard work and constant strain for Bob, but he came through it in good health. He had been fully prepared for the conflict. There were no great surprises or disappointments, no cause for gloom as in 1901. He had carried the load buoyantly, and he took satisfaction in the record of concrete achievement. In addition to the ad valorem taxation law, which promised to add $1,000,000 to the State's income, an inheritance-tax law had passed, the banking laws had been re-vised, and a start made toward a corrupt-practices Act. He was confident the people would adopt the primary at the 1904 election.

John J. Hannan had succeeded Jerre Murphy as private secretary in June, 1903. "Colonel" Hannan, as he has since been known, was a brilliant and experienced young newspaper man interested in the progressive movement. He had a sixth sense for politics. His Irish wit and warm heart made him popular; but when necessary he could be firm, and was an ideal buffer to his chief. He looked the part— tall and stout, but light and quick in movement and alert in mind. His cordiality and good humor pleased all comers, who were likewise impressed with his insight and wisdom. If callers could not see the governor, they went away almost as well satisfied because of their visit with Colonel Hannan.

Henry Huber, subsequently lieutenant governor of Wisconsin, was executive clerk in 1903, taking the place of Alf Rogers. Huber recalls that the governor had a small room in the basement of the capitol where he could work in seclusion. The table, floor, and chairs were strewn with papers which he forbade any one to touch; for in spite of the apparent confusion he knew just where to find what he wanted. Often, when at work on some absorbing problem, or when away speaking, the correspondence would pile up. Henry Huber and Jennie Nelson, an intelligent secretary, would get a stack of letters ready for him to sign. Some he approved as prepared, but most of them he revised, interlining and changing so that they had to be retyped.

One of the things which gave Bob the deepest satisfaction during his second term as governor was the election of Charles R. Van Hise as president of the university on April 21, 1903. He had been the outstanding genius of our class of 1879. My first recollection of him is of a rather countrified-looking student, with high forehead, beak-like nose, large searching eyes, who went to the blackboard and demonstrated with astonishing ease and lucidity the "problem of the rafters," which no one else in the class could do, and which, some of us suspected, even the professor himself could not solve. Van Hise excelled in mathematics and science, but was not a grind. Lessons were nothing to him. He assisted professors in laboratory experiments, and spent hours reading in the library. Yet with all his intense absorption in scientific research, Van Hise never lost interest in everyday life. Bob and Sam Harper often consulted him before anyone else on problems of politics, and he seemed to arrive at a solution with the same unerring facility he showed in solving a scientific problem.

The friendship of our school days had been cemented by intimate association in the years that followed. Charles Van Hise and Alice Ring had been married at about the same time we were. It happened that Bob's mother, Mrs. Van Hise's mother, and Sam Harper's mother, all three remarkable women, became very fond of one another. A spirit of pioneer neighborliness bound the families together. When in reminiscent mood Charles and Bob would tell of having stolen apples from the university orchard on moonlight nights, and other student pranks. Alice Van Hise was a woman of wonderful charm and poise and withal common sense. Her delightful humor was as pervasive as the sunshine she loved. We often had Sunday dinners together. Alice and Bob, with their spontaneous wit, repartee, and storytelling, would keep us laughing until one would think the glass of scuppernong wine had gone to our heads.

Van Hise was democratic and believed in the democracy of education. He upheld the ideals of Bascom as to what the university should do for the citizenship of the State; he also considered it very important that the results of the university's scientific research should be made available to every individual who might want it. I remember his satisfaction over the discovery of a star by a country boy who had taken a university correspondence course in astronomy. He believed in the high educational value of farmers' institutes, housekeepers' conferences, experimental stations, and extension lectures. At the same time he recognized the imperishable place of the classics, the arts, and the professions in education.

The movement to elect Van Hise president originated, as I remember, with the faculty, of whom a few outstanding members like Charles S. Slichter and Frederick J. Turner were the spokesmen. Following the death of President Charles Kendall Adams in 1902, a committee of five of the Board of Regents had been appointed to recommend a successor. William F. Vilas was an influential member of this committee. Up to this time Bob, as governor, had appointed eight regents, only two of whom were on the nominating committee. His appointments had been largely from the alumni of the Bascom era, who would naturally tend to favor Van Hise. Among them was Dr. Arthur J. Puls, a member of our class. Another was Dr.

Almah Frisby, a dear friend, eminently qualified for the position, who was the first woman to serve on the board.

A thinker, a seer, a gentleman, Van Hise was direct in speech and action. He lacked, however, the oratorical gifts and urbanity some of the regents thought essential for a college president. When the nominating committee could not find an outsider who met the approval of the board, Regent Vilas strongly supported the acting president, Dr. E. A. Birge. Birge received three votes, Van Hise eleven. Vilas was so disappointed that he proposed to resign. Bob, who admired Vilas and greatly appreciated his service as regent, was fortunately able to persuade him to reconsider. Afterward, Vilas admitted that he had been mistaken and that Van Hise had administrative leadership and was an outstanding university president.

The state press generally spoke highly of his qualifications, though some charged politics in his selection. Bob gladly and frankly accepted any responsibility that went with the choice of Van Hise for president. After the death of Sam Harper, there was perhaps none of his friends, other than Judge Siebecker and Gilbert Roe, for whom he cared so much or in whom he had such absolute confidence and trust as Charles Van Hise. Yet he used his legitimate influence to make him president from purely disinterested motives, because he believed no one else was so well equipped to carry forward the great work of the university.

Writing of the school he so deeply loved, Bob expressed his own enduring conviction when he cited the declaration of freedom made by the Board of Regents in 1894, at the time that Dr. Richard T. Ely was tried for economic heresy: "We cannot for a moment believe that knowledge has reached its final goal or that the present constitution of society is perfect. . . . In all lines of investigation . . . the investigator should be absolutely free to follow the paths of truth wherever they may lead. Whatever may be the limitations which trammel inquiry elsewhere, we believe the great State of Wisconsin should ever encourage that continual and fearless sifting and winnowing by which alone the truth can be found."[20] Herbert Chynoweth, then a member of the Board of Regents, was the author of the declaration. It was afterward incorporated in a Wisconsin Republican platform as a pledge to sustain academic freedom at the university, and is inscribed on a bronze tablet presented as a 1910 class memorial.

Believing the purpose of the university was to serve the people of the State and bring every resident under the broadening and inspiring influence of its faculty, Bob always supported extension service and adult education. While governor he sought, by the appointment of able alumni as regents, "to build up and encourage the spirit which John Bascom in his time had expressed."[21] For guidance in solving the difficult problems which confronted his administration, he frequently conferred with Professor Commons, President Van Hise, Dr. Ely, Dr. Reinsch, and others. Wherever possible he appointed experts from the university to important state boards.

That the interrelationship of the university and the State, which he had helped to create and foster, would increase and strengthen from generation to generation was one of Bob's fondest hopes.

CHAPTER XV

Bob Launches the Roll Call

For many years Bob had lectured occasionally. He never accepted pay for addresses in Wisconsin, and often spoke elsewhere without remuneration. However, while still practicing law he would receive from $50 to $100 or more for speeches in nearby states. He enjoyed the work, and the extra money helped to meet the ever increasing expenditures of politics and family. Our living expenses mounted year by year. The governorship salary was $5,000. Friends and supporters contributed generously to campaign funds, but in proportion to his means he always spent more freely than anyone. If funds were lacking when he thought it important to send out some political literature, he would pay for it out of his own pocket. If he hadn't the money, he borrowed, and debts accumulated.

That he should go on the Chautauqua platform was inevitable. It offered a wonderful medium for reaching the people and extending his political usefulness. His professional appearance on the Chautauqua Circuit began in 1902 with several speeches in neighboring States. In the summer of 1903 he made an extended tour of the Middle West and went as far east as Maryland and New York. "Representative Government" and "Hamlet" were the titles of his addresses; the latter fitted into Sunday programs or where he spoke twice in the same town.

From his university days he had found diversion in the study of Shakespeare, especially of *Hamlet*. During the course of years he became thoroughly familiar with the best Shakespearean authorities on *Hamlet*. He considered himself only an amateur, but was convinced the critics were wrong who conceived Hamlet as a man with an intellect so disproportionate to his other faculties that the power of action is lost in meditation, reflection, and refining. The key to

Hamlet's seeming indecision Bob found in the conflicting commands laid upon him:

> "If thou didst ever thy dear father love,—
> Revenge his foul and most unnatural murder."

At the same time he is told:

> "Taint not thy mind, nor let thy soul contrive,
> Against thy mother aught."

Starting from this premise, he made a logical argument for Hamlet as a man of action who moves forward with decision and courage to fulfill his purpose of avenging his father's murder when not inhibited by his vow to protect his mother's honor.

Next to Edwin Booth, Bob thought John Barrymore the greatest Hamlet he had seen. Barrymore was interested when he learned Bob had made a study of the character, and asked to see his lecture. After reading it he wrote:

The Ambassador
New York

My dear Senator La Follette

I have read with the greatest possible interest and intense satisfaction your extraordinarily illuminating essays on the subjects of Hamlet and Iago. I am particularly pleased and intrigued by the fact that our ideas about the character of Hamlet—a thing critics have piled exhaustive and misleading Pelions upon Ossas about for centuries—are in complete accord. And naturally from an intellect like your own this subconscious cooperation is a great and joyous stimulant. Thank you a thousand times for your great courtesy and kindliness in sending them to me. You must naturally know what a very great pleasure and honor it was to meet you. No one but myself have seen the manuscripts though indeed they are supremely worthy of wide attention.

Believe me, in the deepest gratitude,

John Barrymore[1]

Bob read this lecture many times to his family and friends before he gave it publicly. It always held the close attention of his audiences whether they had ever read *Hamlet* or not. The cartoonists and reporters sometimes ridiculed the idea of his talking on *Hamlet* to farmers. Only those who heard him could realize that just as he dramatized facts or statistics and made his arguments equally vivid to the expert and layman, so he made the analysis of Hamlet interesting alike to scholars and to those who had never had the opportunity to study Shakespeare.

Bob's address on "Representative Government" was described as "The New Declaration of Independence"[2] after one of his Chautauqua meetings. "Taxation without representation" was, he said, "as much a crime against just and equal government in 1903 as it was in 1776." The gravest menace to our democratic institutions was, he maintained, "the overbalancing control of city, state and national legislatures by the wealth and power of the public service corporations." He analyzed the part the railroads had played in building up the great monopolies, discussed specific legislation to meet immediate problems, and told the story of the Wisconsin struggle as a concrete object lesson of independence won at the ballot box.[3]

Bob believed his Chautauqua lectures were his most practically effective national work for the progressive movement; although, as he said, this work "cannot well be separated from my work as a public official. For it is my work as a public official that has made my work on the platform count."[4] When presented as a part of his actual experience, the issues had a vital interest he could not have given them in theoretical discussion. Always he felt he was working for a cause, speaking as earnestly and measuring results by the same standards as in political campaigns. In a characteristic letter, written after a Chautauqua meeting in Iowa, he said: "I feel very sure that my work is going to do good the country over. Of course I can get in but here and there, and the country seems large. Yet it has already spread out from Wisconsin wonderfully and I am adding quite a number of radiating centers with this summer's work."[5]

The Chautauquas were held for the most part in midsummer; often tents were used as auditoriums. He would come off the platform dripping with perspiration, obliged to change his clothes at the hotel or, if pressed for time, on the train taking him to his next engagement. Travel was hard; trains often late; connections poor. He carried two heavy grips, one of them weighted down with documents to substantiate, if need be, every statement made on the platform. Frequently he could not get simple food and would be ill because of the diet or water. Only his extraordinary vitality and will power made it possible at times to keep on with his rigorous schedule.

In spite of the hardships, he found strength and inspiration in the response his message received from the "real folks." Often he would say, "Belle, the women are interested in these public questions; it is wonderful how well they understand, and how responsive they are in all my audiences." Often he would meet old neighborhood friends, university associates, former political acquaintances. Everywhere he found enthusiastic support for the work he was doing. Though physically weary, he came home from these long, hard jaunts refreshed in spirit.

Bob's speech at Chautauqua, New York, on July 18, was his first invasion of the East and called forth much discussion in the national press as to "La Follette's object." Many suggested that he wished the Vice Presidency. This he never wanted. As reports of his speeches, often garbled, came back to Wisconsin, the stalwart newspapers called him hard, unpleasant names and raised a great cry that the governor was betraying his State, injuring its reputation, and "hurting business." Even when he spoke in Madison at the Monona Lake Assembly, his speech was grossly misrepresented in the press and he was bitterly assailed. Yet when my dear mother said, "Belle, I don't see how you stand all this vilification and abuse of Bob," I replied truthfully, without reservation, "So long as he is doing what he believes to be right, I would be proud of his work though everybody were maligning him."

I do not remember that we ever discussed the matter of Bob's being a candidate for another term. We simply took it for granted that he should lead the fight for the primary law and a commission to control railroad rates, for without this power the taxation law would prove an empty victory. We knew the third term would be his most desperate struggle, but looked upon it as a part of the day's work. The opposition likewise assumed it was a fight to the finish. Bob took no rest after his 1903 Chautauqua lectures. In September he began a round of Wisconsin county-fair speeches, in which the reading of freight rates was the dramatic feature. Standing on a farmer's lumber wagon, drawn up on the race track in front of the grandstand, without protection from the sun, he would speak to thousands of people, mostly from the farms. Citing long tables of parallel freight rates, he would show just how much more the farmers of that particular community were paying to ship wheat, hops, and other products to market than the people of Iowa and Illinois for the same service at places equidistant from market. He would demonstrate that freight charges were in the nature of a tax on production; that while the people of Wisconsin were paying $20,000,000 in taxes for state, county, and municipal purposes, they were paying more than $47,000,000 annually for transportation.

Sometimes when he stopped in the midst of his recital of cold facts to say he must shorten his speech in order not to interfere with the races, there would be cries from the audience. "Never mind the races; let them go over till tomorrow." The crowd would applaud and shout, "Go on." His audience, instead of dwindling, would be larger at the close than at the beginning. While speaking to an immense crowd at the La Crosse Interstate Fair, his figures were challenged by the president of the La Crosse Plow Company, who declared he was getting cheaper rates. Bob retorted that if the manufacturer was getting less than the quoted rates, they must be secret and illegal; in other words, he must be receiving unlawful rebates.[6]

During the winter two candidates for the Republican nomination for governor appeared on the horizon. Judge Emil Baensch and Samuel A. Cook had at one time been personally friendly to Bob and were to some extent identified with him in the public mind. The stalwart strategy was to secure support for each separately at the caucuses as "non-factional" candidates. Then, at the opportune moment they expected to pool their strength, capture the state convention, and in one blow annihilate La Follette, the "agitator" and "troublemaker." Thus the railroads, stalwart newspapers, and the Federal machine united, under the direction of such powerful leaders as Postmaster General Payne, Senators Spooner and Quarles, Congressmen Babcock, Charles Pfister, and Emanuel Philipp, to wage the bitterest, most desperate political battle Wisconsin had ever known.

Bob had the support of the *Free Press,* Hoard's *Dairyman,* and a number of smaller newspapers which gave effective help. He had the backing of a good fighting organization and some strong leaders over the State. But with most of the newspapers against him, Bob's power of reaching the people by word of mouth was, of course, a great asset. It seemed an almost superhuman task to overcome the power, money, and prestige of the opposition in 1904. He did not underestimate the forces he was fighting, yet his plan was to put the Stalwarts on the defensive. He encouraged an aggressive campaign against Babcock's return to Congress, and several progressive

candidates entered the field. Although renominated, and publicly
using a 1902 letter from Roosevelt as an endorsement, Babcock had
a close call in the election, winning by a plurality of 385 in a district
where the normal Republican majority was from eight to ten thousand. Two years later Babcock was defeated by a Democrat.

In his campaign speeches Bob effectively used a preliminary report
which had been made early in April, 1904, on the investigation he
had asked the 1903 legislature to authorize. Railroad Commissioner
Thomas' report proved that during the two preceding years four
railroads had paid Wisconsin shippers over $1,298,000 in rebates and
had failed to report gross earnings amounting to over $400,000,
making a total of more than $1,698,000 upon which they had failed
to pay taxes. It also showed that big Wisconsin manufacturers and
shippers who had opposed legislation to tax or regulate railroads
had themselves annually received rebates amounting to from $40,000
to $60,000.[7]

Dramatizing these facts on the platform, Bob would explain, so
that every man, woman, and child could understand, how the rebat-
ing system gave the railroads tyrannical power, demoralized business,
and robbed the State. He would vividly recount the incident told him
by a large manufacturer who had gone to Madison to help defeat the
railway commission bill because he was receiving a secret dollar
rate upon one of his products when the published rate was a dollar
and a half. The audience relived the brief drama as Bob quoted
the manufacturer who said: "But on my way back after the defeat
of that bill, I learned that two of my competitors were getting a rate
of 85 cents on the same product for which I was paying a rate of $1.
Instead of going home, I took the train to Chicago, called on the
proper railroad official and said to him, 'I have come here to get an
85 cent rate,' and he said, 'Hoity, toity, you have got a $1 rate now
as against the published rate of $1.50.' I looked him straight in the
eye and said, 'I think if you investigate, you'll find that I am
entitled to 85 cents.' He said he would look into it, went out for
a few minutes, came back and said, 'By jove, old fellow, you are
entitled to the 85-cent rate.' Then I understood perfectly how I had
lost certain of my customers to those two rivals in business. They
had had an 85-cent rate where I had had $1. Still, I don't know but
that now I have an 85-cent rate, they've got a 75-cent rate. I have

thought it all out. I want this business open and square and plain, and then I will know where I am and how to make my calculations."

As it became apparent that his county-fair speeches were arousing the people, the railroads grew reckless in their determination to defeat him. A superintendent of the Chicago, Milwaukee, and St. Paul Railroad telegraphed to employees under him: "Come into Madison. Your time goes on. Report to me.—Eldridge." When the men reported to him, "Mr. Eldridge made plain the purpose of his visit. He told the men that Governor La Follette 'had' to be beaten, that every one of them had to get out and work to carry the caucuses of the city of Madison against him. That unless they did so, they could sever their connections with the railroad. That their jobs depended upon their political activity. That the railroad was not going to stand for any fooling on the part of the men, but that every one who could be spared out of the yards, and from the operation of trains must get into the political field and hustle against the governor." Eldridge visited other towns in his special car, making the same speech to the men who answered his call. Some were interviewed individually. It was reported that in these private talks this superintendent said that "every division superintendent in the state was now engaged in this work, that every railroad employee of the state was being harnessed against the governor."[8] The Chicago and North Western Road also called in its conductors, engineers, firemen, yardmen, and others on the payroll to tell them they must see to it that La Follette was defeated. The railroad-employee relatives of a man slated for delegate on the La Follette ticket were notified it meant their "bread and butter" unless he refused. Another employee slated for the La Follette ticket was told he must not only withdraw his name but allow it to be used against the governor. A conductor on the North Western courageously resigned rather than "break faith with La Follette."

Throughout the years of strife I was, of course, aware that Bob ran constant risk of violence. He received threatening letters. When the state capitol burned, we were warned the Executive Residence would burn next. For a time we were harassed at the Executive Residence with strange ringing of bells and pounding on doors, which, though the house was carefully watched, remained a mystery. I tried to accept the hazards of political struggle in the same spirit Bob did: recognizing there was danger in all undertakings; that fear and worry were futile and wasted energy which should be conserved for the work in hand.

The Republican State Convention was to meet at Madison on May 18. Preceding the caucuses Bob initiated a new kind of campaign with what was then a revolutionary tactic, though it is a commonplace today. He began systematically to read the roll call. Going into the senate and assembly districts where representatives had violated platform pledges, he clearly presented the issues at public meetings and then read the legislator's votes on the important measures. The task he set himself was not easy.

It was a new thing to judge public men by their votes instead of by their neighborly conduct and good standing in the community. Before he spoke, his friends would often urge him to omit the roll call, saying people knew the stalwart candidate had voted wrong in the last legislature and didn't intend to vote for him, but that he was personally well-liked, and publicly humiliating him by reading his record could only create sympathy; it would hurt the cause more than it would help. Bob always answered he could make no exceptions; he must hew to the line regardless of the candidate's personal popularity. "This is no time for bouquets or soft words," he said: "we are getting none." I have sat on the platform many times and felt the audience "freeze" as he began to read the ayes and nays disclosing the record of senators and assemblymen to their constituents.

Sometimes stalwart members of the legislature were sitting on the platform. They would find themselves uncomfortable as Bob read their votes, and would leave the hall. Then the crowds would shout their derision. There would be great applause when he would say, "Put the men who have betrayed you on the retired list." Because he never dealt in personalities and held strictly to the record, which told its own story impartially, the roll call carried conviction and was as practically effective as it was dramatic.

The launching of the "roll call" was a daring undertaking in his preconvention campaign. But the election of a legislature which would execute the will of the people when it met in 1905 was, he knew, even more essential to enactment of the proposed reforms than his own election. It was out of his experience and the necessities of the situation that he evolved this plan, which one writer has said displayed "a quality nothing short of genius," whereby he turned the simple reading of the roll call into a weapon which has had far-reaching effect on political history. I have always believed the institution of the roll call, that is, bringing home to the people by specific examples the faithfulness or unfaithfulness of their public servants, was one of the greatest services Bob has rendered.*

Ten days before the state convention, the *Milwaukee Sentinel* practically conceded his nomination. Nevertheless, stalwart leaders ominously continued to claim a majority of the delegates. During the last weeks of the campaign, reports came in that second sets of Republican delegates were being elected under circumstances which could only mean the Stalwarts were "preparing to steal the convention" or bolt it and put up a third ticket.

Bob was having large meetings. His audiences were enthusiastic and deeply in earnest. Excitement ran high. There was fear of violence. He was speaking in Milwaukee on the night before the city caucuses to elect convention delegates. Henry Cochems, who had been working hard and knew the situation, told him there might be bloodshed at some of the polling places next day. Bob replied: "Never mind. Let every man stand firm for his rights. I am still Governor and can exercise the pardoning power."

* In 1933 the *New York Times* began publishing the votes of New York Congressmen.

CHAPTER XVI

Lincoln Steffens Comes to Wisconsin

When Bob arrived home from his speaking campaign on the Saturday morning before the convention, after greeting the family, he said anxiously, "I must get right at work on a speech of acceptance; I haven't given it a moment's thought and must make at least an outline of what I am to say." He sat down in an easy chair in the library. His head sank back. He was fast asleep! I closed the doors and made sure he was not disturbed. In the evening I had difficulty in rousing him long enough to get him to go to bed. The next day, when he awoke, he had the impression he had only been napping; after periods of long strain he would often make up sleep this way.

During the two hectic days that followed, there was no time to prepare a speech. The State Central Committee met at Madison on May 17, the day before the convention, and, according to established precedent, made up the roll of delegates entitled to seats. Due notice had been given that the committee, which was the recognized authority on credentials of delegates, would hear all contests and decide who should sit in the preliminary organization. All contesting delegations were given a full and impartial hearing. By a *unanimous* vote the entire committee, six members of which were Stalwarts, placed enough La Follette delegates on the roll to constitute a clear majority of the convention. A vote of thanks to General Bryant, the committee chairman, for "the fair and impartial manner in which he presided" was also unanimously passed.[1] The leader of the stalwart minority, Marvin B. Rosenberry, later a Justice of the Wisconsin Supreme Court, also personally thanked the majority of the committee for the courteous treatment received. These six stalwart committee members were all experienced politicians, and it must be presumed they fully understood the significance of their cooperation in conceding that a majority of the delegates had been elected for La Follette.

That evening the Stalwarts held an extraordinary mass meeting at the Madison Fuller Opera House, which had been engaged months before. The action of this meeting was unprecedented in Wisconsin history. Inflammatory speeches were made and the State Central Committee denounced. Violence was threatened at the convention next day if the rights of any delegates were "overridden." With uproarious enthusiasm a resolution was adopted that "anti-third term delegates should meet at 11 o'clock the next day and march in a body to the gymnasium and demand their rights."[2] At the appointed time and place about two hundred men met, formed four abreast and, with two large flags waving, marched in a defiant procession from the Fuller Opera House to the gymnasium, a distance of about a mile.

It was known that counterfeit tickets had been printed, and threats made to stampede the convention. Therefore precautions had been taken during the night to protect all entrances to the university gymnasium. A narrow barbed-wire passage led to the door opening into the part of the hall apportioned to delegates, who thus had to enter single file and submit credentials countersigned by the State Central Committee. To prevent a stalwart rush for delegate seats, a plain wire partition four and a half feet high separated the space allotted to delegates from that occupied by spectators. Spectators' tickets were also carefully scrutinized. The sergeant at arms had a large force of university athletes deputized and stationed at strategic places inside and outside the hall.

When General Bryant called the convention to order, the gymnasium was packed with delegates and spectators from all parts of the State. The crowd was tense with excitement. Newspaper correspondents from over the country occupied the long tables in front of the platform, their presence a reminder of the nation-wide interest. With the children I sat on the platform, closely following the proceedings, conscious this was a crisis in the long struggle, but with utmost faith in the outcome. In strict accord with past precedent, the secretary read the roll call, and General Bryant announced that he had been directed by unanimous vote of the State Central Committee to select Lenroot as temporary chairman. It had been rumored that this would be the moment when the Stalwarts might try to capture the convention by force and wrest the gavel from Bryant's hand. While the general was presiding, Rosenberry had come up from the auditorium and taken a seat on the platform directly behind Lenroot. Fearing this might be a pre-arranged signal for action, three husky university men, deputized as guards, took seats directly behind Rosenberry. As Lenroot moved to the front of the platform, he was greeted with cheers and applause. A similar demonstration followed his effective speech prophesying that passage of the primary referendum would make this the last Wisconsin convention to nominate state officers.

When the motion was made to adopt the majority report of the State Central Committee acting as the committee on credentials, Rosenberry, who had served as stalwart leader on the committee, moved to substitute a minority report. This report, signed by himself and five other stalwart members, strangely reversed the position they had taken on the previous day. It now claimed stalwart delegates had been elected in the very counties which had been unanimously conceded to La Follette.

In the debate following his motion, Rosenberry contended that the State Central Committee did not have the power to determine the contests, thus staking the entire stalwart case on the claim that the certificates of the chairman and the secretary of the county committees were the *only* authoritative test of the validity of credentials. This had never been the practice of the party. If this minority contention prevailed, it would absolutely destroy the right of the convention, through the State Central Committee or otherwise, to pass upon the qualifications of its members. Such action was without precedent and would have violated the rule, as old as the law itself, that every representative body is the sole judge of the election of its members.

The first test of strength came on sustaining Lenroot's ruling that all delegates seated by the State Central Committee were entitled to vote on all questions except that of their own right to a seat in the convention. As the great audience listened to the roll call, the only sound that broke the silence was that of the pencils keeping tally. Everyone knew La Follette had a majority unless delegates had shifted during the night under terrific pressure. When it became evident the La Follette forces had a majority, a great outburst of applause broke in on the roll call and swept the convention. The vote was 574 5/6 to 485 1/6.

The 43 contested stalwart delegates seated by the State Central Committee, as well as the 441 uncontested stalwart delegates, participated in the convention proceedings until late afternoon, when it was moved to make the temporary organization permanent. Then a tall stalwart leader, Jeffris, rose and shouted from the floor, "I ask the privilege of announcing that all anti-third term delegates in this convention are requested to meet in caucus at the Fuller Opera House at 8 o'clock tonight!" At the door Jeffris paused and shouted defiantly, "I protest that this convention is not legally organized."[3] An uproar followed. Some of the Baensch delegates left the hall cheering while the La Follette men jeered and booed at them. The Cook delegates sat stolidly in their seats while the bolt was on. They voted on the question of permanent organization and remained until the convention adjourned for the day.

At the Fuller Opera House convention that night and the following day, stalwart notables were seated on the stage and gave the bolters their blessing and official endorsement. Among them were former Governors Upham and Scofield, Congressman Babcock, Senators Quarles and Spooner. Jeffris presided, and a speech by Spooner declaring the convention was "inspired by loyalty to representative government" was given an ovation.[4] The Stalwarts seated 567 delegates,[5] making up the lists in various irregular ways which included drafting of mere visitors from various counties. When a county lacked delegates, Chairman Jeffris would call out, "Who else is here to represent the county?" and volunteers would be sworn in as delegates. Judge Baensch withdrew "in the interest of harmony," and Cook, who had later joined the bolters, was nominated by acclamation as the stalwart candidate for governor. The convention also nominated a full state ticket and adopted a platform. Spooner, Babcock, Quarles, and Baensch were elected as delegates to the Republican National Convention to be held at Chicago on June 21.

It would be almost incredible that politicians and officials of high rank could have given sanction to or taken part in these proceedings if the facts were not of record. Walter Wellman, noted correspondent, and a warm friend of Spooner's, wrote: "It seems impossible for a neutral to study the evidence without coming to the conclusion that the La Follette convention was regular and the other simply a bolting body. I say this much in behalf of the truth of history, and will add that this conclusion is that of most of the neutral men who are familiar with the facts, including many Republican senators and other public men whose sympathies are naturally with Spooner."[6]

The Republican convention at the university gymnasium concluded its work the second day. The platform was read by Herbert Chynoweth, chairman of the Committee on Resolutions, and adopted with resounding cheers. It recorded "unqualified approval of the progressive, patriotic, courageous administration of Theodore Roosevelt," endorsed Governor La Follette's record, the primary, equal-taxation, railroad-commission measures, and approved the investigation which disclosed unlawful rebates; it favored a constitutional amendment authorizing enactment of a graduated income-tax law; denounced the attempt of employers of labor to coerce their employees' votes at caucuses and conventions; promised legislation to protect citizens in the exercise of their rights at the ballot box; and condemned the pernicious activity of Federal employees to defeat legislation pledged in the party platform. The plank on platform pledges, which Bob had inserted because he intended to read the roll call during the coming election campaign, declared they were "sacred obligations binding upon every member of the party" and obligated every candidate for office "to aid in redeeming every pledge in letter and spirit." This plank gave authoritative support to the use of the roll call and reinforced the appeal that only men loyal to platform pledges should be elected.

Bob was placed in nomination by James A. Frear, seconding speeches were made by leading Progressives, and the entire state ticket was unanimously renominated. Bob, Isaac Stephenson, James H. Stout, and W. D. Connor were chosen as delegates to the Republican National Convention. When Bob appeared upon the platform, he was given an ovation. I knew he had not had time to prepare as he wanted to. Though this extemporaneous address was more in his style of campaign speaking, a reporter said he charged the four brief words, "I accept the nomination," with hypnotic power which made the great gathering feel the load suddenly lifted from its shoulders and transferred to his own.

Shortly after the convention it was proposed a representative group go to Washington to present the progressive view of the

Wisconsin political situation to Roosevelt. Bob thought this futile because of the President's personal and political relations with Postmaster General Payne, Senator Spooner, and Congressman Babcock. But friends argued that Spooner had recently presented the stalwart side to the President and that in fairness to Roosevelt the La Follette side should also be presented. Bob reluctantly yielded. He knew the final verdict would have to be at the ballot box in Wisconsin.

The committee to interview the President consisted of Speaker Lenroot, H. P. Myrick, editor of the *Milwaukee Free Press*; Walter L. Houser, Secretary of State; C. C. Gittings, Bob's lifelong friend and supporter; and W. D. Connor, a wealthy businessman who had recently interested himself in the progressive cause. The interview was to no avail. Roosevelt stated with his usual emphasis that it was improper for him to interfere in factional contests. It was a satisfaction to me, however, to learn that our friends had told the President of the activities of the Federal officeholders of Wisconsin who, in violation of the rules and spirit of the civil service, had not only waged persistent warfare on La Follette, but had done their utmost to defeat legislation repeatedly promised in the Republican state platform.

The stalwart plan was to seat the Spooner-Quarles-Babcock-Baensch delegation at the Republican National Convention and bring an action in the Wisconsin Supreme Court which, if won, would place the Cook state ticket in the Republican column on the official ballot—the place to which the lawfully nominated ticket was entitled.

The National Republican Committee began its hearings on the Wisconsin contest on June 17 at the Coliseum in Chicago. Newspapers reported that every train during the morning "brought in Republicans from Wisconsin until the hotels and the Coliseum anteroom put on the appearance of the Madison capitol at state convention time."[7] "The leaders in the great political duel in themselves made the contest nationally famous. . . . The tables for the factions are located on opposite sides of the big hall in which the Committee is meeting. At the head of the anti-La Follette table sat Senator Spooner. Next to him was Senator Quarles and around the table were seated John M. Olin and Harry Butler, the counsel in the case. Governor La Follette presided at the La Follette table and seated with him were attorneys H. W. Chynoweth and Gilbert E. Roe."[8]

Bob described the hearing as a grotesque farce: "While the arguments were being made, the members of the committee strolled about the room or chatted with each other in their seats. The few who gave attention interrupted our counsel so constantly with questions manifestly designed to prevent them from submitting a succinct and intelligible statement of the case, that neither had an opportunity to finish his argument in the time allotted. As soon as that time had expired, without even looking at the documents which had been presented, including the printed briefs, the verified statement of the case, the printed case and the affidavits, the committee refused to permit us to be seated as delegates in the convention."[9]

From coast to coast telegraph dispatches reported the stalwart victory, "Spooner wins: La Follette loses." A well known correspondent commented: "The case of Governor La Follette . . . was lost before the members of the national committee left home. . . . It took the national committee just one minute by the watch to decide the case."[10] This peremptory action convinced Bob that an appeal to the committee on credentials, which was the next step in procedure, would mean only another rebuff. In a conference with friends he said: "We cannot get justice here; the cards are stacked against us."[11] He drafted a statement of reasons for declining to submit the case, which Gilbert Roe presented to the credentials committee. This action was headlined as "Coup By La Follette. 'Fighting Governor' of Wisconsin Hurls Bomb Among Committeemen."[12] The Committee on Credentials promptly reported in favor of seating the Spooner-Quarles-Babcock-Baensch delegation, and the convention adopted the report with loud cheers. When asked what he thought of the action of the convention, Bob answered, "We shall appeal to the people of the State for justice."

During the interval between Bob's nomination and the meeting of the Republican National Convention, the fiftieth anniversary of the University of Wisconsin had been celebrated. It was jubilee year, fraught with happy memories and inspiring events. Former President Bascom delivered the baccalaureate address. Charles R. Van Hise was formally inaugurated president. There was a great gathering of alumni and distinguished educators from over the country. We gladly participated in all the commencement exercises and social functions, giving a large reception at the Executive Residence. Fola graduated at this 1904 commencement. She was greatly surprised when told she had been elected to Phi Beta Kappa, as her university work had been much interrupted by home responsibilities and she had no expectation of honors.

This jubilee year was the twenty-fifth anniversary of our class of 1879, to which Van Hise also belonged. We had a remarkable class reunion. No one entered into the spirit of the occasion with greater enthusiasm than Bob. His deep feeling for old associations and traditions, his vivid memory and spontaneous wit were given full play. Many of our classmates were guests at the Executive Residence. Reminiscences of college days, its pleasures and hardships, the good old times as compared with the present, were sources of gay conversation and laughter. It was heartening to meet so many who had gone out from the university, and to learn how generally they had kept in touch with Bob's work and how ready and eager they were to cooperate.

At the ceremonies incident to President Van Hise's inauguration on June 7, Bob made a simple but singularly effective address. In part he said: "Standing here at the close of the first half century, we turn to meet the increasing responsibilities of the coming years. It is not enough that this university shall zealously advance learning, or that it shall become a great store-house of knowledge into which is gathered the accumulating fruits of research and all of the world's best culture, or that it shall maintain the highest standards of scholarship and develop every latent talent—all these are essential —but the state demands more than all these. The state asks that you give back to it men and women strong in honesty and integrity of character, in each of whom there is deeply planted the obligation of allegiance to the state. That obligation should meet them as they cross that threshold of this institution and go in and out with them day by day until it is a conviction as strong as life."[13]

Soon after the Republican National Convention had excluded Bob as a delegate, Lincoln Steffens came to Madison to interview him. When I learned about it, I was moved to tears. Although I had become inured to the continuous false and ruthless attacks of the stalwart press, still, each time after reading one of Steffens' articles in *McClure's* telling what he had seen in Chicago, St. Louis, Missouri, Illinois, and elsewhere, I would say to myself, "Oh, why doesn't he come to Wisconsin?" It had become a subconscious prayer with me. Of course, I didn't expect him to tell the story as I saw and felt it. But it would be wonderful to have the history of the Wisconsin struggle written up from the standpoint of so expert and impartial an observer. I was confident he had the ability and insight to get at the truth in spite of the maze of lies he would encounter.

When Bob telephoned that Steffens was at the capitol and that he would bring him home for supper, I was very happy. I simply took it for granted he was our friend and gave him a fervent welcome. I was greatly disappointed that he was so unresponsive. It did not occur to me he was still investigating the facts and had not yet reached his conclusions. My assumption that he was on our side of the case—in fact, a wholehearted sympathizer—doubtless impressed him as premature and tactless. He was polite but reserved.

Long afterward I learned why he met my warm greeting so coldly.[14] He had begun the Wisconsin investigation in the belief that Bob was a self-seeking demagogue and troublemaker. His colleagues on *McClure's Magazine* shared his opinion. Before coming to Madison, he had gone quietly to Milwaukee to interview some of Bob's bitterest foes, expecting them to substantiate the charges that La Follette was a dangerous agitator and hypocrite. It was the denunciation by his enemies of the things he was trying to do that gave Steffens the first inkling the Wisconsin governor might be a man of purpose, striving to achieve much-needed reforms and honestly seeking to restore representative government.

Steffens' attitude of mind on his first visit to Milwaukee must have been tipped off to the *Milwaukee Sentinel*, for the laudatory welcome of this leading stalwart newspaper, describing him as a writer whose "evident purpose always has been to speak the truth on all occasions," contrasted strikingly with its later comment *after* Steffens' article on Wisconsin was published.[15]

Steffens proposed that Bob tell him the story of his life, good and bad alike. As Bob was to speak at the St. Louis Fair on June 29 he suggested Steffens accompany us, promising that after his speech he would give all his time to confession. Having accepted the challenge to tell his story without reservation, he made a clean, thorough job of it. He took a stack of documents to verify his case, much as he would if going to court. He had the gift of narrative, and his memory was like a camera; it registered experiences with such exactness and detail. During several days, for long hours, the two men were closeted in a room by themselves, their keen minds searching for the material facts and essential motives, striving to pass unbiased judgment on the record of a life, twenty-five years of which had been spent in politics; Steffens taking notes, asking pointed questions; Bob on his mettle to give a complete, accurate, dispassionate account of his past history.

After this exhaustive inquiry into Bob's version of the fight, Steffens interviewed many representative Stalwarts. He saw Senator Spooner's brother, Philip Spooner, and suggested to this astute politician that he make out a list of Stalwarts to be interviewed in rebuttal. Later, Steffens, accompanied by Mrs. Steffens, went about the State and saw the people on this list. The Steffens article was to appear in the October *McClure's*. I awaited the verdict with anxious heart.

On July Fourth Bob began filling his Chautauqua engagements in neighboring States. Many friends had urged him to abandon these lectures and devote the entire summer to the state campaign. Though he managed to make a number of speeches in Wisconsin, he felt he must earn money to carry on the fight. But he started the organization work early. At this time he had perhaps 100,000 names and addresses, obtained from township leaders, classified according to activity and influence, to whom it was the practice to send campaign literature and appeals for support. A thorough revision and enlargement of these lists on the school-district basis was planned. John M. Nelson ably directed this work. Loyal volunteer workers were urged to stir up interest in every possible school district and bring out the full progressive vote on election day. It was estimated over a million pamphlets were sent from progressive headquarters.

Bob resolved, if humanly possible, to secure a legislature which would enact the platform pledges into law. He went into the crucial legislative districts and "campaigned them as they had never been campaigned before." He spoke on forty-eight days in succession,

averaging eight and a quarter hours a day on the platform. He saw
the advantages of an automobile in mapping out all-day speaking
schedules, and a car had been acquired for his use. It was an
experiment; the auto was not yet in common use and it was regarded as a luxury. Horses were not accustomed to automobiles and
were afraid of them. There were all sorts of risks except the one
that most troubles this generation—traffic. He belittled the objections and suggested having two cars so that in case one broke down
he could use the other. Later in the campaign this plan was adopted.

It was raining heavily when the Winton arrived in the late afternoon of September 1. That night he was to drive to Fond du Lac
and start speaking early the next morning. Bob, Jr., and Phil were
greatly excited about the automobile. They begged their father to
let them go with him. Overwhelmed with joy, the boys started off
with their father and his secretary, Colonel Hannan, on their first
campaign in an automobile. Bob, Jr., was nine, Phil seven years old.
The stalwart press sought to make political capital out of the
governor's use of an automobile for campaign purposes. The
Sentinel falsely charged he had caused runaways and endangered
life, thus proving that he was out of sympathy with the plain
people for whom he pretended to care so much. The stalwart
newspapers also attacked him for earning money on the Chautauqua platform to the neglect of official duties. Although he seldom
replied to this kind of criticism, he turned aside in one of his
speeches to say: "To this cause of taking the government out of
the hands of a privileged few and bringing it back to the people I
will give all there is in me until it is accomplished. . . . You see I
have to put a good deal into the game myself to keep up the cause,
and we must order our living and conduct the business of the state
in a dignified manner. Why, if I didn't have a chance to go out
every summer on the Chautauqua platform and earn $3,000 we
would be in debt $12,000 at the end of four years. We try to live
economically but at that we have put by the chance to lay up anything for our children's future. We understand each other at home;
we have talked it all out and are agreed. I wish to leave something
to the state more lasting than bronze or marble and a better legacy
to my children than mere wealth. And I am not going to be swerved
from my purpose. . . . If I should be defeated on the eighth of next

November, you will find me out early on the morning of the ninth on a new campaign."[16]

The Steffens article in *McClure's Magazine,* which appeared on the newsstands in the last week of September, was a veritable bomb in the camp of the Stalwarts. Although a large edition had been printed, it was sold out by October 2. The *Wisconsin State Journal* said La Follette had hypnotized Steffens. Knowing my suspense, Gilbert Roe had written me from New York on August 10 that the article did for Bob "what Steffens had done for Folk." The *Milwaukee Sentinel,* recanting its former praise of Steffens' integrity and ability in exposing political corruption, now said: "This man Steffens is paid to write ex parte statements under the guise of impartial reports and his publishers prostitute their columns to libelous uses with the hope of reaping financial reward. . . . A more brazen, disreputable prostitution of the power of the press has never been recorded in this country."[17]

Reading Steffens' article a quarter of a century after it was written, I am as moved as when I read it for the first time.[18] It is hard to express what the article meant to us. We knew it would have a profound effect in Wisconsin. For years facts had been misrepresented and motives distorted. This was the first national recognition and impartial interpretation of Bob's work and the purpose of the progressive movement. Other well known writers, attracted by the dramatic conflict, had come to Wisconsin. Their articles, mostly favorable to Bob, appeared in *Collier's Weekly,* the *Outlook, Harper's Weekly,* the *Review of Reviews,* and other publications. The stalwart newspapers were hard-pressed to explain how the Eastern periodicals had been so grossly misled.

Spooner was a magnetic speaker and drew large crowds. He made fierce attacks on the governor, as did his colleague Senator Quarles. But they spoke chiefly in the large cities. The task of following Bob throughout the State was left to their satellites, who made little impression and were soon worn out.

The Supreme Court decision was handed down on October 5, creating great excitement in the State. Most of the daily papers issued extras with big headlines. The decision declared that the La Follette ticket was regularly nominated and entitled to place in the Republican column on the official ballot. The Republican National

Convention was declared without significance in determining title
to place on official ballots, and the bolters were without cause of
action.

When Bob had previously stated that he would carry the issue
to the polls regardless of what the Supreme Court might decide, the
Stalwarts had professed to be greatly shocked. But after the decision
went against them, Spooner, in a public speech two days before
election, said, "I represent here tonight what is called the opera
house platform made by the only regular convention that was held
by the Republican Party in this state this year."[19] However, S. A.
Cook, the stalwart candidate for governor, withdrew from the ticket.
The name of former Governor Scofield was then substituted. But
this was a mere gesture, for the Stalwarts openly concentrated on the
election of Peck, the Democratic candidate, who was running on a
platform dictated by the same reactionary forces that nominated
Rose. The Stalwarts flooded the State with sample ballots showing
how to vote for Roosevelt and Peck, and completely ignoring Scofield, who, in fact, received only 12,000 votes.

A week before election the *Sentinel* reminded its readers "that
the defeat of Disturber La Follette is the paramount issue in this
campaign."[20] The day before election it published two columns of
excerpts from stalwart papers calling for Bob's defeat.[21] The day
after election the secretary of the stalwart State Central Committee
himself said, "The so-called stalwarts to a man supported the national Republican ticket while with almost equal unanimity they
supported Governor Peck, and find no reason for concealing the
fact."

On Saturday night, November 5, 1904, Bob closed his long, hard
speaking campaign with a meeting at the university gymnasium. On
the following Tuesday he was elected by over 50,000 plurality. The
direct-primary law was carried by about the same plurality, and at
last *both* houses of the legislature were safely progressive.

CHAPTER XVII

On to Washington as
United States Senator

In the struggle to prevent Bob's renomination and reelection, the fact that the 1905 legislature was to elect a United States Senator had received relatively little attention. Quarles was a candidate for reelection and would naturally receive the united stalwart support. But he had no such hold on the people of the State as Spooner. Since his name could not be conjured with to confuse the real issues, as Spooner's had been, they charged Bob had secured pledges from candidates for the legislature to ensure his own election to the Senate. Shortly before election Walter Wellman interviewed him as to these rumors. Bob denied them flatly, adding: "You may say for me that I have no wish to go to the United States Senate at this time. I am not and shall not be a candidate. I do not deny that some day or other I may aspire to a seat in the Senate and take one if the people of Wisconsin are willing to give it to me. But mark this: I have set out here in Wisconsin to do a certain work. . . . A part of this work is done, and a part remains unfinished. Until it is all finished I shall remain here at my post."[1] I know nothing could have tempted Bob to swerve from this position. He had instituted the roll call and concentrated his fight on the election of a progressive legislature solely because he believed enactment of platform pledges into law the greatest service to be rendered, and therefore the fulfillment of his highest ambition.

Bob was inaugurated governor for the third time on January 2, 1905. He was in a strong position. The victory at the polls, after ten years of hard fighting, was accepted in the State as decisive.

Lenroot was again elected speaker of the assembly, but in the senate the Progressives had only a small majority. Bob again delivered his message in person. More than a third of it related to the control of railway rates, as the creation of a railway commission was the most important legislative issue at this session. He discussed the relation of transportation to the growth of monopoly and commended President Roosevelt's stand for amendment of the Interstate Commerce Act so that the Interstate Commerce Commission should have "the power to revise rates and regulations." Most of his other recommendations were in line with policies he had previously advocated. But it was in this message that he recommended for the first time a Civil Service Commission and the enactment of a strong civil service law based upon Federal experience and that of Massachusetts and New York.[2]

When he finished his address, John R. Commons, who had recently accepted a professorship of economics at the university, came to me with tears in his eyes and said, "I never expected to live to hear a message like that from the governor of a state."

To Bob's great satisfaction the civil service law, when finally enacted, required all employees then holding office, including his own appointees, to take the regular competitive examination. This provision was in accord with his own stipulation when the bill was drafted.[3] Ernest N. Warner, chairman of the assembly committee in charge of the bill, worked untiringly to secure a model law; he had the valuable cooperation of Professor Commons, who made an extensive survey of the subject both in this country and abroad.

The only menace to the legislative program now lurked in potential animosities and complications that might arise over the election of a United States Senator. The primary law had passed at the referendum, but did not become effective until September, 1906. Before that date Quarles' term expired and a successor must be chosen by the legislature. Following the election, when it became known the Progressives controlled the legislature, various aspirants had developed. Stephenson wished to go to the Senate, and consulted Bob as to his candidacy. Bob said that as far as he knew no legislators were pledged to any candidate, and suggested that Stephenson have some loyal friend canvass the members as to his chances of election.

Subsequently, W. D. Connor became an active candidate, and it was feared the rivalry between him and Stephenson might cause a deadlock in the legislature. Connor came to see Bob and stated that he had enough supporters in the legislature to defeat the La Follette reforms. He bluntly asked if Bob was a candidate. Bob indignantly replied, "No, and I will not be a candidate unless conditions make it necessary to preserve harmony and secure the legislation pledged in the platform." By the time Bob delivered his message, other candidates had entered the field, thus dividing the progressive vote further. It became evident that a Senator must be elected before the legislative program could be achieved. Throughout the State and in the legislature a strong sentiment existed to elect Bob. He was the only man who could be elected without a prolonged, bitter conflict which might engender animosities that would defeat the legislation pledged in the platform.

At a joint session of the legislature on January 25 Bob was elected United States Senator, receiving 100 out of the 123 votes cast. Some of his intimate friends and advisers, most interested in his political future, urged him not to consider the Senatorship. I would not say he was unwilling to be chosen in 1905, but he took no part in bringing it about.

In his address to the legislature he accepted the election conditionally, stating that "if there should appear any conflict in the obligation I entered into when I took the oath of office as governor, and that of United States senator-elect, then I shall ask you to receive it from me and place it in other hands of your own choosing. The selection of United States senator is your prerogative and will, of course, be preserved to you."[4]

This legislative session made an extraordinary record of achievement. Although the railroads fought the railway-commission bill and prolonged the hearings, there was no open attempt to control legislators illegitimately as in previous years. One of the leading stalwart papers said, "This is the 'best legislature' in the sense of personal habits that Madison has ever seen in the memory of the oldest inhabitant." It also observed: "There is much entertainment at the executive mansion these days and stalwarts are in evidence there at social functions. . . . Facile and adapting himself to changing conditions, the idea that Governor La Follette is incapable of throwing off hostilities and making friends of former foes appears fallacious."[5] Bob never allowed political differences to affect his cordiality toward those who had accepted an invitation to his home.

When Bob learned that William J. Bryan was to speak in the State, he consulted the leading legislators of both parties and a resolution was passed inviting him to address a joint legislative session. He made a captivating and effective speech, but some Progressives feared what he said about public ownership might react unfavorably.[6] They were mistaken. His visit tended to create general good will. Bob had the speech printed and sent out, especially in the Democratic districts, where Bryan's influence would be effective.

When the commission bill came up for a final vote, it was passed unanimously by both senate and assembly. This bill was drawn with extraordinary care. Bob and the legislators charged with drafting the measure worked with John R. Commons and other university professors who were recognized authorities on the subject. In addition they got all available outside help.[7] Throughout the long controversy Bob was unyielding for an appointive commission. He argued the commissioners should be the best experts the country afforded, whether residents of Wisconsin or not, and that men especially equipped for the work might not be good campaigners.

Wishing to secure commissioners of the highest order to initiate the work, he appealed to Commissioner Prouty of the Interstate Commerce Commission and other nationally known authorities to accept the chairmanship. Failing in this, three excellent men from Wisconsin were agreed upon: Dr. B. H. Meyer of the university economics department, who has served on the Interstate Commerce Commission since 1911; John Barnes, a foremost lawyer, subsequently a Justice of the Wisconsin Supreme Court; and Halford Erickson, who had rendered valuable service as commissioner of industrial and labor statistics. Expert engineers and contractors were employed many months making a physical valuation of the railroad property in the State. When this task was completed, the commission had the basis for reasonable and scientific rate making, based on the value of the property and the cost of maintenance. It functioned with extraordinary success and benefit both to the public and to the corporations.

Years after the law was enacted, an eminent railroad attorney, making an argument before the Wisconsin Supreme Court, paused to say that while the railroads had strongly opposed a commission to regulate rates, they were now well satisfied that it had relieved them of many sources of trouble and discredit. He also predicted that if it were proposed to wipe out the law and permit a return to their old-time practices, the railroads themselves would be among the first to oppose such change.

From long study of the railroad problem Bob foresaw the menace to the State and Nation of the monopoly of electric power. He sent a message to the 1905 legislature, which now seems prophetic in its bearing on a paramount economic issue confronting the Nation today. In connection with granting franchises for building dams which carried control of water power, he said, "The preservation of our forests and the reforesting of lands . . . are absolutely essential to the preservation of Wisconsin's splendid water powers. The restoration of our forests, and the preservation of our water powers go hand in hand. . . .

"Such investigations as I have been able to make of the subject plainly indicate that many of the grants to construct dams heretofore passed by the legislature, have been secured purely for speculative purposes. In such cases no improvements whatever have been made. The grants have been held awaiting opportunities to sell the same with large profit to the holders, who have not invested a dollar for the benefit of the state, or its industrial development. It is obvious that these franchises may be gathered up, and consolidated with others which have been granted where improvements have been made, and prices advanced until the state, municipalities, and the public will be compelled to pay an exorbitant rate for the power upon which we are likely to grow more and more dependent as time passes."[8]

Foreseeing this, he sought, as was his habit, to express his thought in action, and concluded his message with a recommendation of specific legislation to protect public rights in these great natural resources.

When the legislature adjourned on June 21, 1905, there were written upon the statute books substantially all the important reforms for which Bob and the Progressives had so long contended; the primary-election law; taxation of railroads and other public utilities on the basis of actual physical valuation; the railway-commission law, which included regulation and control of telephone and telegraph companies; a civil service law; anti-lobbying law; labor laws; state-bank law; conservation and water-power franchise laws.

The work in Wisconsin was the rock on which he builded. The sentiment he expressed in regard to the legislation achieved in his State never changed: "If it can be shown that Wisconsin is a happier and better state to live in, that its institutions are more democratic, that the opportunities of all its people are more equal, that social justice more nearly prevails, that human life is safer and sweeter—then I shall rest content in the feeling that the Progressive movement has been successful."[9]

The day after the legislature adjourned, President Van Hise, in behalf of the university, conferred the honorary degree of Doctor of Laws on Carl Schurz and former President Bascom. Bascom delivered the baccalaureate sermon, Schurz the commencement address. The visit of Schurz was a memorable event to the people of Wisconsin. They delighted to recall him as a foremost citizen of the State who had exercised a powerful influence in mobilizing sentiment for freedom and democracy in the decade before the Civil War. It was unquestionably of much significance to the progressive movement that at a critical time in shaping public opinion Wisconsin had come under his leadership. As an exponent of independent political action, he had a profound influence on the State and Nation.

Official duties made it impossible for Bob to meet Schurz at the train. Dr. Ernst K. Voss, professor of German philology at the university, took Schurz to the capitol. Dr. Voss says: "I can still hear the words addressed by Carl Schurz to the young reformer when they met for the first time: 'I am so happy to know that what I have been striving for all my life has been taken up by a younger man. Go on with the good work, Governor, do not lose courage, and may God bless you.'"

The reception we gave in Schurz's honor stays in my memory as perhaps no other social occasion while we lived at the Executive Residence. The university faculty, alumni, and students, state officials, members of the legislature, people from all over the State

—many not in the habit of attending receptions—came to greet the grand old man. He was seventy-six years young—tall, spare, commanding, a vibrant, cultivated voice, his hair and beard only slightly gray, physically and mentally alert. He had a quick sense of humor, a friendly, sympathetic understanding of people. He seemed to meet each individual with special interest and pleasure. In less than a year his heroic life was ended. It was a fitting memorial to the man who had made such a deep impression upon the people of Wisconsin that a Carl Schurz Professorship should be endowed at the university to bring distinguished scholars in all branches of learning from Germany to fill the chair, not only to represent German culture but to be messengers of peace, good will, and common understanding between the two great nations.

Bob had to catch an early train on the morning after the reception to Carl Schurz. I could hardly endure the thought that after months of constant strain he must start off on the wearing summer's work without a moment's breathing spell; but he looked forward, as always, to enjoyment of his lecture engagements in the spirit of the crusader. In my first letter I told him of President Bascom's faith in his future, and that he "seemed anxious only for your *health.*" I added: "That *is* the important thing. What you *have* done is great and *satisfying.* Why should you wear yourself out in further extreme effort."[10] To which he replied: "Belle dear dont worry about me. . . . am taking just as much care of myself as possible. I should really enjoy every hour of this if you were only with me. I think you ought to go part of the time. You see when I get a few of these long range dates off all the work will be in a little radius and travelling expense would be light for two."[11] I did join him at times during the summer when his schedule made it convenient and not too expensive. I was always urging him to conserve his strength and make his speeches shorter. He would promise to do so "next time." But he talked to the multitudes as he would to a jury. When he saw earnest faces looking puzzled, he would repeat his arguments in different form and use further illustrations until he saw they understood and were convinced.

The family had a good laugh, as he intended we should, when we read his letter from Omaha describing how he ran up stairs that were "longer than Jacob's ladder" to catch a train which was an hour late. I realize now better than I did then that these recurring incidents of travel were a tremendous strain on his heart. Later he finished this letter: "The 'Committee' were waiting for me at Jefferson [Iowa] and it was 'plum late' as they say in Wolfville. Hustle to the hotel. Hustle something to eat. Hustle a shave, wash up and change of linnen [sic] and then hustle to the Chautauqua grounds. Good big audience and beautiful day. Talked two and a half hours to people who wanted me to keep it up. But knowing you would not approve I stopped—after telling them I would submit a few remarks in the evening—as I could not get out of town. I threw in two hours and a quarter at night just to make good measure. Had a big crowd at night also & while I did double service it was done in a great cause & I know this portion of our country will long remember it."[12]

At Des Moines, Iowa, he was introduced by Governor Cummins, and reported a fine meeting. From Sioux Falls, South Dakota, where he was the guest of an old university friend, Jesse Boyce, he wrote: "My audience was large. People came sixty miles. The lecture course realized enough on this first No. [number] of their course to pay out their entire course." Bob thought there were encouraging indications that the people were really "going to break the machine" in South Dakota. He wrote that by appointment Coe I. Crawford, anti-machine candidate for governor;* former Congressman Pickler, and eight or ten other gentlemen from different parts of the State had come to the Boyce home to talk with him. They wanted "to engage me to put in twenty to twenty five meetings for them [lectures] making the address I made last night & do it this winter. I told them it was quite impossible but I might get out during the coming year for a week & then we talked over all phases of their campaign, & I gave them the best counsel I could." These men had assured him that South Dakota would be for him "for President in the next convention," and Bob added his characteristically humorous comment to me, "So you see my boom is turned loose."[13]

Although deeply absorbed in his lectures, his letters often referred to the Wisconsin political situation. Whenever he returned for a day or two, he conferred with friends. If he resigned to go to the Senate, the question of an able successor to forward the progressive

* Crawford was elected governor in 1906 and United States Senator in 1908.

program was important and presented many complexities. Lieutenant Governor Davidson would fill out the unexpired term and would then naturally expect to be nominated and elected for the customary second term. Although personally fond of Davidson, Bob felt Lenroot far better qualified by endowment and experience for the work still to be done. Bob is perhaps justly criticized for having encouraged Davidson to run for lieutenant governor if he questioned his capacity to lead the Wisconsin movement independently. I would not claim that in meeting the exigencies of politics Bob was always consistent.

Lenroot was not ambitious to become a candidate for governor, but to many who had borne the brunt of the Wisconsin fight he seemed exceptionally qualified. He had a keen intellect and natural aptitude for politics. In the 1894 Haugen campaign he had become identified with the progressive movement. During his first term in the 1901 legislature, he proved an outstanding leader, and the following session was chosen speaker and unanimously reelected. A lawyer and excellent parliamentarian, he had shown skill in framing and securing adoption of the splendid 1905 legislation. His courage and determination as chairman of the stormy 1904 convention, his work in the subsequent litigation and campaign had played an important part in the progressive victory of that crucial year.

I could see no other available candidate so qualified for the responsibility. I felt about Lenroot as I had felt about Haugen: the people must support him because he was an ideal man for the work ahead. My judgment was also influenced by our intimate personal friendship with the Lenroots. Clara Clough had been a student at the university; had taught school and married her pupil, Irvine Lenroot, some years younger than herself, though she was ever the more youthful and gay in temperament. She was a gifted and charming woman, an inspiring helpmate to Lenroot, whose abilities she perhaps understood and valued better than he himself did.

Appreciating the statesmanship needed for the important task ahead, Bob urged that Lenroot be a candidate to succeed Davidson in the 1906 primary. When Lenroot announced his candidacy, the press interpreted it as foreshadowing Bob's acceptance of the Senatorship.

Before Bob had started out on his 1905 summer Chautauqua tour, we had decided, regardless of whether or not he went to the Senate, to sell our W..t Wilson Street home. It was still mortgaged but had increased in value; with what could be spared from his summer earnings we felt we could buy a farm which would make an attractive home and be a good investment. Five years at the Executive Residence had weaned the children from the old home where they were all born; they were reaching an age when the farm life would mean much to them.

One fine spring morning, when Bob and I were out horseback riding around the Mendota Lake drive, he said as we came to the lane leading in to Maple Bluff Farm, "Let's ride up and ask Sam Marshall what he will sell this place for." Marshall, the son of a prominent banker, was a gentleman farmer who had studied at the Agricultural College of the university. Mrs. Marshall had unusual charm, a merry wit, and was very popular socially. Their children and ours were about the same age. I have never forgotten the lesson I learned from her that very morning. I was bemoaning the fact that children would disagree. "Of course they will," she said, "but I don't take it so seriously. I jump right in and have a good time scrapping with them."

After we had chatted for a little while, Bob asked Marshall: "What will you take for this place?" "Five hundred dollars an acre," said Marshall without a moment's hesitation. There were sixty acres sloping to the south with a quarter of a mile frontage on Lake Mendota. The farm adjoined the golf grounds. There was a beautiful view of the city and a pleasing outlook from every side of the old brick farmhouse. But at that time the price seemed to me far too high, and I rode away laughing at the idea of paying so much. Bob, however, was serious and thoughtful on the way back.

Throughout the summer, with the help of Alf Rogers, I was hunting farm "bargains" near Madison. Whenever Bob came home, we would lay our possibilities before him. Each time he made the same answer, "I don't think anything you have yet found compares with the Marshall place." When my father was visiting us, Bob wrote to be sure and have him look over the Marshall place, because *"he sees everything just as it is."*[14] Maple Bluff Farm had a deep rich soil which he knew would appeal to my father as the first requisite of a farm.

One morning in the fall Bob and I were out for a horseback ride; again we turned in at Maple Bluff Farm drive. Meeting Sam Marshall, Bob again asked, "What will you take for this place?" Marshall again replied, "Five hundred dollars an acre." Bob dismounted; looked through the old house; talked about the age of the wonderful old grape vine which shaded the porch and covered the entire front of the house; discussed the value of lake frontage and other details. But it was more in the nature of a social visit. Our minds were made up. In less than an hour we had reached an agreement to buy the place. The high price we paid was a matter of surprise and comment, but when the transaction was completed I wondered how I had ever had the least hesitation. The children were tremendously pleased. We were not to have possession for some months, but we were all joyful in the thought that Maple Bluff Farm was to be our future home.

We were most reluctant to go to Washington without the children, but as we were uncertain where we were to live it seemed best for them to go to the Hillside Home School for a term. This would give me time to find a suitable home for our next six years in Washington. The Hillside Home School was an unusual school conducted by the Lloyd Jones sisters whom the pupils called "Aunt Nell" and "Aunt Jen."[15] Their brothers owned adjoining farms in this beautiful valley near Spring Green, Wisconsin, and were "Uncle John" and "Uncle James" to all the boys and girls in the school. Occasionally another brother, Jenkin Lloyd Jones, editor of *Unity*, and director of Abraham Lincoln Center, came up from Chicago. In his impassioned way, "Uncle Jenk" would talk to the children when they assembled in the beautiful auditorium of the building designed by the nephew, Frank Lloyd Wright.

Bob had called an extra session of the legislature to meet on December 4. After discussing the subjects of legislation enumerated in the call, he had stated that he would transmit his resignation as governor at the close of this session and accept the "commission as United States Senator." The construction of the new state capitol was the only strictly emergency measure. But before resigning, he was bent on making the most of this extra session to recommend the changes that experience had shown were needed to perfect the progressive legislation. He also thought it vital that the primary law should be amended to provide for a second choice, which he had three times recommended, but it had not been incorporated when the bill passed. Without this second-choice provision he feared that the votes of the people actually in the majority and in accord on a legislative program might be divided among several candidates, whereas the special interests would concentrate on a single candidate. Thus a minority element of the party might nominate its candidate by a plurality vote and defeat the program of the majority. The results of later elections justified his apprehension.

He believed the progressive members of the legislature would unite to fortify the primary law with the second-choice amendment, but he was mistaken. The special session adjourned on December 19 without adopting this amendment or taking favorable action on many of his other important recommendations. The stalwart press interpreted this as proving his loss of power, and predicted that his public career would end with one term in the Senate. Bob did not take his disappointment too seriously; he was sure that when the time came he could take the issues to the people and they would be settled right. There was the new field awaiting him. His resignation took effect on New Year's Day, 1906.

Leave-taking of the Executive Residence cost me few heart pangs. It was a comfortable abode; but to this day a subconscious sense of official obligation is associated in my mind with the fine old place, which Phil himself was to occupy years later as governor.

The last social function I sponsored at the governor's mansion was a reception for Mrs. Davidson. On January 1, 1906, Lieutenant Governor Davidson was formally inaugurated to fill out the unexpired term. Bob was the first to congratulate him. Lenroot wished him well and a happy new year. Davidson replied, "Thank you, Irvine, the same to you and many of them."

The next morning Bob and I were on our way to Washington.

CHAPTER XVIII

"Seats Now Temporarily Vacant
May Be Permanently Vacated"

Bob took the oath of office on January 4, 1906. I awaited the convening of the Senate in a reflective but not unhappy mood. As I watched the crowd gathering in the galleries and the Senators assembling, I recalled that this was the Fifty-ninth Congress; twenty years had passed since I sat in the gallery of the House awaiting the opening ceremony of the Forty-ninth Congress, of which Bob was the youngest Member—twenty hard, trying years, yet in retrospect twenty years of useful effort and concrete achievement. I far better understood now the nature and significance of the struggle than I had earlier. I contemplated the future much more seriously; but I had faith in the outcome.

From the day Bob was elected to the Senate the newspapers had carried many quips and cartoons depicting his reception by that august body, forecasting what would happen when Senator Spooner was called upon to go through the customary ceremony of escorting his new colleague down the aisle to take the oath of office.[1] Within the family circle Bob had joked about walking down the aisle with Spooner. But he arrived in Washington, I believe, without ever having seriously considered the matter of presenting his credentials. He consulted that night with former Senator William E. Chandler as to the customary procedure. Yet on the eve of the event Bob was still in the dark as to Spooner's intention. The next day he presented his credentials to Chairman Burrows of the Privileges and Elections Committee, who indicated Spooner would be glad to present them and escort Bob if requested. Bob replied that he "believed it to be the established prerogative of seniority to take the initiative in any

matter of courtesy to be extended to a junior; that if Senator
Spooner offered to escort me down, his offer would not be declined."
In an intimate letter, marked "strictly personal to our special
friends," Bob humorously described what followed, as he stood in
the Vice President's room talking with Edward Everett Hale, to
whom he had been presented: "Spooner, Reed, Burrows, et al.
swarmed in. Spooner greeted me cordially. I responded likewise.
I made my obeisance to the vice president, and at Spooner's request
accompanied him to the cloak room, Burrows, Reed, et al. following
as a rear guard, lest I might escape. . . . The hour of twelve o'clock
being at hand, we walked into the senate chamber together. The
galleries were filled,—the floor of the senate well occupied with
senators. A murmur crept through the galleries, easily heard on the
floor. . . . I was informed by Spooner that coming late, and being a
new man, I would have to sit on the democratic side. . . . Two
vacant seats remained, one near the door, and one in the second
row from the rear. The senior [Senator], fearful that my occupancy
of the front seat would subject me to a draught, suggested that I
take the *back one*. . . . After the prayer by Edward Everett Hale,
. . . Spooner arose, presented my credentials, stated that I was present, and requested that the oath be administered. The vice president
requested him to present me. He offered me his right wing, I yoked
up with him. The murmur of the galleries smote the ear. We passed
down the center aisle . . . the oath was then administered to me by
the vice president. . . . an audible sigh swept down from the galleries as the tension relaxed. The oath subscribed, Spooner crooked
his arm, we coupled up, filed right, . . . went on around the chamber
to the vacant seat in the second last row. There, as we separated,
I extended to him my hand, and thanked him for his courtesy. The
thing was done."

It happened that we attended the reception to the diplomatic
corps at the White House on January 4, and in the same letter Bob
said that as we approached President Roosevelt "he swore he was
'*dee*-lighted,' 'overjoyed,'—that it was 'one of the greatest pleasures of his life to greet again his old friends,—friends when he was
civil service commissioner, who had entertained him as a guest
when at Madison,' etc., &c., and turning to his wife, and calling her
by her first name, presented Mrs. La Follette with much unction. . . .

"After the receiving line broke up, we were passing through one of the rooms when the great figure of Secretary Taft bore down across the room in our direction. He was exceedingly cordial in his greeting. It is surely fifteen or sixteen years or more since I had seen him at all. He is about one-third larger, but all of him seemed to be an old acquaintance. We met Justice Harlan and many old and new people."[2]

Mrs. Roosevelt greeted each guest with pleasing grace; yet as I read her psychology then and thereafter, her attitude was that of a spectator rather than a participant. She gave generously of her time and strength to official entertainment. Nevertheless, she escaped public attention almost as though she had remained in private life. Nor did it make any difference, as some predicted it would, when Alice Roosevelt, the President's daughter by his first wife, became Mrs. Longworth and passed out of the limelight of the White House.

When I made the calls, then incumbent on a new Senator's wife, I was interested to note some of the changes since 1890. While there seemed to be more wealth, there was less display, and good taste more generally prevailed; homes were more artistic; dress more becoming; manners quieter; voices lower. On the other hand, there were fewer social functions in the nature of open house; on Cabinet and senatorial days you did not see the picturesque throngs of the earlier period. Social life had less color, less individuality; was more conventional, less democratic in spirit and purpose.

When we left Washington in 1891, apartment houses were almost unknown. In 1906 they seemed to have taken possession of the city. Our friend Lulu Daniels Thompson was at the Ontario. She discovered that one of the larger apartments could be rented furnished for $100 a month. She also found a good maid for us, and we were soon comfortably settled. I was amazed at the convenience and quiet of the new mode of living as compared with the boarding-houses of our Congressional days. The occasional howling of the wolves and roaring of the lions at the Zoo, which our apartment overlooked, in a way added to our sense of isolation.

Bob always liked to work at home; but from necessity did much of it there during his first years in the Senate, for his committee room was in the subcellar of the Capitol reached by several flights of dimly lighted stairs and long winding passages. He had been assigned the chairmanship of the Committee to Investigate the Conditions of the Potomac River Front. He said he had visions of cleaning up the whole Potomac River until he discovered that the committee had never had a bill referred to it and never held a meeting.

Bob secured the use of a vacant apartment at the Ontario. Soon all available space was covered with reference material. Colonel Hannan and Nellie Dunn had come to Washington to take secretarial positions similar to those they held while Bob was governor. Nellie made her home with us, and continued to do so during Congressional sessions for a number of years until she married Fred MacKenzie and went to New York. Bob worked long hours preparing for the debate on the Hepburn bill, which dealt with the important question of amending the Interstate Commerce Act of 1887. The primary purpose of this Act had been to create a commission with power to ensure just and reasonable railway rates to the public. For ten years it had assumed the right to fix rates. But in 1897 a United States Supreme Court decision had robbed it of this power and left it useless except to make recommendations. The able commission had repeatedly urged legislation to restore its power to control rates. Congress had turned a deaf ear to these appeals but could no longer ignore the organized protests of the shippers against rebates and unequal rates. President Roosevelt had helped call attention to these discriminations and to create sentiment for a "square deal." The fight in Wisconsin and Bob's speeches in various States had awakened popular protest against abuse of power by the railroads.

By 1906 public indignation had reached a point where even the railroads recognized that some concession must be made. They allowed the Hepburn bill to be reported out from the House Committee on Interstate Commerce. It passed the House and was referred to the Senate Committee on Interstate Commerce. An alliance of two Republican Senators, Dolliver and Clapp, with the Democrats finally succeeded in reporting the bill out, and the debate started. It had a valuable provision for a uniform system of bookkeeping and the examination of railroad books and accounts but, as Bob pointed out, it did not touch upon or even pretend to solve the real question at stake, which was "whether the commission should be given the power to determine what was a reasonable rate, and to enforce its decisions."[3]

For months Bob sat waiting for someone to raise this issue. He was loath to see the bill pass in its imperfect form but, as a new Senator, felt he had little influence with his colleagues. He thought that if Roosevelt exerted his influence, "legislation which would really count could be secured." Although he had known the President for fifteen years, he was aware that when he came to the Senate Roosevelt had been warned he "was dangerous and extreme" in his views and did not feel he could offer any unsolicited suggestions. One evening, after Lincoln Steffens and a few friends had dined with us, Bob was drawn into a discussion of the railroad problem, and spoke with great earnestness of the defects of the Hepburn bill. Steffens said, "I have been seeing the President, and I am going to suggest to him that you have gone all over this question in Wisconsin, that you have been at it for years up there, and it will do no harm for him to have a talk with you about it."[4]

The President invited Bob to the White House for a conference on the rate bill at ten o'clock one Sunday night. They had a two-hour talk. At the President's suggestion, Bob outlined the amendments he thought imperative to secure reasonable rates to the public. When Roosevelt objected, "But you can't get any such bill as that through this Congress," and added, "I want to get something through," Bob replied that if, while the bill was still pending, the President would send a special message to Congress pointing out what needed to be done he could utilize the public sentiment which had been building up for nine years. Then, even if this Congress failed to act, in the next Congress the people would be back of him more strongly. And if he went to the end of his service as President reiterating in messages the true lines upon which this legislation should be written to protect the public, it would be a monument compared to which such a statute as the Hepburn bill would be trivial.[5] Bob had found Roosevelt "a very good listener," and thought he had made some impression. As he left the White House at midnight, he met Steffens going in to see Roosevelt. About two o'clock that morning the telephone rang. When Bob answered, Steffens said, "I have just left the President and he said you did a bully job."[6]

But the President did not send a message to Congress recommending any of the fundamental changes Bob had outlined. No one else was making the fight in the Senate, so Bob decided to expose the essential weakness of the bill and offer the necessary amend-

ments to make it an effective statute. Without Administration
support he knew they could not be adopted, but he thought a right
beginning must be made, as had been done in Wisconsin. Few men
could claim to be better equipped to tackle the problem of railroad
rate control; his interest dated back to the Granger movement and
Chief Justice Ryan's memorable prophecy. It was the subject which
had most deeply concerned him as a member of the House, and it
had been a foremost issue in the Wisconsin struggle.

After weeks of careful preparation, he came to the Senate on
April 19, 1906, with a speech of 148 printed pages. It was just
nineteen years and two months since he had spoken in the House
advocating passage of the Act of 1887 to create the Interstate
Commerce Commission to regulate railroad rates. His speech now
reviewed the history of the subject, presenting facts and arguments
to sustain his amendments restoring to the Interstate Commerce
Commission the power stripped from it by the Supreme Court
decision. His desk was piled high with documents to substantiate
every important statement.

At this time the unwritten rule still prevailed that during his first
year of service a new Senator should be seen but not heard, other
than to answer "Present" and vote Yes or No to the roll call. The
humiliation of the brilliant young Senator from Indiana, Albert J.
Beveridge, for violating this foolish precedent was recent history.
I found the galleries crowded to capacity; people stood in line in
the doorways. There was a good attendance of Senators when Bob
started speaking. That morning the whole world had been shocked
by news of the San Francisco earthquake; also, Senators Tillman
and Hopkins had engaged in a fiery controversy which lasted
beyond the lunch hour. Making due allowances, however, for these
distractions, an observer could not fail to get the impression that
a large group of Senators began talking loudly and moving about
in a disturbing way and soon left the Senate in a body as if by
concerted action.

Bob ignored the exodus until he had completed the particular
subject in hand. Then he stopped for a moment and addressed the
presiding officer in a cool, deliberate manner which arrested the
attention of everyone in the Chamber: "I can not be wholly indifferent to the fact that Senators by their absence at this time
indicate their want of interest in what I may have to say upon this

subject. The public is interested. Unless this important question is rightly settled seats now temporarily vacant may be permanently vacated by those who have the right to occupy them at this time."[7]

After he finished speaking these words, my heart stood still for an instant; then the conviction flashed upon me that his prophecy would come true as it had in Wisconsin. I believed the circumstances justified his calling the attention of the country to the Senate's lack of interest on this momentous question, and I was glad it had become a part of the record. A spontaneous burst of applause came from the galleries, which was quickly stopped by Senator Long of Kansas, who was presiding. That evening, when our little group of friends came together to talk over the day's happenings, some urged Bob to leave the prediction out of the published record, thinking it too extreme to have any chance of being justified by future events. Others argued that its effect upon those who read it in cold type would be quite different from the impression made upon people in the galleries who, having heard what actually took place, were impelled to applaud in spite of the Senate rules. He, however, kept saying: "It is true. It must stand." And it remained in his printed speech "to become," as Lulu Daniels Thompson said years afterward, "one of the best-known examples of well-founded political prognostication," for he lived to see nearly all of them permanently retired by the voters.[8]

By late afternoon of the first day of his speech, it seemed plain to me that the Senators who had returned to the floor were beginning to recognize its significance. A good number on the Democratic side were giving close attention; some Republicans looked serious; others, though professedly reading or talking, were listening with one ear. I felt sure the criticism of the fundamental defects of the bill was making an impression that could not be ignored. Evidently, the Republican leaders came to this conclusion overnight.

The next morning Senator Foraker of Ohio, an aggressive and brilliant debater, started to challenge Bob's interpretation of the Interstate Commerce Commission's recommendations, thus giving him an unexpected and dramatic opportunity to clinch his arguments. After several interruptions and sharp debate, Bob read a quotation from a commission report. Foraker again interrupted and wished to read the remainder of the paragraph, insisting these final omitted sentences supported his contention. Bob answered, "I will read them." As he did so, even some of the "Old Guard" Senators had to laugh, for the entire quotation clearly refuted Foraker. Foraker asked one more question and quit. Later in his speech Bob said: "When any man who cares for his country comes to realize the true significance of the control of commerce upon . . . the economic and social life of the people, with all its consequences to this generation and the generation to come, he will be shocked that it should all be left in the hands of the traffic managers of railroads. . . . It must be controlled unselfishly, controlled with the highest patriotism, upon a broad, national policy. . . . I say to the Senate here to-day that nothing, *absolutely nothing,* can prevent the ultimate government ownership of the railroads of this country except a strict government control of the railroads of the country."[9]

A debate that was a real sparring match developed with Senator Dolliver when Bob began his argument for the physical valuation of railroad property as the fundamental basis for Government regulation of railroad rates. Although they had been good friends in the House, and Dolliver greeted him cordially when he came to the Senate, Bob sensed that Dolliver "was more than a little" against him. Dolliver was a wonderfully gifted man who had imagination, humor, and a remarkable facility of expression. In their first Senate debate each was on his mettle, but throughout each preserved the spirit of good fellowship. Dolliver was the member of the committee in charge of the bill, and at first opposed Bob's argument. Before they finished, however, Dolliver expressed sympathy with the physical-valuation provision.[10] And always afterward he stood with Bob whenever the valuation issue was raised.

In a letter to Fola, I stated that Dolliver had told President Roosevelt that La Follette's speech was doing more to pass the bill than any that had been made. I also mentioned that Senator Bailey, a Democrat, "who had listened throughout the speech," instantly saw the significance of the physical valuation and asked a question that showed he believed "the proposition *sound* and *essential.* This was great backing and established at just the right moment the strength of the position papa was taking. It was the *basic principle* for which he fought all through the remainder of his speech." As the letter has the value of contemporary observation, I quote some of my conclusions, even though they were expressed with the unrestrained enthusiasm of family intimacy: "Papa was as free and at home as though he had been in the Senate twenty years. Each interruption gave him opportunity for driving home his arguments, and he was completely master of himself and the situation. . . . Yesterday [Monday] was not less satisfactory than Friday, except there were no *unfriendly* interruptions. Beveridge and Newlands and Money made inquiries, that served to bring out the points. But the bosses of the Senate did not venture to get into the fire. . . . The conclusion was made in just the right spirit. . . . While he read his speech, he often digressed, and no one could fail to see that he could talk better without notes than with them, and that his manuscript was used for accuracy and definiteness and not from necessity. . . . Many of the senators congratulated Papa and told him it was one of the greatest speeches ever delivered,—it had been an education to them, etc. . . . Knox listened attentively and congratulated Papa; told him it was a very good speech; he did not know that he [Knox] could go so far.

"We all feel very happy. I am deeply satisfied, and you know I am hard to satisfy. My judicial and logical faculty compel me to see both sides. But there is no *other side* to this event, so far as its being a triumph,—an unalloyed triumph for Papa. . . . Whatever comes, he has established himself right in the beginning, as the peer of any man on the floor of the Senate, and a *new kind* of leader."[11]

At the proper time in the debate, he offered carefully prepared amendments to strengthen and improve the Hepburn bill. Most of them had been endorsed by the Interstate Commerce Commission, but that made no difference to the standpat Senators. In speaking for his amendment for the physical valuation of the railroads, he showed that if the same system were applied that had been adopted in Wisconsin it would save the people of the country something more than $400,000,000 each year in transportation charges. Yet on the roll call, this valuation amendment was beaten 40 to 27, with only six Republicans voting for it.

Coming home on the streetcar one day, Bob wondered how far the Senators would go. To test it, he said, "I took a tab out of my pocket and outlined an amendment to the effect that any federal judge should be disqualified from hearing, trying or determining any case for the regulation of railway rates against any road in which he was a stockholder, or whose bonds he owned, or upon which he used free passes. And that amendment was lost 40 to 27. There were only three Republicans who thought that a federal judge ought not to own stock in a road and then hear, try and determine a case involving its interest!"[12]

After failing to get the Administration's backing, he did not expect to pass the amendments at this time; but with Bailey's co-operation he was able to get roll-call votes and place the Senators on record. He knew that on his extensive summer lecture tour he could make people understand the significance of their Senators' votes. A fire could be started on the Western hills and prairies that would make senatorial seats hot in Washington. Although the Senate voted down his amendment relating to employer's liability,[13] he was able, a few weeks later, when its enemies were at lunch and off guard, to maneuver a House bill on the same principle into a position where he could force a record vote. The mere threat of the roll call was enough to make them let it pass, as many Senators did not wish to offend the influential railroad employees' organizations by casting a recorded vote against it.[14]

Watching his opportunity, Bob sprang a bill (S. 5133) "to lessen accident and render travel safer" by limiting the continuous hours of service of trainmen, who were then often obliged to work for twenty-four or even thirty-six hours without sleep. It now seems hardly credible that anyone should have opposed a bill making sixteen hours the maximum for continuous work in this hazardous occupation. But when he brought the bill up for consideration on Tuesday, June 26, late in the morning hour of a hot, muggy day, his motion was opposed. It took five quorum calls and five ballots to convince his tired colleagues who had thought that "mere walking out of the Senate or the declaration of pairs, which removed the names of Senators who were present from the columns of those voting," would dissuade him from holding them until a quorum was registered on the measure.[15]

The bill was discussed during the four following days. On Friday, Tom Carter of Montana alternated with Senator Gallinger of New Hampshire in a prolonged discussion of it which Bob and some newspapers described as a filibuster.[16] That afternoon Bob, who had seen Roosevelt that morning on another matter, wrote me from his seat in the Senate that he was "going out now to Committee room & telephone the President and get him if I can to send me a letter tonight urging the passage of bill to limit hours of ry [railway] service. If I get that I will have a big stick to fight with tonight."[17] Permission to use the "big stick" was given, for in the debate that night Bob said the bill had the recommendation of the President, "who authorized me to-day to say on this floor that it was his earnest hope that the Senate would take action upon this bill, . . ."[18] Although Senators prevented a vote, Bob, by skillful and persistent effort, finally succeeded shortly before adjournment in getting a day set for a vote on the Hours of Service bill at the next session. He planned to make good use of the opportunity when the time came.

The fight for advanced railroad legislation overshadows Bob's other work during this session. Yet the range of his interest and activities is shown in other measures which he initiated and supported. One required committees of all political parties to account for moneys expended in national and Congressional elections; to file statements of receipts and disbursements of these committees, and to prohibit corporations from directly or indirectly contributing to any political committee or any candidate for public office. With the intention that it should go over until the next session, he introduced, shortly before adjournment, a resolution to investigate the grain-elevator trust.[19] He planned "to stir up the country some during the vacation and then put it through in Dec[ember] after the harvest when the Country (the grain country) is hot over the wrong doing of the Elevator Combine."[20] He also got through a bill to turn over to Wisconsin 20,000 acres for forestry reserve, and another which enabled the Menominee Indians, instead of selling the timber on their Wisconsin reservation to lumber companies, to cut, saw, and sell it themselves.

The most important bill then before the Senate Indian Committee, of which he was a member, concerned the settlement of the Affairs of the Five Civilized Tribes in the Indian Territory. One of its main provisions related to the segregated coal lands of the Choctaw and Chickasaw Indians. This bill, as passed by the House, continued and extended the policy of leasing the coal lands to private companies. But when it was proposed in the Senate committee to amend the bill to provide for the sale of the lands, Bob was suspicious and consulted the Secretary of the Interior and Walcott, the Director of the Geological Survey. He learned that bituminous coal of a very superior quality had been located upon over 413,000 acres of this land and that leases covering about 112,000 acres had been taken in the name of private coal-mining companies but were actually controlled by the railroads of the territory. He also found there was little or no competition in prices, and that the transportation rates for shipments were enormously high.

In the committee he therefore vigorously opposed the sale of these lands, but was voted down. He then proposed amendments which were also voted down. Aware that he was regarded as "a crank, a disturber of peace and prosperity," he nevertheless persisted and announced he would reserve the right to oppose the committee when the bill came to the Senate. The committee "smiled a broad smile" which Bob interpreted as reflecting the thought of what the Senate would do to him when he tried to stop the selling of these coal lands.[21] Bob's turn came later. The amendments he offered when the bill was before the Senate led to a two days' discussion.[22] Although these were defeated, the whole subject was so effectively aired in the newspapers as a scheme of the railroads and other special interests to get hold of the Indian coal lands that the plan to sell them had to be abandoned.

The first time he saw the President after this debate, Roosevelt expressed hearty approval of Bob's proposal that the Government take over the Indian Territory coal lands. Later Bob suggested to him the withdrawal from sale and entry of all coal, asphalt, and oil lands by executive order. The President questioned his constitutional power to act without Congressional authority but said he would get Attorney General Moody's opinion. At their next meeting Roosevelt said Moody's opinion left the matter in doubt. Whereupon Bob offered, on June 20, 1906, a joint resolution authorizing the President "to withdraw from entry and sale all public lands known to be underlaid with coal, lignite, or oil and all such lands which, in the judgment of the Director of the Geological Survey, contain deposits of coal, lignite, or oil, and that all such lands be withheld from entry or sale until such time as Congress shall determine otherwise."[23]

On June 30, a few hours prior to adjournment of Congress, he saw Roosevelt in the President's room at the Capitol, and explained he had been unable to get action on the joint resolution; but stated he did not think this Congressional authorization necessary. The President said, "Well, Moody thinks there is some doubt about it, but I'll resolve that doubt in favor of the public, and after Congress adjourns I'll withdraw all government lands known to contain coal deposits." When Bob said he intended to study the subject during the summer and introduce at the next session a comprehensive bill dealing not only with the Indian coal lands but with all the coal lands belonging to the general government, the President replied: "Good. You go ahead, get your bill ready, and I will make it the leading subject in my message to Congress in December. Come and see me as soon as you return."[24] During the summer the President announced the withdrawal of millions of acres of coal lands.

When I went home shortly after adjournment to get the house ready for the children, I found the political situation much more alarming than we had supposed. The Progressives were sharply divided on the nomination of a candidate for governor. In reply to my letter urging him to return at the earliest possible moment, Bob wrote, on June 21: "I am doing everything I can to get away. Everything presses here now. The rate bill conference is still in a wrangle in the Committee. . . . The Standard Oil is flooding the Senate & House with petitions against the pipe line provision nominally coming from independent oil interests really from the Standard Oil. I don't know what I ought to do. . . . the political situation distresses me awfully."[25] That same day he wrote to Gilbert Roe: "I am almost desperate. . . . You see my lecturing begins June 30th out in Iowa. Al & Belle write me ev[er]y day that I must spend some day or so with the party worke[r]s in Milwaukee & as much more in Madison—That I must open headquarters in Madison & prepare a circular address to the Republicans &c. They are nearly wild at thought of my leaving the state But the only way a dollar can be raised for Lenroot's campaign is for me to go out on the lecture platform & earn it. We are in hard lines for money."[26]

Bob stayed in Washington until Congress adjourned on June 30. He had only one day at home before starting on a long season of lectures which, except for several weeks he gave to speaking in the Wisconsin gubernatorial campaign, continued until the following December. Bob's lecture engagements took him into Iowa, Illinois, Indiana, Kansas, Ohio, Minnesota, Missouri, and Nebraska. He immediately launched his long educational campaign of discussing current legislation and reading the roll call on Senators' votes which contributed toward bringing about so many changes in the United States Senate. On July 4, 1906, he wrote from Iowa, after his second speech since leaving Madison, that being at home seemed like a dream, but a dream "to carry with me all the week until I get home again. I tried reading the roll calls on some of my amendments which were 'tabled' to see how it would go. It *goes* & some Senators will find a back fire to look after. I suppose they will think I am the meanest fellow ever to 'go and tell.' "[27]

They did. And the reason for their resentment is evident in the typical reaction of an audience at Evansville, Indiana, where Bob spoke three days later. On his arrival Senator Hemenway of Indiana met him at the train and told him he intended to preside and introduce him at the meeting. Bob warned him that the reading of the roll call might be embarrassing, whereupon Hemenway laughed and answered: "Go ahead, Bob! You can't hurt me. This is my town!" Bob frequently related what followed: "So we rode out together and he introduced me to the audience in a nice speech. He was well received and applauded. Finally, in my speech, I came to the first roll call. I read it exactly as a reader in any legislative body would read it, in a monotone, without emphasis on any name. I could see that the throng was waiting for Hemenway's name. The first time hearing his name listed among those voting wrong, the people turned and looked at one another. As this happened again and again, the crowd began to get warm. The atmosphere grew tense. Presently the people were booing and hissing Hemenway's name. They drove him from the platform. I found him at the back of the tent, at the end of the lecture, walking back and forth. I reminded him that I had asked him not to preside. He was a good sport, 'That's all right,' he said, 'I've no complaint. You were perfectly fair, but if I had known how hot it was going to be, I'd never have gone up there.' "

But few were as "good sports" as Hemenway. In one state after another Bob's unprecedented procedure of ignoring party lines and telling the constituents of both Republican and Democratic Senators how they had voted on recent legislation aroused bitter criticism, was interpreted as an "attack" upon them, and denounced as a violation of traditional "senatorial courtesy." At Salina, Joseph L. Bristow's home, and other Kansas towns he evoked stinging rebuke from the conservative Republican press for his roll call exposure of Senator Long's subservience to the railroad interests.

Toward the end of this hard trip of traveling on crowded day coaches and speaking to large crowds gathered under tents beneath the blazing midsummer sun, he wrote, "I long to get home and yet dread the work before me at once."[28] The work ahead when he arrived home was to put momentum into the Lenroot campaign for governor. It was plain that Davidson had a better chance of success, for he was already governor and his name was better known to the voters. At four successive elections he had been a successful candidate, twice state treasurer and twice lieutenant governor. The Progressives were divided in this contest. Many of Bob's hitherto warmest personal and political friends were active for Davidson, among them former Governor Hoard, General Bryant, and Nils P. Haugen. The Stalwarts, instead of putting up a candidate of their own, were aiding Davidson as against Lenroot. Bob had made his first speech for Lenroot on July 20 at Milwaukee. After two weeks of Chautauqua work in neighboring States, he began an intensive pre-primary campaign on August 14 which extended well over Wisconsin and concluded with a speech the night before the primary election at Madison, where he was introduced by Professor Commons. That same evening, in the Capitol Park, Governor Hoard, W. D. Connor, and others, addressed a large crowd in behalf of Davidson. Bob's audiences had been large and enthusiastic; but it was not possible to turn the tide from Davidson, who was chosen to head the Republican ticket on September 4 by a plurality of 48,438 votes.

Bob made a preelection campaign for Davidson, saying he had supported Lenroot for the nomination, but that he "bowed to the will of the majority." Davidson was elected and reelected two years later. When the legislature convened the following January, Herman Ekern, an outstanding Progressive who had supported Lenroot, was elected speaker of the assembly. Though it took no long step ahead, the Davidson administration is credited with upholding the progressive legislation of the previous administration.

At the time it seemed to me a cruel irony that the candidate Bob supported should be defeated in the first trial of the primary law. He was disappointed, deeply disappointed, but philosophical; he

said we must accept the verdict. I remember that Lincoln Steffens
observed that the outcome of this first primary furnished a far
better argument for the law than if Bob's candidate had won.

We had bought Maple Bluff Farm without any definite plan as
to how it was to be worked and cared for. We did not, of course,
expect it to pay a return on the investment; but Bob was serious
about running it as a real farm. There were eleven acres of cherries
and plums and eleven acres of woods. The rest of the land must be
adapted to these conditions. Bob, Jr., Phil, and Mary were naturally
enthusiastic when their father suggested buying a herd of Shetland ponies he had learned was for sale. They advanced their own
arguments in favor of his project; besides the certain profits in
raising colts, the ponies would be useful in marketing fruit, taking
them to school and fetching guests from town. Caring for the ponies
and breaking the young colts would also be the best sort of work
for them. They admitted, incidentally, they would have a wonderful
time riding and driving.

Somehow, in the midst of all the other things Bob had to do that
summer, he found time to go with Bob, Jr., and Phil to look at the
herd of ponies. After that there was nothing to do but buy them and
start a "La Follette Brothers Shetland Pony Farm." The ponies
had been a feature of a small circus in Wisconsin. They were pure-
bred, high-spirited, and fine travelers. The children could mount
almost any one of them, and sometimes set the pace for their
father's tall Kentucky saddler. No member of the family was more
excited or happy than I when the little ponies came trotting up the
drive from the main highway; there was Dandy, the little black
stallion; Topsy and Gypsy, the smallest pair; Princess and Beauty,
the largest; Jessie and Maitie, in between; like a family of children,
each with its own individuality and special claims on the affections.

I learned that the joys of a pony farm are seldom unmixed with
trouble. One day Rowdy, the Welsh pony, ran away while Mary was
"holding the lines" and the boys were in a store doing the family
errands. But she felt the trying experience was worth while when
her father commended her courage and horsemanship. While Bob
was on the Pacific Coast that year, I wrote him: "The boys do
pretty well about caring for the ponies. It gets us up in good
season to get the chores done and Robert off to school but he does

not complain."[29] We felt our faith in the inestimable value of the farm experience for the children was fully justified when one day Phil and Mary had Topsy hitched to their hand sled, working hard bringing wood from the woodshed to the kitchen wood box, and Mary was heard to say to Phil with great earnestness, "Really, I don't see any use of having lessons; there is so much work to do on the farm, we'll never have any time to read and write."

Shortly after the Wisconsin primary Bob had gone to New Jersey, the Mecca of corporation charters, to help in the primary campaign there. Outstanding leaders of the "New Idea" reform movement were state Senator Everett Colby and George L. Record, whose initiation had enough of the surprise element in it to attract national attention. Colby had recently defeated a prominent political boss for the state senate and Record was a candidate for the United States Senate against the reactionary Republican Senator Dryden. Steffens, who had written several articles exposing political corruption in New Jersey, had added his plea to that of Colby and Record, asking Bob to lend a hand in the campaign to elect Record. During the week that Bob was in New Jersey, from September 17 to 22, he addressed sixteen meetings in ten counties, talking to an estimated 25,000 people, and reaching many more through his widely reported speeches. The reactionary records of Senators Dryden and Kean offered dramatic examples of standpatism for the roll call. The revelation of how these Senators had helped to emasculate the railroad bill brought hisses and jeers for their names. Newspaper reports show the meetings were full of vivid incidents. I remember how encouraged Bob was by the response of the large crowds who came to hear him. He accepted no remuneration for this work, but cared very much for a watch which was sent to him as a souvenir. He carried this watch to the end of his life.

Bob returned to Madison for the Republican state platform convention, spent a week at home, and then left for another two months' trip which took him to the Far West. He had several engagements in Kansas, where his speeches in July had aroused heated discussion and much newspaper comment. At the request of William Allen White, who had gone from New York to see him while he was campaigning in New Jersey, Bob worked in an additional afternoon speech at Hutchinson, Kansas, on October 10. There he again read the roll call and again urged the voters to send Joseph L. Bristow to the United States Senate. Only a month before, Senator Long of Kansas had made a speech denouncing Bob as a Populist, and declaring that the leader of that faith, "Sockless" Simpson, was not so radical as La Follette.[30] But Long was defeated in 1909 by Bristow, who became one of the ablest and staunchest leaders of the progressive group.

By the time Congress convened for the short session, Bob had addressed many audiences and read the roll call in Iowa, Nebraska, Kansas, Missouri, Indiana, Illinois, Minnesota, New Jersey, Oklahoma, Ohio, South Dakota, Colorado, Utah, Idaho, Oregon, and Washington. His speaking dates for the month of November had taken him through Colorado and to the Pacific coast. During the rainy season there he wrote: "Rivers are running high, bridges out & traffic pretty nearly suspended. I am awful sorry to lose any of these engagements. It is so important to make them—but it is a terrible time out here—the like of which has not been in many years if at all."[31] Later he wrote: "Dear Girl dont worry about the finances we will get even after while *sure,* and then do just what we please. There has not been a dollar spent which was not necessary. . . . Heaven bless you, dear heart & keep you & my precious ones safe. Only another week & I shall see you."[32]

CHAPTER XIX

A President "Kerflops"

We seemed hardly to have begun living at the farm when it was time for Bob to return to Washington for the next session of the Fifty-ninth Congress. I thought it wise and practical to stay at home with the children, as this short session began on the first Monday in December and would end on March 4, 1907. Bob could spend the Christmas holidays with us, so the family would be separated for only two and a half months. We agreed to make some permanent living arrangement in Washington for the next year so that thereafter the family would keep together. But for the winter of 1907 he planned to stay with our friends the Thompsons in Chevy Chase; I knew Lu would look after him and that with them he would find comradeship and sympathy in his work.

It had been rumored that when Congress convened, the Senators would punish Bob for his reading of the roll call. Lu and David Thompson went with him to the Capitol to attend the opening session because, as Bob jestingly wrote, they were anxious "to see if I was to be greeted with bricks & hisses. Everything quiet of course. I sat out the reading of the message nearly all of it. Several Senators (mostly dems) came by & stopped & spoke—Senator Knox turned round and was cordial. There is a deal of soreness toward me I hear but I think they are in doubt about how to get at me."[1] The next day he added: "I continue to hear that the subject of 'what we ought to do with LaF'[ollette] has been quite fully discussed & is still under consideration by the men who think they are responsible for the Senate. They have talked and talked with each other and with newspaper men. I think they find it difficult to formulate any proceeding & what they will do probably will be to wait for me in the discussion of some matter and then undertake to chastise me in the regular course of debate."[2]

A few days later he wrote to Bob, Jr.: "My you must have real winter there ice & snow everywhere. . . . As for ice in the Senate— well they have not applied any directly to me yet—and when they do things will warm up so it wont 'stay froze'—I fancy."[3]

Convinced of the power of the roll call, he was constantly trying to extend its use, and wrote to us about an encouraging "lunch at the Willard today with Mr. [Samuel E.] Moffett—who conducts a page under his own name in Colliers. . . . He is to be here a good deal of the time this winter & we are good friends. He says he will adopt my suggestion and run the roll call on important questions. That will be a telling thing to do and will establish a rule which I think the press of the country will have to heed & comment on if they do not copy it. I felt as if I had done a good days work for my country when I had put in three hours with Mr. Moffett."[4] And I trust my readers will note with heartfelt satisfaction, as I do, that today, as a matter of course, the leading newspapers of the country, whether standpat or progressive, publish the recorded votes on all important measures in Congress.

The effect of Bob's roll-call campaigning was evident early in the session. During the previous session he had succeeded in getting his bill limiting the continuous hours of service of trainmen to sixteen hours placed on the calendar so that it became "unfinished business." It was characteristic of him to explain the situation in a letter to little Mary: "I have got one bill that I just have to watch so I wont lose my place. Did you ever play pussy wants a corner? You know if you have a corner & get away from it some one (who is playing pussy) dives in & gets your corner. Well I have got a game like that with a bill. If I get away from my corner some one else will slip in and get the good corner for his bill. So I just have to keep right in my corner every day & watch that bill."[5]

Bob did not attempt to make a well rounded speech when the bill came up. For strategical reasons he deliberately allowed himself to be abused without replying, and yielded the floor whenever the railroad Senators wished to criticize the bill as reported by the committee. Patiently he admitted faults and took their "pounding" while he kept up his sleeve his careful revision of the bill, which he introduced "at the best time" as a substitute.[6] By constant vigilance and skillful management in securing roll calls, he finally won what the *Washington Times* described as "La Follette's sweeping victory" and "a triumph of the *Record*" when, late in the afternoon of January 10, 1907, the Senate passed his Hours of Service bill by a roll-call vote of 70 to 1.[7] As soon as the roll calls began, Senator Spooner had explained that he was paired and could not vote.

In a letter, written in bed at six the next morning, Bob said "fear of the roll call" had entered the souls of Western railroad Senators whose terms were "to expire within two years," Long of Kansas "being about the only exception." Although there were some amendments which Bob wished "were off instead of on the bill," he thought that "On the whole it is a great thing to have gotten through a very good bill . . . about as good as can be framed without further experience in applied legislation."[8] I replied that judging from the *Congressional Record,* the newspaper accounts, and the impression made upon the folks at home it seemed definitely understood as an important victory. Later I wrote: "We all enjoyed and appreciated Moffett's write up of the Hours of Service bill in Colliers. We read it aloud last night. It was fine. The Times write up came at the same time—and I read the Free Press editorials to the children too."[9]

Two days after the bill passed the Senate, the President sent for Bob, but he had left Washington to keep a speaking engagement. Through his office the appointment was arranged for Wednesday morning, January 16. That night Bob wrote home: "Well I called at W.[hite] House today and the Pres. said 'You have done another great piece of work in passing the Hours of Service bill & I am very grateful for it—because I was committed to it & it is right. There was one of the Senators whom I was afraid of last session whom I didn't trust: But I was wrong [.] I trust him now and have every confidence in him—You are that Senator. I was very mad at you for attacking the rate bill but I am coming to see the value of your amendments [.] I am going to support them next session [.] We cannot make it this session but I'll put all my force into it next December [.] I am for the valuation and am going to go into all of this. I am going to address a communication to the Interstate Com[merce] Com[mission] in a few days & I want your help on the things needful to be done [.] I would like you to write me a letter within the next three days setting forth the big things upon which we should concentrate to make the law strong—Will you do it?'*

"He said all this and much more which I can hardly get into a

* On January 30, Bob sent the President a six-page memorandum.

letter i e one letter—We had a good plain talk and are to have more [.] I brought up the Presidential matter & told him things should be moving & that his friends should be allowed to know that they might take hold for him. He put up his hands in protest but not in anger or indignation."[10]

Later President Roosevelt's influence was helpful in securing action on the Hours of Service bill in the House.[11] After a hard fight it was finally enacted into law on the last day of the session.

The inside story of what happened to the coal bill during this same session is told for the most part in Bob's letters, though unfortunately some were lost. Two days after he had arrived in Washington, he called, on December 6, 1906, at the White House to present John M. Nelson, recently elected to Congress. That night Bob wrote me: "The President was exceedingly cordial. Brought up coal business & I asked him for a note to Atty. Genl. Moody, who has been looking up law. He gave it quickly. . . . I went to Moody taking Nelson along. Moody was very nice. . . . He gave me all he had been able to get together on the subject. I shall go to work on it."[12] On Saturday, December 15, Bob saw the President and wrote that Roosevelt "was very effusive in his greeting again but I never know how much he is really *dee*-lighted. The interests, & certain senators & some of the department fellows are planning to give me a stiff fight on the coal and hours of service matters." Roosevelt made an appointment for Monday evening "at six p.m. to talk over the coal bill & other things especially the coal bill."[13] On his return from the White House Bob spent the rest of the day with Steffens. They had "a heart to heart" visit, "one of the times which a fellow always remembers."[14]

On Monday, at 6:00 P.M., Bob saw the President and wrote me that the interview "was the most satisfactory one I have ever had with him. It was quite personal & political—and quite extended and significant."[15] Roosevelt wrote a note on a card asking Charles D. Walcott, Director of the Geological Survey, to give Bob all the information he properly could on the coal business.[16] A broad conservation measure was then prepared which Bob said "was in a large degree the work of the able assistant" assigned to him by Attorney General Moody. It was, he thought, the one bill put before Congress up to 1912 which dealt "with the whole subject in a comprehensive way."[17] Two days before the bill was introduced he wrote: "It will probably be shut out this session but I shall push it now and here-after. It will mean untold good to the American people in all the years to come if it can be put through—and it must be put through no matter how long it takes. Oh there are so many things crying out on every hand. I wish I could accomplish more."[18]

On Tuesday morning, January 22, he went over a synopsis of the bill, section by section, with the President. At every important point "Roosevelt would smite the table and declare his approval with an emphatic: 'Admirable, Admirable! that does the business.' "[19] When they had finished, the President authorized him, if he desired, to announce that it was an Administration measure. That afternoon Bob introduced the bill. Bob knew the bill had powerful enemies, but with these assurances of the President's enthusiastic support he felt confident on Tuesday night that the bill would go through "sooner or later." It was widely reported in the press, certain papers stating it had been submitted to the President and had his approval. It was printed and in the folding room the following morning. There was such a demand for copies that by Wednesday night the supply was exhausted. That evening Bob wrote, "This shows that it has created a great deal of interest in the subject; . . ."[20]

The interest had apparently been so intense that on the same evening Roosevelt made a sudden shift which Bob described as "the President's ker-flop." Yielding to protests against the bill by Spooner, Knute Nelson, and others, he wrote a letter which was delivered to Bob by Walcott, Director of the Geological Survey. Roosevelt wrote that he was now afraid Bob's bill would arouse so much opposition that it could not be put through. He therefore wished to substitute a bill drawn by Walcott. Walcott seemed to expect Bob to comply with the President's request at once and accept Walcott's bill or a combination of it and "a weak sloppy thing which Knute Nelson had introduced a couple of weeks before." Bob told Walcott that he would go over the two bills carefully, that all he wanted was a reasonably effective measure, and that he would not "stick for a bill" because he had introduced it. After studying them, he replied to the President's note by letter because he hoped a careful analysis of the Nelson and Walcott bills would make it clear to Roosevelt that these were not only valueless in themselves but if enacted would actually bring Government control into disrepute.[21]

In his letter to me Bob said: "I suppose they will all pull together to pass some kind—any kind of a bill. The Pres has a passion for getting as many things started as possible. . . . Public sentiment cries out for relief. A good bill can be passed now; but the passage of a makeshift will defer good legislation for ten years & by that time all the coal & oil lands will be gone under weak and shifty leases which influence & the cry of vested property rights will never permit the revocation of.

"Well goodnight dears Dont worry about it. I did at first but am too much of a hardened philosopher to let it nag me long. I shall go in for the right thing[;] not my bill necessarily but a good bill. If they report out a weak defective measure I shall do as I did in the rate bill debate point out its weaknesses and try to amend it. This I suppose will make the Pres mad—(He says the 'attack' I 'made on the rate bill made him awful mad')—but he'll get over it or if he dont it wont matter—it is the course I must follow here and be contented with it."[22]

Two days later, in referring to an attack, led by Senator Carter, which had been made on the President that day in the Senate, Bob added: "It all betokens the spirit here among 'conservative' Senators to 'go after' T.R. . . . And he is such a mixture that they can do it enough of the time to prevent him from doing any *very good* piece of work in the public interest He will always say a lot of good things and half do a good many things—But it all ends rather disappointingly, I am compelled to admit to myself if I dont to others. But it may be the only thing in sight for the day and the hour."[23]

All hope that the President would carry through his promise to support Bob's coal bill was definitely ended by a letter, written on February 5, in which he did not attempt to answer Bob's criticism of the Walcott and Nelson bills, but said he had conferred the previous evening with Senators Hansbrough, Nelson, Carter, and Newlands* together with James R. Garfield, Chief Forester; Gifford Pinchot, Charles D. Walcott, and Joseph A. Holmes, of the Geological Survey. It was evident, Roosevelt said, that it would be hard "to secure *any* legislation on this subject of the coal"; he expressed agreement with an enclosed letter from the Secretary of the Interior giving reasons why the La Follette bill would be less effective than the Walcott bill and asked Bob to support the latter. It was his be-

* Hansbrough was chairman; Nelson, Carter, and Newlands were members of the Senate Committee on Public Lands.

lief, he said, that "to struggle for one particular bill as against all other bills is to play into the hands of the men who wish to do nothing."[24]

Bob's reply reveals the fundamentally different concept these two men had as to what constituted success in legislation: "I am not arguing for the provisions of my bill because I am anxious that the legislation should bear my name. I have no pride of authorship to serve. I do desire that whatever is done be well done. . . . The interests of the public will be better served by temporary defeat of an effective measure dealing with this subject than by compromising on a bill which sounds well in the title but is weak or silent on vital points. . . . You may rest assured that I shall in no case urge nonessentials, and shall at all times be ready to join in passing any measure which will remedy the evil."[25]

Soon after receiving Roosevelt's letter, Bob wrote me: "I have been a good deal disappointed respecting the Pres.—but shall go on in my own way doing the best I can. . . . I shall not oppose the passage of any bill but lay in wait to make it better if I can. . . . I think he knows—must know I am right but the Senate crowd upon whom he must rely to get [it] out of the Pub. Lands Committee as well as the House gang gave him to understand that no bill could pass with La F's name on it. If he would say so frankly to me I'd like him better. But I must take him as he is and do the best I can with him. Beveridge came to me today and told me that the Pres. told him day before yesterday that he the Pres. thought very highly of me & c & c. But you know 'Bev.' I shall always remember how the Pres. threw me down and govern myself accordingly. I wont get caught in the newspapers again by ever letting anyone know that I am relying on him for anything. This is the only safe course to pursue unless you are *strong* enough to command a majority. Then he would be *sure* to stand."[26] After the President decided he could not support the bill Bob introduced, it had no chance of being reported out from the Committee on Public Lands.

Early in this same session Bob had introduced his bill for the physical valuation of the railroads as a basis for fixing railway rates.[27] He had little hope of getting a favorable report from the Senate Interstate Commerce Committee, of which Elkins was chairman, but he kept at it just the same. The President had told him on January 16 that he would support the valuation principle at the next session and that he would write an open letter to the Interstate Commerce Commission soon. In response to his request, Bob wrote a six-page memorandum. On January 30, just a week after the President's "ker-flop" on the coal bill, Bob wrote to me: "I sent the President today a letter setting forth what I think are the most glaring defects in the Rate Law and how to cure them. Lu and David [Thompson] thought it a ripper—but I suppose the Pres will think it a crank production. He [the President] intended to write an open letter to the Inte[r] St[ate] Com[merce] Com[mittee] as to amendments to the bill. But it has in some way gotten out that he would do so favoring a valuation amendment & has raised a storm in Wall Street. The Conservative Senators are warning him that it will produce a panic & beat the party and I shall be surprised if he dont back up. . . . I shall do the best I can to work with him without chasing up and inflicting myself upon him unduly. But at the same time I dont propose to go and jump in the Potomac because he throws me down every day or so—although it is somewhat depressing."[28] Bob's persistent pressure on Elkins and other members finally brought forth a committee meeting. On February 19 Bob wrote: "Today is an important day to me. The Elkins Committee meets on valuation bill. . . . I expected to win before Com.[mittee] but doubt it now. . . . The interests are scared stiff & are putting on the screws. It is also 'reported' that the Pres. has said it was not best to do anything 'now.' He has given up writing his letter to the Inter St.[ate] Com. Com. to open up the subject of amendments to the Rate Law, but will do it 'later in some speeches.' It got out that he was going to & Wall Street threatened him with a 'panic.' The big senators called on him & the 'big stick' which isn't really a big stick at all, was put away."[29]

Bob's letters touched upon many other political questions besides the measures he was sponsoring, and he often commented on the people he saw. After he met for the first time Frederic C. Howe and Ida Tarbell, who called on him at his office in the Capitol on Lincoln's birthday, he wrote, "I was much charmed with her—and with him. She asked me to call on her when in New York."[30] He had read and admired her biography of Lincoln and her articles on Standard Oil when they were published in *McClure's,* and he told her that he was not half so much in awe of her as he had expected.

Another woman he met this same winter and always greatly admired was Lillian D. Wald. From New York, where he was spending a day with Fola and the Roes after a lecture at Plymouth Church, he wrote of a lunch at the Henry Street Settlement with Miss Wald: "She is a wonderful woman, simple, direct, sincere, clear minded with a broad sympathy that wants to help—not for self gratification not to satisfy some sentimental notion but to leave the one helped able to help himself—stronger in character and self-respect."[31]

He always included the children in his letters. Now and then he wrote to each separately. In one of my letters I told him: "Bobbie was pleased to get his letter He read it all through before allowing us to see it. There was a proud look on his face—I said 'You know you have a niche all your own in your papa's heart Don't you?' He understood."[32] In this birthday letter his father had written: "It is hard to let a birthday go by for any of my little ones. It simply emphasizes the broken life we are leading and makes me repeat over and over again that we shall all be under one roof and around one table very soon I hope. . . . You are coming now to the time when each year means a year of important growth in character as well as body. Look well to it that you grow in gentleness and tenderness as well as in strength. . . . The boy Bobbie is a mighty important part of the man. As you are strong and kind as a boy so will you be strong and noble and tender as a man. Every day and hour of life is precious. Every act lays the foundation for another. I love you dear lad—and count on you for many things in the future."[33]

To Phil, who had written that one of the little ponies had lost an eye, he said: "It is too bad, too bad—she is or was such a pretty little thing—such fine spirit too. I never saw a horse that did not seem to be sad and depressed over the loss of an eye—almost as you would expect any human being to be saddened and depressed by such a misfortune. . . . I am sure you did all you could for her and we have to bow our heads to the things we cant help and for which we are in no way to blame. I always feel that when we do our very best being very sure that it is our best to the very last limit that then we must accept without grumbling or kicking whatever comes. Otherwise we should spend a good part of our lives in regretting and mourning about things that have not gone the way they should."[34]

Bob, Jr., went to school in town. I taught Phil and Mary at home.

I wrote that Phil was "learning how to concentrate his thought—and as he is interested and willing, it is a real pleasure to teach him. Mary is making progress. She is not likely ever to have any serious trouble about lessons."[35] "The children seem to be maturing very fast. Little Phil is growing quite reflective. It is beautiful to see how they all love their home. It is not a bad thing for them to spend a quiet winter here and get the perspective of your work and Washington life."[36] "You have a wonderful endowment—such perfect poise with never failing enthusiasm, such clearness of vision, coolness of judgment, courage confidence, and tact. Pervading it all a sense of humor that makes life with you a constant joy. My, but I do miss your company."[37] In reply to Bob's admonition that I must not overdo but rest up and be ready to meet the demands of life in Washington next year, I wrote that I did not dread the social obligations, "those duties seem trifling But the intense interest in you seems too much for me at times."[38] Naturally, my letters often appealed to him to take better care of his health: "It seems to me sometimes as though my life—inner life—was a long prayer that your strength may not give out under the strain to which you have been so long subjected and that the time is not far off when we can feel free to enjoy the time that *is*, not always wait for it to come."[39]

Week end after week end and on holidays Bob went out to read the roll call in neighboring States. His own feeling about this work is expressed in a typical letter: "I had a good meeting unusually good at Greenburg Pa. I only wish that it were possible for me to go out oftener for I know it not only counts locally but reacts on the Senate. . . . The press pretty generally is taking note of my presentation of records and I can see quite a difference among some of the senators about their records. The 'Roll Call' is going to go down in history."[40]

In a letter toward the end of the session, Bob called my attention to an article in the February *Munsey's Magazine*, which told how "the Senators had learned to respect the fighting tactics of La Follette" who had "executed a flank movement which took a number of his hazers by surprise" when he unrolled their voting record to audiences.[41] He also enclosed a special Washington dispatch to the *New York Times* which described the Senators' 1906 "hazing" of La Follette and how he read the roll calls on the Chautauqua Circuit the following summer, "spreading havoc and destruction in the

ranks of the hazers and giving several of them the job of their lives
to get re-elected. The Senate whined and said this was 'not fair.' It
also decided that it would give La Follette a dose this Winter which
would make last Winter's corrective seem like molasses.

"Instead of which, the first important bill that La Follette introduced was passed—a thing that could not have happened last session—and passed despite the fact that two-thirds of the Senate was
praying for an excuse to vote against it, and there was no public
hazing of La Follette over it, either—only some little boarding-
school-girl flings at him. . . . With the session near an end La Follette
is on top. The Senators still snub him in the cloakrooms, but not on
the floor. He is bitterly hated, but also feared. . . . It is the Senate,
and not La Follette, that is being rapidly brought to terms.

"The main trouble with the Senate was that it chose to assume
before ever it clapped eyes on La Follette that he was a lightweight,
a ranting demagogue. The industrious Spooner had spread that reputation for him before he arrived. La Follette does not rant, he is not
a crank, he is extremely level-headed, and such an encyclopedia of
information on every subject he takes up that any man who goes up
against him in debate and has not devoted a couple of years to the
subject is going to retire from the contest much the worse for
wear."[42]

CHAPTER XX

Bob Reads the Roll Call on Congress

Senator Spooner had written a letter to Governor Davidson at the close of the short session, announcing his resignation. Before it was published, Judson Welliver had telephoned the news to Bob at Chevy Chase where he was then ill in bed. The next morning Bob wrote me: "No one yet knows what is behind it. . . . I think the Wisconsin situation taken all together was the underlying cause. Of course when a man takes such a step everything is considered and there are doubtless many things which made up the final judgment. . . . He shrank from the review of his record which he knew was coming. The deadly roll call deterred him. . . . Besides life here in the Senate has changed in the last year. There is a thorn in his side—it is there all the while. There may have been other things—probably were—but these things counted."[1]

Spooner's resignation was to take effect on April 30. Commenting on the contest over the election of a successor to fill the unexpired term, Bob wrote that if our friends stood together they ought to be able to control the situation, but he feared many candidates and "a great mix-up" before it was over with. He added that he would like to see "Uncle Ike" (Stephenson) satisfied but didn't think it could be done. Among other available and desirable candidates in our camp he mentioned Lenroot, Haugen, Cooper, Sanborn, Ekern, Houser, and Hatton.[2] On the same day that Bob wrote, Stephenson had stated in the *Free Press*, "I have decided to become a candidate for the United States Senate, but for the short term only. If elected, it is my intention to retire at the end of Mr. Spooner's unexpired term and not to seek reelection."[3]

A message had come from our friends in Washington telling me Bob was ill with severe influenza. The word reached me after the children were asleep. I wrote them a note explaining, and without disturbing anybody, walked into town, caught an early train, and was in Washington the next day. After I arrived, we naturally discussed the Senatorship at length. I wrote to Bob's sister, Jo, that the situation worried him: "He sincerely believes all his friends should take off their coats for Stephenson for the short term [Spooner's unexpired term] ensuring the election of the right man for the long term—He knows Stephenson will stand and will vote for the right things—from conviction too—If our friends do not support him he thinks Stephenson's friends will unite with Davidson and it will mean bad man for governor weak senator for short and for long term—merging of Sentinel and Free Press and all those disastrous results."[4]

The contest in the Wisconsin legislature was close and prolonged. There were many candidates, and all kinds of conflicting elements. One day after my return to Madison, while the outcome was still in doubt, a group of legislators called on me at the farm. Herman Ekern, as I remember, was the spokesman. After the usual greetings, without any preliminary explanation, the categorical question was asked me: "Do you believe Mr. Stephenson to be a man who can be relied upon to keep his promise?" I replied without a moment's hesitation: "Yes, absolutely." My answer was based on my confidence in Mrs. Stephenson's frank, sincere estimate of his character. Many times, when she had explained to me that his shortcomings were offset by his admirable qualities, she had referred to his inherent uprightness and honesty and had said, "Everyone knows his word is as good as his bond." Afterward, when I related this experience to a friend of Stephenson's, he said it was true that in personal and business relations everybody who knew Stephenson would trust his word as they would his bond; but when it came to politics Stephenson's code of ethics was of a different nature.

Probably the legislature would not have elected him to the Senate, as it did on May 17, except for the understanding that he desired only the honor of serving out the unexpired term and would not be a candidate again. However, in spite of public statements and personal assurances to the contrary, it was evident soon after he came to the Senate that he was ambitious to succeed himself.

A meeting at Milwaukee on May 31, 1907, while Bob was away, was credited with having started the campaign for La Follette Presidential delegates to the 1908 Republican National Convention.[5] There was no money to effect an organization outside Wisconsin, although it was evident popular sentiment existed in other States and some progressive leaders in the Midwest and Far West had early favored him as a candidate. During the winter a leading Kansas editor, who was also a member of Congress, had stated that Bob, if a candidate, could carry the Kansas delegation. A conservative Oregon Senator had surprised his colleagues by saying that "La Follette could count on the Oregon delegation if he were a candidate."[6]

During the summer and fall of 1907, Bob's lecture dates took him into Iowa, North and South Dakota, Montana, Idaho, Washington, Oregon, California, Kansas, Oklahoma, Nebraska, Colorado, Missouri, Indiana, Illinois, Michigan, and Pennsylvania. The title of his lecture remained the same on the program announcements, but people who drove long distances to hear him year after year always knew they would hear a new lecture. For he was telling them what had happened in the recent sessions of Congress, explaining why and how bills had been killed in committee, describing the fight against the special interests which defeated legislation in the public interest, and reading the roll call on the Senators in each State.

As he had only partially recovered from the influenza when he started on his speaking trip, I was greatly relieved when he consented to take Colonel Hannan with him; for this meant his strength would be spared in every possible way. They were good company for each other, and Bob loved the companionship of his friends. After his meetings in South Dakota he wrote: "We came near wiring you yesterday fearing you might see something in the papers about my being sick at Miller. . . . I had a nasty attack due I think to water. . . . The house was full of people. I was determined to go on—& did to the end but I had to excuse myself *often*. . . . John took the best of care of me. . . . He sat by the bed all night."[7] From Billings, Montana, he reported: "A fine meeting last night and then a reception at the Billings business mens Club, I got my audience & I got the town. . . . I have got an *Idea* with a capital *I*. On getting up yesterday morning, it occurred to me to make use of Hannan in this way. I went out and bought a blank book & started John out on a tour of the principal business houses—Merchandise lumber—coal &c to get rates and traffic conditions generally. I got some material which I used last night giving local point to my argument & a fine lot of facts which I can use on floor of Senate to back up my amendments with facts from Montana which will put it up to Senators Carter & Dixon to support the propositions I offer. I got a lot of good stuff & we shall follow this plan at every town where we have time to work it up."[8] In commenting on his meetings in Montana, he wrote: "Every night after lecture I have *had* to go to Commercial Clubs & put in an hour or two in talk equal to another speech. They are all in such distress about rates up here and they want to get all the counsel and help they can. I like them very much & the country & people are full of great promise. They are too eager for wealth & rate it too high. . . . They insist on taking you out in autos & carriages to show you the holes in the ground where they have taken out so *many million* and are sure to get so many more. They say little about their schools which are good except to tell you what it cost to put up the buildings. . . . But they are awakening & a good persistent worker could set up & maintain the right standards."[9]

In Helena, Montana, Senator Carter's home town, an audience of 1,600 gave Bob an ovation. After his speech he had to attend a banquet at the Montana Club, and his former secretary, Jerre Murphy, who owned and edited the *Montana Lookout*, accompanied him. Bob wrote that few club members had attended his lecture, but that the banquet had been arranged as a proper attention to a visiting United States Senator. After listening to them talk for two hours about nothing but the hundreds of thousands of dollars the mines were paying, he was unexpectedly called upon to speak at about 1:30 A.M.: "I told 'em that they had interested & amazed me with their marvelous production of copper but I'd like to know what kind of men they were producing—what kind of citizenship they were building into their new commonwealth. They looked puzzled, then curious, then a little worried, then somewhat interested. Jerre's dark staring eyes never left my face except to steal a quizzical look round the table. . . . I was dead and hardly able to stand when I went in—but came out all right. Jerre said: 'The speech was just what they needed. . .' "[10]

On this return trip to the State of Washington Bob found that his speeches of the previous fall and spring had caused much discussion and aroused bitter opposition. In some places, as at Tacoma, none of the politicians could be induced to present him to the audiences. Bob wrote that his speech at Walla Walla "created a great ruction—because it was the home of Senator Ankeny. He tried to smother me with attention and entertainment. It was their intention to get me to deliver a different lecture or omit the roll-calls. . . . It was next to impossible to get rid of Ankeny He insisted on my going to his home & said he would call & take me to the lecture &c. Remembering the misrepresentation following my Evansville Ind[iana] meeting where Senator Hemenway presided—I firmly declined and went to my room—I then wrote Ankeny a note telling him what I was to lecture upon & that I should go into the records & roll calls & suggesting that he might in his desire to show me attention in connection with the lecture be placed in a position of embarrassment." The note was submitted to President Stephen B. L. Penrose, who said that "if Ankeny did not appreciate it his wife certainly would." But the tactics of these reactionary politicians were offset by President Penrose of Whitman College and President W. E. Wilson of the State Normal School at Ellensburg who telegraphed and wrote ahead enthusiastically about Bob's lectures. President Penrose's telegram was published in local newspapers.

On the train to San Francisco, Bob wrote: "I have scored good results for the cause in all these states. At Albany [Oregon] also a college town—seven feet ahead of me on the platform in the church hung a small disc or receiver & telephones connected with a score or more of homes where people were ill, gave them the lecture perfectly. It was like magic—I tried it the next morning before leaving town. . . . Old Mt. Shasta 14450 feet is above me as I write—white & majestic & awesome—the full round moon hangs over making the everlasting snow melt into the soft clouds above mysteriously. How small it makes man how brief his little flutter of life."[11]

From San Diego he wrote in a retrospective mood: "I have just waked to find the breakers coming at me from the Ocean. It all happened while I slept. When I dropped off, we were in the valley. . . . I slept soundly and then awoke and it was nine years ago. There were the stretches of sandy beach, there were long low roofs & black jagged rocks lifting their heads high against the breakers that foamed & raged around them. . . . It might have been yesterday that we were together here & then—it looked so like old San Diego. It made me very homesick to be here without you. It made life seem so short. It made it seem so wrong to be gone all the time. What is left will go so soon. But this is not the way to write & not the way to feel I suppose."[12]

From San Francisco, where the press reported Bob had an audience of four or five thousand, he wrote: "I talked too long & beg your forgiveness because I know I shall be found out. . . . Except those who had to take the ferry my audience held on till 12 o'clock and would *not let* me stop! . . . As I walked into the hotel on arriving in San F. the first one to greet me was Lincoln Steffens. God bless him He is still doing this part of the country for graft or the open evidence of it. San Francisco is the center now. Heney the great prosecutor is in charge as 'assistant' to the district Atty. He and Steffens have become great friends. One of the rich men Rudolph Spreckles 35 years old millionaire son of Claus Spreckles the Sugar King is the 'chairman' of the anti graft crusade now on. . . . Spreckles is a good man and has ability. . . . Heney has grown fast. He knows more and sees wider every hour. . . . Steffens had Spreckles & Heney up to the hotel & at luncheon with me. . . . I had a nice visit with them—I like them both—& Heney is fine material—quiet, keen relentless, well poised—fearless & a very excellent lawyer all round. Spreckles has the budding of patriotism in him, I think. He only sees San Francisco now and that a point at a time. . . .

"Mr. and Mrs. Heney and Steffens . . . took me to the great barn 'Dreamland Rink' where I spoke. Heney introduced me and did it *right*. It was a fine audience with lots of rep[resentative] people. . . . Steffens told Hannan that Heney's partner, 'a very able man, said it was the longest and greatest speech he ever heard.' I can prove it was the longest. . . . Spreckles sat on the platform & watched me like a hawk with his big wide open brown eyes while I talked of the Crime of controlling a market—as in the case of the Sugar Trust over capitalizing the business, robbing the people & using the money to destroy representative gov[ern]m[e]nt. He shook hands with me a half dozen times before we got away from the auditorium where I spoke. Steffens had warned him that he wouldnt believe a thing I said—but I think he did."[13]

Two weeks later, after speeches in Colorado, Oklahoma, Missouri, Kansas, and Nebraska, he wrote: "The last week was a trying one so far as sleep being possible Long rides with everybody recognizing me & almost no time in bed. The meetings were all large. . . . Kansas is as Wisconsin was eight years ago. In her first enthusiasm of earnest struggle for freedom from the machine. They want me to give a month or two in their campaign. Sooner or later as a result of all this work I shall be obliged to do for Kansas and other states what I did in New Jersey go and help in straight out campaign work. I had a fine letter from Will Allen White. He is beginning. He will see more widely as he gets experience in politics. . . . Kansas will come right in two to four years I trust."[14]

When he wrote this letter, he had only a few more lecture dates before starting on the hunting trip he had planned the year before with Professor John Carlisle. The members of the party also included Cornelius Harper, Irvine Lenroot, Alfred Rogers, and Bob, Jr., who joined him at Glenwood Springs, Colorado. Bob, Jr., recalls: "Dad was not particularly well when we began the hunting trip, yet he stood it better than any of us. He was the first man up in camp in the morning and eager to get the party under way. At night he entertained us around the camp fire, reading as only he could, chapters from Emerson Hough's *Outlaws of the West*, Alfred Henry Lewis' Wolfville stories, and other tales which fitted the spirit of the occasion. . . . One morning, after several days hard riding, Rowdy, the leader of the pack gave cry. Jake, the guide, said, 'That's bear and the trail is hot.' Before long we were the hottest things on the trail. We dashed down the side of the mountain, our horses on the dead run, forded the river, and went on up the mountain to find the dogs had treed the bear. We dismounted, Dad and I walked forward twenty yards, and he gave the commands as though on the field of battle, 'Ready, aim, fire.' As I remember he shot his 33 Winchester twice while I emptied the magazine of my little twenty-two automatic rifle. The bear fell and the dogs rushed in. I was much disappointed to find the bullets from my little twenty-two barely penetrated the bear's hide, but Dad always generously referred to the mounted skin which adorned his study as 'Bobbie's and my bear.' "

In July Bob was lecturing in nearby States, and I accompanied him for a week. His audiences were large, for the people drove long distances to hear him; frequently at the close of his speeches he would have to shake hands with nearly everybody in the audience. He would come off the platform dripping with perspiration, and at times would tell me he had felt dizzy and almost lost the thread of thought while speaking. I knew he was taking serious risk, talking so long on hot days under a tent crowded with people. I tried to persuade him to shorten his speeches and keep within a specified limit—two hours at the maximum.

I bought him an alarm watch and extracted a promise, half serious, half facetious, that he would not speak beyond the two-hour limit. He had lots of fun with the watch. When the alarm went off, the audience would be startled at the strange noise. He would stop suddenly, begin gathering up his papers, and explain in despair that his wife had given him this watch to prevent his talking too long, that he was under solemn oath to keep within the prescribed limit, and that he dared not say another word. The crowd would laugh and cheer and insist he go on; he would yield on condition they promise not to let his wife know.

Once, when he was shaking hands with a long line of people, a woman, speaking in a high-pitched voice which everybody could hear, said, "Mr. La Follette, I wish you would tell your wife for me that I think she wasted her money when she invested in that alarm watch." Afterward Bob, imitating her perfectly, would often tell this story on himself to the great amusement of his audiences.

Colonel Hannan sometimes had great difficulty in getting him to stop speaking in time to catch their train. He tells of a meeting in Los Angeles where he warned him three times that he must leave; but the crowd kept yelling for him to go on speaking. Fearing they would miss the train, Hannan telephoned the station, and the trainmen agreed to hold the train for ten minutes. Hannan returned to the platform, picked Bob up, and carried him off to the waiting automobile. At first he was angry, but finally laughed till the tears came.

Two other meetings stay in my memory as especially vivid examples of the purpose and effectiveness of his use of the roll call. His personal friendship for Senator Julius C. Burrows of Michigan dated back to their service together on the Ways and Means Committee in the House of Representatives. Burrows was a man of real personal charm, but politically conservative. After a speech at Kalamazoo, the Senator's home town, Bob wrote me that "Burrows and his postmaster with the democratic mayor & another leading politician met me at the train with an auto took me to a hotel & there Burrows informed me that he had an engagement & would not alas be able to attend Chautauqua. . . . I told him I thought it was well that he had an engagement that I should take up legislation & the votes of the Senate . . . and I could make no exception for personal friends. . . . I do not believe Burrows will go back."[15]*

I was not present when Bob addressed an Allegheny County Teachers' Institute in the Music Hall at Pittsburgh, Pennsylvania, but I always felt I had been after hearing him tell about it in his vivid way. Before going on the platform, he was warned by the county school superintendent, Samuel Hamilton, who was in charge of the meeting, that he must not make a partisan speech. He explained that his speech was entirely non-partisan; whereupon the superintendent came bluntly to the point: "You might as well understand that you can't read the roll call"; to which Bob replied: "I read the roll call in an unbiased way, following an impartial judicial presentation of the measure voted upon. I never mention anyone's name save as it comes in the course of the roll call." "You can't read it here," the superintendent angrily declared. "You apparently don't know about me; I make my own speeches," Bob said gently, and went on the platform. He immediately told the audience of the colloquy, declared he had no intention of talking partisan politics, urged everyone to rise above party, stand for country first, and then proceeded with his speech.

The superintendent broke in repeatedly with protests against "talking politics" while Bob was denouncing the monopolistic power of the trusts and describing how they controlled the United States Senate, state legislatures, and city councils. Bob took these interruptions good-naturedly and went steadily on with his analysis of how a few men controlled the economic and political destiny of the country through the interlocking directorates of the railroads and the trusts. He told how the railroad officials of Wisconsin, to escape just taxation, had sworn falsely to their earnings to the extent of $11,000,000 in six years, adding: "Of course that doesn't look like much money to you Pennsylvanians. But to we fellows out West who have never had a whole state Capitol stolen in one full swoop, it looks big."[16]

When he finished reading the roll, which showed that the two Pennsylvania Senators, Knox and Penrose, had voted against his amendment to the Hepburn bill for physical valuation of railroads

* Burrows was defeated by Charles Elroy Townsend.

as a basis for taxation, and started to read the roll call on another amendment, Superintendent Hamilton jumped up and insisted that the Senator stop his address, "as the music-hall attendants must get in to clean up for the evening meeting." Bob replied, "I do not wish to encroach on the courtesies of this association, so if it is agreeable to the audience I will go out on the steps and address you." The audience "rose as one person and rushed for the doors. Some crowded on the stage to shake hands with the speaker and escort him to the steps." As Bob went out, "The vast assemblage followed, muttering indignant protests at the treatment accorded him.

"Excitement ran high and for some time threatened to break out in something more serious than verbal protests. Park policemen attempted to keep the audience off the grass around the steps upon which Senator La Follette was standing, but they were swept aside with a rush and the crowd surged as close as possible to the speaker. . . .

"When he had concluded, they crowded around him to shake his hand. A line was formed and as each one passed they commended Senator La Follette on his courage, declared that his words were prophetic and urged him to keep up his fight against the trusts.

"It was a remarkable demonstration. Almost his entire audience was swayed by his no less remarkable speech and showed that they were willing to fight, if necessary, for his cause. Senator La Follette was compelled to remain on the scene for fully 30 minutes after he had concluded his address. The audience lingered to ask questions and the more enthusiastic urged him to continue his speech, even though he had spoken for three hours and 25 minutes."[17]

In telling me of the meeting, Bob said that as he went out of Carnegie Music Hall on to the steps of the library to continue his interrupted meeting he noticed the inscription over the door and made it the introductory theme of his speech:

"Dedicated to All the People."

CHAPTER XXI

A Record-Breaking Filibuster

In the fall of 1907 I had rented a furnished house at 2229 California Street for the coming session. Besides Bob, myself, and the three children, there were Nellie Dunn, Bob's secretary; Emma Gattiker, a dear friend I had persuaded to be the children's companion and teacher; Della Vallen and Laura Sachtjen, daughters of well-to-do farmers who were our neighbors at home. During the summer they had relieved me of all household cares and had come to do the same service because it gave them a few months in the Nation's Capital.

I wanted the children to attend the New Year's reception at the White House. We ordered two carriages; only one came, however, and it was too late to get another—which accounts for the story in the *Chicago Tribune* entitled, "Next President At White House? Roosevelt Enjoys Experience of Receiving Possible Successor in New Year Line." The reporter noted: "Senator La Follette of Wisconsin was pointed out by everyone who knew him to everyone who did not. He brought his wife and children with him, and there were some smiles at the charming democracy of the Wisconsin senator when his party of seven, four adults and three children, emerged from the carriage on the White House portico. They were all received with unction by the president and Mrs. Roosevelt, because it is a fact generally understood here that the Wisconsin senator has a vast deal more of real personal strength throughout the country than many of those who have been prominently mentioned for the republican nomination."[1] Roosevelt was always very cordial in his greetings. The conspicuous warmth of his welcome on this occasion had nothing to do with politics. We were reminded, however, in moving about among the distinguished company which as-

238

sembles at the White House on New Year's day, that Bob was a center of interest as a "Presidential possibility." His record in the Senate, his achievement in Wisconsin, together with his lecture tours and roll calls in so many States, were creating a public sentiment that could not be ignored in Washington political circles.

From New Year's until the Republican convention in June we were frequently photographed, and there appeared in many newspapers and magazines the usual articles about the family of a Presidential candidate. But the children's experience during the years their father was governor had accustomed them to this. The feature stories sent out during the session were on the whole more friendly than those of the governorship period. Thus I recall that the inner life of the family was not overshadowed by anxiety or strain for the first year we were together in Washington. The children were greatly interested in the convening of Congress. Bob, Jr., and Phil never lost an opportunity to attend the sessions, and their interest in legislation sponsored by their father was almost as absorbing as his own. They had access to the Senate floor and were on intimate terms with their father's friends, most of whom they affectionately addressed as "Uncle."

Bob's outstanding fight in the Senate during the 1907-1908 session was against the Aldrich emergency currency bill, finally known as the Aldrich-Vreeland bill. It proposed an issue of $500,000,000 of additional notes to national banking associations, such issue to be based upon state bonds, municipal bonds, and, as reported by Senator Aldrich, also *railroad bonds*. This was the first time railroad bonds had been proposed as a basis for currency issue. In certain ways Bob thought this bill more indicative of the control of legislation by the great financial interests than any bill ever introduced in Congress.

Ever since his amendment to the Hepburn bill for railroad valuation had been voted down, it had been kept bottled up in the Committee on Interstate Commerce. For two years he had been waiting a chance to offer it again. The railroad-bond provision in the currency bill gave him the opportunity. Apparently this had never occurred to the committee reporting out the currency measure; for there was a "flutter of excitement," and "disgust and consternation were plainly manifest" when he promptly offered his amendment providing that "the Secretary of the Treasury should be authorized to accept railroad bonds as security for the emergency currency issue *only after the Interstate Commerce Commission had ascertained the value of the physical properties of the railroads,* upon which the bonds in question constituted a first mortgage; and provided further that no such railroad bonds should be accepted unless the value of the property of the railroad company were found to be ample security for such bonds."[2]

Senator Aldrich introduced the emergency currency bill on January 7, 1908, reported it out of the Committee on Finance on January 30, and made the opening speech supporting it on February 10. While Bob was preparing his speech against the measure, he became ill with influenza and was confined to his home for several weeks. As soon as he recovered, he formally announced he would address the Senate on March 17 and would oppose the railroad-bond provision. Not since the Hepburn bill had he made so important a speech in the Senate. But he was even more alone now than then, for Dolliver disagreed with him and there were fewer Democratic Senators supporting him.

March 17 was a day of excitement and strain for the entire family. I was glad that Gilbert Roe, Netha Roe, and Emily Bishop were visiting us; also that Lincoln Steffens was to hear the speech. We all left home early to make sure of seats in the Senate gallery. Bob, as usual, was working on his speech until the last minute. We jestingly urged him at least to be in the Senate when the hour came for him to speak. After the prayer by Edward Everett Hale, the usual petitions and committee reports were presented. I was listening idly when Aldrich arose and casually stated, as though it were a mere formality, that he had been directed by a unanimous vote of the Committee on Finance to report sundry amendments to the currency bill, one of which was *to strike from the bill all provisions in regard to railroad bonds!*

I knew this railroad-bond provision was the keynote of the argument Bob had prepared against the bill. Quite dazed, I turned to ask if I had heard aright. I noticed that Bob, Jr., had left the gallery. He was soon back again. "I got Daddy on the telephone before he had left the house and told him what had happened," he whispered. The quick wit of his thirteen-year-old son, who had rushed out to warn his father before anyone else recognized the significance of

Aldrich's announcement, gave Bob a chance at the very beginning of his speech to counter the shrewd last-minute move of the Senator from Rhode Island.

When the dull procedure of offering amendments to sundry bills ended at two o'clock, Bob began his speech by declaring that what he had intended to say about the bill had been made even more pertinent by Aldrich's "unexpected announcement" of the "intention to amend it by striking out the provision for the use of railroad bonds as security for emergency currency."[3] Then he went on with his speech as prepared. Later he referred to "the Jack-in-the-box withdrawal of the railway provision,"[4] and accurately predicted that at some stage in the legislative procedure it would be put back.

The first part of his speech was devoted to the centralization of banking and industry. He argued that the only evidence needed to demonstrate the community of interest between banks, railroads, and all great industries was the bare names of the directors of the two great banking groups—Standard Oil and Morgan—given in connection with their other business associations. As printed in the *Congressional Record* on March 17 with his speech, the "List of Men Who Control Industrial, Franchise, Transportation, and Financial Business of The United States With Their Directorships, and Offices in Corporations" covered ten pages. Although Bob had been discussing the concentration of financial control for several years in his lectures and Chautauqua speeches, this was the first time the interlocking character of these directorates had been brought to the attention of Congress. The data he used in his Senate speech had been laboriously compiled from numerous authoritative sources, including John Moody's *Manual* and many directories of directors which had been secured from different friends throughout the country. On the basis of this evidence, Bob asserted that fewer than a hundred men were in control of the great business interests of the country.

Aldrich interrupted to point out that some New York bankers opposed the bill. Bob asked if he knew J. Pierpont Morgan's position. Aldrich answered that he did not, but that he would "be highly gratified" if he "thought Mr. Morgan approved this bill in all its features." Bob suggested in a suave, ironical tone that perhaps "in some indirect way" Aldrich might "be able to find out where Mr.

Morgan stands. But his beaming countenance from the galleries
of this Chamber while the Senator from Rhode Island was making
his speech would rather indicate that Mr. Morgan, the head of one
of these great groups, was not entirely adverse to the propositions
embraced in this bill."[5]

After presenting his "record evidence that less than one hundred
men own and control railroads, traction, shipping, cable, telegraph,
telephone, express, mining, coal, oil, gas, electric light, copper, cotton, sugar, tobacco, agricultural implements, and the food products
as well as banking and insurance," Bob asked: "Does anyone question the overcapitalization of these consolidated corporations which
cover the business of the country? Does anyone doubt the community of interest that binds these men together? Does anyone
question their vital interest in maintaining their overcapitalization
and protecting their stocks and bonds?"[6]

He then told the dramatic story of the 1907 panic, to show it
was not for commercial, but for speculative, legislative, and political
reasons that the Wall Street crash occurred in October of that year.
He charged that the centralized banks of New York City—the
Morgan and Standard Oil banks—did not "give aid and support
to the distressed merchant and manufacturer" but "pursued the
course of the speculating banker. . . . They let great commercial
houses, great manufacturing concerns, . . . down to ruin and dishonor, while they protected their speculative patrons. No better
evidence could be asked to establish the character of this panic or
the character of the men who were in command. By their fruits
ye shall know them!"[7]

A storm of protest, criticism, and ridicule followed his first day's
speech. He was called a demagogue; his statements were denounced
as sensational and false. Between the first day of his speech and its
conclusion on March 24, a week intervened because of adjourn-
ments and other Senate legislation. During this interval a wave of
editorial invective and abuse swept across the country.

At the beginning of the third day of his speech, he said "there
was no occasion for the organs and claquers of the System to become frenzied over any statement" that less than a hundred men
control the Nation's business; the truth of it could easily be proved:
the business of the country was transacted by corporations, and the
control of these rested with the directors, executive committees, and

officers. It was only necessary to analyze the directorates to ascertain the truth. Then he classified the names of the outstanding business directors under three heads: those who gave orders; those who took orders; those who were dummies. Breaking the list down, he showed that *actually* only fourteen men, in cooperation with Morgan and Standard Oil, were in control of the Nation's business. When Senator Chauncey M. Depew's name was mentioned in the "dummy" class, the Senate was amused. And there was outright laughter on the floor when Bob predicted that after the publicity these names had received, there would be more "dummies" listed in the future volumes of *The Directory of Directors*. In naming certain individuals he was not "making war upon these men." He said, "I do not direct my attack against a Rockefeller, a Morgan, a Harriman. They are but types. They but embody an evil. Back of these men is the THING which we must destroy if we would preserve our free institutions. Men are as nothing; the System which we have built up by privileges, which we have allowed to take possession of Government and control legislation, is the real object of my unceasing warfare."[8] This was also true of his attitude toward the reactionary Senators.

Some of the specific objections he raised to the Aldrich bill were: the emergency currency could be used by the great banks for speculative purposes; the centralized financial interests would, because of their power, be able to place severe pressure upon the Secretary of Treasury to induce him to permit the issue of emergency currency "whenever it suits their interests"; by making certain securities the basis of this emergency currency a premium would be placed on these securities—hence the desire to have railroad bonds included.

The most the advocates of the Aldrich bill had ever claimed was, he said, that "it may tend to lessen the danger of a panic, because it is hoped it will tend to lessen the fear of one." And he appealed to the Senate, instead of enacting this "makeshift bill," which would serve only the larger banks identified with special interests, to give its immediate attention to formulating a "comprehensive and thorough plan for banking and currency legislation, specifically directed to restore banking to its true function in the commercial transactions of the country."[9]

Before the bill was finally acted upon, his amendment to prohibit banks from investing in the securities of other corporations or associations with which they had interlocking directorates was accepted by Aldrich and agreed to. Bob's amendment to require examination of the volume of emergency bank notes actually in circulation was also agreed to. But another amendment which he offered to forbid banks to make loans to persons who were officials of the same banks was defeated 37 to 13.[10] Bob and fifteen other Senators, all Democrats except four, voted against the Aldrich bill when it passed the Senate on March 27 by a vote of 42 to 16.

It was seven weeks before the emergency currency legislation was taken up again. Bob was absent because of illness when the House bill, known as the Vreeland bill, came up in the Senate on May 15. It was at once referred to the Finance Committee, of which Aldrich was chairman, and immediately reported back by him. The recommendations of the committee, combined with some amendments, made it practically the *original Aldrich bill* when it passed that same day by 47 to 20 and was sent to conference. The conference report was submitted to the House on May 27, briefly debated under a time limit, and agreed to on the same day by a vote of 185 to 145. Among the Republicans who disregarded the wrath of Speaker Cannon and joined the Democrats in voting against the bill were Cooper, Morse, and Nelson of Wisconsin, Murdock of Kansas, and Lindbergh of Minnesota. These men became the pioneer House Insurgents in the fight against "Czar" Cannon's domination of legislation. During the House debate John Sharp Williams, one of the Democrats who spoke against the conference report, said it "ought to be entitled the 'Cannon-Aldrich political emergency bill.' "[11] Carter Glass, then a member of the House Banking and Currency Committee, described it as "a measure which is 50 per cent House infamy and 50 per cent Senate infamy, thereby making the whole utterly bad."[12]

In conference *the La Follette amendments had been dropped from the bill, and the railroad-bond provision had been restored,* although disguised by rather obscure phraseology. But Aldrich admitted, when categorically asked, that under this provision railroad bonds would be available as a basis of emergency currency. As Bob had predicted, railroad bonds had been sneaked back into the bill, and important amendments had been sneaked out. Three days before the date fixed for adjournment, May 30, this measure was suddenly thrust upon Congress in the form of a conference report, which under parliamentary usage could be debated but *could not be amended in any respect*! Furthermore, in order to bring pressure to bear, those in charge of Senate legislation had held back the public buildings "pork barrel" bill, in which many Senators were much interested—with the warning that it would not pass unless the emergency currency bill passed.

Although Bob had only recently recovered from a severe influenza, he decided to resist passage of the Aldrich-Vreeland bill to the limit of his strength. To him this conference report was such a betrayal of the public interest that he was, as he later said on the Senate floor, "fully warranted in obstructing its passage in any parliamentary way to secure its everlasting defeat."[13] The filibuster was a daring undertaking, for he was the only Republican willing to make a prolonged attack on the conference report. Three other Republicans, William E. Borah of Idaho, Jonathan Bourne, Jr., of Oregon, and Norris Brown of Nebraska, were opposed to the measure and would join the Democrats in a negative vote, but they were not ready to pledge themselves to make a bitter fight against Aldrich and the other Senate leaders of their own party.

Bob felt sure, however, that with the help of three or four Democratic Senators he could prolong debate until the worst features of the bill would call forth such a protest from independent bankers and businessmen that Congress would be forced either to defeat or radically amend it.

When the conference report came up on Friday morning, May 29, Bob had the promise of two Democratic Senators, Stone and Thomas P. Gore, of Oklahoma, to aid him in the filibuster. One or the other was to take the floor when Bob concluded his first speech. Then, after a rest, he expected to continue until Stone or Gore was ready to take the floor again. As the debate was thus prolonged, Bob believed many Senators would hear from their constituents and that a number of them would then decide to aid the filibuster. It was a time-honored rule of Senate procedure that when a Senator suggested the absence of a quorum it was mandatory upon the Presiding Officer to direct that the roll be called. If it be found that a quorum can not be brought in by the Sergeant at Arms, the Senate can be forced to adjourn until a quorum is secured. This right to demand a roll call and thus maintain a quorum in the Senate during debate becomes especially important when a minority is conducting a filibuster. The calling of the roll gives the Senator who is speaking his only opportunity to take nourishment or leave the Chamber for a few moments without losing his right to the floor.

Soon after the Senate convened, while Culberson was making the opening speech against the bill, Bob twice suggested the absence of a quorum. Each time after the roll was called there was an exodus of Senators from the stifling-hot Chamber to the adjoining cloak-rooms. When Bob called attention for the third time to the fact that a quorum was not present, he was amazed to find Culberson actually playing into the hands of Aldrich by asking not to be interrupted and by refusing to yield the floor for a roll call. Bob at once began the parliamentary battle which was the first round in his famous filibuster by insisting that under the rule any Senator had the right to call attention to the absence of a quorum and that it was then mandatory to call the roll. The tactics of Aldrich and his supporters in dealing with this issue foreshadowed the dictatorial violation of rules and precedent which was to break all previous Senate records before the night was over.

Culberson finished his brief speech shortly after twelve. Bob immediately secured recognition from the Vice President and at once called attention to the fact that a quorum was not present. Senators came back on the floor to answer to their names. After the roll call was finished, Bob began his record-making speech at 12:20. I had gone home to Wisconsin a few days before to get things at the farm in shape for the summer. But Fola, Nellie Dunn, and Laura Thompson were in the Senators' family gallery throughout. By insisting on the presence of a quorum, Bob held the floor continuously for 18 hours and 43 minutes. There were 32 roll calls which took from 6 to 7 minutes each. During these intervals he could relax and occasionally take a glass of milk with raw eggs beaten into it. The fight Bob was making against the powerful Old Guard touched the sympathies of the Senate Reading Clerk, John C. Crockett, and although he could read the roll in four and a half minutes he "didn't hurry that night during Senator La Follette's speech."[14]

During the early afternoon a score of Democratic Senators followed Bob's argument closely. But after each roll call most of the Republicans retired to the cloak room. The Capitol was not air-conditioned at this time. The temperature was above ninety, and the atmosphere of the Senate Chamber was stifling. At every opportunity Senators escaped to the balconies. It soon became evident that there would be difficulty in maintaining a quorum. It was equally clear that whenever the necessary forty-seven Senators were not on the floor Bob, or Gore and Stone who were aiding him, would call attention to the absence of a quorum, and the roll would have to be called. Aldrich and a few Republicans remained. Frequently two or three would confer on the Senate floor. When this happened Bob would suddenly pause in his speech, and their conversation would be distinctly audible. He would then ask for order in the Chamber, and laughter would ripple through the crowded galleries.[15] The railroad-bond feature was the chief subject of his attack upon the conference report. Relentlessly he plied Aldrich with searching questions about railroad bonds and stocks being used as securities for the issuance of emergency currency.

Several attempts were made during Bob's speech to deprive him of the floor. Aldrich proposed to keep the Senate in continuous session until the conference report was adopted, which meant that the legislative day was of indeterminate length. A Senate rule provides that no Senator shall speak more than twice upon any one question in debate on the same legislative day. It was not the practice to enforce this rule. But a friendly colleague warned Bob that he must be on guard, for it was proposed to get him to yield to an interruption and then have the Presiding Officer recognize the interrupting Senator as having the floor in his own right. Bob would thus be obliged to secure recognition again from the Chair, which would be counted a second recognition; if after that he yielded the floor, he would not be allowed under the strict interpretation of the rule to get it again.

Early in the afternoon Senator Hale initiated what was apparently the first step in a plan to make it appear Bob had yielded the floor and thus prevent him from making a second speech on the bill later. Just before this, Gore had presented a Memorial from the national committee of the American Anti-Trust League and asked unanimous consent that it be printed in the *Record*. Aldrich objected. Bob and Robert L. Owen, the senior Senator from Oklahoma, both promptly offered to read it into the *Record* for Gore, who was blind and could not do so himself. After a brief colloquy Bob said, "I will yield to the colleague of the Senator from Oklahoma that he may read it." When Owen finished, Hale addressed the Chair. What actually happened can not be found today in the *Congressional Record*. But it was recorded in a page of the transcript of the official Senate stenographer's report of the proceedings which Bob secured. He had this page photographed and returned the original. The transcript of the official stenographer's report read as follows:

Mr. Hale. Mr. President—

The Vice-President. Does the Senator from Wisconsin yield to the Senator from Maine?

Mr. La Follette. I yield to the Senator from Maine.

Mr. Hale. I do not ask the Senator to yield. The Senator yielded the floor; and I secured the recognition of the Vice-President. I only wish to say—

On the original transcript, lines had been drawn through the Vice President's actual words: "Does the Senator from Wisconsin yield to the Senator from Maine?" Above these words which had been crossed out someone had written in longhand a revision which read: "The Senator from Maine."[16] Thus it was made to appear in the printed *Congressional Record* that Hale had secured the floor in his own right.[17] The Vice President's words as actually spoken from the chair had definitely shown that La Follette still held the floor in his own right. Whether the Senate would have approved using this falsified *Record* as the basis for excluding Bob from the floor was never put to the test. The filibuster ended suddenly for a different reason. But it indicates the lengths to which some Senators were willing to go that night in violating time-honored Senate procedure and rules. In fact the *New York Times* noted that "the rulings from the chair were like nothing that ever was heard in the Senate before. Vice President Fairbanks could find anything in the rules that was needed to satisfy one of the Aldrich group."[18]

A few moments after Hale's move to prepare the way for a new interpretation of the Senate rule, another attempt was made to deprive Bob of the floor and contribute to the same end. When Bob remarked that he had to resort to "cross examination" of the Senator from Rhode Island, "for he will not answer frankly," and added that he was compelled to "go over the *Record* to get his position upon this bill,"[19] Foraker promptly invoked rule XIX. This provides that any Senator who imputes to another Senator unworthy conduct or motives may be called to order, made to sit down, and not allowed to proceed until a motion to that effect has passed the Senate. Bob, in compliance with the rule, took his seat. There was great excitement on the floor and in the galleries, for it was evident that the Republicans controlled enough votes "to squelch the little man from Wisconsin then and there."[20] Angry as they were, however, proceedings had not yet reached a stage where they were willing to override the Senate tradition of the right to free speech and the right to debate without limitation. When Gore moved "that the Senator from Wisconsin be allowed to proceed," the motion passed 46 to 1. Foraker cast the negative vote.[21]

The battle over Senate rules and procedure continued throughout the filibuster. It is customary for a Senator, while making a speech, to have the assistance of his clerk. But when it was observed that Bob's clerk was keeping track of whether a quorum was present, he was excluded from the floor at the request of Senator Gallinger of New Hampshire, who invoked rule XXXIII and was sustained in his interpretation by the Vice President.[22] Thus in every parliamentary skirmish Aldrich and his followers had the advantage. The Vice President and the Senators called to the Chair to relieve him from time to time were all supporters of the Senator from Rhode Island, and rendered decisions accordingly. Whenever Fairbanks hesitated momentarily in making a ruling, Aldrich or some member of the powerful inner circle obligingly prompted him.[23]

At 7:05 in the evening Stone suggested the absence of a quorum. The roll was then called for the twenty-third time, and only forty-four Senators answered to their names. The Vice President declared a quorum was not present, and the Senate promptly agreed to Aldrich's motion that the Sergeant at Arms be directed to request the attendance of absent Senators. Immediately thereafter Senators Burrows, Hemenway, and Heyburn entered the Chamber, responded to their names, and the Presiding Officer declared a quorum was present.

Throughout the afternoon and all night the Senate Chamber was a steaming caldron. After each roll call many Senators escaped to the cloakrooms. But Aldrich, although seventy years of age, remained on the floor and took no naps during the filibuster. He was on the alert every moment, conferring with Senators, prompting the Presiding Officer, checkmating motions made by filibusters or pacing about the aisles, "scanning the situation like an eagle."[24] His tall, erect, square-shouldered body, clear-cut features, ruddy complexion, keen eyes, and white hair made him a dynamic and dominating figure as he moved about the Senate. Although many Senators left their seats vacant except when forced back by roll calls, every available space about the walls of the Senate floor was occupied by Representatives, clerks, and Congressional employees who came to watch the unprecedented battle against the powerful Senate leader and his able lieutenants in the Old Guard. The striking figure of Speaker Cannon was seen moving about on the floor. He talked earnestly with various Senators of both parties, and it was rumored that the potent persuasion of different items in the appropriations bill was being used to keep wavering Senators in line.

As the evening session went on, the galleries became packed to suffocation. Outside the entrances long lines of people stood in the hot corridors waiting for a chance to get in. In Washington and many other cities throughout the country, afternoon papers had carried front-page stories of the filibuster Bob was conducting. It was reported that Stone and Gore would join him and that Bryan had telegraphed to a close Washington friend to carry word to Democratic Senators that he hoped they would make the strongest possible fight against the Aldrich-Vreeland bill.[25] During the evening, as Bob had expected, Western Senators began to be bombarded with telegrams asking why La Follette should be compelled to make this fight alone.[26]

Bob was confident these telegrams would bring new recruits to the filibuster if it could be kept up for another twenty-four hours. During the evening he had received intimations to this effect. When he stepped out into the lobby for a moment during the thirtieth roll call, a reporter recorded that he announced "there would be plenty of support for the filibuster," although he "declined to name any of the Senators who would help him."[27] There were also evidences that Aldrich and his group were becoming anxious lest Senators might yield to the bombardment of their constituents. Many newspapers reported that Senators were being warned by

Aldrich and the Old Guard that heavy penalties would be inflicted if they aided the filibuster; appropriations for public buildings in their states might not pass; cloture and reduction of Southern Democratic representation in Congress might be put through. "Proselyting went on in the Senate all night, many Democrats being taken into the Republican cloak room where the situation was made perfectly plain. Senator Aldrich did not hesitate to go over to the Democratic side of the chamber, engage in conversation and then lead a Senator into the midst of the Republicans."[28]

From time to time during the afternoon and evening Bob sent out messages to Fola, who was in the gallery, that he was "feeling tip top."[29] Until late in the evening his strength was holding out far better than he had anticipated. At about 11:30, however, a discerning reporter noted that "it was apparent he was under a great strain. His words did not come anywhere near as easily as they had in the afternoon, and he embraced every opportunity for a slight delay."[30] Some time between ten and eleven o'clock, during the interval of a roll call, Bob had taken a large swallow from a glass of eggs and milk which had been brought to him on the floor. As it went down, he detected a vile, bitter taste. He handed the remaining three-fourths of liquid back to his clerk and said in a voice distinctly audible on that side of the floor, "Take it away," it's "drugged." Soon after that he had been stricken with a severe and painful dysentery unlike anything he had ever experienced before. Subsequently a chemical analysis of the remaining contents of the glass disclosed that it had contained enough ptomaine to have killed him had he taken all of it. At first the pain was so acute and he was in such distress that Bob thought "the jig was up" so far as continuing his speech was concerned. But by forcing several roll calls between 11:30 and 1:30 he managed to leave the floor for a few minutes and get back to his desk in time to resume speaking before each roll call was finished.[31]

At 11:45, during the thirty-first roll call, when it was disclosed a quorum was not present, and later, during the thirty-second roll call, Bob had a few moments' respite. But when he again called attention to the fact that a quorum was not present, Aldrich protested that another roll call was not in order because no business had intervened since the previous one. Bob protested that debate had intervened. But Aldrich maintained, contrary to prevailing

Senate procedure, that debate was not business. The Vice President put the question to the Senate. Bob demanded the yeas and nays and warned Senators "that every precedent you establish to-night will be brought home to you hereafter." There was heated debate over Aldrich's effort to revolutionize long-established Senate procedure in order to win a quick victory over a fighting minority. Aldrich read a few lines from the *Congressional Record* of March 3, 1897, which he alleged was a precedent "exactly on all fours with the present situation."[32]* Many Senators, actually in their seats, abstained from voting because they were unwilling to establish what they believed to be a dangerous precedent. The roll call disclosed that a quorum had not voted. The names of Senators not voting were then called, and two Senators who had previously refrained from voting now voted "nay." But the count was still one vote short of the necessary quorum. As the Vice President started to announce the vote, Aldrich quickly interrupted him to call attention to the fact that Culberson was present and had not voted. Thus prompted, the Vice President did his master's bidding and stated a quorum was present, "the roll call having disclosed that fact."[33] Another time-honored Senate precedent had been violated. But under the Aldrich domination Democratic Senators sat silent.

After the Vice President's decision on what came to be known as the "gag" rule, many Senators concluded there was no danger of further roll calls and went home to sleep. Others slipped off coats and collars, made themselves as comfortable as they could, and took naps on the couches and floors of the cloak rooms. Bob continued his speech for a couple of hours, biding his time until 2:25 Saturday morning, when only a few of the faithful Old Guard were on the floor. Then, after an obvious appraisal of the many vacant seats, he remarked with a polite and pointed emphasis: "Mr. President, I now suggest the absence of a quorum."[34] The Vice President declared this suggestion was not in order. During a parliamentary skirmish two divisions, forced by Bob, and a roll call, subsequently demanded by Aldrich, all disclosed that there was not a quorum.

Bob had a good rest which he thoroughly enjoyed while he watched the discomfiture of the Old Guard until 3:40, when the Sergeant at Arms finally routed enough Senators out of bed and

---

* After the filibuster ended, Aldrich's statement was refuted on the Senate floor.

brought them in to make a quorum. So hastily had they been summoned from their homes, hotels, and the Senate cloakrooms that a number of usually fastidious Senators entered the Chamber with shoes unlaced, suspenders showing, collars and neckties missing. Several sudden and undignified retreats were made into the cloakrooms as Senators discovered their plights before actually taking their seats. After the quorum was finally obtained, and the vote announced which in effect sustained the "gag" rule by 35 to 13, Bob continued speaking without interruption until 7:00 A.M., when he concluded his record-breaking speech by saying: "Mr. President, I am rather reluctant to surrender the floor for the time being, but as others desire to speak and are in waiting, I yield the floor for the present."[35]

As Bob yielded the floor, Stone and Aldrich were both on their feet addressing the Chair. The Vice President recognized Aldrich, who moved that the conference report be taken by yeas and nays, refusing to yield to Stone until the Chair had declared there was a second to his motion. Aldrich had thus astutely gained a parliamentary advantage whereby, at the proper time, the Senate rule could be invoked which provides that after a roll call has started debate is not in order. The bill had been moved forward into a position where he and the Vice President could later cooperate in shutting off debate and jamming the bill through. The Vice President could put the question to the Senate, direct the Secretary to call the roll, and Aldrich could quickly answer to his name, which was first on the list.

After this adroit maneuver Aldrich politely yielded the floor to Stone. Bob had waited beside his desk until he was certain Stone had secured the floor in his own right. Then, gathering up his papers, he went out into the Marble Room, where reporters who talked with him were surprised to find that he did not appear at all fatigued. He told them he could have spoken for hours longer, and that after four hours' rest at home he would return to the Capitol ready at any time to go on with his remarks on the currency bill.

Stone held the floor continuously until 1:30, when Aldrich moved a thirty-minute recess be taken "that Senators may have an opportunity to get luncheon."[36] But a keen reporter observed that "that was not the reason. He wanted to give Democratic leaders, upon whom he exercises almost as much influence as upon his own men, an opportunity to go after Stone."[37]

Later developments indicate that something happened during those thirty minutes. At the end of the recess Stone returned and continued to hold the floor for fifteen minutes more, then yielded to Gore. It had been agreed that Stone was to take the floor again when Gore finished. Bob was to follow Stone. Gore, who was totally blind, made what several reporters described as the best speech of the entire filibuster and "astonished his colleagues by his remarkable grasp of facts and the statistical information he had memorized." He spoke a little over the two hours he had promised and finished at about four thirty. "A few minutes previously Stone had walked over and whispered in his ear, leaving the chamber almost immediately."[38] When Gore ceased speaking, he turned his sightless eyes toward Stone's vacant seat, supposing "that in accord with their previous understanding Stone was on the Senate floor ready to carry on the filibuster." He was "surprised and chagrined when he found Stone was not there."[39]

The astutely planned cooperation between Aldrich and the Vice President brought the filibuster to a sudden end[40] in a way that Bob had not anticipated. There was an instant's pause when Gore finished, and then Heyburn of Idaho, who occupied a seat in the front row near the rostrum of the Presiding Officer, jumped to his feet, shouting for recognition. The Vice President completely ignored him and stated in a matter-of-fact tone, "The question is on agreeing to the report of the committee of conference." Aldrich, profiting by the position he had cleverly maneuvered the bill into when Bob yielded the floor that morning, quickly demanded that the roll be called. Throughout this, Heyburn, his face flushed with anger, was clamoring for recognition. The *Record* plainly shows that he had addressed the chair before the roll call had actually begun and was therefore entitled to be heard. But the clerk, as previously instructed, immediately started to call the roll, and Aldrich instantly answered to his name, which was first on the list. In spite of Heyburn's indignant protests, which rose above the clerk's voice, Aldrich contended that the roll call had begun and could not, according to the Senate rule, be interrupted. The Vice President wavered for a moment, then, after being prompted by

Gallinger and Aldrich, he sustained Aldrich and the roll call proceeded.[41]

Bob had returned to the Capitol in the early afternoon. He was working in his committee room preparing material for another speech which he thought might break the record of the previous day. When he was notified that Gore had finished and that Stone was not on the floor, he rushed to the Senate only to find that the Chamber was in an uproar, and that the magic roll call, which automatically shuts off debate, had actually begun. The excitement was intense everywhere. Senators were rushing to and fro on the floor and crowding in from the cloakrooms. Among them was Stone, who entered in time to vote against the bill.

Although the odds were all against him, Bob fought to the last possible moment, making every parliamentary move to reopen debate. After voting against the bill when his name was called, he addressed the Chair to ask if he could make a parliamentary inquiry. At first the Vice President refused to take notice. But as Bob's repeated shouts of "Mr. President" rang out clearly above the din in the Senate, his voice could no longer be ignored, and the Vice President ruled that a parliamentary inquiry was out of order. In resounding tones which reverberated to the last seat in the galleries, Bob responded, "Then I will take my chances on it, and ask leave to change my vote from 'nay' to 'yea' for the purpose of moving reconsideration." As the clerk went on calling the roll, Aldrich left his own seat in the rear of the Chamber and moved down the center aisle directly in front of the Vice President's rostrum. Bob was in his own seat in the second row from the front on the Democratic side. A Senate rule provides that a Senator must be in his place when asking for recognition. As the roll call finished, showing a vote of 43 to 22 for the conference report, Aldrich and Bob simultaneously addressed the Chair. For different reasons each was trying to use the same parliamentary device of making a motion to reconsider the vote. Bob hoped to use it to reopen the debate, Aldrich to end it definitely. Aldrich won recognition from the Vice President and made the motion to reconsider. Bob, still standing beside his seat, shouted for recognition. Aldrich refused to yield. Hale immediately moved to lay the motion to reconsider on the table. If carried this would end all debate and clinch the passage of the conference report. Bob went on repeatedly demanding the right to be heard on a point of order, indignantly reminding the Vice President and Aldrich, who sought to squelch him, that the Senate rule did not require any Senator should yield the floor for another Senator to raise a point of order. Bob then submitted that under the rule he was entitled to recognition because Aldrich, not having been in his place when he addressed the Chair, was out of order. Although this was obviously the fact, the Vice President ruled Aldrich was in order and had the floor. Bob instantly appealed from the ruling, demanding a roll-call vote. The Senate voted down his appeal 53 to 9, but as he took his seat "the galleries broke into long and continued applause." The Senate refused to reconsider the vote on the conference report, and "one of the most desperate blockades ever seen in the senate chamber came to an end."[42]

The day after the bill was passed, a reporter observed, "There are several Senators who helped to break down his filibuster who will not be happy later in the Summer when La Follette is setting forth their part in it before Chautauqua audiences of their constituents."[43]

Although the filibuster had failed in its immediate purpose, Bob felt the effort had not been in vain. The debate had exposed the character of the currency bill and had called national attention to the methods by which special privilege put through legislation. The applause in the galleries had reflected a popular revolt which the Old Guard would hear later in the roll call.

CHAPTER XXII

"They No Longer Scoff at La Follette in the Big White Building on Capitol Hill"

An article by Lincoln Steffens, reporting recent interviews with Roosevelt, Taft, and Bob, had been published in *Everybody's Magazine* in the latter part of May. It was entitled, "Roosevelt—Taft—La Follette on What The Matter Is In America and What To Do About It."[1] While the currency-bill filibuster was still on, Steffens had written to Bob that among the letters he had received "about the Presidential article, many of the writers express gratification that I 'appreciate' you and your 'lonely fight' in the Senate. You are deeper rooted in the heart of this nation than you think. Health is all I need wish you, you have all else that *we* require of you."[2]

Ten days after Bob arrived home from Washington, the 1908 Republican National Convention met at Chicago. With Roosevelt and the Administration machinery back of Taft, there was little chance of Bob's getting any delegates outside Wisconsin. My heart was set, however, on a solid delegation from our own State, and I was unduly distressed when the Stalwarts elected one of the twenty-six Wisconsin delegates. But Bob accepted the verdict as an incident of politics over which it was useless to worry.

The real object of Bob's candidacy was to bring a progressive platform before the country by presenting it to the convention in the form of a minority report. As the Wisconsin member of the Resolutions Committee, Congressman Henry Allen Cooper, an able and distinguished man who commanded the attention of any assembly, was to present this report. In order to confer with Cooper and

257

others in framing the platform, Bob went to Chicago and stayed in seclusion at the Wisconsin headquarters throughout the convention. Although some reporters "suspected" he was in the city, it was not generally known. Steffens, who was interpreting the convention in a series of syndicated articles, reported that the "machine" ruled the Republicans and that the operations of this convention were the same as in 1896, when Mark Hanna ran affairs. But in 1908 a different man dominated the convention; the old Republican war horses kicked at Roosevelt's rule but they obeyed, and therefore Taft would be nominated. Steffens was probably as unaware as Bob that the week before the convention Roosevelt had written to Lodge, urging "a thorogoing platform as free from the Hale type of reactionary policy as from the La Follette type of fool radicalism."[3]

With banners flying, the Wisconsin delegation and friends marched from the La Follette headquarters at the Grand Pacific Hotel to the opening session of the convention on June 16. Two days later their platform, embodying La Follette's "type of fool radicalism," was presented to the convention by Congressman Cooper. This minority report, which had secured only his vote in the Resolutions Committee, declared for the physical valuation of the railroads as the basis of rate making; election of United States Senators by direct popular vote; publicity of campaign expenses; establishment of a Tariff Commission and tariff revision on the basis of difference in cost of production at home and abroad; effective control and restraint of trusts and monopolies; exemption of labor organizations from prosecution under anti-trust laws, prohibition of the issuance of injunctions in labor disputes. The report was overwhelmingly rejected. Senator Hopkins of Illinois probably voiced the sentiment of the majority of the standpat delegates when he branded the La Follette doctrine as "socialistic."

That same day Henry F. Cochems placed Bob in nomination. Brief seconding speeches were made by Herman Ekern and Charles A. A. McGee. Cochems, who was then thirty-three years old, had already attained wide distinction as an orator, and his speech at Chicago won him national reputation. He was a man of remarkable endowment, brilliant intellect, a student of politics and economics. Over six feet tall, he was handsome and dynamic. As a speaker he had that magnetic power which instantly commands and holds the attention of even a hostile audience.

Cochems' speech and the brief seconding speeches were followed by a spontaneous general demonstration lasting twenty-five minutes,[4] which was extraordinary considering the way the delegates lined up when it came to voting for candidates. While the excitement was at its height, Bob Jr., "who was sitting in the section reserved for the alternate delegates, was picked up and carried on the shoulders of a Wisconsin man to the place where the Wisconsin standard was erected."[5]

As the applause and cheering continued, many recalled that only four years earlier the Republican National Committee had refused to seat the La Follette delegates. Beveridge, who was present, wrote Bob about the remarkable speeches made by young Cochems and McGee which "aroused the only real enthusiasm elicited by any speaker."[6] Walter Wellman reported that "The one dramatic and significant episode . . . of the whole convention, was the splendid and plucky though futile endeavor of radical Wisconsin to point the way to future reforms farther advanced than any yet proposed by Roosevelt."[7] The Wisconsin fight bore fruit not in the choice of candidates but in somewhat influencing the platform which was finally adopted.[8]

Following Taft's nomination, conservative and reactionary Republicans collaborated under the skillful leadership of Speaker Cannon in forcing the selection of James S. Sherman as the candidate for Vice President. Bob promptly telegraphed to Taft: "While the platform is disappointing in some fundamental provisions and omissions, and I shall claim the right to say so, I congratulate you most sincerely, and in the faith that you are more nearly in accord with the great body of Republican voters than the platform I shall do all in my power to insure your election."[9] It was reported that no news had pleased Republican leaders so much that day as "word that La Follette could be depended upon to take the stump in the West for Taft."[10]

In Wisconsin a difficult political situation had developed. Stephenson had gradually allied himself with the conservative Republicans in the Senate. During the fight on the Aldrich currency bill he had voted steadily with the Old Guard. Ignoring his previous pledge not to seek reelection, he announced his candidacy for the long term in the Senate soon after the Republican National Convention. He could count on the support of many Stalwarts. Unfortunately, there were two progressive candidates for the nomination, both men of ability and high standing. State Senator W. H. Hatton had formally announced his candidacy for the long term in December, 1907. In March, 1909, Francis E. McGovern, afterward governor, also came out as a candidate for the Senate.

Throughout the Wisconsin campaign the Progressives severely criticized Stephenson's support of the Aldrich currency bill, but the *Milwaukee Free Press* defended him on the ground that he "was in accord with the views of President Roosevelt and of men engaged in legitimate business everywhere."[11] During August, Bob was lecturing at Midwestern Chautauquas, telling the story of the filibuster. As he read the Senators' votes at different places in Nebraska, men called out, "What's the matter with Burkett?" Apparently Burkett became alarmed, for he wrote to Roosevelt. The President responded with a letter heartily approving the Aldrich bill and stating that "not a single argument worth heeding was advanced against it."[12] The week before the Wisconsin primary, many newspapers carried advertisements appealing for Stephenson's nomination and quoting Roosevelt's letter to Burkett praising the Aldrich currency bill.[13]

The Progressives tried to reach the people through pamphlets and letters, and McGovern made an active speaking campaign. But the sudden camouflaged shift of the *Milwaukee Free Press* and the division of progressive leaders between Hatton and McGovern beclouded the issues and left the voters confused. Stephenson won the preferential primary by a plurality of some 8,000 votes, which assured his reelection by the legislature. When the Wisconsin Republican Platform Convention met, a minority report endorsing legislative policies advocated by Bob was voted down. E. A. Edmonds, Stephenson's campaign manager, was made chairman of the State Central Committee. The anti-La Follette forces were in control.

Our disappointment in the results of the Wisconsin primary was in part offset by the prospect of increased progressive support in the United States Senate. It seemed certain that Governor Cummins of Iowa would be elected to succeed Senator Allison, who had died during the summer. Governor Coe I. Crawford of South Dakota, described as a strong "La Follette man," had won the nomination to the Senate from his State as a progressive Republican. In the Kansas primary Joseph L. Bristow had been nominated for the Senate and W. R. Stubbs for governor. The day after the primary, William Allen White telegraphed to Bob, "Bristow and Stubbs overwhelmingly nominated, you helped wonderfully."[14] An article in the *National Tribune*, a weekly newspaper published in Washington, D.C., echoed the note struck by many newspapers in commenting on these progressive victories: "Men who shape Federal legislation are taking earnest note of Senator La Follette's Summer activities. He has been campaigning in Kansas of late, and has another Republican Senatorial scalp to his credit. For Senator Long's defeat in the primaries for re-election and the designation of Joseph L. Bristow, the man who unearthed the Post Office frauds, is chiefly the work of the indefatigable Wisconsin progressive.

"Two years ago he invaded New Jersey, a Republican stronghold of the 'effete East,' where his ideas are supposed to have obtained but little lodgment. And yet the defeat of Senator John F. Dryden of Newark, for re-election this year is ascribed largely to the Wisconsin Senator's denunciation of him. La Follette has been in a dozen States, calling Senators to book for their legislative deeds—all Senators of his own party. . . . Old-Timers at the Capitol say the like of La Follette's crusade against his colleagues has never before been known in the history of the Senate. . . . The significance of the situation is very great, for Senator La Follette is not far from being able to hold the balance of power. . . . As the Republican majority stands now, 15 Senators of that party, joining with the Democratic minority, could enact legislation. . . . No one can forecast the possibilities of this growing progressive force."[15]

The 1908 Presidential campaign was formally opened in Wisconsin when Taft crossed the state line on September 24 at Beloit, where he was officially met by Governor Davidson and the state officers. Bob had been wired that Taft was coming and was invited to join him. He and B. Cameron, president of the Farmers' National Congress, under whose auspices Taft was to speak, met the distinguished guest at the Madison station and rode in the carriage with him to the university gymnasium. In introducing the candidate, Bob said that from long acquaintance he knew Judge Taft to be "progressive in principle" and "wonderfully equipped in experience."[16]

Taft responded cordially. Bob's public endorsement of Taft, and the fact that they were photographed together were widely reported.[17] From Madison, Taft went to Milwaukee, and Bob rode with him on the special train, where they had a private conversation. Revision of the tariff downward was discussed, and "Taft gave assurances of the strongest sort that his administration would be progressive and entirely satisfactory to the Middle West." In Milwaukee that night Taft publicly declared for "a substantial revision downward" and stated his position in terms which were in accord with his private conversation.[18] Although Bob had been disappointed in the platform, his talks with Taft had been satisfactory, and he went through the campaign believing in him.

Bob gave two consecutive weeks to the campaign in Wisconsin, speaking several times a day to large audiences. On October 17, 1908, at Madison, he introduced Senator Borah, who told the audience that in his judgment "Senator La Follette has been the most original force and the greatest spirit of them all in this great progressive movement to right the wrongs and correct the evils of our industrial life."[19] On the afternoon of November 2 Bob spoke at Youngstown, Ohio, where he also had a brief talk with Taft, who was speaking in the same auditorium that evening. Taft carried Wisconsin by a majority of about 81,000. Davidson was elected governor by about 77,000.

Following the elections there were the usual speculations as to the new Administration. Taft and Roosevelt beamed in photographs and cartoons. The future of the President-elect appeared rosy, although many predicted the overthrow of Speaker Cannon and the passing of Aldrichism. An article in the conservative *New York Times* by Charles Willis Thompson indicates the interpretation of the changes in the Senate, which Steffens had described as a "gentleman's club" when Bob first became a member: "A little council of censors virtually controlled it, and of this council Aldrich was the chief. . . . Now Aldrich is to quit, and only Hale will be left. . . . Slowly, silently, the complexion of the United States Senate has been changing. When La Follette came in from Wisconsin, the old augurs, secure in the confidence born of many years of rule, thought to elbow him aside and make him a laughing-stock. The little, square-built, pompadour-haired fighter went after their scalps—got some of them, Long's for instance—and in the very few years that have elapsed since he made his brick-strewed way into the Senate has seen every election record a supporter of the New Idea. They no longer scoff at La Follette in the big white building on Capitol Hill; they are mortally afraid of him, and as respectful of him as of a rattlesnake.

"Seeing these things, reading the 'Mene, Mene' on the wall, John C. Spooner resigned from the Senate, resigned because he saw that there was before him no future. . . . Now Aldrich follows Spooner, and only Hale is left. . . . He and what he stands for are being elbowed aside by the young, pushing, striving advocates of the New Idea. When he goes the last vestige of the Senate of Hoar's day will have gone too."[20]

Before returning to Washington in December, Bob had decided to start a weekly magazine. Ever since he had owned and edited the *University Press*, he had felt the lure of such an enterprise. The change in policy of the *Milwaukee Free Press*, which gradually drifted over to an openly stalwart position, created an impelling need for a progressive organ in Wisconsin. I think, too, he had a vision of his magazine attaining national scope and influence. No worth-while venture looked too large to him. Yet he attempted only what seemed feasible, and once launched on a course, he adhered to it whatever the cost.

I well remember when it was settled that the first issue of *La Follette's* would be published in January, 1909. One day late in the summer of 1908, a group of Bob's friends had been conferring for hours over the project in the library at the farm. As they were leaving, Lincoln Steffens pulled me aside and whispered: "You mustn't let Bob take on this terrible load. It will kill him." I greatly dreaded the added burden and responsibility. But I answered Steffens' admonition with a laugh; he knew Bob well enough not to expect me or anyone else to stop him when his mind was once made up. Bob habitually overtaxed his strength, always keeping in harness until exhaustion or illness compelled him to stop work. And now he was taking upon himself another tremendous task. The financial obligation alone appalled me. For, however much Bob earned, he put so much back into his political work that we were always hard up. We had been able to pay the interest on the farm mortgage but no part of the principal. We lived modestly, but our current expenses were

LaFollette's
WEEKLY MAGAZINE

YE SHALL KNOW THE TRUTH AND THE TRUTH SHALL MAKE YOU FREE

VOL. I, NO. I   MADISON, WISCONSIN.   JANUARY 9, 1909

The Truth

IN
THIS
MAGAZINE

Lincoln Steffens

PRESENTS

A Remarkable Article

"THE MIND OF A STATE"

HE SAYS:

¶ Cities and states are jelly-fish now. They have a life of their own, but no mind. Nothing but instinct guides them. This is the beginning, then, of the brain of the state.

William Allen White

ON

"THE KANSAS FIGHT"

Next Week

always more than we anticipated. Any attempts we made to adopt a "budget" system failed.

Some of Bob's friends who could afford it had offered to give a certain amount to help start the magazine. Among them was Charles R. Crane of Chicago. A number of well-known writers and economists, such as Lincoln Steffens, John R. Commons, William Allen White, William Hard, Carl Vrooman, Professor Edward A. Ross, Frederic C. Howe, Ernest Poole, Charles Zueblin, and others, had promised to contribute articles. Herbert Quick, brilliant, experienced writer and publicist, was to act as associate editor with Bob. Fred MacKenzie, an able young man, resourceful, tireless, and devoted to the cause for its own sake, was chosen managing editor. Caroline Hunt, for four years professor of home economics at the university, was to be co-editor with me of the Home and Education Department.

Yet as I saw it, in spite of the generosity of his friends and competent assistants, Bob would himself be liable for the greater part of the money to support the magazine, and because of his political prominence he would be subject to criticism for every sentiment and every word of its contents. Moreover, I saw great difficulty in combining the duties of editor and statesman. I argued that the editor must comment on public affairs as they transpire regardless of consequences; whereas the man in public life, to speak most effectively, must often wait the right occasion. Bob answered that his life was "an open book" and that he saw no conflict in his duties as editor and Senator.

All at once I realized that, in spite of the long years we had traveled the road together, I had never before quite understood how inherently frank and unafraid he was.

CHAPTER XXIII

Uniting for Action

After looking about, Fola decided that 1864 Wyoming Avenue would suit our purposes as a Washington residence. The four-story English basement house proved to be well adapted to our needs. As one entered the hall on the ground floor, two large connecting rooms served admirably as offices for Bob. On the second floor were the front and back parlor and dining room. Bob, Jr., Phil, Mary, and Nellie Dunn occupied the third floor. Bob and I had the top floor because it was more isolated. I preferred this, as I took my editorship of the "Home and Education" department of *La Follette's Magazine* seriously and felt I must have a quiet place to write.

We rented the house "unfurnished," but when we took possession it was still completely fitted out with old mahogany and Oriental rugs which we were temporarily privileged to use. This was helpful, as it afforded a standard of replacement and gave time to make selections. I well remember the look Bob gave me and his tone of voice when he said one day: "Belle, I want you to furnish this house completely and comfortably and in good taste. You don't need to skimp and economize. I am earning enough now so we can afford to spend what is needed for suitable furniture and belongings. We never yet have had a house that was furnished right. Let's make a good job of this while we are about it."

Strange, I had never before observed that our commonplace furniture jarred on him. The only time I remembered being dissatisfied with it myself was when he was defeated for Congress and I had noted the deterioration and necessity of repairing all our household equipment. Whatever furniture I bought after that had been merely to meet the needs of our growing family and was adapted to the children's freedom from undue restraint in the home. When we moved from the Executive Residence to the farm, the furniture from the West Wilson Street house seemed good enough for the time being. We had quite a large collection of books. Most of these we had accumulated gradually, but, during his illness when governor, Bob had purchased some $800 worth, including the works of Jefferson, Hamilton, Webster, Clay, Lincoln, and other American statesmen, together with some sets of the best English and American writers. In earlier years he had read and longed to own most of the books he bought when he was governor. He intimated to me that if he failed to get well, he wanted to leave the books for the children to read and remember him by. Thus it was that books overran the library at the farm, occupied the living room and other parts of the house. With the beautiful views of the lake and countryside, with the old fireplace either burning or ready to light, the farmhouse was always livable; I was content to get along with whatever furniture we had.

However, I understood Bob's mandate to furnish the Wyoming Avenue residence adequately, and undertook the task with zeal. I haunted the antique shops and attended Sloan's famous auction sales. When the house was finally furnished to his satisfaction, our friends said it gave the impression of our having always lived there.

We had launched on a larger scale of living. The house was admirably adapted to entertaining. We enjoyed the opportunity for liberal hospitality. Throughout our life together, many of our most precious and lasting friendships had their beginnings when Bob invited guests to lunch or dine impromptu at our home. The four years we lived at 1864 Wyoming Avenue were in this respect especially rich and happy. The dinners Bob gave, with a view of bringing Progressives of the Senate and House together, were helpful in creating a closer personal and political understanding within the group. I tried, incidentally, to make my receptions and other social functions contribute to the same end.

A small group of Senators met at Bob's home on Sunday, February 13, 1909, to discuss their strategy in opposing what they thought was a very bad naval appropriation bill. This was, Bob said, the first gathering of the "so-called Progressives in the Senate for concerted action on legislation."[1] On the previous Thursday Senator Hale of Maine, chairman of the Committee on Naval Affairs, had brought in the bill, which carried an appropriation of something over $2,000,000. He asked unanimous consent for immediate con-

sideration, hoping to pass the bill that same day. Bob politely but
firmly objected, insisting Senators ought to have time to study the
measure. It was a bold move to oppose Hale, "the self-appointed
repository of Senate law and Senate tradition."[2] As chairman of the
Republican Caucus, Hale appointed the Committee on Committees
and was thus the powerful representative of the Old Guard forces
in organizing the Senate. Under Senate rules appropriation bills have
the right of way over other legislation. By holding back big appropriations until toward the end of the session, those in control of the
committees killed off measures they didn't want or, by the same
strategy, rushed other appropriations through on the plea of pressure
for time. It was in protest against this autocratic control of all important Senate legislation that Bob began the fight he was to wage
for so many years by challenging the hasty passage of the naval
appropriation bill on Thursday, February 11.

When Bob insisted the bill should be postponed, Hale admitted
that Senators had "not had much time to examine it," but argued
that this was the condition that met the Senate "at the end of
every session of Congress and especially at the end of a short session, which by law dies on the 4th of March."[3] In the lively tilt
which followed, Hale sarcastically remarked, "I have no doubt the
Senator has in mind a very profound scheme for reforming the
usages, the customs, the practice, the habits of Senators, and the way
of dealing with these subjects." To this Bob retorted with an ironically polite inflection, "I have had the hardihood not only to doubt
the divine perfection of the present arrangement, but almost to believe that if the business of considering the legislation of the Senate
could be distributed among its 92 members instead of being taken
in charge by less than one-third of the body it would be an improvement over existing conditions."[4] During this tilt with Hale, Bob had
sent for documents which were stacked up on his desk in case a
speech were needed to prevent passage of the bill that day. Hale,
perhaps recalling Bob's recent filibuster, heeded the warning and
graciously postponed consideration until Monday.

That evening certain naval officials of highest rank telephoned
Bob to say they were gratified that there was to be further discussion of the bill, and they suggested that important changes were
needed if a navy was to be "built up for the ocean, and not the land."
Bob invited them to meet at his home with certain "associates who
would be selected with the greatest care, and who would protect

them absolutely." They spent the entire Sunday on the bill, assisted by a number of naval officers, determining and sharing among them the items that should be opposed the next day.[5]

In the Senate Bob attacked the inefficiency of the location and the maintenance of the Nation's navy yards. He contended it was due to the fact that a few Senators controlled all the important committees and followed the bad practice of appointing to the Naval Committee so many members from States where appropriations were to be expended. The amendments offered by the little band of Progressives were all voted down, but a start had been made toward uniting them for future action. Bob set store on this beginning. He had been designated the "lonely man in the Senate," yet no one knew better than he that the work ahead was too big for any man to tackle alone with hope of success. The time was now opportune, he believed, for effective revolt against the control of Congress by special interests, typified in the Aldrich-Cannon regime. He had faith that Taft was progressive at heart, and hoped for his cooperation on legislation in behalf of the many instead of the few.

To attain national legislation similar to that won in Wisconsin, Bob knew the progressive Senate forces must be organized. His purpose could be accomplished only through teamwork and by encouraging other members of the group to play the more conspicuous part in the drama. As I watched him in his new role, I marveled at his faith, patience, skill, and diplomacy.

Dolliver of Iowa was one of the first to break away from Aldrich and the Old Guard. When the special session was called in March, Allison of Iowa, who had long guided Dolliver, was dead and had been succeeded by Cummins. Dolliver gave up his place on the Committee on Interstate Commerce to make way for Cummins, because Senate usage did not permit two Senators from the same State and party to serve on the same committee. Dolliver reasonably expected that he would be assigned to the vacancy created by Allison's death on the Finance Committee. He was, however, not only disappointed in this, but Cummins came near being kept off the Committee on Interstate Commerce. A few days after the announcement of the committee appointments, Dolliver agreed to confer with Bob. During a long talk Dolliver said he had often had difficulty restraining himself from an outbreak against Aldrich and the system which dominated the Senate. He had loved Senator Allison and had yielded to the older man's plea when he said: "Jonathan, don't do it; don't do it now; wait until I am gone. I know it is wrong. It has grown up here gradually in the last quarter of a century. I have gone along with it. These men are my associates. I have only a little while left, and I haven't the strength to break away. . . . But wait until I am gone, and then go into this new movement where you belong." Before their talk ended, Dolliver said, in a way that convinced Bob he had changed from conviction: "From this time on I am going to be independent. I am going to serve my conscience."[6]

It was natural that Clapp of Minnesota, a wise, practical statesman, should join Dolliver in the revolt. They were not alike but were close personal friends. The brilliant Beveridge was doubtless influenced by Dolliver's stand. He admired Bob also. I remember once, when he was telling me how highly he thought of Bob, he laughingly remarked: "I couldn't do what he has done. I haven't the courage." Borah of Idaho, Brown of Nebraska, and Bourne of Oregon had shown inclination to act independently, and came from States where there was an awakening. Cummins, who succeeded Allison, had already gained a reputation for progressive leadership. Bristow, a stanch and able fighter, had succeeded the reactionary Long in Kansas. Crawford had been elected as a liberal from South Dakota. They constituted a strong group if they could be brought together on an outstanding issue.

The revolt against "Cannonism" in the House was based on the same principle as was the opposition to Aldrich rule in the Senate. The fight against the Cannon regime was to free the House of gag rule, to divest the Speaker of the power he had usurped and exercised to control legislation in the interest of the few and thus defeat the will of the majority in Congress and the Nation. The Wisconsin delegation was the nucleus of the uprising in the House. A "Roll of Honor" published in *La Follette's Magazine* lists the Republican members who voted against Cannonism and for a revision of the rules.[7]

One of the worst blizzards I have ever known in Washington occurred on inauguration day and necessitated holding the ceremonies inside the Senate Chamber instead of on the Capitol steps as was customary. My contemporary comment on his address noted that "I received a new impression of President Taft from hearing it. The world recognized him as an able, honest, and lovable man. But I had never before seen him when he did not wear that smile,

an intelligent and winning smile, but suggestive of almost too phil-
osophic and too easy a temperament for the aggressive work before him. Perhaps the opening sentence recognizing his responsibility
will *read* perfunctory. But there was something in the simple way
he *said* it that made you feel he *meant* it."[8]

In retrospect, Roosevelt's course in leaving the country immediately following Taft's inauguration, to be gone for more than a
year, seems to me even more significant than it did when I commented on it in a contemporary article. In describing the 1909
New Year's reception at the White House, I wrote that President
Roosevelt was much more quiet though no less cordial in his greetings than I had ever known him to be on any other social occasion.
"He has been gaining in repose these last years. . . . Or perhaps,
the years of responsibility have tempered his nature. Perhaps it is
a different Roosevelt who leaves the White House from he who
entered it. We wish he were not going to Africa. America needs
right now the influence of this strong man, matured and disciplined
by his great opportunity and experience."[9]

How much Taft felt his relatively weak hold on the public, and
the need for such support as Roosevelt might have given him, is
disclosed in a steamer letter he wrote to his former chief when the
colonel sailed for Africa.[10] For several years Roosevelt had been
the close friend and political associate of Taft. It was assumed he
had used his influence to elect Taft President because he wanted
as his successor a statesman capable of securing progressive legislation. Bob felt Roosevelt had prepared the way by stirring up public opinion, but had failed to get the necessary laws because he
lacked a definite economic policy and thus compromised on vital
issues. Taft's judicial temperament and legal training presumably
made him better equipped to cooperate with Congress on legislation. Bob therefore hoped more progressive legislation might be
secured during Taft's Administration. With Roosevelt enthusiastically backing a liberal program throughout the country, it is
easy to imagine the stimulus such teamwork would have given the
progressive cause. It would seem that Roosevelt, knowing Taft as
it is fair to assume he did, should have stood by and backed up
the new Administration in putting over the progressive program.
Instead Roosevelt went to Africa to hunt big game, and President
Taft was left alone to wrestle with big governmental problems.

CHAPTER XXIV

No Longer "The Lonely Man in the Senate"

Roosevelt had, as Bob said, skillfully staved off consideration of the tariff and therefore "that thorny problem fell to the unfortunate Mr. Taft."[1] Ever since 1897 the high schedules of the Dingley tariff, which had contributed so heavily to the profits of many great trusts, had caused increasing popular resentment, particularly in the Northwest. During the 1908 Presidential campaign the rising tide of public sentiment had made it plain that the issue must be squarely faced. Taft recognized this and promised to call a special session to consider the tariff, pledging his Administration to substantial revision downward. These promises had been taken at par value by Bob and the other progressive Republicans who had all supported Taft.

The special session convened on March 16. The next day the President's tariff message was read to the Congress he had called to deal with this long-brewing caldron of special interests. Everyone anticipated a great state paper. The Chamber was crowded, everybody alert as the clerk began to read. At the end of two minutes he stopped. "There was a hush," Bob said, "an expectation that he would resume. But he laid aside the paper. A look of amazement was on every face."[2] The only thing emphasized was the importance of disposing of the tariff as quickly as possible to avoid disturbing business. Bob and the Progressives were disappointed, for they had expected Taft's first state paper "would be a vigorous demand for downward revision of the tariff," but there was not a word about it.[3]

Soon after the inauguration, reports had been circulated that

Taft had gone over to the Aldrich-Cannon rule of Congress. Although disappointed in the tariff message and disturbed by these rumors, the Progressives still held to their faith in the President. A month later, when the House passed the Payne tariff bill in spite of progressive opposition, Bob called upon the President. Taft agreed that the House bill did not comply with the Republican campaign pledges. But when Bob urged him to send a special message denouncing it, Taft replied: "I don't much believe in a President's interfering with the legislative department while it is doing its work. They have their responsibility and I have mine. And if they send that bill to me, and it isn't a better bill than it is now, I will veto it." To Bob's suggestion that this course would be difficult if Taft remained silent until the bill reached his desk, the President answered firmly: "You and your associates in the Senate go ahead, criticize the bill, amend it, cut down the duties—go after it hard. I will keep track of your amendments. I will read every word of the speeches you make, and when they lay that bill down before me, unless it complies with the platform, I will veto it." To emphasize the firmness of his purpose, Bob said the President "brought his fist down on the desk with a thump."[4]

The tariff bill was technically before Aldrich's Finance Committee only two days. Public hearings were not held, but representatives of the larger protected interests were admitted to the committee room for brief conferences. The committee *increased* six hundred of the rates set forth in the House bill. There was no written report, no explanation—only a brief statement by Aldrich. Immediate consideration of this three-hundred-page bill, which most of the Senators had never seen, was requested by Aldrich, who obviously expected to over-ride all opposition. Bob protested that previously the Finance Committee had always submitted a printed report defending each change of duty, and that it had been the established custom to give Senators time to study the changes. No answer was made to his protest. Aldrich's motion was carried, and he also secured adoption of an order that the Senate should meet from ten in the morning until eleven at night without recess.

Nevertheless, the Progressives prepared for vigorous opposition. After they got into the tariff fight, Bob said that they soon began "to know who could be depended upon," and held frequent meetings. He names Dolliver, Bristow, Beveridge, Clapp, Bourne, Cummins, and Dixon as "the group which generally worked together."[5] The Senate was in session through practically every working day during the hot summer months. The Aldrich program forced the progressive Senators to carry on after reaching home at midnight, working until well into the morning, snatching a few hours sleep, and returning to the Senate at ten o'clock.

It soon became clear that a bipartisan combination, including enough Democrats to make up a majority, would resist all important reductions in tariff rates. Even then the Progressives refused to surrender. They kept on exposing the iniquitous provisions of the bill, constantly emphasizing the right of the consumer to equal consideration with the manufacturers.

After a few encounters with the progressive Senators, Aldrich gave up trying to answer their searching questions and repeatedly retreated from the floor. "The Senate boss was," Bob said, "thrown into confusion." He had been accustomed to issue orders—not furnish reasons.[6] Intensive study and discussion of the tariff schedules were divided up among the progressive Senators. Dolliver did a prodigious amount of labor, particularly on the cotton schedules. Bristow took on the lead and sugar schedules, and Cummins made special preparation upon the metal, glass, and other important products of general consumption. Beveridge, who sat near Aldrich, was given a conspicuous role in the debate. He kept the tariff schedules and tabulations before him, following every item and constantly calling Aldrich's attention to the figures. "Time after time . . . he laid bare the fallacies" of the Rhode Island Senator's arguments.[7]

Near Bob, in the section known as the "Cherokee Strip," Bristow sat next to Burton, with Elihu Root directly in front of him. This able and fearless new Senator from Kansas, who had taken Long's place, accurately described the progressive Senators' feeling about the prevailing atmosphere on the Senate floor during the tariff debate: "They [Burton and Root] are absolutely subservient to the Aldrich domination. . . . When I rise, or any other man who is not subservient to the gang that runs the Senate, we are greeted with sneers and insulting remarks from the Aldrich coterie. There never was a machine convention in the worst days of machine supremacy in Kansas that was more intolerant than this Senate machine, and I never have seen a convention in either state or county in Kansas where the participants in political controversy were so discourteous and insulting in their attitude."[8] Only as one lived through the conflict was it possible to realize the tense feeling that pervaded the entire session. Dolliver's superb power held the crowds in the galleries spellbound, and created panic in the Aldrich camp. His arraignment of the bill was masterful.

Bob made two notable speeches on several different days covering the cotton and woolen schedules. He stressed the serious import to the consumer of increased duties placed upon one product after another "until it reaches everything that goes upon his table, everything that goes to clothe and warm his family and provide for their comfort."[9] Although his attacks upon the bill were widely reported as having made "a profound impression," it was as a strategist behind the scenes that Bob rendered the most effective service. The *Record* also shows he was watchful and always ready to back up his progressive colleagues. Bristow, who sat near him, wrote to a friend that La Follette "never wavers or flinches from any contest, be it ever so arduous or disagreeable."[10] Throughout the debate Bob lost no opportunity to fix responsibility for increased tariff duties upon Aldrich and his associates. By insisting upon roll calls he placed them on record. Repeatedly he challenged parliamentary procedure and demanded reasons for the increases, which harassed and embarrassed the Old Guard.

In his speech on the wool schedule, he referred to his previous efforts to expose the influence of special interests in Congress. Warren of Wyoming interrupted to ask sneeringly what the net results of his efforts had been. Bob retorted they had been "pretty good" and would be better: "When I came here I stood alone in this Chamber. Now there are nearly a dozen men who stand with me. . . . The lines of those who wittingly or unwittingly serve great interests will be further broken, not only in the Middle West and the Far West, where great progress has been made, but in the East as well."[11] His answer was like flashing a light on a moving picture. It revealed Bob's achievement, "told what he had been working for, interpreted the roll call, and foretold what was to come." I wrote to Fola about the effect of his reply: "I think the most casual observer saw, as plainly as I saw, what it all meant . . . the coming of a new order of things. . . . The galleries were crowded and listened with that intense interest which Papa commands when at his best. He held the Senate too, absorbed in watching and listening because they could not help it. Then he went back to talking schedules again. It was very telling, and the day as a whole unquestionably defined and strengthened his position and advanced the ideas he has been fighting for all these years."[12]

Two days later Bob had a sharp encounter with Aldrich which one observer thought caused the Senate atmosphere to be "more highly charged than at any time in the debate."[13] When Aldrich insinuated that certain Midwestern Senators would have a hard time explaining the inconsistencies of their votes to their constituents, Bob came back with a scathing review of the Rhode Island Senator's whole handling of the tariff revision. Gallinger promptly requested that the Senate rule be invoked, and the Presiding Officer rebuked Bob for his phrase charging Aldrich "with practicing a legislative trick."[14]

The concluding paragraphs of a letter I wrote to Fola on the day after this encounter with Aldrich tell what the cooperation of the progressive Senators which had come to pass during the fight on the tariff bill meant to Bob and me: "I have never known Papa so moved in years and only a few times in our life as he was last night when he came home. He and Dolliver, Clapp and Beveridge had had a heart to heart talk, and [they] had assured him that they were in the movement to stay. I think they must have said some very comforting and appreciative things to him personally, about what he had accomplished and their belief in him. It meant so much to him that he could hardly tell about it. I know he felt that the goal he had long been striving for had been reached,—that he could rest a bit.

"And he was glad, deeply glad of the fellowship, companionship, and understanding. Dolliver is a tremendous power. I do not see how he has stayed bottled up so long. His attitude is the most significant of all. You feel that he means it; that he will go on now that he is awakened and his change must be of great significance to the whole country. He typifies what all personally honest men must do when they really come to see what is the matter in this country, —take off their coats and go to work to make things right."[15]

When the bill passed the Senate a month later, on July 8, ten Republicans, including a few who were not Progressives, voted against it: Beveridge, Bristow, Brown, Burkett, Clapp, Crawford, Cummins, Dolliver, La Follette, and Nelson.[16] The President's failure to assert leadership and demand downward revision of the tariff disappointed the Progressives, but they still hoped he might do something while the bill was in conference between the two houses. A letter from Steffens in May stating he had it "very direct that Taft means (or says he means) to take a hand in that tariff bill by & by, & on the right side, too" seemed to indicate the same intention the President had expressed to Bob in April.[17] On June 11, just two days after Bob's speech attacking the bill, Beveridge had called on the President and had written his wife: "One o'clock. Just home. Saw Taft—he is with us."[18]

Bob received a similar impression when he called at the White House on July 12. The President himself brought up the tariff question by asking, "What am I to do with this bill?" Bob answered: "Mr. President, you ought to veto it. You remember you said you would unless it was a better bill than when it passed the House. Instead of being a better bill, it is much worse. Hundreds of increases have been made in the Senate." "Well," said the President, "suppose I find that I can't do that. What changes ought I to insist upon in conference?" As Bob outlined the duties which should be reduced, the President made notations. Finally Taft asked Bob to write a letter stating succinctly the things he thought ought to be done.[19] A reporter noted that "Senator La Follette, the hottest fighter for low schedules," had "a broad smile on his face when he left the President and seemed well pleased with what he had said and heard."[20] Although Bob had planned to start for home that day, he stayed on in Washington to prepare a statement of fifteen typewritten pages which he sent to the White House on the following day, July 13, 1909.[21] He urged the President in the interest of the consumer to insist on tariff reductions in many specific schedules below the lowest rates adopted by either House, and submitted precedents to show this would not violate parliamentary usage. The President's only reply was a brief note thanking Bob for his letter.

By the time Bob returned from Wisconsin on July 23, reports indicated the Aldrich forces had won and the Progressives could not support the bill as it would be reported from conferences. After a brief Senate session, Bob attended a meeting with Beveridge, Bristow, Clapp, Cummins, and Dolliver. Each agreed to speak briefly on the bill. That night Bob wrote me he would "do the thing that conscience dictates—being very careful to confine *my attack to the bill*—nothing on the *President* unless it be to commend *if I can* his *effort.*"22

Every device of party pressure was used to force progressive Senators and Congressmen to vote for the conference report. It was threatened that patronage would be withheld, and many post-office appointments had actually been delayed. Preceding the final vote, an effort was made to break insurgent lines by inviting progressive Senators to the White House. Among these were Dolliver, Cummins, and Beveridge. The newspapers speculated openly on the possible effect of this sudden hospitality. One day Dolliver said to Bob, "I was invited up to the White House to a tariff breakfast." And then, with a twinkle in his eye, he added, "the muskmelon he served was not very good." Bob knew Dolliver had not changed. Neither Bristow, Clapp, nor La Follette was asked to sample the White House melons. They were regarded "as hopelessly lost to the administration."23

On the day of the final vote, the situation was tense. Party loyalty was still a fetish in Congress. "The air of the Senate Chamber and cloak-rooms was charged with partisan feeling. It fairly crackled," Bob said.24 Some of the "near" Progressives capitulated, and when the Payne-Aldrich bill finally passed on August 5, only seven Republicans voted against it: Beveridge, Bristow, Clapp, Cummins, Dolliver, La Follette; the seventh was Knute Nelson of Minnesota, who was not a member of the progressive group.

Bob had intended to speak against the bill before the final vote. As a precaution against being excluded, he caused his name to be placed on the list by the Presiding Officer on August 4, and carefully took a copy of that list. The next day he found it had been altered so that his name was further down the list. This strategy was attributed to Aldrich. Various other Senators cooperated with time-consuming, irrelevant speeches and prevented Bob's name being reached before the hour agreed upon for a vote on August 5. Perhaps some Senators saw a vision of Chautauqua tents and thought of the deadly roll call when Bob rose just before the vote to denounce the alteration of the speakers' list. In an ironically suave tone he said he could forego speaking in the Senate with less disappointment, as "I shall have occasion many times to state my views with respect to this tariff legislation between now and the convening of Congress in December next."25

CHAPTER XXV

From the Capitol to the
Pacific Coast

On the day after Congress adjourned, Bob called on the President to say goodbye as was his custom at the end of a session. Dolliver, who was at the White House for the same purpose, joked with Bob about being shut off from delivering his "farewell roast of the bill," saying, "I hope you will have a chance to get rid of that speech before next fall." Bob replied, "Oh, I will, never fear, and soon, too."[1] A week later he began his long summer lecture tour at two Chautauquas in Dolliver's home State.

Without any vacation after the trying summer in Washington, Bob went on into Nebraska, Kansas, and Missouri, speaking day after day to large crowds beneath tent tops under a scorching sun which was pushing the temperature up toward a hundred. From Missouri he wrote: "This hot weather made me do some thinking I tell you. My feet not only blistered but boiled to a turn. So I invested 2½ dollars in some white canvas shoes & I never knew comfort before. They are so cool that my stockings are not even wet when I come off the platform. Then to top off the picture I bou[gh]t two pair of elegant duck, *white duck* pants at a *dollar* a pair and you bet I am the swellest looking fellow that ever came down the pike—white collar, white tie, white shirt, white pants, white shoes. I peel off my black alpaca coat immediately after I make my bow and there I stand as fine a figure as you would see in any restaurant or barber shop in the land."[2]

In another letter he confessed that poor food, alkali water, and hard travel had made him so ill for several days that it "took the last of my strength which the scalding weather had left me."[3] After one of his short visits home, I wrote to him: "I hardly know why the time seems so precious that we spend together and so vacant when separated. I realize the great value of your work and would not keep you at home but I have always the sense of waiting for your coming."[4] He replied to a letter telling him of the children's schoolwork which was made difficult by the change of residence twice a year: "The work in school is preparation for the battle of life boys. Day by day you are forging the armour for the great fight . . . so that like Sir Nigel you will always be ready when any great deed is to be done. [He had recently read *Sir Nigel* aloud to the children much to their delight and his own.] So sweat and tug, no matter how hard it is, just remember you are at work on the armour and weapons with which to wage a great fight against the wrongs which oppress and the evils and ills which afflict the world in which you live. I expect little Mary will have to be locked out of the lesson shop or she will be working on her armour and sword and shield all the while. She will be like her mamma was as a little girl and a big girl too."[5]

His letters on this lecture trip are, as in all his journeys over the country, full of human interest—reports of his meetings, of old friends he met and new ones he made, interpretations of current events and public sentiment. *La Follette's Magazine,* which had published its first issue on January 9, 1909, was now absorbing a large share of his earnings on the platform, but he wrote confidently of its future and was encouraged by the number of people who came up after his meetings to say how much they liked it. Always he regarded every subscriber to his magazine as a special friend.

In September Bob returned to Wisconsin for a few weeks to join Senators Clapp, Page, and others in an investigation of the Menominee and other Indian reservations where it was thought the provisions of his bill for protecting the Indians' forests were being violated. It happened that Elizabeth Glendower Evans of Boston was in Madison, and we met her for the first time. Since then she has belonged to the inner circle of our closest, most helpful, and inspiring friends. She had recently attended a conference of the Women's Trade Union League in Chicago. I insisted she write it up for *La Follette's Magazine,* and subsequently she contributed many timely articles. Later, when *La Follette's Magazine* was in sore straits financially, she helped most generously to tide over the crisis—too generously, I thought.

It was during this visit in September, 1909, that her lifelong interest in Bob's work began. In a published sketch she recorded her impression of the farm, where she visited us so often in the years to come, and her first meeting with him: "The house was a low brick structure with a wide vine-clad piazza standing a little way back from the lake. Between the house and the lake was a herd of Shetland ponies. Behind the house was a barn with horses and cows, the kitchen garden and big orchards of apple, plum and cherry trees. Across the sweep of the lake rose the great dome of the [state] capitol. . . . I became well acquainted with the children—Bobby, a lad of 15, dark-browed, solid in his figure, serious; Phil, aged 13, volatile like quicksilver; Mary, aged 11, blue-eyed and fairhaired, the only one of the children to resemble her father in features. The eldest daughter, Fola, was away from home. . . .

"The first morning, as I sat on the piazza, the senator came and sat opposite me. . . . His countenance was one to arrest attention in any gathering. But it was the expression of his eyes that compelled me. He looked out below level eyebrows with a directness that I felt I had never seen in other mortal gaze. . . . I was longing to get him to talk on politics. He . . . began abruptly, telling me incident after incident of his 10-year fight. . . . There was a solidarity about the La Follette family beyond that of any other I ever encountered. The children took part in every discussion and expressed their opinions freely. There was never an attempt to impose the opinion of the grown-ups upon them. Always they were treated as persons. The right government of the country was the very life of the household, and they imbibed this feeling as the warp and woof of their being."[6]

The first week in October, Bob started out on another long lecture trip which, except for a few days, kept him away from home until Congress convened in December. While he was still in Wisconsin, Taft had passed through the State on a speaking tour. At Winona, Minnesota, on September 17, the President had made his famous speech which aroused such resentment, especially in the West, because he ineptly claimed the new tariff law was "the best bill that the Republican party ever passed."[7] At the time Bob refused to comment publicly on the speech.. But what he and many other

Progressives thought about it was vividly expressed in a letter he
received later from Dolliver. Bob's secretary "squandered special
delivery postage" in forwarding the letter because "it will encourage
and brace you for the battle." Dolliver wrote: "Poor Taft made a
sad mess of it at Winona. I knew he was good natured but I never
dreamed he was so dull. . . . It is like taking candy from children
for Aldrich to confer with Taft. Is he ignorant of the fact that
Aldrich himself organized the proceedings around the textile schedules, every paragraph drawn by the parties in interest, and made
up the bill by attracting a majority, to vote for the *citadel* in exchange for the privilege of naming the other rates? This is not
legislation. It is rank interchange of reciprocal larcenies. I am glad
we are recorded against it, though I do not underestimate the political
peril of being against the President I am willing to quit and go to
farming rather than submit to such a deal."

The feeling of solidarity among the Progressives at this time
was evident in the closing paragraph of Dolliver's letter where he
expressed concern for his colleagues who would be candidates for
reelection in 1910 and might be the first to feel the weight of the
President's displeasure: "Clapp I think is all right; they can't budge
the old man in Minnesota. I feel sure your marvelous faculty of
doing things in Wisconsin will protect your interests from outside
interference. Nevertheless I want you to feel at liberty to send for
me whenever I can get in a good stroke for you. I feel that my life
has been enriched and strengthened by the new light in which I
have had a glimpse of your motives and purposes in American public
life. It is worth a good many sacrifices to come into unincumbered
possession of a farm you have been living on for twenty years as a
tenant or mere occupying claimant. Beveridge we must help. . . . He
is a close question in Indiana on account of the narrow party margin.
We must go to his rescue. . . . Mrs. Dolliver who telegraphed me on
the day the conference vote was taken 'Vote against the report if
you are the only one' joins me in cordial messages to you and
Mrs. La Follette."[8]

Bob found this same feeling of a common purpose among the
Progressives in one State after another as his lecture trip took him
to the Pacific coast and back. He returned to many places where he
had spoken before, and people came up to greet him as an old friend.
After his speeches he often sat up until two and three o'clock to

discuss with progressive leaders the problems they were meeting in their city and state fights. Later, through editorials and roll calls in his magazine, he was thus able to help them in their efforts to nominate and elect progressive candidates to Congress. On this trip his discussion of the concentration of financial control in the hands of a few men, combined with his reading of the roll calls on the Aldrich currency bill and the defeated progressive amendments to the tariff bill, drove home his point with a new emphasis. His vivid and humorous description of how Aldrich, Hale, and other members of the Old Guard secretly controlled legislation through the control of important Senate Committees was written up repeatedly in the local newspapers where he spoke. From the State of Washington he wrote: "It is different than on any other trip. They are keen to know the inside about Taft and everybody seems eager for the breaking up of parties."[9] A few days before, he had said: "It is hard to keep still on Taft and I think with you that we have got to come out ultimately against him. . . . I think our [magazine] policy of attacking his departments and Aldrichism & Cannonism has worked well. But it cannot go on indefinitely without bringing the *responsibility home* to *him as President*."[10]

The day Bob arrived in Spokane, a local newspaper carried a headline quoting Speaker Cannon as saying in a speech on the previous day at Elgin, Illinois, "If Cummins and La Follette are Republicans, I am something else."[11] As Bob got off the train, he was met at the station by a large delegation, headed by Congressman Miles Poindexter, who took him directly to the hotel where a banquet had been arranged. That night Bob spoke to an enthusiastic audience in the largest church in Spokane. When he urged them to send Poindexter to the Senate in the place of the reactionary Republican Senator Piles, "the applause shook the church." After the meeting Bob sat up until two o'clock with Poindexter discussing his campaign and what he could say for him in the other places where he was to speak in the State. Bob was in Oregon when the returns came in from the fall elections, and was shocked at the defeat of Francis J. Heney for reelection as district attorney in San Francisco, where he had been courageously striving to bring the "higher-ups" to justice. Heney had incurred the wrath of the grafters in high places, and they "got him." Bob had hoped to speak in Heney's campaign. But when he found it impossible to reach San Francisco in time, he sent a long telegram urging the voters to support his heroic fight to rebuild San Francisco's civic integrity. The day after the election Bob wrote that it was "sickening to think of San Francisco. What a sink hole it is— An earthquake should swallow it up. I have no words—it isn't a question of being fooled or being indifferent—it's depravity."[12] He hoped that though Heney was beaten in San Francisco, he would at once go back to Oregon and take up the timber cases again.

The defeat of Tom Johnson for reelection as mayor of Cleveland was another great disappointment to the Progressives everywhere. We had watched his ten-year fight for the public welfare, and were sorely disappointed and resentful over his defeat. A few days after the election, Marie Howe telephoned to me that Tom Johnson was coming to Madison to spend a day with her and Fred. She asked if they could come out to the farm to call. I was greatly pleased. He and the Howes had been very kind to Fola when she had been playing with a stock company in Cleveland, and I felt it a privilege to thank him personally for his friendliness.

On the evening of the day Tom Johnson was at the farm, I wrote to Bob, who was in California: "He is one of the greatest spirits we have known. . . . I wish you could have been here to talk with him. There was no call for sympathy in his attitude. But something from a man who could understand, *really* understand would have seemed good to him I believe. I let the children stay at home from school to see him. He seemed to love them each one and he has a great affection for Fola."[13] I met Tom Johnson only once, but I have always felt that Lincoln Steffens' estimate of him was none too high when he said, "I have never ventured to say to any man where I rank him, among the men not only of our day but of all times. It might sound exaggerated to our contemporaries."

Bob's trip through California just after the November elections was full of "hard work and interest." Visiting five different cities in five days, he made ten speeches in the State. Although the *Los Angeles Times* and other reactionary newspapers did not even mention that he was in the State, he spoke to large and enthusiastic audiences and found people alert to the issues he was discussing. In Fresno he met Chester Rowell, editor of an influential progressive newspaper, who was active in the reform movement and, at that time, a great friend of Steffens, Heney, and Spreckels. Bob thought

Rowell was one of "the biggest & bravest & wisest men" he had met on this trip. After his speech at Fresno they sat up until two o'clock while Rowell put the California situation before him "with great clearness." Rowell was interested in uniting the municipal and state reform movements and urged national organization.

When Bob arrived in Los Angeles, he was met at the station by Meyer Lissner, head of the reform organization, and Dr. John R. Haynes, the father of the re-call, which had first been initiated in that city. Bob had a hard but inspiring day there. He made three speeches. The first was to three hundred students at the law school of the University of Southern California. In his brief talk to the students, he "went after them hard to enlist those boys for the state." He wrote home: "It was rather a remarkable little meeting. They pretty nearly hollered the roof off. I shook up the older men too. It was worth while. The boys were ready to put me up on their shoulders judging from the rush they made for me. It made a fellow feel like a boy again. I was glad I had gone to them." At the City Club he addressed an organization of 1,500 professional and business men who "cheered and cheered and applauded" and then lined up to shake his hand. That night he spoke to another large audience in the auditorium which responded in the same way.[14]

Bob finished his lecture tour just before Congress convened in December. The temper of his audiences, the response of people he met on trains and in the towns where he stopped, had made him keenly aware of the revolt which everyone would recognize a year later when the votes were counted in the 1910 elections. Shortly after his return to Washington, a newspaper correspondent asked him if he thought the progressive movement was receding. He answered, "Those who are seeking to stem the tide of the progressive movement . . . are preparing for a flood." From Washington "to the Pacific Coast the masses are aroused."[15]

The state of public sentiment, the degree of interest and enthusiasm of the men and women of the country in government for and by the people was ever the crucial test in Bob's judgment as to whether the movement was advancing or receding.

CHAPTER XXVI

Brandeis Becomes Our Friend

The most damaging blow to Bob's and the people's faith in President Taft as an executive was probably the issue raised in the so-called Ballinger case which held the center of the stage during the session of Congress that convened on December 6, 1909, and ended June 25, 1910. Throughout many years the conservation of natural resources for the benefit of the many rather than their exploitation by the privileged few had been one of Bob's vital interests. Conservation had long been a part of the progressive program in Wisconsin. This movement had gained a strong hold on the public imagination. Roosevelt had emphasized it vigorously and had given great credit for the progress made during his Administration to his friend Gifford Pinchot, who had been Chief of the National Forest Service since 1898. Pinchot was ten years younger than Bob. He was graduated from Yale in 1889 and had studied forestry in France, Germany, Switzerland, and Austria. Inheritance had endowed him with wealth and social position. But he himself had chosen to give his time and expert knowledge to the public service. He was a tall, handsome man, with a distinguished presence and charming manner, who had a wide circle of influential friends.

During the last two years of Roosevelt's Administration, his Secretary of the Interior, James R. Garfield, had been actively identified with carrying out the Roosevelt-Pinchot policies. When Richard A. Ballinger, of Seattle, Washington, was appointed by Taft as Secretary of the Interior, he promptly restored to private entry a large part of the 1,500,000 acres of public lands which Roosevelt had withdrawn to safeguard valuable water-power sites. Bob said that soon afterward "the President began to hear from the public. And then certain of these lands were again withdrawn . . . but not until an opportunity had been given for the water power magnates to get in on the ground."[1]

Furthermore, Ballinger, who had previously served as counsel for the Cunningham land claims, directed Special Agent Glavis, chief of a field division, to bring his investigation of these claims to an end. Glavis appealed to Taft, submitting charges on August 18, 1909, that Ballinger wanted to hasten the decision on these particular claims before their character had been determined. Taft sustained Ballinger. Glavis was dismissed.

Glavis then wrote for *Collier's* magazine a matter-of-fact history of Ballinger's activities in the Cunningham coal-land cases.[2] Two weeks later Bob reprinted part of it in his magazine and published a letter written to him by Francis J. Heney which commended Glavis' integrity and ability in the highest terms. Gifford Pinchot and Garfield strongly supported Glavis. Public interest was stirred. An extraordinary conflict ensued with disastrous consequences to the Taft Administration.

Before Congress adjourned for the holidays, the Senate requested Taft to transmit to Congress all reports, statements, papers, or documents he had relied upon in exonerating Ballinger and dismissing Glavis. That same day, Senator Jones of Washington had a letter from Ballinger to him read to the Senate. It charged that "the pernicious activity of certain officers" of the Forest Service had been the source of the charges "of corrupt and improper practices" relative to "coal lands and other public domain" in Alaska and asked that the Forest Service also be investigated.[3]

After the Christmas recess Dolliver had a letter to him from Gifford Pinchot read to the Senate, on January 6. Dolliver explained it was an answer to an inquiry as to what part, if any, the Forestry Bureau had taken in promulgating accusations against the Department of the Interior. Pinchot conceded that a rule of propriety between Departments had been violated, but he upheld his assistants and approved Glavis' action.[4]

The country was stirred on the morning of January 8 by the news that late the previous night Taft had dismissed Gifford Pinchot because of his "improper appeal to Congress and the public." In a long editorial in his magazine, Bob maintained that the case struck "down too deeply into the life of the American people to be disposed of lightly upon some point of official etiquette." He sharply crit-

icized Ballinger and Taft and defended Pinchot, indignantly pointing out that it was the Ballinger letter to Senator Jones, obviously
written to be read to the Senate, which had "called forth and was
responsible for the Pinchot letter." But the "Ballinger letter received
no public rebuke from the President," whereas the "Pinchot letter
is made the basis of an executive order removing from office a man
of the highest character, whose public service is an enduring monument to his name."[5]

When the Congressional committee to investigate the Interior
Department and Forestry Service met on January 26, 1910, public
interest was intense. It was reflected in the space given the hearings
by the newspapers and the crowded attendance throughout the proceedings. Glavis was the first witness called. It was well understood
that the majority of the committee, including its chairman, Senator
Knute Nelson of Minnesota, who was especially hostile, were strongly
prejudiced against the cause Glavis represented. But those who
anticipated the committee would make quick work of his testimony,
had not reckoned with the lawyer in the case. Louis D. Brandeis
was the driving force, the mastermind back of the Ballinger trial.
Only those who witnessed the dramatic developments as they occurred could appreciate the obstacles he had to overcome and the
genius he displayed in conducting the investigation. Arrayed against
him was the entire Taft Administration backed up by the Old Guard
forces in Congress. Their program was to make it appear that the
charges were in the nature of a conspiracy against Ballinger.

Bob was intensely interested in the case and kept in close touch
with what went on from day to day. At dinner we often discussed
it. We had met Brandeis through Elizabeth Evans, and whenever he
dropped in we listened eagerly to the inside story of the progress
of the investigation. I was personally much absorbed in the subject,
and was among those who gathered every morning long before the
committee-room door opened, standing in line to make sure of a seat.

An adverse majority report by the committee was a foregone
conclusion. Brandeis relied upon the facts reported to the press
for the far more important verdict of public opinion. One particularly
startling disclosure, resulting from his close critical study of the
vast amount of material in the record, went far to undermine public
confidence in the Administration. Among the papers Taft sent in
response to the Senate's request were a report and a summary relat-

ing to the documents Ballinger had submitted to the President on September 6 in answer to Glavis' charges. The Wickersham report was dated September 11. If accurately dated, it meant he had prepared his long report on this mass of confused documents and papers in only five days.

Brandeis noted the extraordinary fact that Taft had not mentioned the Wickersham report when he exonerated Ballinger and dismissed Glavis on September 13. One day, when an assistant to Attorney General Wickersham was on the witness stand, Brandeis suddenly began firing questions at him, such as: "When did you first hear of this report? When did it first come to your attention?" Everybody in the crowded committee room held their breath as he finally asked if the Attorney General's report had not been "antedated." The stillness was painful. We all knew Brandeis had not asked the question except as he had proof to justify it. The witness made an evasive answer, but the implication was plain.

The committee refused to comply with Brandeis' request that Wickersham be called upon for a statement. A resolution introduced in Congress, however, brought an admission from the Attorney General that his report had been falsely dated and had actually been written long after the President had exonerated Ballinger and dismissed Glavis. Subsequently Taft made a like acknowledgment.

Revelations such as this—and Brandeis brought out others equally damaging—proving that fraud and deception were being deliberately used to smother the truth and exonerate Ballinger from the charges against him, did more to wreck the Administration than the actual wrongs committed by the Interior Department. *Collier's, McClure's, Everybody's,* and other less well-known magazines, including our own, were covering the investigation, and even the Administration newspapers could not ignore these startling disclosures which had grave political consequences. The progressive movement was strengthened and solidified in Congress and over the country by Taft's action in the Ballinger case and by his openly reactionary course on legislation during the first two sessions.

It has always been a happy thought to me that, when Louis D. Brandeis came to Washington in the winter of 1910, Elizabeth Evans' introduction cleared the way of all formalities. We met at the beginning on the basis of true comradeship and understanding which has ever since existed between the families. He had a standing invitation to join us at any time, and would often "drop in" for dinner or call later in the evening after the day's work was over. When Mrs. Evans had visited us the previous summer, she had talked much of the Brandeises who were her next-door neighbors. Their friendship dated back to early years when Louis Brandeis and Glendower Evans had been college mates at Harvard. When her husband died, Brandeis helped her through the crisis, awakening her interest and directing her energies to the service of others, implanting in her mind and heart the purpose to work for two—herself and her husband—an inspiring motive that always stayed with her.

Almost from the start of the practice of his profession, Brandeis appears to have consciously given, without any fees, a part of his time and legal services to the public benefit. He and Bob deeply sympathized in the belief that the strong arm of the Government should be used to protect public rights. They had high regard for each other's judgment and conviction. In her reminiscences Mrs. Evans says that after Brandeis' return from Washington, she expressed surprise at the tone of respect with which he spoke of Senator La Follette's opinion on some question of railroad rates: "He knows," remarked Brandeis, "all there is to know. He is a great authority on the subject."

Bob believed that the enormous growth of trusts under the Roosevelt and Taft Administrations was due to the fact that neither President ever took issue with the reactionary bosses, and that when it came to important national legislation they both yielded to the Aldrich-Cannon domination of Congress. Roosevelt's "strongest declarations in the public interest were," Bob said, "invariably offset with something comforting to Privilege; every phrase denouncing 'bad' trusts was deftly balanced with praise for 'good' trusts."[6]

This Rooseveltian policy had created a sentiment among his followers that bigness, mergers, and monopoly were essential factors in mass production and modern business efficiency. With this view Bob emphatically disagreed. In 1912 he wrote: "It will be the impartial verdict of history that the executive could have saved the people from the appalling conditions which confront us today, if all the power of this great government had been put forth to enforce the [Sherman] Anti-Trust law."[7]

He paid no attention to the criticism of friends who, though they admired his fighting qualities, considered him "old-fashioned" in his defense of the Sherman law and wished he was not quite so irreconcilable in his war on monopoly. I was rejoiced to learn that Brandeis' experience and keen intellectual acumen led to conclusions which seem to me as applicable to the business situation now as when they were first published in *Collier's* under the title "Trusts and Efficiency."

Brandeis was greatly interested in the progressive movement. Bob and his colleagues found great satisfaction in consulting him, and his suggestions on legislation and policies were of immense value. Brandeis told me—

> *Belle Case La Follette's manuscript ends on this unfinished sentence. She died on August 18, 1931, a few days after these final pages of her manuscript were written.*

Beginning with Chapter XXVII of the biography, Fola La Follette takes up the narrative where her mother's work was stopped by death. To maintain the continuity of the reader's relation to the story, the author has continued to use the first names of the family as Belle Case La Follette did in her manuscript.

CHAPTER XXVII

"Coming into Your Own After All These Years of Fighting"

The first meeting between Bob and Brandeis had been in connection with the Ballinger case. Brandeis had arrived in Washington on January 25, 1910, the day before the Congressional hearings began, and had gone that same evening to the La Follette home at 1864 Wyoming Avenue. Bob was impressed with the personality of Brandeis from the moment he grasped his hand and looked into his keen, thoughtful face. He came to love and admire him and always found him a genial and fascinating companion. During their first visit, while the two men discussed matters which Brandeis considered very confidential, Bob, Jr., and Phil remained in the room. Their presence troubled Brandeis, and when the boys went to bed about nine he expressed his relief that they had gone. Bob assured him he need not worry, as the boys were accustomed to listening to most confidential discussions and their discretion could be trusted. Years later, when Bob, Jr., became a candidate to fill his father's unexpired term, certain people protested to Brandeis that he was too young and had no political experience. To this Brandeis replied, "Bob, Jr., and Phil have had more experience in politics than any boys since the days of the Roman Senators."[1]

From the time of their first visit until he was appointed to the Supreme Court, whenever Brandeis was in Washington they conferred frequently on the specific work either might have in hand.[2] Although their past experience was different, their values and methods were similar. When confronted with a specific problem, they investigated it; sought first the facts; then devised instruments to deal with it. They never endeavored to solve social and economic problems from the blueprint of Utopian dreams. Neither was doctrinaire; but both had a deep conviction that industry, finance, and government should be organized to serve the best interests of all the people of the country rather than the special interests of a privileged few. From their first meeting until the war in 1917, they were in fundamental accord on the techniques which would best serve this purpose.

Their independent study of railroad and monopoly problems had led them to similar conclusions as to desirable legislative control. Believing that the Sherman Anti-Trust law could and should be enforced, they had both been shocked when Taft's appointee, Attorney General Wickersham, dismissed the cases against the New York, New Haven & Hartford Railroad Company. These proceedings, familiarly known as the New Haven merger case, had been started under the Roosevelt Administration because New England was suffering from the effects of the merger of its transportation, including railroads, trolleys, and steamship lines. The action had been initiated by the Government following an investigation in which Brandeis had assisted the United States District Attorney, Asa P. French. Bob thought the dismissal of the suits by Wickersham was a betrayal of public interest.

Brandeis often dropped in at the La Follette home for dinner during the winter and spring of 1910. He was keenly interested in the insurgent fight. The most bitterly contested legislation during this session dealt with railroad regulation. As the insurgent grapevine brought reports that Taft's railroad bill, known as the Court of Commerce bill, was being drawn and modified by Wickersham with help from prominent railroad executives, Brandeis, Bob, and the Progressives in Congress became increasingly suspicious of the measure. When Elkins reported it to the Senate on February 24, Cummins and Clapp, both members of the Interstate Commerce Committee, joined in a stinging minority report. In the middle of March, Cummins made a four-day speech, opening the fight which cut across party lines as sharply as the tariff and Ballinger issues.

If the bill passed as it came to Congress with the President's approval, Bob was convinced the people would lose all that had been gained in the long struggle with the railroad corporations. The provision for a Court of Commerce was, he said, little more than a mask behind which lurked the real evils of this legislation. As first introduced, it took most of the power away from the Interstate Commerce Commission and transferred it to the Attorney General. This seemed a bold raid on public rights to Bob, who had, as a young man in the House of Representatives, supported the establishment of an Inter-state Commerce Commission and steadily sought to enlarge its power to regulate the railroads. He joined the progressive Repub-licans and Democrats in opposing the measure. They could not pre-vent the creation of the Court of Commerce. But during the three months that the legislation was pending, their attack was so effec-tive, Bob said, that the Administration Senators were "compelled to abandon entire sections of the bill to avoid the humiliation of being overwhelmingly voted down in the Senate."[3]

Bob offered a number of amendments, participated in the running debate, cooperated on strategy, and made four speeches on the bill during the months it was under consideration.[4] For several days he had not even attended the Senate sessions because he was working intensively at home to get a speech out of his system. His first attack on the bill was loaded with the shocking facts regarding the New York, New Haven & Hartford merger. During the investigation of the merger, Brandeis had acquired a detailed knowledge of the whole manipulation, and he gave Bob the salient facts. In a four-hour speech on April 12, Bob reviewed the history of the merger as an example of the evils in railroad financing and monopolistic control of transportation. He expressed the indignation that he and Brandeis shared in his denunciation of the Attorney General for dismissing the Government's case against this merger when it could have been made the strongest suit ever presented under the Sherman Anti-Trust Act.

The denunciation of his home corporations brought Lodge to the Senate floor. He followed the speech closely, sent out for volumes, and conferred with Senator Murray Crane, who was obviously im-patient at the attack.[5] When Bob finished, Lodge came to the de-fense of the New England railroads. Bob's speech was widely reported throughout the country, the New York *Sun* headlining it as a "Whacking for Wickersham."[6] Some newspapers interpreted it as a reply to a prepared address Wickersham had delivered at Chicago, where he made support of the bill a test of party loyalty and "smote the Republican insurgents hip and thigh," practically reading them out of the party.[7]

On June 3, when this bill passed the Senate, Bob stated that, as recommended by the President and reported by the committee, it had contained only four provisions in the public interest and a dozen in the interests of the railroads. "For twelve long weeks," he said, "the progressive Republicans and the progressive Democrats on this floor have made war upon those provisions which were hostile to the public interest. . . . It is no longer the President's bill, or the Wickersham bill, or the Elkins bill. Against all the influence of the railroads, combined with all the power of the administration . . . the administration bill framed in the interest of the railroads has been torn to pieces and rewritten in the interest of the people here on the floor of the Senate."[8] As the bill was on the whole a gain for the public, Bob voted for it.

Another, less sharply defined, contest between progressive Republicans and the Administration developed when a postal-savings-bank bill, approved by the President and supported by Aldrich, was introduced early in 1910. For nearly forty years there had been agitation for some kind of postal-savings-bank system, but the banking interests had prevented action by Congress. Bob favored the establishment of postal savings but disapproved of this particular measure and cooperated in trying to improve it by voting for amendments introduced by Bristow, Borah, and Cummins. Again progressive Republicans and Democrats joined in revising the measure sufficiently so that Bob and all the progressive Republicans voted for the bill when it passed the Senate.[9] But when it came back from the House it was so radically altered by exceptionally effective Presidential persuasion, that Bob joined Bristow and Cummins in voting against it on final passage. Had Dolliver not been paired, he would also have voted against it.[10]

Patronage punishment had been ladled out to the Insurgents in heavy doses ever since they voted against the tariff bill. But it was not until five days after Bob's last speech on the Court of Commerce bill that Taft and his Administration openly joined the forces seeking to prevent La Follette's return to the Senate. The opposition was counting on the fact that the Constitution had not yet been amended to provide for the direct election of Senators. Therefore, even if Bob won at the primaries in September, a hostile legislature could later legally overthrow his nomination and elect another candidate. On June 8, a group of leading Wisconsin Stalwarts held a meeting in Milwaukee. A deliberate effort was made to create the impression that it was an official "Republican State Convention." It was thus reported in many newspapers. The fact was that no Wisconsin Republican convention had ever been called in this manner, and all party conventions had actually been abandoned in the State since the passage of the primary-election law.

Nevertheless, Taft gave the conference the Presidential blessing in a telegram of felicitation addressed to the "Wisconsin Republicans assembled in convention." Former Congressman James E. Watson, a former Cannon leader in the House, addressed the conference, and Vice President Sherman announced from the platform that he was " 'sent here' by President Taft 'because that man is interested in Republicanism, in Republican success in the State of Wisconsin this year.' "[11]

Bob wrote Brandeis that the stalwart gathering "was very misleading to the country but well understood in Wisconsin. It is important as indicating the course which the administration is to take in my campaign."[12] The "convention" was publicly repudiated by his campaign manager, Charles H. Crownhart, later a Justice of the Supreme Court of Wisconsin. The stalwart conference nominated no candidate, but endorsed Governor Davidson and President Taft and strongly approved the Payne-Aldrich tariff law. Taft thus became an issue in the state campaign. "Taft Republican" clubs were organized, and the Stalwarts designated themselves as "Taft Republicans." In Wisconsin the national split was foreshadowed two years before it occurred. Because of the powerful forces opposing La Follette, there was genuine concern among Progressives throughout the country about his return to the Senate. Soon after the Milwaukee conference he received a telegram signed by George Loftus, Lynn Haines, James Peterson, and other Minnesota Progressives offering their support in the coming campaign.[13] Insurgent Senators and Congressmen from other States were planning to speak in his campaign. Steffens, John R. Commons, Fremont Older, Charles Edward Russell, and others had been raising money to help in the Wisconsin fight.

Bob knew that the reactionaries at home and in other States would subscribe generously to a fund for his defeat. Financing his own campaign was a difficult problem. During the past year he had earned money in addition to his salary, but it had gone back into

his work and his magazine. Early in April he had written to Gilbert
E. Roe: "I have *not one dollar* to begin a campaign. The farm is
mortgaged for $12,500. I have had to borrow $2,000 at the Cap[ital]
C[it]y bank to meet expenses *here* which over ran salary to that
amount and some $1500.00 which I earned lecturing this winter went
the same way. . . . But Gil we both know how to fight with our backs
against a wall. We have cut our way out too many times in the
days gone by to go hunting round for a ladder."[14]

Two weeks before Congress adjourned, Belle was called to Wisconsin by the serious illness of her father. She took Mary with her,
but Bob, Jr., and Phil stayed on at Washington to keep their father
company. It was hard, Bob said, to have her go alone, and he sent
"just a line to tell you how we all love you and how lonesome it is
without you. . . . Three gentlemen present here at this moment join
in worshipful adoration to the greatest woman in all the world. In
other words we love you with all our might and send a share to
grandpa."[15]

The insurgency in the Republican Party which the Taft Administration was now endeavoring to punish in Wisconsin actually
represented the growing support for ideas and measures which
Roosevelt had in 1908 characterized to Henry Cabot Lodge as "the
La Follette type of fool radicalism."[16] The movement had grown
rapidly during the colonel's absence, and in the fall of 1909, while
he was still in Europe, Lodge had warned him that "The radicalism
of La Follette and Cummins" seemed "to be rampant" in the States
west of the Mississippi and running down to Kansas.[17]

After fifteen months abroad, Roosevelt returned on June 18, 1910,
and was welcomed home with great enthusiasm. But he soon found
that the political caldron was boiling with trouble. The apparently
united and triumphant party he had left to his heir, Taft, was now,
only a few months before election, split in open dissension. During
his absence the insurgent movement had been organized in Congress
and made articulate throughout the West and Midwest. The fluidity
of party lines, so familiar in those sections of the country, was now
beginning to manifest itself even in the East. His friend Gifford
Pinchot was cooperating with the wild-eyed "lunatic fringe" of
radicals, privately urging that a candidate be nominated against
Taft. On the day the colonel landed, *La Follette's Magazine* printed

three columns reporting an attack on the Administration which Pinchot had made in a speech on June 11, before the Roosevelt Club at St. Paul, Minnesota.[18]

The dynamic and popular former President was in a difficult position. All factions sought his help. Reactionaries and Insurgents besieged him for support. Throughout the summer and early fall he apparently thought it his mission to unite the Republican Party for victory at the November elections.[19] To Bob and the active Progressives, however, Roosevelt seemed unaware of the real forces which were causing the breakdown of strict party lines in so many States. Using the same techniques which had aroused the distrust of the Wisconsin Progressives during his Presidential days, he sought to restore "harmony," and disappointed first one and then another of the opposing groups by refusing to "take sides" in the party primaries and conventions.

Bob was the first of the Progressives in the Senate and House to be received by Roosevelt at Oyster Bay. Certain newspaper reports subsequently implied that he had written asking for the interview.[20] But the meeting was, in fact, brought about by Gilson Gardner, the Washington correspondent of the Scripps newspapers. He was interested in the insurgent movement and participated frequently in the conferences of the Washington group. He was also a personal friend of Roosevelt's, had met the colonel at Khartoum, and returned with him to the United States. A few days before Congress adjourned, Gardner arrived in Washington and urged Bob, in the interest of the progressive cause, to call upon Roosevelt. Bob hesitated, and told Gardner he would think it over because, upon questioning, he found that the colonel had expressed a desire to see some of the Insurgents but had not mentioned La Follette. But on Sunday, June 26, the day after Congress adjourned, Gardner telephoned that he had taken the liberty of writing himself to urge the interview and had a telegram from Roosevelt saying Bob would be received if he came to Oyster Bay the following Monday.[21]

On the same evening Bob attended a dinner for several progressive Senators at Clapp's home, and at midnight he and his sons left for New York. The next morning Bob and Roe took the train to Oyster Bay, arriving at two o'clock. The colonel's chauffeur met them at the station, and they drove to Sagamore Hill. Bob wrote that a Negro attendant showed him into the library, where he waited

until Roosevelt soon "made his appearance, wearing linen knicker-
bockers, and after a cordial greeting said that he had just come in
from pitching hay, confirming his statement by removing a rather
liberal quantity of timothy from his person."[22]

This visit of an hour and a half or two hours was the last Bob ever
had with Roosevelt, whom he had known since 1889. They talked
over the events that had transpired since the colonel had left the
country, especially the legislation of the recent extra session. Bob
asked some searching, direct questions, and never forgot the answers.
In a long, confidential letter to Fremont Older, written only two
weeks after the visit, he gave an account of the talk. "I had gone
there upon a mission," he wrote, "and I sought to impress him with
the fact that the progressive cause had made great strides during
his absence; that nothing could stop or side-track it. Also that T[aft]
had made a mess of things and that nothing short of a miracle could
save the administration. Without quoting him I will venture to
guess that he very much wants to be President again. He is not
greatly changed. He will help some reactionaries on the one hand
and some progressives on the other, being cautious not to aid men
who are regarded as ultra and extreme on either side. This has
always been his idea of a square deal. He is not fundamentally
democratic. His democracy is sentimental.

"He stated that he had accepted an invitation to speak in Milwaukee. I asked him upon what date. He responded 'September 6th
or 7th.' I said to him, 'Our primaries are upon the 6th of September.'
He flashed back, 'Then I will not come until the 7th.'"[23]

From his long talk with the former President, Bob deduced
Roosevelt would "make some speeches,—not too many, just enough
to keep the interest keen," selecting topics "touching many important subjects of general interest," being "very careful how he touches
subjects of legislation, neither endorsing nor condemning except by
implication, but suggesting something ahead." Bob predicted that
he would neither "approve nor condemn the Taft administration
except inferentially."[24] Roosevelt's only comment upon Taft had
been that "sometimes a man makes a very good lieutenant but a
poor captain."[25]

In a confidential letter to Senator Bourne, Bob wrote that he
thought the colonel would "support some men in both camps," and
that the Senators and Representatives in the progressive camp

should, when convenient, call upon him "without invitation," as Roosevelt had suggested at the close of their talk. In this same letter Bob said Roosevelt "is much the same as he was when he went away, with this difference: he was then President. Now he wants to be President, and to be entirely just, in some ways I think he sees more liberally. But he is far from being broadly and fundamentally democratic. I say he wants to be President. Of course you will understand that this is inference upon my part. But when you see him if you do not conclude that he has all the symptoms of a man who is ready and willing, then I shall question your accuracy of judgment and I should not like to do that."[26]

Bob's visit had not been announced in the press. On his arrival at the Oyster Bay station he had successfully evaded the newspaper correspondents. But when he motored back from Sagamore Hill just in time to make the connection to New York, newspaper men boarded the train and rode to the next station, plying him with questions. The meeting of the two men was widely and, in some respects, inaccurately reported in the press; each was quoted somewhat differently in various papers. The following morning the New York *World* and the *New York Times* carried front-page dispatches from Oyster Bay dated June 27. Both papers stated that Bob described Roosevelt as "the greatest living American."[27] The quotation was printed in many papers throughout the country at the time, and was revived later by Medill McCormick and others in the 1912 campaign. But this superlative estimate did not then, nor at any other period, accurately express Bob's opinion of Roosevelt. His own contemporary accounts and the recollections of those who talked with him immediately after his return from Oyster Bay reveal that there was nothing in the visit to have put him even temporarily in so expansive a mood.[28]

After three more days' visit with the Roe family, which Bob remembered as "a comfort and delight," he and the boys left New York, arriving in Madison on July 6. There was an outburst of greetings when they reached the farm and "a rushing away to see the ponies with their new little colts, and the yearlings, most as large as their mothers, and Phil's calf twice as big as when he left."[29] At every home-coming, Bob gave his first attention to the farm, inspecting the stock, fields, orchard, and woods, sharing with Belle and the children the plans for work to be done.

Soon after his return, Bob received a letter from Older asking for confidential information on Roosevelt's attitude toward the insurgent movement. Seeing the newspaper reports of Bob's visit to Oyster Bay and Roosevelt's promise to deliver an address at Milwaukee, Older had published an editorial in the *San Francisco Bulletin* based upon the assumption that if the colonel spoke in Wisconsin he would speak for Bob. In his letter Older said: "I was very much elated over the news, feeling that your fight would be tremendously strengthened by Roosevelt's help. But this morning I find an interview with Lodge in which that gentleman is quoted as saying that Roosevelt is going to campaign for him in Massachusetts. If he says one word for Lodge I feel that the insurgent movement will have to do the best it can without Roosevelt."[30]

In an affectionate letter to Older telling him he was "enshrined in this family from the 'old man' down to little Mary," Bob gave the previously quoted confidential report of his talk with Roosevelt.[31]

Bob's report and Roosevelt's promise to speak for Lodge were a disappointment to Older and the Western Progressives. Roosevelt's privately cordial reception of them at Oyster Bay, followed by public declarations refusing to "take sides" between candidates in the Republican Party primaries, appeared to them as "dodging the issue" and "playing politics." This feeling was sharply intensified when he endorsed the reactionary Lodge and the insurgent Beveridge for reelection. To the Progressives this distinction between party nominations and elections no longer had the reality it still had for the former President. They were demanding now the realignment he was to advocate when he bolted the Republican Party in 1912.

The insurgent Republicans were having a hard fight in California, where Hiram Johnson was a candidate for governor, John D. Works for the Senate, and William Kent for Representative from the Second District. Bob was intensely interested in their campaign. He sent a telegram to be used in Johnson's behalf and supported them in his magazine, which had also published "roll calls" on the records of the reactionary Senator Flint and Representative McKinlay. Fifty thousand reprints of McKinlay's record were distributed in his district, contributing materially to his defeat and William Kent's nomination. In other States, as in California, many extra copies of *La Follette's Magazine* containing "roll calls" on various Senators and Representatives were effectively distributed. They helped to defeat reactionaries and nominate and elect Progressives.[32]

Believing La Follette's reelection was vital to the national progressive movement, and knowing the reactionary forces throughout the country were making a concerted effort to defeat him, thirteen leaders in other States generously came to Wisconsin and campaigned for Bob. They paid their own expenses, made 108 speeches, and covered eleven counties. Those who came were: Senators Borah, Bristow, Clapp, Cummins, and Dolliver, former Secretary of the Interior James R. Garfield of Ohio, Francis J. Heney of San Francisco, Judge Ben Lindsey of Colorado, James Manahan and James A. Peterson of Minnesota, Congressman George W. Norris of Nebraska, former United States Forester Gifford Pinchot of Pennsylvania, and George L. Record of New Jersey.[33] Many Progressives in different States also contributed to the Wisconsin campaign fund.

Bob had expected to "camp in the field," speaking throughout the State during the summer. But Dr. Fox decided Bob was not well enough to carry out this plan, as he had been suffering for several months from intermittent attacks of indigestion and pain. He was not confined to the house, however, and was able to attend some conferences and receive at his home most of the friends who came into the State to help. But for the first time in six years he did not make a single speech in the primary campaign.

Two days before the Wisconsin primary, the Conservation Congress opened at St. Paul, Minnesota. On their way to address the meeting, both Roosevelt and Taft passed through Wisconsin, but neither commented on Bob's candidacy. Belle attended the conference and reported the proceedings for *La Follette's Magazine*.[34] The day before the primary, she wrote to Bob: "I do not feel any anxiety about the election although I am quite prepared for anything in the way of result. It seems to me that personally we have nothing to fear or dread or be disappointed about. We have so much of the best of life."[35]

The closing meeting of the primary campaign was held at Madison on August 31. Senator Cummins of Iowa, Congressman George W. Norris of Nebraska, Congressman John M. Nelson of Wisconsin, and Francis J. Heney spoke to an audience of 1,400 at the university gymnasium, where Bob had twice been nominated for governor. The primary on September 6 brought an overwhelming victory for the entire progressive Republican state ticket which Bob had endorsed. He was renominated by a majority of 102,187 votes over his reactionary "Taft-Republican" opponent, Samuel A. Cook, whom the Stalwarts had nominated for governor at their "Opera House Convention" when they bolted in 1904. Bob received 142,978 votes to 40,791 for Cook. McGovern defeated the "Taft-Republican" candidate for governor by 25,583.[36]

The day after the Wisconsin primary, Roosevelt addressed the Press Club in Milwaukee. This was the "invitation to speak in Milwaukee," mentioned during Bob's visit to Oyster Bay. When Roosevelt reached Milwaukee that day, he gave out his first public comment on the senatorial contest. He said he was unable to believe the statement, made to him since his arrival, "that in spite of Senator La Follette's having carried the primaries in fair open contest, an effort will be made to beat him in the legislature. . . . any such conduct would be," he said, "an outrage" and a "deliberate violation of good faith."[37]

Following the primary, in accord with the Wisconsin law, all the Republicans nominated for state and Federal office attended a state convention at Madison on September 28 and formulated the platform on which they were to stand for election in November. The platform took a definite stand on many of the economic and political issues which were to be the focus of controversy and legislation for the next thirty years.[38] Fred Howe described it as the best political platform ever written,[39] and Ray Stannard Baker wrote Bob that "The Wisconsin platform strikes the top notch."[40] It was widely commented on in the press. The *Kansas City Star* stated: "The great platform of the Wisconsin Republicans was the product of years of drilling in popular political control. . . . Nothing could more clearly demonstrate the values of the direct primary system."[41]

Bob had secured a plank in the platform upholding the liberal policy of the university and asserting that its service to the State "depends upon its freedom to find the truth and make it known, and we pledge the Republican party to the policy of academic freedom so well expressed by the board of regents in 1894, when they declared: 'Whatever may be the limitations which trammel inquiry elsewhere, we believe that the great state university of Wisconsin should ever encourage that continual and fearless sifting and winnowing by which alone the truth can be found.' "[42] The Stalwarts and certain powerful special interests had attacked the university for allowing a faculty member to give expert advice to a committee of the legislature in a report upon the control of water-power rights. At commencement, on June 22, 1910, President Van Hise answered this challenge. In his magazine Bob published the address in full and wrote an editorial vigorously commending the policy of Van Hise.[43]

Two students of the class of 1879, Bob La Follette and Charles Van Hise, profoundly influenced in youth by a great teacher, were now, as mature men, collaborating to sustain former President Bascom's ideal of the relation of a state university to the State.

At the close of the platform convention, Bob, though not well, and aware he might have to undergo a serious operation, made a brief address to the delegates, congratulating them on having "embodied in the platform declarations the ideas and the principles that are so important in the next progressive step to be taken by the people of this country."[44]

The following day he left for the Mayo Clinic, where he underwent an operation for gallstones on October 4. Three days later Belle wrote the children: "I think the doctors believe that practically all danger is passed. Dr. Fox gave out a statement last night. . . . It seemed necessary to make it because people were already beginning to ask and to plan for papa to go into the campaign. They do not seem to realize that time for recuperation is as necessary as time for the operation. And this is what we must impress on papa."[45]

The friends who knew him best realized, as did Belle, that it would be hard to make him take time for a proper convalescence. Two days after the operation, Steffens wrote to Fola: "He owes it to all of us to take all the time there is to get strong and perfectly well. I make this appeal to him personally, because I think that he will respond more to this view than to that of love. And to bring it home to him, I should like to remind him that as things go on our other leaders, one by one, show weaknesses that point more and more to the likelihood that some day we shall have only the one man to head this movement."[46]

As soon as the operation was reported in the papers, letters and telegrams from over the country came to Bob at the hospital. Among them were touching and unexpected messages from unknown people who counted him their friend. To the children Belle wrote, "I enjoy and appreciate them too but I always feel that papa has depths of enjoyment beyond mine."[47]

While Bob was at the hospital, there began that deep friendship with Drs. Will and Charles Mayo which he treasured throughout his life. Although the Mayos did not agree with Bob's subsequent position on the World War, the difference of opinion never clouded their relationship with a shadow of personal misunderstanding. During Bob, Jr.'s, critical and prolonged illness at that period, their generosity in giving their own time for consultation and offering every expert aid of the clinic staff and laboratory helped Bob to meet one of the hardest ordeals of his life.

After receiving a note from Mary, Belle wrote how much every line from home meant and urged the younger children to write more frequently. "The days are long in spite of his numerous letters and frequent visits from the doctors and sisters. He has a great heart hunger for you children. I know you have for him but you must not depend on Fola to express it for you. Write yourselves. Do you not remember the dear beautiful letters he used to write us on his long hot wearisome trips."[48] During his convalescence at Rochester, Bob was shocked and saddened by word of Dolliver's sudden death on October 15. They had become intimate and devoted friends. An editorial in *La Follette's Magazine* on Dolliver and his work expressed Bob's own feeling of deep personal loss.[49] By October 26, Bob was well enough to leave Rochester for home. On the train Belle read aloud to him an article by Ray Stannard Baker from an advance copy of the November *American* which Baker had sent them. Bob thought the appreciation of the progressive movement was splendidly done and was especially satisfied with the picture that had been drawn of Dolliver and glad that Brandeis had been included in "our group."[50] When they arrived at the station in Madison, the children were waiting with their pony cart and drove them to Maple Bluff Farm.

As he was not yet able to make a speaking campaign, and as the election was near, Bob issued a statement on November 3 urging support of progressive candidates on their records regardless of party lines. Invoking the party spirit at this hour in the life of

American democracy "to assure a party victory regardless of the relative merits of the opposing candidates" was, he said, "a surrender of every principle that had made the progressive movement the hope of millions."[51]

Bob's statement expressed the view of those who were counted as the most active Progressives in the various States. It was in sharp contrast to Roosevelt's efforts to bring the regulars and their opponents together and secure "a fairly united" support for the Republican Party at the 1910 elections.[52] Roosevelt's refusal to "take sides" in the nomination contests had distressed many Progressives. In the election campaigns he continued to baffle and disappoint them by following the course of supporting "some men in both camps," as Bob had predicted.[53] They could not understand how he could make the speech he did for Beveridge in Indiana and then endorse Lodge in Massachusetts, Burkett in Nebraska, Warren G. Harding in Ohio, and accept the New York State platform with its eulogy of Taft and his Administration. Some who would have liked to be "his hearty friends and supporters" were puzzled.[54] Others feared "it demonstrates that he is by nature unstable and that no inner conviction is strong enough to hold him to a fixed course."[55] It increased Bob's distrust of the quality of the colonel's progressivism.

The election on November 6, of an overwhelmingly progressive Republican legislature in Wisconsin assured Bob's return to the Senate. The six Republican Congressmen who had voted consistently against Cannon in the House were reelected, as were two other Representatives who had more recently voted with them. Congressman Stafford of Milwaukee, the only consistent supporter of Speaker Cannon in the entire Wisconsin delegation, had been defeated in the primaries by Henry F. Cochems. But at the November election the Stalwarts cut Cochems, who had been closely identified with La Follette,[56] and Victor L. Berger won in the strongest Socialist district of the State by a few hundred votes. Wisconsin thus elected the first Socialist Representative to Congress.

Bob had a deep affection for Cochems, and always thought this young man's exceptional endowment especially qualified him for public service. The defeat was a keen disappointment. In response to a discouraged letter from Cochems, Bob wrote: "I know the thing looks black to you now . . . but faith and power are one. You have great power, and that must be the measure of your faith. Your vision is bound to clear." To persuade the young man he loved and admired that defeat need be only temporary in the work they were doing, he recalled the dark period of his own life which had followed the Sawyer incident. "At just your age," he wrote, "I was the most generally despised man in all the state. Not a dozen men of any political standing dared call themselves my friends. Not a republican newspaper in Wisconsin could afford to print a friendly word for me. I was politically dead and damned. Following that I met three crushing political defeats in succession. You know all the rest. Do not let the word that you will never again be a candidate pass your lips."[57]

Another defeat which Bob found "hard to bear" was that of Charles H. Crownhart. This able young lawyer had generously consented at the eleventh hour to run as an independent progressive candidate for attorney general in a complicated contest. Except for the defeat of Crownhart and Cochems, the Wisconsin election was a sweeping progressive victory. Under Governor McGovern's administration it would be registered in enactment of the "top-notch" Wisconsin platform by the same legislature that would reelect Bob to the Senate.

In the President's home State of Ohio, the Republican candidate for governor, who had been actively supported by both Roosevelt and the Administration—and where the slogan of the last few days was: "A vote for Harding is a vote for Taft"—was defeated by the Democratic nominee, Harmon.[58] Maine, Connecticut, and Massachusetts, then Republican strongholds, were among the twenty-four of the forty-six States which elected Democratic governors. New York and Maryland went Democratic, as did New Jersey, where Woodrow Wilson, candidate on a platform characterized by the *Outlook* as "a Western Insurgent Republican platform," was elected governor.[59]

The results were variously interpreted. In a telegram congratulating Bob, Brandeis said the election seemed "the most complete justification of insurgency. It has cleared the atmosphere wonderfully —the Democratic victories in the East are the results mainly of the absence of Republican Insurgency."[60] Many newspapers called it a "Democratic landslide"; others, in cartoons and editorials, placed the emphasis on the rebuke to Taft or the repudiation of Roosevelt as the next Republican Presidential candidate. As Taft received the returns and the results became obvious, Secretary Knox remarked, "It seems to be a landslide, doesn't it?" whereupon the President replied, "Well, from what you tell me I should say it was not only a landslide but a tidal wave and holocaust all rolled into one general cataclysm."[61]

During a temporary retreat to Oyster Bay, Roosevelt meditated on the elections and wrote to intimate friends about the personal implications. He said the bright spot from his personal standpoint was that it would put an end to talk about his being nominated in 1912, which was beginning to make him very uneasy as he was not responsible for the present situation and did not wish to have to take the responsibility for it.[62] As things stood now, he was convinced that it would not become his duty to accept, for he could not be expected to take command of a ship simply because it was sinking.[63]

In the quiet of his study at Maple Bluff Farm, Bob read his letters and telegrams, carefully analyzing the results. He was convinced the election was not a Democratic Party victory where the Democrats had won. It was a defeat of reactionary Republicanism, condemning the Taft Administration and repudiating "Aldrichism in the Senate and Cannonism in the House."[64] Where insurgent leadership was strong enough to control nominations and make the issue clear, he found it had received support. George W. Norris had been reelected in his Democratic district, which refused to "landslide." Older telegraphed they had "treed the Beast" in California and could rejoice together. Hiram Johnson had been elected governor with a progressive legislature which would send John D. Works to the Senate to replace Flint who had so faithfully followed Aldrich's lead. William Kent had won against heavy odds in the Second District. His exceptional abilities and racy wit would enliven the insurgent counsels. Although elected as a "Republican," he wrote Bob, "I shall cast no party votes" and "look to you as the leader of my sort of party in the Capital."[65] In Ballinger's home state of Washington, a progressive legislature assured Poindexter's election to the Senate.

These and many other direct reports from different States were among the factors which led him to declare in *La Follette's Magazine*: "No progressive leader, however popular, was able to make the progressive vote subservient to any party. Wherever attempted, thousands of progressives withheld their votes in disgust or cast them for Democrats as a rebuke and a warning against any attempts to compromise the progressive cause for a party advantage."[66] Privately he expressed the same conclusion more pointedly. To Bourne he wrote: "The late election has made many matters clear and taught some gentlemen that they cannot be all things to all men. This great progressive movement for popular government will have its way, and no men or group of men is strong enough to stop its progress."[67]

His past experience in Wisconsin led Bob to believe this election indicated a national breakdown in the old party lines similar to that which had taken place years ago in his own State. He attributed the repudiation of the reactionaries in both parties to the work of the Insurgents in Congress and throughout the country. If these dissenting forces could be organized effectively, he hoped the Progressives might ultimately capture the Republican Party, making it the instrument to achieve nationally what had been accomplished through years of work in Wisconsin.

A few weeks after the election, Ray Stannard Baker enclosed an editorial from the *Springfield Daily Republican* in a letter to Bob with the comment: "It expresses a feeling that I have heard quite generally here—that your prestige in the East is growing greatly, that you are coming into your own after all these years of fighting. I was at luncheon at Oyster Bay yesterday, and was surprised and greatly pleased at the warm words in regard to you spoken by Col. Roosevelt. I should like to tell you about them fully."[68]

CHAPTER XXVIII

The National Progressive Republican
League

From the beginning of the insurgent movement, Bob had been the leader to whom the Progressives in the Senate and House had chiefly turned for direction of strategy. The 1910 elections placed him in the strongest position he had ever held in the Republican Party. The newspapers and current magazine articles were now predicting that he would be an important factor in the 1912 campaign. On December 3, 1910, he left Madison with Lenroot to attend the three months' session of the Sixty-First Congress. In Chicago, between trains, Bob had a brief visit with Francis J. Heney and persuaded him to accept an invitation to speak at a meeting of Minnesota Progressives in St. Paul.[1]

His arrival in Washington, as he described it in a letter, was typical of the active tempo of his days during the coming year: "Got in about an hour late and it has been a rush every minute since. Everybody is here and has a large delegation in tow and the telephone rings all the time. . . . I had to go to the Willard to see Spreckels, Older, Governor Johnson, McClure and others. McSween [Washington correspondent of the Philadelphia *North American*] and other newspapermen were here until 1 o'clock this morning."[2]

On his arrival Bob had received a letter from Taft's secretary, Norton, asking that he call at the White House to talk over judicial appointments with the President. His only response to this invitation was a letter to Taft stating he had but one suggestion to offer: that men should be selected who would "construe the Constitution and the law with due regard to the interests of the people," and that those should be eliminated from consideration "whose legislative or judicial record show them biased toward special interests." He added that he would support the President's Administration whenever he could consistently do so and would oppose recommendations only when a conviction of public duty made it necessary.[3] That same day he wrote to Belle, who had been detained at Madison by illness: "My! but I needed you! And I hope you will not be disappointed but I feel that I cannot go. I am sending him enclosed letter instead. I know if I went my position would be misconstrued. . . . He is moving hard to muddy the water and I feel that progressives going there will confuse the public mind as to his true relations to issues.

"Anyhow, I will not be put in the attitude of rushing to the White House where I have been refused admission and where all the plots to destroy me have been hatched, at the very first opportunity offered. I should feel like a sneak and a bootlick to come at the crook of a finger to be advised with about appointments after all that has happened."[4]

After Congress convened, Taft appointed a number of the delayed minor recommendations made by La Follette and the other Insurgents. Bob thought the elections had alarmed the President, who now made it appear the Administration was "in sympathy" with the Progressives and thus sought to "promote the renomination and reelection of Taft." Knowing he must differ with the President on legislation, he did not want to obscure the issue by making a fight on the relatively unimportant matter of patronage. As chairman, he reported some 340 of the President's appointments of census supervisors, although assured by members of the Census Committee that they would reject any Wisconsin appointments not acceptable to him.[5]

When Congress recessed for the Christmas holidays, Bob completed the draft of a constitution for a national league to promote progressive legislation in the different States. For nearly a year the progressive group in Congress had been considering the formation of such an organization with national headquarters in Washington and local centers in the different States. The matter had frequently been discussed informally. At different times Fred Howe, Amos Pinchot, and others had outlined suggestions for a program. The earliest newspaper reference which has been found to the formation of a local Progressive Republican League is in the fall of 1909.

On October 20, at Spokane, Washington, Bob had strongly endorsed Congressman Miles Poindexter as a candidate for the United States Senate. After the speech, he sat up with Poindexter until two o'clock discussing how to conduct the campaign. That night Bob may have outlined the project of local state organizations which should later cooperate with a national league. The next day the *Seattle Daily Times* reported a meeting in Spokane of about twenty editors of country newspapers throughout eastern Washington who met and organized "The Progressive Republican League, which is expected to lead to a statewide movement in arousing people against the Cannon and Aldrich policies."[6] The dispatch from Spokane was telegraphed to Wisconsin newspapers and reprinted in *La Follette's Magazine*.[7]

Later, when plans for the National League were well under way at Washington, the question of asking Roosevelt to join was discussed, and Bob expressed the judgment that he should be invited.[8] Roosevelt had been told about the project by several Progressives, including Gifford Pinchot, who was at this time in frequent contact with the colonel at Oyster Bay and with Bob at Washington. In mid-December when the final details were being worked out, Roosevelt wrote to Bob suggesting he would like to talk over the whole situation with him and one or two Senators like him.[9]

Bob replied that as he was not yet quite "up to standard," he must take the Christmas recess for recuperation, but would certainly see the colonel whenever he could get over to New York during or after the session.[10] Two days after Christmas, Bob received a telegram from Roosevelt inviting him to lunch at Oyster Bay on Wednesday or Thursday or at the *Outlook* office on Friday, and asking for a copy of the 1910 Wisconsin platform.[11] Bob wrote explaining that he must remain at home during the recess to recover from a slight accident which had occurred when he slipped and had caused considerable pain in his side. He added: "I should very much like to have talked over with you the matter of which Pinchot told you last week. I understand that Pinchot wired you that if agreeable to you, Senator Bourne and I (if I was well enough) would see you Wednesday, but as I could not get out and Bourne did not hear from you, he will lay the matter before you in writing. It [the Progressive Republican League] is going to go, and should have your help, if you will permit me to say so. I am enclosing herewith a copy of the Wisconsin platform, several copies of which were sent you from Madison in October, but in your mass of mail were doubtless overlooked."[12]

During the last days of December, Bob submitted his draft of a constitution and declaration of principles for the National Progressive Republican League to Senators Bristow and Bourne. It embodied a program which many informal discussions had indicated most of the active Progressives were willing to support. After some modifications suggested by Bristow and Bourne, the document was prepared for signatures. Copies were sent to certain Senators and Congressmen and to other leading Progressives of both parties in different States.

In a confidential letter to Brandeis, Bob explained that, although he and some others would have preferred a non-partisan title, it had been necessary to include the word "Republican" because "several of the senators and congressmen (good progressives too) decline to be identified at this time with an organization which could be proclaimed a 'third party movement.' These men hold . . . that they would invite almost certain defeat in the coming nominations and elections, and be forced out of public life if they lay themselves open to the charge of starting a third party. These men are prominent the country over as progressives, and their connection with any progressive movement which is to make rapid progress in the several states is almost an absolute necessity. I hope you will decide that you can stand the name and join with us."[13]

As Bob had promised in his letter of December 28 to Roosevelt, Bourne put the whole matter of the League before him in writing, and sent the specific five-point legislative program with an invitation to join. The general plan was to organize state leagues and promote progressive legislation. The national League was to prepare model bills and resolutions for progressive leaders in state legislatures and furnish speakers and literature upon request in order to aid in passing any one of the laws which they might decide to take up in their States. The legislative program which the members of the League agreed to work for was: (1) the election of United States Senators by direct vote of the people; (2) direct primaries for the nomination of elective officials; (3) the direct election of delegates to national conventions with opportunity for the voter to express his choice for President and Vice President; (4) amendment to state constitutions providing for the Initiative, Referendum, and Recall; (5) a thorough corrupt-practices Act.[14] There was nothing particularly new in the program. Three of the proposed laws were substantially planks in the recent Wisconsin platform; the direct primary had been passed while Bob was governor; Oregon already had an initiative-and-referendum law. Both these States had enacted laws for the direct election of delegates to national conventions, and the Oregon law provided the voter an opportunity to express his choice for President and Vice President.

On January 2, Roosevelt replied to Bourne in a two-page letter which he asked be shown to Bob. The colonel said he was in accord with the legislative proposals except for the constitutional amendments for Initiative, Referendum, and Recall. He warned against the danger of becoming a too advanced and therefore ineffective minority, suggested consulting men who were at different stages of the progressive road, specifically mentioning Governors Bass of New Hampshire, Fort of New Jersey, and Senator Cummins of Iowa. In closing he expressed a wish to see Bourne and Bob if either were to be in New York during the next two months.[15]

The following day Roosevelt also wrote a personal letter to Bob, saying he doubted the wisdom of joining the League at the present time. He stressed the need for caution lest it appear to be dictating a program to good people who were not as far advanced as he and Bob. In slightly different form he expressed his reservations regarding the Initiative, Referendum, and Recall, but said he was in accord with the Wisconsin platform and compared the relative progressive accomplishments of Oregon and Wisconsin in terms favorable to the Badger State. He promised an early expression in the *Outlook* of his agreement with the substance of the Wisconsin platform and Wisconsin's leadership in practical progressive state legislation, due to Bob and those he had led.[16]

Two days later Bob received a letter from George L. Record of New Jersey, one of the initial members of the League, saying Raymond Robins had been at his home "the other evening and imparted the rather surprising but very agreeable information, which he claimed to have gotten by authority, that the Colonel was ready to support you as a candidate for president. As the newspapers say: this is important if true."[17]

Later in January Bob and Belle went to New York on short

notice to attend a performance of Percy MacKaye's play *The Scare-crow*, in which Fola was appearing at the Garrick Theater. On his return he found a cordial little note from Roosevelt commending his "yeoman work" in opposing the seating of Senator Lorimer, charged with election through bribery and corruption of the Illinois legislature.[18] Bob replied, thanking the colonel and at the same time answering his previous letter regarding the League. Noting Roosevelt's objection that some States were not ready for the entire program, Bob said, "As practical men we know" it "cannot be jammed through in the different states en bloc." He compared the situation to Wisconsin, where step by step the backward sections were brought "up in line by an organized campaign of education." After explaining the League's plan of work in some detail, Bob closed his letter by saying, "I do not presume to urge you, but do sincerely hope that you will conclude to wire me that I may sign for you."[19]

The National Progressive Republican League was formally organized at a meeting at Bob's home, 1864 Wyoming Avenue, on Saturday, January 21. Most of those identified with the progressive group in the Senate and House attended. Senator Bourne of Oregon was elected president, Representative George W. Norris of Nebraska first vice president, Governor Chase S. Osborn of Michigan second vice president, and Charles R. Crane of Chicago treasurer. Frederic C. Howe of New York became the secretary.

Elected to the Executive Committee were: Senator Joseph L. Bristow of Kansas, Senator Moses E. Clapp of Minnesota, Representative E. H. Hubbard of Iowa, Representative Irvine L. Lenroot of Wisconsin, Representative-elect William Kent of California, Gifford Pinchot of Pennsylvania, George L. Record of New Jersey, and the president, vice presidents, and treasurer, members ex officio. On the following Monday the organization of the League was publicly announced at Washington. Among the signers of its initial declaration were nine United States Senators, one former senator, sixteen Congressmen, six governors of States, and nineteen other men, well known in their own States, and some nationally recognized as active Progressives.[20]

Bob had left Washington the day after the formation of the League, arriving in Madison on January 23. The next day the Wisconsin legislature confirmed the preferential primary nomination and reelected him to his second term in the Senate. On January 25 he appeared before a joint session of the legislature to accept the election, receiving a warm welcome as he entered the crowded assembly chamber, where he spoke for forty minutes. Bob commended Governor McGovern's recent message which he had printed in his magazine, and urged the legislature to redeem "every pledge made in the platform; not in part but to the last line, not in letter but in spirit." The major portion of his speech, however, he devoted to the National Progressive Republican League, reading the declaration of principles and the names of those who had participated in perfecting the organization. He expressed the belief that the formation of this organization was to be "significant in the history of our government."[21] This phrase was not mere rhetoric; it actually represented Bob's feeling as to the potentialities for the whole progressive movement which were symbolized in uniting for action on a definite legislative program these men from different parts of the country.

On his return to Washington, Bob found a reply to his letter of January 19, in which he had expressed the hope Roosevelt would join the Progressive Republican League. The colonel struck a cordial opening note by mentioning his own satisfaction that his son, Ted, then in San Francisco, was an ardent admirer of Bob's. He suggested, however, that he could best help the League by cordial endorsement in the *Outlook* over his own signature, as in the last issue. This would, he said, permit him to express himself at length and make the necessary qualifications. After explaining why he did not at present wish to seem to take prominent part in any political movement, he again suggested that Bob see him whenever in New York.[22]

For some time the active Progressives had believed it was vital to the movement to have a progressive candidate against Taft for the Republican Presidential nomination. During the winter of 1910–1911, E. W. Scripps, owner of the Scripps newspapers, had written to various people suggesting the possibility of all getting together for La Follette in 1912, and had said he could be counted on to a very great extent in any attempted organization.[23] Throughout the winter the leaders from different parts of the country who happened to be in Washington on various missions called upon Bob and urged the importance of a progressive Presidential candidate in order to make a clean-cut alignment against the reactionaries in their own States.[24]

The potential importance of the dynamic former President's own possible candidacy or of his attitude toward any progressive candidate against Taft was naturally never underestimated by the Progressives. Scripps expressed an opinion which was probably shared by many Progressives at the time he wrote on January 2, 1911, saying, "it only requires that Roosevelt, by acts of commission or omission, shall waive his claims in order that La Follette, the only Bob, must be the choice of all for leadership!"[25]

At Washington many conferences were held which included progressive Senators, Congressmen, and others who were interested in the movement. Among those insistent on definite action were Gifford and Amos Pinchot, James R. Garfield, son of President Garfield, and formerly a member of Roosevelt's Cabinet, E. A. Van Valkenburg, editor of the Philadelphia *North American,* then the leading progressive newspaper in the East, and Gilson Gardner, Washington correspondent for the Scripps newspapers and E. W. Scripps' personal representative. These men had a close relationship to Roosevelt. They saw him frequently in New York and acted as the medium of communication with the Progressives at Washington. The question of his attitude toward a progressive candidate against Taft, or the possibility of his becoming a candidate himself, was often raised in casual meetings and also in the more formal conferences. But the invariable answer reported back to Washington during 1910 and early 1911 was that Roosevelt "did not believe there should be a candidate at all; and *as to himself,* it was not to be thought of."[26]

But the men who reported the colonel's position at this time said they did not fully agree with him. They repeatedly expressed the opinion, individually and in conferences, that a fight should be made against Taft's nomination, and that it could not be made without a candidate. Shortly before the close of the session, however, word was received that Roosevelt had become hostile to Taft, although he still did not favor opposing the President's renomination.[27] A cordial longhand letter from the colonel, and a report of a conversation with him, both delivered at his request by Gifford Pinchot to Bob toward the end of February, seemed to indicate a desire to cooperate with the Progressives. In his letter he invited Bob to lunch at Oyster Bay on March 5 or 7 and suggested Bob bring with him Senator Bristow, Congressmen Madison and Murdock of Kansas, and any others he wished.[28]

After talking it over with Pinchot, Bob decided to go over for the suggested conference, and Roosevelt was so advised by Pinchot.[29] But during the closing night sessions of Congress Bob contracted influenza with a severe sinus complication, forcing him to cancel all the lecture engagements he had expected to fill during the recess. When he found he could not go to New York on March 7, as planned, he wired Pinchot asking him to make a "personal explanation" and also telegraphed Roosevelt: "Night sessions brought on another attack of grippe, rendering it unsafe for me to come over. Am very sorry. Gifford will explain."[30]

CHAPTER XXIX

"That Puff of Applause in the People's Gallery"

The special session of the Sixty-second Congress met on April 4, 1911, and as the newly elected Senators took the oath of office some observers recalled the prophecy Bob had made on the Senate floor on April 19, 1906. Then the crowds in the galleries had broken the sacred Senate rule by a round of applause when he paused in his speech on railroad regulation to predict: "Unless this important question is rightly settled seats now temporarily vacant may be permanently vacated by those who have the right to occupy them at this time."[1] "That prophecy has become almost literally true," Ray Stannard Baker observed as the new Congress began its work. "The old guard has vanished utterly before that puff of applause in the people's gallery."[2]

Four days before the fifth anniversary of that dramatic episode when the Senate had been "deliberately abandoned" during Bob's speech, the Philadelphia *North American* printed a long editorial entitled "Three Scenes In the Senate." It quoted the public prophecy and recalled that previously in private "he had said calmly: 'I am alone in the senate this year. Next year there will be two of us. Then there will be six of us, and before six years there will be twelve of us, and on the way to a majority we shall have the balance of power. While alone I can do no more than force a roll-call. But that roll-call will be had.'" The time had come, the editorial said, when the "roll-call" was no longer La Follette's only lever, for now he was "the honored leader of a group" who "hold the balance of power over legislation."[3]

With keen amusement Bob read before publication a part of an

322

article by William Allen White which stated that this Congress "was as different from the Congress that assembled in 1905 as if it had represented a different nation," for now "in the citadel of property thirty-four progressive Senators appeared who wore no messenger boys' caps. Errand boys had been replaced by men."[4] Washington correspondents, interviewing Senators and Congressmen and picking up current underground whispers as they moved about the Capitol corridors, sent out dispatches commenting on the changes. One predicted that "this might mean the nomination of a progressive or insurgent Republican like La Follette for president in 1912," adding that it was worth while "to see the Senate assemble with no Aldrich to hold the reins."[5] Another observed: "The progressive Senators carry on in a manner that indicates their satisfaction with the world." When they "are not conferring in groups on the floor they are in caucus in Senator Clapp's committee-room, planning as to those of their number who shall go on certain committees."[6]

A few days after Congress convened, Bob wrote a friend that it promised "to be a very interesting session. No such political situation has presented itself in half a century. The Senate Republican the House Democratic, and a clear line of division splitting both parties in each branch of Congress."[7] The effect of the 1910 elections was registered at the beginning of the new session in the progressive fight on the organization of the Senate. Bob knew that the election of the President pro tempore was important as a political symbol, both in the Senate and throughout the country. With the retirement of Aldrich and Hale, who had long dominated, the Republican leadership fell to Gallinger of New Hampshire, a loyal member of the Old Guard. When the Republicans met in caucus according to custom, they selected him as their candidate for President pro tempore.

But eight progressive Senators (Bourne, Bristow, Clapp, Cummins, Gronna, La Follette, Poindexter, and Works) did not attend the caucus and refused to recognize him as leader. Bob nominated Clapp for President pro tempore and led a running fight to prevent Gallinger's election, voting against him on seven roll calls in one day.[8] Borah, Brown, and Kenyon had attended the caucus and therefore felt they could not openly support Clapp. But they cooperated by absenting themselves or pairing their votes in a way that counted against Gallinger. When Elihu Root protested the pairing of two

Republican Senators because the effect of it was "to destroy two Republican votes and defeat the candidate of the Republican caucus," Bob stepped into the main aisle and stood for an instant looking at Root. The gallery and floor were suddenly silent. Then Bob's voice rang out in a clear tone as he denied "the right of any secret caucus held outside of the Senate Chamber behind closed doors with no [Senate] reporters present, to dispose of the public business or anything which may exercise an important or controlling influence upon the public business."[9]

This battle was a headline story in both Eastern and Western newspapers because it disclosed that the progressive group when united for action held the balance of power. The *New York Times,* in a comment typical of many others, said, "For the first time that any one here can remember since the Senate was last organized as a Republican body, the old guard to-day failed to carry out its express purpose on the floor, and for seven consecutive ballots found itself in the minority." Its headlines blazoned the facts regarding the encounter: "REGULARS BALKED/FAIL TO ELECT GALLINGER PRESIDENT PRO TEM/INSURGENTS OUT-PLAY CAUCUS/LA FOLLETTE SILENCES ROOT IN CONFLICT OVER RIGHT TO PAIR."[10] After the seven ballots the Senate adjourned "on the motion of Mr. La Follette—for once triumphant in an open vote," growled the same conservative newspaper.[11] But the fight continued until June 5, when further efforts to force Gallinger's election were abandoned. The Senate transacted its business for two sessions without a President pro tempore.*

Bob also led the progressive Republican Senators in a demand for proportionate representation on the important standing committees, where the fate of most legislation is practically controlled either by amendment, substitution of bills, or refusal to report them back to the Senate for consideration. This move was carrying the fight directly to the citadel of that secret, autocratic power he had openly and steadily attacked ever since his daring challenge to the authority of the venerable Senator Hale during the debate on the Naval Appropriations bill in 1907.

To the all-powerful Committee on Committees Bob now presented what must have seemed a revolutionary resolution. It declared there was a division among the Republicans of the Senate, and listed

* Gallinger was eventually elected President pro tempore in December, 1912.

Borah, Bourne, Bristow, Brown, Clapp, Crawford, Cummins, Dixon, Gronna, Kenyon, La Follette, Poindexter, and Works as "Progressive Republicans" entitled to "such proportional representation" upon committees "as their numbers bear to the total Republican membership" of each committee. The assignments of "Progressive Republicans" upon each committee were to be "designated by Senators La Follette, Bourne, Cummins, and Bristow, the four progressive Republican members of the Committee on Committees," and approved and ratified by the Committee on Committees.[12] The resolution was promptly voted down by the Committee on Committees; Bourne, Bristow, Cummins, and La Follette voted for it; against it were Gallinger, Lodge, Penrose, Heyburn, Warren, Smoot, and Bradley.[13]

When Gallinger presented the assignments to the standing committees for adoption by the Senate, Bob protested on behalf of thirteen progressive Republican Senators. In a brief speech, which was widely reported, he gave the reason for their demand and analyzed the meaning of the split which had for several years been developing within the Republican Party in many States. He reminded the Old Guard that "out of the total Republican vote in the Senate more than one-fourth is to-day emphatically progressive Republican. This is a settled and established fact in political history. The country knows it. The Senate can not ignore it.

"The differences which create division in the Republican Party . . . relate to the most important subjects of legislation and the gravest problems which confront the American people. These differences represent not merely conflicting personal opinions of individual Senators. They represent fundamental differences in convictions involving the welfare of 90,000,000 people. If the progressive Republican Senators should fail to represent the progressive public opinion of their States, they would be swept aside and their places filled with men who would faithfully represent that public opinion. If they failed to protest against the denial of representation upon the most important committees in the Senate, they would be remiss in their public duties."[14] The Senate answered this protest by approving the committee assignments. Bob continued as chairman of the Committee on Census, and for the first time was assigned to the important Committee on Finance, where he found an effective medium for projecting his ideas to the country through minority reports.

During the early weeks of this session, Bob introduced a series of bills and resolutions which were to have far-reaching results in the succeeding years. Among them were: a bill to create a Tariff Commission; an amendment to the existing law extending the powers of the Interstate Commerce Commission;[15] the Seamen's bill, which he reintroduced;[16] a resolution, which was agreed to, directing the Secretary of the Interior to transmit to the Senate a list of all claims upon lands which had been withdrawn from the national forests in Alaska under Secretary Ballinger's regime;[17] a bill providing for the valuation of coal and asphalt lands on Indian reservations;[18] a bill to create a Public Utilities Commission for the District of Columbia;[19] a resolution for an investigation of the Washington Gas Light Company.[20]

Three days after the extra session convened, Bob had introduced a resolution to reopen the investigation of Senator Lorimer's right to his seat. Toward the close of the previous session, Lorimer had been seated as Senator from Illinois in spite of the vigorous opposition of the Progressives and an eloquent protest against his admission by Senator Root. Bob had made repeated efforts to obtain specific information as to the alleged "slush" fund of more than $100,000 raised for Lorimer's election. Subsequent to the Senate's vote seating Lorimer, new evidence had developed. During the recess Bob sought details from various people in Illinois. He also conferred with Professor Charles E. Merriam, Charles R. Crane, and Walter Rogers of Chicago, who came on to Washington to discuss the possibility of reopening the case with him and with the President.[21]

Bob's resolution provided that a special committee should conduct the investigation and that five newly elected Senators who had not previously voted on the case should be appointed to the committee. Leading newspapers headlined the story from coast to coast. Many dispatches noted the indignation of Lorimer supporters and Old Guard Senators at this violation of precedent. They stated that "Never before in the history of the Senate has an individual member sought to name a committee of investigation touching upon the right of a Senator to retain his seat—or for any other matter."[22] The resolution was introduced while a committee of the Illinois senate was investigating the charges against Lorimer. On May 17 it found that he had obtained his seat in the United States Senate by bribery and corruption. On May 22 Bob began a four-day speech in the Senate, reviewing the history of the case, and referring to the evidence recently produced in Illinois. He demanded that the case be reopened and that the investigation be made by a special committee elected in open session by the Senate.[23] A bipartisan reactionary combination indirectly defeated the La Follette resolution by passing a substitute,[24] which was referred to the Committee on Privileges and Elections.[25] The leaders of both parties agreed upon, and the Senate approved, a committee of eight, a majority of whom might be expected to vindicate Lorimer.[26] The investigation dragged on for months, and brought many sensational disclosures, but the committee finally voted 5 to 3 in favor of Lorimer. Finally the Senate, on July 13, 1912, repudiated both the committee's and its own previous decision. "There was a deathly silence in the Senate Chamber while the roll was being called."[27] By a vote of 55 to 28 the Senate evicted Lorimer because "corrupt methods and practices were employed" in his election.[28] In his magazine Bob ran a roll call analysis of the Lorimer case, which, he said, "stands out as one of the blackest pages in our national history."[29]

The investigation aroused such public indignation that it became an important factor in bringing about a Constitutional amendment providing for the direct election of United States Senators. Bob had favored this amendment for years. A resolution providing for its submission to the States had passed the House several times but had been blocked in the Senate. At this session, however, the Senate adopted the resolution by a vote of 64 to 24 only a few weeks after Bob had demanded that the investigation be reopened. It passed the House at the next session and became a part of the Constitution on May 31, 1913.

While Bob and the progressive Republicans were aggressively challenging the old order in the Senate, Roosevelt had been on a six weeks' speaking trip. Returning from the West, he visited Madison on April 15, making three speeches, one of which was before the Wisconsin legislature. Arriving on an early train, he was Governor McGovern's guest at a breakfast in his honor at the Executive Residence. A letter to Bob, written the next day, reported that as the colonel rode down to the capitol after breakfast he said to McGovern that he wished he had time to talk politics with him, and "dropping his voice to a confidential tone" added: "I cannot tell you how very much I am disappointed in Taft. But it is not time yet to form a new party,—it would be a section of the party. We are not ready for that. I would very much like to see and talk with La Follette."[30]

In his speeches at Madison, the colonel advocated modified initiative and recall legislation, thus going further toward support of the League's program than he had in his *Outlook* editorial or his letters to Bourne and Bob. A well known participant in the Wisconsin movement wrote Bob the next day: "All your friends here were most agreeably surprised at Ex-President Roosevelt's frank and strong endorsement of you and of what Wisconsin has done under your leadership. . . . his declaration for you by name, both at the Capitol and at the Gymnasium was clear and emphatic. Every one with whom I have talked since say[s] that Roosevelt has now definitely and irrevocably placed himself on the progressive side. He is with the progressives on both feet."[31]

Shortly before this letter about Roosevelt's Madison visit reached him, Bob had received reports from two friends who had talked with him in California. From San Francisco, where the colonel spent several days, Rudolph Spreckels wrote: "T.R. is just as certain as I am that Taft cannot win the election, but thinks his nomination is sure. . . . Governor Folk has been with us for a few days, he told me that if Taft & Harmon are candidates you could win on a third ticket easily."[32]

In a strictly confidential letter which Bob was not permitted to show even to his co-workers, Fremont Older wrote: "I had a long talk with Roosevelt while he was here and I feel quite certain that he is looking forward to something happening which will cause his renomination for president. He doesn't like Taft, but will not say so, openly and publicly, although he told me that he didn't like him. I told him that I thought you ought to be president, and he said that you could not be elected. I don't think he will ever stand for you, because I think he feels way down deep that you would make good, and in that event he would never see the White House again. I may be doing him an injustice in making this analysis, but I want you to know just how I feel about it. He told our little group here that we ought to work for the defeat of Taft's nomination, and he didn't add that we ought to work for you . . . Governor Johnson says that if it were left for him to pick a candidate for president, he would pick you without any hesitation. That is the feeling we all have here."[33]

Bob wrote on April 18 thanking Older "for your good letter. Be sure it will be held strictly with me. It puts Mr. T.[eddy] just where he belongs and confirms many other things which have come to me. He wants *it*—wants it *now*—if not now, *soon*. He has encouraged me through P. [Gifford Pinchot], has said he would support me 'quietly'—couldn't support me 'openly'—it would be regarded as 'another attempt to name a man' etc. etc.

"He is willing to have some one do the Light Brigade Act, stop Taft, and get shot about the right time. . . . The progressive cause is the only hope of the country. It should not be permitted to foozle because no one has the courage to go up against the Administration forces and the solid south. The party about whom you wrote me wont do it, but would be very glad to administer upon the estate of the man who does undertake the job.

"I stand ready to go to the front and take all the chances on beating the administration and any near progressives who would take a mournful delight in probating my political estate. But I am not willing to undertake the job, nor is it for the future good of the progressive cause that any one should stand *until* and *after* a campaign fund is—not promised, but in the hand. I cannot go out and ask that it be put up. So there you are Freemont [*sic*]; you asked me to write you fully and freely. I have done so and place this in your hands with the same reservations which you made regarding your letter to me."[34]

After an absence of seven weeks, spent chiefly in the insurgent territory, where he encountered the "fluid" conditions of party lines, the colonel returned to Oyster Bay on April 16. Only seven days after his speeches at Madison, while the progressive glamour of Wisconsin was still vivid, Gilson Gardner had lunch with him.[35] When Gardner returned to Washington, he reported his talk to Bob and also gave a full account of it to a group of Progressives who met at Senator Bourne's office in the Capitol on Sunday, April 30. Among those who attended this meeting were Senators Cummins, Clapp, Bourne, Gronna, La Follette, and Poindexter; Representatives Lenroot, Hubbard, and Norris; Professor Charles E. Merriam, State Senator Clyde Jones, and Walter S. Rogers of Chicago; Angus McSween, representing Van Valkenburg of the Philadelphia *North American*, Gilson Gardner, ana a number of others. During the conference Gardner told of his recent interview with Roosevelt. This report, although generally accepted as accurate at the time, subsequently became the subject of bitter controversy.

In a written account, which is corroborated in substance by Irvine L. Lenroot, who was also present, Bob has recorded that Gardner said Roosevelt "had entirely changed his mind regarding a Progressive candidate against Taft; he *now* believed that the Progressives should put forward a candidate, that *I should be the candidate*, and that I should get into the fight *at once*; . . . He said that he was still inclined to believe that Taft could not be beaten; that he (Roosevelt) could not openly oppose him as a candidate because he had made him President; that he could not, for the same reason, openly advocate my candidacy against Taft; but that he would, if I became a candidate, commend my work from time to time in *The Outlook* and help along in that way; that while visiting the legislature in Madison he had spoken there and strongly endorsed my work; that he did it, having in mind the possible announcement of my candidacy, with the idea that it would be useful and helpful as an expression of approval. He said further that if Taft could not be beaten for the nomination, as he was still inclined to believe, I could, nevertheless, stand as a candidate, and if defeated in the convention, I would not be weakened before the country."[36]

Practically everyone present at this conference participated in the discussion, and there was unanimity that the Progressives must unite upon one of the progressive leaders as a candidate against Taft. Cummins said, "There is but one man who should be considered as the Progressive candidate, and that is Senator La Follette." When asked as to his own candidacy Cummins replied, "I shall not be a candidate; it is out of the question." He also promised to do everything in his power in Iowa to elect as many delegates as possible to support La Follette in the convention if he would consent to be the candidate.[37]

When asked if he was willing to become the progressive candidate, Bob repeated what he had previously said to individuals and small groups in conferences: that he thought the Progressives of the country could not support Taft for renomination; that he would support any thoroughgoing Progressive who would come out and make a clean-cut fight, or that he was willing to make the fight as the candidate if the Progressives thought he should do so, provided men could be found to meet the necessary expenses. There was agreement of opinion that Bob should be the candidate against Taft, and when the conference concluded those present apparently considered the matter of his candidacy settled provided the one condition of a campaign fund was met.[38]

Bob thought that if $100,000 was assured for the pre-convention campaign, a creditable showing could be made which would advance the progressive cause whatever the outcome might be in regard to the Presidential nomination. On April 6 Charles R. Crane had dined at the La Follette home; Fred Howe had also been a guest, and William Kent had dropped in later. They had talked over the work of the League, the reopening of the Lorimer case, and the general political situation. Before Crane sailed for Europe, two days later, Van Valkenburg had seen him in New York and Crane had said he would subscribe $25,000 provided La Follette was the candidate.[39] A few weeks later Kent pledged $10,000 and began writing to others for contributions.[40]

Other members of Congress also pledged support of Bob's candidacy. Among them were Senators Bristow of Kansas, Works of California, Crawford of South Dakota, Representatives Victor Murdock of Kansas, C. A. Lindbergh of Minnesota, John Nelson, E. A. Morse, and W. J. Cary of Wisconsin. Senator Borah said there were complications in Idaho which he thought could be best taken care of "by making no open declaration at the time, but gave assurance that the delegation from his state could be depended upon for support in the convention."[41]

The day after Gardner discussed La Follette's Presidential candidacy at luncheon with Roosevelt, President Taft also speculated out loud on the same subject during his afternoon stroll with his secretary, Charles D. Hilles, and Major Archie Butt. Taft expressed the hope that his recently appointed Secretary of the Interior, W lter L. Fisher, might not "find himself advocating the nomination of La Follette for the Presidency," although from what he heard this would not surprise him at all. Archie Butt records in his diary that "Hilles said he had talked with him [Fisher] only the day be-

fore at luncheon at the Metropolitan Club. 'And did you reach the
conclusion that he would support La Follette for the presidency?'
[asked the President] 'Well, not exactly that,' said Hilles, 'but he
told me that La Follette was not the demagogue that some people
thought him and that he felt him to be one of the biggest statesmen
of the period.' "[42]

But apparently, either shortly before or after the conference at
Senator Bourne's office, some one else had seen the colonel and
brought back a report which conflicted with Gardner's. This evidently again raised doubts as to the former President's intentions.
For Elizabeth Evans, who was a house guest at the La Follette
home, wrote Alice Brandeis that it appears Roosevelt "is wilfully
now for renomination & La Follette is about to put it up to him,
straight, that he himself will run against any candidate who does not
come out, now, & campaign at the head of the progressive forces,
prepared to take defeat, if need be as their leader. It is Roosevelt's
plan to keep himself dark till the last moment & then try to rush the
Convention; & that plan La Follette is determined to prevent. He
will stand aside himself & back up T.R. if the latter will enter the
lists now. But from now on he takes the stand that he that is not for
the Cause is against it, & will ram that home. His talk is as compelling as a verdict of Fate. We talked last night I am ashamed to
say till after midnight. There were folks in, & I guess none of us
knew the hour.

"Then at lunch today there was company, Jud.[son] Welliver
among others, & *such* good talk, with the Senator brilliant & jovial
as I have never before seen him."[43]

The very next day, however, brought still another report regarding
Roosevelt's position toward his own and Bob's candidacy which
seemed authoritatively to confirm the one Gardner had recently
made. Van Valkenburg arrived in Washington after an extended
conference with Roosevelt in which the colonel had read to him the
article he had prepared on Wisconsin for the *Outlook*.[44] On Saturday, May 6, Van Valkenburg had a three-hour talk with Bob the gist
of which was recorded in another letter Elizabeth Evans wrote the
following day to Alice Brandeis: "I cant quite keep back the news
that T.R. says that LaF. is the logical Progressive candidate &
should come out *now*, & that he, T.R. will back him up, & agrees not
to be a candidate himself! He has just *discovered* Wisconsin, says

he was blinded by prejudice before & could not recognize La F's true
character,—that if he had done so it would have been better for his
own administration—that La F. has educated his state into a true
democracy & tried out there on a sound basis the policies that other
states are experimenting in blindly, etc. Said he is writing an article
on La F. for the Outlook—for which look out. All this in a 3 hours'
talk with Van Valkenburg yesterday, & reported to this house last
night about midnight."[45]

A meeting was held at Bob's home on Tuesday night, May 9, at
which it was "decided to start the ball rolling as soon as $100,000
was in sight." Also, the opinion of the group seems to have been
that Gifford Pinchot "would be the best man for running mate."[46]
The following night Van Valkenburg told a group of Progressives
at Washington that Roosevelt was "definitely and completely out of
the running," and the next day William Kent, who was present, communicated Van Valkenburg's statement to the colonel in a letter.
Kent also wrote that he was "of the impression that we shall get
together and start something in the matter of running Senator La
Follette for the Presidency" and that "those present seemed to think
that Gifford Pinchot was probably the best man for running mate."[47]
In his reply Roosevelt cordially invited Kent and his mother to
motor out to Oyster Bay for lunch, but neither confirmed nor denied
Van Valkenburg's report.[48] Kent did not go to Oyster Bay at this
time.

What Roosevelt actually said to the different men who talked with
him alone could be known only to him and to them. But there is
reliable contemporary, documentary evidence, in addition to the
testimony of individuals of exceptionally accurate memory, that
Gifford Pinchot, Gilson Gardner, and Van Valkenburg repeatedly
reported that Roosevelt was not and would not be a candidate, also
that Gardner's and Van Valkenburg's talks with the colonel, as recorded by Bob, were actually in substance thus reported to him and
to others at Washington. There is also the documentary evidence
that the colonel was informed Van Valkenburg had reported he
"was definitely and completely out of the running."[49]

As a master of the game, Roosevelt appears to have delighted in
"playing politics" and to have skillfully observed the ancient rule of
putting nothing in writing which could be communicated by word
of mouth. This method suited his temperament and his concept of

the proper and effective method of dealing with a difficult situation. Some who talked with him about his own Presidential candidacy and that of La Follette may have shared in an understanding as to subtle verbal shadings which were not communicated in their reports at Washington. Others doubtless accepted the messages at their face value. It is also probable that Roosevelt's own attitude changed according to the political weather.

Plans had reached the point where a call for La Follette's candidacy was actually being drafted by Lenroot and Kent,[50] when it was reported to Bob that some of the Chicago Progressives might decide after all that it was expedient to support Taft because of his recent appointment of Walter Fisher and others to his Cabinet. The reaction of the La Follette family to this possibility is accurately and frankly recorded in a letter Belle wrote to Elizabeth Evans stating that Gifford "Pinchot was here last evening conferring with Bob. He is in good fighting feather, quite unchanged. But there are indications that the Chicago group (This is surmise and confidential) have been pulled off. Probably not Mr. Crane, but those with whom he works. As I told you and Mr. Brandeis, they were very confident and cocky when here last, but it looks to me as though Mr. Fisher had captured the group since. If this proves true I think it will relieve Bob of the responsibility of being a candidate. I was glad to have the assurance that it would be a great relief to him just as it would to me to feel that he was free to go on with his fight without the undertaking of a great campaign. If the progressives are united and determined enough to stand for and back up him or any other candidate he will lead or support some one else."[51]

Bob had expressed this view frequently in conference, and recorded it a little later in a confidential letter to a friend in Nebraska when he wrote: "I am in favor of uniting our support behind any progressive who will make the run and who has the confidence of the progressives generally. Or I am willing to do the other thing. What I want is a strong cohesive force as the basis, making the fight for the things we have been contending for."[52]

In weighing the advisability of his own or another progressive candidacy against Taft, he never thought the deciding factor should be the immediate chances of winning or losing the Presidential nomination in the 1912 convention. For him the vital test was the relation of any such candidacy to the long-time objectives of the progressive movement. He did not think the campaign should be undertaken at all unless the active Progressives were agreed upon a candidate. But once initiated, he believed the contest should be carried through for that candidate until the final ballot at the convention. He stated this clearly to those who urged him to run, and stressed it particularly to Gifford Pinchot because of his close friendship for Roosevelt.[53]

Only ten days after Gifford Pinchot, "in good fighting feather, quite unchanged," had been at the La Follette home, Roosevelt's promised article appeared in the *Outlook*. Both Gardner's and Van Valkenburg's reports of the colonel's privately expressed intention seemed to be given definite confirmation in his published account entitled "Wisconsin: An Object Lesson for the Rest of the Union." The article was superlative in its praise of the constructive, practical accomplishment in Wisconsin. It should be read in full by anyone interested in evaluating the import it had for Bob and the Progressives at this time. In his personal reference to La Follette, Roosevelt said: "I doubt whether American students of social economics fully realize the extraordinary work that has been accomplished during the last decade, and is now being accomplished in the State of Wisconsin under the lead of Senator La Follette and of the group of entirely practical and at the same time zealously enthusiastic workers who have come into active control of the State mainly or largely because of the lead he has given them. . . . After my visit I felt like congratulating Wisconsin upon what it had done and was doing; and I felt much more like congratulating the country as a whole because it has in the State of Wisconsin a pioneer blazing the way along which we Americans must make our civic and industrial advance during the next few decades."[54]

In his magazine Bob reprinted the article in full.[55] His usual skepticism as to the colonel's verbalism appears to have been swept aside by this unqualified public tribute to the constructive achievement in Wisconsin due to many years of collaboration by State and university under his leadership. Temporarily, at least, the former President's early cooperation with the reactionary Spooner, Payne, and Babcock forces seems to have slipped into the background.

Bob appears to have accepted the declaration in the *Outlook* as an expression of a sincere and enduring evaluation rather than as a possible move on the political chessboard.

CHAPTER XXX

From "Lone Crusader" to "Leader"

Bob had been present in the historic old Supreme Court Chamber of the Capitol when the famous decision in the Standard Oil case was rendered on May 15, 1911. It gave a new construction to the Sherman Anti-Trust Law which had been on the statute books since 1890. He thought it was a dangerous decision with implications which menaced our free institutions. By reading into the Sherman Act the construction that only "unreasonable" restraints of trade were prohibited, the Court had reversed a long line of precedents.[1]* With intense feeling, which must have been revealed in his expressive blue eyes, he heard Justice John Marshall Harlan, in the small Supreme Court Chamber, deliver his emphatic protest against the decision. Later, as Bob awaited a street car at the east front of the Capitol, he encountered Justice Harlan. The Justice had noticed him as he pronounced his dissent from the bench. "It is an outrage!" Harlan exclaimed to Bob, his voice still shaking with emotion. "What the Court has done today it has done by usurpation, nothing less."

Bob agreed with Harlan, and said so frankly to the press, declaring: "The court has amended the Sherman anti-trust law just as it was attempted over and over in the Senate to do it. What they did not get in the Senate they have now got from the court. . . . I fear that the court has done just what the trusts have wanted it to do and what Congress has refused steadfastly to do."[2] In his *Magazine* Bob published Justice Harlan's dissent and severely criticized the Supreme Court decision.[3] Bob thought the decision was "a crisis,"[4] and telegraphed Brandeis: "We need you to consider next important step

* This decision subsequently found popular interpretation in the distinction between "good" and "bad" trusts advocated by Theodore Roosevelt and J. P. Morgan.

in view of decision yesterday. Come immediately if possible."[5] Brandeis was equally concerned, and left Boston the following night, arriving in Washington on Thursday, May 18, for a conference to which Bob had invited Francis J. Heney, who happened to be in town, and a number of others, including Members of both Houses of Congress. After a thorough discussion that evening, Brandeis, Lenroot, and Heney were asked to prepare a draft of a bill to supplement the Sherman Anti-Trust law. They did this. Then, during the weeks that followed, these drafts were discussed and letters exchanged regarding them. On May 23 Brandeis sent copies of his revised draft to Bob and Lenroot. A letter from Bob, enclosing one from Lenroot covering certain points, crossed Brandeis' in the mails. Later Brandeis sent Bob additional memoranda which took up the suggestions in detail.[6] This interchange of ideas was typical of the way these men worked together at this time.

Later, in a speech to a group of businessmen, Brandeis said: "La Follette knows this [trust] problem by heart. He has never theorized about it. He has always, by tremendous work and the aid of a marvellous memory, secured cold facts about the evils of trusts. He has dug down to bed rock in the trust matter and, in a cold, businesslike, analytical way, he has discovered the truth about them."[7]

While they were still consulting about the details of the amendments to the Sherman Anti-Trust Law, the Supreme Court rendered another decision on May 29 which reaffirmed the doctrine of the recent Standard Oil decision that only "unreasonable" restraints of trade were unlawful.[8] Justice Harlan again delivered a vigorous dissent. This "judicial usurpation of the legislative function," asserted twice within two weeks, increased the criticism of the Courts which had been steadily growing. *La Follette's Magazine* had persistently denounced "the tendency to judicial legislation," and it again commended Justice Harlan's opinion. In the next issue it began publication of a series of articles by Gilbert E. Roe entitled *Our Judicial Oligarchy*, which were subsequently published as a book to which Bob wrote the introduction.[9]

On June 6 Bob attended a public reception of some 20,000 people who assembled at the Fifth Regiment Armory in Baltimore to honor James Cardinal Gibbons. Among the prominent speakers were President Taft and Colonel Roosevelt. Bob had hoped to have a word with Roosevelt after the meeting, as he wished to thank him personally for his article on Wisconsin. But this proved impossible, so he wrote a little note expressing his appreciation and explaining, "It was my misfortune to get wedged in away back of you and try as best I could it was not possible to get out until you had been carried off by some of your friends."[10] The colonel replied that he was pleased Bob had liked the article, and added, "I felt that I owed it to Wisconsin, and, my dear Senator, that I owed it to you."[11]

At the cardinal's reception Taft and Roosevelt had greeted each other cordially and had had a few moments' conversation. This was played up in the newspapers, some asserting positively but inaccurately that during this brief talk Roosevelt had promised his support to the President.[12] During the following weeks a series of inaccurate reports was sent out from Washington asserting there was dissension and division among the Progressives in regard to supporting La Follette for the Presidential nomination. One story went so far as to announce that Gifford Pinchot and Garfield had gone over to Taft.[13] In response to an inquiry from Minnesota Progressives, Poindexter replied: "There is no change of opinion among the so-called insurgents here with reference to the presidential nomination. I think without exception they would all be delighted to see Senator La Follette nominated and would do everything they can to bring about that result."[14] It was definitely known that certain of these stories had been written by reporters who covered the White House.[15] These false reports finally went so far that Congressman George W. Norris openly charged they had "originated at the White House" and that it was generally understood the information came from the President's private secretary.[16]

No authorized announcement of Bob's candidacy was made, although a story appeared in many newspapers throughout the country on June 17 and 18 which was thus interpreted. The fact was that a Washington reporter, Clyde Tavenner, who represented a syndicate of 1,240 weekly papers, had sent out a dispatch stating La Follette would be a candidate. Hearing of this, Gilson Gardner feared he would be "scooped" and sent out a story that the formal announcement of La Follette as the progressive candidate for the Republican nomination could be expected almost any day.[17] As Gardner's close connection with La Follette and the progressive group at Washington was well known, John Snure and others stated in their signed stories that these announcements were based upon the "highest" authority.[18] The result was that newspapers called up Bob's office "all day Saturday at intervals of about five minutes." Hannan wrote Gifford Pinchot, "We simply said, 'nothing to say' "; but he predicted with some concern that the announcement made in this way "will bring a flood of letters from all parts of the country, and it will be necessary to equip ourselves immediately to answer these."[19]

Four days after this newspaper story appeared, Clapp publicly declared for La Follette. Other active Progressives, including most of the progressive Senators, Congressmen, and governors, made similar individual announcements during the summer and fall. Borah made no public declaration, although he had given private assurances of support. Week by week the opposition to Taft within his own party thus became more sharply defined throughout the country. It was also increasingly evident in Congress, where the President had to depend upon the standpatters to pass legislation unsatisfactory to the Progressives.

In June, Bob led another legislative battle against the Administration forces when the reciprocity agreement with Canada was reported to the Senate from the Finance Committee by Penrose. Although the agreement involved a treaty with Canada, it had been submitted by President Taft in his call for the extra session in the form of a bill requiring passage through both Senate and House. During the Sixty-first Congress it had passed the House by a large majority, but had failed to reach a vote in the Senate before adjournment on March 4. In general the bill provided that certain goods manufactured in the United States should be admitted duty free to Canada, and raw materials and farm products from Canada should be admitted duty free to the United States. For years the agitation for reciprocity had received strong backing from Eastern manufacturing states.

Although Bob believed in the principle of tariff reciprocity with Canada, careful study led him to oppose this particular bill because he thought it was not true "reciprocity." He was convinced it would sacrifice American farmers to Canadian competition, while actually strengthening our trusts by giving them cheaper raw materials. Ultimately he thought it would place the Canadians at the mercy of American trusts. With his minority report from the Finance Committee, he also filed on June 13 a statement of his reasons for opposing the bill and gave notice that he would offer amendments for the reduction of tariffs in the interests of all consumers, including farmers, "who are compelled to carry all the burden of the President's lopsided pact."[20]

On June 21 Bob made his first speech against the bill.[21] The debate during the day revealed that the progressive Republicans would have the aid of Senator John Sharp Williams and other Democrats. Their combined strength proved such that many newspapers described the conflict as one of the most dramatic that had occurred in the Senate in years. Fola, who was in Washington at the time, noted, "Yesterday afternoon's battle was regarded here as a very significant victory for insurgency."[22] Reading the accounts in the Boston papers, Brandeis wrote Bob, "You seem to have done great things yesterday, and indeed generally since I saw you."[23]

But the Old Guard viewed it differently. The day after Bob's attack on the bill, Archie Butt, personal aide to the President, noted in his diary that Senator Brandegee gave the President a "ludicrous account" of the method of the Insurgents in the Senate. Brandegee thought "nothing would be more ironical than the fact that the old committee rooms of Senator Aldrich should now be the headquarters of the insurgents. He said that the insurgents met two or three times a day in these rooms, which are very close to the Senate Chamber, and that all Senator La Follette had to do was to walk out of the Senate Chamber and hold up his finger, and he would be followed by the whole thirteen of the insurgents. Unquestionably Cummins is becoming jealous of La Follette, but the latter's power is such that he not only called them into caucus in this way, but also recorded what they had to say and their votes."[24]

An editorial in the *New York Times* had severely criticized Bob for stating that the suppression of news against the Reciprocity measure was a black page in our history.[25] A few days before the final vote Bob again declared in the Senate that the press had a duty to the country in all matters of public concern, but that a false impression regarding the bill had gone forth because the press had "a direct money advantage in it." As evidence of their financial stake in the legislation, he cited an editorial in the Philadelphia *North American*, which had now swung into opposing the Reciprocity measure but frankly admitted it had approximately $40,000 to $50,000 dependent upon its passage. He also quoted from a letter sent to newspapers throughout the country by Herman Ridder, president of the American Newspaper Publishers Association, declaring it was "of vital importance to the newspapers that their Washington correspondents be instructed to treat favorably the Canadian reciprocity agreement, because print paper and wood pulp are made free of duty by this agreement."[26]

Bob offered an amendment to reduce the wool and cotton schedules of the Payne-Aldrich Act, but it was voted down. The Reciprocity bill passed the next day by 53 to 27. But all the progressive Republicans except Brown of Nebraska, Poindexter of Washington, and Works of California voted with Bob against the bill, which was signed by the President. Although it thus became a law in the United States, popular disapproval in Canada prevented its ever being put into effect. Nevertheless, angry American farmers remembered it had been the President's pet baby, and it had disastrous political consequences for him.

The day before Bob had made his final speech against the Reciprocity bill, Archie Butt commented on the very long message to Congress the President had just prepared and was reading to his Cabinet that afternoon. Butt noted that Taft was "really out after La Follette. He hates the Wisconsin man with a consuming hatred."[27]

While the Reciprocity battle was still on, Brandeis came to Washington to confer with Bob about another matter. A few days later Belle wrote: "We had a 'homey' visit with Mr. Brandeis. He always makes us feel double our strength in love, capacity and futurity."[28] Another friend they both especially enjoyed, who was also frequently at their home during this summer and fall, was Ray Stannard Baker. Following a suggestion Baker had made, the *American Magazine* asked Bob to write a series of autobiographical articles. For a long time Bob had been considering doing such a series, and negotiations had actually been under way for a number of months with *Hampton's Magazine*. He therefore had some forty or fifty thousand words of basic material in rough form before the matter was taken up and the contract actually signed on July 6 with the *American Magazine*. By arrangement with John S. Phillips, publisher of this monthly, Baker was assigned to assist in editing the articles Bob prepared.

Although Bob thoroughly enjoyed the work, signing this contract meant he had added another obligation to the heavy load he was already carrying. He always insisted that writing was a relaxation. But to his family and intimate friends it seemed that these articles and the editorials for *La Follette's Magazine* meant spending many hours at his desk which should have gone toward the vacations he failed to take. He believed his magazine was an important factor in the educational work of the progressive movement, for the subscribers were widely distributed throughout the country, and the magazine went into many communities where there were only reactionary newspapers. But the subscription was only a dollar, and at this time there was a loss of a little over a thousand dollars a month. At intervals Bob was forced to dig into his own pocket or to give time to raising money to meet the deficit and prevent suspension of publication. Such a crisis developed in August because an attack of influenza in the spring had forced him to cancel speaking engagements which he had counted on to meet the extra expenses. The advance on his first article enabled him to tide over until his anxiety was relieved by the generous contribution of a friend who gave twice the amount which it was estimated would be necessary before new subscriptions began to come in.

It was a help as well as a great satisfaction to Belle to be able to add something herself to the family income at this time. A week before Bob's contract was signed, the North American Press Syndicate, which supplied material to one hundred newspapers in every State in the Union, had telegraphed acceptance of a number of brief articles she had submitted, under the title of "A Thought For The Day."

During the hot summer there were amusing incidents and pleasant social interludes which were a relaxing accompaniment to the exacting legislative work. Occasionally the Progressives combined strategy conferences with dinner at Bourne's, Clapp's, or Bob's home. After all-day sessions, when the evenings were especially oppressive, Bourne would take some of them for a drive in Rock Creek Park. On one occasion, while the reciprocity battle was at its height, Bob, Clapp, and Kenyon were driving with Bourne when his car suddenly encountered the President's automobile at a sharp turn in the road. Taft's companions were the four reactionary Senators Penrose, Murray Crane, Smoot, Wetmore, and the President's aide Archie Butt. Butt said that they could almost hear the comments of the men in the other car and that he thought those in Taft's car looked pretty guilty, as if caught doing something wrong. He had no doubt the insurgent newspapers would broadcast the President's joy ride with the standpatters.[29] What the newspapers missed were Bob's inimitable descriptions of this and similar encounters to his intimate friends and family.

Immediately after the Reciprocity bill passed, Penrose, as chairman of the Finance Committee, reported to the Senate a measure which had already passed the Democratic House, revising the famous "Schedule K," the wool schedule of the Payne-Aldrich Tariff. A few days later, on July 27, Bob presented a substitute bill. It was substantially the same as the amendment the Senate had voted down when he previously offered it to the Reciprocity bill. In a speech that same day, he attacked the duties on wool then in effect under "Schedule K." The Senate adopted his substitute by a vote of 48 to 32.[30] The next day Belle wrote to a friend, "Bob is feeling fine and has his hand on the helm."[31] He was appointed to the Conference Committee and shared with Representative Underwood the leadership in working out a conference report which was reported to the Senate and passed on August 15 by a vote of 38 to 28.[32] Before it passed, Bob called the Senate's attention to the fact that for the first time in history tariff duties had been discussed and determined by the Conference Committee with doors wide open and press reporters present. He added that he hoped this method, which had been initiated on Senator Bailey's motion, might become a precedent for all committee action on public business in the future.[33] He thought this was the most important achievement in the entire fight.

Bob was also appointed to another Conference Committee on a bill which placed on a free list agricultural implements, boots, shoes, and many necessities of life which farmers bought but did not sell. He submitted this conference report on August 16 and it was agreed to without a roll call vote.[34] Another bill, lowering the duties on cotton, was also passed by Congress. These three measures revising the Payne-Aldrich Tariff, popularly known as the "Pop-Gun" tariff bills, were promptly vetoed by Taft on the ground that such legislation should await the report of the Tariff Board.

But the farmers thought differently. The correspondence which began flowing into Bob's office indicated swift fulfillment of a prophecy made by Frank Harrison, editor of the *Nebraska State*

Capital, that if the President vetoed the wool bill and the farmers' free list "there will be a storm in this western country that will be so loud and strong that all the postmasters and federal brigadiers will rush for cover and stay there."[35] An active worker in the Grange who had been a Republican all his life reflected the sentiment expressed in many letters when he wrote Bob from Ohio: "It is a wonder how unanimous the farmers are; not a man has talked to me who will vote for Mr. Taft under any circumstances and not one but what will support you."[36] The same man warned the editor of the Ashtabula *Beacon Record* that "the machine may be able to nominate Mr. Taft again but it will never be able to elect him. Mr. La Follette is the man whom the farmers want for President and if he is not nominated you may expect the election of a Democrat."[37]

Throughout the spring and summer of 1911, special articles in newspapers and magazines reflected the growth of the progressive movement and the importance that was being attributed to La Follette's leadership as the opposition to Taft and the reactionaries became more pronounced and effective in Congress. From Boston Mrs. Evans wrote Belle with some amazement of "a capital article on the Senator, really appreciative," which had appeared in the conservative *Boston Evening Transcript*.[38] In June, *Harper's Weekly* printed "A Talk with La Follette" in which "The Senator From Wisconsin Discusses His Fellow-Senators New And Old."[39] In the *Saturday Evening Post* of June 10, the leading article by Samuel G. Blythe, entitled "The Lonely Man of the Senate," vividly told the story of the change in La Follette's position from "a lone crusader" to a "leader." Chase S. Osborn, the governor of Michigan, who had formerly lived in Wisconsin, was sufficiently impressed to write Bob that, after watching his work for more than twenty years, he applauded every word although he did not think even this masterly writer did his work justice.[40]

The July *World's Work*, then edited by Walter Hines Page, carried a ten-page illustrated article by William Bayard Hale. The title alone was enough to make the standpat Senators writhe if they read it: "La Follette, Pioneer Progressive, The Story of 'Fighting Bob,' The New Master of the Senate And Candidate For The Presidency."[41] When an illustrated article by Henry Beach Needham entitled "La Follette's Ideas, An Interview With the Leader of the Progressives," appeared in the *Saturday Evening Post* on July 8, the interest of the younger members of the family centered on a photograph taken at Maple Bluff Farm. The children had gone home early in June to spend the summer at Madison, and Belle wrote asking Phil if he didn't think "it fine that The Saturday Evening Post published the picture of your ponies? It ought to advance the market value."[42] This fiction of potential profits from ponies was always maintained. But even when Bob discussed increasing the circulation of *La Follette's Magazine* through pony prize contests, he and every other member of the family knew that if an unknown purchaser actually appeared some good reason would be found why that particularly beloved animal could not be sold.

As the adjournment of Congress drew near, Bob wrote John R. Commons about doing some research on the legislative aspects of the articles for the *American Magazine*. Commons was coming East to attend an economic conference, and he stopped off for a day at the La Follette home to talk over the work. They also discussed the political situation and Roosevelt's attitude toward the La Follette candidacy. Commons took the midnight train to New York on Thursday, August 17. The next day he had lunch with Roosevelt. Returning to his hotel immediately afterward, Commons wrote Bob a brief longhand note saying: "Dear Bob [:] Lunched with Roosevelt and A. P. Moore, editor & owner of Pittsburgh Leader—latter red-hot progressive—has been running daily big head line—'For President 1912 Theodore Roosevelt.' is organizing Progressive League—Roosevelt will write him letter not to boost him for president—Both of them say you ought to run—T.R. not very emphatic—Moore very insistent—is ready to come out for you when he had published T.R.'s letter—But the interesting thing is what he says of Flynn [William Flinn]—former boss—says he is red hot progressive—especially for initiative, referendum and recall (with question mark after judges). They want Flynn to be head of the Pennsylvania Progressive League. Is eager to have you meet Flynn & I told him I would do my best.—Wish you would make inquiry about him if you do not know already."[43] The meeting then suggested by Alexander P. Moore and "T.R." actually took place four months later.

A few days before the extra session adjourned, Bob introduced the bill to amend and strengthen the Sherman Anti-Trust Act. At the next session Lenroot introduced the same bill in the House. It was based on the fundamental concept that monopoly could be prevented and competition maintained by proper enforcement of a clearly defined law. The bill provided that every restraint of trade should be presumed to be unreasonable in which it was shown that certain business practices were followed, thus placing the burden of proof upon those the Government sued. This was a direct reversal of the majority decision recently handed down by the Supreme Court which had been approved by both Taft and Roosevelt. The bill also gave private parties alleging injuries at the hands of trusts and combinations the right to intervene as parties to suits brought by the Attorney General or any United States District Attorney for violation of the Sherman Act.[44]

Immediately following the reading of the bill, Bob made a speech reviewing the history of the Sherman Act and the Supreme Court decisions relating to it. He discussed the proposed bill in detail and urged the necessity for its passage because of the recent decisions.[45] The President's "consuming hatred" was probably intensified by this speech, for Bob pointed out the inconsistency of Taft's recent approval of the Standard Oil and Tobacco Trust decisions,[46] and his previous position as expressed in his message to Congress on January 7, 1910. At that time Taft had disapproved of writing the word "reasonable" into the statute because this would be "to thrust upon the courts a burden that they have no precedents to enable them to carry, and to give them a power approaching the arbitrary, the abuse of which might involve our whole judicial system in disaster."[47]

During this special session Brandeis and Bob cooperated on another measure designed to protect the public from exploitation by monopoly interests. The Administration's policy in Alaska had been under insurgent fire when it reopened to public entry lands which had previously been included in the national conservation program. A resolution introduced in the Senate by Poindexter called upon President Taft for information as to the opening of the shore of Controller Bay to a railroad company.[48] This grant aroused suspicion because it appeared to give the railroad company a monopoly of the harbor. The Alaskan question threatened to become a political issue. Taft took it seriously and wrote an exceptionally long message which was sent to Congress on July 26.[49]

Brandeis had been counsel for one of the House committees which had carried on an investigation and frequently discussed the matter with Bob. That they were in complete accord on the policy which should prevail in Alaska was natural, for their thinking had been along similar lines long before they met. As early as 1906 Bob had introduced a bill in the Senate protecting the Government's rights to coal and other minerals on public lands. Although it had failed of passage when President Roosevelt withdrew his support, Bob had persistently introduced it year after year when the opportunity offered. After several long conferences about Alaskan policy, Brandeis, at Bob's request, dictated a memorandum for him.[50] On his return to Boston, he tersely expressed the pith of their program when he wrote suggesting this slogan:

> Alaska: the Land of Opportunity
> Develop it by the people, for the people.
> Do not let it be exploited by the Capitalists,
>   for the Capitalists.[51]

On August 19, three days before Congress adjourned, Bob introduced a resolution Brandeis had drawn which formulated their conclusions. It provided that "the Government should own and operate all railroads, docks, wharves, and terminals, make provision for operating mines and leasing mines at reasonable royalties, with suitable safeguards for prevention of waste and security of life, and, in general, provide for proper conservation and development of the natural resources of Alaska, to be administered by a board of public works, to be appointed by the President and confirmed by the Senate."[52] At Bob's request this resolution was laid on the table with the intention of taking it up at the next session. But the day before Congress adjourned, he discussed the proposed law, calling the Senators' attention to the fact that it incorporated an Alaskan policy which had been adopted in the Wisconsin Republican platform of 1910.[53]

The extra session of Congress adjourned on August 22. Bob had written Brandeis while the Reciprocity debate was in full swing, "These be awful rushing times with me just now."[54] This phrase accurately described the heavy pressure under which he had worked throughout the entire winter and summer. Bob had spoken at length on every leading question before the Senate. This meant an enormous amount of "digging" in preparation for each speech. His assistants and the experts to whom he always turned for specialized information gave him invaluable help. But he never took his speeches on important legislative matters "ready made" from another hand. His incisive answers to hostile questions and his quick response in sharp debate revealed the hours that had gone into mastering the details of a subject. For a time he had attended daily meetings of the Finance Committee in addition to the regular Senate sessions. By dictating at night after he got home, he had completed, and sent off on August 20, his first article for the *American Magazine*. Only a few days after Congress adjourned, he wrote his brother-in-law, "I stood the work of the session very well, and am ready for it as fast as it comes."[55]

Bob stayed in Washington after Congress adjourned on August 22, 1911, to complete the series of articles he had contracted to write for the *American Magazine*. These were subsequently published in book form with three additional chapters under the title of *La Follette's Autobiography*. The first of the series was published in the October issue. Theodore Roosevelt read it with interest, and wrote Bob that he thought the first article was "capital." He expressed particular satisfaction with a sentence in which Bob had said that a proper attitude toward public affairs was more important than any definite views a man might hold.[56]

"It was good to know," Bob replied, "that you had read the beginning of my story and like it. I hope it may help a bit in the direction in which we are all moving. Never before have I done anything that gave me the real pleasure I get in this review of our work in Wisconsin.

"Yes, Colonel, the right attitude, with resolution and judgment behind it is basic. The tools of democracy are necessary, but there is little good in loading men down with them before they are willing or ready. The bungler may give a good set of tools a bad reputation because he does not know how to use them. Everything worth doing takes time and the years teach us all patience."[57]

Thus Bob addressed Roosevelt in a personal letter for the last time.

CHAPTER XXXI

"Shifting the Scenes"

At the La Follette home on October 29, 1911, Fola and George Middleton, a well-known young dramatist, were married by the Senate Chaplain, Reverend Ulysses G. B. Pierce. It was a simple wedding, the family and a few intimate friends being the only guests. Mary was bridesmaid, and Paul Kester, with whom Middleton had collaborated on a play for Julia Marlowe shortly after being graduated from Columbia University, was best man. Soon after his marriage "Mid," as the family called him, became literary editor of *La Follette's Magazine,* writing a regular column under the title of "Snap Shots."[1] Through the years Bob followed the production and publication of Mid's plays with as keen an interest as this young dramatist had in his father-in-law's work in the Senate.

By the fall of 1911, the issues of the 1912 campaign were clearly defined. The progressive movement was at high tide and the conservative leaders in both parties were on the defensive. In the spring and summer of 1911, Governor Woodrow Wilson had been received with great enthusiasm on speaking trips through the Northern States. During the early months of 1911 he had, with the cooperation of George L. Record and other progressive Republicans of New Jersey, secured the enactment of a primary-election law, a corrupt-practices Act, a bill to regulate public utilities, and a measure enabling the cities of the States to adopt the commission form of government. In the fall of 1911 Wilson appeared to be the most likely progressive candidate for the Democratic Presidential nomination. Throughout the country progressive Democrats began to rally to his support as against Governor Judson Harmon of Ohio.

On September 14 President Taft left his summer home at Beverly,

Massachusetts, for a 13,000-mile speaking trip which took him to the Pacific coast. He strove to rally the rank and file of the Republican Party to the slogans which had been effective in previous campaigns, but he was coldly received throughout the West. Canadian Reciprocity, the Payne-Aldrich Tariff, and the President's recent veto of measures to revise that unpopular law had created a glacial atmosphere in the insurgent territory which even his genial smile could not melt.

As Taft's weakness became more evident, some of the "regular" Republicans and many Federal officeholders began to meditate on the possibility of a candidate with better chances of election. By September Bob's candidacy had developed a strength which was evoking comment in both Eastern and Western newspapers. Medill McCormick, who had called upon Bob earlier in the summer and volunteered his services, was in charge of publicity at Washington headquarters. The reports which came in from over the country during September and early October indicated that the Progressives of the West and Midwest were enthusiastically pledging their support.

Senator Clapp had been on a successful speaking trip in California which had included "a round up meeting" of Progressives in San Francisco. On his way back home he stopped off at several places to address meetings, and was surprised at the enthusiasm he found for La Follette even in Senator Smoot's home. He wrote that during his speech at Salt Lake City, when he casually mentioned La Follette's name, "they simply stopped me with their response."[2] Early in September George W. Norris had predicted that North Dakota, the first State to hold a Presidential primary, would be for La Follette by from five to one to ten to one.[3] He now wrote to Washington headquarters from Nebraska that Clapp's speech at Lincoln had been "masterly"; although not published in full in the newspapers, "it had percolated through the state" and "caused a great deal of favorable comment everywhere." Norris reported "very good success in Nebraska" and was "satisfied we will get this state."[4] The governor of Nebraska, Chester H. Aldrich, was equally optimistic, and had previously announced "La Follette is the choice of our people" and "could carry the state."[5]

In Senator Cummins' State, one of the leading agricultural papers of the country, the *Homestead*, published an editorial in September criticizing Taft and urging Republicans to nominate La Follette for President. The owner of this paper, James M. Pierce, had written Bob in May that all three of his publications, the *Homestead*, the *Wisconsin Farmer*, and the *Farmer and Stockman*, having a combined circulation of 280,000, would support him for President in 1912.[6]

More than three hundred Progressives from different parts of Minnesota had gathered at Minneapolis on September 7 to hear Congressman Lenroot, Professor Charles E. Merriam, and James Manahan, who was elected Congressman at Large from Minnesota a year later. A resolution was presented to the meeting by Leonard Erickson, seconded by Hugh Halbert, and adopted by a rising vote. It endorsed La Follette as the leader of the progressive movement, the logical nominee of the Republican Party for President, and closed with the phrase, "We pledge ourselves to work for his nomination and election first, last and all the time."[7] A week later Clapp returned from his Western trip and gave out a statement predicting that "there would be but one candidate representing the progressive element of the country at the next Presidential election and that a vote for progressive principles would have to be cast for Robert M. La Follette."[8]

At Los Angeles, California, on September 12, Senator Works told members of the Union League that "Taft and La Follette are destined to face each other in the next Republican national convention, and if it were left to popular vote today La Follette would be nominated, and easily too."[9] On the evening of that same day progressive Republicans of South Dakota met at Huron, endorsed La Follette for President, pledged him "unswerving support," and heard Senator Coe I. Crawford and R. O. Richards join in acclaiming him as the progressive leader.[10] Senator Clapp spoke there the next night and wrote Bob's secretary that "things are shaping up fine Crawford has his fighting suit on and I look to see the fur fly."[11]

Reporting to Washington headquarters on the political situation in the Sunflower State, William Allen White wrote: "Kansas Republicans are for La Follette. If we can get a presidential primary we can get the delegation. In a convention Taft will win—most of the delegates—say 11 out of 16. [Governor] Stubbs is frankly for La Follette." White said he hoped Stubbs would "convene the legislature and pass a presidential primary law. Then it will be clean sailing."[12]

The day Taft started on his Western trip, Rudolph Spreckels had arrived in Washington with encouraging reports from the California Progressives. Governor McGovern of Wisconsin had been Roosevelt's guest at lunch in New York on September 19, and Spreckels saw the colonel at Oyster Bay eight days later. The next day Spreckels wrote a brief longhand letter to Medill McCormick reporting that Roosevelt had "said he would take no active part and that Governor McGovern of Wisconsin had told him that he thought it would hurt our cause to have him, (T.R.) come into the fight—T.R. says he thinks if we can get $500,000—in hand to organize with LaF. can be nominated but he thinks we cannot elect him,—says a democrat is almost sure to win."[13]

By the middle of September, the campaign had developed such impetus that it seemed advisable to bring the leading Progressives of the country together for a conference. A call was issued by Walter L. Houser from the National Progressive Republican headquarters at Washington, and three hundred Progressives representing thirty States assembled at Chicago on October 16. The conference was called to order by Medill McCormick. George L. Record of New Jersey presided as permanent chairman. It had been generally understood that the conference would endorse La Follette for President.[14] As the "keynote" speaker, Senator Clapp said "Senator La Follette is in himself a platform that represents the progressives."[15] The conference unanimously adopted resolutions declaring: "The record of Senator La Follette in State and nation makes him the logical candidate for President of the United States. His experience, his character, his courage, his record of constructive legislation and administrative ability meet the requirements for leadership such as present conditions demand.

"This conference indorses him as a candidate for the Republican nomination for President, and urges that in all States organizations be formed to promote his nomination."[16]

These resolutions had been drafted by Edward P. Costigan of Colorado, Charles E. Merriam of Chicago, James R. Garfield of Ohio, Amos Pinchot of New York, and J. E. Little of North Carolina. They had been revised by Congressman Lenroot of Wisconsin and Garfield, who had been Secretary of the Interior during Roosevelt's Administration.[17] Garfield had hesitated about attending the conference to such an extent that McCormick had finally telegraphed

Gifford Pinchot not to let Garfield spoil his record by failing to take part in the movement to nominate a Progressive.[18] But it is probable that another voice was even more persuasive than either McCormick's or Gifford Pinchot's. For on October 10 Garfield had called on Roosevelt at the *Outlook* office in New York, and it was after this that he signified his intention of attending the Chicago meeting.[19]

Although the progressive delegates from thirty States had unanimously endorsed La Follette, Garfield had vigorously protested this action in the Resolutions Committee sessions. After some discussion he had reluctantly agreed to the resolution as drafted. On his return to Cleveland, he promptly wrote Bob that he thought the endorsement of any single individual was a mistake and that he had only accepted the resolution with the understanding that he intended to regard it as a recommendation, not a pledge. He also made the extraordinary suggestion that it would be a great help to the general movement if Bob himself would make a similar statement.[20] Garfield sent a copy of this letter to Roosevelt.[21] He also read it to at least two of Bob's supporters in Ohio, Herbert Williams and John D. Fackler. Both these men had participated in the Chicago conference. Williams, who was active in the Grange, reported to La Follette headquarters in Washington that Garfield had said he was not a Presidential candidate himself and had also given the reasons why Roosevelt did not feel like being a candidate. Williams therefore concluded Garfield would be "all right" as to La Follette's candidacy.[22] Fackler, who was subsequently in charge of the La Follette headquarters in Ohio, wrote urging Bob to ignore Garfield's letter, and assured him they would take care of the gentleman in Ohio by going ahead without him if he did not come across as they expected he would.[23]

In Bob's files there is a carbon copy of a reply to Garfield's letter on which is marked "not sent" in his manuscript.[24] Other notations on the letter indicate it was drafted by Walter Houser and Medill McCormick. Bob probably refused to write or sign any answer to Garfield's strange suggestion. He and others at his Washington headquarters were convinced that Roosevelt's influence was responsible for Garfield's efforts to prevent a La Follette endorsement at Chicago. This interpretation was based upon a chain of circumstantial evidence. Shortly before the Chicago conference Fackler had written to Washington headquarters that Garfield was hesitating about participating.[25] Bob had also been informed a few days later that Garfield had gone East "to consult the Oracle at Oyster Bay."[26] This visit was reported in the newspapers, and much was made of it when Garfield arrived in Chicago in a noncommittal mood regarding the endorsement of La Follette.[27] Bob knew Garfield had decided to attend the conference after seeing the colonel.[28] Therefore Bob interpreted the effort to prevent his endorsement as indicating that Roosevelt desired to keep the field open for his own candidacy and that the two men had an understanding as to tactics. Soon after the conference an editorial in the *Outlook* seemed to echo Garfield's attitude by declaring, "This indorsement is to be regarded as a recommendation rather than the committal of the movement to any one man."[29]

Two weeks after the conference a special dispatch to the *New York Times* quoted William Allen White as stating "Taft Can't Win" and endorsing La Follette. Under the title of "Shifting the Scenes," an article by White was printed in *La Follette's Magazine* which said, "Wall Street sees that Taft cannot win," and predicted that "La Follette will carry the West. Nothing can stop that. Wall Street knows it. Wall Street's feet are so cold that its toes clink! That's why it is dumping Taft and preparing for some new political maneuver. La Follette sentiment is growing. The Taft trip has proved that he cannot regain the people's confidence—that he does not know their language, that he cannot hold their allegiance. Something must be done to stop La Follette's rise as Taft sinks. Something will be done. The scurrying feet of the stage hands behind the curtain foretell coming events."[30]

Just prior to the Chicago conference Gilson Gardner, on behalf of the Scripps newspapers, had visited a number of the Midwestern States traversed by Taft. In the communities Gardner visited he was regarded by the active Progressives as an emissary of the group at Washington. To a friend who had asked for confidential information on the political situation, Bob had accurately described this relationship in a letter introducing Gardner as "a close personal friend, with whom you can talk as freely and confidentially as you would with me . . . he is an important factor in the advisory counsel [*sic*], so to speak, of our progressive group here in Washington. He is therefore by far the best man I can send to you as my personal representative for the confidence suggested."[31]

When he reached Minneapolis, Gardner wrote the La Follette headquarters saying, "Have been to Iowa, Nebraska, South Dakota, North Dakota, and Minnesota and find the farmers ten to one against Taft. I don't think anything can prevent solid La Follette delegations from these states (except possibly Minnesota). If the rest of the country feels anything like this Northwest, it is a landslide. Taft can't get the nomination."[32] That same day he also wrote Roosevelt that the farmers of Iowa, South Dakota, and Minnesota were ten to one against Taft because of reciprocity.[33] The following day, at the Odin Club in Minneapolis, Gardner talked to twenty-seven Hennepin County Progressives who had gathered at a luncheon to hear him. One of the men present subsequently stated that "Gardner told us of his personal interview with Colonel Roosevelt. He said that Roosevelt told him that there should be no delay on the part of La Follette or his friends in having him announce his candidacy, and that he was given that message to take to Senator La Follette's friends.

"The question then came up whether the colonel would be likely to be brought into the race himself. Mr. Gardner then made the most positive statement that had yet appeared, saying that the colonel told him he not only would not enter the race, but that in no circumstances would he accept the nomination if tendered to him."[34]

Gardner attended the Chicago conference, and on his return to Washington he said to Bob, "I have come definitely to the conclusion that you now have a fair chance to win the nomination in the convention," and also announced his intention of going to New York "to acquaint Roosevelt with the situation as he saw it, and urge him to a more active and more open support" of Bob's candidacy.[35] Gardner made an appointment by telegram to see Roosevelt at eleven o'clock on Friday, October 20.[36]

Upon his return to Washington, Gardner said to Bob: "Roosevelt is not only surprised at the development of your candidacy, but he is disappointed as well. . . . Roosevelt wants to be President again, but you know it has heretofore been his judgment that Taft could not be beaten. However, he now believes that he will be beaten. This change of opinion is not due alone to my report of the conditions in the west, but others have seen him; and then this

Chicago conference had been very informing to him. He begins to
see that this Progressive movement is a whole lot bigger than he has
ever believed it to be. Now you are developing such strength that
being nominated in 1912 becomes a possibility. And even if you
should fail of the nomination, your leadership of the Progressive
movement would become so established that you would be in the
way in 1916."[37] Others had been ahead of him, Gardner said, in
reporting the decline of Taft's strength and the development of
the La Follette candidacy. "Dan Hanna of Ohio, son of the late
Mark Hanna, and Nat Wright, his editor of the Cleveland *Leader*,"
had urged that it was time for the colonel "to 'cut the string' and
turn his candidacy loose. Roosevelt had received also a report in
writing from [John Callan] O'Laughlin, correspondent for the Chicago *Tribune*, who had been with Taft on his 'swing around the
circle,' and he reported Taft a 'dead one,' and urged upon Roosevelt that it was time for him to get in. 'Still,' Gardner said, 'he
will not do it. He cannot come out as a candidate against Taft. He
knows it. He has said so himself again and again.' "[38]

A little over a month later, following a visit of Dan Hanna to
Roosevelt, the Cleveland *Leader* published an editorial entitled
"Will Roosevelt Lead?" and another Hanna paper, the Toledo
Blade, became steadily more pronounced in his support. Bob thought
the tone these newspapers struck so soon after the owner had seen
the colonel indicated that although Roosevelt had not yet "cut the
string" he had "loosened it, giving his friends an opportunity to
start here and there an 'insistent demand' that he should be the
candidate of the Progressives."[39]

Following the Chicago conference, enthusiastic reports regarding the La Follette candidacy continued to come in at Washington
headquarters throughout October and the first ten days of November. The strength of the progressive movement was revealed
day by day in the response which the returning delegates met in
their different States.[40] Encouraging as this was, Bob clearly recognized that so long as Roosevelt chose to remain available for the
nomination by making no public statement his actual entrance into
the field could disrupt the progressive forces. This last report from
Gardner regarding the colonel's changed attitude renewed doubts
as to Roosevelt's real intentions. Late in October Bob said to a

member of his family that he thought he might win the Republican nomination if Roosevelt "didn't mess things up."*

In November Taft's home State of Ohio became the first battle-ground for the Republican Presidential nomination. Here the forces and the strategy were revealed which later directed the pattern of action in other States. On the evening of November 3, Senator Clapp was the principal speaker and guest of honor at a dinner which a Cleveland newspaper described as "one of the most significant political gatherings this city has witnessed in recent years." The spacious banquet room was filled to capacity. "Gathered there was a body of men, many of whom have never actively participated before in political organization." The stage facing the diners was decorated with pictures of Presidents Lincoln, Garfield, McKinley, and Roosevelt. But nowhere was there a picture of Taft. In "the center of the group was a picture of Senator La Follette. On the tables were found expensive likenesses of the Wisconsin senator."[41]

Judge R. M. Wanamaker of Akron presided and introduced Clapp, who "turned a withering invective upon the reactionary leaders and champions of special privilege within his own party." He closed his talk with a eulogy of La Follette and was cheered by the audience when he ended with the statement "that an epitome of all the best thought in the progressive movement was carried in the name of the Wisconsin leader."[42] As Clapp took his seat, several men simultaneously addressed the chairman, while the cheers were "still reverberating." But Judge Wanamaker recognized Walter W. Pollock, who had attended the Chicago conference as a delegate from Cleveland. Pollock had grown up in Grant County, Wisconsin, where he had known Sam Harper and had cast his first vote for Bob's election to Congress. On his motion a temporary organization of the Ohio Progressives was formed. Wanamaker was made chairman and John D. Fackler, a well-known Cleveland attorney, was named secretary. James R. Garfield's name was not among the guests listed at this dinner. But the reporter did note as present

* Henry F. Pringle, in his biography *Theodore Roosevelt* (New York, Harcourt, Brace & Company, 1931), p. 548, states: "It lay in Roosevelt's power, as the events of those turbulent years unfolded, to make La Follette the nominee. It is improbable that the Taft forces could have blocked his selection."

a prominent Cleveland lawyer, John J. Sullivan, former United States District Attorney, who was to play an important role at another banquet in Youngstown, Ohio, just seventeen days later.

In the interval between these two banquets, the elections on November 7 confirmed Bob's estimate as to the unexpected strength of the progressive movement among the rank and file. In Ohio Newton D. Baker was elected mayor of Cleveland as a disciple of Tom Johnson, who had been defeated in 1909. Brand Whitlock was elected mayor of Toledo, and the Progressives won an overwhelming majority of the delegates to the state Constitutional Convention which was to be held early in 1912. Garfield was, however, defeated as a candidate for delegate. Some newspapers and some La Follette supporters in Ohio attributed this defeat to the loss of progressive support due to Garfield's previous vacillation.[43]

The Ohio victory in Taft's home State had special significance and was received with rejoicing by the Progressives everywhere. It jolted the Old Guard and set in motion waves of political maneuvering which reached from Ohio to Massachusetts, Washington, D.C., New York, Oyster Bay, and back again to the Buckeye State. It was regarded as a forecast of what would happen in the States where there were Presidential primaries for the election of delegates to the national convention. The day after election, Senator Atlee Pomerene was reported in a dispatch from his home at Canton, Ohio, as predicting that La Follette would be the Republican nominee.[44] At Washington, D.C., Senator Cummins gave out a statement on November 10 declaring he believed "it improbable that President Taft will be the nominee of the Republican party in 1912," and stating "I am for La Follette for the Republican nomination and will do all I can to bring about the nomination."[45] A little later Governor Hiram Johnson and a gathering of five hundred Progressives in a meeting at San Francisco came out for La Follette for President. The movement for a progressive Republican organization in Massachusetts was also given an impetus by the Western victory.

But the regular Republicans and Federal officeholders were as much alarmed by the Ohio elections as the Progressives were elated. Republican National Committeemen and Old Guard leaders began looking to their fences and seeking a candidate with better chances to win than Taft. They saw the progressive straws in the wind and knew the Lodges and the Burtons wouldn't do. They feared La Follette, and there was a "Shifting" of "the Scenes" as William Allen White had astutely predicted. Aware of Roosevelt's great popular appeal to many rank-and-file Progressives, they also knew he was remembered in the inner Republican circles as having worked harmoniously during his Presidential years with the senatorial "Big Four," Aldrich, Spooner, Allison, and Platt. The trend was clearly revealed in the report that even an Old Guard Senator like Murray Crane of Massachusetts had deserted Taft's sinking ship and written offering his support to the colonel.

In Ohio, after the election, Walter F. Brown, the sagacious Republican National Committeeman, was one of the many sudden converts to progressivism. He was soon openly advocating Roosevelt's nomination as the salvation of the Republican Party. Joining with those Progressives who were under the spell of the glamorous former President, Brown and "regular" Republicans of his type steadily and astutely encouraged the demand for Roosevelt. An editorial explosion from the *Outlook* suddenly aided these combined forces in their plan to prevent an endorsement of La Follette on November 17 at the scheduled meeting of the Ohio progressive organization. The timing of the editorial, which came off the press on November 16, the day before the meeting, may have been fortuitous, but it was effective. For it was interpreted by newspapers and politicians as an attack on the Taft Administration and the opening gun of Roosevelt's Presidential candidacy. In a signed editorial the colonel arraigned the government policy toward "business" as "chaotic," and recommended that the Nation adopt "a progressive policy" akin to that which had been so successfully put into actual practice in Wisconsin, where the State did justice to the corporations and in return exacted justice from them toward the public.[46] Telegraphic dispatches from Washington to Ohio newspapers reported that politicians were predicting Roosevelt would be a Presidential candidate with La Follette as his running mate.[47] The day after the colonel's editorial appeared, Ohio Progressives from ten counties met at Cleveland. A declaration of principles was drawn up, but La Follette was not endorsed, and it was expressly stated that the organization was in behalf of a movement rather than any particular candidate. What Garfield had not been able to accomplish at the national progressive conference at Chicago in October had been achieved at Cleveland in November.

A few days before this meeting Garfield had informed Roosevelt that Ohio Progressives would follow the plan he had urged at Chicago. In this same letter he told of a talk with Walter L. Houser, La Follette's campaign manager, when the latter had recently been in Ohio. Garfield reported that Houser was satisfied with this plan, that La Follette was in accord with the suggestions made in Garfield's letter to him, and that La Follette would so declare in his first speech.[48] If Houser made such statements, it was without any authorization. In fact he had every reason to know they were entirely inaccurate. He also knew that the implication of such a plan was contrary to La Follette's repeatedly expressed determination to enter into no combinations and to continue as a candidate himself until a nomination had been made at the Republican National Convention.

Following publication of Roosevelt's editorial, reports began coming into Washington progressive headquarters that division was being created in the progressive ranks by some of Roosevelt's friends who were giving out that La Follette's candidacy "was really in Roosevelt's interest and at the right time he would be brought out as the real candidate" or that delegates elected for La Follette "would be delivered to Roosevelt in the convention."[49] These rumors were picked up and enlarged upon by Democratic newspapers or those favorable to Taft.[50]

Bob thought the confusion and difficulties which were being created in the progressive organizations in the different States could easily be stopped by a few plain words from Roosevelt. When Bob bluntly expressed this opinion in conferences at Washington, however, Gifford Pinchot and Gardner continued to insist "that Roosevelt did not intend to be a candidate."[51] At La Follette headquarters everywhere this "Roosevelt situation" became, as Bob said, "the most trying of all." From Chicago headquarters the secretary, Walter S. Rogers, reported that the colonel had made himself the center of the stage and there was Roosevelt talk everywhere.[52] On the same day, from the same city, Medill McCormick telegraphed that Roosevelt had taken a good deal of wind out of La Follette's sails.[53] A letter written immediately after Houser left the La Follette home probably reflected Bob's own words in the phrase "that the Great

Hunter is playing the game and playing it with high cards."[54] For the previous night the subterranean activities had finally burst forth in open fireworks on November 20, at the annual banquet of the Garfield Republican Club in Youngstown, Ohio.

As Bob read the morning papers, they seemed to offer definite evidence that the underground activities of the preceding weeks had been carried on with the colonel's blessing. Among the prominent speakers reported to have assailed Taft's record as President in their prepared addresses were James R. Garfield, who was regarded as Roosevelt's spokesman in Ohio, and Judge R. M. Wanamaker.[55] Reporters noted that there was no picture of La Follette at this banquet and that his name was scarcely mentioned. Seated next to Garfield at the speakers' table was a well-known Cleveland attorney, John J. Sullivan, who was described by one of those present as a "jury-swaying, poetical, flamboyant type of lawyer."[56] Sullivan attacked Taft's Administration and made an impassioned appeal for Roosevelt to become the candidate for the Republican Presidential nomination. As Garfield had recently seen Roosevelt, Bob had no doubt that both men knew in advance about the speech Sullivan had planned to deliver at this banquet.[57]

The day after this banquet Gilson Gardner was sufficiently concerned to telegraph the colonel that certain Progressives at Washington felt the use of Roosevelt's name, though unauthorized, was likely, unless checked by some public announcement, to divide the progressive strength and cause serious trouble. Gardner asked if there was anything Roosevelt wished him to do about this.[58] The colonel replied that there was nothing he could add to what he had said on several occasions in letters and authorized statements, which it would be foolish to keep repeating.[59] Three days later Gardner saw Roosevelt at his office in New York.

On Saturday, November 25, there was a conference at Washington which was attended by Ray Stannard Baker, Walter Houser, Gifford Pinchot, and Gilson Gardner, who was just back from his talk with Roosevelt. That evening Baker and Brandeis dined at the La Follette home.[60] The gist of Gardner's report and the conclusion Baker came to during that evening's talk were recorded in his brief diary entry the next day: "T.R. will not say I will not be a candidate, but he does say 'I am not a candidate.'" Baker noted it as his opinion that Roosevelt could get the progressive following from La Follette while La Follette bore the brunt of the fight.[61]

Two days after this dinner at Bob's home, the Philadelphia *North American,* on the morning of November 27, printed what purported to be an "authoritative statement" reiterating Roosevelt's previous statements that he "was not in the remotest sense a candidate for the nomination" in 1912.[62] That same day an afternoon newspaper at Madison received a dispatch from Washington which may have been sent by Gilson Gardner, since he often reported political news for the *Wisconsin State Journal* at this time. Certainly it came from someone who had inside information. It reported that progressive leaders at Washington were "frankly elated" over the statement in the Philadelphia *North American* because it was based on a letter Roosevelt had written the previous week to the editor, Van Valkenburg. A New York dispatch printed under the same headline quoted Gifford Pinchot as saying: "The authorized statement from Col. Roosevelt in the Philadelphia North American merely repeats what his friends have known all along. The Colonel has a habit of meaning what he says. I am glad the statement was made, because it will settle for good, all doubt in the public mind, make the issue between La Follette and Taft perfectly clear, and greatly encourage the progressives. Nothing could be better."[63]

That evening Gifford Pinchot spoke before the Insurgents' Club in New York. Although he had publicly announced his support of Bob's candidacy long before, the *New York Times* headlined its story of the meeting, "Pinchot Comes Out For La Follette." In his speech Pinchot said that "since this morning the crystallization is going to proceed faster than ever around 'Bob' La Follette." When reporters asked if this statement had anything to do with the published announcement that Roosevelt had been eliminated as a Presidential possibility, Pinchot replied, "I mean that since Col. Roosevelt has eliminated himself Senator La Follette is his logical successor." Although Pinchot disclaimed being "Roosevelt's messenger," his close relationship to the colonel led many to interpret his statements as an authorized indication of Roosevelt's intention.[64]

Ten days later, on December 7, Gifford Pinchot addressed a luncheon meeting of four hundred Progressives at the Grand Pacific Hotel in Chicago. He declared that Taft's renomination was "either impossible or extremely improbable" and that La Follette had "a mighty good chance to capture the flag." On the same night, in a speech to the Chicago Press Club, he said: "If Col. Roosevelt had not made his recent statement, and I am in a position to know he means what he says, he might have been the candidate. I do not assert that La Follette is yet sure of the nomination, but, now that circumstances have made Mr. Taft's renomination either impossible or extremely improbable, the attention of the country is turning swiftly and eagerly to Bob La Follette of Wisconsin."[65]

On Saturday morning, December 9, two days after Gifford Pinchot had spoken at the Chicago Press Club, Bob received a letter which had a definite influence on his subsequent action. On Friday afternoon Ray Stannard Baker had talked with Roosevelt in New York. Immediately afterward Baker went to The Players club and reported his conversation to Bob in a four-page letter. Baker said he thought the colonel had "*progressed* a good deal since Gilson Gardner saw him. More people have been to talk with him about permitting the use of his name. He said today: 'I am *not* a candidate and I don't want the nomination, but I can see that things might so shape themselves that it might be my duty to accept a nomination—provided there was an unmistakable call from the country.' . . .

"He was evidently greatly pleased at what [Walter F.] Brown, the old war horse out in Ohio, has been saying about his candidacy & something that Gronna has been quoted as saying also pleased him.

"You know, Senator, I have been rather inclined to feel as Pinchot evidently feels or felt, that he really was not in it; but it seemed absolutely plain to me today that if the demand is loud and long enough, and if the prospects seem right, that he will certainly jump into the game. He thinks Taft's prospects are gone, he evidently thinks you cannot command enough strength to be nominated—therefore—!!

"I thought you would like to know this promptly—though I am sure you have not been deceived at any time."[66]

The day he received this letter Bob wrote Baker: "Your interview with that gentleman leaves no doubt as to his course. It is not only the latest word, but sounds the clearest note which has yet come to me. It will have a most important bearing upon my course. I am most grateful to you for it all. It is my political judgment that it will not be best for the progressive cause in the long run to play any candidate as a stalking horse. I shall study and plan to make this fight an open one, with every important figure in plain view where the public can see every incident and rightly interpret the action of every candidate or possible candidate."[67]

But there were many factors at work which made it difficult to make the fight "an open one." A study of the public statements, private correspondence, and underground activities of many men soon after they had seen or received letters from Roosevelt or Frank Knox in late November and early December shows they were drawing the same conclusions that Baker had reported to Bob after his interview with the former President on December 8. With the unanimity of a trained chorus, organization Republicans like Walter F. Brown of Ohio, E. Mont Reily of Kansas City, Missouri, and Colonel Yeiser of Nebraska sang the tune which had for many months been the theme of Frank Knox, that astute newspaper owner, politician, and Rough Rider, who had been devoted to the colonel since the days of the Spanish War. They steadily repeated that Roosevelt did not want, and his true friends did not want him to have, the nomination for the Presidency unless it came to him in an entirely genuine and spontaneous manner. His "true friends," genuinely devoted admirers, and the Republican officeholders who were now certain Taft was "a dead one" all united in speeding up the previous organization of the spontaneous demand.

During the first weeks of December some of the Progressives who had publicly declared for La Follette were privately assuring Roosevelt and others that they would add their voices to the demand at the proper time. William Allen White, who always had a sharp ear for underground political activity, wrote admonishing Roosevelt to remember he was still a La Follette man, but advising him to get his ark ready for the early flood that was coming.[68] With keen amusement the colonel read this letter to some friends as the opinion of a strong La Follette supporter from Kansas.[69]

At about the time Roosevelt was chortling over this letter in his office at the *Outlook,* a shrewd Washington correspondent sent a signed dispatch to his newspaper reporting that none of the progressive Senators supporting La Follette would discuss the colonel publicly. But they had, he said, privately expressed the conviction that "Roosevelt is playing a game of shadow" and would continue to do so until certain "whether victory or defeat would be his portion should the national convention stampede for him." If the game should continue right up to the convention, and if at that time he became "convinced there was no possibility of Republican victory, he could produce a wagon load of documentary evidence in proof of the contention he never was a candidate and never intended to be."[70]

In spite of Roosevelt's public denials, underground reports that he would be a candidate continued to create confusion among Progressives and brought a stream of inquiries to the La Follette headquarters at Washington. To meet this baffling situation, Houser had proposed to Bob that a letter be written to Roosevelt which would compel him in his answer to say definitely whether he would in any circumstances be a candidate. Bob replied that he could not consent to write a letter, or to allow a letter to be written, which would in any way bind him to support the colonel. But he also told Houser that it would do no harm to call a conference to be attended by Gifford and Amos Pinchot, Gardner, and others to discuss the matter.[71] The conference was accordingly called. It met at Gifford Pinchot's residence in Washington two days after Bob had received Ray Stannard Baker's confidential letter. Among those present were Brandeis, Lenroot, Gardner, McCormick, Houser, Kent, La Follette, and Gifford and Amos Pinchot. Lenroot recalls that "From the very start La Follette was dubious about the proposal," but had consented "to have a conference." The discussion lasted some time, as several drafts were presented. Throughout the conference La Follette's attitude "was that the proposition necessarily involved a contingent pledge that he would support Roosevelt should he become a candidate, and that he was not prepared to make such a promise." As a result the whole matter was dropped.[72] After the conference Lenroot walked home with Bob, who "expressed his distrust of Roosevelt in stronger terms than he had at the conference," while Lenroot maintained that "if Roosevelt should become President, he would not betray the Progressive cause."[73]

After the disillusioning experiences with Roosevelt as President, Bob had never counted on his promises, and realized that if it suited his purpose the colonel might swiftly "change his mind." But when Bob agreed to become a candidate, he had relied on the continued and loyal support of Gifford Pinchot, Garfield, Gardner, Van Valkenburg, and the other men who had been most insistent in urging him to lead the Progressives in what then seemed a losing fight against Taft. But during November Bob's steadily increasing doubt as to certain of his supporters was shared by Brandeis, who wrote his brother not long after the conference at Gifford Pinchot's home that he had "been deep in Progressive counsels" and had "an ever-growing admiration for La Follette."[74] Years later Brandeis said he had "thought definitely at the time" and still had "a clear impression that Roosevelt directed and manipulated the men and the situation." In "late November and early December 1911" Brandeis "had no question that McCormick, Gifford Pinchot, Garfield and others were being directed by and working with Roosevelt. At first when this became manifest to him he was surprised."[75]

For Bob it had been hard at first to doubt the men he liked and had trusted. But the conference at Gifford Pinchot's residence strengthened his doubts, and they were confirmed that evening when Pinchot called at his home. In his *Autobiography*, written less than a year after the event, he recorded that Pinchot had informed him "that, following the conference, he, Gardner, and Medill McCormick had conferred together, and that he desired to notify me that there must be no break with Roosevelt; that should one come, he and the other two had decided they would go to Roosevelt."[76] Pinchot again reiterated his previous statements "that Roosevelt was not and would not be a candidate," that "if nothing were done to oppose Roosevelt he would ultimately support me openly," and that "I had no right to question his motives or his good faith."[77]

During their plain talk Pinchot argued that Roosevelt had the thing in his own hands and could do whatever he liked about it. Bob agreed there was no way to prevent him from coming into the campaign as a candidate, but warned Pinchot the colonel would be confronted with his record if he did so. Bob added: "I am not seeking any break with Roosevelt. I have no doubt he could take a large Progressive following with him because he is accepted by many people unacquainted with the details of his record, as a Progressive. He is probably in a position to divide the Progressives and destroy all chance of success in this campaign. But I say now, that if he undertakes such a course, he will surely fail. I know your strong friendship for Roosevelt, and I appreciate the support you have given me. I sincerely hope you are not mistaken when you say that Roosevelt has no intention of becoming a candidate and that he will, as you say, ultimately openly and actively support me for the nomination. . . . But there is no other way for me than to go on making the best fight I can."[78]

A few days after this frank talk, Gifford Pinchot, George L. Record, and Governor Bass of New Hampshire spoke to "a great crowd" which manifested "tremendous enthusiasm" at Tremont Temple in Boston on December 16.[79] Preceding the meeting, Roosevelt had been in Boston for two days. After a conference with several progressive Republicans, including Matthew Hale, who were forming a local organization, the colonel sanctioned a statement that he had urged Governor Bass to speak.[80] Medill McCormick had been active in organizing the meeting. The newspapers described the audience as "a reflective, representative gathering of voters, with several hundred women."[81] It was elaborately explained to the audience that the meeting was for a policy and not for a man. Elizabeth Evans and several of Bob's friends who attended were surprised that his name was mentioned only once in a brief reference made by Gifford Pinchot.[82] They were unaware that the omission of his name was in accord with a policy previously agreed upon and reported to Roosevelt in advance of the meeting.[83] Bob himself noticed, however, in the newspaper accounts that Pinchot omitted from his address, otherwise similar to the one he had delivered at Chicago, his positive statement that Roosevelt would not be a candidate. Bob inferred this omission meant "that Roosevelt no longer wanted Pinchot emphasizing this statement by repetition."[84]

This inference was based upon Bob's certainty that after their "very plain talk" Pinchot had seen Roosevelt in New York and communicated the substance of it.[85] Within forty-eight hours thereafter, Bob said, "there came a pressing invitation over the long distance telephone for Houser and Lenroot to meet Roosevelt with Gardner and Gifford Pinchot at the residence of Amos Pinchot in New York, on Sunday, December 17th." Bob declined to permit Houser to go, suggesting that William Kent go instead, because he was unwilling that "any beaten pathway" should be established between his headquarters at Washington and Roosevelt's offices in New York.[86] Bob knew that Houser had gone to Boston for the Tremont Temple meeting and that he would be there at the same time as Gifford Pinchot and Medill McCormick. He therefore took the extra precaution of having his secretary telegraph Houser not to attend the meeting with Roosevelt at Amos Pinchot's home the next day.[87]

On Sunday, December 17, Roosevelt, Lenroot, Kent, and Gardner met at Amos Pinchot's home in New York. There is a conflict of recollection as to whether Houser attended this meeting. If he did, Bob never knew it. Amos Pinchot is positive Houser was present at some time while Roosevelt was there.[88] Lenroot is equally certain Houser was not present.[89] It may be that contrary to Bob's specific instructions, Houser met Roosevelt at Amos Pinchot's home after Lenroot, Kent, and Gardner had left the conference.[90]

Immediately upon their return to Washington, Lenroot, Kent, and Gardner saw Bob. He has recorded the substance of the colonel's statement as reported to him by these three men: "Roosevelt said he was not a candidate, but he should never again declare that he would not be a candidate; that he did not think he ought to make such an announcement anyway, because if it were found in the convention that I could not beat Taft, it might be necessary for him to permit his name to be presented to the convention; that even then he could not do so, if upon the whole situation it appeared that he might be beaten in the election; that he could not afford to be beaten in the election, as it would spoil his place in history, but that a defeat would not injure me; that I should go ahead with the campaign, and if I could be nominated, all right; that if it were found in the convention that I could not make it, then he might come in; but that 'under no circumstances ought we to permit the wires to be crossed' or any division or contention come between our friends in the campaign. . . .

"Gardner expressed great satisfaction at the result of the interview, contending that Roosevelt was acting in perfect good faith; that he was not a candidate and did not intend to be a candidate. Kent agreed that they would be justified in reaching that conclusion if Roosevelt's word could be relied on; but thought that notwithstanding his repeated assurances he might be expected to break in at any time and attempt to carry off the nomination; that he certainly would do so if he thought he could get away with it and win in the election against a Democrat. After Kent and Gardner had gone, Lenroot gave it as his opinion that, notwithstanding all Roosevelt had said, he was at that very moment a candidate, but that he would never come out in the open until he had secured such pledges of support as would insure his nomination and also felt sure that he could win in the election."[91]

On the same Sunday that Roosevelt, Lenroot, Kent, and Gardner met at Amos Pinchot's home in New York, another conference took place in Toledo, Ohio. A newspaper reported that Walter F. Brown and John D. Fackler of Cleveland, "manager of Senator La Follette's campaign in Ohio, held a secret conference. . . . While this conference was private, sufficient information concerning it was given out to indicate that state and county organizations of progressives undoubtedly will work together and that their forces may be massed behind Col. Roosevelt instead of Senator La Follette for the Republican nomination for president at the national convention in Chicago next June, should the Roosevelt strength warrant it."[92]

While these conferences were going on, Bob was attending brief Senate sessions, preparing speeches, and completing some of his articles for the *American Magazine* which had to go to the printer before he left to open his speaking campaign scheduled during the holiday recess. On December 14 he telegraphed Gilbert Roe, who had suggested bringing Steffens when he came down to help Bob clean up some of the work: "Better not bring anyone this trip as I have only four days, and minutes are diamonds."[93] But printer's deadlines and Presidential campaign engagements suddenly became unimportant when he received a telegram from Madison later in the day telling him the little chestnut mare Maidie was "very ill with pneumonia." Although "minutes were diamonds," he dropped everything to draft a telegram to the veterinarian who had for so many years cared for the animals he owned: "Little Maidie is out of Nut Brown Maid, she out of Gipsy, and she out of Old Kit, a Green Mountain Morgan mare, with which I plowed and worked as a boy on the farm. She is the last of her line and represents many precious associations. It will be hard to forgive you if she dies. I have waited to breed her, because I could not find a suitable mate. I want to preserve the family very much."[94]

CHAPTER XXXII

An Underground Campaign
Bubbles to the Surface

On the night of December 20 Bob left Washington for Pittsburgh, where he spoke the next day before the Equal Franchise League. The Philadelphia *North American* reported that as he left the train former State Senator William Flinn greeted him by saying: "Senator, I am for Roosevelt and La Follette for first and second places in the national government. . . . I am for either of you, or, better still, for both of you."[1] That evening Flinn entertained Bob at dinner at his home and sat on the platform of Carnegie Music Hall throughout the speech. The following day he sent a thousand-dollar contribution to Bob's campaign, although he must have known at this time that Roosevelt was the "receptive" candidate he would soon be openly supporting.

The night after Christmas Bob, accompanied by John Hannan, left Washington for Youngstown, Ohio, where he was to make the first speech of his Presidential campaign the next day at noon. Although they arrived in a heavy snowstorm, he was greeted as he stepped off the train by a delegation of twenty men which included many city and county officials and Judge R. M. Wanamaker and John D. Fackler, who had come over from Cleveland to meet him. Throughout the morning there had been persistent reports that an attempt would be made to stampede the meeting for Roosevelt. In a recent speech in Cleveland, Wanamaker had devoted most of his time to Roosevelt and had told reporters afterward that he was for Roosevelt first and La Follette second.[2]

Bob had been warned to be on guard as to Wanamaker. Before the meeting Wanamaker and Fackler called on him at his room in the Todd Hotel. The judge suggested "it would be a fine thing" if Bob "would mention the names of former Presidents Garfield, McKinley, and Roosevelt, as it always had a good effect upon an audience and tended to promote enthusiasm to refer to the old-time Republican leaders of the party." Bob answered that he "was not much given to talking about individuals" and intended to discuss what the Progressives proposed to do to remedy the present-day evils oppressing the people.[3]

At the main door of the theater where Bob spoke, men passed out printed cards bearing the inscriptions "The Republicans of Ohio are for Theodore Roosevelt for president," "Hurrah for Teddy! We want Teddy!" But in spite of these elaborate preparations, the anticipated demonstration did not take place.[4] "With his opening sentence" Bob won the close attention of the audience and "held them with ever-increasing intensity until his conclusion." He was "compelled to hold a reception, and hundreds of men crowded about him and expressed their absolute agreement with his doctrines. One man, voicing the general feeling, said: 'This man has got Billy Sunday beaten to death. I have seen Sunday convert a lot of them, but this man converts his entire audience.' "[5]

After his speech at Youngstown, Bob left for Cleveland, accompanied by Hannan, Fackler, and Wanamaker. A local paper reported that Cleveland "became the political center of the United States" when "the most brilliant radical in the United States Senate" invaded Taft's home State, stepping down from an Erie train at 4:15 P.M. "with a smile on his face, a soft brown hat on his head and his travelling bag in his hand." He was whirled off to the Hotel Euclid for a reception which was attended by hundreds of people, although a blizzard had been raging all day. That night he talked to five thousand people who crowded into Gray's Armory, the largest hall in the city. Long before eight "every seat in the gallery and on the main floor, except those reserved for delegations from out of town, was taken. People were standing two and three deep in the galleries. Around the seats in the auditorium men and women stood five and six deep."[6] Among those who came through the blizzard to hear him was Newton D. Baker, the mayor-elect. When Bob appeared upon the platform, accompanied by Garfield and Fackler, "Men and women waved hats and handkerchiefs in the air and yelled themselves hoarse." At the close of his speech "There was a rush for the platform, and hundreds greeted him personally before he could escape to rest for another arduous day of Ohio campaigning against an Ohio president."[7]

The next night at Toledo, the "home town" of Walter F. Brown, an audience "packed every available inch of space," and it was "estimated 2000 or 3000 people were turned away."[8] For safety the police closed the doors of the hall three-quarters of an hour before Bob arrived. While he was "electrifying" this audience by a speech which was headlined as a "Denunciation of Trusts and Court," Walter F. Brown called upon Hannan at the Boody Hotel in Toledo. "He made a proposition that the delegates be divided half for Roosevelt and half for La Follette." Hannan told him "No." Immediately after the speech Hannan saw Bob "and reported Brown's proposition and the definite negative answer given." Bob expressed emphatic and "complete approval."[9]

The following day Bob traveled more than a hundred and fifty miles through Ohio's oil-field territory. Throughout his Ohio tour, which he closed in Cincinnati on December 30, he met the same tumultuously enthusiastic reception. Before leaving Ohio he recalled, as he always did on December 31, his wedding day, and telegraphed Belle: "Dear Girl, My heart is with you and the dear ones on this our anniversary day. Blessings on you all. It seems an age since I left. Hope for some word from you tonight. Trip has been remarkable. Great meetings both day and night and great enthusiasm everywhere. Am tired but standing work in the same old way."[10]

The Ohio State Conference of Progressives was scheduled to meet at Columbus on Monday, January 1. Walter W. Pollock, who was to be a delegate from Cleveland, had attended Bob's meeting at Cincinnati on Saturday night. At that time he was certain they had enough delegates to endorse La Follette, although he knew Garfield, Wanamaker, and Pinchot might try to prevent it. On Sunday morning Pollock saw Hannan in Cincinnati, told him they had a majority of the delegates, and asked who would be in charge of La Follette strategy at Columbus. Hannan told him to follow Houser's instructions.[11] That same morning a dispatch was published in a Cincinnati paper which Bob may have read before leaving for Michigan. It reported that in a statement on the previous day Fackler had "declared that the delegates would indorse the Wisconsin Senator for the Presidency."[12]

But many things happened in Columbus during the brief interval before the delegates met. The day before the conference Wanamaker arrived from Cincinnati, where he had spoken with Bob the previous night. He told reporters he was more than pleased with La Follette's tour of the State. By an early train Gifford Pinchot came from Mentor, where he had been a guest in Garfield's home.[13] That same Sunday Houser also arrived and had a talk with Pinchot.[14] The next morning Walter F. Brown of Toledo, chairman of the Republican State Central Committee, held a long private meeting "with Pinchot, Houser, and Fackler, and worked with them on the resolution which finally was adopted" by the conference.[15] What took place in that room will probably never be known. An alert reporter also noted as "a significant happening of the day" that Brown, Houser, and Pinchot had breakfasted together.[16] Subsequent developments indicate that in these private meetings Houser became a party to a program of procedure which both he and Pinchot knew Bob had opposed at all times.

That same morning, before the battle started in the conference, Pollock and several loyal La Follette delegates called upon Houser. For many years the two men had known each other in Wisconsin. Pollock told Houser they had enough delegates to endorse La Follette, were prepared to go through with the fight, and asked what the strategy should be. Houser was "non-committal" and stressed the importance of not offending Roosevelt's prominent friends. Throughout this interview Pollock had an intuitive impression that Houser was not being sincere.[17] Houser probably gave similar advice to other La Follette delegates.

When the conference of one hundred or more delegates from practically every county in Ohio met at the Hartman Theater, Fackler presided as chairman and was elected president of the permanent organization. At first the effort to endorse La Follette was "overwhelmingly favored." Senator Works of California, Clapp, Brandeis, and scores of delegates made forceful speeches for the declaration. "There was not the slightest doubt of the temper of the large majority of the delegates." A reporter wrote that "in the quiet but highly remarkable speech of Brandeis there was a gripping, throbbing appeal for the strongest support the delegates could give 'the man whose fight for many years was made alone but always for the people.' Had the question been put to a vote after these speeches it would have been a runaway for the Wisconsin man."[18]

But a hot debate ensued which was closely followed by two silent, interested observers. Matthew Hale had come all the way from Boston "to study the Ohio movement."[19] Walter F. Brown occupied an inconspicuous seat at the back of the theater. The opposition, led by Pinchot, Garfield, and Wanamaker, prolonged the battle into the late afternoon. Thus before the vote was taken, some delegates, as well as Clapp, Works, and Brandeis, who were speaking elsewhere in Ohio that night, had to leave to catch trains. A delegate recalls that the Roosevelt supporters were not out in the open for him, but argued effectively that it would be unwise to estrange his following.[20] A reporter noted that "those who worked to prevent the indorsement cheerfully announced themselves as thoroughly willing to vote for the Wisconsin man, but doubting the wisdom of tying to him at this time."[21]

Pinchot had just made two widely reported speeches in Ohio endorsing Bob for President. He now said to the delegates that "it would be foolish not to crystallize the Roosevelt progressive sentiment and the progressive sentiment of all other men, whatever candidate they may prefer, so that we can get delegates to the Chicago convention who will vote for the progressive candidate, which we know will be Mr. La Follette."[22]

It was nearly five o'clock when Wanamaker rose to make a final appeal to the delegates "not to go into the presidential campaign by going against the advice of such leaders of the National Progressive League as Pinchot, and Walter Houser, secretary of the National League and Manager of the La Follette campaign."[23] The vote was taken immediately after his appeal. The resolution, introduced by Delo E. Mook, which endorsed La Follette and named no other man, was defeated. But by a vote of 52 to 32 the conference passed the resolution on which Walter F. Brown, Pinchot, Houser, and Fackler had collaborated that morning. It opposed the renomination of President Taft, and declared the "purpose of the Ohio Progressive Republican League" was "to work in harmony and unison to nominate a Progressive Republican for President, recognizing as fellow-Progressives all who hold the principles for which we stand, whether they be for the presidential nomination of Robert

M. La Follette or Theodore Roosevelt, or any other Progressive Republican."[24] Then, as a "personal expression" of the delegates, another resolution was adopted, by a vote of 81 to 11, naming La Follette as "the living embodiment of the principles of the progressive movement and the logical candidate to carry them to successful fruition."[25]

This "personal expression" was, however, poor consolation to men who had gone to Columbus confident they had enough delegates to endorse La Follette unequivocally. They had been outmaneuvered by Garfield, Pinchot, Wanamaker, and Walter F. Brown.[26] Subsequently there was great bitterness toward Houser in Ohio among the loyal La Follette men for the part they believed he had played in bringing about a result so satisfactory to the Roosevelt supporters.[27] The Ohio conference set the pattern for the Roosevelt supporters to manipulate the situation in Colorado and other States. It was followed up by a persistent campaign through letters and unfounded newspaper stories, all designed to make it appear La Follette was working closely with Roosevelt and would later either receive his support or withdraw in the colonel's favor.

The day after the conference the *Washington Times,* owned by Frank Munsey, who became a munificent Roosevelt backer, printed an editorial entitled "Roosevelt Becomes The Progressive Candidate." The same issue carried a front-page story, signed by Judson Welliver, with the headline "ROOSEVELT NOW CANDIDATE, TAFT BEATEN IS BOAST." Welliver also predicted, "It is probable La Follette's name will be withdrawn as a Presidential aspirant."[28] This story was probably inspired by information received at a little dinner in Washington where Walter F. Brown and George W. Perkins, generous contributor to Roosevelt's campaign, were the other guests, and Frank Munsey was host.[29] On the same day that Welliver's story appeared, Perkins, manifesting an interest in progressive ideas, telephoned Gilbert Roe at the latter's office in New York requesting copies of La Follette's principal speeches, stating he wished to make a study of them.

Bob had arrived in Detroit from Cincinnati on Sunday evening, December 31, the night before the progressive conference at Columbus. In a happy mood after his successful Ohio tour, he sat up in his room at the Cadillac Hotel with Walter S. Rogers "discussing middle west politics for more than an hour after the bells tolled out the old year and tolled in the new.[30] Early the next morning newspaper men found him in the coffee shop, where he was having breakfast before taking the train for the first speech of his Michigan trip. They reported he was beaming with optimism and "appeared in the pink of condition" after his strenuous Ohio tour.[31] Traveling in day coaches and by trolley, he made three speeches on New Year's day, all in districts of standpat Congressmen who had been ardent supporters of Speaker Cannon. At Flint, Bay City, and Saginaw the halls were packed and hundreds of people turned away. After his speeches the crowds surged to the platform to greet him with the same enthusiasm that had been manifested in Ohio.

Although Bob never knew it, his next day's schedule was deliberately upset by his devoted friend and secretary, John Hannan. After his speech in Saginaw, Bob expected to spend the night there, leave at an early hour for a morning meeting in Owosso, and make his principal Michigan address at Grand Rapids that evening. Between trains he was scheduled for an afternoon meeting at Lansing, the state capital. Local Progressives had asked Governor Chase S. Osborn, a former Wisconsin resident, to introduce him. This seemed a natural choice since Osborn was second vice president of the National Progressive Republican League. When the invitation was extended, Osborn said "that he would regard the privilege as an honor and that he was in full sympathy with Senator La Follette and the progressive policies."[32] After accepting, the governor prepared a long "Introduction" which he gave to the press in advance of the Lansing meeting.

A friendly reporter sought Hannan out in Saginaw and confidentially tipped him off as to the content of Osborn's speech. Hannan told no one but made his plans accordingly. He was an expert on train schedules, and Bob always left all travel details to him. There were two railroad stations in Saginaw with trains leaving at about the same time. The newspaper men who were accompanying Bob on his Michigan trip walked to the station, expecting to join him on the train for Owosso. After they had gone, Hannan and Bob left the hotel in a hack. Hannan directed the cabman to go to the wrong station. Arriving late, as Hannan had planned, they boarded the train without tickets. It was some time before Bob discovered what he supposed had been the cabman's mistake. His comments are not recorded. But reporters who found him in the town of Holly far from his destination noted that "He tried to secure a special train, an engine or any old thing that would get him to the capital, but there was nothing doing."[33]

Meanwhile the governor was busy at Lansing "trying to locate the guest from Wisconsin. He had his fine automobile at every train. . . . The trains came but with them no La Follette." Long before the hour scheduled for the meeting the hall "was crowded to the very doors."[34] When Osborn finally learned that Bob could not reach Lansing, he went to the Masonic Temple, mounted the platform, and asked the privilege of delivering his own speech which had previously been given to the press. Announcing he did not believe the rumors he had been hearing that La Follette was dodging him, he proceeded with one of the strangest "introductions" ever prepared by a governor to "welcome" a visiting Presidential candidate. The reading of this twelve-page typewritten manuscript would have consumed at least a third of the time Bob's train schedule had originally allowed for this meeting. What was later described as Osborn's "savage attack"[35] must be read in its entirety to appreciate how skillfully it escaped libel by an interlarding of doubtful compliments.[36]

The governor stated La Follette could not be elected, expressed the hope he would not be nominated, but promised to support him if he were. Making the most of his former residence in Wisconsin, Osborn declared he had known "La Follette and of him" ever since "his fight for district attorney of Dane County against the machine of Boss Keyes," had "always believed him to be entirely honest" and believed him to be "honest now." Then he went on to flay Bob by misrepresenting different episodes in his public career. Beginning with a garbled sketch of the Sawyer affair, he subtly implied a lack of integrity and sincerity of purpose throughout his life. "In every campaign," he said, "Senator La Follette has spoken boldly, has been a potent agitator and has always landed in a place of distinction and good salary. I have always believed he chose to make a profession of politics. I have always believed he had his interests primarily at heart."[37] At first the audience was stunned and baffled by the attack, but as innuendo followed innuendo there were interruptions. It became evident "some in the crowd were getting restless. In the rear of the room, members of the La Follette committee were

mad clear through."[38] Frank Robards, Michigan manager for La
Follette, nearly "broke up the meeting" by yelling out, "Who is
paying for this hall?"[39] Although the question was repeated, Osborn
continued and climaxed his diatribe by asking La Follette and Taft
to withdraw and permit the Republican Party to "settle upon Albert
J. Beveridge or Theodore Roosevelt as candidate for president."[40]

When Osborn finished, Robards rushed to the platform and declared to the excited crowd that "the governor's speech, when he
should have shown the spirit of host," was "shameful." He charged
that "in the presence of two witnesses the governor had once declared he was in entire accord with La Follette and for this reason"
had "been invited to introduce the senator."[41] After the audience
was gone, Osborn and Robards "had it out." Robards "was mad"
and "called it a cowardly attack." The governor answered that he
"meant every word" and regretted La Follette "could not get here"
so he "could say it over again to him." The governor "went out
laughing." On the train to Grand Rapids, where Bob was to speak
that night, Robards "made dire threats against the governor."[42]
Robards probably gave Bob a vivid account of the Lansing performance. It must have seemed to Bob a strange attack to come
from Osborn, who had written him only a few months before expressing unbounded admiration for the twenty years of public service
he now condemned.[43] Evening papers carried the story of the governor's speech in front-page headlines. But when reporters sought
Bob out, his only reply to a barrage of questions was: "I discuss
issues, not men. I have absolutely no comment to make."[44]

That night at Grand Rapids a responsive audience packed Powers
Opera House, but any who went expecting the fireworks of personal
invective must have been disappointed. For two hours and a half
Bob held his audience in rapt attention while he analyzed the
economic problems confronting the country and discussed the progressive program for dealing with them. At times they were "so
silent that one could almost hear him breathe, then right on top of
such a dramatic situation he turned the crowd to laughter." But
"not once did he evidence that he had ever heard of such a man as
Michigan's governor or his statement."[45]

The night Bob spoke at Grand Rapids, a dispatch was telegraphed
from that city by someone who apparently held cards in the same
game Osborn was playing. It had no basis in fact, but sending the

dispatch from the place where Bob was speaking helped to make it appear authentic. Variously headlined in different papers, the purport of the announcement was that after consulting "intimate friends" La Follette was "seriously considering withdrawing as a candidate for president in favor of Theodore Roosevelt."[46] A Washington correspondent sent a similar tale to a Chicago paper.[47] That same day Gilson Gardner telegraphed a signed story from Washington stating La Follette would remain a candidate, that Roosevelt was his chief supporter, and that the two men were "working in harmony to control the National Republican Convention."[48] The next day a dispatch from Lansing, Michigan, reported that Frank Knox, state chairman of the Republican Committee, had expressed hearty approval of Governor Osborn's speech.[49] The following day Gardner sent out another signed dispatch repeating the La Follette-Roosevelt harmony theme, but suggesting Roosevelt might respond to "an overwhelming demand," and predicting the convention would choose the candidate "who is most likely to lead the cause to victory."[50] Experienced men with a fine sense of timing were laboring in the vineyards of Michigan and Washington.

The reports of Osborn's speech were headlined on the front pages of the Chicago newspapers, and one leading daily printed the story of La Follette's withdrawal in favor of Theodore Roosevelt on the morning of the day Bob was to speak there. But before Bob left Kalamazoo, where he made the final speech of his Michigan tour, the telephone wire to Chicago had been busy. Houser had been directed to issue immediately a formal statement over his signature declaring that La Follette had no intention of withdrawing, that his friends would not withdraw his name, and that the campaign for his nomination would continue until the gavel fell "declaring who is the nominee of the Republican convention for President."[51] When Bob arrived in Chicago that afternoon at five o'clock, reporters bombarded him with questions and begged repeatedly for answers. But he merely smiled and replied that he could not comment as he was giving out no interviews on this trip.[52]

That night, before his speech, he was the guest of honor at a dinner arranged for him by Dr. Albert J. Ochsner, the distinguished surgeon. Ochsner was a former Wisconsin man, born at Baraboo, the little town which had been Belle's home before her marriage. Ochsner and Bob were devoted friends throughout their lives, each vitally interested in the work of the other. Fifty friends and former University of Wisconsin students attended the dinner and helped to give Bob a friendly welcome when he came upon the platform at Orchestra Hall for the first speech of his Illinois tour. The Chicago *Inter-Ocean* reported it was "the largest and surely the most enthusiastic political gathering ever held in Orchestra Hall. Every seat in the hall was occupied before eight o'clock and about a thousand persons were turned away. . . . He talked two hours and a half, and the audience seemed willing to remain indefinitely."[53] All the reports indicate Bob was in fine form and made one of his vivid and stirring speeches. But during the night he suddenly became nauseated and developed a temperature. After his meeting he had eaten an oyster stew, and the attack of ptomaine poisoning brought on violent vomiting and dysentery which persisted during the next two days. In spite of his acute and distressing indisposition, which he knew was only temporary, he insisted upon filling all his engagements. But the reports sent out by some newspapers were so exaggerated that he thought it necessary to telegraph Belle the facts.[54]

Early on the morning of January 4, Bob left Chicago for a trip through central and southern Illinois. Traveling for two days by train and trolley with the temperature below zero in a record-breaking cold wave, he made seventeen speeches, addressing crowded meetings at Joliet, Peoria, Bloomington, Decatur, Springfield, East St. Louis, Danville, and smaller towns of the state. From East St. Louis, where he concluded his Illinois tour, on January 5, he turned back to Washington, stopping in Indiana to address a meeting at Terre Haute. Fred MacKenzie, managing editor of *La Follette's Magazine*, commented on Bob's trip in a letter to an intimate friend, "I went across Illinois with him when he was in the West, and everywhere there were evidences of the same revival spirit that characterized the people of Wisconsin in the stirring campaigns of ten years ago."[55]

While Bob was touring in the West, Brandeis had been speaking in Ohio, Minnesota, Wisconsin, and Illinois, urging La Follette's nomination and declaring that "only the revolutionary and Civil wars had surpassed in importance the progressive movement now before the people." The "struggle for industrial liberty is now on," he said.[56] At Chicago he talked to a large luncheon of businessmen on the same day Bob spoke at Orchestra Hall. In all his speeches Brandeis discussed the bill Bob had introduced at the extra session of Congress to meet the Supreme Court's interpretation of the Sherman Anti-Trust Act in its decision of May 15, 1911. To the large audiences that gathered to hear him at the university gymnasium in Madison and elsewhere, he said of La Follette: "What he has done in his State and what he has done in Congress he would do in every position of trust in which he may be placed, and no position, in my opinion, can be too high for a man who understands as he does the needs of the American people, who feels as he does brotherhood with them, and the great brotherhood of them in a way that I believe no American has done since Abraham Lincoln."[57]

Bob arrived in Washington on the afternoon of January 7 as leading Democrats reached the Capital to attend a meeting of the Democratic National Committee and the annual Jackson Day dinner. A week after Bob's return, Belle wrote to a friend: "He came home very tired, but in a few days was feeling himself again. It always gives him new strength to go among the people and find how much in earnest they are."[58] Without any vacation or rest he took up his work again. In addition to attending Senate sessions and trying to complete his articles for the *American Magazine,* he had to deal with a succession of harassing problems from day to day. Immediately on his return, he learned from Belle and John R. Commons that while he was away an attempt had been made at his Washington headquarters to undermine his candidacy.

Commons had been a guest at the La Follette home while helping to prepare campaign material. Among other things he had worked on a biographical pamphlet which reviewed Bob's public record. A fund had been set aside to cover the cost of printing and distributing. When completed on December 21, this manuscript had been sent to Houser at Washington headquarters[59] and turned over for printing to the publicity department which Medill McCormick was directing. Shortly before Bob left for Ohio, he had asked for copies of this pamphlet and was surprised to find it had not been printed. He spoke to Congressman John M. Nelson about the importance of getting the document out immediately. Bob had asked Nelson to take charge at headquarters during his absence, as he did not wish McCormick to be the only person in authority when Houser went to the Ohio conference.

After Bob left, McCormick handed Nelson "a copy of what Nelson supposed was the approved manuscript. It developed, however, that a manuscript written by McCormick himself had been substituted for the original."[60] Upon reading McCormick's manuscript, Nelson's suspicion was aroused because it contained flattering references to Roosevelt so phrased that had it been sent out from La Follette headquarters it would have committed Bob to. Roosevelt as a thoroughgoing Progressive if the colonel later became a candidate. Nelson went straight to McCormick and asked "why a eulogy of Roosevelt was to be sent out ostensibly in the interest of La Follette's candidacy."[61] Nelson told McCormick that this manuscript could not be printed and sent out with his consent while La Follette was away.

McCormick took the manuscript and subsequently directed the clerk at headquarters to have it put in type, telling him to offer the printer a bonus of $200 for rushing the printing of the document. Shortly afterward McCormick left for Chicago. From the West he telegraphed Nelson urging that publication of ten thousand copies of the campaign book be rushed.[62] If the printing had gone through as McCormick had directed, it would have made such a deep cut in funds that the original manuscript could not have been printed. The only choice would have been to send out his or none at all.

But fortunately the clerk to whom McCormick gave his manuscript took it to Nelson and informed him of the offer McCormick had authorized making to the printer. Nelson submitted the McCormick manuscript to Belle and Commons, who decided that under no circumstances should it be printed. They directed that the original manuscript should be printed at once.[63]

McCormick had intermittently spent a good deal of time at Chicago headquarters and had been there during the latter part of Bob's speaking trip. While in the West Bob had received disturbing reports about what was going on at that headquarters and elsewhere. The Saturday after his return to Washington, he telegraphed asking his friend Professor S. H. Clark of the University of Chicago to get him a list of five leading progressive Republicans in each county in Illinois.[64] He asked that this be done without using his name. In a confidential letter he explained: "I cannot go fully into my reasons, nor is it necessary to say more to you than this: There are those in the Headquarters at Chicago who are giving more attention to encouraging sentiment for another candidate than they are to organizing the sentiment for the candidate for whom the headquarters were opened and are being maintained."[65] On the same Saturday he telegraphed Edward P. Costigan of Colorado making a similar request for that State.[66]

During Bob's Western speaking trip it had become evident that Roosevelt's candidacy would soon be launched. The steady underground work which had been carried on for weeks by experienced Republican committeemen[67] and others had bubbled to the surface in rumors, newspaper stories, straw votes, and personal reports which eventually found their way to Washington. Day by day it became evident that men who had urged Bob's candidacy and given both private and public assurance of support were shifting to Roosevelt. On January 10, three days after Bob returned to Washington, an editorial appeared in William Allen White's newspaper, the *Emporia Daily Gazette,* which was reprinted in many newspapers and interpreted by them and by Bob himself as a declaration for the colonel.[68] The original editorial analyzed recent special Congressional elections and concluded with the prediction that as far as the success of the Republican Party was concerned "It's Roosevelt or bust."[69] The day after the White editorial appeared, Frank Munsey, publisher and owner of the *Washington Times,* printed a front-page editorial predicting that "If the call does come," Roosevelt "will buckle on his armor."[70]

The drive for uninstructed delegates, or for a combination whereby delegates would be instructed for both Roosevelt and La Follette, was now speeded up. In spite of Bob's repeated refusal to enter into any such combination, and Hannan's categorical negative to Walter F. Brown's proposal made at Toledo on the night of December 28,[71] the activity along this line did not stop. In Colorado the Progressives had planned, until a few days before their state conference on January 16, to endorse La Follette alone.[72] But they changed their resolution to include Roosevelt when they received a letter from Gifford Pinchot which was written without Bob's knowledge and was directly opposed to his repeatedly expressed determination. Pinchot wrote that personally he was strongly for La Follette and believed the wisest plan in his interest was to "follow the same course as the Ohio Progressives." He added, "So does Mr. Houser." Pinchot also assured them there was "'a community of interest' among all

Progressives, and that when Colonel Roosevelt and Senator La Follette have put their heads together and decided what is best for the Progressive cause, then we shall all fall in behind their decision."[73] The letter gave a totally false impression of speaking authoritatively for La Follette and misrepresented him by implying he was a party to the plan. The Colorado Progressives naturally followed Pinchot's advice.[74] It is possible similar letters were sent to other States.

To Bob's surprise a visit was received at his Washington headquarters on January 14 from John D. Fackler, who came with a proposition from Walter F. Brown and Dan Hanna. They proposed that the campaign be carried on in Ohio with La Follette as the candidate, but that one Roosevelt delegate should be placed upon the ballot with one La Follette delegate in each Congressional district. Roosevelt was not to be known as an open and avowed candidate. The inducement offered was that "they would furnish all the money for the campaign in Ohio, but they stipulated that the La Follette Progressive literature which had been supplied from Washington," and was on hand at Ohio headquarters, "should be destroyed, and no more sent out into the state."[75] Subsequently two Washington correspondents sent stories about this visit to their newspapers which differed as to the amount of money offered, but agreed that an offer had been made and flatly refused.[76]

Bob himself said: "Fackler was told that I would enter into no deal or combination with the man who stood for the very things in politics to which I was opposed . . . Fackler returned to Ohio with directions to say to Brown and Hanna that their offer was rejected; that we should continue to make a straightout fight for Progressive principles and for my candidacy, and that we would enter into no combination of any character whatsoever."[77]

Similar specific directions were also sent to the La Follette headquarters at Chicago because Bob was apprehensive that McCormick had been doing everything he could from that headquarters, as well as from Washington, to undermine the La Follette candidacy. Bob sought no quarrel with anyone. But he was determined to make "the Roosevelt men" in his camp "show their hands" so that there would be "no more double work going on" in his headquarters.[78] Bob's insistence that no alliances should be made brought the issue to a head. A few days after Bob's emphatic refusal of the proposal Fackler brought from Ohio, a conference was called at Washington headquarters by Gifford Pinchot. Among those Bob recalled as being present were Gifford and Amos Pinchot, William Kent, Walter S. Rogers, Lenroot, Hannan, and Gilson Gardner. McCormick was there at the beginning, but withdrew later because Bob declined to participate if he were present. Heney happened to be in Washington at this time and attended in response to the urgent request Bob made after he learned the conference had been called.

At this meeting Gifford Pinchot still advocated continuing the La Follette campaign, but insisted upon following, in Ohio, and elsewhere, the scheme proposed by Walter F. Brown and Dan Hanna of putting Roosevelt delegates on the ticket with La Follette delegates. He reiterated his statement that Roosevelt was not and would not be a candidate, but contended this method would win additional votes. Heney and Amos Pinchot opposed the plan. Bob was also firmly against it, and Gifford Pinchot was voted down. At the conclusion of the conference, Amos Pinchot remarked to his brother: "Gifford, I think you will sleep better tonight now that it is settled that we are not to be tied up with representatives of machine politics and the Steel Trust."[79]

Gifford Pinchot apparently acquiesced in the decision, and Bob thought the matter was finally settled.

A reliable contemporary document records that on Thursday, January 18, Roosevelt took definite action toward making a statement that he would accept the nomination for the Presidency if it were tendered to him as the result of a popular demand. An entry in the diary of a member of the *Outlook* staff notes this as the day on which the colonel made the "crucial decision" when he telegraphed Frank Knox to come from Michigan to New York. Two days later, on Saturday, January 20, at the *Outlook* office, Knox, Nat C. Wright, editor of the Cleveland *Leader*, Everett Colby of New Jersey, William Fellowes Morgan, and Mark Sullivan conferred with Roosevelt. The plan was submitted to Knox, who approved. A letter was drafted for the six governors who were to petition Roosevelt to become a candidate in response to the popular demand. Knox took a copy of the letter, which he was to present to the governors as soon as possible.[80]

Gifford Pinchot had been present at the beginning of the interview while the colonel told his view of the situation, but left, at the colonel's suggestion, before the real business of the conference began.[81] The proprieties were thus observed in relation to a man who had been one of the prominent initial supporters of La Follette and who was now in the embarrassing position of having to introduce him as a Presidential candidate at Carnegie Hall two days later.

On the same day that Roosevelt collaborated in drafting the letter to be signed by the six governors, Fackler, who had come to New York from Cleveland with Nat C. Wright, saw the colonel at the *Outlook* offices. Roosevelt told him he was going to be a candidate.[82] From New York Fackler telegraphed Houser that he would be in Washington that evening and would call him on arrival.[83] He probably saw Houser that night. The next day, Sunday, January 21, Fackler and Clapp had a long talk with Bob. Both men urged him to withdraw his candidacy and come out for Roosevelt. This he refused to do.[84] Knowing Fackler had come to Washington by way of New York and had seen the colonel, Bob interpreted the urging of his withdrawal "as reflecting Roosevelt's attitude."[85]

For weeks Bob had been convinced that Roosevelt was an active if not an avowed candidate. Only the politically naïve could have had any lingering doubts as to the colonel's intentions after reading the newspapers on the Saturday and Sunday following the "crucial decision" reached at the *Outlook* office on Thursday, January 18. On Saturday the Pittsburgh *Leader* restored to the masthead of its editorial page the slogan "For President, 1912, Theodore Roosevelt." The fact was widely reported in a dispatch which noted that the slogan had been eliminated four months before at the colonel's request.[86] The *Leader*, edited by Alexander Moore, was said to be partly owned by William Flinn,[87] who had seen the colonel the previous day.[88] Bob probably read the report in the Philadelphia *North American*, which he saw daily. It must have had a special significance for him because of John R. Commons' letter describing the luncheon with Moore and Roosevelt the previous August when they had said to tell La Follette to go ahead with his candidacy.[89] That same Saturday, January 20, newspapers carried a prophetic dispatch from Kansas City regarding another of Bob's supporters who had recently seen the colonel. George L. Record of New Jersey had spoken in Kansas City and was reported to have said in an interview that Roosevelt "must be drafted."[90]

The New York *World* commented the next day that since his visit to the colonel "Mr. Record in public speeches and statements has practically come out in support of the Roosevelt boom."[91] On Saturday, January 20, Bob had, as he said, been "reminded that 'nothing weighs lighter than a promise'" when Cummins announced his candidacy for the Presidential nomination.[92] Bob refused to make any public comment. But he wrote a detailed confidential letter to Judge Kenesaw M. Landis in which he stated: "Responding to your inquiry with reference to Senator Cummins' announcement, I can say that it was not made with my consent."[93] Discerning newspapers interpreted Cummins' action as a blow to Bob's candidacy in that it was a definite sign the colonel would soon enter the field.

Weeks previously a meeting had been arranged for January 22 at Carnegie Hall in New York, where Bob was to make the most important speech of his pre-convention campaign in the East. A few days before this meeting Gifford Pinchot had proposed that while Bob was in New York a luncheon should be arranged at Amos Pinchot's home where he should meet Roosevelt. Bob refused because he was determined not to be drawn into a situation which could later be misinterpreted to mean that he had an understanding with Roosevelt or had accepted him as a candidate who represented "real Progressive principles."[94] But in spite of Bob's precautions, it was later falsely reported in at least one newspaper, on authority "from unimpeachable source," that on the afternoon of the day he spoke at Carnegie Hall La Follette had "agreed to withdraw in favor of Theodore Roosevelt 'when the time comes.'" Gifford Pinchot was said to have been the intermediary in making the deal between La Follette and Roosevelt.[95]

Bob left Washington on Monday morning, January 22, with Bob, Jr., and Phil. Arriving in New York at 4:45, they were met at the station by Gilbert and Netha Roe, Frederic C. Howe, Ray Stannard Baker, Amos Pinchot, Francis J. Heney, Lincoln Steffens, and George Middleton. From the station Bob and the boys went directly to the Roe home on Riverside Drive.

Before going to meet Bob, Amos Pinchot had seen Roosevelt that afternoon at about three o'clock at the University Club. Pinchot had made the appointment earlier in the day. In a written account of what took place he says: "I told him that we came in the interest of La Follette, that while no one disputed his, Roosevelt's right to enter the race for the presidency at any time, yet a point had been reached where it was exceedingly unjust that La Follette should be kept in ignorance of the Colonel's intentions, and that in any case our La Follette group considered itself pledged to the Wisconsin senator until he released us of his own accord. Roosevelt replied frankly that he had not decided whether he would run or not; that he admired La Follette and considered his work during the Taft administration of the greatest importance; that in his opinion La Follette had no chance whatever of beating Taft and that if he, Roosevelt, should enter the race for the nomination, Taft would probably win anyhow. At the moment, he did not believe he would run, but he might change his mind, only, however, if there were a really strong public demand for him."[96]

Bob knew nothing about this interview until later. That evening, after a quiet family dinner at the Roe home, Bob, Phil, and Bob, Jr., drove to Carnegie Hall with Gilbert and Netha Roe. Because of repeated press reports that he was about to retire and that Roosevelt would soon become a candidate, many of Bob's friends thought his meeting might be a failure. He himself admitted fearing they would arrive only to find the large auditorium, where he had spoken once before, practically empty. Roe had told him that the newspapers had not given his meeting a particle of help. As they approached they were amazed to find that Carnegie had been packed ever since "8 o'clock and the reserves of two police stations . . . called out to take care of the crowds that were jammed into Seventh Avenue for several blocks north and south of the hall."[97] As they drove up, "at least a thousand who could not gain admission to the meeting hemmed in" Bob "and would not let him pass"[98] until he had made two speeches from the automobile to those who had been waiting for an hour outside. The *New York Times* reported that "Carnegie Hall never held a bigger nor a more enthusiastic audience" than that which waited for him inside. It was "made up of men and women from every walk of life. There were politicians there, both Republican and Democratic; ministers, lawyers, merchants, laborers, while the women formed at least a third of the number that packed the hall."[99] More than two hundred members of the Insurgents' Club, of which Frederic C. Howe was president, were seated on the stage. Among them were Ray Stannard Baker, Francis J. Heney, Gilbert E. Roe, Lincoln Steffens, and Amos Pinchot. As Bob came through the aisle between the closely ranged chairs, "the great audience jumped to its feet and let loose cheer after cheer," giving him a welcome he said he would never forget.[100] In the course of a long and gracious introduction, Gifford Pinchot told how he had come to enlist under the La Follette banner. "Five or six years ago," he said, "a Senator about whom I knew and cared for but little, began to drop into my office in the Forest Service. He came of his own accord to help the service and it was not long before his help began to count. He was a solitary man in the Capitol, feared and disliked by the old leaders, for he represented a point of view that had fewer followers in the Senate than is the case to-day. Even those who should have been his friends failed to understand him at first, and I was slow in getting his measure because I was prejudiced against him." Then, as he came to know him better, Pinchot said he discovered that "La Follette had courage and common sense," was "lovable as well as strong," and nine times out of ten "exactly in the right"; that "in the broadest sense of the word he was a constructive statesman."[101]

Reports differ as to the closing line of Pinchot's introduction. The *New York Times* quoted him as saying, "I therefore have the great honor and the pleasure of introducing to you Robert Marion La Follette of Wisconsin," but noted that this differed from the advance copy of his speech, which read, "The pleasure of introducing to you the candidate I support for the Republican Presidential nomination, Robert Marion La Follette." The reporter added, "The omission, however, did not appear intentional."[102]

As Bob stepped to the front of the stage, he rested his hand lightly on Pinchot's arm for an instant in acknowledgment. Then, taking from a thin little black portfolio two sheets of manuscript, he read a tribute to Gifford Pinchot, who, he said, would "hold an unique place in the history of our Government. Out of office he has been as great a public servant as in office." As Bob spoke he "faced tier after tier of well-dressed men and women reaching from the footlights to the last seat in the top gallery." Although he began reading from manuscript, he soon tossed it aside. He "got on good terms with the audience at once and never lost it during his speech."[103]

Warned in advance that a New York audience would not listen to serious discussion for more than an hour, their spontaneous response to his argument soon led him to tell them they were "just like Wisconsin folk." For two hours this audience followed him with the same intense interest as people had on his Western speaking trip. Throughout his speech the audience frequently broke in with spontaneous applause and cheers. At the close hundreds gathered near the stage to greet him and kept him shaking hands for an hour after the speech was over.

After the meeting, which Ray Stannard Baker recorded in his diary as "a great success," a small supper party was given for Bob at the Plaza Hotel by E. Clarence Jones. Among the guests were Baker, Heney, Amos and Gifford Pinchot, Roe, and Steffens.[104] Bob rode to the hotel with Amos Pinchot, who told him of his talk with Roosevelt that afternoon. As Pinchot recalls it, Bob "replied that he was now, more than ever, convinced that Roosevelt intended to draw off the support he had gathered; that, much as he hated the idea of being a stalking horse for Roosevelt, he would stay in the race in any event; that he considered Roosevelt to be a more or less unconscious instrument of Morgan and the Steel crowd; that he believed that we would some day discover he had always been tied hand and foot to Gary and the Steel people."[105]

Bob spent the night and most of the next day at the Roe apartment. At four in the afternoon, a conference began at Roe's office which was continued at his home through dinner and until eleven that night. Those present in the afternoon were Baker, Bob, Heney, Roe, and Steffens. In the evening Frederic C. Howe joined the group. Baker recorded the reason for the conference as being that "Roosevelt has so nearly become a candidate, is indeed a candidate while denying it." During the conference Bob himself clearly stated the two courses open to him, and these were discussed from many different angles. But the possibility of his supporting Roosevelt was evidently not among the alternatives considered because it was accepted that should the colonel be elected "he could not be depended upon to carry out the program of the Progressives as La Follette sees it." Baker noted: "Whichever horn of the dilemma La Follette accepts he is sure to meet serious difficulties. In any event he has small chance of being nominated and of course knows it perfectly well." Commenting upon Bob's attitude, Baker wrote the next day, "I believe first that La Follette's interests are primarily in the cause itself—in advancing progressive measures and a progressive program, but he also has an ambition, and a proper one, to be President, that he may help to carry out that program."[106]

Heney and Steffens had both seen Roosevelt and undoubtedly contributed their views to the conference. The next day, in a letter to a relative, Steffens described the way he felt about the situation: "It looks bad at the moment. The Colonel is mussing up the whole Progressive situation with his 'to be or not to be.' And he won't make a statement. He talks to us privately, but not convincingly; at least not to all of us." Steffens added: "La Follette is bully. He is for the cause, not himself, and wants to act, at once, and in the best interest of ultimate results."[107]

After the conference Bob took the midnight train for Washington. Upon his return he was surprised to find that, without consulting him, a conference had been called for January 29 at Washington headquarters. He supposed this had been done by Gifford Pinchot, and so stated in his *Autobiography*.[108] Although he did not know it at the time, others had cooperated, and the campaign files show that Houser signed some of the letters and telegrams calling the conference.[109]

The day Bob arrived, newspapers over the country printed dispatches from different places reporting evidences of the intensified political activity which had been radiating from Oyster Bay and the *Outlook* offices. Bob probably read the series of dispatches in the Philadelphia *North American* which included one from Pittsburgh, reporting that state Senator William Flinn said he expected Roosevelt to announce within a fortnight that he would accept the nomination.[110] Returning to New York City that day from a trip to Missouri, Ormsby McHarg, who had "helped corral the Southern delegates for Taft," was quoted as saying, "Col. Roosevelt will be nominated and will accept." McHarg also threw out the warning "that any man who stood in the way would get hurt."[111] From Missouri, Governor Hadley announced he was for Roosevelt, and Governor Stubbs of Kansas made public a telegram he had sent the colonel urging him to respond to the demand. In different States men who had been actively working for Roosevelt's nomination were reported to be talking of letters they had received from the colonel indicating he would accept a nomination in response to a demand.[112]

The New York *World* gathered up a few bits of evidence, including excerpts from Gifford Pinchot's introduction at Carnegie Hall, and interpreted them in an editorial describing Bob as "A Decoy Duck": "The plan is working well," the editor wrote. "Mr. Roosevelt is playing fast and loose. He will not deny that he will take the nomination. Roosevelt headquarters have been opened in Chicago, in charge of a former United States Attorney. Roosevelt clubs are being organized throughout the West. . . . George W. Perkins of the Steel Trust and the Harvester Trust and formerly Mr. Morgan's partner does not deny that he is financing a Roosevelt campaign. . . . With Taft out of the way the road is clear for Roosevelt and a stampeded convention. That is the real work that La Follette is doing. Consciously or unconsciously, he is the Roosevelt decoy duck."[113]

Day by day the underground campaign for Roosevelt, combined with the false announcements published about the La Follette candidacy, had rendered it increasingly difficult for Bob to carry out the plan he had determined upon when he wrote Baker on December 9 that he intended "to make this fight an open one, with every important figure in plain view where the public can see every incident and rightly interpret the action of every candidate or possible candidate."[114] But in spite of the odds against him, he kept working on his plan. Through his magazine, and the posting of letters and literature to individuals, he apparently hoped to keep the issues clear and offset newspaper misrepresentation as he had so often done in Wisconsin. When he wrote to Professor Clark thanking him for the list of Illinois Progressives, he said that through these names he would "reach out for others, because I do not propose to have anyone play me for a stalking horse for anybody. I do not fit the part.

"This game of stampede by a lot of old liners and some of the very new liners may succeed, but I reckon it will be a bit hard to sustain for five months."[115]

The day he wrote to Clark he also directed the manager of *La Follette's Magazine* "to search the pages of the forthcoming number of the magazine and be certain that neither Roosevelt's nor Cummins' name, nor any reference to their candidacies appears in any way." This was to be "a standing order until further notice."[116] The order was evoked by the fact that the "News Worth Remembering" column of the previous issue had reprinted a part of Gilson Gardner's Roosevelt-La Follette-working-in-harmony dispatch. Although Bob did not criticize the over-burdened staff, he must have been greatly distressed that his magazine had thus inadvertently seemed to sanction this deliberately inaccurate dispatch.

A letter he wrote to Charles McCarthy at Madison two days before the conference at Washington headquarters indicates he expected that almost any tactics might be invoked. After mentioning that he "had a ripping meeting in New York," he asked McCarthy to tell John Commons "not to believe anything he sees about me in the papers until I tell him it's so. There is a game on for a stampede, but I am too old to shy at noise."[117] That same day he wrote thanking Amos Pinchot for his generous part "in giving me one of the most successful political meetings I ever had. I perfectly understand just how, in your quiet strong way, you stood back of everything. Whatever comes out of this game now being played in violation of every rule of honesty and decency, nothing can shake my confidence in either your loyalty or your insight."[118]

CHAPTER XXXIII

"There Wont Be Any Funeral Unless It's a Real One with Music and Flowers"

Ever since his return from the West, Bob had been carrying a heavy working schedule at Washington. In addition to attending the Senate sessions, he was trying to complete his articles for the *American Magazine* by working late nights at home. The threatened disruption of his organization from within, as revealed on his speaking trip, and during various conferences in New York and Washington since his return, was a constant source of anxiety. After retiring he often found it impossible to sleep and returned to his desk to work until the early hours of the morning.

Monday, January 29, 1912, was a tense and trying day in the La Follette household. It was then they learned that Mary, the youngest child, must undergo a critical operation, and that same afternoon Bob attended a conference which had been called at his Washington headquarters without consulting him.[1] Present at this conference were Gifford and Amos Pinchot, Charles R. Crane and his secretary, Walter S. Rogers, the manager of the Chicago campaign headquarters; Professor Charles E. Merriam, Louis D. Brandeis, William Kent, Irvine L. Lenroot, Gilson Gardner, Angus McSween, Washington correspondent of the Philadelphia *North American*; Walter L. Houser, John J. Hannan, and Medill McCormick. The discussion took up most of the afternoon and was marked by plain speech all around. Two alternatives were submitted in writing by those who now favored Roosevelt: One was "That

394

La Follette shall withdraw in favor of Roosevelt, with reservations as to differences of opinion, and continue to stump." The other proposed "That La Follette shall withdraw, but not in favor of anybody, and continue to stump, leaving the individuals of the group to take what course they choose."[2]

Bob went to the headquarters that afternoon, but in order to ensure the fullest and freest possible discussion he did not enter the conference room. Shortly before five o'clock, while they were threshing the matter out in conference, Bob was called to the telephone by a representative of the Associated Press, who informed him that the *Chicago Daily News* had published a story that afternoon to the effect that Medill McCormick, Crane, Gifford Pinchot, and others were holding a conference at Washington headquarters, and that a statement would be issued announcing La Follette's withdrawal.[3] This dispatch had obviously been sent out before the conference had taken any action. Evidently someone among his former supporters had assumed that the withdrawal of financial support would force Bob to accept one of the alternatives they intended to present. As part of the story headlined "La Follette to Quit, Washington Report," another dispatch from New York was printed under the subtitle "Roosevelt to Obey Demand."[4]

Immediately after leaving the telephone, Bob called Houser out of the conference and drafted the following statement to be signed and given out by Houser: "Washington, D.C., January 29, 1912. —Once for all I want to settle the rumors in circulation that Senator La Follette contemplates withdrawing as a presidential candidate. Senator La Follette never has been and is not now a quitter. When he entered the contest for the nomination he assured those who induced him to become a candidate that he would go through to the end, and that is his determination. He will be there until the gavel falls in the convention announcing the nominee. Senator La Follette is making this campaign to promote the principles in a national way for which he has stood and fought in his own state and in the United States Senate. He will make a campaign in every state to elect delegates pledged to those principles, and to his candidacy as the Republican nominee for President, first, last, and all the time."[5]

Various accounts of what took place on this afternoon of January 29 were subsequently published. Bob recorded, a few months after

the event, his own recollection, which agrees in substance with that
of Brandeis and Lenroot, who were both present.[6] Before giving
any statement to the press, Bob said he called Crane, Merriam, and
Rogers out of the conference "and informed them of the Chicago
story which I believed had been given out by McCormick before
leaving Chicago; that the Associated Press had called for confirmation or denial, and that I had prepared the only statement which
I could consent to have issued on the subject. I knew from what
Houser had reported as to the proceedings in the conference that
the Pinchots, Gardner, and possibly some others, had already decided to desert, and I submitted this statement to Mr. Crane. I had
never for one moment believed that he would abandon me. He is a
man of few words, but with great constancy of purpose. He had
been in the conference with the Pinchots for hours, and subject to
as strong an appeal as it was possible for them to make, and I
watched his face with keen interest as he read the statement. There
was no change of expression. He returned it to Houser, saying very
quietly: 'I think that statement is all right.'

"So I knew that I would at least have one strong supporter to
the end. With Crane, Merriam, and Rogers I then joined the conference. [Gifford] Pinchot at once entered upon a review of what
he had said to the conference regarding my candidacy and that of
Roosevelt. In order to bring the discussion directly to the point, I
called up the alternative statement which Houser informed me had
been under discussion, regarding my withdrawal in favor of Roosevelt. I told them that I had but one answer to make; that I had
never played that kind of politics and never would; that I did not
recognize Roosevelt as standing for Progressive principles; that
I had resisted from the time of its proposal every effort on the
part of Pinchot and others to make me serve as a stalking horse
for Roosevelt's candidacy; that I had not sought the support of
Pinchot or any one else, and had not made myself the Progressive
candidate; that they had joined in urging me to stand; that I had
made a clean fight for principle which had tremendously strengthened the Progressive movement all over the country, but now, when
there seemed to be some prospect of success, it was proposed to turn
everything over to Roosevelt; that if this were done the campaign
would be converted into a contest to nominate Roosevelt rather
than advance a cause; principles would be compromised or wholly

ignored, and the Progressive movement suffer untold injury; that Pinchot had pledged his support to me as long as I continued a candidate; that I could not prevent his withdrawal of that support, but that I would say nothing which he could construe to be a consent or release from his obligation to continue his support. The Pinchots, Gardner, and McCormick then withdrew, but Crane, Merriam, Rogers, Kent, Lenroot, and all of the others assured me that they would go through with me to the end. It was a great relief to have it settled and over with. For weeks the strain had been severe."[7]

The day after this conference, Houser wired Frank Robards, who was doing active organization work in Michigan: "Keep to the helm. Will write you fully. The fight goes to a finish."[8] The next day a three-page typewritten letter to Robards emphatically recapitulated the position Bob had taken at the conference and also stated: "Whatever the papers have said, or may say in the future, this is definitely determined. La Follette will be a candidate until a nomination is made. He will not be a candidate in partnership or in combination with any other person, nor will we campaign for delegates who are for La Follette for second choice, or for first choice and a second choice that they are hoping to go to at the first opportunity."[9] This letter, although signed by Houser, accurately summarizes Bob's program for action. It was probably written at his specific direction or dictation. Subsequent testimony which has come to the author from reliable sources indicates that although Bob was unaware of it, Houser was at this time suggesting to several people in Washington very different tactics.[10]

On the day of the conference at Washington, Governor Johnson of California, who was on his way to New York, had stopped off for a few hours in Chicago to see Heney. That day, after he left, Heney wrote a longhand letter to Bob reporting that Johnson was absolutely sound on the La Follette candidacy and thought Bob was not being fairly treated by others. Heney gave "in a nutshell" the three propositions which the governor intended to put up to Roosevelt: first, that they were in honor bound to support Bob to the end should he desire to remain in the fight; second, that Roosevelt was morally obligated to take his name off the ballot and publicly urge his friends to support the delegates; third, that under no circumstances would Johnson join forces with the reactionary

Republicans who were already out for the colonel in California. Heney added that they were both personally fond of Roosevelt and admired him, but thought his present course was not justifiable and would not promote the best interests of the progressive movement or the American people.[11] When Bob received this letter, he immediately telegraphed Johnson at the Waldorf-Astoria Hotel in New York: "Have seen U'Ren. His report most gratifying. I feel that in the interest of the progressive mo[ve]ment I must go through to the end. Shall never forget your uncompromising loyalty."[12]

Three days after the last conference Amos Pinchot ever attended at the Washington headquarters to which he had contributed so generously, he wrote Bob saying: "I want to thank you for your generous letter of the 27th, about the meeting at Carnegie Hall. It was certainly a superb meeting, but the credit of its success was due to you alone. I regret as much as you do Colonel Roosevelt's attitude toward the nomination. But, more than I can tell you, I fear that the course which you decided on at our conference on Monday will help the nomination of a reactionary at Chicago, and in the meantime split up the Progressives throughout the country. But whatever happens, nothing will change my personal feeling of affection for you."[13]

The opinion expressed in this letter was undoubtedly shared by Lenroot and several others who preferred Bob as a candidate, regretted Roosevelt's entry into the field, but accepted it at this time as inevitable and frankly stated to Bob that they thought the Progressives should now unite on the colonel because they could thus defeat Taft and win the election.

Some weeks previously Bob had promised to attend the annual banquet of the Periodical Publishers' Association at Philadelphia on February 2. He and Governor Wilson were to make the principal speeches. Preparation of this address was an additional burden at a time when he was already working night and day. John R. Commons had been a guest at Bob's home while preparing campaign material, and he also helped to prepare the press release for this speech.

Only four days before the dinner Belle wrote: "Mr. La Follette is dreading the publishers' dinner, as he always does a new audience. His time is so interrupted that it is almost impossible for him to do anything more than outline his ideas for the occasion. I wish he could prepare definitely what he is going to say, so as to be sure and keep in the time limit."[14]

Following the conference of January 29, Bob and Belle had taken their youngest daughter Mary to Providence Hospital. A surgical operation for the removal of a gland near the jugular vein had been ordered by Dr. William F. Mitchell and set for the morning of February 3. When he learned how critical the operation was to be, Bob wished to cancel the Philadelphia engagement. But late in the afternoon of February 2 he finally yielded to the advice of friends who insisted his failure to appear would be interpreted as confirmation of the persistent reports that he intended to retire in favor of Roosevelt.

He left for Philadelphia on an evening train, accompanied by Hannan, Congressman Victor Murdock, and a few other friends from Washington. En route he worked on his speech which, as it came from the typist, was a document of many pages. He marked cuts on this manuscript and found that, as cut and read aloud to Hannan, it could be delivered in thirty-seven minutes.[15] But it was too late to have the text retyped, and he was obliged to take the total manuscript into the banquet hall. At the Bellevue Stratford Hotel, where the Publishers' Association had engaged a room for him, he was met by his son-in-law, George Middleton. During the day Bob had been suffering an attack of indigestion, and had therefore eaten no dinner. Upon his arrival at the hotel room he ordered a hot chocolate. As he drank it he remarked that it was only luke-warm and nauseating. After changing his clothes, and before leaving the room, he took a drink of whisky, as he sometimes did prior to going on the platform when fatigued. Then he, John Hannan, and George Middleton went to the banquet hall, where the dinner had been in progress since eight o'clock.[16]

Among the six hundred who attended the banquet were leading magazine publishers, writers, newspaper correspondents, and many other distinguished men of the day. Alexander Graham Bell, Rear Admiral Peary, Walter Hines Page, Amos Pinchot, Oswald Garrison Villard, Ray Stannard Baker, Lincoln Steffens, John S. Phillips, and several of Bob's close friends in the Congressional progressive group, including Senator Bristow, Congressmen Murdock and Len-root, were present. At the speakers' table sat, left to right, facing the diners, Dr. S. Weir Mitchell, Governor Wilson, Cyrus Curtis, Don Seitz of the New York *World*, who was toastmaster, Mayor Blankenburg of Philadelphia, and William J. Burns. A place between the toastmaster and Mayor Blankenburg had been reserved for Bob. As he entered the banquet hall about eleven o'clock, Wilson was concluding a brilliant address admirably suited to the occasion. Adapting to the late hour, the governor had given his prepared speech to the press and made a charming, tactful, impromptu forty-minute talk which captivated the audience. After Wilson finished speaking, Bob joined the party at the speakers' table. "He and Governor Wilson shook hands warmly and sat talking together for a few minutes . . ."[17]

The speech, as Bob had prepared it to deliver at the banquet, emphasized the importance of newspapers and magazines as educational agencies in a democracy, and stressed the danger of a growing subtle domination through the centralized control of banking credits and advertising. He contrasted the subserviency of the newspapers to special interests with the great educational service rendered in recent years by the more independent weekly and monthly periodicals. The speech closed with a warning of the new peril to the freedom of these publications in the centralization of national advertising which would increasingly seek to gag them.

It was after eleven o'clock when Bob rose to speak. The Philadelphia *North American* reported that "the fighting Senator got a heartening reception. His opening was good-humored and graceful, and gave no hint of the painful scenes that were to follow. When he remarked that if a Democrat were to be elected president he hoped it would be Governor Wilson there were appreciative cheers for the handsome compliment for a political rival."[18]

After the extemporaneous reference to Governor Wilson, Bob picked up the pages of his prepared speech. Something, probably the expression on the toastmaster's face, made him realize this uncut version might appear a formidable document.* Apparently endeavoring to explain the use of the manuscript, he remarked, "For fear there may be some here who will not report what I say

* The toastmaster, Don Seitz, said in an interview two days later: "He [La Follette] held in his hand what must have been 60 closely written pages of manuscript. I looked aghast when I saw he intended going through them all."

correctly, and because I am going to say some things I consider important, I want to have a record of them."[19]

This unfortunate phrasing of his apology for using manuscript lost him the sympathy of his audience at the very beginning of his speech. He had thought it necessary to explain why he was reading his speech, but the explanation, probably unconsciously due to the fact that he had often suffered misrepresentation, was especially inept on an occasion where so many of the distinguished guests were newspaper editors and publishers. George Middleton recalls feeling "instantly the tactlessness of his remark," and adds, "I am sure he also felt the quick unfavorable reaction of the audience. . . . He struck an aggressive note at the beginning and this put them in an aggressive attitude toward him. He got off on the wrong foot and he never got back. As an experienced speaker he intuitively knew he had lost control of the situation at the outset; had he been less fatigued he might even then have adapted himself and his material to the occasion. Instead he went doggedly ahead, determined to make the audience hear him though it was clear, as he went along, that he knew he was failing in a crisis."[20]

As usual on such occasions, many of the diners had been leaving and returning to the banquet hall throughout the evening. But arriving only in time to speak, Bob was unaware of this and misinterpreted these comings and goings as indicating he was losing his audience. He put down his manuscript, which he had started to read in its deleted form, and tried to gain their attention by talking extemporaneously. This departure from his formal address, however unsuited the material may have been to the occasion and the late hour, was a disastrous mistake. He was suffering from acute indigestion and was too worn and fatigued to meet that most exacting test of a speaker: the quick reorganization of a new speech in the presence of an audience.

In the Senate or on the platform he would, if he sensed an audience was becoming restless, put aside his manuscript and effectively focus attention by driving home a point in a brief digression. He apparently attempted to do this in the banquet hall. Harassed by the impression that he was losing his audience, instead of wooing them back, he further alienated them by the aggressive tone which was a manifestation of his own tension. As he returned, from time to time, to read from his hastily cut manuscript, he elaborated points that had already been covered extemporaneously. In his effort to recover a situation lost in the first few minutes of his address, he lost all sense of time. For an hour and a half or two hours[21] he continued speaking in spite "of cynical retorts to his rhetorical questions. At one point, after painting a picture of conditions, he asked, 'Is there a way out?' and some one cried 'We hope so.' "[22]

The reporter for the *Public Ledger* noted: "The face of Wilson was a picture as La Follette went from one blunder to another. He was the most attentive listener the Wisconsin radical had from beginning to end. At first he took notes of what Senator La Follette said but soon desisted. His face grew graver and graver and men who recalled said yesterday that he, perhaps, understood better than anyone else in the room what terrible blunders La Follette was making. Governor Wilson was looking on a tragedy, in a way, and his face showed it."[23]

The climax of what many of those present still remember as a painful ordeal came during the last fifteen minutes of his speech. In preparing his address, although aware it might subject him to criticism from some reactionary newspapers, neither he nor any one working with him foresaw that there might be guests at this dinner who would interpret his analysis of conditions as a personal attack. Many of the facts on which he based his conclusions had come to him from Will Irwin and other newspaper and magazine men. During the two years of its existence *La Follette's Magazine* had frequently attacked the subtle processes by which the news was controlled and distorted in many publications.[24] In writing his talk for the Philadelphia dinner, Bob thought of himself as the publisher of a magazine speaking to publishers "who knew, many of them from bitter experience, the powerful influence" which was exerted "directly and indirectly over the publisher through the centralized control of great national advertising agencies."[25]

But to his weary auditors he was not a publisher. Many had previously known him only through the cartoons and newspaper descriptions of an "Insurgent Senator." Had his address been brief, his manner gracious and persuasive as it often was, the effect might have been different. But fatigued and harassed by the strain of the past weeks, unable to sleep properly, he became the victim and not the master of his failure to win his audience. His tone was strident, and what had been intended as an analysis of a situation by a member of a profession to fellow members of the same profession appeared as a personal attack to many of those present. Almost thirty years later one newspaper publisher, who sat opposite the speaker, still recalled with intense emotion that La Follette "looked directly at me and shook his finger."[26] The length of his speech, his tiresome elaboration of his argument, and the tone of his delivery undoubtedly intensified the personal interpretation which was made by the toastmaster, Don Seitz, and many in the audience.

Even if Bob had read in his best form, early in the evening, the thirty-five-minute version of his address, the audience might have resented the content of the latter part as a premeditated attack. For, though he was unaware of it, this part struck a note directly counter to the purpose of the dinner which had been arranged that year to bring together the newspaper and magazine publishers. The publisher of the *American Magazine*, John S. Phillips, who was present, said: "It should be borne in mind that we had invited many newspaper men; more than ever before. They were our guests. Don Seitz who presided was a newspaper man. It was very late when Senator La Follette spoke. His speech was long and attacked the newspapers; it was inappropriate and long. The newspaper men were our guests."[27]

To these newspaper men and their hosts, the publishers, Bob read the conclusion from his manuscript precisely as he had prepared it. Subsequently he published the entire speech in his *Autobiography* and in *La Follette's Magazine*.[28]

Newspaper reports and individual recollections regarding the behavior of the audience during Bob's speech differ. Some record mocking interruptions with sharp reproof from Bob while the toastmaster repeatedly rapped for order. One publisher who was present recalls that he thought the audience was "patient and courteous, considering the lateness of the hour and the length of the speech." Among the audience "there were those who said, some in joy, others in sorrow, this speech would end his chances for the presidency."[29] According to one report, when Bob sat down "Don C. Seitz, the toastmaster, publisher of the *New York World*, rose to his feet. He spoke slowly, deliberately and distinctly in the silence. 'I want to apologize to the newspaper press of the country in general,' he said, 'for the foolish, wicked and untruthful attack that has just been made upon it.' Then he introduced [the next speaker William J.] Burns."[30]

Throughout Bob's speech Wilson scarcely moved. He sat at the speakers' table with his hands in his pockets, occasionally leaning slightly forward or backward. "After Burns had spoken, and the meeting was over, Wilson and the Senator chatted for a moment."[31] Among the few in his audience who came up to speak to La Follette were John S. Phillips and Congressman Victor Murdock. Two days later Bob wrote Phillips: "It took nerve to greet me as you did Friday night—or—rather Saturday morning. While sorry you were there I appreciate your coming up under the circumstances."[32]

As soon as the meeting ended, George Middleton left his seat at the rear of the large banquet hall and went up to Bob. He recalls: "Hardly any one spoke to him. I walked with him to the elevator. When he entered the room, he went immediately to the bath room and vomited. Lenroot was there, crouched in a chair. Steffens came in. But the Senator made no comment. He hardly spoke. I went with him and John Hannan to the station where he caught a late train for Washington in order to get back in time for the operation on Mary."[33]

Belle had remained at the hospital overnight with Mary. There Bob joined her shortly after his arrival. He was present in the operating room while Dr. Mitchell performed the protracted and delicate operation of removing three glands near the jugular vein which necessitated keeping Mary under ether for two hours and twenty minutes. Throughout most of the day he stayed on at the hospital with his daughter. This was reported in the Washington press and other newspapers.[34]

The newspapers reported the publishers' dinner the next morning, but printed only brief excerpts from Bob's speech and few made any particular comment. Probably most of the accounts had been written before the conclusion of his address. The Philadelphia *Public Ledger* was one of the few to foreshadow on the morning of February 3 the devastating blast that was to follow. It quoted extensively from Wilson's address and compared the two principal speakers, noting that they "were both applauded before their speeches, and Governor Wilson was applauded after his speech." This report also commented, "If La Follette and Wilson may be contrasted as they were last night, they both in a sense, went after the same thing, but Wilson was a rapier and La Follette a club."[35] The afternoon papers of February 3, however, reported an interview with Don Seitz, the toastmaster, which was carried throughout the country in the Sunday-morning newspapers on February 4. He attributed the length of Bob's speech to "his broken-down mental condition," but at the same time held him responsible for the portion of the text prepared in advance and read at the banquet, which was characterized as developing into "an infamous slander of the newspapers and the wallowing, sycophantic praise of the magazines." Seitz expressed the opinion that "the Senator, not knowing the relationship between the magazines and newspapers, came to the dinner with the idea of attacking the latter and currying favor with the magazine publishers."[36] In the same issue which carried this interview, the Philadelphia *Public Ledger* printed an editorial entitled "Mr. La Follette's Methods." After caustically flaying both the content and delivery of Bob's speech, the editorial concluded: "The toastmaster was wholly justified in taking the extraordinary step of reproving his attack upon the newspapers of the entire country as mendacious and foolish, but the reproof was unnecessary. Mr. La Follette is not suffering, as Mr. Seitz says, from some sort of aberration due to overstrain; he is suffering from too much La Follette."[37]

As reports of the Philadelphia dinner came over the wire to the San Francisco *Bulletin* the editor, Fremont Older, like so many of Bob's friends outside Washington, was greatly disturbed. He paced up and down his office and kept repeating: "La Follette must have been ill. Why did they let him speak? They shouldn't have let him speak."[38]

From coast to coast on February 4, and for days after Seitz' interview, newspapers headlined stories of La Follette's "collapse" and "mental-breakdown" coupled with announcements of the withdrawal of his Presidential candidacy, many claiming that these reports were based "on the highest authority" or "unimpeachable sources." These false statements about his lamentable failure at Philadelphia were to continue throughout his life and persist even after his death. In 1916, when he was a candidate for reelection to the Senate, the *Philadelphia Inquirer* published an editorial about his speech which Bob's former law partner thought was ground for a libel suit.[39] During the war hysteria of the First World War,

Rupert Hughes, Gertrude Atherton, and other prominent writers elaborated on these tales and cited them as evidence of mental instability. In 1930 Owen Wister, in a magazine article, referred to the Philadelphia-dinner episode as a characteristic revelation of La Follette.[40] False reports that Bob, at the conclusion of his address, had fallen across the table were repeated by Wister and other writers for years after the event. As late as 1939, when the La Follette papers were not available, a careful historian, who astutely noted that Bob's "collapse" was "temporary," was nevertheless sufficiently misled by false reports to record that "his friends hurried him to a sanitarium."[41] Equally untrue statements that he had frothed at the mouth, wandered incoherently, and spoken in a drunken condition were published in the newspapers and circulated in letters and whispering campaigns immediately following the dinner and throughout the 1912 campaign for the Presidential nomination.[42]

While in the West Brandeis had read the newspapers, and on the train from St. Louis to New York he wrote a little note to Belle. "My thoughts have been much with you and Bob and the children," he said, "and I long to be East where I may hear something authentic. Only make Bob take the rest he needs and make a pleasure trip out of this necessity. When he comes back we will take up the good fight again together. With much love."[43]

In the midst of misrepresentation and desertion, it was a comfort to Bob and Belle to have this assurance of love and loyalty.

Typical of messages that came from men and women in many States was a longhand letter written in Cleveland on February 5, signed by C. R. Williams and Delo E. Mook, who had introduced the resolution endorsing La Follette at the recent Ohio State Conference: "Our Dear Senator, We have fought for your endorsement at all times both at Columbus Convention of Progressives and also at League Meeting at Cleveland. We will continue this line of action until you tell us to stop. We deplore your present illness but can await your recovery."[44]

Bob's failure on an important occasion at a critical moment was a harrowing experience for a man who was capable of lying awake at night, tossing and turning because he thought he had made a poor speech to a small audience in some obscure little town. But it was never his habit to verbalize over unhappy events unless talk might lead to constructive action. What must be accepted as unalterable failure or sorrow he worked out in silence and solitude as he had so many problems in his younger days on the farm when he followed his horse behind the plow. Although he did not discuss the Philadelphia speech with his family or close friends at Washington, his letter files reveal that he realized the anxiety distorted newspaper reports might cause those who had not seen him. At the first opportunity he wrote to his sister and a few intimate friends. As soon as possible he and Belle both responded to the inquiries which came from many others.

At no time, either before or after the Philadelphia dinner, did Bob either contemplate or sanction the withdrawal of his Presidential candidacy. But because he himself recognized that his failure at Philadelphia was due to extreme fatigue and nervous exhaustion, he did authorize the cancellation of his immediate speaking dates. At first he had insisted on keeping at least the one important engagement to speak at the progressive banquet in Jersey City on Monday night, February 5, before taking a much needed rest. But he was persuaded to let someone else take his place. Subsequently, when the distorted stories of his "collapse" and "mental break-down" at Philadelphia were published, Belle and his daughter Fola thought it would have "been better if he had gone to New Jersey."[45]

Thinking Phillips might be anxious about the *Autobiography* articles after reading the newspapers on Sunday, February 4, Bob dictated a letter that night assuring him he would "send final revise on the April (No. 7) article by Tuesday." He added, "It is my present intention to take at least a couple of weeks off. This will not be to the disadvantage of The American, because the completion of the series will be a first mortgage on as much of that time as I give to work of any kind."[46] This was the same letter in which Bob thanked Phillips for coming up to greet him after his speech at the Philadelphia banquet.

Following the exaggerated reports in the newspapers, anxious inquiries poured in from friends throughout the country. From Chicago the distinguished surgeon Dr. Albert Ochsner wrote Belle inviting them to be his guests on a trip to Mexico.[47] To Dr. Ochsner and other friends Belle gave the facts as frankly as she did in a letter to Mrs. Charles Mayo at Rochester when she wrote a few weeks later: "Bob's condition has been grossly misrepresented in the newspapers. He is suffering from lack of sleep and is in need of rest. He realizes it, and has let go of his work for a while and is already much better."[48]

To several close friends who had expressed concern and inquired about the continuation of Bob's candidacy, Belle explained the situation as it seemed to her and Bob when she wrote: "The political situation has been a trying one. As you may know, he became a candidate at a time when it was generally believed Taft could not be beaten in the Convention, and when no one else would undertake the burden of making the contest; yet it was important for the Progressive Movement, unless it was to disintegrate, that someone should assume the leadership. When the aggressive campaign disclosed that the movement had a deep hold on the people pressure was brought to bear to force Mr. La Follette either to combine with Roosevelt or to get out of the field altogether. This he refused to do because he has always been open and frank with the people and never entered into any deals or compromises which might confuse the issue or sacrifice what he considers fundamental principles. The persistent reports that he has withdrawn and misrepresentation as to his health are a part of the plan to make him yield."[49]

In the meantime the newspaper reports and the tales that were industriously circulated by other media contributed to the further disruption of the progressive organizations which had been built up around his candidacy and had endorsed him either before or after the progressive conference at Chicago on October 16. A comparatively mild report of what was going on was sent to Madison to Dr. George Keenan by a physician in St. Paul, Minnesota, who wrote: "Up in our neck of the woods, they are giving out that La Follette has withdrawn from the Presidential race, on account of his health, that he is suffering from chronic trouble, and has but a short time to live. Minnesota and the Northwest, in general, were strongly for him, but they are taking the above as gospel truth, and unwillingly going over to some other candidate." The writer closed with the plea, "if you take any interest in his political welfare tell me about him."[50] But most of these false rumors as to Bob's physical and mental condition did not reach those who could refute them from direct personal and professional knowledge as Dr. Keenan did in his reply to this letter.[51]

Undoubtedly some of Bob's friends sincerely believed his failure at Philadelphia indicated a long rest was imperative when they urged him to take an ocean trip, to go to Egypt or some place in Europe. Others, who were not alarmed about his health, honestly thought that in order to avoid a split in the progressive forces he should now yield to the inevitable, permit Roosevelt to assume the undisputed leadership, and withdraw his own candidacy. But there were other men, in Washington and elsewhere, prominently identified as having advocated his candidacy from the beginning, who were now determined he could and should be retired from the Presidential campaign regardless of the consequences to him personally. Having transferred their support to Roosevelt weeks or months before, they now made the most of the Philadelphia dinner debacle as an occasion for the public announcement of an act long consummated. Some of these announcements, made by men who had reason to know their statements were inaccurate, deliberately implied that La Follette was mentally incapacitated.

A careful study of the contemporary documents and the subsequent correspondence available to the author, combined with the testimony gathered from those who participated in these conferences which followed the Philadelphia dinner, indicates that decisions were made and action was taken in matters which vitally concerned Bob without even consulting him. Some of the facts he never knew. Some became known to his intimate friends only long after his death.

Although Bob was unaware of it at the time, there is reliable evidence that during late December, 1911, and January, 1912, as it became more evident Roosevelt would be a candidate, Houser had expressed to others his agreement with the opinion of Gifford Pinchot and McCormick that the thing to do was to shift to the colonel and thus win the nomination from Taft. In talking to Congressman Nelson immediately after the Philadelphia dinner, Houser assumed that La Follette's candidacy was ended, and emphasized that he "had been right in his opinion that the thing to do was to support Roosevelt."[52] There is also evidence that Houser talked to others in a similar vein. His assertions probably led to assumptions on the part of some La Follette supporters which were not in accord with the facts and which had never been authorized by Bob. This may have been responsible for many of the bitter and inaccurate assertions made later in the campaign by some of the men who had originally urged Bob to become a candidate.

It was Nelson's opinion that Houser never "had any deliberate intention of betraying La Follette or being disloyal to him. But that McCormick and Gifford Pinchot and others worked on him; that he was impressed and perhaps flattered; that Houser loved playing the game of politics, and probably persuaded himself that La Follette would ultimately come over to Houser's opinion; that then Houser's judgment would be confirmed, and he would be in a fine strategic position in relation to Roosevelt."[53]

The correspondence in the files of La Follette's Washington headquarters and the author's interviews with many people tend in general to substantiate Nelson's analysis. There is, however, documentary evidence that in at least one instance Houser expressed definitely conflicting opinions to Bob and McCormick in regard to writing a letter to Roosevelt. Other testimony indicates that Houser was influenced at times to advise action which was contrary to Bob's expressed instruction.

It appears that early on Sunday morning, February 4, while Bob was still at the hospital with Mary, Senators Clapp and Bourne and John D. Fackler, who was in charge of the Ohio headquarters at Cleveland, all met in Walter Houser's private office at Washington headquarters in the Evans Building. According to the recollection of one of the men present, Houser stated that the La Follette campaign was over and started to put through a telephone call to Roosevelt at Oyster Bay to say that because of La Follette's illness his campaign was called off and his supporters were coming out for Roosevelt. Clapp dissuaded Houser from putting through this telephone call, suggesting that they should not attempt to deliver La Follette's supporters to anyone.[54]

On the afternoon of that same day, another conference was held at the Washington headquarters which was attended by Houser, Bourne, Bristow, Lenroot, Angus McSween, and John D. Fackler. Probably Medill McCormick, who was in Washington at this time, and a number of others also attended the meeting. John J. Hannan, Bob's confidential secretary, was in and out of the conference room, although he was not there constantly. "The advisability of having La Follette withdraw and transferring the support of the La Follette organization to Roosevelt was discussed." Bristow stated "he would not be for such procedure unless it were acceptable to and authorized by La Follette."[55] Clapp apparently took the same position.

McSween announced that Van Valkenburg, the publisher of the

Philadelphia *North American,* had directed him to say that on Monday morning, February 5, his paper was coming out for Roosevelt. John Hannan, Lenroot, and others recall that this conference, without any authority from Bob, drafted a statement of the withdrawal of the La Follette candidacy.[56] While the conference was still discussing the form of withdrawal which was to be issued, Fackler put in a long-distance call to Cleveland, and then left to catch the 6:35 train for that city.[57] Apparently some of the conferees were confident Bob would, or at least determined he should, sign on the dotted line. That same night, Sunday, February 4, Medill McCormick telephoned from Washington and told Amos Pinchot in New York "that La Follette was about to give out a statement of final withdrawal."[58] McCormick may have made similar statements that night to other individuals in different parts of the country.

The following morning, Monday, February 5, there was another meeting at headquarters. The conferees drew up a statement of La Follette's withdrawal from the Presidential race which it was intended he should sign. While the conference was on, Bob, who had not been invited to attend, dropped in at headquarters. He did not, according to Lenroot's recollection, enter the conference room. But those who were present must have known he was there because the statement was taken out and submitted to him for his signature. He read it and handed it back, saying he would sign no statement without consulting Belle. This answer was reported back to the conferees, and they designated Lenroot, Hannan, and Houser as a committee of three to submit it to Bob and Belle at their home.[59]

That same day the committee of three went to the La Follette home at 1864 Wyoming Avenue, where they submitted the statement to Belle and Bob. She read it and answered she would rather see Bob in his grave than have him sign that statement.[60] As so often throughout the years these two traveled the road together, a similar sense of values brought independently and spontaneously a complete accord as to choice of action. The following day Belle recorded her reaction in a longhand letter to Gilbert Roe: "When I learned of the humiliation Bob had suffered in Philadelphia I longed for you Gilbert[.] And it is you and Alf who are needed here or men like you—if there are any. The impression he made must have been pretty bad[.] I should judge it was pitiful and yet the way Hannan & Lenroot and Houser have been willing to make a funeral of it, rouses my ire. They are telling how slowly he works, how he has not done anything new for a long time[.] Lenroot is particularly aggravating along this line[.] I could not but ask him who made the fight and won the Lorimer investigation the speech in Alaska on the tariff & so on last session[.] I know Bob suffers from brain fag all the time because he will not try to rest but to hear these men talk you would think he had been a dead man for several years instead of carrying the whole load of the progressive movement[.] It needs a man to talk back to them[.]

"Yesterday they came up here with a statement that Bob withdrew from the race *unless* Wisconsin *wished* to name him[,] that he was going away for prolonged rest, must be shielded from all strain and so on[.] If it had gone to the country no one would have doubted that he was a wreck for all time." She told this friend, from whom they never withheld anything, "I want you to know he is, in spite of his suffering bravest of us all[.] Determined as ever to fight it out and down as other obstacles."[61]

On Monday, February 5, the same day that Bob dropped in at Washington headquarters and refused to sign the statement which was handed to him, Medill McCormick telephoned to Amos Pinchot in New York that "La Follette was too ill to make a statement but that there would appear in the next morning's papers one by his manager, Houser, to the effect that he had definitely retired."[62] That night McCormick also sent a telegram to the Illinois Progressive Republican League, which was printed the next morning in the *Chicago Daily Tribune* and other newspapers as part of a Washington dispatch, announcing that La Follette had virtually withdrawn from the race and that "action had been taken by his supporters which will result in the support of the Roosevelt movement by progressive[s] in all sections of the country, including Illinois." McCormick's telegram contained the following statement: "Considering all the circumstances, including Senator La Follette's physical condition, in the opinion of the overwhelming majority of progressive Republican members of both houses of Congress, progressives in Illinois must unite to send Roosevelt delegates to the national Republican convention."[63]

Soon after the Philadelphia dinner, probably at the time of these conferences, Lynn Haines, who had been working at the Washington headquarters, came home and said to his wife, "This is a terrible thing La Follette's friends have done to him."[64]

The evening of the day Bob refused to sign the statement of withdrawal which the committee had submitted, he went to the Providence Hospital to see Mary. On his return home he wrote to his sister at Madison: "Whatever you may see in the papers dont you get fooled nor allow Bob or Billy to think for a moment that I am worn out physically[.] I have not been in better trim in years. I have not had sleep enough in months and am tired that way. A few weeks will make a world of difference with me. I am in a game where the cards are stacked and some 'friends' have a cold deck or two under the table But I shall play my regular game— all the cards on the table—nothing concealed from the public. No one shall use me or my delegates. Playing it this way I shall not have so many delegates as though I would let some of the *friends* of T.R. play as my partners but I'll come through with a clean score with the people."[65]

Bob also directed Houser to issue a statement this same evening stating La Follette would take a few weeks' needed rest but definitely declaring he would not retire from the campaign; that his name would be presented to the Republican National Convention and that delegates would "make an aggressive contest for his nomination, and for a strong platform."[66]

The next day Bob wrote to Gilbert Roe, with whom he was always entirely frank: "Dear Gil: I am likely to be attacked in every conceivable and underhanded way by the friends of another candidate in order to force me to quit the field. Since returning from New York I have had the screws applied to me, but have stood against it. Since my flunk at Philadelphia, everybody here (outside of the immediate household) has been on my neck to force me out. Last night I made my final answer, and REQUIRED Houser to issue the statement which you have no doubt read. I did it in the face of threats, or suggestions which amounted to threats, from the Philadelphia North American, and while I have not seen the paper this morning, I understand that they have begun to strike below the belt.*

* That morning on the front page, the *North American* had carried a Washington dispatch, signed by Angus McSween, with the headlines: "La Follette, Ill/Is Virtually Out Of Presidential Race/Fight For Delegates Dropped Except in Wisconsin." The first lines of the dispatch read, "Senator La Follette's virtual withdrawal as a candidate for the presidential nomination was announced from progressive headquarters tonight."

"I have been in sore need of a few friends who were not in politics, and should have asked you and perhaps Fred [Howe] and Stef[fens] to come over, but it seemed unreasonable to do it when I know how busy you are. . . .

"There is not a thing wrong with me, excepting that I find myself dead tired. I think a couple of weeks spent mostly in sleeping will put me right. I have not been in better physical condition in years. Let us know about Janet, Gil. With a world of love for you all, Bob."[67]

In response to a telegram received on Monday, February 5, from his friend Will Colver, who was in Chicago, Bob drafted in his own manuscript the following night letter: "No chang[e] Bill. Always remember I never quit. But I find I must have a few weeks of sleep and rest in order to catch up. Didnt know I was really in need of it. There wont be any funeral unless it's a real one with music and flowers."[68]

"La Follette Never Authorized Either the Withdrawal of His Candidacy or a Transfer of His Support to Roosevelt"

As distorted stories swept across the country, Bob's friends grieved. But some former supporters, who had already privately gone over to Roosevelt, made the most of the situation by deliberately spreading the impression that Bob was incapacitated. In Washington, Senator Gronna was among those who were told La Follette was so completely broken physically and mentally that he could not even be seen. After refusing to sign a commitment to support Roosevelt, which had been submitted to him, he went to Bob's home to call and express sympathy to his wife. To Gronna's amazement Bob himself opened the door, welcomed him warmly, and invited him to his study, where he had been dictating to his secretary. When Gronna returned home he walked the floor in anger, denouncing what he thought was a deliberate campaign of deception and telling his wife that he would fight to the finish to carry North Dakota for La Follette.[1]

From Nebraska Frank Harrison wrote to say that a report that Bob was "under restraint" in a private hospital was being "quietly circulated" and had become quite general even in Wisconsin.[2] Personal letters could not catch up with garbled press reports and underground whispering campaigns. Misrepresentations of fact followed swiftly one upon another. Knowing the futility of verbal denials through the press, Bob submitted in silence until the oppor-

Suggestion to Pinchot: Wouldn't it be safer to quarantine him or lock his clothes up in the fumigator?

J. N. Darling, in the *Globe and Commercial Advertiser*, New York, Feb. 17, 1912.

tunity came to refute them effectively by action in the North Dakota campaign. Then, so far as he was concerned, the humiliating failure of his speech at the publishers' dinner slipped into the background in due proportion to the totality of his life and work.

From the office of the *Outlook* letters signed by F. K., and dated February 8 and 9, 1912, were sent out stating that La Follette's physical breakdown made his early retirement likely and that the writer was certain Roosevelt would accept the nomination if tendered. Each recipient was advised to get in touch with a specific individual in his State.[3] Only a few progressive leaders communicated directly with Bob as Gronna had. Some, accepting these false tales as fact, immediately repeated them in letters and public statements.[4] Others continued to reiterate them in correspondence even after they had been refuted by Bob's intimate friends and by his own active speaking campaign in North Dakota. Gronna was the only one of the Senators originally endorsing Bob's candidacy who continued to campaign for him after Roosevelt announced he would accept the nomination.

The deliberate falsehoods circulated by some of Bob's former supporters received effective collaboration from certain newspapers. The statement issued by Houser at Bob's direction on the night of February 5 had been prefaced by misleading headlines and distorted interpretations to make it appear that La Follette was a broken man and had actually withdrawn his own candidacy. Under a front-page headline, "LA FOLLETTE, ILL, IS VIRTUALLY OUT OF PRESIDENTIAL RACE," the Philadelphia *North American*, which had been one of his strongest supporters, said: "The construction certain to be placed upon this statement, and which is expected, is that Senator La Follette realized that his present condition eliminates him as a possible candidate."[5] The actual statement issued by Houser had presented very different facts when it announced that a temporary indisposition made it necessary for Senator La Follette to take a few weeks' rest but that delegates to the convention would make an aggressive contest for his nomination and for a strong platform.[6]

On the same day that Houser's statement was published, many newspapers throughout the country carried a New Jersey dispatch announcing that La Follette had withdrawn in favor of Roosevelt. In mid-December Bob had accepted two invitations to speak in

New Jersey on Monday, February 5. One was at a Hudson County Progressive Republican League dinner in Jersey City; the other at a luncheon in Trenton before the annual meeting of the New Jersey State Editorial Writers' Association. When these engagements were canceled, George L. Record had telegraphed Washington headquarters early Monday morning asking Lenroot to take Bob's place.[7] It had been so arranged. But later that morning, when Bob had dropped in at headquarters and refused to sign the statement of withdrawal which the conferees had drafted, Lenroot had been chosen as one of the committee to submit it to Belle and Bob at their home. Senator Clapp had then been selected to substitute for Lenroot and had taken the train for Jersey City.[8] That morning Hannan had predicted to the conferees and to a reporter that La Follette would refuse to withdraw. That same afternoon the *Newark Evening News* published a statement by Hannan that La Follette would not withdraw his candidacy.[9]

That night, at about the time an extraordinary announcement was made in Jersey City at the Hudson County Progressive Republican League dinner, Bob was writing his sister from Washington not to be alarmed by newspaper reports and explaining that he was "in a game where the cards are stacked and some 'friends' have a cold deck or two under the table."[10]

At the dinner reporters noted that an atmosphere of excitement pervaded the large room where six hundred people had gathered to hear Record and Clapp. The New Jersey Progressives had held a number of conferences, and the shift toward Roosevelt among the "Essex group" of leaders had been on for some weeks. It was expected that an effort would be made to swing this meeting to his candidacy. A number of Bob's supporters had deliberately stayed away because they did not wish their presence to be misinterpreted. They knew Record had told Gilbert Roe the previous evening at the latter's home, in the presence of Governor Hiram Johnson, that he felt he must leave La Follette, as others in New Jersey had already gone and he could not make the fight alone.[11]

When the guests had finished their "dollar dinners," they moved nearer the speakers' table. As George Record rose, there was an expectant hush. He had been the most prominent New Jersey delegate and the permanent chairman of the first Progressive Republican League Conference at Chicago which had endorsed Bob's candidacy in October, 1911. Whatever he said at this dinner would inevitably be an important factor in both the New Jersey and the national campaigns. Opening his speech with a tribute to La Follette's long, unselfish public service, he recalled how much his campaigning in New Jersey in 1906 had meant to the progressive movement of that State. After elaborating this theme and expressing regret at Bob's absence as the guest of honor, he added, "I am able to say to you with infinite pleasure, that a few minutes before I came into this hall that I received—over the telephone—from Washington, the information that we will be able to go into this fight under the united leadership of Theodore Roosevelt! . . .

"Senator La Follette has but added another to the long list of sacrifices that he has made for this cause. He is ill—unable to go on. He must go abroad or else we fear that his health will be permanently lost. . . ."[12] Record explained that his long-distance telephone conversation had been with Walter L. Houser, one of La Follette's managers, and that the Senator had "withdrawn in favor of any other candidate" that might "be named by the Progressive Republican party"; that he had done this on "the advice of friends and physicians following his breakdown in health in Philadelphia on Friday night." He added that Congressman Lenroot of Wisconsin was among those who had persuaded him to take this step and that the news which had just come to him "over the telephone wire" from Houser in Washington meant "all obstacles can be removed" and "we can now all join for Roosevelt, the Progressive Republican candidate."[13]

If Record understood Houser correctly and reported the telephone conversation accurately, the facts were grossly misrepresented. Many years later Lenroot said: "Houser had no right to make any such statement. La Follette never authorized either the withdrawal of his candidacy or a transfer of his support to Roosevelt."[14] Record's own statements as to the actual content and the time of Houser's telephone communication to him are conflicting.[15]

But there can be no doubt as to the immediate effect of Record's announcement, which was widely reported in the press. The funeral meats baked that night for Bob's candidacy furnished forth the Roosevelt progressive wedding feast which had been planned for New Jersey. But "all obstacles" could not be so easily removed. In spite of apparently overwhelming difficulties, James E. Pope,

Frank Sommer, and a loyal group of La Follette supporters obsti-
nately carried on his campaign and brought him into the State to
speak to large audiences the week before the New Jersey primary.

Five days after Record's announcement at the new Jersey progressive dinner, Gifford Pinchot sent a telegram from Jersey City
to Hugh Halbert, a member of the executive committee of the
Minnesota Progressive Republican League, which was given to the
newspapers and sensationally interpreted. The fact that Pinchot
had been a La Follette supporter and a generous contributor to his
campaign had been widely publicized. Although his support had
been transferred to Roosevelt many weeks before, this was not
generally known. Therefore whatever Pinchot said about Bob still
carried a note of authority, and it was inferred that he had "inside"
information when he telegraphed Halbert saying that "in my judgment La Follette's condition such [that] further serious candidacy
impossible."[16] The publication of this telegram a few days after
Record's announcement probably contributed more than any other
single factor to the belief that Bob had been seriously incapacitated.
Pinchot was regarded by many Progressives throughout the country
as the disinterested Sir Galahad of the movement. Therefore many
who would have discounted ordinary rumors and newspaper reports
were persuaded to believe the tales which were being circulated in
a well organized whispering campaign to the effect that Bob had
lost his mind or was a victim of an incurable disease.

During the days that followed the publishers' dinner in Philadelphia, many things were done in the belief that the end justified
the means. Bob never knew of some of them. But among those that
came to his knowledge he thought Gifford Pinchot's telegram was
one of the hardest hits below the belt. Belle wrote to their classmate
Jean Bascom, daughter of President John Bascom: "We have had a
hard siege, and all the publicity and exaggeration have made it difficult to bear. Bob's courage and iron resolution do not desert him,
however; nor his sense of humor. So long as his spirit is not broken by
all that he has to endure, I feel that I should be grateful whatever the
outcome."[17] To another intimate friend Belle wrote that "Even
Bob's closest friends have advised him to retire from the race and
endorse Roosevelt. This he could not do, and will not; so he is again
a lonely man. I think the breaking down of the Progressive alliance,

which as you know took him so long to build up, is the hardest part of the situation."[18]

Four days before Pinchot wired Halbert, leading Progressives had held a conference in Minneapolis, and George Loftus, president of the Minnesota Progressive Republican League, had telegraphed congratulating Bob on his refusal to withdraw.[19] On the same day that Pinchot wired Halbert from Jersey City, Congressman Lindbergh had telegraphed from Washington to George Loftus that La Follette would "be in shape to take hold in a few days. His constructive legislation in Wisconsin is the best material to show what can be done by a Progressive executive. I believe any shift at this time would weaken the Progressive work generally."[20] The next night, at the request of Halbert, a meeting of the Minnesota executive committee was called. There was a stormy session. Halbert made a speech insisting La Follette was so ill that he was out of the running, and read Pinchot's telegram to prove it. When this did not prevent adoption of resolutions unanimously pledging continued support to La Follette, Halbert resigned and came out for Roosevelt.[21]

At Bob's direction Houser had gone West to get in touch with those who were in charge of campaign headquarters in the different states. Stopping off in Ohio, he telegraphed that "Fackler had gone to Cleveland to betray us. His speech took the Cleveland League to Roosevelt." Houser added that nevertheless some of the La Follette people would "fight to the end" and tickets would "be put in the field in the two Cleveland districts."[22]

Similar conflicts were on in other States. Governor Stubbs of Kansas and Governor Aldrich of Nebraska had publicly announced transfer of their support to Roosevelt. As late as the morning of February 8, Johnson had assured Gilbert Roe that he would stand for La Follette.[23] But the following morning he had arrived at Roe's home in a state of great agitation. After pacing the floor for some time and finding considerable difficulty in coming to the point, he finally told Roe that he was obliged to go over to Roosevelt.[24] On Sunday, February 11, he had gone to Washington to ask Bob for his release because he had decided to support Roosevelt.[25] The day after Bob talked with Johnson, he wrote to a close friend outlining his own plan "to fight for delegates in Minnesota, North Dakota, South Dakota, Nebraska, Oregon, and probably California—no matter how many governors back up, nor how many La Follette Leagues or Clubs surrender their charters. And before the convention meets in June the people of this country will understand the difference between the kind of progressives we are, and the sort that are ready to chase any old band wagon."[26]

In one State after another efforts were made to capture the organizations which had originally endorsed La Follette. Prominent Progressives who had gone over to Roosevelt expecting the former President to sweep everything before him were surprised and harassed by the splits that developed in their States. Men who had urged Bob to become a candidate and had for months lauded him in their speeches grew increasingly resentful and began to blame him for the division in the progressive forces because he would not retire in favor of the man they were convinced could win. Bitterness crept in. Friends who had worked together for years became enemies. Animosities developed against Bob which were to endure as long as he lived.

Foreseeing something of what would happen, William Kent called on Bob at his home on Sunday, February 11, to present the situation as he saw it. Kent had contributed generously to Bob's campaign and had stood by him loyally during the trying period when others were privately going over to Roosevelt. On this particular Sunday, Kent had what he described to Amos Pinchot as "a rather painful interview" with Bob.[27] The next day, after "much hard thinking," Kent wrote a frank, sincere letter presenting his view of the "very acute" California situation. He urged Bob to request that his name be taken off the California primary ballot and, for his own sake, not to oppose Roosevelt and "thereby accumulate as enemies those who are naturally your friends."[28] Bob replied to this "dear friend," for whom he had an abiding affection all his life: "Out of the group of those whom I love and trust, there is not one whose counsel would be more carefully considered than yours,—not one, the loss of whose friendship and esteem would leave a more lasting wound. But I should be unworthy of the regard of all men of right standards, if I did not follow my conviction in this as I have in all things. I am everlastingly sure of the righteousness of my resolution to fight straight on, never halting, never turning one single step aside to bargain with sham success. Every day strengthens that resolution and the future will vindicate my course. For the present I must endure the pain and mortification attending upon the loss of political followers and even personal friends. But out of many trials I have been taught the lesson of fortitude and patience. Whatever befalls me believe me sincerely grateful for your past support and confidence."[29]

The day that Governor Johnson gave out a formal statement in New York announcing he was for Roosevelt, Chester H. Rowell telegraphed Bob's Washington headquarters that he agreed with Johnson's course and would resign the presidency of the California La Follette League at a meeting to be held the following week.[30] With Rowell went the support of one of the leading progressive newspapers of the State, which he edited. The next day a telegram from Fremont Older, editor of the San Francisco *Bulletin*, was received at the La Follette headquarters in Washington. It showed what was happening in California and revealed the difficult personal situation which had developed for Older as it had for many others in the States where the governors and Senators formerly supporting La Follette had shifted to Roosevelt: "Of course I think Roosevelt's treatment of La Follette is not only the crime of one century but all centuries. Everyone has gone over here. What can I do? Rowell, Lissner, and Earl are all out for Roosevelt. I am helpless."[31] On March 25 Francis J. Heney called on Bob at his home in Washington. Heney said that his heart was with Bob, who was doing right in staying in the fight; that Roosevelt was responsible for any division jeopardizing the progressive movement; but that he felt compelled to stand with Johnson or get out of politics in California.[32] But Rudolph Spreckels, who had been closely associated with all these men in the long fight against political corruption in the State, refused to transfer his support to the colonel. Although a personal friend of Roosevelt's, he stood steadfastly by the La Follette candidacy and made it possible to continue his campaign in California.

The day before Governor Johnson made his announcement, Gifford Pinchot had issued a statement in Washington publicly declaring that he was for Roosevelt. Pinchot explained that he had "of course, taken no part in advocating the nomination of Col. Roosevelt" until he had notified Senator La Follette. The letter of notification had been delivered to Bob the previous day. Among the reasons Pinchot gave in his public statement for transfer of his support to Roosevelt was "the ill-health of Senator La Follette, which all of his friends so greatly deplore."[33]

On February 21 Roosevelt spoke at Columbus before the Ohio State Constitutional Convention. Drafts of the address had been submitted to Gifford and Amos Pinchot, Governor Johnson, and E. A. Van Valkenburg.[34] This speech, in which Roosevelt came out for the recall of judicial decisions, brought enthusiastic response from many Western Progressives, but it shocked Roosevelt's more conservative Eastern supporters. As he passed through Ohio on his return trip to New York, he said to a reporter, "My hat is in the ring!" Three days later, in a letter replying to a call signed by seven governors, Roosevelt publicly declared, "I will accept the nomination for President if it is tendered to me, and I will adhere to this decision until the convention has expressed its preference."[35]

Public declarations for Roosevelt were now made day after day. Most of the progressive Senators, Congressmen, and governors who had previously endorsed La Follette followed the glamorous Rough Rider's hat into the ring. Gronna never wavered, and, with the exception of Lenroot, the Wisconsin delegates to the convention seemed ready to support La Follette to the end. From the first Bob insisted he wanted only delegates who could be "found facing one way all the while, and stand until the last shot is fired."[36] Lenroot thought he ought to support Roosevelt for second choice. Although he had dined recently at Bob's home, he did not talk the matter over with him but took it up by letter and messages sent through Hannan. After an exchange of letters he decided he could not serve as a delegate.[37] To a close friend Belle wrote, "Nothing that has happened has been so hard for me. We have managed to keep the personal relation but I realize that Bob and Irvine can never be the same to each other as before. It is a relief to have the matter decided. I think Bob feels better than for some time. He has realized that Lenroot disapproved of his course and was in full sympathy with Pinchot, Kent, and the rest in leaving him. This has worked on Bob and while he has accepted Lenroot's criticism in the friendly spirit it was made, now that Lenroot has made the issue and they have agreed to disagree Bob feels the decks are cleared and whatever delegates he has from Wisconsin will know what they stand for."[38]

Bob had consented to take a vacation, and really intended to keep his promise. But this holiday, like so many others he had planned, was postponed and finally dropped. Before taking any rest, Bob felt he must finish his articles for the *American Magazine*. Also, now that "the deserters" were "weeded out," he thought it imperative to set his campaign "going in a clean cut way" in States where his supporters wished to continue the fight for delegates.[39] From different parts of the country approval of his refusal to withdraw had been indicated by telegrams from "many people who would have felt they were betrayed if he had taken any other stand."[40] Charles R. Crane, Elizabeth Evans, Rudolph Spreckels, James E. Pope, William La Follette, and others, together with many volunteer workers, made it possible to keep his headquarters functioning and pay the expenses of speakers. A few days after the publishers' dinner, Crane had sent word to Bob that his continued support could be counted on. Shortly after this he had come to Washington to see Bob. As Belle wrote Mrs. Crane soon after this visit, "That Mr. Crane should support him so generously financially and so unquestionably as a friend when his personal feeling might have led him in another direction, is the supreme test of unselfishness and loyalty that helps us to forget all else that has happened."[41] Although aware that many of Bob's friends did not understand his course, Belle thought it "the only one he could follow and not belie his convictions. Perhaps time will vindicate his action in this crisis as it has in times past when he has stood alone. But whatever happens he has been true to himself, and that is the only guide we can follow in the complexities of politics."[42]

The first Presidential primary to be held in the United States was scheduled for March 20 in North Dakota. Senator Gronna was confident Bob would win, but he took no chances and went out himself to speak and to work among his friends. Also, the chairman of the executive committee of the Progressive Republican League, E. M. Tucker, did an excellent job in organizing the campaign. Reports coming in from Michigan, Nebraska, Oregon, and California indicated that there was "a lot of sentiment, which if the leaders had stayed by," as in North Dakota, might have made it easy to carry other States. Between dictating the final chapters of his autobiography to meet publication dates for the *American Magazine*, Bob was making important decisions regarding the campaign and sending telegrams to friends in Wisconsin, Minnesota, and elsewhere asking them to fill speaking dates in North Dakota. With remarkable generosity these men paid their own expenses, postponed their personal affairs, and jumped on trains to meet the schedules which were being booked for them. Belle wrote to a dear friend that in spite of the few hours' sleep that Bob had and "the strain of all that has happened, he seems to gather strength and power. Perhaps from those deeper resources—second wind of which [William] James speaks."[43] In another letter she wrote with penetrating insight, "He feels better always when things are straightened out and the decks seem cleared for action, no matter how big a fight he has on his hands."[44]

He was in fact already preparing for action himself. In response to urgent telegrams from Senator Gronna and Walter D. Corrigan, Bob interrupted his work on the articles for the *American Magazine* and left Washington on March 12 for North Dakota. When Gronna and Corrigan had arrived in North Dakota to campaign for Bob, they found that intimations were being deliberately circulated that "La Follette was mentally wrecked."[45] They were convinced that the only effective way to defeat such tactics was for him to speak in North Dakota himself. It was evident that the fight for delegates was actually between Roosevelt and Bob, for the old-line Republican organization had practically abandoned Taft and was backing the colonel. Bryan, who was keenly aware of this, had sharply criticized Roosevelt's record in a recent speech at Fargo and declared that when it came to progressive Republican candidates he was "pledged to Bob La Follette who was a progressive before Roosevelt could spell the word." He reminded North Dakota voters that he had gone into Wisconsin and campaigned for La Follette and had also refused to go there to campaign for Democrats who were against him.[46]

Roosevelt's campaign in North Dakota had been opened the first week in March by Gifford Pinchot. He was followed by Garfield, Governor Stubbs, and other prominent speakers. Frank Knox of Michigan, who had been so active in the underground campaign for Roosevelt, also came into North Dakota to help organize. While fervently advocating Roosevelt's nomination, Pinchot explained his desertion of La Follette's candidacy in a laudatory epitaph. Referring to the Wisconsin Senator as a friend of long standing, he expressed admiration for his courage and service to the progressive cause, but likened him to a disabled engine. Then, arguing that "the train of progress must not stop," he declared that "another human engine, Roosevelt, must take the progressive train on to the terminal."[47] Pinchot repeated this description in a speech at Minneapolis, and was reported to have said in an interview that even if nominated "Senator La Follette would be physically unable to make the campaign."[48]

The day before Bob left Washington to begin his campaign, Belle, who accompanied him, wrote that she had encouraged his going to North Dakota as it was "the best way to give the lie to these deserters who are going about claiming they left him because he was disabled. I don't mind those who came out in the open so much and said they left him because they believed T.R. could win."[49] Bob opened his campaign in North Dakota with two long speeches in Valley City, one at the normal school, the other at the armory. On the walls of the armory there was a large banner which read, "Our Motto: North Dakota for Fighting Bob."[50] He began both speeches by saying he had been told that he had recently been described as "a disabled steam engine" and had come to demonstrate "my fire box is all right, my drive wheels strong, and my sand box isn't empty."[51] This was the only public reference he made throughout the North Dakota campaign to the false tales that had been circulated or to the assertions and denials regarding Roosevelt's encouragement of his candidacy which had been capturing the headlines during the last few days. After this impersonal comment on what Pinchot had said, Bob proceeded to discuss what he regarded as the important issues of the campaign. He reviewed both Taft's and Roosevelt's legislative records on the economic and political problems which he believed must be met and solved if representative government was to survive in this country. His discussion of Roosevelt's record as President was variously described in different newspapers as a "beautiful tribute"[52] or an "arraignment" and "the most stinging criticism,"[53] according to the individual reporter's reaction.

A newspaper commented that "The Senator had his fighting clothes on, and plunged into the North Dakota campaign with a vigor which has given him an added right to his title of 'Fighting Bob,'" and noted that he finished the final speech of the first day "strong and vigorous, with all the old time resonance in his voice, and the old time animation in his manner."[54] During the remaining three days of his North Dakota campaign, he made two or three long speeches and a number of short ones each day. Hundreds of men and women gathered at railway stations or came in from distant farms and ranches to hear him. At some places the business houses were closed during his meetings. On the edge of "the cow country," within a hundred miles of the old ranching home of Roosevelt, ranchmen filled the halls, "clambered about the stage, stood in the aisles and yelled themselves hoarse for 'Fighting Bob,' "[55] Everywhere he had packed auditoriums, and overflow meetings were frequently necessary. Gilbert Roe preceded Bob when he had to address two meetings in the same town.

At the close of the four-day campaign, the Washington correspondent of the *Minneapolis Tribune*, who had covered the trip, wrote that La Follette "is unique. Supposedly coming from a sick bed, the Wisconsin senator looks anything but a sick man. He is tense, vigorous and full of fighting ire. Picture this 'little giant' with the bushy head of hair, tramping up and down the platform, face, hands and figure in nervous action as he drives home his points. Picture him leading carefully up to his arraignment of the popular idol of the day and as one prominent North Dakotan described it, 'getting away with it,' and you have 'Bob' La Follette on the stump.

"His present course means that he has broken with old friends. . . . His household has turned against him. He has found traitors in his camp. He has broken with Pinchot, with Garfield, with Clapp, with Johnson of California and many others with whom he has tasted the fruits of victory, and with whom he has consoled in the hour of defeat. But it must be said to his credit, that he is apparently unafraid. There is no shrinking in his manner. He is already laying his plans for 1916 and means to carry on the fight. There is an indominitable [sic] something in this little fighting man that evokes admiration whether willing or unwilling."[56]

The day before the primary, Bob left North Dakota, returning to Washington with Belle to complete his articles for the *American Magazine*. On the train they learned that he had won a sweeping victory in the first Presidential primary to be held in the United States. Out of a total of 49,264 votes in the Republican primary, La Follette received 28,620, Roosevelt 19,101, and Taft 1,543.[57] Headlined reports and amusing cartoons broadcast the results of the primary from coast to coast. In the Wisconsin primary on April 2 the La Follette ticket carried the State by almost three to one over Taft. There was no Roosevelt ticket in the field, and the colonel received only 628 votes.

Early in April Bob started out on another speaking trip which took him into the States where prominent progressive governors, Senators, and Congressmen had shifted their support to Roosevelt and local organizations originally pledged to La Follette had been disrupted. He began a five-day campaign in Nebraska on April 5. The man chiefly responsible for arranging and carrying it through was Frank A. Harrison, an original and dynamic individual who owned a weekly newspaper and the Antiquarian Book Store in Lincoln. Following in the early American tradition, he ran his little paper in a vigorous personal way, sending out additional pamphlets and special pages when he thought the occasion demanded. He had supported Bob's candidacy from the beginning and had taken an active part in organization work in his own and other States. When Governor Aldrich, Congressman George W. Norris, and other prominent Progressives in Nebraska joined with a number of reactionary Republicans in shifting to Roosevelt and taking over the Nebraska Progressive Republican League organization, it merely spurred Harrison to greater activity for La Follette. He promptly wrote, printed, and sent out to the state newspapers a series of cards comparing the records of the two men and asking pertinent questions which brought forth editorials and stirred up discussion. In sending the cards to individuals, he enclosed self-addressed envelopes on which he had printed across the top, "I WANT THE NAMES OF ALL WHO ARE READY TO FIGHT FOR LA FOLLETTE TO THE END. If you are standing for principle instead of chasing 'band wagons' and federal pap, let me hear from you."[58] He received many immediate responses, and the day after the North Dakota victory men came flocking into his office in the Antiquarian Book Store to find out how they could help in the Nebraska campaign.[59]

Thus, through the volunteer help of many men and women who were not politically prominent, meetings were organized, and people gathered at the stations and packed the halls to hear Bob. Belle attended his meetings and the receptions which were arranged for her. Later, in Oregon and California, she proved a persuasive advocate of votes for women at many meetings sponsored by the suffrage organizations. Although she did not speak in Nebraska, Bob's references to her in endorsing votes for women and the impression she made on those who met her evoked a friendly editorial entitled, "Two La Follettes."[60] From Nebraska she wrote her children: "Papa is having great meetings. Crowds everywhere And yet there is something different than North Dakota It may be the management or it may be that the politicians are tied up. No one seems so confident of the result. And yet neither Taft nor Roosevelt seem to have much doing. I am puzzled by the situation."[61] During the first day in Nebraska Bob made a dozen speeches, a number of them brief talks from the rear platform of the trains. That night, in Bryan's home town of Lincoln, he spoke in the spacious auditorium which "was packed to the doors" so that "many persons were unable to gain admission."[62] He repeated this program the following day when Fola, who had been speaking for woman suffrage in the Midwest, joined her parents and traveled with them. That night Bob spoke to another huge crowd at the auditorium in Omaha, but his daughter heard only the latter part of his speech, as she was "expounding the doctrines of woman suffrage" to another audience in the same city.[63] The day after Bob left the State, the newspapers announced that La Follette's talk had "angered" the colonel and that the Nebraska Progressive Republican League was arranging a Roosevelt speaking trip.[64]

Bob went from Nebraska to Oregon. His opening speech was made from the steps of the city hall at Pendleton on April 13. A thousand people stood in the street for two hours listening to him. A reporter noted that "when the meeting ended in a round of cheers the street was strewn with Roosevelt badges, which had been proudly worn by many prior to the La Follette speech."[65] In Portland a thousand people gathered at the Union Depot to greet him as he arrived in that city on his way to Eugene, where he spoke at the University of Oregon the next morning. He was introduced by an instructor in history, Dr. Joseph Schafer, who was a graduate of the University of Wisconsin. That night at Salem, the capital of Oregon, "an audience of nearly 3,000 people jammed the Grand-Opera-House, clogged the streets and hundreds were turned away."[66] He delivered a brief address outside to over five hundred people who could not get in but had waited until he arrived. The regular Republican organization had taken "steps to keep prominent Republicans from introducing him." When the progressive Democratic governor of Oregon, Oswald West, heard of this, he "volunteered to introduce him."[67] West had been a member of the Oregon Railroad Commission from 1907 to 1910. In presenting Bob to the audience he said: "I am an admirer of our visitor—because he is loyal to the people and because he is one of the best equipped men in public life today. To him the credit is largely due that we have an effective interstate commerce law and commission. To him is due most of the credit for our having effective railroad legislation and commissions in this and a number of the other states. It was he, more than anyone else, who brought order out of chaos—beat the railroads at their own game and blazed for the people a trail through the jungle of the big interests. We are indebted to him for much of the progressive legislation which is found on our statute books today. I believe in credit where credit is due."[68]

The next night, when Bob spoke in Portland, he had an audience of ten thousand people at the Gypsy Smith auditorium. Many had been unable to gain admission, as the entrances had been closed fifteen minutes before he began his two-and-a-half-hour address. After speaking for about an hour, he abruptly announced that he ought to have a thorough understanding with his audience before proceeding. The audience was hushed and expectant during the brief pause. Then he announced, "I am a candidate for the Republican nomination for President." A bombardment of applause swept the auditorium before he could go on to say: "I ran five times for Governor of Wisconsin and you may just as well make up your mind to elect me President next November. . . . I shall continue to be a candidate for President until our Government is entirely restored to the people. I would rather have the place in history as the man who led such a fight than to have been one of a score of Presidents whose names you cannot remember tonight."[69]

As Bob and Belle left for California on the night of April 18, they expected he would carry both Oregon and Nebraska, which were to hold their primaries the following day. His meetings "had been as large and enthusiastic as North Dakota," and although they "felt the lack of organization," especially in Nebraska, they "thought it would not make so much difference in the primary." In Oregon they had encountered little Roosevelt sentiment, and it had seemed to them "like a contest between Bob and Taft with the people for Bob, and the machine for Taft." Therefore it was a shock when they learned in San Francisco, the morning after the primaries, that Roosevelt had swept Nebraska and had run a little over six thousand ahead of Bob in Oregon. To an intimate friend Belle wrote, "It was a body blow to get the news from Nebraska and Oregon this morning. In spite of all my experience in politics it took me, and the rest of us too, entirely by surprise."[70]

Bob's campaign in California provoked bitter controversy. Governor Johnson and some of Bob's other former supporters resented his coming into the State. Newspapers which had been advocating his nomination for President a few weeks before greeted his entry into California with scathing editorials. They charged him with splitting the progressive vote, described his mission as "one of selfish ambition, selfish revenge, and selfish disregard of the progressive cause."[71] While Bob was still in Nebraska, the California papers had printed stories containing a statement signed by Governor Johnson and several telegrams to him signed by Medill McCormick, Gifford and Amos Pinchot, William Kent, Gilson Gardner, George L. Record, and John D. Fackler. In substance these men reiterated, with added details, previous versions of statements that they had transferred their support to Roosevelt because Houser had informed them that La Follette had withdrawn his candidacy. They also denied recent public statements by Houser that Roosevelt had encouraged Bob to become a candidate.[72] These telegrams and Johnson's signed statement were widely reported throughout the country. The next day at Fremont, Nebraska, Bob received a telegram saying that Will Colver of the Scripps papers wanted him to wire immediately to their editor, Robert F. Paine, at San Diego, California, an answer to the question, "Did you or did you not sign or authorize type-written withdrawal from race?"[73] Bob drafted the following telegram in his own hand and had it sent off to Paine: "I never signed and never authorized any withdrawal as a candidate for the presidency. I refused at all times to withdraw or compromise."[74]

He also sent a long telegram to Rudolph Spreckels in San Francisco with the understanding that it was to be given to the newspapers. This was one of the few times in his life that Bob ever answered this type of personal attack through the press. His telegram gave the lie direct to certain statements. He named names, cited specific conferences at which several of these men had actually informed him that their connection with his candidacy was ended a number of days before the date they alleged Houser showed them a typewritten copy of the withdrawal of La Follette's candidacy. The tone of the opening paragraphs of Bob's long telegram reveals the indignation which made him violate his life-long habit by responding to Spreckels' request for a public answer. "The attempt of any of my former supporters to justify their desertion of my candidacy by making Houser their scapegoat is," he said, "a cowardly perversion of fact. They know that no one had authority to withdraw me as a candidate and that no one ever professed to have such authority or ever attempted to assert it. And they know, one and all, that I persistently refused to withdraw in favor of Roosevelt or any one else and stated to them again and again that having once entered the contest I would not back out. They furthermore know that I refused to permit Roosevelt's candidacy to be coupled with mine or to combine with him in any way."[75]

When Bob and Belle arrived in San Francisco, about two weeks after this telegram had been published, Rudolph Spreckels met them at the station and accompanied them to the Palace Hotel. The entire organization of the Progressive Republican League of California, which had endorsed Bob in November, had been taken over to Roosevelt by Governor Johnson, Chester Rowell, Meyer Lissner, and others when they swung their support to the colonel. But Rudolph Spreckels, William E. Smythe, Robert F. Paine, Irving Martin, and hundreds of individual members in different parts of the State had refused to join the stampede. Spreckels had taken charge of Bob's campaign, was financing his trip through the State and paying the expenses of many speakers from Wisconsin and other States. The Scripps papers in California and the Stockton *Record*, owned by Irving Martin, continued to support him.

Newspaper men bombarded Bob with questions on his arrival and recorded their disappointment at learning his campaign was to be made on "principles" with "no personalities." They lamented that he was "not going to 'swat' Governor Johnson, or 'smash' Editor Rowell, or kick Francis J. Heney aroun'."[76] But Bob also warned them he "would not give bond to keep the peace under abuse."[77] Later, while he was having lunch in the grill of the Palace Hotel, a reporter saw Heney come in and expected the two men to glare at each other. Instead he noted that "as soon as Heney saw the little Senator with the iron grey pompadour he went over to his table," shook hands cordially, talked with him, and said afterward: "I like Bob La Follette. I think a whole lot of him, and I wish things had shaped so I could be for him this time, but they didn't."[78]

Although Heney, Governor Hiram Johnson, Gifford Pinchot,

Medill McCormick, Senator Albert J. Beveridge, and others were touring the State for Roosevelt, Bob drew large crowds everywhere during the three weeks he was there. He made several speeches a day and closed his California campaign in San Francisco, where William E. Smythe introduced him to an audience of five thousand people. The meeting was held the day before the primary at the Dreamland Rink, the auditorium where Heney had introduced him in 1907 and where Rudolph Spreckels had heard him for the first time. Although the reporters recorded no change of expression on Bob's face, he must have smiled inwardly when Smythe opened the meeting by saying: "Hiram Johnson is a good man, but good men frequently go to New York and get buncoed. I don't say Hiram blew out the gas when he went down there to talk politics in February, but he was held up and robbed of his convictions and handed a gold brick all gilded with United States steel. Don't let him drop that brick on you tomorrow."[79]

From California Bob went to Ohio, New Jersey, and South Dakota, speaking a few days in each State. Gilbert Roe, who had postponed all his law cases to campaign in California, went with him to New Jersey and South Dakota. Everywhere Bob had the same enthusiastic meetings, but Roosevelt swept California, defeated Taft in his home State, and won most of the delegates in the States where Presidential primaries were held. A few days after the California primary, Belle wrote Netha Roe that she had received a telegram from Bob, who was then in Ohio, saying "he was proud of the result, that every vote was a conviction and that he was feeling well and game." She added, "When the smoke rolls away it will all stand out clear perhaps and at any rate we shall all be glad that we did not deviate from the way that to us was the only one."[80]

During the New Jersey campaign Bob met the Presidential candidate who was to win the 1912 election in November. On the night that Bob spoke in Newark, James E. Pope gave an informal little dinner for him before his meeting. Just as they were seated, a message came from Governor Woodrow Wilson, who was a dinner guest in another private dining room in the same restaurant, saying he would consider it a great privilege to meet Bob. He was invited to come up, and Pope recalls that in the course of Governor Wilson's "conversation with Senator La Follette he made the statement that

'Record's action in the Roosevelt affair was the most dastardly piece of political treachery he had ever known.' "[81]

Bob had predicted in his speeches in New Jersey, Ohio, South Dakota, and California that Roosevelt and Taft would go into the Republican National Convention so evenly matched that a mere handful of delegates would hold the balance of power. He believed that if Taft did not have enough delegates to nominate him on the first ballot, the thirty-six delegates from North Dakota and Wisconsin instructed for La Follette might be the deciding factor. Preceding the convention many newspaper correspondents made similar predictions. Although Taft and Roosevelt each claimed enough delegates to assure his nomination on the first ballot, the discrepancies between their claims were so great that it was generally assumed neither candidate knew just how many he could actually count upon. In one State after another the Roosevelt faction had charged "fraud" in the election of Taft delegates. Bob suspected, and it was later admitted by Judson C. Welliver, correspondent of one of Frank Munsey's newspapers, that many of these early contests were started merely for "psychological effect, as a move in practical politics," so that a tabulation of delegate strength could be put out to "show Roosevelt holding a good hand in the game."[82] This tactic was used to prove Taft a "dead one" and influence the band-wagon Republican politicians to swing to Roosevelt in the later Presidential primaries of the Western States. The result of this Roosevelt policy was that an unprecedented number of contests was presented to the Republican National Committee when it met in Chicago on June 6.

While the committee was hearing these contests, Hugh Gordon Miller, a candidate for Congress on the Roosevelt ticket, and George B. Cortelyou called upon Gilbert Roe in New York to suggest a combination of La Follette-Roosevelt delegates to control the temporary organization of the convention and to offer him their support for temporary chairman. Roe replied that he was not a candidate and that although the La Follette delegates might have a candidate, they "would keep absolutely clear of anything that could look like a combination with either Roosevelt or Taft." A day or two later Roe was again approached by Miller, who had in the meantime seen the colonel. Roe was invited to "have a conference with Roosevelt personally." He declined, and reported both talks to Bob, who was in Washington working on his platform and writing the final chapter of his *Autobiography*.[83] When Bob received Roe's letter, he wrote at once to his friend Alfred T. Rogers, who was national committeeman from Wisconsin, warning him to be on the alert at Chicago. Another Roosevelt supporter, Governor Hiram Johnson, also asked Roe to act as temporary chairman.[84]

Failing to get Roe, the Roosevelt people sought to make the next best deal they could. A few days before the convention met, Bob received word from friends in Wisconsin that Governor McGovern would be the Roosevelt candidate for temporary chairman.[85] Bob immediately sent his secretary, Hannan, to Madison. Hannan saw the governor at night at the Executive Residence and appealed to him not to permit the use of his name as a candidate because it would be interpreted as evidence that La Follette had a secret alliance with Roosevelt. McGovern refused to yield, said it was the greatest opportunity that had ever come to him to make a speech, and insisted that his candidacy for temporary chairman would be in La Follette's interest. After leaving the Executive Residence, Hannan telephoned Bob at Washington and reported his talk with the governor.[86] Hannan received instructions to go to Chicago, stay there throughout the convention, and do everything possible to prevent the delegates who were pledged to La Follette from taking any action which might be interpreted as a working agreement with either Roosevelt or Taft.

During the week preceding the convention, the Republican National Committee held hearings on the contested elections of delegates. Bob thought it was evident from the beginning that "each candidate was trying to seat a sufficient number of fraudulently credentialed delegates, added to those regularly chosen to support him, to secure control of the convention and steam-roll the nomination."[87] When the decisions of the first few days were rendered in favor of Taft, Bob thought it began to look as if the President might be nominated on the first ballot. With the exception of States which held Presidential primaries, all the delegates had been elected by precisely the same methods Roosevelt had sanctioned in 1904 and 1908 when he controlled the national committee. The committee of 1912 was deciding contests according to its usual custom, but now Taft supporters were in control. Some of the Roosevelt claims were

so flimsy that Roosevelt members of the committee actually con-
curred in voting to seat Taft delegates. But from Oyster Bay the
colonel denounced decisions in favor of Taft with charges of "fraud"
and "treason," finally taking the train to Chicago to direct the battle
against the man he had made President by similar methods in 1908.
Vast crowds welcomed him and cheered his speeches. His followers
hoped he would stampede the convention. Instead, his dynamic
presence constellated adoration and wrath. Tempers reached the explosion point. Men who had worked together for years hurled angry
epithets at each other in hotel corridors and through the columns of
the press. Violence was feared. There were threats that Roosevelt
would bolt the convention if his delegates were not seated in the
contested elections. Bob had been informed of this but thought it
was "bluffing" to "frighten the Taft organization into giving them
some delegates which they were not entitled to."[88]

The first test of actual strength would come on the "seating" of the
contested delegates for the temporary organization and on the vote
for temporary chairman. In such a close contest any move indicating
La Follette had made "a deal" on the temporary chairmanship with
either Roosevelt or Taft might suddenly bring enough band-wagon
votes from other States to stampede the convention to a victory. By
long-distance telephone Bob was keeping in close touch with the
situation at Chicago through John Hannan, Gilbert E. Roe, Alfred T.
Rogers, Walter L. Houser, and others.[89]

The night before the convention the Wisconsin delegation,
headed by Governor McGovern, held a tense session in room 200 of
the Grand Pacific Hotel, where Bob's headquarters were. Henry F.
Cochems made a motion that the delegation should present the name
of Governor McGovern as its candidate for temporary chairman of
the convention. Several delegates argued for the motion. Others
vigorously opposed it. Finally, after hours of heated debate, the
meeting adjourned. Cochems and James A. Stone, secretary of the
delegation, were appointed to confer with La Follette by telephone
and report back to the delegation the next day before the convention
met.

At about 8:15 the next morning a telephone call was made from
Cochems' room in the Grand Pacific Hotel which Bob answered at
his home in Washington. Throughout the telephone conversation
Cochems was present, but he asked Stone to do the talking because

he was "hoarse." Stone reported briefly what had taken place the night before. Bob answered that he considered it vital that the Wisconsin delegation steer clear of any agreement or combination which would give any color to the claim that there was a combination between La Follette delegates and the delegates of either Taft or Roosevelt until both Taft and Roosevelt had been compelled to show just what strength they had. Bob also asked that John Hannan and Alfred T. Rogers be invited to make statements regarding information that had come to him. Stone then turned and asked Cochems if there was anything else to be said. Cochems replied, "Yes, say to Bob if he presses this motion to a vote it will result in a split in the delegation." Stone repeated this to Bob, and the answer came back, quick and decisive: "Let the split come then, and say to him and to the delegation for me, if any man on the delegation desires to vote against me or against my judgment on any proposition to come before the Convention, I beg of him to go on the first ballot. I want every delegate to vote for me until I release him, or go at once."[90]

Stone reported the conversation to the delegation which met at ten o'clock, and Cochems verified his report. Hannan was invited to appear, and told them of Roe's refusal to accept support of the Roosevelt forces as a candidate for temporary chairman. The Cochems motion that the delegation present McGovern as its candidate was voted upon and defeated fifteen to eleven. The meeting adjourned and the delegates went over to the Coliseum to take their seats in the convention under the La Follette-for-President banner.

That afternoon, when nominations for temporary chairman were declared in order, members of the Wisconsin delegation were amazed to see Cochems mount the platform and name McGovern as a candidate. The vast crowd listened in silent attention. The resonant voice which rang out through the Coliseum had a special portent for the delegates. It was the same voice many of them had heard nominate La Follette as a Presidential candidate in 1908. Bob's daughter, watching the scene from the gallery, felt keenly what Cochems' action would mean to her father, who had loved and admired this extraordinarily gifted young man since his student days at the University of Wisconsin. A dramatic tension swept the auditorium as Governors Hadley and Johnson, William Flinn, John J. Sullivan, Albert Bushnell Hart, Heney, and other Roosevelt supporters jumped to their feet in rapid succession to second the nomination. Reporters turned to each other in the press gallery to ask if it meant La Follette really had a secret deal with Roosevelt. A group of Roosevelt supporters in the audience stood up shouting, "Hurrah! Wisconsin has come under our banner!" As the seconding speeches were greeted with resounding cheers, the Taft delegates watched the demonstrations anxiously, fearing this might be the beginning of a stampede.

But cheers and speculation were quickly halted. As the Roosevelt supporters concluded their seconding speeches for McGovern, Walter L. Houser stepped to the front of the platform. Many expected he would also second the nomination. Instead he sprang the dramatic sensation of the afternoon as he shouted in a voice that carried to the farthest corner of the huge auditorium: "This nomination is not with Senator La Follette's consent. We make no deals with Roosevelt. We make no trades with Taft."[91] This declaration robbed the Roosevelt supporters of the psychological band-wagon advantage they had hoped to gain by uniting on McGovern. The convention knew that delegates instructed for La Follette would not go to Roosevelt on the ballot for President.

When the votes were counted, McGovern had 502 and Root 558, which elected him temporary chairman by the narrow margin of only 18 more than half the convention. It was an important victory for the Taft forces, but Bryan and other special correspondents thought the Presidential nomination was still in doubt.[92] A similar impression prevailed that night at La Follette headquarters, where they were "feeling good" over the result of the day.[93] The intense animosities between the supporters of the two leading candidates made the situation complex. The fight seemed so close that no one could tell what would happen, and the 36 Wisconsin and North Dakota delegates instructed for La Follette were needed by both sides. It was reported that on a second ballot some of the delegates instructed for Roosevelt would go to La Follette. Newspapers predicted a deadlock which might finally result in the nomination of Governor Hadley, Justice Charles Evans Hughes, Cummins, La Follette, or a "dark horse."[94] Bob's wife read these dispatches on the train for Wisconsin, where she had suddenly been called by the critical illness of her father. She telegraphed and wrote Bob suggesting that if an unexpected opportunity came he should start a move to nominate Senator Bristow or some other Progressive he could heartily support.[95]

The second day of the convention a demonstration started for

Governor Hadley, who was acting as the Roosevelt floor leader. But a few moments later it was shifted to Roosevelt when a woman leaned over the edge of the balcony waving a huge lithograph with the colonel's portrait. Chanted shouts of "We Want Teddy" swept the galleries and found a frenzied response from his delegates, who formed in lines, waving their banners and cheering as they marched about the floor of the Coliseum. The demonstration lasted about forty-five minutes, but there was no stampede. The Taft, La Follette, and Cummins delegates sat silently in their seats and joined no processions.

During the sessions of the convention which continued intermittently for five days, the Roosevelt delegates made speeches hurling angry charges of "theft" and "burglary" at the Taft forces, claiming that the Republican National Committee and the Credentials Committee were wrongfully excluding many of their delegates. The number varied at different times, ranging from over 100 to a final 72, but it was always enough to have scant control over the Presidential nomination. At meetings in the Auditorium and elsewhere, Roosevelt thrilled huge throngs with impassioned speeches. Denouncing the decisions of the national committee, he formulated his famous campaign battle cries of "Thou Shalt Not Steal" and "We Stand at Armageddon, and We Battle for the Lord."

Shortly after three o'clock on the afternoon of June 22, the report of the Credentials Committee was adopted and the permanent organization completed with Root as chairman. Test votes of the two preceding days had made it evident that the anti-Roosevelt forces were in control. Following the reading of the majority platform by former Vice President Fairbanks, Walter C. Owen, the Wisconsin member of the Resolutions Committee, presented the La Follette platform as a substitute. Bob had hoped to put the convention on record through a roll call on his platform. The Wisconsin and North Dakota delegates had gone begging for help in every direction, but they could not get the necessary one-State delegation to join North Dakota in seconding the adoption of the platform. It was therefore impossible to force a roll-call vote. The galleries greeted Owen's reading of the platform with frequent applause, while the Old Guard Republicans on the platform looked on with bored indifference. But none rose as in 1908 to denounce it as advocating "doctrines of Socialism." In 1912 they merely listened in discreet silence and quietly laid the La Follette platform on the table.

The names of only two candidates were presented to the convention. Warren G. Harding made the nominating speech for Taft, and Michael B. Olbrich for La Follette. Seconding speeches for both candidates followed, and then the roll was called. Roosevelt's strategy prevented any test of what would have actually happened had all the delegates voted on the first Presidential ballot. Obeying the colonel's orders, 344 of his delegates sat beside their Roosevelt banners and refused to vote. The result announced was: Taft, 561; Roosevelt, 107; Cummins, 17; La Follette, 41; Hughes, 2; and 344 delegates not voting. That night the delegates who had refrained from voting joined with other Roosevelt enthusiasts in pledging their support to him at an indignant protest meeting in Orchestra Hall. "Thou Shalt Not Steal" was the opening phrase of Roosevelt's speech in which he made the sacrificial promise to lead a third party "if only one State should support me."[96]

Newspaper correspondents noted that Senator Borah, who had been one of the prominent Roosevelt leaders in the convention, was not present at the Orchestra Hall meeting. Immediately after Taft was nominated, Borah had gone to Roosevelt's room in the Congress Hotel and had urged him not to accept the endorsement which had been arranged for the meeting that night. Roosevelt had replied that the movement could not be stopped because these men were in earnest and determined to nominate a leader.[97] "If they do not nominate me, they will nominate La Follette."[98]

Three days after Taft was nominated, the Democratic National Convention met at Baltimore, where Bryan led the progressive forces in a prolonged battle to purge his party from the corrupt influence of Tammany Hall and the domination of special privilege as represented by great magnates like Thomas Fortune Ryan. When the national committee met, he openly opposed the move to select Alton B. Parker for temporary chairman of the convention. From Washington Bob was following every move of the contest with intense interest. His friend Frank Harrison, who knew Bryan well, had come from Lincoln, Nebraska, to report the convention. The night before it convened, Harrison telegraphed Bob that the national committee had named Parker and that Bryan "requests you to come tomorrow morning says the circus will be good to see."[99] Bryan had decided to allow his name to be presented as a candidate for temporary chairman against Parker. This decision meant foregoing any chance of his own nomination for President.

The next day Bob arrived at the convention too late to hear Bryan's famous speech but in time to see him defeated for temporary chairman by a vote of 579 to 506. That night he wrote to Harrison that it was hard to see Bryan "go down before the representatives of privilege, who seem to have the convention in control. I know he will not be discouraged, but will fight on to the end. . . . Greet our friend for me, and tell him I very much want to see him after the ball is over."[100] In another letter to Joseph E. Davies, who was the Democratic National Committeeman from Wisconsin, he said: "I sat in the convention when Wisconsin cast her votes for Bryan for temporary chairman, and was proud to see the old state make a clean progressive score. I came away saddened, but not discouraged, and I am sure that you and those fighting with you, will go straight through to the finish."[101]

When the newspapers discovered Bob had been in Baltimore, it was reported he had held a secret conference with Bryan. The fact was that the two men had not met in Baltimore, but messages had been exchanged through Harrison and others. It had been arranged that if Bryan lost out at Baltimore and a reactionary were nominated, they would get together for a conference.[102] But the brief skirmish on the temporary chairmanship was the only battle Bryan lost. From that time on he dominated the convention.

On June 27 Bob made another trip to Baltimore. Throughout the dramatic night session he sat among the newspaper men and heard Bryan make the winning fight for his famous resolution declaring the Democratic Convention was "opposed to the nomination of any candidate for President who is the representative of, or under any obligation to J. Pierpont Morgan, Thomas F. Ryan, August Belmont or any other member of the privilege-hunting and favor-seeking class."[103] The overwhelming victory on this resolution assured the nomination of a progressive candidate. The sessions continued for five days until the afternoon of July 2 when Woodrow Wilson was nominated on the forty-eighth ballot.

At Chicago Roosevelt had bolted. At Baltimore Bryan had dominated his party and forced the nomination of a man with a progressive record as governor of New Jersey.

Bob admitted to a friend that work on the final chapter of his *Autobiography* had been suspended during the period of the two conventions because "in the excitement" he found it hard to stick to his "knitting." A week after it was all over he wrote to Gilbert Roe, "Well these be great times and are evoluting after their own fashion in large measure as is always the case with the working out of great events."[104]

CHAPTER XXXV

Progressive Senators Swing into Line Again on the Roll Call

Soon after the Democratic Convention Bob wrote to an intimate friend that he had decided to move slowly in regard to Wilson. He thought his recent experience in depending upon "half baked" Progressives of the Republican brand justified him in "going a little slow" on a Democrat who had only been progressive for about eighteen months and had not "shed his milk teeth yet."[1] Although admiring Wilson's record as governor, Bob thought all his previous writings and addresses indicated he had formerly been "a pronounced conservative if not an out and out reactionary." Therefore he considered Wilson's nomination the second-best thing that could have come out of the convention in Baltimore, and regretted that it had not been Bryan, who seemed better qualified by long experience to deal with the reactionary opposition which any fundamentally progressive economic legislation would meet in Congress. If Wilson was elected and proved to be a really progressive President, Bob believed he would soon be subjected to the severe test of a conflict with a standpat Democratic Congress aided by the Republican reactionaries.

There were disturbing "whisperings" in Washington that Bryan was not to be taken into Wilson's councils, and it was reported that Wilson would keep as manager of his election campaign William F. McCombs, who had been his preconvention political manager. McCombs had for a time been Gilbert Roe's law partner. Bob knew him, and feared his reactionary economic views might have considerable influence. Furthermore, the Democratic platform had been disappointing to Bob, especially on the important issues of trust and currency legislation. It seemed weak and vague as compared with the platform presented at Chicago by the Wisconsin delegation.[2] All these factors combined to make Bob decide upon a policy of "watchful waiting" rather than the public endorsement he would undoubtedly have given had Bryan been the Presidential nominee.

In a long conference with Senator Luke Lea on July 12, Bob urged Lea to advise Wilson not to appoint McCombs as his election campaign manager or as chairman of the national committee. Bob explained frankly to Lea that he did not expect to support Wilson actively but that he hoped nothing would arise which would make it necessary for him to attack Wilson's candidacy. All this Lea reported in a letter to Wilson.[3]

Bob thought that Wilson was the only candidate who had any progressive attributes and that there was greater hope of genuine constructive legislation under him than if Roosevelt became President. He believed "everything should be done to prevent true progressive republicans from joining the Roosevelt party" because his success meant "disaster to the progressive cause and to the country."[4] Bob's letter files show that wherever his personal word counted or his counsel was asked, he replied in accord with this deep conviction. He was confident Wilson would be elected, and content with the part he believed his own Presidential campaign had contributed toward assuring this result. In a letter to Charles R. Crane, Bob summed up his own estimate of what the continuation of his candidacy had actually meant: "If I had gone out of the field in February, Roosevelt would have been nominated 'hands down' and if I had not campaigned Nebraska, Oregon, and California those states would now be counted for Roosevelt. If I had not had an 'iron brigade' (though a small one) at Chicago—again the Bull Moose would have had his way. Perkins would have been another Mark Hanna, and political history would be somewhat different. It has not been all in vain. And though the country calls it a defeat, and it was defeat for the time, I like to believe, and hope you can in some measure share in the belief that in a broad way, it was a very substantial victory."[5]

Bob planned to give all the help he could through his magazine and on the platform to the election of progressive Republican candidates to Congress and to state offices in States where they had a worth-while progressive program. He thought this would help to preserve and possibly strengthen the little band of Progressives in the next Congress. Then if Wilson proved progressive, these men could be of real service to him in the event that too many reactionary Democrats failed him on progressive measures.[6]

To unite the progressive Republican group as an effective legislative force, Bob had to deal with men who had been largely responsible for his Presidential candidacy and had then abandoned him. Many had publicly denounced him when he refused to withdraw in favor of the colonel. But Bob made up his mind "to forget all this to the extent necessary for cooperation on progressive legislation."[7] He said little, but waited his opportunity, which came about a month after the Republican Convention. A series of bills revising the Payne-Aldrich tariff schedules had passed the House. When they came up in the Senate, Bob seized upon this opportune parliamentary situation and offered an amendment as a substitute.[8] His amendment was in precisely the same form as the wool bill for which all the Progressives except Borah and Bourne had voted the previous year. Bob had consulted with the Democrats and reached an understanding for cooperation along the same lines as before. But he had not discussed his plan with the progressive Republicans and did not know what they would do. As he listened to the vote, he was delighted to hear "every man of them, except Cummins," swinging into line on the roll call and, with the Democratic vote, making it possible to pass his amendment as a substitute.[9]

Two days later Belle wrote, "It has established friendly relationship with the progressives, made the Democrats feel good, and the reactionaries, though mad, are conscious of his power. All doubts are removed, and he is in the same position in the Senate that he was a year ago."[10] In a letter to Rudolph Spreckels Bob said, "You should have seen the progressives. They were as tickled as a lot of runaway boys who had found an easy way to get back home."[11] Although this tariff revision was subsequently vetoed by President Taft,[12] the vote on the wool schedule had served to bring the progressive Republicans together in the Senate. To his friend Crane, Bob wrote that it was gratifying to find he could pull the progressive group together again on legislation even if he "could not hold them against the call of the Bull Moose."[13]

During the hot summer months Bob put in long hours at work. In addition to attending Senate sessions and participating extemporaneously in the running debates on legislation, he wrote editorials for his magazine, completed the final chapters of his *Autobiography,* prepared and delivered several speeches. One of the pledges in his Presidential platform had been a proposed constitutional amendment for an easier method of amending the Constitution. At the earliest opportunity he characteristically sought to convert his platform pledge into a legislative act. On August 5 he introduced as a joint resolution this constitutional amendment which had been drafted after extensive research by his friend David Thompson, who was then Law Librarian of Congress.[14]

Early in August Bob delivered a widely reported speech for an amendment to the Post Office Appropriations bill. The amendment was designed to prevent the penalization and discharge of postal employees either for forming their own unions or for affiliating with national labor organizations such as the American Federation of Labor. He maintained that postal employees were entitled to the same rights as other government workers. In his speech he severely criticized certain rules and regulations promulgated during the Roosevelt and Taft Administrations, charging that they had been used for political ends and were actually depriving Government civil-service employees of certain fundamental constitutional rights. He said his statements were based upon a personal investigation he had made in 1911 when he sent a series of questions to some 12,000 or 15,000 railway mail clerks. This inquiry had aroused the displeasure of the Post Office Department, and his mail had been opened by those sufficiently interested in the testimony of the railway mail clerks to use a method of espionage that was "almost Russian." Bob had on his desk in the Senate a package of envelopes, similar to hundreds he had received in the same condition, showing unmistakable signs of having been opened and resealed. His speech evoked extensive editorial comment.[15] The amendment passed the Senate and became a part of the law governing the removal of employees from civil service.

As the time for adjournment approached, Bob's parliamentary strategy helped pass another resolution. It was an election year, and so many Senators had gone home that during the final hours of the session there was not a quorum in Washington. This created a situation which enabled Bob by insistence on a quorum and intimation of a filibuster to force through a resolution directing the

Clapp Committee, then investigating the 1904 and 1908 Presidential campaign expenditures, to include the 1912 campaign. This resolution, introduced by Penrose, specified that the committee should inquire into correspondence and financial transactions between John D. Archbold, president of Standard Oil, George W. Perkins of the Harvester Trust, Theodore Roosevelt, and Members of Congress, and ascertain expenditures made by or on behalf of all Presidential candidates. For years Bob had advocated detailed publication of campaign expenditures, and this had been one of the planks in his 1912 platform. Addressing the Senate "on a question in the nature of personal privilege," as one of the 1912 Presidential candidates, he urged his colleagues to pass the resolution.[16] Several newspapers credited his strategy with forcing it through shortly before Congress adjourned on August 26. He had previously conferred with the Democratic member of the investigating committee, Senator Atlee Pomerene, and had arranged to give him as much information as possible regarding the contributions to the Bull Moose campaign.[17]

While Congress was still in session, delegates from different States had responded to the call of the Bull Moose and assembled in Chicago on August 5 to form a third party which was still nameless. Destined to an early death sentence from the man who fathered it, this short-lived child was finally christened the Progressive Party. Senator Beveridge opened the convention with an oration which set a high emotional key for the colonel's followers. The next day Roosevelt delivered his twenty-thousand-word "Confession of Faith." The convention nominated him for President with Governor Hiram Johnson as his running mate and adjourned to the singing of hymns. A platform was drawn up with the assistance of Charles McCarthy of Wisconsin. The major expenses of a spectacular campaign were paid by George W. Perkins, Frank Munsey, and a few others.

Leaders of the new party soon launched intensive speaking tours. In the fall, Beveridge, Gifford Pinchot, and several of Bob's former supporters carried the battle into Wisconsin, where they joined forces with Governor McGovern and Henry Cochems. In many other States complete tickets for state offices were placed in the field at Roosevelt's insistence. In some States this split the progressive vote and led later to the defeat of Bristow and others who had been leaders in the progressive movement but had refused to join the new party. It was reported Roosevelt had declared that "unless La Follette gets in line for the Progressive party he will stamp himself a reactionary of the deepest dye."[18] Bob refused to comment on this statement.

When he returned home on September 15, the election campaign was in full swing. For a week Belle and Elizabeth Evans had been speaking at the county fairs advocating passage of a state referendum to give Wisconsin women the right to vote. McGovern had been renominated for governor in the Republican primary on September 3, and the new Progressive Party had held a state convention at Milwaukee on the 11th with Governor Hiram Johnson, Medill McCormick, and Henry Cochems among the prominent speakers. After stormy conferences the delegates decided it was unwise to nominate a state ticket in Wisconsin. This was tantamount to an endorsement of McGovern even though he had refused to follow Roosevelt in the formation of the new party. McGovern, on his return to Madison after the Republican Convention in June, had insisted in public statements that his candidacy for the temporary chairmanship had been in the interest of La Follette's nomination. For over two months he managed to maintain a discreet silence regarding the new party. Then, about two weeks after he had been safely renominated in the Republican primary, he issued a public statement attacking both Taft and Wilson and endorsing Roosevelt and the new party. This brought the long-simmering indignation of many progressive Republicans to the point of openly refusing to support him. His attack upon Wilson caused a similar reaction among progressive Democrats. In a State where party lines had ceased to be rigid on important issues, McGovern needed the progressive votes of both parties.

Bob knew that if the intention to punish McGovern for his action at Chicago were carried through, it would mean the election of the reactionary Democratic candidate, John C. Karel, a former football hero familiarly known as "Ikey" Karel. Karel had been nominated in the primary through a combination of reactionary Republican and Democratic votes. As a member of the assembly in 1901, he had voted against all important progressive measures and subsequently became associated with the tory elements of both parties. If he became governor, it would mean wrecking the progressive legislative program. Bob used all his influence to assure

McGovern's reelection. He pulled no punches on what he thought of McGovern's motion at Chicago or his endorsement of Roosevelt. But through signed editorials in his magazine and a state-wide speaking trip he persuasively argued that although he had as much cause as any one to resent McGovern's action, this did not stand in the way of supporting him for a second term because his reelection was vital to the progressive cause in Wisconsin.

Because of this critical situation Bob confined his speaking campaign to Wisconsin. Although he did not publicly endorse any Presidential candidate, his widely reported speeches were frequently interpreted as being for Wilson.[19] The course he steadily followed from the time the new party was formed undoubtedly helped to swing many progressive Republican votes away from Roosevelt to Wilson. In his speeches and his magazine, which had a circulation well distributed over the country, he vigorously attacked Roosevelt's past record in relation to the great trusts and monopolies. Repeatedly he described the trust plank of the third party's platform as a device to bind the Government to the perpetuation of the Steel Trust. As a featured article, with Brandeis' photograph on the front page, he published a severe arraignment of the "Roosevelt-Perkins-Steel-Trust-Party." This article was an address Brandeis had recently delivered before the Massachusetts branch of the American Federation of Labor. Summarizing the past record of the great trusts, Brandeis declared that labor could hope for nothing from this new party with a platform which stood "for the perpetuation and extension of private monopoly in industry."[20] In the same issue the "News Worth Remembering" column noted that the hearings before the Clapp Committee had recently revealed the large contributions made to the 1912 Roosevelt campaign by George W. Perkins, a director of the Steel and Harvester trusts, and Frank A. Munsey and Dan R. Hanna, large stockholders in the Steel Trust.

The previous week *La Follette's Magazine* had published the first of a series of five articles which were widely quoted because they told the dramatic inside story of the Presidential campaign from Bob's own point of view as frankly and accurately as his knowledge of the facts at the time permitted. Subsequently these articles were included as the final chapters in his *Autobiography* when it was published six months later in book form.

Bob had written the articles during the summer. He wished to deal fairly with all the participants and tried to write the story not only for the judgment of the day, but for the years to come. In a letter to a friend he admitted that after his recent experiences with some of the men it was a bit of a strain to deal with them in that spirit.[21] While he was in the midst of this work, Elizabeth Evans was a house guest for a few days. On the train returning home she wrote frankly expressing her fear that he could not write the story objectively because he was still too close to the events which had given him just cause to feel bitterly toward Roosevelt.[22] When the articles were completed, Bob sent them on to Ray Stannard Baker and waited anxiously for the candid criticism he valued highly. After several days Baker wrote that he had read the manuscript with intense interest and had found it "a remarkably clear, calm and convincing narrative."[23] Belle sent a copy of this letter to Elizabeth Evans, and Bob wrote Baker that the verdict rejoiced him and "took an awful load off."[24]

The last two articles, published just before election, attacked Roosevelt's record on anti-trust legislation and told the story of his hostility toward the early progressive movement in Wisconsin. The Democrats in Wisconsin and elsewhere made the most of the three-way split in the Republican Party. In several speeches Wilson digressed from his arraignment of the Republican record to express his love for those "lonely figures" climbing the "ugly mountain of privilege" in order to take away from this citadel the captured rights of the people of the United States. He doffed his cap to Bob La Follette, "that indomitable little figure" who had "never taken his eye for a single moment from the goal he set out to reach" and had "walked a straight line to it in spite of every temptation . . ."[25] Bryan, on his Western speaking tour, repeatedly described Bob as the pioneer progressive of the Republican Party, declared Roosevelt was "not worthy to unloose his shoes," and reminded audiences that the colonel was an eleventh-hour progressive—though hardly that— since he had not arrived until five minutes to twelve, when he had demanded the whole thing.[26]

Roosevelt ignored the criticism of his early attitude toward La Follette and the progressive movement until he entered Wisconsin. Then, in a widely reported speech at Oshkosh, he defended his record and denied that he "did not take sides with the La Follette people in their campaign in Wisconsin in 1904."[27] Two days later he was scheduled to speak in Milwaukee. For this large meeting he had prepared a long typed manuscript, answering his critics and quoting from earlier public statements in which La Follette had praised him. A friendly crowd which had gathered in front of the colonel's hotel greeted him enthusiastically when he entered the automobile with Henry Cochems and his secretary, Elbert E. Martin. As he stood up in the car, responding to the cheers of the crowd, an insane man drew a pistol and shot him in the right breast. Martin disarmed the maniac, turned him over to the police, and Roosevelt ordered the chauffeur to drive to the auditorium. In spite of the protests of his friends, he insisted he would "make this speech or die." With the bullet still in his breast, and the extent of the wound unknown, he went upon the platform and talked for more than an hour. Fortunately the force of the bullet had been diminished by the manuscript of his speech and his spectacle case. Subsequent examination indicated that the wound was not critical, but his physicians ordered rest to prevent complications. Among the hundreds of telegrams he received expressing profound regret and wishing him a speedy recovery was one from Bob. Sixteen days later Roosevelt addressed a huge audience at Madison Square Garden in New York.

The night before election Bob closed his campaign at the university gymnasium in Madison. It was the first time he had spoken there since he had introduced Taft from the same platform in 1908. On the final night of this bitter 1912 campaign, the huge auditorium was packed to the doors as it had been when the Republican State Convention renominated Bob for governor in 1904. People were standing in the halls and on the stairs. Young men had climbed up on the beams and remained perched there throughout the meeting. Many university students were in the audience and their "sky-rocket" for Bob resounded above the applause as the friendly crowd welcomed him home. Belle preceded Bob with a thirty-minute speech for the woman-suffrage referendum, as she had at a number of his other meetings in the State. Throughout his campaign he had supported the referendum, and the home-town audience applauded the tribute he paid to Belle, as he came forward on the platform to address them at the close of her speech. They laughed heartily, too, when he alluded to an old tale of his enemies by saying that the reason he allowed her only thirty minutes was because they might otherwise find out who was the author of the speeches he had been delivering for the past twenty-five years.

The next morning at 9:35 Bob and Belle arrived together at the town of Madison polling place in Wingra Park. Bob entered the booth, cast his vote, and then went to his office. Belle stood outside during the day, at the required legal distance from the booth, trying to persuade men to vote for the referendum giving Wisconsin women the right to vote.

That night Bob, Belle, and the children, together with a few intimate friends, gathered about the fireplace at the farm to listen to the returns. Before eleven they knew that, as expected, the split in the Republican Party had elected Wilson. In many States Taft ran a poor third, but in the normally Republican State of Wisconsin it was Roosevelt who played that role, with Wilson as victor by 33,634 over Taft. For a time it looked as if McGovern had been defeated by the reactionary Democratic candidate, Karel. But later returns showed McGovern had pulled through with a majority of 12,019 as against an average majority of 22,675 for the balance of the state ticket. The next morning Bob called at the Executive Office to congratulate him. An editorial in the leading progressive newspaper of the State, entitled "Saved At The Switch," attributed his victory to the campaign Bob had made. A few days after Wilson's election Bob telegraphed to Brandeis, "All happy here."[28]

A month later, on the morning of December 1, Bob, Belle, and the children arrived in Washington. Andrea Synoia, an intelligent young Swiss boy, who had relieved Belle of many household cares, had preceded them by one day. Although it was always hard for the family to leave the farm at Madison, Andrea had made the transition easier for them this year. When they entered the house at 1864 Wyoming Avenue, which they had occupied for four years, they found the fires lighted in the open fireplaces, the table set for breakfast, and the sun streaming in the windows. Belle wrote that the place seemed more like home than she had ever thought any rented house could.

Three days after they arrived in Washington, the Sixty-second Congress met for its final session, which would end automatically at noon on March 4, 1913, and be followed immediately by the inauguration of Woodrow Wilson as President. During this final session Bob was in a strategically important position which was recognized in the passage of legislation he had long advocated and which brought an unsolicited benediction from regular Republicans. As Bob had predicted during a speech in the Senate seven years before, many seats then temporarily vacant had been or were about to be permanently vacated.[29] The overwhelming defeat of Taft led the Old Guard to make concessions to the progressive Republican faction. La Follette and Cummins were appointed to serve with Oliver, Root, and Smoot on the Republican steering committee of the Senate. The committee announced that it had agreed upon five bills which would be given consideration before adjournment on March 4, and this program was endorsed by the Republican Party Caucus. Three of these five bills had been introduced by Bob, and a fourth provided for legislation he had been advocating ever since he made his maiden speech in the Senate. The press recognized his extraordinary victory and noted that "the adoption of the complete legislative program which the Wisconsin senator espouses is the accomplishment suddenly wrought up by the man who less than eight years ago was hazed when he arose to address the body of which he is now a member."[30]

From the Senate gallery Elizabeth Evans, who was a house guest in the La Follette home at this time, watched Bob through her opera glasses as he sat at his desk during the counting of the electoral vote. She wrote Alice Brandeis that he "looked as jolly & as carefree as a college boy,—chumming with everybody, cracking jokes on Murray Crane—Senators leaning over & passing the word to him. He said at dinner—'I don't know what possessed me during that hour—I felt like a boy.' Different from the days in the Senate when he had to eat his lunch all alone!"[31]

Each of the five bills endorsed by the Republican caucus represented some aspect of Bob's long-continued legislative interests. The bill to limit the issuance of injunctions he considered important to labor organizations.[32] The bill to create a legislative drafting bureau and to establish a legislative reference division in the Library of Congress[33] was modeled on those in Wisconsin which had been inaugurated while he was governor. A similar bill had previously been introduced in the House by Congressman John M. Nelson of Wisconsin.[34] It had been drafted in cooperation with Charles McCarthy, who had a distinguished record of public service in the State as legislative librarian. The bill to regulate the hours of employment and safeguard the health of women in the District of Columbia embodied principles Bob had long advocated.[35] Among those who collaborated closely with him on this bill and appeared at the hearings were Mrs. Florence Kelley and Josephine Goldmark. In two preceding Congresses he had introduced a bill to create a tariff commission.[36]

The fifth bill, introduced in the House by a Democratic Representative, William C. Adamson of Georgia, provided for the physical valuation of railroad property as a basis for fixing railroad rates.[37] Legislation to this effect had been passed in Wisconsin while Bob was governor. In 1908 a physical-valuation plank had been included in the minority platform which Congressman Cooper of Wisconsin read to the Republican National Convention at Chicago. Then it had been greeted with shouts of "Socialist," "Take it to Denver," and other terms of derision. From the delegates to that convention it had received less than 30 votes out of about 1000.[38]

For seven years Bob had been trying to get a physical-valuation bill through Congress. After first introducing it as an amendment to the Hepburn bill in 1906, he had persistently offered it at each succeeding session whenever it was pertinent to legislation under consideration. The bill introduced by Adamson had passed the House on December 5, 1912,[39] and came to the Senate in essentially the same form as the amendment Bob had introduced seven years before.[40] When the Senate referred it to the Interstate Commerce Committee, Clapp, who was chairman, appointed Bob chairman of the subcommittee to which it was then referred. Bob immediately sought to improve the bill through amendments based upon investigations, court decisions, and valuations which had been made since he had introduced his amendment to the Hepburn bill. He was assisted by other members of the committee and also secured the help of Professor John R. Commons, who had worked with him on legislation when he was governor, and Professor Edward W. Bemis, a leading utility expert. Night after night he worked with Commons until one in the morning, but a friend who was a house guest noted that Bob was "down early in the morning, at it again. And as bright as a lark, all the time."[41]

The amended physical-valuation bill was reported favorably to the Senate[42] only a few days before Congress adjourned automatically on March 4. On the morning of February 24 it began to look as if prolonged debate on appropriation bills might delay it beyond March 4. Bob rose to call the Senate's attention to the importance of the bill and warned Senators "without a note of taunt or bluster, but with a quiet *white heat* determination" that some of the appropriation bills might go over to another Congress.[43] The bill was soon allowed to come up for consideration. In discussing it, Senator Newlands, who was a member of the Interstate Commerce Committee, commended the valuable aid of Professor Bemis and Professor Commons, commented on the "great care and precision" with which Bob always moved "in matters relating to economic legislation," and expressed the opinion that this bill could be regarded "as fairly perfect."[44] At the request of Senator Smith of Georgia, Bob explained the purpose of the measure in a brief speech, pointing out that it authorized the commission to ascertain separately the elements of value to be taken into consideration in determining the fair value of the property. Thus the commission would be able to ascertain just how much of the total amount had been invested by the railroads and how much had been contributed by the public. The separate values to be ascertained were: the original cost to date, the cost of reproduction new, the cost of reproduction less depreciation, and certain intangible values which the courts might take into consideration, such as going value and franchises. He frankly stated that the primary purpose in establishing these values separately was "to put into the possession of the commission and upon record the data which will enable us ultimately to try out the question and determine the right of the railroads to capitalize the unearned increment" and over-capitalize the investment and the rolling stock. The purpose was in other words to prevent the practice of watering railroad stocks.[45]

Not long after Bob finished speaking, the bill passed the Senate unanimously and Senators gathered about his desk to congratulate him. Later that evening there was rejoicing at home as Bob gave his account of the day, and Phil, who had been in the gallery, reported that his father had never spoken better.[46] Three days later the bill passed the House without a dissenting vote. President Taft signed it as one of the last acts of his Administration. Thus in 1913 a Congress still dominated by a Republican majority enacted a law that had been greeted with jeers in 1908 when presented by Congressman Cooper of Wisconsin to the Republican National Convention which nominated Taft for President. The next day, in an editorial in the *Wisconsin State Journal*, Richard Lloyd Jones wrote that Taft's signature on this bill had put him, on one important measure at least, "ahead of his partially progressive predecessor, Theodore Roosevelt, who, while President, did all in his power to embarrass Senator La Follette in his labors for this most important bill which will save this country not less than $400,000,000 annually."[47]

A contemporary estimate of the importance of this law was expressed in an article by Professor Commons in which he said: "The victory of Senator La Follette is as surprising as it is complete. No piece of legislation of greater importance to the people of the country and to the greatest property interests of the country could be proposed."[48] In commenting on the fact that not one Senator had voted against the bill, a number of newspapers referred to Bob's maiden speech in the Senate when he had predicted that seats temporarily vacant would be permanently vacated. One experienced Washington correspondent noted that "A great many 'permanent vacancies' have come to pass since that day, and to that fact is due in large part the passage of the physical valuation measure . . ."[49] An editorial in the New York *Globe*, which was reprinted in *La Follette's Magazine*, observed that in 1906 Senators had "insulted him by running for the cloak room when he arose to speak, thus leaving him to address empty chairs. . . . As a thinker of good ideas first and as a converter of violently hostile opponents few men in public life have surpassed this Wisconsin Senator. The abuse of him seldom slows up, but year by year he discovers himself vindicated. It is this that keeps him, in spite of the hard knocks he gets, an unconquerable optimist."[50]

CHAPTER XXXVI

A Minority Senator

Bob's legislative victories during the final weeks of Taft's Administration had placed him in a position which evoked much newspaper speculation as to what the attitude of this leading progressive Republican would be toward the new Democratic Administration in a Senate where the party margin was so close that on some issues he might hold the balance of power. Congress would, under the Constitution at that time, adjourn automatically at noon on March 4. Wilson would then become President, with the Democratic Party in full control of the Federal Government for the first time since Cleveland's Administration. The House was safe by a large majority, but the Senate was close. For the first time Bob would be a minority member in a Democratic Senate.

During the years that the Republicans controlled Congress, he had never been a strict party man. He had cooperated with progressive Senators of both parties in his persistent effort to secure legislation to meet the economic and political problems created by our rapid transition from an agricultural to an industrial economy. Since 1906 he had been reading to large audiences throughout the country the roll call votes of Republican and Democratic Senators on important legislation, urging their constituents to defeat or to reelect these representatives on their records regardless of party labels. Ever since 1909 *La Follette's Magazine* had carried on a similar roll-call campaign which had contributed toward the election of both progressive Republicans and progressive Democrats in the Senate and House. As a United States Senator he had thus followed the course he had initiated as governor in Wisconsin early in 1900 when he had read throughout the State the roll call votes on legislation in the assembly and senate. The progressive achievements, which had become known as "the Wisconsin idea," had been the product of progressive Republicans cooperating with "fair-minded" or progressive Democrats uniting against the reactionary forces in both parties.

Although elected as a Republican Senator to serve in a Republican Congress, Bob criticized and refused to be bound by what he considered the iniquitous custom of framing legislation in the secret party caucus. He supported Taft and Roosevelt when he thought they were advocating wise, effective legislation. He opposed both these Republican Presidents when he thought their policies were wrong. To Bob the fact that Wilson was a member of a different party seemed unimportant since Wilson had repeatedly indicated he would advocate a progressive program. If it included legislation to break the growing power of monopolies and the centralized control of capital and credit through interlocking directorates, Bob was certain that Wilson would have a hard fight and that it would include opposition from the reactionaries in his own party. Since the Democrats had only a small margin in the Senate, Bob believed that the President would therefore need the help of progressive Republican Senators to put through any fundamental measures on these vital issues.

This opinion was shared by Brandeis, Crane, and many other progressive-minded men in both parties. Brandeis and Crane had supported Wilson, and the press had repeatedly reported that they would probably be in the new Cabinet. Therefore a statement by either was news. In mid-January Brandeis was visiting Crane in Chicago, and when they went to Milwaukee their trip to Wisconsin "stirred speculation." A reporter interviewed Crane while he and Brandeis were having breakfast at the Hotel Pfister. Crane was quoted as saying: "Progressives everywhere should get together behind Wilson. There should be no such thing as a Democratic Progressive or a Republican Progressive." He predicted that Wilson's Administration would be successful, but added that it could not be "unless all Progressives get together determined to help him." When questioned as to the position La Follette would occupy during the next four years, Crane replied that La Follette's opportunities would be greater than they had ever been because for the first time he would have "a president in sympathy with his ideas" and that he had "been too long identified with the Progressive cause to hang back now because of party differences. It is not necessary that he follow Wilson. He can work on an independent program, for there is not much difference between the two men."[1]

A speech Wilson made ten days later, at a farewell banquet given to him in Atlantic City by the New Jersey state senators, seemed to indicate that he would welcome Bob's counsel and help on legislation. He told the senators that in recent years New Jersey had built up a reputation for progress "surpassing even Wisconsin which used to have the leadership, and which had produced such strong men as Bob La Follette."[2] Analyzing the Senator's qualities, Wilson said: "He is strong because he studies every angle of every question. When he gets up to speak, he knows what he is talking about. When he has finished speaking, it is difficult for a man to vote against him and give any convincing reason for doing so because La Follette has presented the case from the standpoint of the man who knows. The only way a man can justify voting against La Follette is to know more about the subject than La Follette knows."[3]

When Bob was questioned by the Washington correspondent of the *Milwaukee Journal* about Wilson's speech, Bob replied, "Nothing could be more gratifying than this report that the man who is to be president of the United States is advising his associates to secure the most complete and reliable information to be had before they begin legislating upon matters vitally affecting our people and our civilization." The same dispatch reported that progressive Senators were "pleased by President-Elect Wilson's tribute to Senator La Follette and his method of preparing for legislative duty."[4]

Bob thought that this was the method Brandeis had used for years and that Brandeis was the man best qualified to assist the President in formulating and enforcing legislation "to make our institutions better serve the needs of our time." Bob and many other Progressives hoped that Wilson would have the wisdom and the courage to ignore the attacks on Brandeis and appoint him Attorney General. Soon after Wilson's tribute to Bob, Crane said, in a letter to the President: "A recent visit to La Follette at Washington brings up a matter that I feel I should write to you about. La Follette has made up his mind to devote himself to progressive legislation. He has great talents for this sort of work, he is in fine physical condition and believes that with you at the White House and Gore to work with in the Senate, he has the best of opportunities to serve the country. He is, however, like all other progressives, most anxious to have Brandeis to work with. He has worked with Brandeis for several years and greatly prizes Brandeis' wisdom, patience and sympathy. He also believes that Brandeis, more than anyone else, in Washington and in authority can pull together the progressives—whether La Follette, Democratic or Bull Mooser—and harmonize progressive legislation." In the same letter Crane added his own testimony as to Brandeis' "real patriotism, sweet reasonableness and clear foresightedness."[5]

Norman Hapgood, who had been especially active in presenting facts to refute the false charges he knew were reaching the White House, had also conveyed to the President Bob's hope that Brandeis would be appointed. Although Bob was not aware of it, Colonel House had previously suggested to Wilson that either Brandeis or Crane be included in the Cabinet, but not both since this would be too much La Follette.[6]

Preceding the inauguration Elizabeth Evans, who had been an ardent Wilson supporter, was a guest at the La Follette home. On February 16, in a letter to Alice Brandeis, she said, "Belle is persuaded that Louis is *in* the Cabinet," and added: "We hear that the pressure against him on Wilson is something terrific, & from sources best calculated to undermine his confidence in L. But Spreckels reports that Wilson told him, very recently, that his confidence in L.D.B. had in no way wavered."[7] Two days later Belle wrote Alice Brandeis that all the family had enjoyed her daughter Susan's recent visit and closed the letter by saying: "We are expecting you to be in the official family after the fourth of March. If for any reason you do not come, it will be a body blow to the administration, and oh, such a disappointment to your friends."[8] Late in February Mrs. Evans wrote, "It is hard to live till we learn Wilson's Cabinet. The Senator is on the anxious seat."[9] One rumor followed another.[10] On March 2 the *New York Times* reported, "There was much opposition to President-Elect Wilson's understood intention to invite Mr. Brandeis to take a Cabinet seat," and noted that a delegation of "prominent Massachusetts Democrats" had called upon Wilson at Trenton to protest.[11] The Cabinet appointments were not made known officially until the last hour of the very last day. Years later Mrs. Evans still remembered that on the night before inauguration Bob came home and announced "that the names of the incoming Cabinet had been given out—and that Brandeis' name was not upon the list. He was mad right through to his backbone."[12]

That night a well-known Washington correspondent sent out a dispatch reporting there was a feeling among all the Progressives that the new President had started his career with a mistake in excluding "Brandeis after there had been so many assurances" that he was to be a member. The regret was not because Brandeis the man had been excluded, but "the fact that Brandeis typifies the best and most progressive thought in the Democratic party, the thought which Mr. Wilson as a candidate made a feature of [in] most of his campaign speeches, and that in some manner this thought is being suppressed and is denied expression and representation by its most able and conspicuous exponent." This correspondent stated that it would not be possible for Wilson, even if aided by Brandeis himself, "to entirely eradicate the present belief that Mr. Brandeis was excluded from the cabinet because of privilege, working through organization politics, and that Mr. Wilson has yielded to the pressure brought to bear upon him by these influences."[13]

Bob was present when Wilson took the oath of office. In the inaugural address the new President sounded a note "of aspiration and of idealism" to which the vast throng in front of the Capitol responded with an enthusiasm that was echoed later in the press.[14] His inauguration was heralded as marking the "beginning of a political epoch." It was predicted that the United States had "entered upon a new phase of popular government, and no man can foresee the outcome."[15] Another newspaper observed: "He takes office after public opinion has been aroused and crystallized by twelve years of agitation and education." Consequently "The public conscience is awakened and ready to support any sound remedy for existing evils which he may offer."[16]

Bob made no public comment on the address, but the day Wilson was inaugurated he telegraphed Brandeis: "Everybody understands you are now absolutely free to go forward using your great abilities for the public good as you have for so many years. I look forward to your cooperation in this independent work with high hopes. All join in sending you and Mrs. Brandeis all abiding love."[17] Two days later, however, Bob expressed his disappointment more frankly when he wrote to his sister: "Wilson's cabinet is only half-way. Brandeis turn down breaks all our hearts—but I propose to wait for his [Wilson's] measures & support all that are right. But I thank the lord I had the foresight to maintain my position of independence[.]"[18] Brandeis wrote from Boston thanking Bob for his telegram and saying, "I long to see all the La Follettes."[19]

Although Bob loved Brandeis, his disappointment was not merely personal. He knew that Wilson, after his nomination, had twice consulted Brandeis[20] and had apparently been in general accord with him regarding legislation to deal with monopolies and the centralized control of capital and credit. Failure to appoint Brandeis Attorney General raised doubts among the Progressives as to the policy of the new Administration on these issues. Bob believed that as a private citizen Brandeis had rendered public service during "the last half dozen years so important and far-reaching in its present and potential value as to make him one of the greatest figures of his time." Therefore it seemed to Bob that "the President lost a great opportunity when he failed to enlist the services of one of the few men with a real genius for the very problems which his administration must master if its work is to endure."[21]

Rudolph Spreckels, who was in Washington for the inauguration, shared Bob's disappointment, and the two men discussed the possible reasons for Wilson's failure to appoint Brandeis. A few days later Spreckels saw the President and wrote Bob a note saying: "I had a very satisfactory interview with the gentleman yesterday, and while his explanation concerning failure to appoint our friend was, in my judgment, incorrect reasoning, it was not due to [the] campaign made against him by the agencies that we gave credit to. I spoke very plainly, both as to what has happened and what might happen, and somehow I feel, from the assurances given me, that there is very little danger of many serious mistakes being made in the future. He also said he hoped that our friend would permit him to consult with him concerning the things with which he is most familiar, as he valued his opinion and counsel, and believed in him as a man."[22]

Spreckels had talked with Wilson on the afternoon of March 7, and that evening Brandeis saw the President at eight o'clock at the White House.[23] While in Washington, Brandeis also had a visit with Bob. On his return to Boston he wrote to Bob's son-in-law, George Middleton, saying: "I am inclined to think that so far as I personally am concerned the disposition which has been made of the Cabinet matter is best. The Senator and I are planning to do some legislative work together, of which we are very hopeful."[24]

On March 13 Washington correspondents telegraphed widely carried dispatches announcing that the President had invited La Follette to confer with him the following evening at six o'clock. The *New York Times* proclaimed in its headline, "La Follette to Act As Wilson Adviser," and commented, "For the first time in the history of the United States, a Republican Senator is going to be one of the chief advisers of a Democratic Administration."[25] Sumner Curtis, a veteran Washington correspondent, observed, "Nothing since the Democratic administration was installed a little more than a week ago has so emphasized the change in the political atmosphere at the national capital as this prospective visit of the pioneer progressive upon the executive head of the government."[26] Another correspondent said that the summoning of La Follette to the White House was "the biggest political topic at the Capital today. It indicates that President Wilson looks upon the Wisconsin Senator as the real leader of the Progressives."[27] White House interpreters were reported to have emphasized that the purpose of the President's invitation was to discuss the legislative program, not patronage matters.

Bob arrived at the White House at six o'clock on the evening of March 14. It was the first time he had been there in three years. The President received him in his study and the two men had an hour's talk. When he came out, the reporters were waiting to question him about his widely publicized conference with Wilson. They recorded that although he would not talk about his visit, he was "in high good humor" when he departed. In answer to a question he said: "This is my first visit in three years to the White House. I came once after a special tariff session called by President Taft, but I wasn't received." When asked, "Well how do you feel now?" he answered, "Fine" as he stepped into his automobile. As the reporters crowded about the car "to hear why he was feeling so fine after a reappearance at the White House and a long talk with a Democratic president," he repeated, "Fine," and added, "I never felt better than I do now." And then recalling the false reports that had been circulated, he added, "I have been in excellent health for two years."[28]

Neither the President nor Bob made any public comment on their talk. But newspaper reports, apparently inspired by White House "interpreters," stated that they had discussed a progressive legislative program, including the tariff, trusts, currency, physical valuation of railroads, development of Alaskan coal resources, and that on these subjects "the two men found themselves virtually in agreement."[29] Although the newspapers did not mention it, the fact that they had discussed the Seamen's bill was recorded in a letter the President wrote the day after Bob visited the White House. In this letter to Spreckels, Wilson expressed genuine interest in the bill and said that he had not known of it in any detail until Senator La Follette called it to his attention. Wilson's response to Bob's presentation of the bill can be inferred from the fact that the President also told Spreckels he hoped Congress would take it up at an early date since it seemed to him of capital consequence.[30] This was undoubtedly one reason why Bob left the White House "in high good humor."

Soon after seeing the President, Bob was called to Madison by the illness of his brother, William. While there Crane came to see him. The next day Crane wrote Wilson from Chicago saying: "Yesterday I had some two hours with Senator La Follette at Madison. He is happy about his talk with you and the prospect of working with you."[31] In this hopeful mood Bob approached the special session the President had called for April 7 to begin work on his legislative program. Bob left no doubt as to his own policy. In a front-page signed editorial in *La Follette's Magazine*, which many Senators and Representatives read, he warned Republicans that this was "no time for trifling or playing politics, or trying to put the Wilson administration in a hole." It was "no time for the Roosevelt-Perkins Party or the Republican Party to maneuver for 1916. The American people demand that money and credit and transportation, and the market place where labor and the products of labor are bought and sold, be freed from the control of powerful interests.

"If the Wilson administration offers legislation which will best accomplish this result, it is the duty of the minority to support that legislation. If not, it will be the duty of the minority to offer better legislation instead. No greater opportunity was ever presented for patriotic statesmanship. The field is open to the minority as well as to the majority."[32] Throughout the eight years that Wilson was to be President, Bob, as minority Member of the Senate, steadily followed the principle of action he had outlined in this forthright warning to his own party.

The week Congress convened, Bob and Belle set aside their work for a few days to take a brief vacation they had long planned with their beloved family physician, Dr. Phil Fox, and his daughter Kate.

Bob, Jr., and Phil accompanied them on the trip that covered the ground Dr. Fox had traversed as a young surgeon during the Battle of the Wilderness forty-nine years before. His vivid recollection of the tragic suffering of the men in both armies made an enduring impression on them all. Battlefields which in schoolbooks had been mere names recording which side won suddenly became realities. Belle wrote that "the anxiety, sorrow, and suffering, the havoc and destruction" rose before them "like Ingersoll's Dream." In her article about the trip she said: "We are grateful the nation survived; that slavery was abolished. But we pray that such a thing may never happen again. We long for the fulfillment of Christ's teaching, for the coming of the universal brotherhood. And I know of no way of impressing the lessons of peace, like a visit to battlefields,—with one who served as a surgeon there, who has lived a life of service fifty years since."[33]

When the special session met on April 7, Bob introduced his Seamen's bill,[34] which he hoped might become a law at this session since Wilson had privately expressed keen interest in its passage. The following day the President read his message in person to a joint session of Congress, thus renewing a procedure abandoned ever since President Adams had read his fourth message to Congress in 1800. When Wilson first announced that he would deliver the address himself, many of his own party had sharply criticized him. But interest in the unusual event drew unprecedented crowds to the galleries and floor of the House Chamber. The enthusiastic response he received dissolved the brewing hostility toward the idea and created converts to what henceforth became an established procedure. Bob listened attentively to the brief message from a seat in the third row near the center of the Chamber. It was printed in *La Follette's Magazine*, but no record has been found of any comment Bob made on it publicly or privately.

The same issue of Bob's magazine which carried the President's first message to Congress also had a full-page advertisement announcing the publication of *La Follette's Autobiography* in book form. At the top of the page was a quotation from Wilson's future biographer, Ray Stannard Baker, describing the autobiography as "A Stirring And Convincing Story." During the next four months this quotation appeared nearly every week as the lead in a full-page advertisement which included comments from other individuals and excerpts from newspaper and magazine reviews. The book was advertised to sell for $1.50. But by enclosing $2.00 and filling out the form which was a part of the advertisement, a subscriber could buy the book and receive *La Follette's Magazine* for fifty-two weeks.

The fact that the book was published by the Robert M. La Follette Company, Madison, Wisconsin, must have surprised many regular subscribers who had read previous announcements during the fall of 1912 and as late as January 4, 1913, that it would be "Published by Doubleday, Page & Co., New York." Bob made no statement as to why the contract with this firm had been canceled by mutual consent two months before the book was published. The story behind the cancellation of this contract illustrates the courage with which Bob could meet keen disappointment.

Soon after the first chapter of his autobiography had appeared in the *American Magazine*, Bob had received attractive offers from leading publishers to bring it out in book form. Several offered substantial cash advances, and one also proposed the unusually favorable terms of 20 per cent royalties. Some made their first approach through Baker, others wrote directly to Bob.[35] Walter H. Page, later appointed Ambassador to England by Wilson, then head of Doubleday, Page & Company, wrote Baker that his firm was deeply interested, not mainly for financial reasons, but because they were in sympathy with a book which was their kind of gospel.[36] On October 19 Page went to Washington to see Bob. Baker was also there when they discussed not only the publication of the autobiography, but an edition to be sold with *La Follette's Magazine* and the possibility of bringing out later a special boys' edition and a Chautauqua edition. After his return to New York, Page wrote that all his associates shared his enthusiasm for the book and that Bob would therefore have the conviction and moral earnestness of the whole staff in its fortunes. He enclosed a tentative draft of a contract and asked Bob to suggest modifications or anything else he desired.[37]

An important factor in Bob's final decision was that he knew of Baker's very satisfactory relationship with this firm as publishers of his books under the then secret pseudonym of David Grayson. Bob had also liked Page personally and had been favorably impressed with his enthusiasm for the various aspects of the project. He therefore replied that if they could agree upon certain changes in the contract, he would like Doubleday, Page to publish the book.[38] At Bob's request Gilbert Roe formulated the desired changes and talked them over with Page, who also made certain suggestions. Roe rewrote the contract several times in order to embody all the suggestions made by both Bob and Page. The contract was finally agreed to by both parties toward the end of February, 1912.[39]

In April Bob sent to Doubleday, Page the last three chapters of his autobiography which completed the story as it appeared in the *American Magazine*. At the suggestion of Doubleday, Page it had been mutually agreed that Bob should write additional chapters for the book, frankly telling the truth as he understood it about the 1912 Presidential campaign.[40] During the summer he completed the last three chapters of the book as finally published. These chapters were serialized in *La Follette's Magazine*, the first installment appearing on October 5, the final one on November 2, 1912. The proofs of these chapters were sent to Bob by the publisher early in November, and the book was thus ready to go to press as soon as they were returned with his final corrections.[41] Up to this time no question had been raised as to the content of these chapters or the terms of the contract.

But what Bob described as "days of tribulation" regarding publication of the book soon began. On November 18 Gilson Gardner wrote Page that he would hold the firm responsible for libel if they published "the malicious and untrue things" La Follette had recently published about Gardner in his magazine and in newspapers.[42] Although Gardner had been frequently mentioned in the chapters published in *La Follette's Magazine* and widely quoted in newspapers, he did not specify what he now objected to as "malicious and untrue." When Bob received the Gardner letter from Page, he sent it to Roe saying: "You will see from the enclosed copy of letters that Gilson Gardner is getting gay. I take it that this is a bluff, but possibly not. He doubtless could have Perkins' financial backing, or the backing of the Pinchots, to make me trouble. I do not want to take out anything from the matter as it has been published in the magazines which, in so far as it relates to Gardner, is exactly the same as the final proof sent in to Doubleday Page & Co. By reading over the portion of the magazine article which relates to Gardner, you can at once see what is said without waiting for the

page proofs. I think we will have no trouble to prove every statement regarding Gilson Gardner, Kirby, et al."[43]

About three weeks later Doubleday, Page received a letter from
Governor Francis E. McGovern of Wisconsin protesting that the
account of his action at the Republican National Convention, published in *La Follette's Magazine* on October 26, was untrue in almost every statement and conveyed an utterly false impression so
far as it related to him. He did not actually threaten a libel suit,
but offered to give the publisher a correct and accurate account of
the incidents.[44] Page sent copies of this letter to Bob and to Roe
and asked how it should be answered. Roe suggested that Page say
he would be glad to have any error of fact pointed out. In his letter
Roe also said, "If either this material or any part of the book con-
tains an error, both yourself as publisher, and Senator La Follette
as author, are more interested than anyone else in having such error
pointed out in order that it may be corrected."[45]

McGovern's and Gardner's threats disturbed Page. There was no
libel clause in the contract both Page and Bob had signed, and the
question had never been raised in the preliminary discussion of
terms. Page now protested and sought to change the contract so that
Bob would be liable.[46] An extensive correspondence ensued throughout November and December, 1912. Roe refused to alter the contract but stated that Bob would try to meet Page's apprehension by
revising any specific statements the publisher feared might make the
firm liable. He wrote Page that Bob believed his account of the
Presidential campaign was true and accurate; that he had shown his
willingness to assume personal liability by publishing these final
chapters in his magazine, and that no one had sued him. Page suggested only minor modifications in a few paragraphs, and these were
all made. Roe himself made a few revisions with Bob's approval.
A cordial letter from Page on January 9, 1913, seemed to indicate
his complete satisfaction with the cooperative spirit in which Bob
had responded to his suggestions.[47]

But a few days later Bob received a letter signed formally by
Doubleday, Page & Company informing him that they planned to
publish a first edition of only a thousand or fifteen hundred copies.[48]
This was contrary to previous plans, and it seemed to Bob that such
a small first edition by this prominent firm would be a mere token
publication. He concluded that they had lost interest and that pub-

lication by this firm would now be equivalent to a quiet burial of the book. It was a keen disappointment, but he wasted no time in mourning. As the legislative situation did not permit him to leave Washington, he asked Belle to go to New York to help work out some other plan. She and Roe talked the matter over in detail with Page on January 23. A new agreement was reached and formulated the next day in a letter dissolving the previous contract by mutual consent. Bob bought the plates and paid Doubleday, Page & Company to print the book, thus becoming the publisher of his autobiography.[49] To raise the immediate cash necessary to pay for a first edition of 2,500 copies, he and Belle placed a mortgage on their farm. After harassing delays the book finally came out on April 10, 1913. Orders had been received for 674 copies to be sold in connection with subscriptions to *La Follette's Magazine*, which had at that time 33,708 paid-up subscribers.[50]

As author and as publisher Bob thus assumed a double liability for any libel suits. After the book appeared, a number of people continued to call him unpleasant names in private letters and to write about plans for publicly refuting his account of the 1912 campaign.[51] But no one ever sued for libel.

Bob's facilities for distributing the book were very limited. He could not afford extensive advertising nor had he the usual trade exploitation agencies. A form letter signed by him went out to about two thousand book dealers announcing the publication date, and a small circular was enclosed with letters sent from his office, but none were ever put in mail sent by Government frank. The first edition was soon exhausted, and he ordered a second of 2,500 copies.[52] Other editions followed. A third edition was printed by the Blied Printing Company at Madison, and a sixth edition was later printed by the Homestead Printing Company at Des Moines, Iowa. The book was persistently advertised in *La Follette's Magazine*, and through the years many copies were sold in connection with subscriptions. The records of these transactions have been lost, but Fred Holmes, who as managing editor supervised several editions, estimated that considerably more than forty thousand copies were sold.[53]

The book received much wider press comment than could have been expected when Bob decided he must publish it himself. Most reviews were favorable. They tended to stress the chapters dealing with the recent Presidential campaign, but most reviewers accepted

Bob's account of these events as an accurate, frank narrative from his point of view. Some thought, however, that his attempt to interpret Roosevelt's mental processes entered a realm beyond his knowledge and might therefore be erroneous. In the *New York Times* Charles Willis Thompson quoted at length from Bob's account of the different conferences preceding Roosevelt's announcement of his candidacy and commented that La Follette had told his side of the case as completely as possible, "with a savage frankness" which made it "a mighty interesting contribution to history" and cleared up "to a great extent the mystery that has hung over that cloudy year." Thompson found that the rest of the book was "extremely interesting as a record of a long, gallant and single-handed fight" told with "simplicity and force" and that "its account of his solitary battle in Wisconsin and of the formation of the Progressive group in the Senate makes a great story."[54] The New York *Globe and Commercial Advertiser*, in a long review by Mrs. Nell Dawson, evaluated it as "a remarkable and inspiring story."[55] The New York *Evening Mail* thought the book fell too frequently to "the level of a political harangue," and hoped that La Follette would not leave it as his definitive account of this remarkable period and "of the brilliant services which he has rendered" but that in calmer times "it will be treated by him as material for a better considered, a broader, a more moving volume."[56] The *St. Louis Post-Dispatch* reviewer said the "book ought to be an inspiration to any young man who aspires to a career of public service; not alone an inspiration, but a guide, a philosopher and a friend."[57] The *Literary Digest* considered it "a valuable addition to biographical as well as to political history."[58] The conservative *Springfield Daily Republican* found it "one of the most interesting and important of the political documents of the time" and commented that its literary form was "simple, vivid, but not rhetorical."[59] The *Political Science Quarterly* reviewer said that the book was "in some respects disappointing" and the earlier part "of more permanent interest," but that "No where else are the methods of the lobby or the procedure of committees presented in a more graphic way."[60] The book was also reviewed in Canada and in England.[61]

In Washington the *Evening Star* described it as "a spirited narrative, open and fearless" and "an important study of political history."[62] Soon after the book was published, Bob received a favorable review written by Clyde H. Tavenner, a recently elected Democratic Congressman from Illinois, who wrote that this review was sent out to 2,600 weekly Democratic newspapers, and 1,000 daily Republican and Democratic newspapers.[63] A few weeks later Tavenner reported that the book was "being much read by politicians in Washington, but by none with more interest than those from Iowa."

Among the many letters Bob received about his autobiography, there were two which meant so much to him that he included excerpts in a draft for a circular. Soon after the book was published, he sent inscribed copies to Charles A. Beard and Ray Stannard Baker. He had high regard for Beard's work and was looking forward eagerly to reading his forthcoming book on the economic interpretation of the Constitution which he had ordered from Brentano's in advance of publication.[64] In a two-page letter to Bob about his autobiography, Beard wrote that it was a pleasure "to see how quickly you get to the main point and illuminate every big problem in American politics by your own story. I shall certainly make my students in Politics read it next year, for in it they will find the inner history of the rise of the progressive movement."[65] Baker wrote that he was "impressed again with the fine sincerity of the thing. It will become one of the standard autobiographies of this most interesting period in our history: and besides that it will surely be of great value to many struggling young men, who aren't sure yet that the long fight is the one that wins—really wins."[66]

Meanwhile Bob had been attending Senate sessions and working on various aspects of the Legislative program outlined by the President in his post-election speeches and in his message to Congress. Since the opening of the special session, the House had been revising the Payne-Aldrich tariff. When the new bill, drafted by the Democrats, passed the House by 281 to 139, most of the progressive Republicans, including six of the Wisconsin Representatives, had voted against it. When this bill, known as the Underwood-Simmons tariff, reached the Senate on May 9, Senator Simmons, moved that it be referred to the Committee on Finance of which Bob was then a member. Penrose immediately offered an amendment instructing the committee to hold public hearings on the bill.[67] This amendment was supported by the Republicans and opposed by the Democrats.

Throughout his service in the Senate, Bob had repeatedly protested against the secret action of Congressional committees on public business and had steadily maintained his right to discuss in open Senate and elsewhere all legislative proceedings, including those in executive sessions. In his speech supporting the Penrose amendment, he recalled that four years ago, when the Republicans were in power, he had protested against the secret procedure of the majority members of the Finance Committee in drafting the Payne-Aldrich tariff. He urged that the committee members of both parties and newspaper reporters should have the right to be present at the tariff hearings. He declared that "even the caucuses of political parties, when they deal through their representatives with public business, should be open to the public" because "all legislative business is public business."[68] He also offered an amendment providing that those who appeared before the committee to protest the proposed duties of the pending bill should be compelled to answer under oath sixteen specific questions as to their profits, costs of production, and wages. Penrose accepted Bob's amendment which was thus combined with his for public hearings. The two were voted on together and defeated 41 to 34. Although defeated on the roll call vote Bob had requested, his sixteen questions were included in the questionnaire the Finance Committee sent to manufacturers.[69]

The Democratic chairman never called a meeting of the full committee. After the ten Democratic Members had revised the House bill, they followed what Bob thought had been the "bad example of the Democratic majority of the House" and called a party caucus of Democratic Senators to act upon it. In a signed editorial entitled "King Caucus," he protested that this method of legislation meant that the bill would be "debated behind closed doors" where secret votes would be taken which would be considered binding upon all Democratic Senators when the measure came before the Senate. Bob thought revising a tariff bill or any other bill in party caucus was secret control of legislation. Trades, deals, dickers, and corruption thrive best in the dark, he said. "To take the public business into a corner to be transacted under a seal of 'confidence' is the first step toward public betrayal."[70]

On May 26 the President issued a statement to the press declaring: "Washington has seldom seen so numerous, so industrious, or so insidious a lobby . . . There is every evidence that money without limit is being spent to sustain this lobby and to create an appearance of a pressure of public opinion antagonistic to some of the chief items of the tariff bill . . . Only public opinion can check and destroy it."[71] The President's direct appeal to the country brought swift action. The Senate passed a resolution instructing the Judiciary Committee to make an investigation, which Bob succeeded in having broadened and strengthened. In urging the Senate to "insist upon the fullest, most searching, and thoroughgoing investigation," he said there ought not to be "any partisan lines drawn on this resolution" because the President, for whom he had "the greatest respect," must have had a basis for his statement.[72]

Later, in an editorial, Bob said: "The country is indebted to President Wilson for exploding the bomb that blew the lid off the Congressional lobby. He hurled his short-fuse missile directly at the insidious interference with tariff legislation but it resulted in uncovering the whole works. . . . I have for years exposed the sinister work of these evil forces, in controlling Congressional legislation and the administration of government at Washington. Congress sneered. The interests cried demagogue. The public believed. The case is proved."[73]

The resolution for an investigation of the lobby had also provided for an inquiry as to the financial interests of Senators. On June 3 Bob testified under oath before a subcommittee of the Senate Committee on Judiciary. After describing the cruder lobbying methods that had existed when he was a member of the House, he cited as an example of his long interest in legislation to curb improper lobbying, the Wisconsin statute recommended when he was governor. He listed as his personal investments *La Follette's Magazine*, Maple Bluff Farm, and some shares in zinc-bearing lands in Wisconsin, and stated that because of these shares he had asked to be excused from voting on the Payne-Aldrich tariff schedules relating to lead and zinc.[74] The next day a Washington dispatch to the *New York Times* noted that he had asked to be excused from voting in 1909 because he held a few shares in a zinc mine and predicted that his example would "undoubtedly be quoted as a precedent."[75]

The following week Brandeis came to Washington to consult with the President about the proposed currency legislation. Predictions and rumors that tampering with the financial structure would bring on a panic had been circulating for some time. Stocks dropped early in June, and credit was tight. Many considered the situation alarming, and it was argued that currency legislation ought not to be pressed. Bob thought that there was no business reason for a panic, but that special interests were manipulating the situation to exert influence on the currency bills which were being framed. On the day that Brandeis saw the President, he wrote his brother, "The administration is having pretty hard nuts to crack with the crumbling stock market."[76] He talked with Bob before and after his appointments with Wilson[77] and told him of the favorable response he had received to his opinions, which the President had asked him to formulate in a memorandum. This was encouraging news to Bob since he and Brandeis agreed on the fundamental provision essential for any effective legislation dealing with banking and currency.

At this time Brandeis and Bob were also cooperating on trust legislation. On June 13, 1913, Bob introduced a bill that was a revised version of the bills he and Lenroot had introduced in the Senate and House in 1911 and 1912 to supplement the Sherman Anti-Trust Law.[78] This last bill, like those that had preceded it, was, as Brandeis said, "the outgrowth" of a conference Bob had called in May, 1911, and represented "the contributions in thought and suggestions of a very large number of people."[79] Brandeis, Lenroot, Heney, Bob, and others had worked on the actual drafting of the different portions of these various bills, seeking each time to clarify and improve their provisions. Late in May, 1913, Bob had sent Brandeis a copy of the bill he had introduced in January, 1912 (S. 4931), asking for suggestions as to changes and additions. Brandeis made a redraft of the bill, incorporating a few changes, and sent it to Bob.[80] Possibly they made further changes during Brandeis' visit to Washington shortly before it was introduced. The day after the bill was presented to the Senate, the *New York Times* described it as the "most complete and sweeping definition of the phrase 'unreasonable restraint of trade' yet proposed," and declared that if adopted it "would put an end to the famous 'Rule of Reason' announced by the Supreme Court in the Tobacco Trust and Standard Oil decisions."[81] *La Follette's Magazine* printed the bill in full and briefly summarized its purpose by saying: "This bill aims to protect law abiding business against aggressions of the trusts. It establishes order out of business chaos. It is a guide to tell businessmen what they may do and what they may not do under the law. It takes the doctrine of *reasonable* restraint of trade laid down by the Supreme

Court in the Standard Oil and tobacco cases and enumerates all acts that are to be regarded as unreasonable."[82] Bob was unable to get the bill reported to the Senate from the Committee on Interstate Commerce, but a printed copy reached the President. Penciled notes on the margin in Wilson's handwriting indicate that he read it.[83]

The tariff bill was reported to the Senate from the Finance Committee on July 18, and on the following day Simmons opened the debate. The chief theme of Penrose, Smoot, Lodge, and other standpat Republicans was that dire panic would follow enactment of the proposed reductions in the Payne-Aldrich schedules. After listening for ten days to this reactionary echo of the 1909 Aldrich tariff fight, Bob arranged a conference at his office with Senators Bristow, Borah, Clapp, Cummins, Crawford, Gronna, Kenyon, Norris, Sterling, and Works.[84] In 1909 four of these progressive Republicans, Bob, Bristow, Clapp, and Cummins, together with Beveridge and Dolliver, had made up the progressive group who had dared to violate party discipline and vote against the Republican Payne-Aldrich tariff on its final passage.[85] At the 1913 conference the eleven Senators formally decided not to follow the standpat Republicans in their almost solid opposition to the Underwood-Simmons tariff. Instead of supporting the amendments offered by Smoot and other reactionary Republicans, they planned to vote for what they believed were wise downward revisions of the Payne-Aldrich tariff and to try to improve through their own amendments certain other schedules which they thought were the unfortunate products of haste and the secret Democratic caucus method.[86]

The dry routine of the tariff debate was interrupted at the end of July when a joint resolution proposing a woman-suffrage amendment to the Constitution came before the Senate. For months suffrage organizations had been working toward this end. Bob had been much interested in the intensive local campaign during January and February when Belle, Elizabeth Evans, Mrs. William Kent, and other women he knew had spoken at meetings in Baltimore and Washington. Belle had expected to head the homemakers' section of the parade at the National Capital the day before Wilson's inauguration. But shortly before the event her daughter Mary became ill with scarlet fever, and both were quarantined at home. She was well represented, however, by her two sons, Bob, Jr., and Phil, who marched up Pennsylvania Avenue to the Capitol in a parade which included some men and thousands of women. The La Follette family had also been interested in the woman-suffrage parade in New York on May 6, 1911, when Fola had carried the banner for the actresses' division and Gilbert Roe and George Middleton were among the eighty-seven men who joined in the march up Fifth Avenue.[87] But this parade had not produced the disgraceful scenes that took place in Washington in 1913 when the police failed to protect the women from insults and attack at different points along the line of march. Senators and Representatives received vigorous protests from many States calling for an investigation.[88]

On April 7, when Congress met in special session, another suffrage parade marched up Pennsylvania to the Capitol. From start to finish the women received courteous treatment. Five hundred and thirty-one women, two from every State, and one from each Congressional district, carried petitions asking Congress to pass a constitutional amendment. A group of Senators and Representatives met them in the rotunda of the Capitol. Bob was there to greet his daughter Fola, who brought the Wisconsin petition. Later, from the Senate gallery, she and her mother heard Senator George E. Chamberlain of Oregon present a joint resolution proposing a constitutional amendment extending the right of suffrage to women. It was referred to the Senate Committee on Woman Suffrage.

When the committee granted a hearing on April 26, Belle and Mrs. William Kent were among the prominent speakers introduced by Dr. Anna Howard Shaw, president of the National Woman Suffrage Association. All the speakers were well received, and the committee members joined in the applause that greeted the different arguments.[89] Among those present was Joe Mitchell Chapple, editor of the *National Magazine*, published in Boston. As his home had been in Wisconsin, he was especially interested in Belle's speech. Later he sent her the galley proof of his monthly editorial on "Affairs at Washington." Bob read it aloud to the family at the breakfast table.[90] In his article Mitchell said that "Mrs. La Follette made a remarkable and forcible address" and that she resembled her husband "in her manner of speech and appearance." He noted that as she spoke "one of the men auditors burst out admiringly, 'Isn't that just like Bob!' "[91]

On June 13 the Senate Committee unanimously recommended passage of the constitutional amendment granting suffrage to women.

Suffragists, traveling in automobiles and holding meetings on the way, began to converge on the National Capital. They brought petitions from every State with signatures representing almost two hundred thousand men and women. Arriving in Washington on July 31, they were welcomed by sympathizers who rode out to meet them. As the procession wound its way up Pennsylvania Avenue many observed that members of the Senate Committee on Woman Suffrage rode in one of the automobiles. At the Capitol the women delivered the petitions to their Senators and then went to the Senate galleries. Many Senators made brief speeches urging passage of the joint resolution.

In presenting the Wisconsin petitions, Bob said: "I can not remember a time, Mr. President, when I was not in favor of extending the suffrage to women. I have always believed in cosuffrage, as I have always believed in coeducation, equality of property rights, and, in short, sir, equality of opportunity for men and women alike; that civilization is best and most advanced where men and women cooperate and mutually respect each other; that democracy is safest where its entire citizenship is most enlightened, most interested, most alert. If the ballot educates men in citizenship and is a source of power and protection to them, surely it is of equal value to women.

"Government is organized, Mr. President, for the good of society; and the very basis and foundation of all organized society is the home. Every act of government reacts for good or evil upon the home. The tariff now under consideration, the laws regulating trusts, the statutes for the control and regulation of banking and currency, the laws regulating interstate transportation, and all legislation of like character strikes directly at the home life, because it bears directly upon the cost of living and the ability to maintain the home. The women of this country are as directly interested in everything pertaining to the economies of government and of the home as are the men. They understand it as well as do the men, and their potential influence, even when handicapped by the denial of the right of suffrage, has been felt in the Halls of Congress. The long struggle to write upon the statute books legislation protecting the home and the life of the family against the adulteration of food products would have been going on to this hour except for the organized effort the women of the country put back of that great reform movement.

"And, so, Mr. President, just as it is essential that we should have the cooperation of the women of the country in the development of the home life, so we should have the cooperation of the women of the country in the legislation which underlies the home life and is foundational to all our social reforms."[92]

The petitions were referred to the Senate Committee, but no further action was taken at this session. For several years the constitutional amendment granting suffrage to women continued to be an issue which Bob and Belle steadily supported.

From the time that the House tariff bill had been referred to the Senate Finance Committee, Bob had been working on the complicated measure. The committee had assigned experts from the Treasury Department to the Democratic and Republican Members. As Bob's views on the tariff were not in accord with either of these extremely partisan groups he had requested an expert for himself, and thus secured the able assistance of William S. Culbertson, whom Wilson subsequently appointed in 1916 to the permanent Tariff Commission which Bob had long advocated. Culbertson had served on the Tariff Board under Professor Henry C. Emery of Yale University, who had been appointed chairman by Taft after passage of the Payne-Aldrich tariff. This Board had been created by an amendment the progressive Republicans had obtained to the Payne-Aldrich tariff.

Bob thought it was a weak substitute for a permanent Tariff Commission, but he knew the able experts on its staff had assembled valuable economic data. Therefore he had been keenly disappointed when the Board had been quietly put out of existence by the failure of the new Democratic Administration to appropriate funds. Although the offices had been abandoned and the staff scattered, he finally traced the files to a store-room in the Treasury Department. Knowing that McAdoo had no authority to release them, he went to see the President. He told him that the vaults of the defunct Tariff Board contained an immense amount of information, in the form of reports and investigations, and that "since they were doing nobody any good locked up in those vaults" he would like to have access to them. Wilson readily granted the request which promptly brought a dray load of statistical and economic data to Bob's office.[93]

At Bob's request Professor Emery came to Washington to indicate the material that would be most helpful. Bob also consulted with the available experts of the Tariff Board's staff who had worked on the investigations. With Culbertson's assistance he put in weeks studying the facts that had been assembled. This material he used during the debate and in drafting the amendments he offered as substitutes for the Democratic caucus schedules on cotton, wool, earthenware, glassware, iron, steel, grain, and sugar.[94]

When the income tax provision came up in August, Bob, Bristow, Borah, Cummins, Norris, and several other progressive Republicans offered amendments to raise the rates. The *New York Times* had previously predicted that Bob would have a great deal to say about this feature of the bill as he was practically "the originator of income tax legislation in Wisconsin whose laws are conceded to be the best income tax legislation in the country."[95] His amendment provided for a graduated tax increasing in proportion to income.[96] He cited the excellent results of the Wisconsin law which had been pledged in the 1910 platform and enacted in 1911. Bob's and Bristow's amendments increased the rate from 3 to 10 per cent on incomes over $100,000.[97] After thirteen reactionary Republicans had joined the caucus-bound Democrats in voting to defeat the Bristow amendment, Bob expressed regret at the failure of his own party to equalize the tax burdens.

Although Bob's income tax amendment was also defeated the next day, it caused a rift in Democratic solidarity which created the first real excitement in the Senate tariff debate and stirred newspaper speculation for several days.[98] Vardaman was the only Democrat who actually broke the caucus rule by voting for it, but at least three other insurgent Democratic Senators had alarmed party leaders by threatening to do the same. Ashurst, Reed, and Thompson interrupted the roll call to say they would have voted for the La Follette amendment had they not been assured that the income tax provision would be changed by Democratic members of the Finance Committee.[99] An acute Washington correspondent predicted the La Follette amendment would "be revised by the Democrats and rewritten in a way to give it the semblage [*sic*] of an original Democratic measure."[100] The increase agreed upon in the Democratic caucus was less than Bob and Bristow had asked, but even these revisions meant that a progressive minority had again forced a forward step in legislation to meet changing economic conditions.

From the time the bill was introduced until the last day of the debate, Bob sought to improve it by amendments. The intense partisanship of the Democratic caucus defeated some that might otherwise have passed.[101] The day his income tax amendment was defeated he wrote Gilbert Roe that "the attitude of the whole democratic organization towards the Progressive Republicans who assisted directly and indirectly in Wilson's election, is really very exasperating."[102] The intensely partisan policy of the Wilson Administration had disappointed and irritated the progressive Republicans[103] who, during the Taft Administration, had cooperated with the Democrats in opposing the excessively high schedules of the Payne-Aldrich tariff. These progressive Republicans were therefore expected to revert to strict party lines on the final vote. Since the Senate Chamber had never been so evenly divided on the tariff, the newspapers predicted that the slim Democratic margin would place tremendous power in the hands of one individual Senator. A special dispatch to the *Springfield Daily Republican* said that the tariff question of the moment was "What will La Follette do?"[104] The New York *World* reported that active negotiations had been in progress between Democratic leaders and La Follette with the hope of obtaining his vote but that the Wisconsin Senator refused to state his position, saying it would depend on the number of amendments he was able to have incorporated.[105]

On September 8, the day before the final vote, Bob discussed the rates on wools and offered his amendments to the famous "schedule K." Throughout his speech Gilbert and Netha Roe and Professor S. H. Clark of the University of Chicago were in the gallery with Belle and Bob, Jr. Belle wrote her daughter that although Bob was not at his very best "he made a remarkable impression and held the attention of the Senate on the much worn theme late in discussion. It was an achievement to be proud of. Mr. Clark was I think very much impressed from the standpoint of his profession as a critic of public speaking." The next day Bob introduced additional amendments and presented detailed arguments for adoption, but they were defeated. The Senate floor was crowded with Representatives from the House, and all the galleries were filled. Belle and Bob, Jr., again heard him from the family gallery. They both regretted that under the time limitation previously agreed upon, his detailed discussion of his amendments forced him to stop abruptly and crowded out the conclusion of his speech.[106]

Late that afternoon the debate ended and the Vice President put the question on the final passage of the bill. As the names were called the first progressive Republicans on the roll, Borah, Bristow, Clapp, Cummins, and Kenyon voted "Nay." The roll call proceeded deliberately until the clerk called "La Follette." Bob, who was seated in the front row, "leaned forward a trifle and vigorously answered, 'Aye.' "[107] A reporter noted that "instantly the dignified Senate was transformed into a scene nearly approaching disorder. Women and men, in the galleries and on the floor, clapped their hands for two minutes in acknowledgment of the action taken. The only ones not sharing in this demonstration were the regular Republicans and the Progressive associates of Mr. La Follette."[108] Later Senator Poindexter, of the Roosevelt Progressive Party, voted for the bill and the demonstration was renewed. No Republican except La Follette voted for it. Thus the Payne-Aldrich tariff law was repealed and the Underwood-Simmons bill passed 44 to 37, with 14 Senators not voting.[109]

That evening the President learned that the first major bill of his legislative program had passed the Senate. When informed that La Follette and Poindexter had voted for it, he expressed his admiration "for their conscientious independence and courage."[110]

Bob's vote was highly praised in the Democratic press but severely condemned in many of the Republican editorials. The newspaper edited at Albany, New York, by "Boss" William Barnes contemptuously referred to "La Follette, of Wisconsin, who, though elected as a Republican, has departed so far from the principles of the Republican Party that he is no longer to be counted among its members." This comment and excerpts from many other newspapers were published in *La Follette's Magazine* with a parenthetical phrase designating the political alignment of each newspaper and indicating whether it was progressive or "tory."[111]

The Washington correspondent of the Philadelphia *North American*, who had followed the tariff debate closely, reported that "La Follette's vote was undoubtedly based upon the exercise of greater intelligence, upon stronger convictions, and greater independence than that of any other vote cast." He also stated that the Wisconsin

Senator's speeches had "made evident to everyone that La Follette had voted for the bill because it is better than the existing law but that he voted for it with keen regret that it could not be made a better bill."[112] An editorial in the *Springfield Daily Republican* noted that he had staked "his political future on a vote" for a Democratic revision "which indicates his willingness to risk the unpopularity and disaster, so far as Wisconsin is concerned."[113]

Some of the independent national periodicals commented favorably on Bob's non-partisan vote. An editorial in *Harper's Weekly*, which was probably written by Norman Hapgood, said that "to one man falls the greatest share of glory for independence, because it cost him most. Especially did Senator La Follette's situation require strength of character; not only has he always been a Republican, but he had, since the Roosevelt split, come to be looked upon as likely to dominate the party in the future. As progressiveness seemed needed to save it from destruction, La Follette's influence had suddenly been multiplied. In voting for the Democratic tariff, he gave a final proof that no consideration can prevent him from following always his conviction. This man has fought the straight fight all his life. Often the sacrifice has been great. He has given up friends, money, comfort, party praise, easy advance. He has stood abuse and suspicion. Nearly always the country and his party have come around finally to La Follette's position."[114]

CHAPTER XXXVII

Trying Times

Three weeks after the tariff bill passed, the La Follette family had to move from the house at 1864 Wyoming because the owner wished to occupy it. But fortunately they found a larger house at 3320 Sixteenth Street for the modest rent of $100 a month. This was their Washington home for the next decade. The spacious rooms were well arranged for entertaining, and Bob enjoyed the informal dances and impromptu parties this house made possible for the children on week ends and during the holiday season.

When Bob, Jr., left Washington to ·enter the University of Wisconsin, the entire family accompanied him to the train. That night his father wrote him that "no one wanted to go back to the house, so we drove until bedtime to drive away the 'lonesome devils.' You are close to our hearts, laddie."[1] When Bob, Jr., became a candidate for president of. the freshman class, on an "all state" ticket,[2] his father wrote, ". . . I know you will make a *clean* fight and take the result win or lose *just the same.* You remember that Hamlet describes Horatio as 'A man that fortune's *buffets* and *rewards,* hast ta'en with equal thanks.' You have inherent strength and will not lose your head in victory, nor be weak of heart if you are defeated. A game man is a good winner and a good loser. . . . I love you, my dear boy."[3] Later, when Bob, Jr., was elected president of his class, his father telegraphed, "Congratulations from Dad[.] Be nice to the fellows who were beaten and now remember what your real job is[.] With worlds of love I am yours to count on."[4]

Following the passage of the tariff bill, the legislative situation was such that Bob felt free to arrange a brief speaking trip through the South and Midwest. A few hours before taking the train, he wrote Belle, who was in Boston speaking for suffrage: "Dear heart

I shall not see you till I come back about the tenth of November. By that time I'll have earned enough to beat the wolf for a while anyway. The big house seems lonesome without you."[5] When Bob spoke at Raleigh, North Carolina, on October 29, under the auspices of Meredith College, he was introduced by Chief Justice Walter Clark, whom he greatly admired. After responding to Justice Clark's tribute to his work in Wisconsin and recalling that North Carolina had been the home of his mother's family, Bob turned to the problems confronting Congress. Here, as elsewhere, he discussed the Seamen's bill, trust legislation, and the pending currency bill, stressing the importance of strengthening the measure that was then before the Senate Committee. He dramatically described the growth of the trusts and his fight on the Aldrich-Vreeland currency bill in 1908. So many people requested further information that John Hannan wrote, "You ought to curtail the promises to your audiences with respect to sending them the speech containing the list of interlocking Directorates. We only have 75 left. They cost about $58. a thousand. At the rate at which the requests are coming we have got about enough left to last a week. It is my opinion that you have other uses for the proceeds of the lectures than to pay for printed matter for distribution in the South."[6] The letters that came to Bob's office, his own letters, and the newspaper reports indicate that during his first trip South the audiences responded as they had for many years in other parts of the country.[7]

By mid-November he had spoken in North and South Carolina, Georgia, Tennessee, Kentucky, and Ohio, and had delivered his lecture on Hamlet at the University of Wisconsin. On his return trip he also spoke in Ohio, New Jersey, and Pennsylvania, arriving in Washington for the opening of Congress on December 1, 1913. The following day he heard the President read his "the state of the Union" message in which he called for prompt action on the pending banking and currency bill and for the strengthening of the Sherman Anti-Trust law.[8]

In a previous message to Congress the President had said that a reform of the banking and currency laws was "imperative" to set businessmen free and give them the "tools of action." Bob was in accord. He had long contended that a reform was necessary. For years he had studied these problems. In 1908 he had opposed the Aldrich-Vreeland currency law as "a makeshift bill" and had urged the Senate to take the time to formulate comprehensive legislation, "specifically directed to restore banking to its true function in the commercial transactions of the country."[9] During the Senate debate in 1908, he had raised a storm of denunciation and denial when he drew attention for the first time in Congress to the fact that through a system of interlocking directorates fewer than one hundred men controlled the credit of the country. The accuracy of Bob's analysis was subsequently confirmed by irrefutable authorities in addition to the testimony and evidence the Pujo Committee brought together when Brandeis served as counsel for its investigation of money and credit. While Brandeis and Bob sometimes differed, they were in complete accord on the menace of this control of credit and the legislation needed to deal with it.[10] Bob also had reason to believe the President shared their views. He knew Wilson had consulted Brandeis about the proposed currency legislation and had asked him to submit a written memorandum of his views as expressed in their talk. Therefore he had hoped that the bills sponsored by the Administration would include Government control of Federal Reserve banks and the prevention of interlocking directorates, two provisions he and Brandeis considered essential.[11]

Bob was therefore keenly disappointed when the Administration's currency bill passed the House without any provision to prevent interlocking directorates. Although an amendment to this effect had been offered by a progressive Democrat, it had been defeated by the Democratic majority which controlled the House. It was reported that this had been done with the President's approval.[12] The House bill had been before the Senate Banking and Currency Committee for two months. As Bristow was a member of this committee, Bob had heard about the hearings where leading bankers had testified, and he also knew about the sharp differences that had arisen among the members of the committee on the issue of private banker or Government control of the new system.[13] Since the committee was evenly divided, two reports were filed representing the point of view of each group.

As the bill finally came to the Senate from the committee, Bob thought it was "a big bankers bill" which legalized the concentration of capital that had developed during the previous fifteen years and put the control of industry "in the hands of a few men."[14] During the debate he sought to improve the bill. One of his amendments, providing that no member of Congress could serve on the Federal Reserve Board or be an officer or director of a Federal Reserve bank, passed without opposition and is today a part of the law.[15] But his amendment to prevent interlocking directorates, which he regarded as absolutely essential to the control of investment banking and the concentration of capital, was defeated.[16] On the final vote fifty-four Democrats and Republicans joined in passing the bill. Bob was one of the thirty-four Senators who voted against it because he believed that ultimately "it would work out great loss and harm to the American people."[17] The bill was signed by the President, and the Federal Reserve System came into being on December 23, 1913.

On January 20, 1914, the President delivered a long message to Congress which Bob thought presented the most "important and far-reaching" legislation Wilson had proposed since his inauguration.[18] His five-point program to make the Sherman Anti-Trust law more effective included: a clarification of the policy and meaning of the Sherman Act; prohibition of interlocking directorates; establishment of a Federal Trade Commission to advise and inform business; supervision and regulation of the financial operation of the railroads; punishment of individuals rather than of business itself for violations of the law.[19] Bob was in general accord with all these recommendations except the proposal to regulate the financial operation of the railroads, which he thought unwise.

As Bob listened to Wilson's message, it seemed to him that at last a President was advocating legislation which, if effective, would include the essential provisions of bills and amendments he and other Progressives had been trying to get through Congress during the preceding Republican Administrations. For many years after the Sherman Anti-Trust law was enacted, Bob had maintained that it could curb the vicious practices of monopoly if vigorously enforced. But subsequently, during the period of swift industrial expansion, he came to the conclusion that the Sherman law alone was not enough to deal with these evils. He thought the failure of the Roosevelt Administration to enforce this law during these years had permitted such a rapidly growing concentration of quick capital in the hands of a few men, combined together through interlocking directorates and intertwining interests, that additional legislation was needed. After the Supreme Court decisions in the Standard

Oil and American Tobacco cases, he thought it was imperative. In commenting on how they had emasculated the Sherman Act, he once said, "The Supreme Court decision pulled its teeth, I am in favor of putting spikes where the teeth were."[20]

Shortly before Wilson delivered his message, a Washington newspaper dispatch had predicted that "what corporations or individuals can do in interstate commerce will be based largely upon the La Follette anti-trust bills of three years ago."[21] The Democrats formulated and introduced five separate bills to carry out the program the President had outlined. After careful study Bob concluded that the Administration's bills were "flabby and without teeth." He thought they might be "strengthened and patched up" but that it would "take a lot of bracing work." In a letter to Spreckels he explained why he thought the President's legislative program had been so ineffectively formulated: "The fact is, the men who are working on these bills have tried to go ahead independently of Progressives who have spent years on these subjects. The Democrats have become slaves to the party caucus. They want every measure with a party brand on it for political capital. And most of them haven't been long enough interested in progressive principles, especially those involving economic issues, to be ready for the work. They have taken some bills introduced in previous sessions by Progressive Republicans, and not wanting to follow literally, have cut and pieced without chart or compass, until their work is almost a joke. This they have begun to realize in the last few days and are quite at sea. They may be willing later to consent that the bills shall be made in open committee and reported by the Committee to the House and Senate, instead of being sent to a caucus to be recast as political bills."[22]

The evening after this letter was written, Bob and Belle dined at the White House. Although he did not mention the occasion in either diary or letters, he undoubtedly shared the feeling Belle expressed in a note to their son Bob, Jr., saying, "We had a truly good time. The dinner was to the Speaker. We were next in honor[,] as Mrs. Clark could not be there *I* sat next to the President. Phil nearly fell over when he learned of it."[23]

Two days later the *New York Times* reported that the President had conferred with the chairman of the Interstate Commerce Commission. At the White House it was stated that the pending rate

cases had not been discussed; that the President had sought information regarding the commission's investigation of the physical valuation of railroad properties, and the opposition to confirmation of
his two recent appointments to the commission, Winthrop M.
Daniels and Henry Clay Hall.[24] Bob had been greatly disturbed
by these appointments, and the press reported that he would oppose
confirmation.[25] After reading this newspaper report, Daniels wrote
the President suggesting that his name be withdrawn if the situation was embarrassing.[26] Wilson replied that no opposition in the
Senate would be embarrassing to him and that they were looking
forward to having Daniels in Washington.[27]

The opposition to Daniels was neither personal nor partisan. Bob
and many Senators in both parties believed his decisions as a member of the New Jersey Public Utilities Commission during Wilson's
administration as governor indicated a definite reactionary bias
on the problem of valuation. They were apprehensive that this bias
would affect his decisions in the pending cases dealing with the
railroads' demand for a 5 per cent increase in rates. This demand
had been made soon after Bob's Railroad Valuation bill had been
enacted and before the Interstate Commerce Commission had time
to make the physical valuation of their properties which this law
provided should be the basis for fixing rates. Brandeis had appeared before the commission as a representative of those who
opposed the rate increase. It was estimated that if the advance
was granted, the transportation charges to the public would be
increased at least $50,000,000 annually.

Bob thought that granting these increases would be a concealed
first step toward undermining the Railroad Valuation law. Information he had received from economists and specialists made him fear
that Daniels would be predisposed to favor these increases.[28] Bob
wrote Spreckels that "Wilson's appointments make those who want
to be friendly with his administration sick and disgusted. Two
[men] appointed Interstate Commerce Commissioners—Hall of
Colorado and Daniels of New Jersey—are hard to understand. Hall
is said to be a railroad attorney and Daniels is a member of the
New Jersey Public Utility Commission, that gave the Passaic Gas
Company a good round value on all its property, and then *added
thirty percent for intangible value,* allowing them to earn 8 percent
on this moonshine, into which, of course, they never put a dollar.

I suppose they will put Daniels over, and we shall get his blue sky views refelced [*sic*] in railroad valuation. Isn't that a pretty raw deal? And yet, Wilson is a great improvement on Roosevelt and Taft."[29]

When Daniels' nomination came before the entire Senate, it was debated in executive sessions on three successive days. Bob and other Senators made repeated unsuccessful efforts to have the proceedings thrown open to the public. It was reported that the battle behind closed doors was not fought along strict party lines, but that Walsh, Vardaman, and other Democrats agreed with La Follette. On the second day's executive session, when "Democrats were lining up hourly with the La Follette-Cummins-Bristow opposition," it became evident that if a vote were taken Daniels would be defeated. One newspaper reported that at this time he would not have received ten votes on a roll call. The Administration's leaders forced a recess to stave off defeat and gain time to withdraw the nomination.[30]

But when the Democratic leaders consulted Wilson, he insisted the nomination be put through. He was reported to have told Senators that the time had come to "let up on the railroads." At the executive session the next day, a number of progressive Democrats who had previously opposed Daniels were either absent or "changed their attitude" on the roll call and joined the Old Guard Republicans in confirming the nomination by 36 to 27.[31] Thirty-two Senators did not vote. The *Congressional Record*'s only report of the executive sessions is the statement that "the injunction of secrecy was removed from the vote by which the Senate confirmed the nomination."[32] This action had, in fact, been taken on Bob's motion.[33] The next day the *New York Times* disclosed that nine Senators, "headed by Senator La Follette, openly revolted against the proceedings behind closed doors tonight after the executive session. Senator La Follette declared on the floor that he proposed to defy the rules of the Senate in the future and discuss publicly legislation not affecting foreign relations. Senators Bristow, Cummins, Clapp, Kenyon, Norris, Jones, and Gronna (Republicans) and Poindexter (Progressive) maintained the same attitude. The revolt created somewhat of a sensation and there was much speculation as to the effect it would have upon future executive sessions."[34] Ultimately they succeeded in having open sessions for such confirmations.[35]

In an editorial Bob questioned whether this appointment and the President's position on currency legislation foreshadowed a retreat from the militant progressive leadership he had indicated in his speeches. Bob noted that nine progressive Democrats had firmly resisted the Administration's appeals and had stood to the end against Daniels' confirmation. In analyzing the strange alliance that had finally put the nomination through, he said, "What an inspiring spectacle to the millions who voted for Wilson as a true Progressive to see him in one short year triumph over progressive Democrats and progressive Republicans by securing the support of about all that remains of the old Aldrich Oligarchy in the United States Senate. It reminds thoughtful men of the beginning of the second year of the reign of one William Howard Taft."[36]

After the Senate battle on Daniels' appointment was over, the legislative situation was such that Bob was free to join Belle, Fola, and the Roe family for a few days' vacation at Atlantic City before Belle left for a month's cruise in the Caribbean as Elizabeth Evans' guest. For many months Bob and her intimate friends had been concerned about the heavy work load Belle was carrying. In addition to her regular household and social responsibilities she had been editing her "Home and Education" department in *La Follette's Magazine* and helping in the suffrage campaigns. She had also been writing articles and making speeches in Washington and elsewhere in protest against the policy of segregation which had been quietly revived in Government offices under the new Democratic Administration and was being openly advocated for the public transportation service in the District of Columbia.[37] But efforts to persuade her to go away for a rest had failed until Bob offered the bribe of joining her in a brief vacation before she left for the trip which she later described in a series of articles.[38]

Bob returned to Washington feeling more like work than he had for months and saying that he would be able "to make a good showing."[39] After Belle sailed from New York, Fola wrote her father that "it was a pull for mother to push off from the shore where her beloveds were."[40] In a little goodbye note Belle told Bob that she had no apprehension about the trip but that "if anything *should* happen . . . I want you all to get the largest happiness out of life possible and whenever or whatsoever befalls me I know you will make up to each other what I should do for you."[41] Soon after Belle left, Bob wrote: "Dear heart I shall miss you. There will be vital things turning up ev[e]ry day now. The lines are going to tighten ev[e]ry hour from this on. I will keep a grip on myself and be as sure of my ground as possible before I take any *next step*—but you feel it in the air that things are going to move rapidly."[42]

A few days later he wrote that he had done some good work on the Indian Affairs Committee, where a stiff fight had been put up to get rid of the Indian Commission "composed of a dozzen [*sic*] high class non-salaried men who visit Reservations & look for wrong doing against the Indians. For years they have been crippled with a meager appropriation of $4000 for travelling expenses. I made a hot argument & not only defeated the move but carried a motion to increase their appropriation to $25000 . . . to make even more thorough investigations.

". . . I also attacked (later) the unconscionable attorney fees allowed to shyster attorneys out of Indian funds—and established in two cases the rule of fixing $15000 as a minimum fee" and provided "that the Secty of Interior should fix it as much less" if he felt it just. "It is a *mile* post."[43]

The same letter said that John R. Commons had brought him "an invitation from Mrs. Harriman to lunch at her home to meet Col. House to discuss Wilson[']s recent flirtations with the railroads and other interests." Among the guests were Louis Post and Felix Frankfurter. Bob sat next to the colonel and liked him "very much and had a good plain talk with him. I think he is genuine and really understands. I put him on to a number of things and he promised to stick some pins in the right places on several matters of importance."[44]

One evening, after talking on the telephone with Brandeis, who was in Boston, Bob wrote: "I am very anxious to see Louie & find out how things are going with him. He said over the phone tonight, 'well some pretty important things have been happening over the country.' Meaning—as I understood the recent elections. He said it with a good deal of satisfaction as it seemed to me and I am sure that he is feeling very deeply on the subject of the President[']s interference with the work of the Commission."[45] Two weeks later Bob wrote Belle: "It is a great thing to have

Louis at hand to talk things over with. He is thoroughly critical of the course which things are taking."[46]

Bob had learned that a prominent official in the Treasury Department, presumably in close touch with White House policy, was saying that the Interstate Commerce Commission should grant the demands of the railroads. This same informant also told Bob it was "common rumor that the raising of the rates would be acceptable, in order to bring prosperity to the railroads."[47] Further investigation convinced Bob that many railroad-inspired appeals for increased rates were being addressed to the President and forwarded by him to the Interstate Commerce Commission. Bob was shocked at this procedure, as he believed it would inevitably be interpreted as indicating the President's approval.

Bob was also concerned about a propaganda campaign organized by those who were parties to the proceeding in cases then before the commission. In an editorial he declared that "no such disgraceful spectacle had ever before been witnessed" to hammer the commission into rendering a decision favorable to the railroads.[48] He regarded the commission as a judicial body subject to the same rules as governed a court and therefore thought that testimony should be presented only under the rules and regulations it prescribed. To this end he introduced a bill making it a misdemeanor to attempt to influence the action of the commission except at regular hearings in a pending case. Concrete evidence which he used in his argument for the bill was secured through two resolutions he introduced. One directed the commission to transmit to the Senate all evidence introduced and all exhibits received at hearings in the rate cases.[49] The other called for transmission to the Senate of all communications the commission had received designed to influence its decisions on these cases.[50] When he spoke for his bill, he read from a mass of material that had been sent to the President and transmitted to the commission. He also had printed in the *Congressional Record* a diagram indicating the sources of the organized propaganda.[51] His bill was referred to the Interstate Commerce Committee, of which he was a member, but he was not able to get further action on it.

Bob was widely berated for his speech, but a prominent Washington correspondent reported that in view of all that was known at the Capitol it was impossible to question that the President had "exerted himself" to obtain rate increases "regardless of facts and without any knowledge" as to whether the railroads were entitled to them.[52]

Many newspaper editorials and even some of Bob's friends criticized him severely for his implied criticism of the President. But other friends and many progressive Republicans and Democrats agreed with the opinion expressed by Judge Charles F. Amidon, of the United States District Court of North Dakota, who wrote Bob: "I have often thought how easy and pleasant the road has been for President Wilson because of those who have gone that way before him, and done the fighting. No public man has ever entered into the labors of others more truly than the President, . . . Those whose judgments have not been made strong and wise by the fight are in charge of the work of embodying the progressive movement into measures of government. They are almost sure to compromise and wash out its real, most distinctive features. I am glad you are on the ground . . . to point out how far the performance falls short."[53]

Although critical of what seemed to him a regression in the President's former progressive position on currency and railroad legislation, Bob had throughout 1913 vigorously defended Wilson's policy of non-intervention in Mexico which had been bitterly criticized by Lodge, Penrose, and many other Republicans. He had also commended Wilson's two public statements concerning our diplomatic relations with South America, which he interpreted as giving notice that our State Department was no longer to be used "as the agent of high finance."[54]

The President had inherited problems in relation to Mexico which were due to the internal conflicts that followed the fall of Porfirio Díaz. Insurgency and civil strife led to depredations on persons and property in Mexico and at times along the border. The great landowners and also citizens of the United States and other countries who had large investments in Mexico were calling for intervention to restore order. Victoriano Huerta, one of the revolutionary leaders who had established himself in a part of Mexico, had been recognized as the head of a *de facto* government by most of the European and Latin-American powers. But Wilson had refused recognition and had adopted a policy of "watchful waiting." Bob publicly supported this policy, and declared in an editorial that the efforts of some newspapers and certain American politicians to force the Administration to recognize the Huerta government or to embroil us in a war with Mexico was "reprehensible in the last degree. Back of this organization are powerful interests ready to coin the lives of our soldiers or the honor of our country into the fortunes which they have at stake in their Mexican concessions."[55]

In a brief address to Congress on August 27, 1913, Wilson had expressed his confidence that if this country maintained a strict neutrality, the Mexicans would solve their own domestic affairs satisfactorily in their own way. To this end he announced a complete embargo on arms and requested that all United States citizens leave Mexico because it was "imperative that they should take no unnecessary risks."[56] Bob listened to this address with profound approval. Belle, who was also present, wrote that as she left the gallery she heard "on all sides approval of the President's attitude." She thought "there was no mistaking the general sanction of his policy to *secure peace with peace*. And there was general rejoicing that no danger of jingoism threatened the nation." It seemed "like the dawning of a new era—not of sentimental talk about peace, but of *actual enforcement of the peace principle*." Bob published the entire address in his magazine, which stated that Wilson "had contributed a state document to history that will assuredly prove a beacon toward World peace."[57]

Early in April, 1914, shortly after Belle left for her trip with Mrs. Evans, an "incident" occurred in Mexico which suddenly altered the President's policy of "watchful waiting." While the Atlantic fleet was off the coast of Mexico after its spring maneuvers, a group of sailors in a small boat flying the United States flag landed at Tampico to buy supplies for their ship. They were arrested by an officer in Huerta's army but were soon released. Huerta formally expressed regret and promised to punish the offending officer. But Admiral Henry Mayo, who was in command of the fleet, demanded a formal apology with the hoisting of the United States flag and a salute of twenty-one guns. Huerta agreed provided the American fleet raised the Mexican flag and returned the salute. Acting upon instructions from Washington, Admiral Mayo refused, since this might imply recognition of the Huerta government. Thereupon Huerta refused to salute as demanded.

The President summoned Congress in joint session to hear a special message dealing with the Mexican crisis. Bob was one of the committee appointed to wait upon Wilson in the Speaker's room and escort him to the House Chamber. After briefly stating the facts, the President expressed the earnest hope that war was "not now in question." He said he had no doubt he could do what was necessary to enforce respect for our Government "without recourse to the Congress" and yet not exceed his "constitutional powers as President," but that he "did not wish to act in a matter possibly of so grave consequence except in close conference and cooperation with both the Senate and House." Therefore he had come to ask their approval to "use the armed forces of the United States in such ways and to such an extent as may be necessary to obtain from Gen. Huerta and his adherents the fullest recognition of the rights and dignity of the United States . . ."[58]

The joint resolution requested by the Administration was quickly passed by the House but acrimoniously discussed in the Senate, where Phil followed the proceedings with keen interest. He wrote his mother that he had missed two days of school listening to the debate but "it was worth it."[59] While the resolution was still being discussed, the President ordered Admiral Frank Fletcher to seize Vera Cruz. During this action four American marines were killed and twenty wounded; 126 Mexicans were killed and 195 wounded. This made the passage of the joint resolution inevitable, but Bob sought to limit it to the immediate emergency. He offered an amendment providing that "the United States hereby disclaims any disposition or intention to exercise sovereignty, jurisdiction or control over Mexico or any portion of the same, except for the pacification thereof, and asserts its determination, when that is accomplished, to leave the government and control of Mexico and every portion thereof to its people."[60]

Bob's amendment was defeated by the narrow margin of three votes. Bristow, Norris, Bob, and ten other Republicans then voted against the joint resolution. Bob did not believe that the facts as presented to Congress justified approval of the President's use of the armed forces. But he stated editorially that after action had been taken it could no longer be a question of supporting or opposing the President's Mexican policy since it could "only create division where we should be united." He believed, however, that it should at once be made known "in every capital of the world that the

President has the support of a united country at his back" and that we should proclaim "our fixed purpose to withdraw the armed forces of the United States from Mexico at the earliest possible moment consistent with national honor."[61]

In a long letter to Belle, Bob said, "We have had strenuous times here and plenty of excitement day and night. . . . There is a *remote* possibility that we may yet be saved the disgrace & crime of carrying on war with Mexico but it is exceedingly doubtful. It has been a very trying time & everybody feels the strain & wear of it all. While it would have been a great comfort to have you here —I am glad you have escaped it—for it has been continuous."[62]

Additional warships were ordered to Mexican waters, and American marines occupied Vera Cruz. Huerta promptly demanded their evacuation and gave passports to the American Chargé d'Affaires at Mexico City. It seemed that war was at hand. Then, on April 25, the President accepted an offer of mediation from Argentina, Brazil, and Chile. The crisis passed. Subsequently Huerta resigned, and war with Mexico was avoided.

Belle and Mrs. Evans had returned from their trip on May 11. A week later Mrs. Evans wrote from Boston saying she had quite a talk with Alice Brandeis "this morning about public affairs, & all she told was bitterly hard to bear. But the net result, *in me*, has been the realization that I have not been open-minded about Wilson —& in my longing to believe in him, have refused to see."[63] To this letter Belle replied with her customary tolerance, "You glorify the people you admire so much that when they fall short you are crushed with disappointment. It is a tremendous task to be President of the U.S., and every man has his limitations. I strive to believe that Wilson is true to himself and it is my best judgment that in spite of his mistakes and shortcomings he has set the stakes quite a bit in advance of his predecessors. That is, on the average he has done better and the country will expect more of future presidents because of the Wilson administration. I think Louis Brandeis has more reason to suspect and denounce the course that has been pursued than any one else, but he finds more to commend and is more tolerant than any of the rest of us. Unless Wilson sums up better than Roosevelt, then your Senator [Bob] made a mistake in not joining the Bull Moose party. These are difficult times politically and there are doubtless undercurrents that we do not see or understand. All we can do is, to help along the surface manifestations that appear to be moving in the right direction, contribute what we can to the betterment of the situation."[64]

Soon after Belle reached home, she had written Bob, Jr., that his father had been doing effective work "in the Senate, on the floor and in committee" and that he seemed to be "feeling in good spirits and in good physical condition." She added that he had been taking "a two or three mile walk every night before going to bed and some vigorous exercise every morning."[65] Therefore it came as a shock when Bob was suddenly stricken ill during an intense heat wave in June. For many weeks his doctors did not permit him to go to the Senate. They assured him that his illness was due to overwork and predicted a complete recovery. Although he himself was confident, he was well aware that the grave symptoms which accompanied his sudden digestive disturbance meant that rest was imperative.

A week after Bob was taken ill, Belle had to leave with Mrs. Evans to fulfill a contract for a two months' trip on a Midwestern Chautauqua circuit to debate with an anti-suffragist the question of granting votes to women. Shortly after she left, Bob wrote his daughter Fola, who was also away from home on a speaking trip, that, "Mamma found it hard to go—but she could not cancel without giving some *big reason* & she smothered her feeling and went out because it was necessary to protect me from publicity on this—and publicity would of course come—if at all—in its worst & most sensational form." In the same long letter, written in pencil on scratch paper, he said: "Now, dear, a word to *you* about myself—and this I feel so sensitive about that you must not mention it to Mid, Gilbert or any one else. I *think* my trouble is due to toxic poisoning—I *believe* the Doctors think so. I am *certain* that I shall be my normal self in a few weeks—but just now I am somewhat knocked out—partial loss of feeling on one side—a little impaired motion on the other. I cannot quite walk right—that is my left leg is a little off. Now these conditions have improved vastly in the week since they first came on. Should the use of my left leg improve as much in another week I don't think *it would be noticeable in my walk.*

"Now the reason why this thing seems not so horrible—is because I believe it to be toxic that is a deadening of nerve centers

through poisoning & irritation and congestion resulting therefrom
—and *not a leakage,* (a blood clot a rupture of an artery) is just
this: (1) My doctors say my arteries are not hardened but soft.
(2) It came on with a severe billious attack, vomiting bile for a
day. (3) Its behavior since shows many evidences of toxic poisoning. (4) The *large area affected,* argues for poisoning rather than
some *spot* of *pressure.*

"Beloved one I have given it to you straight. You were entitled
to have it that way. You are my girl and you will meet it whatever
it is. But I feel it so keenly that I dont want anyone to know
except the bone of my bone & the flesh of my flesh. I have had a half
dozen of the best specialists and they all agree with what I have
given you. Also they all agree that it will pass in a few weeks or
months at most. They say I have twenty years of reasonable work
in me yet—with reasonable periods of application and rest."[66]

Late in July Phil sailed for England with David and Laura
Thompson, and Mary left to spend the rest of the summer in
Madison. Bob remained in Washington with Bob, Jr., in the large
house where he told Belle it was "so lonesome" you could hear it
"without whispering." He lived on buttermilk, bran bread, and
Granola. His son, who was then eighteen, answered the telephone,
did the marketing, and counseled with his father on all the important decisions that had to be made during the summer. His
father wrote Belle that their son was "one fine manly fellow, with
a great head on him. He would make a smashing good writer and
I think is a natural orator . . . I wouldnt take anything for this summer with Bobbie."[67]

In his letters Bob related to his absent family the little happenings
at home, the financial problems of his magazine, his opinions on
pending legislation, and the political turns in Congress. He eagerly
awaited the almost daily letters from Belle and his children, which
they usually shared with one another. He was worried over the difficulties Belle was having on her long Chautauqua tour through a
dozen States, speaking on hot days to audiences beneath tents and
in crowded halls.[68] Knowing the conditions, he wrote, "Poor Girl
this has been one awfully gruelling summer. How you have stood
up under it I dont understand . . . My but you are a great woman[.]
I love you."[69] He kept Belle's and Fola's letters which record the
conditions of campaigning for woman suffrage on the Chautauqua

circuit at that time.[70] In a note to Fola, Bob said, "I cannot destroy letters that are a part of someone I love."[71]

Bob's illness had forced him to cancel some $8,000 worth of speaking engagements he had contracted for in the vicinity of Washington where he could return on night trains in time to attend Senate sessions the following day. He had undertaken this additional work to help meet expenses and the deficit of his magazine. Therefore the burden of financial anxiety was added to that of illness. In a letter to Belle he said, "I'm so hard up that it dont make any difference any more. But I'm going to get strong & sound so I can work off my debts when I do."[72] He followed the doctors' orders faithfully, limiting his activities to writing his editorials, taking his favorite drives in Rock Creek Park, and seeing only a few friends. He wrote Belle of his visits with Brandeis, Commons, Lenroot, Alf Rogers, Roe, George Rublee, and Andrew Furuseth, who kept him informed on the progress of the Seamen's bill which was still bottled up in the House.

One evening when Brandeis came to dinner, they "had a good old talk." The next day Bob wrote Belle that Brandeis had seen Crane before his appointment at the White House and had urged Crane "to talk with the President about getting back some of the real progressives—the earnest ones—for whom he has had apparently little time and to whose utterances he has given very little heed. It is hard to see him lose ground when you must believe he wants to do the right thing. And it is made harder by the apparent return of the old reactionary crowd—Penrose, Gallinger, Foraker, Brandegee, Cannon[,] Roosevelt—and prosperity. Wilson[']s clearness of mind makes him cocksure and stubborn while his inexperience and ignorance of more than the merest smattering on the problems and his intense political partisan feeling renders him almost impossible. It just breaks ones heart to see him throw away chances for good things & swallow bad things with good labels, while the old Republican and old Democratic devils chuckle."[73]

Bob's talk with Brandeis that evening confirmed his own views as to the unsatisfactory situation in the Senate on the bill regulating the financial operations of the railroads, and he wrote Belle that "It makes me 'have' to get into the fight; and nothing but the fear of the Lord keeps me back—& I dont know how long that will."[74] But the doctors were firm in their orders that he should not return to the Senate until fall, and he was therefore continuously absent after June 20. He had made "plans for a lot of things"[75] and was deeply disappointed that he could not contribute directly to the pending legislation dealing with the trusts, railroads, and other economic problems he had worked on for so many years. He followed the proceedings closely, however, and commented on some of them editorially. It was a satisfaction to him that, as finally passed, the Clayton bill, designed to clarify the Sherman Anti-Trust law, included a provision to prevent interlocking directorates and also exempted labor organizations from anti-trust laws. With keen interest he followed Lenroot's efforts as a member of the Committee on Public Lands to preserve the essential purpose of a resolution Bob had introduced in the Senate in 1911 providing for a Government-owned railroad in Alaska and the opening of coal lands there under a leasing system. Bob told the readers of his magazine that Lenroot's "steadfast and brilliant fight" on matters of importance had "beaten down the privilege seekers" and protected the public interest in the measure that was finally passed.[76] He also described Lenroot's part in securing approval by the House of an amendment Bob had been able to tack onto an appropriation bill when it was in the Senate shortly before he became ill. This amendment provided for $25,000 to enable the Library of Congress to make a beginning in its Legislative Reference service and thus take "an important and necessary step toward rendering the business of law making more efficient, more exact, economically sound and scientific."[77]

During the last week in July, Bob read with increasing anxiety the European dispatches reporting the diplomatic tensions between Austria and Serbia that followed the assassination of Archduke Franz Ferdinand at Sarajevo. On July 31, three days after Austria had declared war on Serbia, Bob, Jr., wrote his mother, "The trouble in Europe is the absorbing topic of conversation at our little table."[78] On August 2, Bob wrote her that "The outlook for general European war is very black at this time. There is a chance for it to clear in the next 24 or 48 hours. If the thing dont change soon it will drift beyond control. . . . Of course this whole thing may quiet down and the war dogs be sent growling to their kennels inside a week. It would seem as if it could not be otherwise. But we are all cave men under the surface I guess."[79] Two days later Bob wrote Phil, who had arrived in London, that no one could "forecast the outcome of this thing" and that it would be difficult "to do ancient towns & castles & highways and scenes of historic interest when you are in full view of the stage where with lightening [*sic*] like rapidity is being performed the world's greatest drama."[80] As his father anticipated, Phil had in fact deserted ancient castles and secured admission to a closed session of Parliament through the courtesy of T. P. O'Connor.

On August 4, Germany and England exchanged declarations of war, and the Kaiser's armies marched into Belgium. The President proclaimed United States neutrality and, as official head of one of the powers signatory to the Hague Convention, offered to act in the interest of European peace.

A few days later Belle wrote from Michigan, where she was speaking on the Chautauqua Circuit: "I suppose Washington is in mourning. What a shock Mrs. Wilson's death must be. How terrible this war. It does *seem* as though all this Peace sentiment ought to avail in some way. It seems as though there was only one point of view regarding war. You hear only one among the people. I think Wilson administration is intrenched if it keeps us out of war. I hear only praise for the President because he kept us out of war. Roosevelt's day is done men say. It is strange how things work out."[81]

Wilson emphasized his formal proclamation of neutrality by issuing on August 18 an "impassioned appeal" declaring: "The United States must be neutral in fact as well as in name during these days that are to try men's souls. We must be impartial in thought as well as in action, must put a curb upon our sentiments as well as upon every transaction that might be construed as a preference of one party to the struggle before another."[82] Bob responded to this appeal with wholehearted and sustained support. It was published in full in *La Follette's Magazine,* which declared that "Wilson's course in the present world crisis is high statesmanship and splendid patriotism."[83]

From the beginning of the European War, Bob was convinced that if the United States was drawn into it, the struggle for democracy in this country would be set back a generation. Apparently Wilson was also apprehensive as to what failure to maintain neutrality might mean, for he told Secretary Daniels that, "Every reform we have won will be lost if we go into this war."[84] Soon after the European War began, Bob expressed anxiety as to how special interests might utilize the war to undermine progressive legislation. The La Follette Seamen's bill was still in the House, where opponents were making an indirect attack upon it by claiming that its safety provisions might affect Wilson's program to rehabilitate the merchant marine. To counteract this insidious opposition, Bob published a series of editorials and articles in his magazine to arouse support for the Seamen's bill.[85]

He was also concerned about the partisan attacks reactionary Republicans were making on Wilson's neutrality policy. Fearing the impact they might have on the approaching Congressional elections, he wrote a long, signed editorial as an appeal to progressive voters who might respond to his interpretation of the Administration's foreign policy. He commended the twenty Arbitration Treaties which provided for investigation and an attempt at adjustment before the contracting parties resorted to war over differences. He paid tribute to both Wilson and Bryan for "their great service to the human race" in "making international agreements which constitute at least the beginning of peace negotiations between the United States and the civilized world." Bob also declared that, "Because of his course in dealing with the European war, President Wilson today holds a supreme place in the confidence of the people of the United States. In the estimation of his character and service all other subjects are subordinated to the one great fact that everywhere finds spontaneous expression in the simple phrase: 'He is keeping us out of war' . . . every move for peace, every act for strengthening neutrality, has the stamp of sincerity, of wise caution, and fearless purpose. Full in the eyes of the world he maintains a calm and poise in direct ratio to the responsibility that rests upon him."[86]

In this same nonpartisan spirit Bob wrote editorials endorsing progressive Republican and Democratic candidates for the Senate in the approaching primaries and the election. Among them were Senator A. J. Gronna, Senator Joseph L. Bristow, Francis J. Heney, Representative William Kent, Senator Robert L. Owen, Raymond Robins, Representative Raymond B. Stevens, Judge Charles A. Prouty, Senator George Chamberlain, and H. L. Loucks.[87] Copies

United States Senate,

COMMITTEE ON CORPORATIONS

ORGANIZED IN THE DISTRICT OF COLUMBIA,

WASHINGTON, D. C.

Sep 28 – 1914

Dear Frank —

Some time ago Kent wrote Hannan that something in LaFollettes would help your fight for the Senate. I also had a letter from Chris Runckel making a like suggestion. I am just recovering from a real case of sickness or would have responded sooner.

Last week – Sep 26 – I ran a criticism of Knowlands record – and this week Oct 3 are running enclosed as a signed Edion the front page. If you wish to publish you can give it out to the papers on receipt – of this simply stating that "La-Follette will say in a signed Editorial this week in his magazine the following" — or something of the sort – introducing it as you like.

While you were pretty mean two years ago I would forget it and if I were well enough come and speak for both you and Kent —

I sincerely hope you both will

Always just the same —

Bob.

Hon. Francis J. Heney

San Francisco

California

Bob endorses Francis J. Heney for United States Senator

of his magazine were distributed widely in their respective States. The Heney endorsement was requested by William Kent, who wrote Hannan that "something in La Follette's would help Heney's fight for the Senate." Bob wrote a strong editorial and sent a copy to Heney, before publication, with a longhand letter in which he said, "While you were pretty mean two years ago I would forget it and if I were well enough come and speak for both you and Kent. I sincerely hope you both win. Always just the same Bob."[88] Later endorsements were made in his magazine of some thirty-two candidates for Congress, "irrespective of party designation," which included Republicans, Democrats, and "Bull Moosers."[89]

The reports Bob had been receiving on the political situation in Wisconsin were disturbing. The progressive Republicans had not been able to unite on candidates for the September primary when men were to be nominated for governor, state officers, and a United States Senator to succeed Stephenson. This gave a tremendous advantage to the Stalwarts who united in supporting for governor Emmanuel Philipp, the bitter opponent of progressive legislation ever since Bob's first term as governor. Early in May Bob had written his former secretary, Jerre Murphy, that "It looks as though we would have to make our fight over again or at least a part of it."[90] Conditions had grown steadily worse. Five progressive Republicans had entered the field for the governorship, and six candidates were seeking the Republican senatorial nomination.

Governor McGovern was one of the candidates for United States Senator, but the Wisconsin progressive Republicans could not unite on him. His conduct at the Republican National Convention in 1912 had alienated many of his friends. Bob had nevertheless supported him for governor against Karel, the reactionary Democratic candidate. But after election to a second term as governor, it seemed to Bob that McGovern had repeatedly ignored the public interest in playing a game of personal politics which "belittled and besmirched everything." For purely factional reasons he had attempted to oust from office Herman Ekern, who, in Bob's opinion, was "the ablest insurance commissioner in the country." This and other unwise acts had engendered antagonisms that destroyed cooperation on legislation and made it impossible for Bob and others to support McGovern for the Senate.[91] In an effort to unite the progressive Republicans,

Bob endorsed Thomas Morris, an able man who had unselfishly and courageously served the progressive cause since 1904, as state senator, president of the Normal School Board, and lieutenant governor.[92]

The result of the Wisconsin primary was a severe blow. The split in the progressive Republican forces had enabled the Stalwarts to nominate Philipp for governor, although the official returns showed that out of 125,000 Republican votes he had received only a third. All the other state officers were renominated over their reactionary opponents. McGovern won the senatorial nomination over Morris and the other candidates by barely a third of the total Republican vote.[93] The primary was widely interpreted in the press as a personal defeat for Bob and the end of the progressive movement in Wisconsin.

In a letter to Elizabeth Evans, Belle said: "The Wisconsin political situation is incredible. It seems as though it must be just an ugly dream. . . . Not only were Phillipp [*sic*] and McGovern nominated, but the legislature is reactionary. Karel was nominated for Governor by the Democrats. He is as bad as can be." She added that Paul Husting, the Democratic nominee for United States Senator, was "a true Progressive and sound to the core we believe. But thus far that is the only ray of light we have."[94] Since the legislature was reactionary, Bob thought it would be a calamity if either Philipp or Karel became governor, and that it might mean "*the end of progressive* Wisconsin for a *decade.*" In that event he feared that a "pretense of economy" might be used as an "easy and popular method of destruction" to undermine the Wisconsin commissions and laws that Philipp had fought as a lobbyist and Karel as a member of the legislature when Bob himself was governor.[95]

To prevent this calamity he outlined a strategy which he hoped might defeat the reactionary nominees in both parties. Two days after receiving the report of the devastating primary, he wrote to Alf Rogers in Madison. On the assumption that there was "still a number of good fights in our fellows," he urged that they should have "an independent ticket" for the legislature and all state officers "in every case where a progressive republican is not nominated" except when a combination could be made with the Democrats "in cases where an out and out progressive democratic candidate has been nominated." He said he thought that perhaps Wisconsin was ordained to "lead on to a union of the progressives of both parties" to prevent a reactionary victory and suggested that they could give the Democrats "some pretty strong tentative assurances on the national side to *save* the *progressive cause in the good old state.*" With full understanding of the hard blow they had received, he added: "I suppose our fellows are mostly in the hospital. But for that very reason it is a good time to patch up their wounds and pull them onto their feet and start something."[96]

The first response to his plan was an appeal for him to resign from the Senate and become a candidate for governor. The Wisconsin leaders thought he was the only man who could overcome party regularity and win as an independent. They undoubtedly believed he could later be returned to the Senate, but seemed unaware of what it would mean to lose the seniority that had contributed to his influential position on important committees, which gave him "power in shaping legislation" and therefore "*opportunity* for *public* service." Rogers wrote that he thought one of Bob's old-time speaking campaigns might defeat Philipp. In a long letter Bob replied that "as I analyze the situation and my feeling I find that Wisconsin is dearer to me than all the rest and I believe in our scheme of democracy with her lead in fundamental legislation that she is the most important interest in the whole field." He said that the people of the State were not to blame for the situation that had developed. "*Our own people are to blame.* If I can save Wisconsin and am the only one who can, I want the way opened for me to do it. I shall know before this reaches you what my doctors think about my ability to do it."[97]

While Bob was going through this intense inner conflict as to what he should do, Bob, Jr., had to return to the university. Belle wrote him that she had seldom seen his father so depressed and that "It was hard to let you go; your absence makes [me] realize more keenly than when you were here—if that is possible—how much you have been to us this summer. Whatever comes we have a brainy young man ready to share all our responsibilities." She said his father did not "feel equal to the kind of campaign called for and realizes how difficult the situation must be if a whirlwind campaign is the only way to win. . . . But, oh, it is so hard for him to adjust to the thought of letting the situation go by default, of not doing the thing that has the greatest chance of saving the state. He did not sleep last night and his mind is on the subject all the while."[98]

Bob was also harassed at this time lest his inability to meet the financial obligations of *La Follette's Magazine* should force him to stop publication. In an attempt to save it through a combination with the *Wisconsin Farmer*, Roe made a special trip to Des Moines to see the owner, James Pierce. When Roe stopped off in Madison, he was alarmed to learn that Wisconsin friends were urging Bob to become a candidate for governor and make a whirlwind campaign. In a letter that undoubtedly influenced Bob, he said: "Even if you can get a grudging permission from your Doctors, there is still a tremendous element of risk which you have no right to take; Secondly: the State of Wisconsin like an individual has got to stand on its own feet and be left to settle its own destiny. You cannot constitute yourself guardian of the state. The present reaction in Wisconsin is natural and is to be found in every state and city that has gone through anything like a similar fight. . . . I could write a book on the subject, but I should always come back to the conclusion above expressed, that you should take counsel of your health, which means as well your family, and your opportunity for years of useful service to the country, and furthermore you will render a better service to the State of Wisconsin by letting it have its little debauch, than you will by attempting to save it at the fearful cost you will have to pay."[99]

In a longhand note, which revealed what was for him an exceptional state of despair, Bob replied: "Your good heart to heart letter came to us this morning. Alf had wired so we were prepared for the Pierce turn down. Evils are coming upon us in swarms: political disaster—financial destruction—friends growing critical and exacting—and sickness dogging me for months. Against it all your devotion warms me about the heart. On top of all that has befallen, to announce the failure of the paper [*La Follette's Magazine*] makes the end seem pretty near. I will write again in a day or two when I get pulled together."[100]

Two weeks later twenty progressive Republicans met in Wisconsin and authorized a telegram to Bob, signed by Richard Lloyd Jones, demanding an answer as to whether he would become an independent candidate for governor. The verdict of Bob's doctors had been "dead against" any strenuous campaign, and they had given only a "reluctant consent" to his making a few speeches later; one a day "with careful diet and necessary rest."[101] Bob wrote Jones giving the reasons why he would not be a candidate. This letter was published, and John J. Blaine, an able progressive Republican, who had been state senator, announced his candidacy as an independent against the reactionary Republican and Democratic nominees for governor.[102] These progressive Republicans did not put up a candidate against McGovern, but whatever influence they and Bob had undoubtedly went to the Democratic nominee, Paul Husting.

Ever since Bob had been forced to cancel his speaking engagements because of illness, the future of *La Follette's Magazine* had been in jeopardy. Through his lecture fees and the assistance of friends, who believed in the contribution the magazine was making to the progressive movement, he had hoped to continue to meet the financial deficit as he had in the past. He knew that an independent publication dealing with political and economic issues must frequently attack vested interests and could not therefore expect an income from the large advertisers which sustained popular magazines. His thought on this subject was recorded in two long letters which state the problems as clearly for the present time as they did then.[103]

In fearlessly serving the public, he was aware that such a publication must rely upon subscriptions plus the "small pickings" of independent advertisers. To raise subscriptions to a point where they covered costs would make the price prohibitive to most readers. The only way to meet the inevitable deficit and keep the magazine free was by donations from those who believed in its educational work and by money he could earn through his lectures. He thought that no magazine of this type had a right to exist unless it served a public purpose, and it was on this basis alone that he had asked and received financial help. Over 500,000 copies a year had been printed, and with the usual estimate of five readers for each copy Bob thought the value of its public service had been far-reaching.

Now in its sixth year, with a circulation just under forty thousand, *La Follette's Magazine* had a pressing financial deficit of $10,000 which his illness made it impossible for him to meet. His farm was mortgaged to the limit, and he had no other personal security to borrow on except his life insurance. Some friends, who had given more than generously in the past, were committed to other publications and causes which made them feel they could not help now. A few frankly said they thought his work for the magazine, with the inevitable problem of meeting the deficit, was too great a strain on him and that he should concentrate all his energy upon his legislative work in the Senate.[104] They had tried to work out a plan to put the magazine on a permanent basis with a fund pledged to meet the deficit of $1,000 a month. When they were unable to raise enough money for this project, they offered to help take care of the outstanding obligations on condition that Bob would consent to stop publication.

But Bob could not accept this alternative. He believed the magazine made an important contribution to his work in the Senate as its subscriptions were widely distributed throughout the country, and his editorials were quoted in many other publications. He knew, too, that through the years the roll calls on men and measures and his editorials had repeatedly been effective aids in defeating reactionary candidates and electing progressive Senators and Representatives to Congress. In Wisconsin his magazine had some twenty thousand regular subscribers, and during the last few years, when the special session had kept him almost continuously in Washington, it had been his only medium for clarifying national and state legislative issues to the voters. He had known a period when there was no large newspaper in Wisconsin which would give the progressive cause a fair presentation. At this time the two leading Republican newspapers in Milwaukee were extremely hostile. He also remembered vividly how the voters had been misled and the issues confused when a progressive newspaper had suddenly turned reactionary in response to orders from its owners. Bob prophetically foresaw that this might happen again. To stop publication of his magazine after the nomination of Philipp and Karel, two ancient enemies of the progressive movement, seemed to him a complete surrender to reactionary forces that were trying to destroy everything known as the "Wisconsin idea."

During the months that he was ill, Bob had been exploring, with the help of Gilbert Roe, Alf Rogers, and John Hannan, every possible way of continuing the magazine. Roe wrote Rudolph Spreckels that he had never fully appreciated "how the burdens of the paper weighed him down. At the same time next to his family and friends, the paper is the dearest thing to him in life. I think the problem is to save both him and the paper if we can; but of course, if we can only save one the paper has to go."[105] Roe had sought to negotiate a combination of the magazine with the *Wisconsin Farmer*. When that failed he had tried to arrange to retain a page in another publication where Bob would be free to write his signed editorials. When none of these combinations could be made, Belle suggested that Bob should tap his only remaining source and borrow enough on his life insurance to persuade his creditors to wait and let him pay the rest as fast as he could earn it through the future speaking engagements he then had under contract. Meanwhile he intended to test out the experiment of reducing costs by turning the magazine into a monthly.

After they had made this decision, Belle wrote Elizabeth Evans that Bob "feels to quit now is a declaration of surrender and failure which is worse than death to him. He looks forward to the time when he can earn the money." The next day, in another letter to this same "Beloved Elizabeth," she said: "I believe you know that I deeply appreciate the generous help of our friends for the magazine while at the same time I recognize that we have no right to expect them to continue their support longer than their judgment approves, and especially if they do not think the paper is rendering service. . . . True Bob undertakes more work than he should. He sees the end and not the difficulties and obstacles. But it is his faith and persistence that have sustained him through his long struggle. He has to live and act according to his light."[106]

During October Bob's health improved sufficiently so that the doctors thought he could safely go to Wisconsin to speak for Blaine the last few days before election. He arrived in the State on October 28, and spent the day in conferences. That night an itinerary was made out, and telegrams were sent to friends in each town requesting them to arrange the meetings as scheduled. Although people were given such short notice, large and enthusiastic audiences turned out for all of the sixteen speeches he made, which varied in length from two hours to ten minutes. But a special dispatch from Milwaukee to the *New York Times* falsely reported that some of Bob's meetings were canceled because of "lack of attendance" and others because he was "in no condition to speak." It was headed:

"LA FOLLETTE BREAKS DOWN
SENATOR JUMPS INTO CROWD AND SECRETARY STOPS
HIS SPEECH"[107]

On the very night that this report was telegraphed from Milwaukee, Bob sent a telegram to Belle saying, "Fifteen speeches old time audiences with time could reach any result conditions unprecedented anything may happen tell nellie to mail prof[essor] Roe's letter and Blanks am pretty tired expect to start back tuesday all well. love."[108]

Since Bob still had his magazine, it was possible for him to refute the Milwaukee report. Under the heading "A MALICIOUS LIE," he printed the Milwaukee dispatch and followed the quotation with a signed statement categorically denying these false assertions and insinuations which had been widely carried in the press.[109] After reading many variations of this dispatch in different newspapers, Roe wrote Bob that he thought they were "all clearly libelous" and "probably sent by some one in Milwaukee who had it in for you."[110]

On November 3 Philipp defeated Blaine for governor and announced the following day that his victory was "a complete repudiation of the much-heralded Wisconsin idea."[111] An editorial in the *New York Times* commented that the Wisconsin election had "ended La Follette."[112] Although Roosevelt had endorsed Blaine, McGovern had refused to support him. In a letter to Roosevelt after the election, McGovern said that his own defeat for the United States Senatorship was due to the Blaine candidacy and La Follette's influence in persuading progressive Republicans to vote for Husting.[113]

Bob arrived in Washington the day after the election. Belle wrote Bob, Jr., that his father had "stood the strain almost better than we could expect," but that "his heart is sad and heavy. Of course nothing could ever make your papa believe that Wisconsin or the country is going to be always reactionary. He says one better die than lose faith. But the time ahead at best looks short to people of our age. It is a great comfort to feel that you children will be ready to do your part."[114] That same day Belle wrote Elizabeth Evans that *La Follette's Magazine* would be changed to a monthly beginning with the next issue and added, "When I suggested to Bob this morning that we quit it altogether he said, 'well if I do I will announce that I am going to quit politics altogether. It is all there is to depend on in Wisconsin.' "[115]

Two weeks later Bob began earning the money to meet the most pressing magazine debts by filling some of the lecture engagements he had under contract. While he was speaking in Texas, Illinois, Iowa, and Michigan, Belle remained in Washington with Phil and Mary, who were attending school there. Bob, Jr., had returned to the university. His father had been concerned over difficulties his son was having with some of his studies and had sent a set of postal cards with the request for brief daily reports which would put it "up to you each day *to look yourself in the face* and take stock of what you have *done that day*."[116] Before leaving for his speaking trip, he wrote Bob, Jr., recalling that "It is just forty one years today that I drove a farm team—hitched to a lumber wagon—loaded with cordwood—a cow tied behind from Primrose to Madison. It was one of our loads. We were moving so I could go to school and as soon as prepared—should enter the University. I was a little peaked but hardy country lad, brim full of ambition and grit. Think of hauling a load of wood 22 miles to save buying it. I sawed that wood—and milked that cow. I had four years of the hardest kind of work. That cold, snowy November day I never forgot nor the up-hill fight for five years to get through the University—yet it was nearly six. It seemed tough when I looked about and saw other boys having it easy nothing to do but get their lessons. But oh it was fine to *make myself* go over the rough road with a big burden on my back.

"You dont have to make yourself do outside things in order to buy wood and coal and clothing and supplies and pay house rent—but you have a chance to make yourself do your *job* and do it better than any man in your class. Do it so that the faculty, your class-mates, your fraternity will all have to say 'Bob La Follette is the ablest man in his year. He proves that the second generation can be better than the first' . . . I love you Bobbie and Im bound you shall be a *winner* on your *own* mettle. You are just getting into form. Keep it up . . . Yours always and always Dad."[117]

Later Bob, Jr., wrote his father that "Things are going all right here but I *miss* home   I miss you each one. I dont think I will ever be contented except at home   I miss politics and the big men that come to the house. I got more out of one conference with Mr. Brandeis and John Commons than I will ever get out of a years work in geology."[118] Although a protracted illness later prevented Bob, Jr., from completing his studies, the university subsequently granted him an honorary degree.

Bob delivered the final lecture of his trip on December 7, at Ann Arbor, Michigan, and reached Washington the following evening. At noon on December 8 the President read his message to a joint session of the Sixty-third Congress. During the preceding weeks prominent Republican leaders had been persistently attacking the Administration for its failure to put the Army and Navy on a war footing. Various organizations, including the Army and Navy League, had also been clamoring for a huge military program popularly known as "preparedness." Although the President began his address with a discussion of domestic legislation, it was evident that the European war was already creating difficult problems within our own economy. Among his recommendations were the establishment of a Federal shipping corporation with power to build and buy merchant ships for foreign trade and immediate confirmation by the Senate of the London Conference proposals for greater safety at sea, which later became a menace to the passage of the La Follette Seamen's bill.

Belle heard the message from the gallery of the House Chamber and undoubtedly reported her impressions to Bob that night when he reached home. With deep satisfaction she heard Wilson oppose the type of "preparedness" program demanded by his critics when he declared that we were "champions of peace and of concord" and that "We never have had, and while we retain our present principles and ideals we never shall have, a large standing army." In discussing our policy he advocated strengthening the National Guard, and stressed the point that we had always regarded a powerful Navy "as our proper and natural means of defense." But he said that anything more than this would mean "that we had lost our self-possession, that we had been thrown off our balance by a war with which we have nothing to do, whose causes can not touch us, whose very existence affords us opportunities of friendship and disinterested service which should make us ashamed of any thought of hostility or fearful preparation for trouble."[119] Belle thought that "a warmth and enthusiasm" and an exceptional "depth of affection" went out to the President from the audience. She noted that "His peace utterances met with a great wave of approval which found expression in tears as well as applause. However divergent the views may be of its policies, few will question that the Administration's ideals of Peace have kept us out of war."[120]

When Bob arrived that night from his speaking trip, he was "in good health and spirits." Everyone felt a remarkable change in him. The next day Belle went down to the Senate to see him take his seat again after his long absence. From the gallery she observed that "The Senators gave him a cordial welcome, except Gallinger, who did not speak to him."[121] Probably Gallinger had read Bob's editorial reviewing the Senator's long, reactionary record in detail and urging New Hampshire Progressives in all parties to unite in defeating him by electing Raymond B. Stevens, a progressive Democrat.[122]

During the Christmas holidays sorrow touched the La Follette home when Bob's twenty-six-year-old nephew, Billy La Follette, was stricken by Bright's disease. After the death of Bob's brother, William, his son had come on to Washington to make his home with his uncle. Billy's excellent mind, keen wit, and fine character had endeared him to every member of the family. Although he seemed to gain a little and came downstairs for a good part of Christmas day, the doctors considered his condition critical. Bob did everything possible to ease the last days of his nephew, whom he loved deeply. After the young man's death he wrote to the brothers and sister that "Billy knew he was very sick" and had "told Bobbie when they were alone that he doubted if he ever got out of this . . . He awoke out of a doze the morning he died . . . and called out to me: 'Uncle Bob, I'm afraid.' I was sitting by holding his hand. He wanted me by him a good deal of the time. I knew what was in his mind, sleeping and waking. I said to him, 'Billy, there is nothing you need fear. I think you are coming through all right.' (I had to tell him that, though I had about given up hope) 'But, Billy if you dont get well, there is nothing for you to be afraid of. You've lived a clean straight life. You've been honest and square. Don't be afraid Billy. You are all right; you're all right.'

"He dropped off to sleep again—and awoke soon calling out to me. 'Im all right, Uncle Bob; I'm all right.'

"And he is all right. Nothing can be more certain than that."[123]

Early in January Colonel House had indicated through Fred Howe that he would like to meet Gilbert Roe. An appointment was made, and for a half-hour the three men discussed people, policies, and politics in a general way. No special mention was made of Roe's possible appointment to the Federal Trade Commission, although his name had been suggested to the President by several people. That same day the colonel wrote the President that Roe had impressed him more strongly than anyone he had seen in connection with the Trade Commission; that he seemed a man of marked ability and that his name would be received with enthusiasm by both Progressives and progressive Republicans.[124]

The President invited Bob to call on him at the White House on the evening of January 12 after dinner. Immediately on his return home Bob wrote Roe saying: "This is graveyard to you and Netha. It is ten o'clock, and I have just come from an interview with the President. He sent for me, as I wrote you today, and I spent an hour with him. He said that he had two or three sets of men under consideration for the Trade Commission and he wanted to know about you. I cannot at this time go into detail nor is it necessary; indeed it probably would not tell you very much, even if I could fully. I am rushing to catch the last collection. Suffice it to say that you are most seriously under consideration beyond any question, and I hazard the opinion that you are in great danger of being struck by lightning.

"He also wanted to discuss with me matters of legislation, and urged me to come and talk with him about legislation from time to time without waiting to be called, as he believed we had much the same point of view and desires regarding service to the public.

"I conclude by saying that it looks good to me, and I think is likely to come to a head very soon."[125]

At the time Bob saw the President, Colonel House was a White House guest.[126] When the appointments to the Federal Trade Commission were given out, it was a great disappointment to Bob and Belle that Roe was not named.[127] Nevertheless, when Wilson appointed George Rublee to this post Bob vigorously supported his confirmation during the fight that developed against him.[128]

A few days before Bob had been invited to call at the White House, he had written Spreckels that "President Wilson has disappointed me in many ways. He has compromised with the System on legislation and on many appointments. The folly of such a course should have been so apparent as to have saved him from it. He can never have the help or confidence of the Special Interest crowd. They would be against him because he has tried to do some things for the public, and the man who lays hands on them at all is never forgiven. But, on the whole, Wilson has done some good things, and at least is entitled to the credit of having dealt with the subjects that his predecessors allowed the interests to run away with."[129]

The last week in January Bob wrote his son that although the Conference Committee was "doing a little work from time to time on the Seamen's Bill," all legislation was being held up by the filibuster on the ship-purchasing bill.[130] This measure, which Wilson had recommended in his message, provided funds for the government to buy and to build ships to carry our products to foreign ports. Its purpose was to replace in part the vessels that had been suddenly withdrawn from the sea because of the European War. The only ships available for immediate purchase were merchant vessels owned by German companies which had taken refuge in our harbors.

The filibuster against the bill was led by Republicans who argued that it was "socialistic" and that in purchasing ships owned by German companies the President might be leading us into war against Great Britain. Bob, who had long favored building up our merchant marine, supported the bill and denounced the attacks made upon Wilson by prominent Republican Senators. In a signed editorial he declared that the same Senators who had recently arraigned the President for his Mexican policy of "watchful waiting" were now trying to make "the country believe that back under cover, behind this bill, the President has some dark and sinister plan to force a war with the Allies." Bob quoted from the President's plea that the United States "be neutral in fact as well as in name," and said: "Wilson will not plunge this country into war. At the head of the nation that stands for peace, he has guarded our neutrality with noble care." Bob took the position that for more than a century the United States had maintained the doctrine that a neutral nation had the right to buy merchant vessels just as it had the right to buy merchandise from the citizens of any country in time of war as in time of peace. Since this right of a neutral nation had been sustained by the opinions of the ablest jurists and an unbroken line of decisions in our courts, Bob thought it should not be surrendered now.[131]

Powerful private shipping interests were opposing the bill through every medium at their command. Although the filibuster had been initiated by Republicans, party lines broke down later in the debate. A Democratic Senator, Hitchcock of Nebraska, offered an amendment placing an embargo on the shipment of arms and ammunition for which Bob voted. It was defeated by 51 to 36, although it had been supported by fourteen Administration Democrats, all the progressive Republicans, and Senator Gallinger, the Republican minority leader. Bob also offered an amendment designed to restrict the term of lease of vessels acquired by the Shipping Board and to give it power to fix rates.[132] It was reported that this amendment embodied the kind of compromise which had been considered at a White House conference.[133]

The next day Belle wrote Bob, Jr., that his father was "conferring with the White House and other democratic brethren on the shipping bill." She added: "Every little while your papa jokingly refers to his being read out of the party and I think he realizes that something may be sprung on him in that nature. It may work out that he will have to be an 'independent.' "[134] On a crucial test vote Bob was the only Republican who joined the Administration Democrats in voting against abandoning the bill.[135] But the filibuster nevertheless prevented it from coming to a final vote.

Bob offered a resolution on February 8 which he hoped would contribute toward the President's purpose of maintaining our neutrality and help toward an early peace. It became known as the La Follette Peace Resolution because it called for a conference of neutral nations to seek an "early cessation of hostilities" in Europe by issuing a joint offer of mediation to the warring nations. Bob thought such a conference would be a practical step toward protecting neutral rights, limiting the region of warfare and hastening the return of peace. But he went beyond these immediate objectives and sought to establish more permanent international cooperation. His resolution suggested that the conference consider rules for limiting armaments and nationalizing the manufacture of military and naval equipment, as well as the regulation of exports of war supplies from one country to another. It called for the ultimate establishment of an international tribunal to pass upon international disputes and proposed that the conference consider plans for a federation of neutral nations to safeguard the peace of the world.[136]

The resolution immediately received wide newspaper attention. From New York Roe sent Bob two clippings with a note saying the "editorial is unusually friendly to you for the Sun and the Sun of last night and this morning both carried a copy of your peace resolution in full."[137] This editorial commented that the resolution "deserves in its general intention and scope the sympathy and support of every American—of every neutral . . . A congress of Neutrals for the benefit of the rights of neutrals and for peace, if peace can be made: what well-founded objection lies to such a body for such a task?"[138] The Baltimore *Sun* said it had "much to commend it, not only as a general proposition, but as an immediate need."[139] The New York *Evening Post* described it as "a move in the right direction" that would show what power we still believe to reside in moral forces."[140] In a brief speech for the resolution Bob said, "Mediation has well been called 'applied brotherhood,' " and he therefore maintained that "The neutrality of the United States can not and should not be that of selfish indifference." A conference of neutrals was important because the situation was "filled with menace. Who can say at what moment the dark curtain that veils so much of the struggle may be swept aside by uncontrolled forces that will fasten upon the peaceful nations and draw the whole world into the vortex of war?" In concluding he said it would be "folly to pretend that the mere calling of the proposed conference will end hostilities. But it is little short of an international crime for Congress to withhold from the President the authority and the necessary appropriation enabling him" to "aid in bringing peace to the nations now at war. We can no longer avoid our responsibility. The balance of the world at peace awaits on this Government."[141]

Many of the President's admirers thought this plan would appeal to his imagination since it was in accord with his plea for neutrality, his lofty ideal of service to humanity, and his offer of mediation. But he was adamant when approached on the subject. The resolution was referred to the Foreign Relations Committee, where there was no hope of action without the President's approval. Bob always believed that a conference such as he had proposed offered one of

the greatest opportunities that could come in all history to a man
possessing the supreme power Wilson then had.[142]

Throughout this long session Bob and Furuseth had worked persistently to get a satisfactory Seamen's bill through Congress. On
the last day they learned that Furuseth's long, uncompromising devotion to freeing the sailors from involuntary servitude and protecting
the safety of travelers at sea had been rewarded by victory. But
in all the disheartening years of the long fight, Furuseth had, as
Bob wrote, "so effaced himself that the public had little opportunity
to know the man. Even the measure that represents his great life
work, the Seamen's Act, bears, by Congressional usage, not the name
of Furuseth, but of—La Follette!"[143]

CHAPTER XXXVIII

The La Follette Seamen's Law

Andrew Furuseth, president of the Seamen's Union, first came to see Bob in December, 1909, with a letter of introduction from Francis J. Heney. Later, in an editorial, Bob drew a vivid picture of the "tall, bony, slightly stooped man, with a face bespeaking superior intelligence and lofty character," who called that day because he "wanted to interest me in the cause of the American sailor. He was a sailor himself, he said, and he wanted to 'be free.' I did not know what he meant. I questioned him. Surely there were no slaves under the American flag. Bondsmen there were,—but Lincoln changed all that. And it had been written in the amended Constitution. 'Yes,' he said, 'but not for the sailor. All other men are free. But when the amendments were framed, they passed us by. The sailor was forgotten.'

"I asked him to tell me about it. Sitting on the edge of the chair, his body thrust forward, a great soul speaking through his face, the set purpose of his life shining in his eyes, he told me the story of the sailor's wrongs. He said little of himself, excepting as I drew him on to speak of the long, long struggle of which he was the beginning . . . He spoke with a strong Scandinavian accent, but with remarkable facility of expression, force and discrimination.

"He knew the maritime law of every country; the social condition, the wage level, the economic life of each sea-faring nation. He was master of his subject . . . He was logical, rugged, terse, quaint, and fervid with conviction.

"Born in Norway, the call of the sea came to him as a lad of sixteen. He stood upon the cliffs and looked out upon the infinite. The life of the sailor, like the ocean, must be wide and free. He felt its mysterious spell. He would be a 'free seaman,' with all the world an open door. . . .

521

"His dream was shattered early by the hard realities of life before the mast. First in the boats of Norway and later on the decks of the merchant marine of every great maritime nation he served as a seaman, and everywhere conditions were the same. He found himself a common chattel! He was owned by the master of the ship!

" 'I saw men abused,' he said, 'beaten into insensibility. I saw sailors try to escape from brutal masters, and from unseaworthy vessels upon which they had been lured to serve. I saw them hunted down and thrown into the ship's hold in chains. I know the bitterness of it all from experience.'

"He had seen over-insured and undermanned ships go down at sea, with appalling loss of human life, all because greedy owners would not furnish skilled seamen to sail them, or provide lifeboats for passengers and crew." Furuseth "would not submit to slavery. He could not abandon his beloved sea-calling."[1]

He studied the history of the sea and found out that the seamen of northern Europe had at one time been the freest of all workers but that when land laborers were freed from the soil the sailors had continued to be bound to the ship. For six centuries admiralty courts, laws, and treaties had confirmed the sailor's status of a chattel. They were bondmen, and the master of the ship was absolute master of the seamen. He deliberately planned to get one great nation to provide by law a haven where seamen could escape tyranny and maltreatment aboard ship. One country where a sailor could lawfully leave his ship would serve to elevate the condition of labor at sea throughout the world. Furuseth selected the United States as his battle ground, and in parts of the Pacific coast he helped organize the International Seamen's Union.[2]

From San Francisco he came to Washington, where he lived for fifteen years in shacks and sailors' boardinghouses, refusing to accept more than seaman's pay. In the corridors of the Capitol, the committee rooms, about the hotels and streets of Washington, wherever he went, he carried his appeal for freedom. As Bob worked with Furuseth he found this Viking seaman's "whole personality was articulate with the cry for justice that would not be denied. Beaten again and again, like all leaders who win final victories, he was only stimulated to better fighting by defeat."[3] It was inevitable that the human elements in such a cause should appeal to Bob and lead to an enduring friendship between the two men, which the family shared. Almost every Sunday, from the time of their first meeting, "Andy" came to the La Follette home for breakfast throughout the long struggle to put through the Seamen's law.

During one of their intimate talks Bob touched upon Furuseth's future and asked, " 'When you can no longer work, what provision have you for old age? . . . How much have you been able to lay up against failing power?' His keen eye mellowed and a placid contemplative expression smoothed out the seams of his weather beaten face as he said, 'When my work is finished, I hope to be finished. I have no provision against old age; and I shall borrow no fears from time.' "[4]

Long before Bob was elected to the Senate, Furuseth had been haunting the halls of Congress urging legislation to protect the seamen. He had helped to secure passage of the Maguire Act in 1895 and the White Act in 1898. This legislation had improved conditions, and had given American sailors the legal right to quit their ships in United States ports. But in reality this country had continued through its commercial treaties with many nations to sanction the binding of sailors to their ships. From 1898 to 1904 Furuseth had steadily led the fight to perfect further domestic legislation and to "realize the goal of freedom for seamen of all nations."[5] Although improvements were secured, the over-all legislation Furuseth desired was first introduced by Bob in 1910 and again in 1911.[6] But the opposition was so powerful that Furuseth and Bob could not force action on these bills.

In April, 1912, the country was shocked by a disaster at sea when a luxurious White Star ship, carrying many internationally famous passengers, went down after striking an iceberg. The terrible loss of life on the *Titanic* was due largely to inadequate safety provisions. In an editorial comment on this disaster Bob said, "Every soul on board would have been saved had there been a sufficient number of life boats and a sufficient number of able seamen to launch and man such boats. Two hours elapsed between the time of the collision with the iceberg and the sinking of the vessel. The sea was smooth as glass. Not a life need have been lost."[7] There were 2,201 people on the *Titanic* of whom 885 were crew. The ship had some rafts and collapsible lifeboats. But it had only some 14 standard lifeboats, each capable of carrying 65 persons, that is, less than half the people on board. These facts so shocked people that an International Conference for Safety at Sea was called to meet in London. On May 12 an excellent Seamen's bill was introduced in the House by Representative William B. Wilson, who had worked closely with Furuseth in behalf of the seamen's cause. Later he became Secretary of Labor in President Wilson's Cabinet. The recent *Titanic* disaster made it impossible for the opposition to bottle up this bill in committee. After prolonged debate it passed the House on August 3, 1912, and went to the Senate, where it was held in the committee for nearly eight months.[8]

Bob repeatedly protested this delay. Finally he threatened a few days before the automatic adjournment of March 4, 1913, to hold up the appropriation bills unless the Senate acted upon the Seamen's bill.[9] This warning forced the committee to report the bill. Bob blocked Senator Knute Nelson's attempt to delay consideration and forced an agreement for a vote on March 2. When he finally succeeded in getting the floor, however, there was little time left to debate the bill, which Senator Burton had managed to change in committee so that the essential purposes of Representative Wilson's bill as passed by the House were actually defeated.

During the bitter debate that followed, Bob clashed continually with Nelson and Burton. He succeeded in placing in the *Congressional Record* the specific pledges of both the Republican and Democratic 1912 platforms for legislation to protect life at sea and to free seamen from involuntary servitude. Bob also offered amendments to restore the original provisions to the House bill. Two of five were adopted by roll-call votes. But the bill passed the Senate practically as reported from the committee.[10] An equally unsatisfactory conference report was sent to President Taft, who refused to sign it forty minutes before he quit office. Bob and Furuseth were greatly relieved because they thought its most important provisions were "less acceptable to seamen than the harsh terms of the existing law."[11]

Ten days later, when Bob had talked with Wilson on the evening of March 14, the President had assured him that the Seamen's bill would have his sympathetic support. On April 7, the first day of the special session called by Wilson, Bob had introduced his Seamen's bill. A portion of it was substantially in the form of the bill that had passed the House in August, 1912. But new clauses had been added covering safety provisions which were Bob's special contribution.[12]

On June 26, Furuseth sent the President an eight-page typewritten analysis of the bills which had been offered by Nelson and Burton in the Senate, and by Representative J. W. Alexander in the House.[13] The only bill that had Furuseth's support was the La Follette bill. Wilson replied that he appreciated the deep significance of the seamen's cause and pledged his support in every way possible.[14] It was therefore a bitter disappointment to Furuseth and Bob when the Senate Committee on Commerce favorably recommended the Nelson bill on October 2, 1913. Although nominally under the authorship of Senator Nelson, the bill was modeled on the previous Burton bill and practically identical with the one Taft had refused to sign.[15] Nelson had long been in political alliance with James J. Hill, whose vast railroad interests were bound up with the ship companies operating at sea and on the Great Lakes. If the bill became a law, Bob said "it would enable Hill to continue to supplant American seamen with Chinese on his Oriental lines."[16] In reporting the Nelson bill the committee also recommended that no final action should be taken on it until the results of the International Conference for Safety at Sea were known. Although it would not have altered Bob's strategy, he apparently did not know that this desire to postpone action until after the conference, which would not convene until November 12, was shared by the President and Secretary of Commerce Redfield.[17]

When the bill was reported, the Vice President followed the committee's recommendation and announced that it would go on the calendar and be "postponed until the regular session of Congress." Bob promptly objected to "the bill being laid aside for the session," and it then went on the calendar to be taken up in regular order. Furuseth was, as Bob wrote to a friend, "down the banks" and "ready for the first time to quit and go home," although "I have assured him for months that the Seamen's bill could pass this session."[18] On October 7 Bob took advantage of a lapse in the desultory debate and moved to proceed to consideration of the Nelson bill. The motion carried, and the bill thus became the unfinished business.[19] That night Bob explained his strategy in a letter to Bob, Jr., saying: "This will bring it up automatically every day there is a session at two o'clock and at least gives us a *show* to get something through this session. It will impose some additional work on me—but it is 'good work' in more than one sense. I have not seen Furuseth since it happened but know he will feel pretty good over it."[20]

Two days later, when the bill came up, Bob saw there were many empty seats and noted that the Senators he confidentially described as "the 'objectors' who serve the steamship companies" were absent. Seizing this strategic moment, he secured unanimous consent that consideration of the Nelson bill should begin on October 16 and that it should be voted upon not later than four o'clock on October 23. This parliamentary victory prepared the way for Bob's next move. Now that the date for a vote was definitely set, he could safely carry out his plan to substitute his bill "for the bad one which the Senate committee reported."[21] Belle wrote Bob, Jr., "It makes this life seem worth all the strain if something like this goes through that is a real service to humanity."[22]

The day that Bob won this victory another terrible sea tragedy occurred. When the *Volturno* burned and sank off the coast of Newfoundland, 136 passengers perished. The newspaper reports convinced Bob that precise information about the disaster would prove valuable as evidence of the need for the safety legislation provided in the La Follette Seamen's bill. He immediately asked Furuseth to have someone waiting in New York to see any of the rescued people who landed there to "ascertain the conditions upon the Volturno, the sort of seamanship there was there, and particularly to interview any of the sailors, if any would be willing to give statements."[23]

On October 16 Bob gave formal notice that he would offer the La Follette bill in the form of an amendment as a substitute for the Nelson bill.[24] Burton protested and urged that no final action be taken until after the International Conference for Safety at Sea.[25] Bob thought this argument was merely strategy for delay in the expectation that the recommendations of the conference could be used against the La Follette bill. Furuseth, who had been appointed as a delegate by the President, had astutely warned Wilson that no help would come to the seamen from the London Conference because "The ship owners of Europe and the United States will take care of that."[26]

Bob's substitute bill directly challenged the world-wide system of involuntary servitude. Under it an American sailor could leave his ship in a foreign "safe port" (one where cargo is taken on or discharged) ; and a foreign sailor could leave his ship in a like American port. He was also given the right to demand half his earned wages when he quit. A standard of efficiency was set up with decent living conditions on board ship. It provided greater safety for crew and passengers. As finally perfected during the debate, it required that all vessels at sea and on the Great Lakes, above a certain tonnage, should be equipped with a sufficient number of seaworthy lifeboats to carry at one time every passenger and every member of the crew. Each lifeboat had to be manned by at least two men with the rating of "able seamen" or higher, who were trained in lowering and handling lifeboats. The bill also directed the termination upon due notice of any existing treaties which might conflict with its provisions.[27]

When the formal debate was about to begin on October 21, an early roll call showed the absence of a quorum, which, if continued, might be used to prevent the vote on the bill, set for October 23. The next day Bob and several other Senators censured the absentees. After another roll call revealed that a quorum was still lacking, Bob moved that the Sergeant at Arms be directed to notify "all absent Senators to return immediately and attend upon the sessions of the Senate." A quorum was thus obtained and a possible danger averted.[28]

The opposition to the La Follette bill was again led by Senator Theodore Burton, who had in both branches of Congress presented the arguments of the shipowners and opposed legislation desired by Furuseth and the Seamen's Union. Burton was an able lawyer and a resourceful, adroit debater. Among those who conspicuously enlisted on Bob's side were Senators Harry Lane, John Sharp Williams, Morris Sheppard, and George Sutherland, later Justice of the Supreme Court, who all rendered valuable assistance on the floor and behind the scenes. But the opposing forces were personalized in the duel that developed during the debate between Burton and Bob.

Bob analyzed his substitute measure and contrasted it with the Nelson bill which Burton was supporting: "Of course," Bob said, "I am a landlubber and have to take my tutelage from those men who have been at sea. I never shall be able to express my very great obligation to Andrew Furuseth, who for the last four years has called upon me almost every Sunday morning to talk with me about this legislation." Describing Furuseth as "one of the most intelligent men it has ever been my good fortune to meet," Bob pointed to the gallery as he said, "For 19 years he has been sitting up there in that corner of the gallery waiting to be made free. Whatever I happen to know about this subject I have acquired from talking with him." To illustrate what would happen in an "hour of supreme danger" during a storm when the man on the bridge had to give orders, through interpreters, to lower and handle the lifeboats, Bob contrasted such a situation under the stringent requirements of his bill and the Nelson bill. Just think of it, he said, "in a lifeboat, perhaps one into which, say, your daughter or your son is to go, you can not go with them; the conditions may be such that they must go alone, with the fury of an ocean storm all about them, with the vessel every moment settling lower and lower; they must go over the side into a lifeboat in the crew of which there is a Turk, a Chinese, a Jap, a Greek, a Negro from South Africa, a Hungarian, and an Arabian." Under the committee bill there will be two men who are not "able seamen, not men experienced at sea, but men who have passed the drills; one man in the boat who can interpret between the commanding officer and all the languages represented there. Some of them may understand, to some of them it may be gibberish, for all the interpreter has to do is to pass the scrutiny of the inspector." And Bob asked if you "had a boat of that kind on one side of the vessel," and on the other side there was a boat "manned by two able seamen, two men who had had three years at sea, and a crew who understood the language of the officers," which would you prefer? . . .

"You can lower away a boat in a very high gale, and if you strike the water at just the time that judgment and experience and intelligence will tell you is a proper moment, you drop it in a comparative calm; you drop it at a time when you catch the wash just right, and the boat does not crash against the side of the vessel and crumple like an eggshell; she goes where she should go; she gets away. . . . You have to look the sea in the face to know it; you have to study the sea and the sky together to know the sea; you have to observe the sea in all her moods . . . to know how to grapple and wrestle with and overcome her." The facts Furuseth had gathered regarding the recent *Volturno* disaster were now effectively used by Bob in answering Burton. The report of survivors showed that the loss of life had been largely due to lack of efficient men to handle the lifeboats. The ship carried only eight able seamen. Therefore the handling of the nineteen lifeboats and their passengers had been left to the steward's department consisting of men with "hardly any experience at all, and unable to speak and understand the English language." The only lifeboat that got away was in charge of the second mate. It was manned by two able seamen, precisely the crew specifically required by the La Follette Seamen's bill for each lifeboat aboard a ship.[29]

On the final day of the debate it took an hour to get a quorum. Bob wrote that the lobby opposing the bill "was on hand in big force" and that telegrams were pouring in from "Boards of Trade and Chambers of Commerce and big shippers."[30] Senators were bombarded with pleas to delay action until after the London Conference. Burton had held the floor for over seven hours of the limited time allowed for debate. He had clashed repeatedly with Bob and Lane of Oregon, who had eloquently supported the La Follette bill with testimony out of his own experience as a seaman on the Pacific Ocean.[31] In the last hours before the time set for the vote, Bob discussed the provisions of his substitute, which he said Burton had from the beginning of the debate "misstated, distorted and misrepresented." When Bob had called the Senators' attention to where Furuseth was sitting, he had also noted the representatives of the Great Lakes shipping interests and had referred to them in "blistering terms" as "the lobby in the gallery."[32] The close allies of this visible "lobby in the gallery" were, he said, the great shipowning corporations not only of this country but all those whose commerce came to our shores.

Before tracing the history of the legislation affecting the status of the American sailor since 1790, Bob said: "I place above and before any bill which merely concerns business interests and property rights this measure which involves the rights of thousands of men to be free men . . . the safety of the lives of hundreds of thousands of men, women and children. . . . The attempt to secure legislation for the emancipation of the sailors from serfdom and the safety of human life at sea repeats the history of every attempt to secure legislation against organized corporate power, no matter how urgent the need." He then recalled the forty years' opposition of bankers to postal savings, of the express companies for a quarter of a century to parcel post, of the seventeen years' effort before even an adequate pure-food law could be passed, and the long fight Bob had made to force the railroads to adopt safety devices and to ascertain and enforce reasonable freight and transportation costs. "We now come," Bob declared, "to another test of corporate power arrayed against human rights."[33]

During the debate Bob incorporated in his bill perfecting amendments which he thought greatly strengthened its safety provisions.[34] All opposition amendments were voted down, one of Burton's by 36 to 12 and another by Bacon, against the abrogation of any treaty provision, by 33 to 15. Late in the afternoon of October 23, 1913, the La Follette Seamen's bill, with its perfecting amendments, was agreed to without a roll-call vote.[35]

Bob wrote Belle, who was in Boston speaking for suffrage: "Yesterday was really one of my best days in the Senate. That is, it brought probably the best results which I have achieved since I came here—the railroad valuation bill excepted—and on the human side it is far and away ahead of all else. I speak of it as my achievement. Of course, I would never have gotten into it far enough to have it seize hold upon me if it hadn't been for Furuseth. . . . We all felt good. Gompers sent Holder around to 'hug' me. Many telegrams have come from sailors' associations today expressing appreciation. Poor fellows—it is a keen satisfaction to have been able to help them."[36]

Among the many messages Bob received was a treasured longhand letter from Andrew Furuseth, who said, "permit me to thank you for myself and for those whom I more intimately represent." Of the 1,693,000 seamen and coast fishermen in the Caucasian world, "not one of these yet in early manhood, but will be profoundly affected and benefited in his daily life through your bill, when it shall become law . . . They are following the strugle [*sic*] with bated breath: they know of your victory . . . and their hearts are full of gratitude, which like myself they know not how to express. From the depth of my soul, thank you. May God bless and keep you and yours."[37]

The day after the bill passed, Bob wrote Bob, Jr.: "You should have seen Furuseth. Phil had taken him into the Senators' gallery for the finish. I held the floor for nearly an hour at the end & the opposition who have beaten him for 19 years got what was coming to them. I spared no one and gave Furuseth credit for the long fight. When the bill passed—He sprang up ran out of the gallery into the upper corridor, crying out: 'This finishes the work Lincoln began.' Tears were running down his cheeks. He put his hands to his throat saying: 'I am choking, I am so happy.' "[38]

Although Bob rejoiced in winning this first battle, he knew that the passage of the bill by the Senate did not assure final victory. He wrote Bob, Jr., "there is still work to be done to beat the steamship co[mpanie]s who will now transfer their fight to the House to try & kill it or hold it up there."[39] In an editorial for the next issue of his magazine he charged that "the great shipping combinations" were "rushing their trained lobby agents to Washington to block it in the House of Representatives." He predicted, "The onset on the House will be a thing, the like of which has not been witnessed in years. DELAY! DELAY ON EVERY PRETEXT WILL BE THEIR FIRST METHOD OF ATTACK! They will argue that it will disturb treaty relations with foreign nations; that it will impose too great hardship on the smaller water transportation lines, anything, everything to gain time to bring pressure to bear upon members of the House."[40]

Bob's prediction proved correct. The bill was held in the House committee for many months, during which *La Follette's Magazine* kept up a barrage of editorials and articles, including a series of letters by Furuseth refuting attacks on different specific provisions of the bill.[41] As Bob had foreseen, the pretexts for delay echoed Burton's arguments in the Senate that no action should be taken until after the London Conference. When that issue ceased to be pertinent, the opposition subtly and successfully prolonged the delay by persuading influential men in high places that passage of the bill would endanger treaty relations with foreign nations.

Less than six weeks after the bill passed the Senate, the President delivered a message to Congress on December 2, 1913. He noted that questions of safety at sea were then under discussion in London and told Congress that as soon as the conclusions of this convention were known we ought to address ourselves "to the prompt alleviation of the very unsafe, unjust and burdensome conditions which now surround the employment of sailors. . ."[42] Although Furuseth had little hope that the sailors would receive help from this conference, he had gone abroad as one of the American delegates appointed by Wilson. It remained in session from November 12, 1913, to January 12, 1914. But when it adopted recommendations which were below the safety standards of the La Follette bill, Furuseth became convinced that the convention "was packed in the interest of the ship owners."[43] He cabled his resignation to the President on December 22, 1913, returned to Washington, and on January 12, 1914, sent him a critical analysis of the proposed recommendations.[44]

On March 17 Wilson transmitted to the Senate an authenticated copy of the proceedings of the International Convention for Safety at Sea, as signed in London on January 20, 1914, with its regulations, final protocol, and *voeux* to "receive the advice and consent of the Senate to ratification." This was printed, with Furuseth's adverse report to the President, as a confidential Senate document. Secretary Bryan urged early consideration as it had to be ratified before December 31, 1914.[45] After reading the recommendations of the London Convention, Bob agreed with Furuseth that they were "all the steamship companies could desire."[46]

For months the Senate took no action on the recommendations of the London Convention for Safety at Sea, which now had the status of a treaty waiting for ratification. Meanwhile the La Follette Seamen's bill languished in the House with only an occasional spark of life. Furuseth kept in close touch with Bob, who advised him on strategy.[47] The House finally passed it on August 27, 1914, with amendments proposed by Representative J. W. Alexander.[48] It then went to a Conference Committee composed of Members of both Houses. During the months that it lingered there, Bob and Furuseth were anxious as to what might happen behind the doors of the committee room because a conference report can not be amended.[49]

In December, 1914, while the bill was still in conference, the Senate took up in executive sessions the London Convention recommendations, which Great Britain and Germany had already ratified. John Sharp Williams presented an amendment which embodied Furuseth's suggestions. The amendment reserved the right of this country to impose upon vessels in the waters of the United States such higher standards for safety and protection of seamen and passengers as the United States "shall enact for vessels of the United States." Thus, even if the Senate ratified the London agreement, the Williams amendment left the way open for enactment of the La Follette bill, which had higher standards. The Senate adopted the amendment by 49 to 20. The proceedings of the executive sessions were not printed in the *Congressional Record*, but the *New York Times* reported that the London Convention for Safety at Sea was ratified with the amendment on December 16. The dispatch interpreted the overwhelming vote for the amendment as meaning the La Follette Seamen's bill would be pressed at an early date.[50]

The Seamen's bill was finally reported out from the Conference Committee on February 22, 1915, and as printed in the *Congressional Record* it filled sixteen columns.[51] Fifteen months had elapsed since the Senate had passed the La Follette bill on October 23, 1913. Now only a few critical days remained before Congress automatically adjourned on March 4. Unless passed by both Houses and signed by the President before noon on that date, the bill would die, and Furuseth would have to begin his long fight all over again. Bob was disappointed in certain aspects of the bill as it came from the conference, but the report could not be amended. Belle wrote Bob, Jr.: "It is pretty good for the sailors, but weak on safety provisions. Still it is an improvement on no provisions at all and papa will support it on that ground. I hope it goes through."[52]

The House approved the conference report without a record vote.[53] In the Senate, however, it was opposed by Root, Lodge, Burton, and Smith of Georgia. Bob did not enter the debate while they were attacking it. On February 27 the Senate accepted the bill without a record vote.[54] But Smith then made a last-minute effort to defeat it by moving to have the vote "reconsidered." Sensing the danger of this maneuver, Bob took the floor to defend the bill. He moved to table Smith's motion to "reconsider" and warned Senators that if debate were prolonged it would not only jeopardize the Seamen's bill but also appropriation bills, thus forcing an extra session. Bob's motion passed by the narrow margin of 39 to 33, with 24 Senators not voting.[55] This disposed of all efforts to prolong debate and prevented another vote. Only the President's signature was now needed to complete enactment of the Seamen's bill.

From the time Bob had first talked with the President about the

Seamen's bill, there had been no doubt that Wilson favored the humanitarian aspects of this legislation. But Bob had reason to believe there was now grave danger that the President might not sign the bill.[56] It was known that Great Britain, Germany, and other nations with which the United States had commercial treaties had filed protests against the measure with the State Department. Since the outbreak of the European War, repeated violations of our neutral rights by Germany and Great Britain had made our diplomatic relations with both countries increasingly difficult. Bob feared that Wilson might therefore be persuaded by the arguments of the opposition that the enactment of the Seamen's bill would disturb existing treaties and cause disorder in our commercial relations with grave consequences.

The day the Senate agreed to the conference report Bob telephoned the White House. He asked the President's secretary, Joseph P. Tumulty, to request an opportunity to be heard in case the President had any intention of vetoing the measure. Tumulty recommended the appointment, which was arranged for March 1, but subsequently postponed until the evening of March 2.[57] Furuseth wrote the President on March 1, recalling Wilson's previous expressions of "kindly sympathy with the efforts being made to improve the condition of seamen" and persuasively answering out of his own experience an apprehension the President had expressed, regarding possible international complications, during an interview with the Executive Board of the American Federation of Labor.[58]

Meanwhile Bob decided to try to clear up any apprehension that might be lurking in the State Department regarding the effect of the Seamen's bill on existing treaties. On the afternoon of the day he was to see the President, he went with Senator Robert L. Owen and Furuseth to call upon Secretary of State Bryan. But Bryan sent them to Robert Lansing, then Counselor to the State Department. In writing of this visit Bob said, "We felt that Lansing was distinctly unfriendly and, after a brief talk with him, we returned to Bryan, telling him he would have to hear us." Each of the three men presented his arguments, and it seemed to Bob that Bryan was deeply touched by Furuseth's appeal.[59] Although the Secretary of State was impressed with their arguments for the bill on its merits, he nevertheless shared Lansing's apprehension regarding the treaties. When they left, Bryan wrote the President, suggesting how

Wilson might tactfully veto the bill or postpone operation of it until after the war, when circumstances would be more favorable.[60]

After seeing Bryan, Bob returned to the Senate until it was time to go to the White House. Although the appointment had been requested only for himself, he decided to take Furuseth with him. When they arrived at eight o'clock, Bob asked Wilson if he would be willing to hear Furuseth for ten minutes. Gilbert Roe's recollection of Bob's own account of the interview records that "Andy went down on his knees to the President. He begged him to make him a freeman who had a right to walk the streets and live his life as other citizens did, which right he did not have as a seaman." Bob said, "Wilson was moved by this appeal as he had never seen him moved on any other occasion." When Furuseth was asked years later what happened that night, he replied: "I can't remember what I said or did. That doesn't matter. It was La Follette's job. I was very much stirred up. I was all aflame . . . The President asked me some questions and I answered them. There were tears in La Follette's eyes. He was awfully moved . . . Then I was dismissed from the room. I was told to wait until the Senator came out. He was in there for twenty minutes or more."[61]

When Bob left the White House to return to the Senate, he knew Wilson had been deeply moved by Furuseth's plea, but he was uncertain whether they had succeeded in overcoming the grave apprehension the President had expressed regarding the treaties. Therefore he decided to make one further suggestion which he hoped would appeal to the President as removing "every possible risk of foreign complications." In his letter to Wilson Bob pledged that if, during the next Congress, additional time should be needed to adjust all differences with the nations concerned, he would "aid to the uttermost in passing a joint resolution extending the time limit on the treaties."[62]

Bob remained at the Capitol throughout the night. Except for a few hours' recess, the Senate was in continuous session until adjournment at noon on March 4. Bob entered the debate on the Indian appropriation bill and succeeded in getting through an important amendment in behalf of the Indians. While the Senate was in session, he was called to the telephone by the President's secretary. Tumulty told Bob that the President had telephoned him saying: "Tumulty, I have just experienced a great half-hour, the tensest since I came to the White House. That man La Follette pushed me over tonight on the Seamen's bill."[63]

At ten o'clock on the morning of March 4, the President came to his room in the Capitol near the Senate Chamber. While he was signing the bills that had passed during the night, Senators came in to greet him. As Bob shook hands with him, Wilson "leaned close and whispered, 'It's all right. I think you will be satisfied.' "[64]

Shortly after Bob told Belle of the President's whispered message she wrote Bob, Jr.: "Your papa has just come home from the Senate which adjourned at twelve o'clock without turning back the clock. One great big victory has been won—the Seamen's Bill is signed. It had a narrow escape. I think it was your papa's presentation to the President that persuaded him, and convinced him that any fears he might have as to international complications should not stand in the way. You can imagine how Furuseth feels."[65]

CHAPTER XXXIX

"We Have Ceased to 'Be Neutral in Fact as Well as in Name'"

Two weeks after the Sixty-third Congress adjourned on March 4, 1915, Bob left Washington on a speaking trip which took him into Pennsylvania, Iowa, Michigan, Minnesota, and North and South Dakota. On his way to Dakota he stopped off in Madison and was alarmed to find that Bob, Jr., was ill with a streptococcic infection which had developed after an attack of tonsillitis. Dr. Evans and the other physicians decided that Bob, Jr., ought to return with his father, and they arrived in Washington on April 12. Although Bob, Jr., improved at first, the infection flared up again later and he remained critically ill throughout the summer.

Soon after Bob returned to Washington, he received a six-page typewritten letter from Secretary Bryan with several enclosures. Bryan expressed appreciation for the word he had received that Bob was planning to write an editorial answering the barrage of criticism directed against the Secretary during recent months. Bryan mentioned certain facts which might be stressed, and emphasized that in dealing with the overwhelming international problems confronting the Wilson Administration there had been no differences of opinion among the President, Lansing, and himself in preparing the State Papers. He also suggested that the editorial should stress the great difficulty of maintaining neutrality as between the belligerents in Europe because of the numerous instances which had arisen requiring prompt consideration and decision.[1]

Bryan and Bob believed that the observance of strict neutrality as between the belligerents was a first essential in preventing the United States from being drawn into the European War. But in-

creasing violations of neutral rights had made them both apprehensive lest some disaster might occur which would inflame public
opinion.[2] For months American shipping interests had been angered
by the British violations, which had gone so far as to prevent access
of American ships to neutral ports with neutral cargoes. Our protests had proved ineffectual, and indignation had steadily increased.
In retaliation against the British attempt to prevent both contraband and noncontraband goods from entering Germany, the German
Government announced on February 4 the establishment of a war
zone in the waters surrounding the British Isles and proclaimed the
use of submarine warfare against all enemy merchant vessels found
in those waters after February 18.[3] The nature of the submarine
made it practically impossible to observe the established principles
of first ascertaining by visit and search the belligerent nationality
of the vessel and the contraband character of its cargo and then
ensuring the safety of passengers and crew before destroying the
ship. Therefore this announcement contained a menace to neutral
cargoes and neutral passengers on enemy ships. Furthermore, if
the British used neutral flags as a ruse of war, then neutral vessels
might be mistaken for belligerents in disguise.

The day after the German announcement, the captain of the
British merchant vessel *Lusitania* ordered the American flag hoisted
as the ship approached the Irish coast. The use of a neutral flag in
the war zone caused great excitement on the ship. Among the
passengers was Colonel House, who had undertaken the first of his
many confidential missions as the President's personal representative. The colonel recorded in his diary that on his arrival reporters
from every newspaper in London questioned him about the British
captain's hoisting of the American flag but that fortunately he had
not been an eyewitness and was able to say he knew of it only
from hearsay.[4] On February 10 the United States protested to Great
Britain against this use of the American flag,[5] and on that same
day notified Germany that the German Government would be held
to "a strict accountability" for acts against American citizens and
their vessels.[6] In the Senate two days later Bob, while urging passage
of his resolution calling for a conference of neutral nations, had
declared that the safeguards of peace demanded a clearer definition
of neutral rights under modern conditions and that delay was "filled
with menace."[7] Seeking to eliminate these increasing menaces to

neutral rights, the United States sent identical notes on February 20 to Germany and Great Britain. These notes suggested that the two countries agree to abandon the use of floating mines, the use of submarines to attack merchant vessels, the use of neutral flags as *ruse de guerre,* and also proposed that Great Britain agree not to place foods on the list of absolute contraband.[8] In his letter to Bob, Bryan had enclosed copies of these identical notes. Germany accepted the principal proposals of the American note on March 1, but asked that other imports besides food should be free from blockade.[9] Great Britain waited until March 15 to reply and then declined the American proposals.[10]

On March 28 the British ship *Falaba* had been sunk by a submarine, and an American citizen, Leon Thrasher, had been drowned. The President drafted a note to Germany in regard to the Thrasher case and submitted it to Bryan on April 22.[11] Bryan thought the note placed us in a position which was not neutral and was therefore likely to bring on a crisis. He reasoned that American citizens who sailed on enemy ships were no differently situated than those who stayed in a belligerent country and assumed the risks of their location.[12] He persistently urged the President to warn Americans against traveling on belligerent ships.[13] The correspondence between the two men during the next few weeks records their first serious differences of opinion as to what the United States should do to maintain neutrality and avoid war.[14] But even a few days in advance of receiving Wilson's draft of the note to Germany, Bryan seems to have been unaware that a divergence of opinion was imminent since his letter to Bob on April 17 gave the impression there was complete accord. This letter evidently strengthened the confidence Bob had frequently expressed in the President's determination to maintain neutrality and avoid involvement in the European War.

On Saturday morning, May 1, the day the British ship *Lusitania* sailed from the port of New York, an advertisement appeared in many American newspapers in which the German Embassy warned against the risk of traveling on the ships of Great Britain and her Allies through the waters Germany had declared a war zone.[15] That same day an American tanker, the *Gulflight,* was torpedoed by a German submarine.[16] The President had gone to Williamstown to attend the christening of his first grandchild, but returned to Washington on May 3. That evening Bryan, who was extremely apprehensive, went to the White House "for an extended conference." The following morning he had another long talk with the President before the Cabinet met.[17]

Three days later, on May 7, the *Lusitania* was sunk off the coast of Ireland without warning by a German submarine. Throughout the country people were profoundly shocked as they read the reports of the sinking of this huge, luxurious ship which had carried so many international celebrities on its trips to and from Europe. For days the tragic stories of the survivors filled the newspapers. The ship had gone down eighteen minutes after it was torpedoed, and 1,198 of the passengers and crew, including 128 American citizens, had lost their lives.[18] A report of the ship's cargo, printed in the *New York Times* the following day, led Bob and others to wonder whether the unusually swift sinking of the ship and consequent heavy loss of life might have been due to an internal explosion set off by the torpedo igniting the munitions listed in the cargo.

Intense excitement pervaded Washington. Congress had adjourned, and there was much speculation as to whether the President would call a special session. The newspapers obtained comments from prominent men, including a number of Senators and Representatives. Germany was almost universally condemned for not giving sufficient warning before sinking the *Lusitania* to allow passengers and crew to leave the ship in lifeboats.

But there was sharp divergence of opinion as to what the United States should do about the loss of American lives. Many pointed out that the *Lusitania* was a British ship carrying munitions of war and that those who sailed on her assumed some risk, especially as they had been warned by Germany. Representative A. Mitchell Palmer of Pennsylvania, later Attorney General, thought the sinking did not call for immediate drastic action and certainly ought not to embroil us in the European War as "The Lusitania was flying the British flag, and carrying munitions of war for the support of a belligerent." Senator Hoke Smith of Georgia denounced the "heathen destruction of lives," but did not anticipate serious international complications between Germany and the United States since "It was an English vessel carrying munitions of war." Senator Thomas J. Walsh of Montana saw only two alternatives, "Our citizens must yield to the warning given to keep out of the waters around Great Britain or we must take the other alternative and make war." He said he was "not yet prepared to declare that either interest or honor" required "that we choose the latter."[19] Former President Taft counseled patience and reminded Americans that war was not the only way to make a nation accountable.[20] Few who had supported a policy of neutrality advocated action that would involve the United States in the European War. Bob told reporters that he had "the utmost confidence in the ability and wisdom of President Wilson and Secretary Bryan to handle with credit to the country and themselves the grave situation in which we are placed by the sinking of the *Lusitania*."[21] But Theodore Roosevelt and others who had been harsh critics of Wilson's policy in Mexico and Europe clamored for immediate action.[22]

At the time the *Lusitania* was sunk, Colonel House was still in London on his confidential mission for the President. A dinner had been arranged in his honor at the American Embassy for May 7. That night, as bulletins arrived reporting the extent of the disaster and the appalling loss of lives, the American Ambassador, Walter H. Page, read them aloud to the guests. House said to Page, "We shall be at war with Germany within a month."[23] Two days later he cabled the President, "We can no longer remain neutral spectators."[24] Page, who had been living in the hope that we would join the Allies in battle so that we might have standing and influence when the reorganization of the world began,[25] shared the freely expressed unofficial British feeling that "the United States must declare war or forfeit European respect."[26]

Three days after the sinking of the *Lusitania*, the President spoke in Philadelphia. He did not refer directly to the tragedy. But in discussing the elevating influence of peace and the example that America must set, he said: "There is such a thing as a man being too proud to fight. There is such a thing as a Nation being so right that it does not need to convince others by force that it is right."[27] As Bob interpreted the speech, it seemed to him to express the wisdom and ability he had told reporters he expected from the President and Bryan in meeting the grave situation created by the sinking of the *Lusitania*. He thought it indicated Wilson was determined to resist the demands that the United States rush into war because American lives had been lost on a belligerent ship, and intended to solve the crisis by other means. Bob was among the callers received at the White House the day after Wilson's Philadel-

phia speech. The *New York Times* and other newspapers reported
Bob had told the President that he wanted the United States to
take a firm stand but that he was opposed to war.[28] His talk with
the President apparently gave him confidence that the crisis would
be solved satisfactorily both to the German and to the American
people without the horrors of war.[29]

Two days after Bob had talked with the President, the United
States sent a note to Germany protesting against the loss of American lives and insisting upon the right of Americans to travel in
safety upon unarmed merchant vessels. Since it was practically impossible for submarines to capture belligerent vessels and take them
into port, the note in effect demanded that Germany abandon the
use of submarines against unarmed merchant ships in the war
zone around the British Isles.[30] Although Bob did not know it,
Bryan had joined in this document with "a heavy heart" because he
thought it meant relinquishing the hope of acting as peacemaker
between the belligerents—a role which required "the retention of the
confidence of both sides."[31]

As Bob had left Washington on May 20 for the first of fifty
lectures in Southern States, he was not at the Capital when the
German reply was received on May 31. It maintained that the *Lusitania* was not an unarmed merchant vessel but had been built as an
auxiliary cruiser; that she carried guns and a cargo of munitions
and that the German Government believed it acted "in just self-
defense" when it sought to protect the lives of its soldiers by destroying ammunition destined for the enemy.[32]

The evening of the day this reply was received, the President
drafted another note to Germany which he read aloud at the Cabinet
meeting the following morning. There was little discussion of the
note itself, but a heated argument occurred over whether a protest
should also be made to Great Britain against interference with
neutral shipping. Bryan thought it should. The President came out
definitely against it. At the close of the meeting Bryan told the
President he thought it unfair to all concerned for him to remain
in the Cabinet. Wilson, wishing to avoid an open break, asked Bryan
to submit new suggestions as to a course of action.[33]

Bryan went over the draft of the note to Germany carefully,
and was so disturbed at the content that he wrote two letters to the
President on June 3, analyzing it in detail and submitting sugges-

tions.[34] Apparently the more he thought about it, the greater his anxiety became, for on June 5 he wrote another longhand letter renewing his suggestions and urgently expressing his belief that the note as outlined by the President at the Cabinet meeting would be likely to cause a rupture of diplomatic relations which might rush the United States into war in spite of all we could do.[35] Although convinced the President did not wish war, Bryan thought this note might lead to it. On June 8 he wrote Wilson that he felt the issue involved was of such moment that to remain a member of the Cabinet would be unfair to the President and to the cause nearest Bryan's heart, "namely, the prevention of war." The resignation was promptly accepted, and Bryan ceased to be Secretary of State in the Cabinet of the man he had done so much toward making President. In his reply the President wrote Bryan that "Even now we are not separated in the object we seek but only in the method by which we seek it," and added, "We shall continue to work for the same causes even when we do not work in the same way."[36]

Bob received the news of Bryan's resignation in the little town of Humboldt, Tennessee, where he was speaking at the Chautauqua. Before he had had an opportunity to read Bryan's statement, he was interviewed. He was reported to have "vigorously expressed the shock which the resignation gave him and also the esteem and confidence in which he held both President Wilson and Mr. Bryan." The reporter quoted Bob as saying: "I believe that one desires peace as much as the other, but I know that Bryan is especially committed to a policy of peace. His framing of the peace treaties and getting them signed was, to my mind, one of the greatest pieces of work that has been accomplished by any secretary of state and I had an idea that the question between the President and Mr. Bryan was whether or not a suggestion of arbitration should be made."[37]

From Washington that same day Belle wrote Bob she had "never known such political excitement as that stirred up by Bryan's resignation." Although she found that "the Washington folks" all seemed to be "anti-Bryan," she could not believe the President expected to get the United States into war. A few days later she wrote that Bob's secretary had reported that the newspapers were "lambasting" Bryan but that he thought the majority of the newspaper men were with him though none of them were "saying so— out loud."[38]

During the months that Bob was away on his speaking trip through the South, Bob, Jr., was critically ill. When Bob, Jr., first returned to Washington, he had seemed to improve under home care. But soon after his father left, the virulent streptococcic infection renewed its attack, affecting the muscles and lymphatics, causing swelling and constant, excruciating pain. Although there were intervals of improvement, he was critically ill for months. Week after week his temperature would go up to 103 and 104. At that time there was no specific treatment known for this treacherous infection which often proved fatal. The only hope was that his resistance would be strong enough to overcome the invasion. Belle wrote or telegraphed almost every day, sending reports on Bob, Jr.'s improvement or relapse as the fever chart registered the changes in his battle with the infection.

Although Bob had to speak six days a week and make long trips on day coaches in order to get from one engagement to another, he wrote home almost every day. Two weeks after he left Washington, just as he was going on the platform at Madisonville, Kentucky, he received a telegram telling him that Bob, Jr.'s temperature had gone up, that his face was swelling and he was suffering acute pain. Bob wrote: "It was mighty hard to make a speech on top of that. When I got off the platform the telegraph office was closed and I could neither get word nor send any. It was a good thing that I could not get at the telegraph office till I had time to thresh it out as I walked the floor of my room as I did all night long. . . . But towards morning as daylight came (it is a great steadier) I prepared some night messages which I had arranged to be sent that morning."[39]

A week later he wrote Bob, Jr., "As I look back over the hours and days and months since . . . we went to see Dr. Evans—it was Sunday the 21st [March]—it seems ages ago. . . . That is *fourteen weeks yesterday.* Up and down—back and forth, coming and going. . . . How this thing will stand out in your whole life! How often will you hark back to it. Bobbie this has been a year of great disappointment to you. A bitter, trying, grilling year. But laddie, it has been the year of your greatest growth, your greatest development of character and strength, and power and patience. It seems a cruel thing to consider a bed of wearing, grinding, pain and confinement as a place in which we grow the elements which make for achievement. But it is. A fellow takes stock of himself—in a long stretch of sickness as he never has before. It's all so different, so disciplining. He is tied up with himself as he never was before. He cannot get away. He has to talk it out face to face with all his foibles, his mistakes. He takes his own measure over and over again. He sizes up his resources his reserves. I think it is the one time when in a calm sure way in a long period of illness when he is not to[o] sick to think—I think it is the one time when a fellow obeys the mandate 'Know Thyself.' Of course I would not prescribe a case of streptococic [*sic*] sickness as a course of training. A fellow would prefer to work it out some other way. But in a way Bobbie its been a big year. . . . you have been doing the biggest and bravest and hardest things of your whole life since you were sick. It will all count in your larger growth."[40]

Throughout Bob, Jr.'s long illness he looked forward eagerly to the daily letters his father wrote giving a detailed account of the meetings and often relating with a humorous touch amusing incidents which occurred. On this Southern trip Bob found his audiences keenly interested and responsive. Everywhere the managers told him he was drawing the largest audiences at each Chautauqua. Many people called on him at his hotel before his lectures. From Arkansas he wrote he had "been receiving the whole Town this morning, ladies as well as men." He found the women were "alive for suffrage" and "making the men pay attention."[41] He was surprised to find that nearly all the Southern Republicans were progressive. He also found that people were aware he had supported some Democratic measures, particularly the shipping bill, and that the Democrats wanted to "adopt" him.[42]

Belle replied they were all glad "to feel your message is getting across, and that you are awakening another section of our country to civil consciousness. . . . As I see it, you and Bryan have a distinct place in history because of your power to arouse the plain folks —who are the basis of democracy, to a sense of patriotic responsibility to the work of our time. In addition, you have your constructive legislative record, which will stand out more and more clearly as years go by. How much greater than merely being President. . . ."[43]

The Georgia legislature was in session when he was in Atlanta, and Bob was invited to address a joint session on July 1. Senator

Thomas W. Hardwick and Congressman William C. Adamson escorted him to the Speaker's rostrum. The press reported that he "was cheered to the echo when he appeared, and also at the conclusion of his speech." For an hour and a half he told the Georgia legislators about the long fight in Wisconsin and counseled them to build up progressive legislation gradually and scientifically, constantly working to perfect it, and then to guard it carefully to prevent it from being broken down.[44]

Twice on this long trip Bob managed to get home to see the family. By traveling all day on a local he arrived in Washington at ten-thirty on the evening of July 11, and left at four o'clock the next morning. Belle wrote to Mary in Madison that he looked well and that his tour had given him "that same fine reaction which he always gets from his speaking campaigns."[45] Later in the month he again had two days at home before starting on another trip through a number of Northwestern States. On his way to these engagements, he received news at Columbus, Ohio, on July 24, of the tragic loss of lives through the sinking of the overloaded steamer *Eastland,* as it lay at the dock in the Chicago River. The next day he stopped off at Chicago to investigate the causes of the disaster, but found it was impossible as the streets were "packed for blocks with excited people seeking information about relatives and friends."[46] Later, when he happened to meet Judge Kenesaw Landis on another train bound for Chicago, Bob learned authoritatively about the gross negligence which caused the tragedy. Landis, who had convened the grand jury, was "full of the Eastland disaster" and "talked like a house afire." He told Bob that on the morning of the tragedy when he made the order he had said to his clerk "that he would put a crimp in the rascals who were trying to beat La Follette's seamen's law."[47] A few weeks before the disaster the manager of the company which owned the *Eastland* had written Secretary Redfield pleading for exemption from the safety provision of the Seamen's law due to go into effect on November 4. For the August issue of *La Follette's Magazine* Bob wrote an editorial entitled "A Sacrifice to Greed," excoriating the policy which had caused the disaster and declaring that if the Seamen's law had been in effect on July 24 the *Eastland* catastrophe would in all human probability not have happened.[48]

After five months of almost continuous speaking, Bob returned to Washington on August 30. Early in September he went to Madison, where he spent many weeks gathering material on state issues and preparing a series of speeches which he intended to deliver at intervals throughout Wisconsin. He had been distressed at the way Governor Philipp's reactionary regime was curtailing and undermining many of the agencies set up during the preceding progressive administrations. Philipp had brought about drastic changes in the policies of the Tax Commission and the Insurance Commission. Under the popular façade of "economy" he urged the abolition of the Legislative Reference Service and recommended large reductions in the appropriations for the university, where he charged half-baked theories were being taught in the classrooms which intimidate capital and close factory doors. In denouncing their extension service he declared, "This university-on-wheels business has got to stop."[49]

Bob realized a new generation of voters had arisen since he had discussed these issues in practically every town and village of the State. It was imperative to get the facts to the people again so that they could be thinking about them and discussing what progressive government actually meant in their daily lives. The value of the progressive laws in the saving in indirect taxes from high freight rates, high gas, electric, and insurance rates must be kept constantly before the people to refute the specious charges of "wasteful extravagance."[50] From past experience in his county-fair campaigns, Bob knew that this kind of educational work could be carried on more effectively in an "off year" than during the heat of an election campaign. Therefore, immediately after his return to Madison he set about the task of mastering the facts. Day after day he was at his office from eight thirty in the morning until after eleven at night, reviewing the work of the Philipp administration and "wrestling with the problems of state finances." His desk was "piled high" with reports of the Railroad Commission, the Tax Commission, and the Industrial Commission.[51] He put in long hours with John R. Commons, Herman Ekern, Charles Crownhart, Joseph D. Beck, and progressive members of the legislature, gathering facts and analyzing their impact on the lives of the people in the State.

He was particularly concerned about Philipp's attack on the "extravagance" of the university in the drive to cut down its appropriations. One evening he dined with his former classmate,

Charles R. Van Hise, who was still president of the university. The following day Bob wrote Belle that after dinner they had gone into the library, where Charles "got out his documents and briefs," going over them thoroughly and giving him material for several days' work. Bob thought the case of the university should be a speech in itself; that it ought to be made in a hundred towns in the State, as the people were wholly without the facts and anyone could therefore make political capital by "lambasting the university for its extravagance." He added that he wished he "had nothing to do but champion the university for three months."[52]

Late in November Bob began his educational campaign on state issues. At intervals during the winter he carried on this work for a few days at a time whenever he felt the legislative situation permitted him to be away from the Senate. One of his typical meetings was vividly described in a letter Belle received from a friend of Zona Gale's who wrote from Portage after hearing him for the first time: "I have never save occasionally when Miss Gale has been holding small groups, felt such affection in an audience, for a speaker. Of course you know all this—know how they crowded about the door and the street and the auto to be near him as he came out—know how they laughed and applauded—and nearly— or quite wept. And how best of all they thought with him, clear headedly and convincingly. . . . I've never seen such a way with an audience as his. The sweetness of his spirit, his infinite patience, his delicious humor, his courage and force and bigness. We did not know any *one* person could be like that. Having heard him, it is easy to understand why democracy came to its real birth in Wisconsin."[53] As Bob traveled about the State, he found his audiences responding in this enthusiastic old-time way to his closely knit factual speeches analyzing how Governor Philipp's administration was undermining progressive legislation. But he was troubled by the lack of organization, and thought a great deal of work needed to be done in the State before the primaries. After making a number of speeches in late November, he had to go to Washington for the opening of the Sixty-fourth Congress, but he planned to return later.

In the fall Bob had been much concerned about a change in the Administration's policy which he believed menaced maintenance of our neutrality. It had been announced that the Anglo-French Financial Commission, headed by Lord Reading, had obtained a loan of $500,000,000 through J. P. Morgan and Company, the fiscal agents of the Allies in this country, and that the bonds were to be sold to the American people. This was a reversal of the Government's position as declared in August, 1914, when Secretary Bryan, after consulting the President, had telegraphed to J. P. Morgan and Company that loans by American bankers to foreign nations at war were "inconsistent with the true spirit of neutrality."[54] Bob wrote a signed editorial for his magazine criticizing the loan as a violation of that neutrality which President Wilson had asked the American people to maintain when he appealed to them in August, 1914 to "be neutral in fact as well as in name," to "be impartial in thought as well as in action," to put a curb upon "every transaction that might be construed as a preference of one party to the struggle before another" and thus keep our Nation "fit and free to do what is honest and disinterested and truly serviceable for the peace of the world."[55] In his editorial Bob asked: "How long can we maintain a semblance of real neutrality while we are supplying the Allies with munitions of war and the money to prosecute war? . . . With our manufacturing interests extending enormous credits to the Allies, with our money interests committed to keep the bonds of the allied governments good, we are underwriting the success of the cause of the Allies. We have ceased to 'be neutral in fact as well as in name' and are no longer 'fit and free to do what is honest and disinterested and truly serviceable for the peace of the world.' "[56]

Maintenance of our neutrality was also seriously threatened during the summer and fall by the continuing controversy over submarine warfare. In August diplomatic correspondence had reached a point where Secretary Lansing was writing the President about the probability of breaking off relations with Germany and speculating on how war with that country would affect the position of the United States as a party to peace negotiations. The tension on the submarine issue was temporarily eased, however, when von Bernstorff wrote on September 1 that instructions from his government concerning an answer to the last *Lusitania* note stated, "Liners will not be sunk by our submarines without warning and without safety of the lives of non-combatants, provided that the liners do not try to escape or offer resistance."[57]

Throughout the country the feeling against Germany had been greatly aggravated by reports published in leading newspapers and periodicals describing a system of German espionage in this country designed to blow up vessels carrying munitions to the Allies and to dislocate, by sabotage, industries serviceable to them. A few days before Congress convened, Lansing asked for the recall of Captain Karl Boy-Ed and Captain Franz von Papen, naval and military attachés at the German Embassy in Washington, for complicity in these plots.[58]

On December 7, 1915, Bob attended the joint session when the President delivered his annual message,[59] reversing the policy he had advocated the previous year in his annual message of December 8, 1914. Bob was greatly disturbed as he heard the President advocate legislation providing for a strong preparedness program which Colonel Roosevelt, Senator Lodge, the Navy League, and other critics of Wilson's foreign policy had been demanding since the early months of the war in Europe. The President also asked for immediate enactment of an espionage law. Anxiety regarding the implications of this message caused much speculation among the Members of Congress in both Houses. It cut across party lines. Several Democratic Senators sought information from Senator Stone, chairman of the Committee on Foreign Relations. Stone wrote the President asking for an early appointment to discuss our foreign affairs so that he might know more definitely what Wilson's policy was. He explained that several Democratic Senators were "quite seriously disturbed" about our diplomatic policy with respect to the European powers but that he himself knew nothing not generally known through the press and was as much confused as those who came to him.[60] Although Bob shared this anxiety as to what might be taking place behind the diplomatic curtain, he made no public comment on the message nor did he refer to it when he spoke a few days later in St. Paul, Minnesota, before the Convention of the American Society of Equity to an audience of seven thousand influential farmers from North and South Dakota, Iowa, Montana, Wisconsin, and Minnesota.[61]

From St. Paul Bob went to Wisconsin, where he made a series of speeches during December and the first weeks of January. While in Madison he wrote an editorial supporting Wilson's policy of non-intervention in Mexico and declaring the President would "not be

forced by the American Congress into war with Mexico."[62] Between
his engagements he went to Washington to spend Christmas with
his family. Throughout his speaking trip he discussed state issues.
His audiences responded so enthusiastically that he telegraphed
Belle, "Wisconsin surely coming back."[63] On January 19 he returned
to the Senate to participate in the heated debates that were brewing
in Congress because of conflicting views on the maintenance of
neutrality and because of anxiety regarding the President's diplomatic policy.

On January 27, 1916 the President began a speaking tour in
which he assumed "the leadership of the movement for preparedness
that had been started by his opponents."[64] Although Bob did not
know it, Wilson had directed Lansing two days before this to
threaten the German Ambassador with the breaking off of diplomatic relations unless a more satisfactory note was submitted in
the *Lusitania* case. The following day von Bernstorff had submitted
another draft which the President and Lansing both pronounced
satisfactory.[65] On his speaking trip Wilson's emphasis as to the
reasons for immediate, enormous increases in Army and Navy
varied somewhat in different cities, but his general theme was
similar in talking to the immense audiences that greeted him. In
Cleveland he told them we were "daily treading amidst the most
intricate dangers" which were "not of our making" and "not under
our control" and that no man in the United States "knows what a
single week or a single day or a single hour may bring forth." In
this same speech he joined reassurance with warning when he said,
"You may count upon my heart and resolution to keep you out of
the war, but you must be ready if it is necessary that I should
maintain your honor."[66] At St. Louis he emphasized the enormous
stretch of coast line and declared the United States ought to have
"incomparably the greatest navy in the world."[67]

On the day that the President began his tour in favor of the
preparedness program, Bob publicly expressed the opinion that the
plain people of the country were opposed to it. The occasion for his
brief extemporaneous speech arose during the debate after a huge
petition had been presented by Kenyon, who said it was so large that
if joined together it would reach some 15½ miles. The petition had
been circulated by the Organization of American Women for Strict
Neutrality and had been signed by more than a million citizens

distributed through every State in the Union.[68] It favored an embargo upon the exportation of arms and ammunition for use in the European War. Among those who spoke for it were Clapp of Minnesota, Hitchcock of Nebraska, Clarke of Arkansas, Martine of New Jersey, Ashurst of Arizona, Works of California, Lane of Oregon, and Townsend of Michigan.

In closing the debate Bob emphasized the vital importance of the Constitutional right of petition and vigorously condemned the Senate rule and practice which, without reading or debate, swiftly sent "petitions representing the arduous labor of months, expressing the hopes and convictions of thousands of people," to "the lasting silence of the committee's rubbish room." Declaring that the subsidized press was no indication of what the plain people were thinking, he said the largest possible consideration should be given "to any other avenues of expression of which people avail themselves."

As further evidence of sentiment which was not being played up in the headlines of the metropolitan press, he told of recently addressing a convention of seven thousand representative Northwestern farmers at St. Paul who had spontaneously and unanimously "adopted resolutions condemning the preparedness program," thus voicing what he believed to be "the calm judgment of the agricultural population of the Middle West." Also, in the many different States where he had spoken during the summer he had found the almost universal sentiment of his audiences to be "gratitude that we have been kept out of war, and a no less universal desire for some other way of settling international troubles than war.

"The average man does not understand why the United States Congress and this administration are so indifferent to the world situation. I fully realize the enormous difficulties, but I believe that history will hold us accountable for our contribution to the general holocaust, and I think it will be hard for future generations to understand why the neutral powers kept aloof; why they did not unite, under the leadership of the United States, in an effort to restore peace and order. I believe, too, that if one-tenth part of the energy and time now directed in agitation and investigation of preparedness were to be turned toward other means of settlement of international problems for the future we should restore the confidence of the people and redeem our place in history."[69]

CHAPTER XL

"The Will of the People Shall Be the Law of the Land"

As reports of the President's speeches reached Washington, many Senators and Congressmen became alarmed lest his demand for immediate huge increases in the Army and Navy might be due to some unknown development in our diplomatic relations with Germany. They realized that the resumption of unrestricted submarine warfare against belligerent merchant ships might at any time precipitate a crisis. The *Lusitania* case had not yet been settled, and American lives had been lost on other belligerent ships. Sentiment had been steadily growing in Congress for legislation warning American citizens against sailing on these vessels. Bob was in favor of this policy because he "regarded it as unjustifiable and unpatriotic that a few contending for a debatable right should voluntarily assume risks that might imperil the peace of the Nation."[1] He had supported the President's policy of warning Americans to leave Mexico in order to avoid the possibility of involving the United States in war through the loss of their lives. He and many other Senators and Representatives of both parties thought that this precedent should be followed and that for the same reason American citizens should be warned against travel on belligerent ships.

Bryan, at the time of his resignation, had urged the President to take some such action in the *Falaba* case, and was still advocating legislation to that effect. Early in January Senator Gore, after consultation with Bryan, had introduced a resolution to prohibit issuance of passports for use on belligerent ships and another to prevent neutral vessels from transporting Americans on ships with contraband of war cargoes.[2] Subsequently resolutions were introduced by other

553

Senators. The proposed legislation, initiated by Democrats, was not in accord with the position the President had taken and was interpreted in the press as a revolt in Congress and a demand that he change his policy.

On February 8 the German Government issued a memorandum announcing that "enemy merchantmen armed with guns no longer have any right to be considered as peaceable vessels of commerce. Therefore the German naval forces will receive orders, within a short period, paying consideration to the interests of neutrals, to treat such vessels as belligerents."[3] Immediately following this announcement some newspapers predicted on the "highest official authority" that Americans would be warned against sailing on armed merchantmen.[4] On February 15 Secretary Lansing told newspaper men that although the Government thought the "rule of international law permitting belligerent vessels to arm ought to be changed," there was no present intention to warn Americans from traveling on belligerent vessels armed solely for defense.[5] That same evening at the White House, Miss Ida M. Tarbell, who was a dinner guest, remarked to the President that it was an anxious time. He replied: "No one can tell how anxious it is. I never go to bed without realizing that I may be called up by news that will mean that we are at war. Before tomorrow morning we may be at war."[6]

In Congress, as anxiety over the possibility of war increased, the demand for legislation to warn Americans to refrain from traveling on belligerent ships grew. On February 17 Representative Jeff McLemore, a Democrat from Texas, introduced a resolution in the House requesting the President to warn Americans against traveling on armed merchant ships.[7] A few days later he introduced another resolution, and Bryan telegraphed endorsing it.[8] Tumulty and two members of the Cabinet told Wilson that unless he intervened the resolution would pass.[9] The President summoned Senators Stone and Kern and Representative Flood, chairman of the House Foreign Relations Committee, to a conference at the White House. There was plain talk. Stone informed Wilson that Members of both Houses were deeply disturbed by what they read and heard, some fearing the President had pressed his preparedness program to meet just such a crisis as this; that he himself found it difficult to consent to plunge the Nation into the vortex of the world war because of the unreasonable obstinacy of any of the Powers or the foolhardiness of our own people recklessly risking their lives on belligerent vessels.[10] The President made it emphatically understood that he was opposed to the Government taking any definite action to prevent Americans from traveling on belligerent armed merchant ships and that he would hold Germany to strict account if American lives were lost.

Various accounts of what Wilson had said were conveyed to the Members of both Houses. Several newspapers reported there had been a dramatic and stormy scene in the President's study.[11] Anxiety increased in Congress. Many were convinced that Wilson intended to maintain his position even at the risk of war. A non-partisan revolt grew among those who thought his policy was unneutral and therefore inevitably leading toward war. Democrats and progressive Republicans met in excited conferences. Speaker Clark telephoned the White House for an appointment. The following morning Clark and Representatives Claude Kitchin and Flood saw the President and informed him that the McLemore resolution would carry two to one or three to one.[12] But Wilson remained adamant, insisting that any interference from Congress would hamper his negotiations with Germany.[13] He continued his vigorous intervention to prevent action by Congress. The previous evening he had made public a letter he had written to Senator Stone defining his position.[14] All the usual machinery for exerting pressure on Congress to "stand behind the President" was set in motion. Intricate parliamentary maneuvers were planned to table the resolutions and thus defeat direct action on the issue in the Senate and House.

Senators and Representatives from both parties were summoned to the White House. In talking to two Republicans on the House Rules Committee, Irvine L. Lenroot of Wisconsin and William S. Bennet of New York, Wilson "expressed the opinion that if the resolution was passed, or was not tabled by a vote of the House, it would contribute to forcing the country into war."[15] This argument and the ruthless coercion of party discipline finally brought many Democrats back onto the Democratic reservation. Then, after almost a week of intense pressure to prevent Congressional action, the direction of the President's intervention appeared to shift abruptly.[16] It culminated in an extraordinary letter to Representative E. W. Pou, the ranking Member of the House Rules Committee, asking for an early vote on the Gore-McLemore resolutions in order that there might be "an immediate opportunity for full public discussion and action upon them" so that our foreign relations might be "once more cleared of damaging misunderstandings."[17] In taking this action, Wilson disregarded all known precedents of communication between the Executive and Congress.[18] The irritation and resentment of Democrats who favored a warning was not concealed. Many considered the letter a definite slap at Chairman Flood, Speaker Clark, and the Democratic floor leader Kitchin.[19] Commenting on the letter the next day, a well known Washington correspondent said: "Never before in the history of the country has the President of the United States asked Congress to approve or disapprove of his foreign policy. That is what Mr. Wilson did today."[20]

Bob read the President's letter and the reports of his various conferences with Members of Congress in the newspapers at Madison, where he had been since February 21. He had gone to Wisconsin to attend a conference and make two speeches at meetings of some four hundred progressive Republicans who had come to Madison from different parts of the State. Because of the illness of his son Phil, who was a student at the university, he stayed on in Madison to be with him during an operation and until the doctors were certain all danger was past. When Bob returned to the Senate on the morning of March 3, he asked to have printed in the *Congressional Record* several telegrams representing groups of citizens in Wisconsin urging support of resolutions warning Americans from sailing on belligerent ships; also one from a group in California which expressed amazement at the President's attitude and urged that the precedent created by Wilson's stand on warning Americans out of Mexico should be adhered to in the present crisis regarding travel on armed merchantmen.[21]

Following the presentation of petitions and bills, Senator McCumber of North Dakota offered an amendment requesting Americans to refrain from travel on armed merchantmen as a substitute to the Gore concurrent resolution to the same effect. Then the Gore concurrent resolution came before the Senate. Although the President in his published letter to Pou had requested free discussion and a direct vote on the issue, it was soon evident that the Administration forces had privately worked out a combination of extraordinary parliamentary tactics to shut off debate and prevent a direct vote on the issue in the Senate. Senator Ollie James immediately made a motion to table the Gore resolution and all substitutes for and amendments to it and demanded the yeas and nays on his motion. The Vice President ruled that the motion to table was not debatable. Thereupon Gore modified his resolution in a way that entirely changed it.

Bob and Borah both sought recognition from the Chair, but the Vice President ignored them and ordered the roll call. The Senate was gagged, and the modified Gore resolution was tabled by a vote of 68 to 14. Bob, Norris, Jones, Gronna, McCumber, and Sherman were among the fourteen who voted against tabling.[22] They would all have supported the original Gore resolution. Had there been enough votes to prevent tabling the modified resolution, the parliamentary situation would then have permitted bringing the question directly before the Senate again by substituting the McCumber resolution requesting Americans to refrain from travel on armed merchant ships. But the Administration prevented a direct vote on the issue in the Senate, and a few days later it succeeded in tabling the McLemore resolution in the House after limited debate. Norris, Bob, and many others thought the resolutions would have passed by large majorities in both Houses if Congress had not been coerced by the President.[23]

During the debate in the House a number of Representatives predicted that the President's policy would lead the country into war. A Democratic Representative, Robert N. Page, brother of Ambassador Page at London, was so convinced this would be the inevitable result that he announced on March 6 that he would not be a candidate for reelection.[24] In an editorial in *La Follette's Magazine*, Bob referred to Page as a Member "of high standing serving his seventh term in the House," and quoted from Page's statement that the President had not been satisfied with "an unreserved expression of confidence on the part of Congress" but had demanded a vote upon the warning of American citizens to refrain from using armed vessels of belligerents and asked that it be voted down.[25]

The day after the McLemore resolution was tabled in the House, Bob gave notice that on the following Friday he would address the Senate "upon the issues raised by resolutions in connection with warning Americans against traveling on armed merchant ships of the belligerents."[26] On March 10 he spoke for about an hour. When the Senate convened, the galleries were filled with people expecting a dramatic debate on the new crisis in Mexico which had arisen because Francisco Villa, a Mexican insurgent, had crossed the American border the previous day in a raid at Columbus, New Mexico, resulting in the death of twenty-three American citizens. Knowing Bob was to speak, Belle was in the gallery. She noted that there was a good attendance on the Senate floor when he began and that throughout his speech "he held the close, interested attention of a much larger number than is usual these days. The galleries remained filled throughout. He spoke from manuscript, but the large number of citations and the importance of accurate and exact statements made its use quite natural."[27] In opening his speech he expressed the belief that in spite of the newspaper attacks and the violent individual assaults on Wilson, the majority of our people felt a deep gratitude that we had a President who had striven to keep us out of war, and so far had succeeded. Bob said he wished it clearly understood that it was in no carping spirit that he took issue with the President in his recent extraordinary demand that Congress should vote down resolutions warning or requesting American citizens to refrain from travel on belligerent vessels. This demand had "raised an issue of the gravest importance to the future well-being of our Government." Bob explained that as he understood the pending controversy the President assumed it "to be the exclusive prerogative of the Executive to pursue any foreign policy, whatever the issue, independent of any suggestion from either or both branches of Congress.

"The peremptory manner in which the Administration forced action upon the resolution in the Senate, the extraordinary proceedings by which the resolution was changed and tabled, without opportunity for debate or explanation, warrants the belief that the President denies Congress the right to express its opinion upon a matter which lies within its constitutional authority quite as much as that of the Executive.

"We must infer from what has transpired that the President in his personal conference with Senators and Representatives made it understood that he considered the whole matter so exclusively within the field of Executive authority that he regarded the introduction and consideration of resolutions advising our citizens to refrain from travel upon armed merchantmen as an interference with his prerogative. Congress was made to understand that a vote of confidence would not suffice, and that nothing less than a complete denial of any intent or purpose to express an opinion or offer advice on the part of Congress would satisfy the Chief Executive."[28]

Bob then quoted a passage from the President's book, *Constitutional Government in the United States,* in which Wilson, five years before he became President, had expressed the view that "The initiative in foreign affairs, which the President possesses without any restriction whatever, is virtually the power to control them absolutely. The President cannot conclude a treaty with a foreign power without the consent of the Senate, but he may guide every step of diplomacy, and to guide diplomacy is to determine what treaties must be made, if the faith and prestige of the government are to be maintained. He need disclose no step of negotiation until it is complete, and when in any critical matter it is completed the government is virtually committed. Whatever its disinclination, the Senate may feel itself committed also."[29]

In commenting on this quotation from Wilson's book, Bob expressed a fundamental difference of opinion regarding the constitutional limitation of Presidential power which later, when translated into action, often brought the two men into direct conflict. In the Senate that day Bob said, "If there is warrant to believe that President Wilson may, on the verge of a great world crisis, predicate vitally important and decisive action on that declaration, then, sir, it ought not to go unchallenged. . . .

"If the President is clothed with such unlimited power, if in conducting foreign affairs he can go unhindered of Congress to the limit of making war inevitable, and if the Congress has no alternative but to accept and sanction his course, then we have become a one-man power, then the President has authority to make war as absolutely as though he were Czar of Russia." Bob declared he did not believe that the framers of our Constitution ever intended to invest a President with such power "either directly or as an incident to any power directly conferred upon him." Citing historical precedents to support his opinion, he challenged the view that either the Constitution or the statute creating the State Department conferred "such unlimited and unconditional authority in the President that it becomes an offense for Congress to take such action as has been proposed in the Senate and the House." Bob reminded Senators that during the Civil War when Secretary Seward had asserted that American policy in dealing with the French attempt to set up a monarchy in Mexico was a purely Executive question, the House of Representatives by a vote of 119 to 8 had passed a resolution declaring that "Congress has a constitutional right to an authoritative voice in declaring and prescribing the foreign policy of the United States as well in the recognition of new powers as in other matters; and it is the constitutional duty of the President to respect that policy, not less in diplomatic negotiations than in the use of the national force when authorized by law."[30]

In concluding his speech Bob said: "I believe it to be vital to the safety and perpetuity of this government that Congress should assert and maintain its right to a voice in declaring and prescribing the foreign policy of the United States. . . . Democratic control of foreign policies is a basic principle of all organized effort looking for the future establishment of permanent world peace. . . . Shall we in this crisis of the world's history fail to assert our constitutional rights and by our negligence and default permit the establishment in this country of that exclusive Executive control over foreign affairs that the people of Europe are now repenting amid the agonies of War? . . . There never was a time in history when it was more fundamentally important that we preserve intact the essential principle of democracy on which our Government is founded—that the will of the people is the law of the land."[31]

From the gallery Belle noticed that when Bob finished speaking a number of Senators came up to speak to him. She was delighted when she heard later what they had said. All agreed that he had made "a very important contribution" and that it was "a splendid thing to have done." That afternoon Congressman Clyde H. Tavenner of Illinois and Henry Ford's Washington representative called on Bob. The latter authorized Bob's secretary, John Hannan, to order 150,000 copies of the speech, the printing to be paid for by Henry Ford. The following day Senators Borah, Hoke Smith, Gronna, and Congressman Frear ordered several thousand copies for distribution. During the day many Senators and Congressmen told Bob how highly they thought of the speech after reading it in the *Record*, and said "they believed his position sound and right."[32]

The day Bob spoke, the front pages of the afternoon papers carried reports of the President's official announcement, made after the Cabinet meeting, that a punitive expedition was being sent into

Mexico to capture and exterminate Villa and his lawless band.[33] Although Wilson publicly declared three days later that the pursuit was "deliberately intended to preclude the possibility of intervention,"[34] the potentialities of the situation were so dangerous that American consuls were directed to warn Americans in Mexico to leave for the border or nearest port.[35] Critics of Wilson's Mexican policy attacked him, charging that the Villa raid proved he should have intervened long ago. There was a degree of tension in Congress which made Bob fear that if our troops ran into general fighting in Mexico, a declaration of war would come quickly. He was so deeply concerned that on March 13 he telegraphed Gilbert Roe asking him and Steffens, who had recently returned from Mexico, to come over that night for a conference, but neither was free to leave New York.[36] In a letter to Roe he explained: "I really needed to confer with you. Indeed the situation may at any time take a turn where one should have the best counsel at hand in order to be of much service or to feel sure enough to go to it & even try to serve. I have no one here whose judgment counts as yours would. I would give half of the time left me if we could only work in hailing distance of each other."[37]

On the same day that he wrote this letter, Bob saw the President at the White House at twelve fifteen.[38] There is no record of his talk with Wilson, but it seems probable that he discussed the concurrent resolution which he introduced in the Senate the next day. It incorporated the terms of an agreement with the de facto Carranza Government in Mexico which had been arrived at through diplomatic correspondence.[39] The resolution noted that the President had ordered or was about to order armed forces into Mexico, and that Congress approved this action. But it added that Congress assured the *de facto* Government that the sole purpose of the expedition was to arrest and punish the band of fugitive outlaws who had recently entered the United States from Mexico and committed outrages on American citizens at Columbus, New Mexico. It also stated that Congress joined with the President in declaring that the military expedition should not encroach upon the sovereignty of Mexico or interfere with the domestic affairs of the Mexican people. In presenting the resolution, Bob said he thought that after hearing it the Senate would agree that it should be considered at once and passed without debate. When the Senate Clerk finished the reading, it was agreed to unanimously.[40]

The next day Bob returned to Wisconsin, where he remained from March 19 until after the primary for the election of delegates to the Republican National Convention of 1916. Bob had announced his Presidential candidacy on February 22 at a meeting of progressive Republicans in Madison. He told them that he was a candidate for precisely the same reasons that he had been in 1908 and in 1912. In presenting his program he had advocated the nationalization of the manufacture of all munitions of war; an embargo on the exportation of arms and ammunition; a conference of neutral nations to co-operate for peace among nations and to consider the establishment of an international tribunal for the settlement of international disputes. His address was printed in full in the *Wisconsin State Journal* with a comment by the editor, Richard Lloyd Jones, who stated it was "one of the greatest speeches ever made by the senator."[41] Bob's name had also been filed in the North Dakota primary, which he carried on March 21 by 13,000 majority, receiving two-thirds of the votes cast.

Bob did not expect to carry any other States in 1916. But previous experience had demonstrated that even this small group of delegates instructed to vote for La Follette could force presentation of a minority platform to the Republican Convention. This had proved an effective way to bring the issues before the people and create a public sentiment which later contributed toward enactment of needed legislation in Congress.

The Stalwarts campaigned for an uninstructed delegation to be headed by Governor Philipp as one of the delegates at large. Bob knew that the Wisconsin primary on April 4 would be interpreted as a test between the reactionary, stalwart element of Governor Philipp's administration and the progressive Republicans. The Stalwarts were boasting that it was "Bob's last fight." Although Bob had large and enthusiastic audiences at his meetings, he was troubled about the lack of organization, especially in Racine and Kenowsha counties where there were many factories manufacturing munitions. He was so doubtful about certain districts in Milwaukee that he telegraphed John Hannan to come on from Washington. A few days before the primary he wrote Belle that he thought it would take another month to make a good canvass of the State on national issues.[42]

The returns from the primary came in slowly on April 4. Late that night Bob telegraphed the family at Washington that scattering returns indicated a divided delegation. Shortly after 2:00 A.M. of April 5, he sent another wire informing them that things looked better.[43] But from Milwaukee hostile sources were sending out dispatches on the night of April 4 and the early morning of April 5 which led newspapers in New York, Chicago, Washington, and other large cities to print headlines announcing, "La Follette Loses State," "Wisconsin Turns Down La Follette," "Repudiation of 'Wisconsin Idea' As Advanced by Senator Seen," "Senator Gets No More Than Five of Twenty-Six Delegates To The Convention."[44] It was also falsely reported that Bob's campaign manager admitted the defeat of twenty-one delegates. Editors who had long been eager to write La Follette's political obituary made the most of these false reports. The *New York Times*, in an editorial entitled "Fall of the Badger Boss," chortled: "The little Giant of Primrose is fallen. Wisconsin is untrue to her La Follette. . . . His defeat on Tuesday merely registers a fact that has been palpable for some years. Wisconsin is sick of the boss who has ruled her personally or by his substitutes since 1900."[45]

Reading these accounts in the newspapers and hearing nothing further from Bob, Belle assumed the reports must be correct and telegraphed him that the result showed there was great need of work in the State and that he had "probably never made a campaign of greater service." The following morning Bob telegraphed: "I ran six thousand ahead of my delegates in Milwaukee and probably forty thousand ahead of them in State, also that many ahead of Philipp. Voters marked my name but neglected to mark my delegates. Except for this mistake would have swept the State."[46]

The final returns showed Bob had received 110,064, while Governor Philipp as delegate at large had 70,813. Of the total of 26 delegates, 15 were instructed for La Follette. Of these, three were delegates at large. The Stalwarts elected 11 uninstructed delegates. Subsequently it was learned that many county clerks had issued ballots which did not carry the designation "La Follette" after the La Follette delegates' names as prescribed by law. Also, throughout the States thousands placed a cross opposite the name La Follette, thinking that was sufficient. This error cost the La Follette delegates thousands of votes.[47] An article in the *New York Tribune Magazine*, by Frederic C. Howe, analyzed the vote and concluded that La

Follette "had achieved a remarkable victory, in many ways the most remarkable victory of his life."[48]

When Bob arrived in Washington on April 8, the Senate was proposing to limit debate in order to rush through the preparedness measures. Newspapers were reporting alarming tension with Mexico and speculating on the new crisis that was developing with Germany over the recent torpedoing of the unarmed French channel ship *Sussex*. Many of the passengers and crew had been killed by the explosion, and three Americans had been injured, although no American lives had been lost.[49] On April 10, in reply to demands for an explanation, the German Government sent an unsatisfactory note which aroused resentment.[50] In a public address at the annual Jefferson Day Dinner, the President indicated that he believed the crisis might mean war.[51]

Shortly after this, Ray Stannard Baker, who had been present at the Jefferson Day Dinner, spent an evening with Bob at his home and talked over the whole situation. Baker noted in his diary that Bob had said he would go immediately to call upon the President to see if Wilson would "support a resolution in Congress to call a conference of neutrals and get something constructive under way." Baker found that Bob was strongly against war and "setting his whole weight against preparation based upon hysteria and panic."[52]

There is no record that Bob called at the White House. If an appointment was requested, the President was probably too occupied to arrange it, for he was then preparing a virtual ultimatum to Germany. On April 18 a note was sent which threatened to sever diplomatic relations unless Germany immediately abandoned "its present methods of submarine warfare against passenger and freight-carrying vessels."[53] The following day Bob attended a joint session of Congress and heard the President review the submarine controversy with Germany and state the terms of the note which had been sent the previous evening.[54]

It was generally understood this ultimatum would mean war unless Germany accepted its terms. Bryan's anxiety was so great that he immediately came to Washington to urge Democrats in the House and Senate to take a firm stand against war. Although the President's message received widespread newspaper approval, Members of Congress expressed diverse opinions. Lodge and a number of others who had previously been hostile toward Wilson's foreign policy commended his action in sending the note. Many of the Senators and Representatives who had favored resolutions warning Americans against travel on belligerent ships publicly criticized the President's position or stated they did not think Congress should go to war on this message or this issue. Among these were: Senators Norris, Gore, Sherman, Kenyon, and Representative Cooper, ranking Member of the House Foreign Relations Committee.[55] Senator Kenyon commented that if war should grow out of the present situation, "the first line of American defense should be made up of those Americans who started all the trouble by taking passage on belligerent ships."[56]

Although Bob made no public comment on the President's message, he was fully aware of the grave international crisis it might bring. He had never been a pacifist, but he did not think this country should resort to war on the issue the President had raised with Germany—the right of Americans to travel freely without risk on belligerent merchant ships. Bob thought war the most ghastly experience that could come to any country, and that it was always "the people—not the handful of men in positions of power—who must pay the full price." Therefore he believed that those who must "do the fighting and the dying" should be consulted on the gravest issue that could come to a Nation. To make this possible he devised the best legislative instrument he could for immediate use under the limitations of the Constitution. On April 29 he introduced a bill authorizing an advisory referendum to be conducted under certain conditions by the Bureau of the Census. It provided that if the President should sever diplomatic relations with a foreign country, and 1 per cent of the qualified electors of each of twenty-five States thereupon filed petitions with the Bureau of the Census calling for a popular vote, an advisory referendum should then be conducted by mail and the results reported to Congress. The measure was designed to assist in giving force and vitality to "that enduring principle 'The Will of the People Shall be the Law of the Land.'" Bob believed that if this bill could be passed, it would provide for the expression of popular sentiment "in such an authoritative manner as would 'give Congress pause.'"[57]

At Bob's request the bill had been referred to the Committee on the Census, of which he was a member. No objection was made to this procedure at the time. But apparently the Administration subsequently became aware of the meaning of the bill. A few days later Senator Stone entered a motion to have the Committee on the Census discharged from further consideration of the bill and to refer it to the Foreign Relations Committee. Bob, Norris, and Clapp all participated in the debate, insisting that the bill had been properly referred to the Committee on the Census. The issue did not come to a vote, as Stone requested that the matter be laid aside.[58]

On the same day that this debate occurred, a note which the German Government had sent on May 4 was made public. It stated that orders had been issued to the German naval forces that both within and without the naval war zone merchant vessels should not be sunk without warning and without saving human lives, unless these ships attempted to escape or offered resistance. The note added, however, that if the United States should be unable to obtain from Great Britain observance of the rules of international law universally recognized before the war as laid down by the United States in notes to Great Britain on December 28, 1914, and November 5, 1915, the German Government would then be facing a new situation in which it must reserve complete liberty of decision.[59]

Four days later the President, through Secretary Lansing, informed the German Government that scrupulous observance of its altered policy would remove the principal danger to the good relations between the United States and Germany. In an additional paragraph the President reasserted in substance the position he had taken in the *Lusitania* note by stating that the United States could not for a moment entertain, much less discuss, a suggestion that respect by German naval authorities for the rights of American citizens upon the high seas should be in any way "contingent upon the conduct of any other government affecting the rights of neutrals and non-combatants."[60]

War with Germany had been temporarily averted. But the death of a number of Americans in bandit raids along the border had brought another crisis with Mexico. The situation was so serious that the State Department was again issuing instructions to United States consuls to be prepared to advise Americans to leave Mexico immediately.[61] In the Senate cloakroom and about the Capitol Bob heard certain Senators openly threatening that intervention would be forced. His own interpretation of the menacing tension between the two countries was confirmed by the report Steffens brought back at this time after spending months in Mexico and traveling about the country on General Carranza's special train. Steffens knew Carranza dreaded war, but Carranza had been told and believed that President Wilson wanted war for his American purposes.[62] Toward the end of April Steffens had come on to Washington hoping to present the facts he had gathered to the President. In Administration circles he found the impatience with Carranza keen, and the interventionists "getting in their fine work." An article he had written on Mexico had just appeared in *Everybody's Magazine*. It had aroused great interest, and those who knew him were eager to hear the full story of his investigation, which they realized he could never tell in a published article. One of the first reports he made was to his old friend Secretary of War Newton D. Baker, whom he had known when the latter was closely associated with the work of Tom Johnson as mayor of Cleveland. Steffens found that Baker, "being a Tom Johnson man," could understand it all, and he was encouraged to learn that the President was wiring the troops every day, warning them to avoid conflict. Steffens spent that evening with the La Follette family and another guest, Andrew Furuseth, who helped in effective ways to win cooperation from other labor leaders and organizations. Within the next few days Steffens saw all the members of the Cabinet one after another and told his story to each, "man to man."[63]

During the next two months Steffens spent a great deal of time in Washington, and kept Bob and Belle constantly informed of the progress he was making. They both cooperated with him in every possible way. A meeting was arranged at the La Follette home under the auspices of the Washington branch of the Woman's Peace Party. Mrs. William Kent presided and introduced Steffens to an audience that crowded the spacious rooms of the large house on Sixteenth Street. Belle wrote up the meeting for the May issue of *La Follette's Magazine* which carried Steffens' story about Mexico to thousands of people in different States throughout the country.[64]

Throughout the winter and spring of 1916, Bob and Belle had followed with intense interest and cumulative indignation the bitter controversy that raged over the confirmation of Brandeis as Associate Justice of the Supreme Court. A vacancy had occurred when Justice Joseph R. Lamar died on January 2. Bob was in Wisconsin at the time but returned to Washington on January 19. Soon after this, Attorney General Thomas W. Gregory sent for Bob and told him he believed the President might be induced to name Brandeis. Aware that both conservative Democrats and Republicans would oppose him, Gregory wished to know if there would be enough progressive Republican votes to assure confirmation. Bob made a careful canvass of Senators and reported to Gregory that it would be safe to assure the President that although a hard fight would be made against Brandeis, enough votes could be counted on to confirm him.[65]

On January 28 the President sent the Brandeis nomination to the Senate. Two days later Bob wrote Phil: "We are all very happy over the Brandeis appointment. I had something to do with it— (Sub rosa on this) Will tell you when we meet. There is going to be a big fight over the confirmation. *But he will be confirmed.*"[66] Brandeis did not know that this canvass of Senators had been made in behalf of his nomination until many years after Bob's death.[67]

Hearings were held on the nomination, which was under consideration before the Senate Judiciary Committee for four months. Bob never doubted that Brandeis would finally be confirmed, but the scurrilous charges against the man he admired and loved roused his indignation. In editorials in his magazine he reviewed Brandeis' long service in behalf of social justice, and denounced the attacks that were being made upon him[68] by the great financial and privileged interests of the country, "organized as never before to defeat a judicial appointment." Their campaign had, he said, "descended to the low level of widespread defamation and falsification of a long and honorable private legal career." In one of his editorials Bob predicted that the time would come when even Brandeis' enemies would be forced to "concede his greatness and recognize the epoch-making event of his appointment to the Supreme Bench." The people of the United States owed "a great debt to President Wilson for this appointment. In Brandeis he selected the ablest and truest and best-equipped servant of this day and generation for this high service. And the country is indebted, also, to the President for the brave, unflinching fight which he made for the confirmation of Mr. Brandeis."[69] In a letter to Belle, soon after the first editorial appeared, Alice Brandeis said that what Bob "wrote about Louis was the best possible, so discriminating and so just. I loved every word of it."[70]

Although several progressive Republicans were absent when the final vote came in the Senate, Cummins was the only one to vote against the nomination when Brandeis was confirmed on June 1, by 47 to 27. Bob had worked hard to win Cummins' support, and thought his defection so outrageous that he wrote a scathing editorial analyzing the reasons for this particular Senator's persistent opposition to Brandeis. He went even further in a letter to Gilbert Roe which Brandeis greatly enjoyed reading many years later when Bob's daughter showed it to him. Describing as "Six Big Burglars," the lawyers who had signed a "Holy Horror" letter declaring Brandeis "unfit," Bob excoriated the "soft shell progressives" who had the audacity to suggest that such false charges should be answered.[71] Belle wrote Elizabeth Evans that she thought it was the "most cowardly treachery" she had "ever known for the so called progressives to give these old reactionaries the excuse and sanction for their fight on Louis."[72]

The night before Brandeis was to be confirmed by the Senate, Belle had written Alice Brandeis: "I am thrilled with the thought that Louis is to be confirmed tomorrow and Monday he will take his place on the bench. Then there will be an end to all this wicked business. As soon as Louis is a member of the Court his enemies will take to cover[.] I suppose some of them will be claiming they made him Judge. The fight has been a bitter desperate one but it will end with the oath of office[.] There is that advantage over a political position[.]" She urged Alice Brandeis to come on to Washington for the ceremony on Monday, June 1, and added: "We will have a quiet dinner. Quiet to the outside world but we will draw the shades and dance on the table and do whatever we feel like doing in the way of jubilation."[73] To the end of her life Alice Brandeis remembered with vivid pleasure this "quiet dinner" at the La Follette home on the evening of the day Brandeis became a Justice of the Supreme Court.[74]

CHAPTER XLI

A Mandate from the People

Bob was in Washington during the sessions of the Republican National Convention which met in Chicago on June 7, 1916. On one of these evenings Justice and Mrs. Brandeis and Frederic C. Howe were at the La Follette home listening with Bob, Belle, Mary, and Bob, Jr., to the news from the convention, which in those days, before radio, was telephoned and telegraphed to them from Chicago.

The Progressive Party, which was certain to nominate Roosevelt, had arranged to hold its convention in the same city at the same time. Early in April, following a private luncheon in New York attended by Roosevelt, Lodge, Elihu Root, and Major General Wood, a succession of newspaper dispatches had predicted that Roosevelt would be the Presidential nominee of both conventions. Roosevelt and some of his supporters apparently hoped he might be chosen by the Republicans, and were quietly working to bring it about. During the spring while Steffens was in Washington and seeing a great deal of Bob, he wrote a letter saying: "La Follette has been sounded to see if he will support T.R. at the Republican Convention, and he sounded very hollow. He won't, of course. T.R. must be anxious to ask it."[1]

Soon after the Republican Convention met, it became evident that the reactionary element was in control. Senator Warren G. Harding of Ohio presided as both temporary and permanent chairman and delivered the keynote address. After Senator Lodge had submitted the platform, adopted by a majority of the Resolutions Committee, the minority report was offered by the Wisconsin delegate Edward J. Gross. Although no other State furnished the necessary seconding motion to force a vote, Gross followed the Wisconsin precedent of two preceding conventions and read the minority platform presenting many of the issues on which Bob had recently campaigned in Wisconsin. As in 1908, boos, hisses, and derisive laughter greeted this platform. Phil heard this hostile demonstration from the press section, where he was reporting the convention for a Wisconsin paper. He wrote his father that he was never prouder to be his son "than when Ed Gross made his fight on the platform planks amidst the scoffing of the galleries and delegates."[2] Commenting later on the hostile reception of this 1916 minority report, Bob predicted: "The delegates who mocked and derided the declarations of that platform will pass and be forgotten. The principles enunciated in that platform will ultimately find a permanent place in national legislation." He also noted the fact that, although rejected by previous Republican Conventions, the Wisconsin minority platforms of 1908 and 1912 had been adopted by Congress within eight years and almost bodily written into Federal Statute.[3]

The names of ten candidates were presented to the convention. Senator Fall of New Mexico placed Roosevelt in nomination late on Friday afternoon, June 9, and his speech was followed by an enthusiastic demonstration lasting thirty minutes. Then Michael Olbrich nominated Bob. The galleries were disposed to jeer, but they were rapped to order, and the delegates rebuked them by calling to Olbrich, "Go on; you're all right." The disturbers then quieted down, but there was no demonstration when Olbrich finished.[4] Bob's nomination was seconded by Robert M. Pollock of North Dakota.

After taking two ballots, the convention adjourned late that night without nominating a candidate. During a conference which followed in a hotel room, it became evident that Republican leaders would not accept Roosevelt as their candidate. They thought he was so identified with favoring United States entry into the European War that his nomination would focus the campaign on this issue and Wilson would win. At two o'clock on Saturday morning Nicholas Murray Butler telephoned Roosevelt at Oyster Bay to tell him he could not be nominated and to ask whom he would suggest.[5] When the convention met at noon that day, a letter from Roosevelt was read suggesting the nomination of Lodge. But as the roll was called, it became evident the convention had overwhelmingly nominated Charles Evans Hughes. Only seven delegates had taken the colonel's advice and voted for Lodge. That same day the Progressive Party Convention nominated Roosevelt. The colonel declined the nomination and subsequently endorsed Hughes, thus signing the death warrant of the party he had brought to birth.

In letters to the family and intimate friends, Belle wrote that Bob "was glad that Roosevelt was squelched—yet there was not much satisfaction in Hughes and Fairbanks and the platform."[6] She thought it was evident Hughes could not "win on a Teddy Roosevelt platform," and predicted that if he took issue with Wilson on the policy of having kept us out of war in Mexico and Europe, Wilson would be the next President.[7]

As had been anticipated, Wilson was renominated by acclamation on June 15 at the Democratic Convention in St. Louis. The intention of the leaders had been to make Americanism the focus of the demonstrations at the convention. But the delegates, who came from all over the country, unexpectedly altered that plan by "one of the most dramatic scenes in the history of national conventions." Spontaneous outbursts of "wild, uncontrollable enthusiasm" interrupted the keynote address of the temporary chairman, Martin H. Glynn, former governor of New York, as he cited significant precedents during 140 years of our history to support his argument that "the policy of neutrality is as truly American as the American flag," and declared that "the United States is constrained by the traditions of its past, by the logic of its present and by the promise of its future to hold itself apart from the European warfare, to save its citizens from participation in the conflict that now devastates the nations across the seas."[8]

Repeatedly, when Glynn assured his audience that Wilson stood where Washington, Jefferson, John Adams, and other Presidents had stood who had saved America from involvement in European war by maintaining the traditional American policy of neutrality, delegates jumped up on their seats, waved American flags, cheered, and paraded in the aisles. By their spontaneous response to this part of Glynn's address, the delegates themselves struck the keynote for the Democratic campaign to reelect Wilson which resounded across the country in the terse, compelling phrase, "He kept us out of war."

Three days after his renomination, the President mobilized the National Guard of the United States for service on the Mexican border where intermittent raids continued to bring demands for intervention. Within a week a clash occurred in Mexico between American and Mexican troops. Twenty-three American soldiers were taken prisoners. A formal demand was made for their release, and Carranza, who had previously issued an ultimatum demanding the withdrawal of American troops from Mexico, was asked for a statement of his intentions.[9] On June 22 the President wrote Colonel House that he thought the break had come and that all his patience seemed to have gone for nothing.[10]

The newspaper headlines seemed to indicate that war was imminent. After brief debate Congress passed a joint resolution authorizing the President to draft the National Guard into the military service of the United States.[11] Bob had offered an amendment that this service should not in any event be longer than during the period of actual hostilities, but it was defeated.[12] He had supported Wilson's policy of non-intervention in Mexico and was perplexed by what appeared on the surface as a sudden shift of intention. He thought that the border should be protected but that our troops should be withdrawn from Mexico, as there would be inevitable clashes beyond Carranza's control if they remained there long.

When this new crisis with Mexico developed late in June, Steffens hurried to Washington. After he had spent an evening at the La Follette home telling the family about the situation as he understood it, Belle wrote that if the country was not already at war with Mexico the Administration seemed to be traveling fast in that direction.[13] Steffens had talked with the Mexican representatives in Washington and had tried to get an appointment with the President but Wilson had refused to see him. Cabinet members told him he was too late, and Secretary Baker said war had been decided upon. The President had been informed that Carranza wanted war to rally the Mexicans to his regime. Steffens knew this was not true, but realized that reliable documentary evidence might be needed to prove it to the President.[14]

From the law offices of Carranza's attorney in Washington, Steffens secured private telegrams which proved that Wilson had been misinformed. After reading these, Steffens went to the White House. Knowing he could not see the President, he dictated a message to Wilson saying he had documents which the President should see, and added, "A war due to irresistible causes is bad enough, but a war made by misinformation is unforgivable, and, I, for one, will never forgive it." Later, when Steffens returned to his hotel after going to the Senate, he found that the White House had been calling him. He was requested to see the President early the next morning, July 5, at the White House—not the office.

Steffens spent the evening of July 6 at the La Follette home. In his vivid way he told Bob, Belle, and Bob, Jr., of his visit to the White House that morning, describing how Wilson had received him at the head of the stairs and taken him into the library as he demanded what the information was. Steffens' exceptional ability to report the exact phrasing as well as the overtones of a conversation made them all feel they had shared this important talk with the President which Steffens recorded many years later in his *Autobiography*. Steffens quoted to the President several of the private telegrams from Carranza to his attorney and related what he himself had learned of the man while traveling with him on his special train through Mexico. When the interview was over, the President escorted Steffens to the head of the stairs, paused, and told him he had brought very valuable information which prevented a war.[15]

The following day Belle wrote that Steffens had been "wonderfully pleased with his interview" and thought that Wilson was "by far the most progressive President we have had in many long years." Steffens had "a lot of influence with both sides," and it was "great work."[16] The next day Bob wrote to a friend, "No one knows—that is but few know—the real inside of the Mexican affair but it was a close shave—and very much to Wilson's credit on the whole."[17] A few weeks later the President agreed to a proposal, made by Mexico, for the appointment of a commission to negotiate directly with the Carranza Government for a peaceful settlement of the dispute over the presence of the Pershing expedition in Mexico.[18] Steffens stayed on to see that the commission was agreed on, safely appointed, and well started on its work. From Washington he wrote a friend that the La Follettes had been "awfully good" to him.[19]

The debate on the large appropriation bills for the Army and Navy held Bob in Washington for another six weeks. For months a skillfully organized agitation for a huge preparedness program had been carried on throughout the country. The day before the President was renominated, he had marched up Pennsylvania Avenue at the head of sixty thousand people, including men from the Army and Navy, Cabinet members, Senators, Representatives, and other civilians. In heading and reviewing this parade, which a newspaper described as among the grandest spectacles ever seen in Washington, Wilson symbolically took "command of the forces in the country demanding preparedness."[20] This demonstration endorsing what then seemed a huge Army and Navy program for the United States took place on Bob's sixty-first birthday, but he did not celebrate it by marching in the parade.

From the beginning of the agitation for preparedness, Bob had opposed increases in the Army and Navy except for defensive purposes. When the Administration decided to back these appropriations, which naturally had the support of leading Republican Senators who had long advocated such a program, it was evident the bills would be forced through. Nevertheless Bob persistently presented amendments which he believed would remove some of the most dangerous potentialities of the legislation. One amendment he offered to the Navy bill was debated for two days and attacked by Senators of both parties as an encroachment upon the President's power as Commander in Chief.[21] In its final form as presented for a vote, after Bob had modified it at the suggestion of Senator Norris, the amendment provided that "no battleship, battle cruiser, scout cruiser, torpedo-boat destroyer, or submarine herein appropriated for shall be employed in any manner to coerce or compel the collection of any pecuniary claim of any kind, class, or nature of any individual, firm, or corporation, or to enforce any claim of right to any grant or concession for or on behalf of any private citizen, copartnership, or corporation of the United States."[22]

That afternoon Bob began an impromptu speech which he continued the next day, holding the floor for over seven hours. The speech and the debate it evoked filled forty columns of the *Congressional Record*, and was widely reported in the press. David Lawrence noted in the New York *Evening Post* that "The Wisconsin Senator . . . held the attention of a comparatively crowded chamber," while "many Senators listened to every word of it some of them, no doubt, appreciating full well that only political expediency had brought about the extravagance of both parties in their plans for military and naval enlargement. . . . the warning will, of course prove ineffectual, for a majority of both parties are victims of the preparedness hysteria, and the Naval bill will pass substantially as reported by the Senate Committee. It was not without profit, however, to have the Wisconsin Senator place in the record some sincerely non-partisan remarks on the subject, the wisdom of which future history undoubtedly will vindicate."[23]

In opening his speech Bob said that the proposed military program would impose the greatest tax burden that had ever been known in any country at peace with all the world. "There is not a man in the United States Senate who would have had the hardihood one year ago to propose such an increase or to suggest an appropriation of such magnitude for military purposes. And there is not a Senator on this floor who would have dared to vote for such an appropriation—not one. And yet one year ago the European war was at high tide."[24] He declared that this change of sentiment in Congress had been brought about by an organized campaign in motion pictures, magazines, advertisements, and editorials alleging that our country was in danger of attack from a foreign foe. He cited statements of Army and Navy officers who had testified that the United States was impregnable against attack and adequately prepared for defense. He quoted the testimony of General Nelson A. Miles and General Erasmus Weaver, a member of the General Staff, of the Board of Ordnance and Fortifications, and of the Joint Army and Navy Board.

In discussing the Navy appropriation, he read testimony from naval experts before the Committee on Naval Affairs showing that the United States Navy was second only to that of Great Britain and that the plans of the admirals would place on the American people "the enormous burden of a navy equal to that of England." Admitting that the measure would probably pass, he said: "Twelve months ago, the Secretary of the Navy denounced it. Twelve months ago the President of the United States was against it. He was plainly against any program of this sort. With the financial power of the great nations of the earth weakened, if not broken, there is every reason why we should not have this program forced through Congress. It is unjust; it is a great wrong. It is the beginning of a greater wrong. When we once start upon a plan of this sort, I do not know how we are ever to get back to a basis that is rational."[25]

Through quotations from H. N. Brailsford, Norman Angell, Frederic C. Howe, and others, Bob portrayed the competition in armaments, the conflicting economic interests, and the secret diplomacy which had led up to the war in Europe. Declaring that for four years financial interests had sought to bring on war with Mexico, Bob explained that his amendment was designed to restrict the Navy from being used to collect the debts of speculative investors in Mexico and in Central and South American countries. "Back of all modern war is practically the one policy, financial imperialism . . . It is behind the present war in Europe; it is the underlying cause of that which has converted almost all of Europe into a human slaughter pen."[26]

When Senator Lewis interrupted to ask whether Bob approved of President Wilson's course in Mexico, "he did not mince words, but threw . . . partisan politics to the winds"[27] by replying: "I do most emphatically. I sincerely hope that the standard bearer of the Republican party in this campaign . . . will not under any circumstances take the position that it is the duty of this Government to put the flag of the United States behind the investment of speculators in Mexico or elsewhere. Mr. Wilson declared in his speech at Detroit that he would not stand for that policy, that he would not become the collecting agent of investors in Mexico. The American people, if that issue is made between the Republican candidate for the Presidency and President Wilson, will, in my opinion, overwhelmingly stand with President Wilson on that issue. . . .

". . . I BELIEVE EVERY DOLLAR THAT GOES INTO A FOREIGN COUNTRY AND EVERY MAN WHO GOES INTO A FOREIGN COUNTRY WITH HIS MONEY, LOOKING FOR PROFITS, SHOULD ACCEPT THE LAWS OF THE COUNTRY AS THE ARBITER TO WHICH HE WILL APPEAL FOR JUSTICE IF HE FEELS AT ANY TIME THAT HE IS REQUIRED TO PROTECT HIS RIGHTS IN THAT COUNTRY."[28]

In closing his appeal for passage of the amendment, Bob said, "Believing in democracy, in the right of self-government—ready to defend the precious heritage of our own sovereignty—let us here and now resolve and declare that we will never permit the armed forces of the United States to be used to despoil our sister republics of their property, interfere with their right to govern themselves according to their own standards, or violate their sovereignty—as sacred to them as American sovereignty is to us."[29] Bob's amendment was defeated by a vote of 44 to 8.[30]

Steffens had been in the Senate press gallery during part of the discussion, and wrote Gilbert Roe that: "Bob's speech rattled the bones around here. I heard about two hours of it, then heard the correspondents talk about it among themselves at the capitol & told the officials at the War, Navy & State Department about it."[31] A few days later Belle wrote Mary that her father had "done some good work since he made his long talk; yesterday an amendment adopted providing for the families of the national guard and the day before the age of enlistment restored to twenty-one. We are all very happy about it."[32] The task of correcting proof on his long speech occupied the entire family and took all of Bob's spare time for several days. It was not printed in the *Congressional Record* until August 5. That same day he left Washington by train to make a speech at a Chautauqua meeting in Indiana, returning the next day so that he would not miss the vote on the Keating child-labor bill. After voting for it, he left on August 12 for Madison, accompanied by Belle and Bob, Jr., to enter the hotly contested primary campaign for his renomination. The Stalwarts were predicting this would be the end of La Follette.

In the spring Bob's campaign manager, Charles H. Crownhart, had made a survey of the State through letters to leading progressive Republicans. The reports had been that a hard fight would be made against Bob, and that if there were two progressive candidates for governor nothing short of a political earthquake could prevent a repetition of the disastrous 1914 primary when Philipp had won the nomination.[33] When Bob returned to Wisconsin, there were two progressive candidates for governor, William H. Hatton and Francis E. McGovern. After this split in the progressive forces, which Bob had tried to prevent,[34] it seemed probable that the stalwart candidate, Governor Philipp, would be renominated in the primary.

Bob began his 1916 primary speaking tour on August 14. His opponent, M. G. Jeffris, had already delivered many speeches in different parts of the State. This was the same Jeffris who had led the bolting stalwart Republican delegates when they had marched from the university gymnasium in 1904 to hold their rump convention at the Fuller Opera House in Madison. On July 12, 1916, the stalwart Republicans had held a convention in the university gymnasium, at which they had endorsed Hughes for President, Philipp for governor, and Jeffris as their candidate to run against

Bob. In a speech at this convention Jeffris had sounded the keynote of the campaign by reverting to the type of vituperative personal attack he had used in the 1904 campaign. Declaring La Follette had been a destructive force in Wisconsin in both parties, Jeffris attacked his vote for the Democratic Underwood tariff and challenged his right to run on the Republican ticket. He denounced Bob's opposition to the preparedness program, his proposals for an embargo on arms, a referendum on war, and his support of Wilson's non-intervention policy in Mexico. The possibility of a libel suit was carefully avoided in the climax to his tirade by quoting an editor of a Democratic Virginia newspaper who had stated that La Follette "talks and acts and seems to think like a lunatic in an asylum or an idiot in a home for the feeble minded."[35]

Bob opened his campaign at Sun Prairie, a small village near Madison. On this tour he traveled by automobile, and was accompanied by Phil and Bob, Jr., who took turns in driving a new Ford at what was then regarded as the high speed of forty miles an hour over rough country roads in order to meet the heavy schedule of many speeches each day. Without ever mentioning Jeffris' name, Bob took up the issues that had been raised and clarified his position on them in his own vivid way day after day to the large crowds that gathered to hear him. Repeatedly he pledged his continued support of American neutrality and his opposition to entrance into the European War. Throughout his campaign he endorsed the candidacy of Hatton for governor and the entire progressive ticket.

In this campaign, as in 1910, Bob had the help of men from other States. They were strategically booked in different parts of Wisconsin, traveling mostly by automobile to cover meetings at crossroads and villages by day and the larger towns at night. Among those who came to speak for him were Senators Clapp, Gronna, Kenyon, and Norris, former Congressman James Manahan, and Andrew Furuseth. Clapp, Furuseth, and Kenyon came into the State for both the primary and the election campaigns. Kenyon told his audiences how profoundly his thought had been influenced as a young man by hearing La Follette speak at the Chautauqua. Describing him as "the most influential political power in the country," he said that "it would be a blow to democracy if Wisconsin failed to send him back to the Senate."[36] When Norris spoke at Ripon, he replied to telegrams he had received from certain

Wisconsin citizens criticizing him for coming into the State by saying: "I have felt that the question before the people of Wisconsin in the primaries was one in which every person in the United States who has a genuine concern about government has a vital interest. It is a question of national importance, for if Senator La Follette is not returned to the United States Senate it will be the severest blow that could be dealt the progressive movement throughout the country. It is a question in which the people of my own state of Nebraska are as keenly interested as are the people of Wisconsin."[37]

A few days after Jeffris had made his bitter attack on Bob at the stalwart convention, William Allen White had published an editorial in his newspaper, the *Emporia Gazette,* declaring: "The election of a President is no more distinctly a national matter than the re-election of Senator Robert M. La Follette in Wisconsin. For no public official in the White House, on the Supreme Bench or in Congress in a generation has been more truly and worthily a national public servant than Senator La Follette . . . His record vote is a guide in the Senate to the brave wise statesmanlike course in every crisis."[38] White's editorial was published in full in the *Wisconsin State Journal* and *La Follette's Magazine.* It was also printed on the back of letters sent out from campaign headquarters at Madison.

The national aspect of the campaign was further emphasized by communications from Francis J. Heney of California and Senators Bristow and Borah which were published in the *Wisconsin State Journal.* Borah had intended to speak in the Wisconsin campaign, but when legislation important to his own State made it impossible for him to leave Washington he wrote a long letter of endorsement which Bob's campaign manager thought was a "corker" because it was just the right kind to carry weight.[39] Among those from other States who helped, through generous contributions, to meet the expenses of speakers and organization work were Mrs. Louis D. Brandeis, Charles R. Crane, Elizabeth G. Evans, Congressman William Kent, William T. Rawleigh, and Rudolph Spreckels.

Toward the end of August a nation-wide strike was ordered by the four railroad brotherhoods whose demands for an eight-hour day had been rejected by the railroad executives. Bob, Gronna, and Clapp were all speaking in Wisconsin at the time, and were ordered

by the Sergeant at Arms to return to Washington. Although Bob
had been campaigning for only two weeks, he had been making
seven or eight speeches a day averaging about an hour each. When
the summons to return reached him at Fond du Lac, he took the
first possible train for Washington. His important dates were filled
by Andrew Furuseth, who had been campaigning very effectively in
the labor districts where he had asked to be sent. Bob arrived on
September 1 in time to vote for the Adamson bill which made an
eight-hour day on interstate railroads compulsory and called for a
commission to study the effects of such a law. The bill was drafted
on the same principle Bob had asserted when he succeeded in passing the 1907 law limiting the hours of continuous service to sixteen
hours—the shortest day it was possible to get at that time. As early
as 1913 he had publicly declared that the wisdom of legislation providing for an eight-hour law for both men and women was no longer
a debatable question.[40] The President had recommended the Adamson bill. But the Republicans attacked it. Bob believed the measure
was vital to the public welfare, and he was the only Republican to
vote for the bill when it passed the Senate.[41] The bill was approved
by the President on September 3, just before the strike was to
begin. Bob also participated in the debate on the Revenue bill
which increased taxes on incomes, instituted an inheritance tax to
provide for the preparedness program, and set up a Tariff Commission. When the bill passed on September 5, Bob, with five other
progressive Republicans, joined the Democrats in voting for it.
On that same day he was renominated in the Wisconsin primary.
The total vote was very light, but he received 100,396 to Jeffris'
66,569, carrying sixty counties to Jeffris' ten.[42] The split in the progressive forces due to McGovern's candidacy defeated Hatton and
assured Philipp's reelection.

When Bob returned to Wisconsin to begin his campaign for reelection, he met the strongest Democratic opposition he had encountered since he had been in the Senate. His opponent was William F. Wolfe, an able lawyer from La Crosse, whose parents had
been born in Germany. He thus had a command of two languages,
and in communities where it might make a special appeal he spoke
in German. Even in the primary campaign he had attacked Bob's
position on preparedness and on warning American citizens off
armed merchant ships. He also criticized him for his failure to

"stand behind President Wilson," and accused him, as Jeffris had, of "pulling for the German vote in Wisconsin" by advocating an embargo on arms.[43] Thus Bob's non-partisan position on national issues drew forth the same verbal fire from the conservatives of both parties, who began in this campaign to hurl the ugly charge of pro-Germanism against him because he continued to advocate policies which he believed essential to maintain neutrality.

Throughout his campaign Bob met these attacks, as he had so many others in the past, by talking over with the people of Wisconsin his reasons for the position he had taken on legislation during the recent sessions of Congress. He was determined, in so far as it was within his power, that his record on these important issues should not be misinterpreted or glossed over. Covering the State as he had in the days when he was governor, he frequently made seven or eight long speeches a day. People drove great distances to hear him. In the northern part of the State he made forty-five speeches in fifteen days, going to communities where he had not spoken for twelve years. A newspaper correspondent who covered this tour wrote: "Every speech of Senator La Follette's varies and yet they seem to all cover the same subjects. It is because of this variety that frequently the same men are seen in the audiences in different places. . . . Everywhere it has been the same story. Great crowds, interested crowds, men who hang upon every word; who crowd about the Senator at the end of the meeting. Pledges of support come not only from members of his own party but from Democrats and from independents. At every La Follette meeting there are political conversions."[44]

Once again issues were cutting across party lines in a State where many voters had learned to ignore them. When Hughes spoke in Milwaukee and made a trip through the State, he was welcomed and introduced by Governor Philipp. Soon after the Republican Convention, Bob had published a signed editorial severely criticizing the platform but stating that Hughes would be acceptable to the great body of progressive Republicans and that probably no other man could have brought so many Republicans of all elements to join in his support. But soon after, when Hughes began his campaign, the newspaper reports seemed to indicate that he was allying himself with the reactionary Old Guard Republicans in the different States. In Wisconsin and elsewhere he denounced the

Underwood tariff and the Adamson eight-hour law which Bob had supported. Following the line of the platform, he drew to his support those who had been openly hostile to Wilson's policy of non-intervention in Mexico and Europe.

In Wisconsin the stalwart Republicans, who controlled the State Central Committee, used every device to force Bob to make a declaration for Hughes, but he steadily refused. This was interpreted as a tacit endorsement of Wilson, and undoubtedly helped to swing many votes to him. The *Wisconsin State Journal*, then recognized as the leading progressive daily newspaper of the State, was actively supporting Wilson for President, Bob for the Senate, and Burt Williams, the Democratic candidate for governor.[45]

Since it was a Presidential year, the campaign inevitably centered on national policies. But in 1916 the issue of war or peace became the theme that dominated and climaxed many speeches. Nowhere was the claim that Wilson's reelection would mean keeping the United States out of the European War more strongly emphasized by the Democrats than in Wisconsin. The Democratic candidates for state offices followed the lead of the President as reported in his speeches. After Wilson's speech at Shadow Lawn on September 30, the Democratic candidate for lieutenant governor declared that at last the issue had been made a clear-cut one, "a vote for Hughes means war; a vote for Wilson, peace."[46] Senator Husting, Bob's colleague, sounded a similar note, while Senator John Sharp Williams stated in a speech at the Madison high school, "I say that Wilson has kept you at peace, he has kept peace with honor and is entitled to your appreciation."[47] Although there is no press report of the occasion, Senator Williams had lunch with Bob at Maple Bluff Farm. In preparation for the visit, Bob, Jr., had been instructed by his father to buy the best bottle of whisky available in Madison for the guest. The beverage was choice, but Williams declined to partake on this occasion.[48] Two weeks before election Bryan also came into Wisconsin to campaign, and declared that one of the two great issues was whether this nation would "rebuke or approve President Wilson's success in keeping this country out of war."[49]

A few nights before election, Bob was interrupted by a question from the audience while addressing a large meeting in Milwaukee. He had been discussing his reasons for supporting an embargo on arms and other legislation which he thought would help to maintain strict American neutrality and thus bring us to a place at the head of the peace table with an impartial influence among all the belligerents. He believed this would enable us to lead the way to arbitration rather than to war in the settlement of international difficulties. After expressing regret that Congress had not followed the same course that it had taken in relation to Mexico, when it authorized the President to put an embargo on things that kill, he went on to say that he wished President Wilson had followed the example of George Washington and issued a proclamation which in substance told greedy citizens who sold arms to a belligerent on the high seas that "they need not look to this country for protection because they would not get it." At this point a newspaper reporter noted the following dialogue:

"Will the other fellow remedy that?" cried a voice.

"What other fellow?" La Follette asked.

"Hughes."

"I don't know. You are as capable of judging that as I am. So great a responsibility hangs on this election, the result of which may mean the peace of our country that I believe every man must decide his vote, between himself and God."[50]

Bob closed his campaign on Saturday night, November 4, with a meeting in the little village of Loyal, where he had never spoken before. More than a thousand people gave him "a rousing reception. The hall was jammed to the very window sills and even the aisles were blocked."[51] After the meeting he returned to Madison to spend Sunday and Monday with his family. On Tuesday he cast his vote. That night, before the glowing wood fire in the dining room at Maple Bluff Farm, he, Belle, Bob, Jr., Phil, Mary, Alfred Rogers, and a few other intimate friends heard the election returns as they were relayed from town by telephone. Wilson's election was in doubt for several days, but before midnight Bob's return to the Senate was certain. The final count, including the votes of the Wisconsin soldiers on the Mexican border, gave him 251,303 to Wolfe's 135,144. His plurality was at that time the largest that had ever been given to any candidate in Wisconsin. He carried 69 of the 71 counties in the State. Governor Philipp was reelected by 63,263 votes over Burt Williams, the Democratic candidate, who carried many of the progressive strongholds. Bob ran more than 30,000 ahead of Hughes and over 28,000 ahead of Philipp.

Wilson lost this normally Republican State by only 29,459. In analyzing these complex returns a few days after the election, Bob's secretary, John Hannan, wrote that if the Democrats could have held their normal vote in the German Democratic counties the State would have gone for Wilson. ". . . Wilson's big vote in Wisconsin came from Progressive Republicans and labor unions."[52]

A dispatch printed in the *Wisconsin State Journal* appraised the significance of Bob's personal victory by noting that he was "the only Republican leader of national reputation who has been sustained by the voters. His indorsement by his party was decisive."[53] At that moment none of the subscribers to this leading progressive newspaper in Wisconsin could have foreseen that the editor, Richard Lloyd Jones, would soon be rivaling Bob's ancient reactionary enemies in virulent attacks upon him.

Bob's interpretation of Wilson's victory was similar to the report the British Ambassador made to his Foreign Office when he wrote that "the elections have clearly shown that the great mass of the Americans desire nothing so much as to keep out of the war. It is undoubtedly the cause of the President's re-election."[54] In a long signed editorial entitled "Jingoism Rebuked," Bob said: "Woodrow Wilson's reelection has tremendous significance. First of all, the plain people throughout the country registered their approval of his worthy efforts to keep this nation out of the maelstrom of war.

"Of even more significance is the smashing of the great political machines that have so long dictated national elections. The West reelected Wilson. . . . Every precedent was broken when a President of the United States was put in the White House by voters outside of the great financial and industrial centers of the nation. . . .

"The President must accept the outcome of this election as a clear mandate from the American people to hold steadfastly to his course against war."[55]

Bob believed that his own reelection by an overwhelming plurality meant that the people of Wisconsin had also given him a mandate to hold steadfastly to his course against war.

CHAPTER XLII

"An Important Hour in the
Life of the World"

Bob returned to Washington alone on December 4, 1916. Throughout the winter Belle stayed on at Maple Bluff Farm with Bob, Jr., Phil, and Mary. Their Washington house at 3320 Sixteenth Street had been sublet furnished to the families of Representative William L. La Follette and Captain Walter K. Wilson, a West Point graduate and regular Army officer then on duty at the War Department. Bob had arranged to make his home with them during the winter. This plan had been adopted both for economy and because it seemed unwise to break up the children's schoolwork, since Bob expected to be in Washington for only two months, as the short session of the Sixty-fourth Congress would adjourn automatically on March 4, 1917.

Congress met in joint session on December 5 to hear the President deliver his brief annual message. Bob noted that as Wilson entered the Chamber he was greeted with cheers which continued until "stopped by the Speaker's gavel." The message proposed nothing new, Bob thought, except legislation, based on the Canadian law, to prohibit railroad strikes until after the Government had investigated. He recalled that last autumn John Commons had sent him word "not to get caught on that."[1]

That evening Bob dined with Brandeis. His visits with friends were shared with Belle and the children in the longhand letters he wrote them almost every night. He told of the "homey" times he had with the Brandeises when they were alone, and also wrote of special occasions when there were interesting guests. On a Sunday evening early in December he described "a nice little dinner"

586

where the guests were Elizabeth Evans, Mrs. George Rublee, Associate Justice John H. Clarke, and Mr. De Haas of Holland. "I like Clarke *very* much," Bob wrote. "He is sincere modest—but sure. He & B[randeis] love each other and it is a great thing to have put two such men on the bench. More power to Wilson in filling up the bench." He added that he had a good visit that day with "Commons from 11 A.M. till 5:30 P.M. at my Capitol office. . . . He is well and dearer than ever. Thank God for such good friends."[2] That same week he and Commons spent another day working on a plan to initiate the Government ownership of railroads. Bob thought it was "comprehensive and thoroughly scientific." Money for a strong bureau working on a three-year plan would be needed. They hoped that Crane and Spreckels might be interested enough to give backing for a splendid working force.[3]

Action on the important legislation pending in Congress moved slowly. The Federal Corrupt Practices Act, blocked during the previous Senate session by a filibuster of Old Guard Republicans, was withdrawn by Administration leaders. An immigration bill, vetoed earlier in the year by the President because it provided a literacy test, was revived. When the bill passed on December 14, Bob helped defeat an amendment which he declared would have excluded such political refugees as "Garibaldi, Kossuth, General Franz Sigel and Carl Schurz" had this provision been in the law at the time they came to the United States.[4] He wrote his family that he "got in on the immigration bill and helped kill a few snakes."[5]

Bob left Washington on December 20, two days before Congress adjourned, to join the family in Madison for the Christmas vacation. During the preceding week the newspapers had carried front-page dispatches reporting German overtures for peace parley and speculating on the outcome. Germany and her associates, Austria-Hungary, Bulgaria, and Turkey, had proposed that the United States Government communicate with Great Britain and her Allies about the possibility of entering into peace negotiations. The German note had been transmitted to the Allied Powers on December 16 by Secretary of State Lansing.[6] Two days later, before any of the Allied Powers had replied officially to the German note, the President, through Secretary Lansing, sent a note to all the belligerents suggesting that they communicate their peace terms.[7] This note was carried on the front page of the newspapers on the morning of December 21, and it seems probable that Bob read it on the train. Although he apparently made no public statement, he heartily approved it. The note requested a statement of specific peace terms and also contained a proposal for cooperation of neutral powers and a declaration for a future league to preserve world peace. Bob's resolution, introduced on February 8, 1915, calling for a conference of neutral nations, had made similar proposals.[8] From the beginning of the war he had hoped that neutral mediation might bring about a negotiated peace by strengthening the masses of the people of each belligerent country against the imperialistic military groups in their countries which were intent on a crushing victory. Bob had not returned to Washington when a resolution approving the President's note passed the Senate 48 to 17, but it was announced by Senator Kenyon that had he been present he would have voted for it.[9]

The day after Christmas, while Bob was still in Madison, the German Government's reply to the President's note was made public. It failed to state Germany's peace terms, but proposed "the speedy assembly, on neutral ground, of delegates of the warring states," thus excluding the presence of neutrals.[10] The Allies promptly rejected the Central Powers' proposal for a peace conference. Then, on January 10, the Allies replied to the President's note rejecting his proposals and suggesting as necessary conditions of peace territorial, political, and economic adjustments in Europe which it was evident could not be won at that time.[11] Thus the attempt at peace negotiations in January, 1917, ended in failure.

On January 15 Bob returned to Washington. Soon after his return, Bob, Jr., came on for a few days' visit. His father met him at the station, and delighted in every hour of their companionship, which broke the loneliness he always felt when away from the family. On the night his son left for Madison, Bob wrote Belle that "the visit was a joy to me with the sting of parting with him at the end of it that must go with most of our happiness. I know how very keenly he felt it because I know how it made my heart ache to have him go. My! if everything goes well with us what a good time we'll have all together at the farm next summer—and its not such a whale of a long way off either."[12]

A week later Bob made a two-hour speech protesting against a cut of $109,000 which the Senate Committee had made in an appropriation for the Children's Bureau as it came from the House. This cut was a hard blow. Bob reviewed the work the Bureau had done under Julia Lathrop's able direction, and pointed out that the appropriation was to be used to continue and extend an important study of the causes for the high death rate among children in the first year of infancy. It had been shown, he said, that this death rate of one baby out of every eight bore a relation to the wages of fathers and the conditions under which the children were born. After Bob had, as he wrote the family, given "the Committee hell" for about two hours, the roll was called, and the appropriation was saved by a vote of 31 to 17.[13] That evening Julia Lathrop telephoned Bob to express her appreciation. Many years later she wrote that it did her "soul good to remember it" and that she wished, when his biography was written, "there could be a little footnote to tell how generously and modestly he protected the Children's Bureau!"[14]

In the midst of Bob's speech on the Children's Bureau, President Wilson had been escorted to the Chair to address the Senate. From his seat in the front row of the center aisle, Bob followed the President's historic address advocating a "peace without victory" with intense interest and approval. The President stated the general conditions which he thought would justify him in asking our people to help "guarantee peace and justice throughout the world" at the end of the war. The treaties and agreements must, he said, "embody terms which will create a peace that is worth guaranteeing and preserving, . . . not merely a peace that will serve the several interests and immediate aims of the nations engaged." Therefore, "it must be a peace without victory," since only a peace between equals could last. He described at some length what that equality meant. It included the recognition of the rights of small and weak nations equally with those of the large and powerful nations, freedom of every people to determine its own life, government by consent of the governed, free access to the seas for all peoples, and moderation of armaments. These, he concluded, were "American principles, American policies" and "also the principles and policies of forward looking men and women everywhere, of every modern nation, of every enlightened community. They are the principles of mankind and must prevail."[15]

The *New York Times* correspondent noted that as the President concluded, "a sharp round of applause broke out in the galleries and on the floor . . . The applause on the Democratic side was general. The man who started the hand-clapping, however, was Senator La Follette of Wisconsin, Progressive Republican, who has voted frequently with the Democratic majority since the beginning of the present Administration."[16]

The Senators and spectators rose as the President left the Chamber. Bob, before resuming his interrupted speech, said: "I know how difficult it will be to bring the Senate back to a consideration of the pending question. I think we must all feel, sir, that we have passed through an important hour in the life of the world."[17] In an editorial the New York *World* quoted this reference to the President's address and stated: "Senator La Follette did not exaggerate the facts. . . . Our own belief is that President Wilson has enunciated the broad principles of liberty and justice upon which alone a durable peace is possible . . ."[18]

When Bob started the applause at the conclusion of the President's speech, these two men were, in so far as their public statements had revealed, in accord as to what the position of the United States should be toward the war in Europe, and the peace by which it should be terminated. Bob had publicly endorsed Wilson's appeal for strict neutrality. Both men desired a just peace and were apparently convinced that it could only be arrived at by fair, mutual agreement. Both believed that any other peace would, as the President said, be accepted in humiliation, under duress, and therefore could not last. Both realized that any enduring peace must be based upon an agreement among nations to limit armaments to the minimum necessary to maintain order and to forbid such as would be used for aggression or conquest. Both had declared for freedom of the seas and the establishment of some international tribunal through which the problems that would inevitably arise among nations could be considered and adjusted by mutual agreement rather than by resort to war. Bob had designated the suggested tribunal as a "Commission" rather than a "Court." But in some respects he had gone even further than Wilson in the powers he thought should be delegated, particularly in his proposal to prohibit traffic in arms and munitions of war between private individuals and governments. The fundamental differences between the President and Bob were not in the objectives they both passionately desired, but in their conflicting opinions as to the means by which these desired ends could be achieved.

Although Bob was in accord with the President's declared objectives at this time, he thought Wilson had made certain serious mistakes in the means used to achieve the apparently desired ends. Bob regretted that the President's note to the belligerent nations requesting a statement of peace terms had been so long delayed, and wished Wilson had previously taken a more aggressive action toward peace by calling a conference of neutral nations. The fact that the President had not maintained the strictly neutral policy he had so wisely advocated at the beginning of the war was, Bob thought, the chief reason for the failure of his effort at mediation. Bob believed this lack of real neutrality had led the Allies to hope the United States could be drawn into the war on their side, thus turning the tide for a dictated peace. His opinion was necessarily based upon the public documents available to Senators at that time. Few, if any, Senators were aware how far the President had actually been led from the path of strict neutrality while Colonel House was abroad.

The year before, in February, 1916, House had, under the skillful guidance of the British Foreign Minister, Sir Edward Grey, worked out a memorandum defining "as precisely as could be done in advance" the action the President would be prepared to take. This memorandum had committed Wilson to proposing at some indefinite future time a conference to end the war, and then, if Germany should refuse, "the United States would probably enter the war against Germany."[19] The memorandum had been drawn up on February 22, and confirmed by the President on March 8, 1916, after House had returned to Washington. The only revision the President made was to insert the word "probably."[20] With the confidential House-Grey memorandum in their archives, the Allied governments knew that their refusal to enter into peace negotiations in January, 1917, made it probable that the United States could be brought into the war on their side with the President committed to peace terms "not unfavorable" to them. Had Bob known this memorandum was in the Allied archives, he would have been less hopeful as to the effectiveness of the President's appeal on January 22.

Many individuals in this country and in Europe responded to

Wilson's speech with the same hope and enthusiasm Bob had expressed. The French Socialists approved,[21] and the Russian Foreign Office endorsed it.[22] But a program for peace without victory did not stir enthusiasm among the dominant leaders of the belligerent governments which had entered into secret treaties based upon the ancient doctrine and practice that to the victors belong the spoils.

A week after the President made his peace-without-victory speech, Bob dined at the White House. That day he had been detained at the Senate and did not reach home until seven. In a letter to the family he gave an amusing account of how he had "to hustle to dress and get to the White House by eight o'clock" in time for the large formal dinner given to the Supreme Court. He found that his vest had come back from the cleaner still smelling "to heaven of gasoline—which caused a convocation of the whole family. They put the vest in the oven and baked the gasoline out of it. Will was ready to loan me studs. Capt. Wilson did loan me a neck scarf. I wore Bobbie's silk hat & take it all round was quite fixed up. By standing on the rear platform of the street car on the way down & letting the wind blow through me I eliminated enough gasoline so that I did not take fire when I scratched a match to light my cigar." Although Bob disliked formal dinners in anticipation and avoided them if possible, he usually managed to have a good time after he arrived. The lady designated as his partner that evening was not exciting. He described her to the family as "a nice fat old girl" who didn't "believe in womens voting or anything else excepting Prohibition." Although bored with this Congressman's wife, whose "father had never tasted liquor beer tea coffee or tobacco," Bob had a pleasant hour later in the East Room, sitting on a couch with Brandeis listening to a musical program. Bob thought Paul Reimers had "one of the sweetest" tenor voices he had "ever heard." After the music ended, Bob and his colleague from Wisconsin, Senator Husting, said good night to the President and Mrs. Wilson and "hiked for home."[23]

Two days after Bob had dined at the White House, the morning papers reported that a note had been received from the German Government announcing that in accordance with the freedom of action reserved in its note of May 4, 1916, unrestricted submarine warfare would be resumed on February 1 in the war zone except in certain lanes for a limited number of passenger vessels.[24] No one knew what action the President would take. The following night Bob wrote the family a letter which recorded his impression of the atmosphere that had pervaded the Capitol during the day. "One cannot shake off the feeling that an awful crisis [is] impending," he said. "I have felt impelled to try and break through & see Wilson. But it is given out that he is 'locked up alone' & seeing no one. He came to the Capitol late this afternoon & was closeted with Stone in the rooms of the Committee on Foreign Relations. I think something will come in the morning. The Old Line Republicans are all eager[.] The headlines of the papers are blatant for war to begin. You can only stand and grimly wait for a chance to fight the devils off. The White House & State Dept. have been sealed up tight as a drum. No one has gotten a hunch so far. The Democrats are saying little—just waiting for orders."[25]

The next morning word was received at the Capitol that the President had handed the German Ambassador his passports and would address a joint session of Congress at two o'clock.* As Bob talked with Senators after this message was received, he found "Stand Pat Republicans were sneeringly charging that Wilson 'knew it would be popular & was playing the game.' " Bob did not hear a single "expression of regret from a standpatter," but he found "all of the Progressive Republicans & Democrats were sick at heart." Stone, chairman of the Committee on Foreign Relations, told him confidentially that he regarded the President's action "as a blunder worse than a crime."[26]

Reports that the President would address Congress spread rapidly throughout Washington. Gallery tickets were in great demand. Bob gave his to Charles R. Crane. The Capitol was soon crowded and the feeling tense. Promptly at two the President entered the Chamber of the House of Representatives. His face was " 'drawn' set in 'grave lines,' " showing the intense strain he had been through as he had sought in "agony of spirit" to reach his final decision.[27]

Directly in front of the President, in the first row of the seats assigned to Senators, Bob listened with intense anxiety and growing dissent as he heard Wilson give his view of the prolonged submarine controversy and announce that Germany's declaration had left him "no alternative consistent with the dignity and honor of the United

---

* Passports were handed to the German Ambassador and his staff as the President began his address to Congress.

States" but to break diplomatic relations.[28] To Bob this drastic action seemed a grave diplomatic error which brought us dangerously near war. But he noted with apprehension that a majority of Senators and Representatives applauded, and some Democrats cheered. He found it hard to sit out the address. When the President finished, Bob went to his office, where he could be alone, as he "did not want to see anybody."[29]

Late that afternoon he went to see Bryan, who had telephoned asking him to come to his room at the Hotel Lafayette. The previous night Bryan had addressed a huge peace meeting in New York under the auspices of the American Neutral Conference Committee. Anxiety about the diplomatic crisis led him to stop off in Washington. He had prepared a statement to give out that night. He thought the President's action bore out the fears he had expressed when he resigned and that the United States was near war.[30] When Bob arrived at the hotel, the two men talked over what might be done to prevent the disaster they both feared. Bryan proposed holding a mass meeting, but Bob thought this would not be effective. He suggested that Bryan call in as many Democrats as he could the next day while he himself saw the progressive Republicans in an effort to unite the two groups on a well considered resolution which would start a discussion that could run along for a few days "in the hope of things cooling off." Bob, remembering the incident which had precipitated war with Spain, was keenly aware of the danger that at any moment " 'the Maine will be blown up'—and we be carried into a declaration of war—by the Jingoes in spite of everything."[31]

During the next two days Bryan and Bob kept "plugging away" at their plan in the hope that they might "get some fellows braced up to resist being rushed into war."[32] Bryan wrote his wife that it was "distressing to see so many men afraid to act" although he had "already strengthened several."[33] When Bryan left Washington, Bob thought he was quite discouraged so far as Congress was concerned. But Bob counted every day a gain so long as it was possible to get by without some dire event upon which the war makers might seize. He wrote that he had started work which was "beginning to stir things up" among "the constituents of this flock of congressional sheep" and that he was doing everything he could to prevent "its taking on any pacifist brand." He found the labor organizations, the Farmers' Equity, the Farmers' Union, and the Grange all showing "an encouraging readiness to respond," and he thought a week or ten days of lee-way would help tremendously.[34]

Bob was impelled to all this day and night work because he still believed, as he had from the beginning, that for the good of this country and the entire world the United States should keep out of the European War. But his plan to "get some fellows braced up" proved more difficult than he had anticipated. He was surprised and disappointed when Stone, who had told him confidentially on Saturday, February 3, that Wilson's action was a "blunder worse than a crime," suddenly reversed his opinion publicly on Monday, February 5, by introducing a resolution "approving the President's course in severing diplomatic relations." Bob prevented immediate consideration of the resolution in order to discuss it with his colleagues. In a letter to the family he said: "A lot of fellows—ours—mostly dont want to vote for it—but I expect they will. I dont see how I can. It was unnecessary for him to have taken that step & it puts us in a perilous position where it wont take much to push us clear over the line."[35]

The resolution was debated on Wednesday and passed 78 to 5.[36] Of all the progressive Republican and Democratic Senators who had not wanted to vote for it, the only ones who finally joined Bob in voting No when the roll was called were Gronna, Kirby, Works, and Vardaman. Lane would have voted against the resolution except for the fact that when he returned to the Senate Chamber after a brief absence during the debate he found the doors locked and could not enter.[37] That night Bob wrote his family that his mail was beginning to grow "quite heavy with protests against war." He ended his letter with these lines: "Good night dear hearts. You must be prepared for me to get some criticism for my vote. I expect it as a matter of course—but feel that I could not vote otherwise."[38]

That astute Republican leader, Senator Lodge, who had long been hostile to Wilson's policy of trying to keep the country out of the European War, had deftly aided passage of the resolution because he was certain it led directly toward his own goal of active participation in the conflict. That same day he wrote his intimate friend, Theodore Roosevelt, that he had urged the Democrats to bring in the resolution approving the President's action because he wished "to get the Senate wholly committed to the break with Germany. That seemed to us the first step." In commenting on the five Senators who had voted against it, he said the two Democrats, Vardaman and Kirby, were "rabid Bryan pacifists" and that he would not attempt to describe La Follette, who appeared on the list as a Republican but always voted with the Democrats.[39] Roosevelt replied, commending Lodge's speech for the resolution as "exactly right," and expressing the opinion that "La Follette as a type is considerably inferior, in morality and capacity, to Robespierre." The colonel added that he had already applied for a division of troops and that if Wilson gave him one and sent him to war he would serve the President "with single-minded loyalty."[40]

Among other prominent Republican leaders who had appealed to the public "to stand behind the President" were former President Taft and Charles Evans Hughes.[41] Following the break with Germany, the governors of many States announced their readiness to respond to any demands the President might make.[42] The Bethlehem Steel Company, the United States Steel Corporation, the Remington Arms Company, and J. P. Morgan and Company sent word they would place their resources at the service of the Government.[43] Henry Ford, who had previously refused to manufacture munitions for Europe, now offered his factories and private fortune to the Government for war purposes. The German-American National Alliance adopted resolutions approving the break with Germany and offering to raise regiments for war against Germany.[44] Many metropolitan newspapers made predictions similar to that of the New York *World*, which editorially declared, "The American people might as well make up their mind that war with Germany is inevitable."[45]

During these weeks of intense anxiety, Bob admitted in his letter home that at the end of the day he was tired, depressed, and lonesome. He wrote that he dreaded what would happen if American lives were lost on either American or belligerent ships sunk without warning, as he knew there would be a terrific clamor for war. "It keeps one in a state of tension here just as it does at home—but we dont know anything you dont get daily from the dispatches. . . . I miss you all so much It is hard not to be able to talk things over with you Belle day by day as we always have."[46]

Soon after severing diplomatic relations with Germany, the President invited neutral countries to take similar action.[47] None of the European neutrals followed his lead. In their replies some referred to his refusal to respond to their previous efforts at cooperation. All confined their action against Germany to diplomatic protests of unrestricted submarine activity in the war zone and continued to maintain their neutrality.[48] This was what Bob thought the United States should have done. He believed that whatever violation of rights or commercial sacrifice Holland, Denmark, Norway, Sweden, Switzerland, Spain, Central and South America might tolerate without sacrificing their dignity and honor the United States was "strong enough and brave enough to endure for the sake of saving the world from being drawn into this dire catastrophe."[49]

After publication of the German note, many American ships had remained at anchor in the ports of the Atlantic seaboard rather than risk taking cargoes through the war zone. American shipowners were talking of arming merchant vessels themselves or were joining with representatives of big industrial interests in clamoring for government protection. Bob thought the arming of merchant ships for the purpose of protecting them by firing upon belligerents would rob them of their neutral status and the right that status gave them to certain immunities. Firing upon a belligerent would in itself be an act of war which he thought might take this country into the war through the order of a ship's captain without even waiting for Congress to pass upon the issue as provided in the Constitution. If the United States was drawn into the European War, Bob believed it would hazard the peace of this Nation for all time by linking the destiny of American democracy with the ever menacing antagonisms of foreign powers. He thought it would be criminal to risk hurling this country into the European conflict to maintain our technical right to travel and to commercial profits. As an expression of his own individual opinion, and with the hope that it might start thought along this line, he introduced a joint resolution on February 12 making it unlawful when this country was not at war for any armed merchant vessel of the United States to leave the ports of this country or any of its territories for foreign countries.[50] A week before this resolution was introduced, he had written his family that if he were President "not a ship should clear from an Atlantic port or any other for a European destination. In 60 days the war would be over."[51]

On the day that Bob introduced his resolution, delegations of several hundred men and women representing many organizations in different States arrived in Washington. They had come to plead with the President and Congress to keep the country out of war. During the day speeches were made and resolutions passed at several conferences held in committee rooms at the Capitol and at Washington hotels. The meetings attracted crowds of people "who applauded and cheered the arguments against war with a fervor almost religious." Among the delegates were Mrs. Henry Villard, chairman of the Emergency Peace Federation; Professors Emily Greene Balch of Wellesley, William I. Hull of Swarthmore, David S. Muzzey of Columbia, Harry Allen Overstreet of the City College of New York, Rev. Norman M. Thomas, C. A. Sorenson, representing Western Granges and peace societies; W. T. Creasy, Secretary of the Pennsylvania Grange; Edward Cassidy of the Central Labor Union of New York, and Joseph D. Cannon, representing the Western Miners' Union. Members of the delegation went to the Capitol, where they called on Bob, Works, Wadsworth, and other Senators and Representatives. Senator Stone received the entire delegation in the Marble Room just off the Senate Chamber. A reporter noted that he listened to their speeches with deep interest and "seemed to be visibly moved by the sentiment of the addresses." From the Capitol the delegates marched down Pennsylvania Avenue in a biting, cold wind to the White House. The President was "out." But Secretary Tumulty graciously received them and their petitions. Mrs. Villard made a brief extemporaneous speech, and Norman Thomas read resolutions pledging loyal support to the President in his efforts to settle international disputes by peaceful means and urging Congress to take no irrevocable step toward war but in case of such a crisis "to seek, through an advisory referendum, a direct expression of the will of the American people." That evening a mass meeting was held at All Souls' Unitarian Church, where various speakers advocated keeping Americans out of the war zone and a referendum vote on the issue of war.[52] In talking with the delegates at the Capitol, Bob had found that they seemed to know about his bill for an advisory referendum on war, which he had introduced at the previous session, and were all "boosting for it."[53]

The previous week, when the Chicago branch of the Woman's Peace Party had passed resolutions asking for a conference of neutral nations, a referendum vote on war, and keeping Americans out of the war zone, Belle had written Bob calling his attention to the fact that they were supporting the things he had long been advocating. In Wisconsin, Belle had been continuing her work with the Woman's Peace Party by speaking at various meetings. After she had addressed a gathering at the City Library in Madison, Bob read in the *Wisconsin State Journal* a scathing editorial about the meeting by Richard Lloyd Jones.[54] Bob wrote her that it was "a nasty thing Dick Jones did. But dont mind him. Nothing matters so long as we are doing what is right. Thats the only thing that lasts." A few days later he said he hoped the editorial would not make her so uncomfortable that she would "pass up any invitations to speak. Lets have peace if we have to fight all Hell to preserve it."[55]

Bob had a feeling that something more was coming soon from the President, and dreaded the result. Night after night he worked on different aspects of the international situation. Not knowing what might come up suddenly in the Senate, he wanted to "get in shape for any quick turn."[56] He planned to offer his advisory referendum on war as an amendment if any bill came up in the Senate to which it was germane. Through this strategy he hoped to bring it before the Senate and force a roll-call vote on the issue.[57] To meet another possibility he wrote to John Bassett Moore, Edwin Borchard, and other authorities on international law asking their opinions on the right of any merchant ship to claim the immunities of a merchant ship, including warning, if the ship was armed. He thought "it might count in a crucial hour" if he could get from them a declaration that "the sinking of an *armed merchantman without warning*—even if attended with loss of American life" was "*not a cause* for war." Having studied the correspondence of the State Department on this question, he noted that "it squints both ways & leaves the matter in doubt."[58]

Although no official statement was given out from the White House, the Washington newspaper reports indicated that the President's thought and Bob's were moving in opposite directions on the question of arming merchant ships. On February 14, two days after Bob had introduced his resolution, a double-column headline announced: "Cabinet Split Over Arming Merchantmen to Resist 'Sub' War/Practically Certain, However, That President Soon Will Provide American Ships Protection/Daniels Opposes The Project But Lansing Backs Wilson In Belief That Vessels Should Be Armed." The next day another headline shrieked, "President Likely To Call

Joint Session Any Day And Ask Authority To Use Force of Arms."[59] None of the men Bob talked with seemed to know what the President's plans were. Therefore these and similar newspaper reports influenced the decision and action of many Senators. On February 16 Bob said in a letter to his family, "If the President springs any war stuff we will debate it (at least a few of us) until the last gasp."[60]

Subsequent developments indicated that the newspapers had received inside information. Tremendous pressure was, in fact, being brought to bear on Wilson to arm merchant ships.[61] The issue had come up in the Cabinet meetings and was creating stormy sessions. Wilson maintained that ships might arm but that he must have authority from Congress to put Navy guns and gunners on them. Several members of the Cabinet were insisting upon action to a point that came near open revolt and resignations.[62]

On Saturday, February 17, Bob had a call from Arthur Brisbane, editor of Hearst's newspapers, which increased his anxiety. Brisbane was much worried over the situation. He had seen several Cabinet members who had told him they were for war and believed it was "sure to come."[63] The following morning Bob read the newspaper reports stating that the President had gone to the Capitol late Saturday afternoon to discuss with Stone and a number of other Senators the advisability of asking Congress for authority to protect merchant ships against German submarines.[64] He also read that on Saturday Lenroot had made a speech in the House denouncing pacifists as a "peril" to the country and attacking any war referendum on the ground that it might bring on civil war and that there were some issues too important to be delegated to the people. Bob thought this attack was designed to take a shot at him and his bill for an advisory referendum on war, but he assured the family that it would not mar his and Lenroot's "cordial relations." Bob spent Sunday alone at his office in the Capitol "looking up things bearing on the foreign situation," while his two secretaries, Hannan and Grace Lynch, worked in the office downstairs answering the stacks of letters and telegrams which had come from different parts of the country urging that the United States keep out of the European War. When he wrote to the family that night, Bob noted that these letters were all one way, and then added, "I suppose there are hosts of people who want war and sustain the President, but naturally they dont write to me."[65]

The legislative jam had become so great that the Senate held a night session on Monday. Although Bob was watching every move on the floor, he broke away long enough to go to the station to meet his son, Bob, Jr., who had decided to follow Dr. Phil Fox's advice and get out of the severe Wisconsin climate for the winter. From the station they returned to the Capitol. That night, when the Senate adjourned, the "two boys," as Belle called them, went home to share the bedroom where Bob had written his long letters to the family. Each morning they went to work together. The daily companionship of his twenty-two-year-old son was a great comfort to Bob during this period of intense anxiety and hard work. To an unusual degree he relied on his son's clear thought, objective judgment, and exceptional executive ability. In taking a position as his father's clerk, Bob, Jr., had access to the Senate floor and assumed many office responsibilities which lightened the burden his father had been carrying.

The day after Bob, Jr., arrived, the Revenue bill, providing half a billion dollars to meet the greatly increased appropriations for the Army and Navy, came up in the Senate. Only fourteen days of the session remained before Congress would automatically adjourn. Debate on the bill occupied the Senate for several days. Bob, Jr., wrote home that his father was hard at work on amendments which would place the burden of taxation on those best able to pay it.[66] On February 23 Lodge presided over a Republican caucus which included, among others, Penrose, Smoot, Weeks, and Brandegee of the regular Republican faction, and Norris, Bob, and Poindexter of the progressive group. The press noted that this was the first time Bob had attended a party caucus in many years, and that there was "perfect harmony between the two Republican factions." For totally different reasons they had united in a decision to prolong debate on the Revenue bill and force an extra session. Lodge and the Senators who shared his views wished Congress to remain in session because they feared the President might retreat in the march they thought he had started along the road to war. Bob, Norris, and a number of others wanted Congress in session to prevent Wilson from going further in that direction.[67]

When the Republicans returned to the Senate Chamber after their caucus, a reporter noted that "all the indications pointed to a well-organized filibuster. It was whispered that Senator La Follette, who has a reputation as a long distance speaker, was prepared to take the floor on call and consume the better portion of two or three days."[68] Democratic Senators openly charged the Republicans with filibustering. John Sharp Williams took the floor to inform his colleagues that he had noticed the unprecedented spectacle of a private conversation between La Follette and Penrose, which corroborated the report he had read in the morning papers that the Republican Party had "made up its mind to filibuster in order to have an extra session."[69] Many hours were consumed in debate on amendments which Bob and others offered. The *New York Times* noted that the Republicans sided almost to a man with the Wisconsin Senator and that the Democrats were treated to a further exhibition of the "unanimity of Republican purpose by seeing Republican after Republican consult with Senator La Follette and then offer another amendment and demand a roll-call."[70]

On Saturday night a truce was reached in the Republican filibuster when the Democrats agreed to put off the vote on the Revenue bill until the following Wednesday. Bob felt that those who wanted an extra session had made a good bargain in this arrangement because it held the vote off for about forty-eight hours longer than he thought they could have been certain of doing by continuing their filibustering tactics.[71]

Some time during the morning of Monday, February 26, Bob, Jr., wrote his mother, "There seems to be no doubt now but what there will be forced an extra session *in case* the President asks for authority to use the army & navy as 'He' thinks fit."[72] Before this letter was finished, word was received at the Capitol that the President would address a joint session of Congress in the House Chamber at one o'clock. Shortly before the President arrived, Senators went over to the House and took the seats assigned to them near the front of the Chamber. The galleries and floor were crowded, and the mood that pervaded the audience was tense as Wilson read his brief Armed Neutrality message. Sitting near the front, Bob listened with arms folded across his breast. He did not move until the President asked Congress for authority not only to supply merchant ships with defensive arms, but "to employ any other instrumentalities or methods" that might "be necessary and adequate to protect our ships and our people in their legitimate and peaceful pursuits on the seas."[73] A friend noted that Bob was so shocked at this demand for unlimited authority that he "threw up both hands instinctively as though hope were gone."[74]

CHAPTER XLIII

The Famous Armed Ship Filibuster

When the President finished reading his Armed Neutrality message, he walked quickly out of the House Chamber. The applause gave way to the reverberations of excited discussion among Senators and Representatives on the floor and along the corridors of the Capitol. Bob did not linger to talk with his colleagues but went directly to the Senate restaurant, where he had lunch with his son and Senator Hoke Smith of Georgia. Soon after lunch Bob, Jr., continued the interrupted letter to his mother: "Well the President has been down and asked for everything he needs to pull off a little war all his own." He added that his father was determined to do everything he could to force an extra session, and that Smith's comment indicated the Georgia Senator would "do nothing unusual to prevent an extra session."[1]

The following day the Armed Ship bill was introduced in the Senate. It gave the President the powers he had asked. Bob delayed consideration of the bill for one day by refusing to alter a previous unanimous consent agreement that the Revenue bill should remain constantly before the Senate until it was voted upon.[2] When questioned by a reporter as to his reason for doing this, he replied that he wanted the public to know about the bill before it was acted upon.[3] Study of the Armed Ship bill convinced him that it meant war and that if it did not confer the power to make war entirely in the President's discretion, there were no words in human language which could accomplish that result. He thought it violated the letter and the spirit of a fundamental provision of the Constitution "which expressly vests the war power in Congress," a provision without which "the Constitution could not have been adopted."[4] Furthermore, he believed that, if enacted, the measure would prove inadequate and ineffective, since all the available evidence pointed to the futility of such armament. It seemed to him that the loss of life and tonnage on armed merchant ships of the Allies had already demonstrated that placing guns on merchantmen did not afford effective protection against submarines. Only two days before this bill was introduced, the armed British merchant ship *Laconia* had been torpedoed twice and sunk without a chance to fire a shot. In view of all the evidence Bob thought it would be criminal to arm our merchant ships and lure them "to embark on a voyage fraught with such imminent peril" in the belief that they might resist attack.[5]

The bill had been drawn by Wilson himself. He had presented it only six days before the Sixty-fourth Congress would, under the Constitution, automatically end at noon March 4. Bob was therefore convinced that in asking for this power so late in the session, and attempting to force the bill through before adjournment, the President revealed his desire to be left alone to exercise extraordinary autocratic power during the nine months before the new Congress would meet.*

To Bob, Norris, and the other Senators who fought through to the end to defeat the bill, the issue was fundamental to the preservation of democracy because they believed it was a menace to the liberty of a people to place the war-making power in the hands of any President. Bob's letters record that before February 16 he and a few other Senators had agreed to debate "until the last gasp" any move the President might make which they believed would permit him to take the United States into the European War.[6] A day or two after Wilson's February 26 address to Congress, he told his young cousin, Suzanne La Follette, that the Armed Ship bill meant war and must be blocked.[7] He warned her that he was organizing a fight to defeat it and she must be prepared to hear him called a traitor.[8]

When the Senate met at eleven on Friday morning, March 2, to debate the bill at the first moment permitted under the rules, Bob had a list of the Senators ready to help defeat it. The time each would take had been carefully calculated. Those he feared might yield to the inevitable Administration pressure during the final hours

---

* The day before the President addressed Congress, Secretary Lane wrote his brother that the President did not want an extra session, but wished to be "alone and unbothered" and would probably not call Cabinet meetings if Congress adjourned. *Letters of Franklin K. Lane,* p. 240.

of the session were encouraged to speak early. The last names on the list were Clapp, Gronna, Lane, Works, Norris, and La Follette. Excepting Lane, all were progressive Republicans.

Bob counted on ten Senators, besides himself, to speak against the bill.* Frequently, on the floor and in his office, Bob talked with these men, one or two at a time. There was not an hour during the two days and nights the Armed Ship bill was before the Senate when some member of this group was not ready to take the floor. There were also several others who might help in ways that would not publicly identify them with the opposition.

Under the Constitution at this time the Sixty-fourth Congress would end on March 4. There remained, therefore, only forty-nine hours before the automatic adjournment, at noon Sunday, to consider all the important legislation still pending. Bills carrying appropriations of $1,500,000,000, including the largest Army appropriation bill ever presented, with its provision for universal military training, had not yet passed the Senate. Although this congestion of the calendar made an early extra session appear inevitable, the Administration insisted the Senate should pass the Armed Ship bill before adjournment.

For several days there had been rumors the Administration program might be blocked and an extra session forced. The press reported, "La Follette loomed up as the great unknown quantity," but kept "an ominous silence" and refused to be sounded out by newspaper men or inquiring Senators.[9] Although Bob made no public statement, his strategy was well formulated. He hoped to block the bill, forcing it over to the new Congress, thus giving time for the anti-war sentiment, which he knew existed throughout the country, to register on Congress and defeat the measure. This plan, however, suddenly became more difficult than he had anticipated. The publication, in an exclusive Associated Press dispatch, of the Zimmermann telegram on March 1, the very day the Armed Ship bill

---

* Other Senators opposing the bill were Cummins, progressive Republican; Jones of Washington, a regular Republican; Stone, Vardaman, O'Gorman, and Kirby, Democrats. Though Kenyon, progressive Republican, had previously conferred with the anti-war group, he did not cooperate in defeating this bill. Gore, an anti-war Democrat, who might have helped, was ill and absent.

first came up in the Senate, abruptly shifted the emphasis of the debate.

Bob and Senator Stone were convinced the release of the telegram had been carefully timed and suddenly sprung to inflame public opinion and influence Congress.[10] Many newspapers also took this view.[11] Even Stone, chairman of the Senate Foreign Relations Committee, had known nothing of it until after the story had been given to the press.[12] The content and mysterious manner of publication evoked excited debate that day in the Senate and House.

The telegram, signed by Zimmermann, the German Foreign Secretary, carried instructions to Eckhardt, the German Minister at Mexico City. It announced the intention of beginning unrestricted submarine warfare on February 1, but also endeavoring, in spite of this, to keep the United States neutral. If neutrality could not be maintained, and war came, it offered to make an alliance with Mexico: Germany to give financial support and Mexico to reconquer her lost territory in New Mexico, Texas, and Arizona. In the event that war with the United States finally came, then it was to be suggested to the President of Mexico that he communicate with Japan proposing adherence to this plan.[13] Had Germany desired to inflame American opinion, a better document could not have been devised. The press comments generally assumed that although our Government did "not admit having instigated the publication," there was no doubt it had "tacitly consented."[14]

The exclusive Associated Press dispatch, carrying the Zimmermann note to the country, also announced: "This document has been in the hands of the government since President Wilson broke off diplomatic relations with Germany [February 3]. It has been kept secret while the President has been asking Congress for full authority to deal with Germany and while Congress has been hesitating."[15]

To Bob this statement implied that the President had been deliberately withholding from Congress important documents regarding the belligerents' action and releasing them through the press at the opportune moment to force legislation giving the Chief Executive further powers. Already deeply concerned over the President's lack of real neutrality, Bob's distrust was increased. During the violent debate which ensued, he asked how long the note had been in the Government's possession,[16] and whether it had been given out by the Administration or any of its Departments to be first communicated to Congress through the press.[17] In a memorandum among his private papers there is a penciled question, "Why was it given to the public in the manner it was?"[18]

The answers to some of his questions were publicly revealed many years later. The fact was, this note, sent in cipher from Berlin, had been intercepted by the British Naval Intelligence Service on January 16.[19] A month later the English translation was transmitted through Ambassador Page and was received at the State Department on Saturday evening, February 24.[20]

Although the President's first impulse had been to make the note public immediately, he had been persuaded to wait and consult with Lansing, who was out of town when it arrived. On his return on Tuesday morning, Lansing suggested the telegram be made public indirectly to protect the State Department from the charge of influencing opinion on the Armed Ship bill.[21] After a private view of the contents, Colonel House added his persuasive word in a letter to the President, urging it be published the following day, as it would "make a profound impression both on Congress and on the country."[22] The next afternoon, when the President telephoned that he thought it wise to give the telegram to the morning papers, Lansing again suggested it be made public indirectly, as "this would avoid any charge of using the document improperly and would attract more attention than issuing it officially." The President agreed to this plan.[23]

That night Lansing, under pledge of secrecy as to the source of information, gave a close paraphrase of the telegram to E. M. Hood, an Associated Press reporter. The startling story broke in flaming headlines the next morning. But it never has been explained why this inspired dispatch included the inaccurate statement that "this document has been in the hands of the government since President Wilson broke off diplomatic relations with Germany." The plan worked out as anticipated. A few hours before the House was to vote on the Armed Ship bill, Lansing and the President confirmed the authenticity of the telegram.[24] The disclosure undoubtedly changed many votes and contributed to the large majority of 403 to 14.[25] In the Senate it broke down party lines, shifting to the President's active support Lodge and others who had long favored entry into the European War.[26]

All this suddenly rendered the fight Bob and the others had agreed to make against the bill infinitely more difficult. As anticipated by Lansing, the Associated Press dispatch was a front-page story with sensational headlines. Leading newspapers in Wisconsin, as well as the East, became more virulent in their attacks on the Senators who were opposing the Armed Ship bill.[27] As it approached a vote in the Senate, the *Milwaukee Journal* declared that Bob and his colleagues were misrepresenting and humiliating Wisconsin. "Newspaper after newspaper," it stated, "that has stood staunchly by La Follette in his battles in Wisconsin now comes out in rebuke of his present stand. . . . He may not heed the warning, but he knows today, that in this he does not represent Wisconsin."[28]

Shortly after the Senate met at eleven on Friday morning, March 2, Stone moved to take up the Armed Ship bill (S. 8322). The motion was agreed to by a vote of 64 to 15.[29] Bob voted "No," thus again registering publicly the opposition he was to maintain steadily until adjournment. The beginning of the debate, however, was delayed until four to permit final consideration and a vote upon the Navy bill in accord with a unanimous-consent agreement made the previous night.[30] Thus supporters of the Armed Ship bill themselves agreed to the loss of four hours which might have been available for its debate.

According to customary procedure, Stone, as chairman of the Foreign Relations Committee, would have been in charge of the bill. But after he announced his opposition, Hitchcock, of Nebraska, the next ranking Democrat on the committee, took charge. He had previously opposed American entrance into the war, as Bob and other Senators ironically reminded him later. Forty Senators had, in 1915, voted for his amendment, declaring it an unlawful breach of neutrality for any American to furnish arms or ammunition to belligerents in Europe.[31] It was also reported that he had opposed the Armed Ship bill in committee, but after seeing the Zimmermann letter "he accepted the responsibility forced upon him by Mr. Stone's desertion."[32]

In opening the debate Hitchcock admitted the bill did not entirely represent his own judgment, but argued the President should be given the power he asked because he could be better trusted than Congress to keep the country out of war. He reminded the Senators that as recently as February 26 the President had told them that he was as much opposed to war at this time as he had ever been. Hitchcock added that he was ready "to take the President of the United States at his word upon his record."[33] Lodge made the principal Republican speech for the bill, suddenly becoming the President's advocate. Believing he had the previous day adroitly "tied the German note to Wilson" and caught him "in the grip of events" which would force him into war,[34] Lodge, with his particular impassioned elegance, urged the Senate to "confer upon the President the powers he asks."[35]

After more than seven hours of debate, Hitchcock asked unanimous consent to lay aside the Senate bill (S. 8322) and take up the similar bill which had already passed the House (H.R. 21052).[36] He sought to eliminate the parliamentary necessity of returning the Senate bill to the House by securing a direct vote on the House bill. Several hours would thus be gained in rushing the bill to final passage. Bob recognized the strategy and objected. This blocked Hitchcock's maneuver, but intensified the growing rage against the Wisconsin Senator.[37]

Soon after midnight Hitchcock repeated his request for unanimous consent to take up the House bill. Norris suavely said he did not want to object if he could avoid it, and would like to consult with his colleague.[38] Hitchcock assented, and Norris went over to consult briefly with Bob.[39]

This unanimous-consent agreement was finally bought by the Administration leaders at the high price of consenting to the recess which Bob, Norris, and their group had been trying to force.[40] Bob withdrew his objection to substituting the House bill, and the Senate agreed to recess until ten Saturday morning, March 3.[41] This recess cut the fighting time for the little opposition group by nine hours. It was the beginning of defeat for the President.[42]

Two Senators, riding home together that night, felt they had done a good day's work toward keeping their country out of war. Norris said to La Follette: "We've got them beaten. We can hold them now: we've enough speakers to filibuster from tomorrow on."[43]

As the Senate met Saturday for its final twenty-four-hour session before automatic adjournment, a telegram from Belle brought a word of understanding to Bob: "My faith in the clearness of your vision, in the rightness of your action, was never stronger than in this hour of national peril. Strength be with you."[44]

That morning, while Brandegee and Fall were speaking, Bob retired to the cloakroom to rest, leaving Norris and Stone to guard the floor. These "cat naps" were an ominous sign. They were known to be part of his previous "filibustering expeditions." A Senator asked his intentions, but Bob, stretching out on the couch, turned his face to the wall, indicating he resented questioning. Soon he was lost in restful sleep—a preparation for his battle to keep the country at peace.[45] Meanwhile on the floor, Brandegee, a Republican member of the Foreign Relations Committee, and Fall, of subsequent Teapot Dome fame, were openly advocating war with Germany and admitting the effect of the President's bill would be to take the United States into the European War.[46] Bob later, in his magazine, quoted these Senators and similar assertions made by Lodge, Reed, and Walsh. "The Armed Ship bill meant war," he wrote. "The public need not rely on opponents of the measure for proof of this fact; supporters of the bill in the course of the debate again and again specifically stated that it meant war."[47]

Early Saturday afternoon Stone, a prominent Democrat, began his attack on the bill. He had been a member of the House during the same three terms Bob was. In the Senate since 1903, he had joined in the famous filibuster against the Aldrich-Vreeland Currency bill, adding his six- or seven-hour speech to Bob's more than eighteen-hour talk.[48] Then the fight had been against the dominant Republican regime. But now Stone was breaking on a crucial issue with the President of his own party whom he loved and admired.[49] He and Bob had conferred frequently. Both men believed the bill meant war, and were determined to defeat it.

As Stone spoke, many sensed the personal tragedy his decision meant: "For nearly four years I have worked by the President's side, and have enjoyed both his friendship and his confidence. . . . If the question to-day were one only of faith and trust in him, I would not hesitate; . . . I can not take part in committing what I believe would be an unpardonable and perilous mistake."[50] He recalled the President's neutrality proclamation of August 19, 1914, and his proclamation of September 8, 1914, for a day of prayer for peace. Referring to his own support of Wilson's peace proclamation, he said: "Following the President's leadership, I stood for honest neutrality between these warring nations. . . . I have not changed. I can not change. I have no reason to change."[51] He reminded the Senate that even as late as the previous Monday the President, when asking for power to arm ships, had in effect stated that "so far we had no just cause for war."[52]

He discussed Wilson's speech of January 22, 1917, which Bob had spontaneously commended immediately after the President addressed the Senate.[53] Reading an excerpt, which included Wilson's statement "that it must be a peace without victory," Stone commented in terms which also accurately expressed Bob's position: "I thought the President was right then; I think so now. . . . I stand to-day where the President stood one month ago. . . ."[54]

As Stone continued hour after hour, Democratic leaders recognized he was definitely aiding the filibuster.[55] The serious situation started discussion of harsh parliamentary tactics, although, at 6:15, when Stone concluded his four-and-a-half-hour speech,[56] only three Senators had spoken against the bill while eight had argued for it.

During the evening, however, Hitchcock repeatedly sought unanimous consent to limit speeches and fix a definite hour for a vote. Each time he was blocked by objections from Cummins, Clapp, Gronna, Norris, and Works. When Hitchcock finally revealed his determination to identify and thus punish those who had "a deliberate intention to filibuster the bill to death," Norris replied frankly and accurately, "I would not hesitate to kill the bill if I could. . . . But the fact is that most of the time has been taken up by those who favor the bill."[57] This defiant declaration was ominous. Debate became more bitter. Supporters and opponents of the bill each openly charged the other with filibustering.[58] Threats began to circulate in the cloakrooms.

Early in the evening Sir Cecil Spring-Rice, the British Ambassador, was among the anxious observers in the diplomatic gallery, where foreign representatives were watching the outcome. At intervals several Cabinet members were seen on the floor. It was whispered the Administration was turning on heavy pressure. Throughout the night the galleries remained crowded, though at times during the debate the Senate floor appeared almost deserted. But Senators did not go home. In nearby offices and cloakrooms bipartisan conferences on how to break the filibuster and punish opposing Senators were keeping the President's supporters awake.[59] A well informed Washington correspondent reported doubt was being openly expressed "that La Follette could be headed off. He has it in his power to kill the bill unless he can be caught off his guard or 'strong arm' parliamentary tactics are used."[60]

Throughout the continuous night session Bob remained at the Capitol, where he had two offices. The one in the sub-basement looking out on a little grass plot was occupied by his secretary and intimate friend John J. Hannan and his clerk Grace Lynch. The other, directly above, was his private office, where he slept that night as best he could when not watching the parliamentary situation, conferring with people, and preparing material which he expected to use in speaking Sunday morning. Bob, Jr., was, at this time, his father's assistant clerk, and thus had the privilege of the floor. Neither he nor Hannan slept that night. One or the other was constantly watching the floor and keeping the Senator informed.

Shortly before three o'clock Sunday morning, Bob was hastily called to the floor by a warning of a new attempt to break the opposition. Gronna, who had aided the filibuster since 1:30, was still speaking. Toward the end of his speech an observer counted nine Senators in the Chamber; he noted, however, that "Republicans and Democrats were shouting with laughter in the Democratic cloakroom over imitations of Senators by Joseph O'Toole, Chief of Pages."[61] But as Hitchcock suddenly appeared in the Chamber and announced he had a statement signed "by nearly 80 members of the Senate,"[62] the cloakroom doors immediately swung open, as if at a signal, and at least 75 per cent of the weary Senators took their seats. Ollie James, ardent Administration supporter, and a powerful man to be relied on in emergencies, was now in the Chair.

The round robin, actually bearing seventy-six signatures, had been drawn up and submitted, during the night, to each Senator present. This statement, Hitchcock now announced, was to be put in the *Record* to show that nine-tenths of the Senate wanted to vote for this bill, but were "being prevented by 12 Senators."[63] Robinson, at Hitchcock's request, read the statement into the *Record*. Obviously angry and much excited, he stumbled over some of the illegible signatures. Although Bob was in the Chamber, he made no recorded comment. But an unfinished note, penciled during the debate, gives his immediate reaction and certain facts which were then well known to Senators, but little known to the public: "The Tory Republicans who have spoken on this bill—and signed the statement [round robin]—were and have been playing a game—They supported this measure because it makes for war[;] some of them have declared their readiness to vote for a declaration of war—but they were ready—to force an extra session."[64]*

The presentation of this round robin, more than eight hours before adjournment, was openly denounced by two of the men who had signed it with the understanding it would be used only as a last resort.[65] Gronna, who had refused to sign, expressed the mood of Bob and those opposing the bill when he boldly declared that he was not afraid to have the country know it and that Hitchcock would find there were others who could not "be bulldozed by the Senator from Nebraska."[66]

John Sharp Williams quickly came to the defense, warning that it would be "one of the most humiliating spectacles in the course of American history" if Congress adjourned and the bill was defeated by the Senate.[67] He spoke with an emotional intensity which reflected the growing anger on the floor and in the cloakrooms. Fatigue and frustration were steadily brewing bitterness. Seeing the Wisconsin Senator in the Chamber, Williams finally asked whether anyone present objected to unanimous consent for a vote at nine o'clock Sunday morning. Bob promptly replied, "Well, Mr. President, reserving the right to object to the request when it is presented finally, I will say to the Senator, to save time, that I shall object when it is made."[68] He thus carefully phrased his answer to protect his right to demand later that the rule be enforced and the unanimous-consent agreement submitted in writing. By this parliamentary tactic he could perhaps gain the floor; it would certainly cause further delay.

In the early morning hours Works, a man of great dignity and quiet power, after repeated efforts, secured the floor. Formerly a Justice of the California Supreme Court, he had been elected to the Senate as a progressive Republican in 1910, but had not been a candidate for renomination. Believing the bill would "amount to a declaration of war," he made his final Senate speech on this issue.[69]

---

* This refers to their earlier cooperation toward forcing an extra session by their dilatory tactics on the Revenue bill.

He agreed with Bob that certain Senators were advocating passage of the measure on that very theory.

Stating he had received thousands of letters "from good American citizens protesting earnestly against this step toward war,"[70] Works denounced the newspaper campaign to involve the United States in the European conflict. He had read into the *Record* an excerpt from the London *Daily Chronicle* expressing England's gratitude: "The debt that England owes the newspaper world of America can not be estimated. The editors of the best journals have been fearless and very shrewd champions of the allies' cause. . . . We have no better allies in America than the editors of the great papers."[71]

Following Works, at about six Sunday morning, the genial and much loved Clapp, who had been waiting on the floor since midnight, delivered his final Senate speech against the bill. With deep feeling he protested he could not abdicate his "function as a Senator and delegate to another the power to declare war."[72]

Lane of Oregon, whom Bob loved deeply, and whom he knew to be fatally ill, made a brief speech. The basis of the fundamental understanding which had existed between the two men from the time they first met was revealed in his words that day. In opposing the bill, he spoke as a representative of the "hundreds of thousands" who had never "received a salary large enough to keep them from crowding the edge of hunger and starvation all their lives." He, like Bob, was "no man of peace," and "would fight to the last ditch . . . against anybody or any nation that attempted to invade this country"; but he did not wish to protect citizens who travel around the world during wartime selling munitions when so many of our own citizens were in distress. Declaring the terms of this bill would lead to war, he uttered the prophetic words he was to live long enough to see realized: "I would not be at all surprised now if 30 days should bring a great calamity to this country."[73]

About 7:30 Sunday morning, with Vice President Marshall presiding, Norris began the last opposition speech before Bob expected to take the floor. Answering the repeated charges of filibustering, Norris said that "some careful student will some day look up the *Record,* and he will find that those who favored the bill have taken the most of the time in its discussion."[74] Within a few days two Senators did precisely what Norris predicted.[75]

As the session entered its final hours, feeling grew more heated and menacing on the floor, in the cloakrooms and corridors of the Capitol. Some of the majority Senators willfully omitted the usual greetings of "senatorial courtesy" toward their colleagues. It was evident rage and hatred were swiftly replacing normal tolerance. An editorial in the Sunday morning *New York Times* foreshadowed the press vituperation the minority must expect. It denounced Stone and La Follette as participating in "an evil endeavor, in which no loyal American would have engaged,"[76] and reported in the news columns that the filibuster was "largely incited if not directed by Mr. La Follette."[77]

The pressure was intense, but none of those who had agreed to make the well planned fight failed. The "little group held back their ammunition and filled in the last hours of the time." There were also some Senators who wanted to see the bill beaten "but would not filibuster so it could be seen."[78] At least two prominent Democratic Senators wanted the "filibuster to win," but thought "they could not afford" to oppose the bill openly. However, after confiding in Norris, they followed his suggestion and assisted "in consuming some of the time" by speaking in its favor.[79]

Parliamentary dangers were imminent; any tactical slip, through inexperience or lack of seasoned floor leadership, might be disastrous. During the final forty-nine hours of the session there was always a member of the opposition on the floor ready to speak and prevent a vote. Fully aware, from his own previous experience in filibusters, that the bitterest denunciation would inevitably be directed against the last speaker, Bob accepted the responsibility. He agreed to follow Norris and hold the floor for the last four or five hours, or as much longer as might be necessary until final adjournment. "Some one had to speak last. It was the hard place," and Bob "took it."[80]

Whenever pressure was strong for a chance to speak on an important measure, it had become the custom for the Presiding Officer to make out a list and recognize Senators in the order noted. Bob had, therefore, taken the precaution Saturday to ask the Vice President to put his name upon the list of speakers. The Vice President had replied that "he had torn up all lists and should keep no more as it caused criticism. He had kept no list the last 24 or 36 hours on the Armed Ship bill."[81]

The following morning, some time after the "round robin" had been presented, an incident occurred which Bob recorded in a family letter: "About 4 or 5 A.M. Sunday morning [March 4] I received a *confidential* note unsigned as follows:

" 'A tip—It has been privately communicated to me that a scheme is hatching to have the Presiding Officer ignore or refuse to recognize you when you rise to speak & go forward "ruthlessly" to put the Question and force a vote. Ask no questions but depend upon it that that scheme is afoot.' "*

Bob added, "I was told by the messenger who sent the note."[82]

This warning, written on a pink "Senate Memorandum" slip, was definite evidence that Senators were planning to violate what Bob believed were important constitutional rights. It increased his determination to invoke every parliamentary device to get his message to the country. He was convinced the American people did not want war.

During the debate telegrams had been pouring into his office. Four out of five urged defeat of the bill. However, most of those advocating passage insisted that the President should be given this power in order to maintain peace. Bob was convinced that if the country once understood, what most Senators knew, that this so-called "Armed Neutrality" actually meant war and the end of any real neutrality, there would be an overwhelming pressure on Congress to defeat it at the extra session which the filibuster had now clearly made inevitable. With this determined purpose he went on the floor to make the final speech against the bill.

The Senate could have no doubt as to Bob's intention, for while Norris was still speaking, Hannan and Bob, Jr., had carried in the volumes of diplomatic correspondence and other material he expected to use. These were piled high upon his desk and the one adjoining when he entered the Chamber about eight thirty, ready to ask recognition as soon as Norris finished.

He was surprised to find that Senator Luke Lea had replaced the Vice President as Presiding Officer. Lea signaled him to come to the desk, explaining that he had been called to the Chair by the Vice President, who *"had handed him* a list containing the names of

* This note, written on a "Senate Memorandum," is with the La Follette Papers.

United States Senate.

MEMORANDUM.

A tip:— It has been privately communicated to me that a Scheme is hatching to have the Presiding Officer ignore or refuse to recognize you when you rise to speak — & go forward "ruthlessly" to put the question & force a vote. Ask no questions, but depend upon it that that Scheme is afoot.

At about 4 A.M. March 4, 1917, Bob received a confidential warning on a pink "Senate Memorandum" slip

617

Owen and Hitchcock who were to be recognized in that order when Norris yielded—". Bob told Lea it was a trick to shut him out. Only the day before, the Vice President had stated he was keeping no more lists. Lea said he must enforce the list if he remained in the Chair, but offered to refuse to be "a party to recognizing" it if Bob "protested then and there." As it was better for him to have Lea in the Chair than anyone else, Bob answered he would *assume* that Hitchcock and Owen would not occupy all the time and requested that his name be entered on the list following Hitchcock's. Lea did this. Bob then went to Owen and asked "if he could tell me how much time he would occupy. He replied that 'he did not know.' I saw then that I was to be shut out—and boiled within."[83]

Lea also undoubtedly warned Bob of the cloakroom talk threatening violence against him. For, following this talk with Lea, Bob, Jr., recalls his father instructed him to go down to his office and bring up his little traveling bag "and put it in the corridor just back of the Vice President's desk. I knew he had the gun in the bag and I consulted with Colonel Hannan and we decided to take the gun out of the bag."[84] This small black bag Bob usually left at his office, packed, ready for travel. For many years he had carried the revolver for protection on speaking trips. To meet engagements he was often forced to use "accommodation trains" and other means of travel necessitating long waits at lonely stations during the night. He was a crack shot, and this assured protection.

Bob, Jr., brought the bag up and put it in the corridor just outside the door. He remembers that when he came into the Chamber his father called him over and asked where he had put it: "I told him. He did not ask me anything about the gun and I did not volunteer the information that I had taken it out of the bag. At no time during the situation did he ask for the bag or go out to the bag. When things got tense I felt perhaps we had made a mistake in taking the gun out of the bag because I did not know but what violence would develop and I was afraid I had left him defenseless."[85]

Late the previous evening, although Bob did not then know it, Lane had told Hannan "there was liable to be trouble on the floor of the Senate as some Senators were beside themselves with rage at those who opposed the bill . . . their 'rage' was centering entirely on 'Bob,' " and Lane said he "was ready for them no matter what might occur."[86]

As Norris finished at about nine thirty in the morning, both Bob and Owen addressed the Chair. The Presiding Officer, Lea, following the list, recognized Owen, who spoke for the bill.[87]

While Owen was still speaking, Saulsbury, the President pro tempore, supplanted Lea in the Chair. Bob immediately informed him what the Vice President had said and done about the lists, and asked whether Saulsbury intended to follow the list or give recognition from the floor under the rule. He warned Saulsbury that "as a member of the Senate" he had constitutional rights and that if "denied them some one would get hurt." Saulsbury refused to disclose his intention or discuss the matter further. Bob returned to his seat, and waited.[88]

During the last hours of the session, Bob, Jr., was standing near the door on the left of the Vice President facing the Chamber, about fifteen or twenty feet from his father, who had the first seat in the first row. Although the *Record* entirely omits the fact that La Follette addressed the Chair, Bob, Jr., recalls that before Owen concluded his father "was on his feet, shouting, 'Mr. President,' before Hitchcock did so."[89] Saulsbury ignored Bob but made the parliamentary error of failing to recognize Hitchcock in his own right when he asked, "Does the Senator from Oklahoma [Owen] yield to the Senator from Nebraska [Hitchcock]?"[90] Owen tried to "pass the floor to Hitchcock by saying, 'I yield to the Senator from Nebraska.' "[91]

Bob, outraged at this violation of the Senate rules, turned indignantly to Saulsbury, charging him with the parliamentary error and insisting one Senator could not yield the floor to another in that way. Hitchcock immediately asked for the floor "in his own right," and Saulsbury declared, "The Senator from Nebraska first addressed the Chair and is recognized."[92]*

For what seemed a minute or two Bob stood out in the center aisle shouting that he was not going to be denied his rights. His son recalls that while his father was defying the Senate to take him off his feet "a sort of a rush and movement started on the Demo-

* The *Record* shows [p. 5012] that La Follette's effort to protest the Chair's ruling that Hitchcock had the floor, was shut off by Hardwick's suggesting absence of quorum, which was followed by a roll call.

cratic side" in which Ollie James and several others were leading. Standing there, Bob, Jr., did not know but "there would be a riot right on the floor of the Senate."[93]

Norris recalls that Lane, alarmed by threats he had overheard, walked down the aisle behind another Senator, prepared, if necessary, to use a rattail file, which had a long sharp point, to protect Bob from personal violence on the Senate floor.[94] Aware that at least one Senator was armed on the night of the third and morning of the fourth of March, Lane, who was a physician and knew anatomy, told Bob and his son a few days later what had actually happened: "I had this file in my office and I slipped it my pocket. . . . If you slip this file down inside a man's collar bone on the left side you can reach his heart with one thrust and he will never move again. When you were trying to get recognition and Hitchcock was recognized, Ollie James, who was carrying a gun, started across the Chamber toward you with his hand under his coattails, but he would never have drawn that gun. Before he could have done so I would have stopped him with this file. I was right within reach of him all the time. I knew he was armed because as he got up and was moving forward I saw his gun."[95]*

Bob was entitled to the floor, under the rule, since he had been on his feet before Owen concluded, and the Presiding Officer had, in fact, failed to recognize Hitchcock in his own right after Owen finished. But his further protest was shut off by the suggested absence of a quorum. As the roll call ended, Hitchcock tried to begin his speech, but Bob interrupted with "a parliamentary inquiry" as to whether the list upon the desk before the Presiding Officer was to be observed or disregarded. He succeeded in getting into the *Record* a brief statement of what the Vice President and Saulsbury had done about the lists before Robinson began an angry, insistent protest that he was not stating "a parliamentary inquiry."

Bob moved out into the center aisle and down into the well before the clerk's desk. Directly addressing Saulsbury, he defiantly shouted: "I am stating a parliamentary inquiry. . . . I will continue on this floor until I complete my statement unless somebody carries me off, and I should like to see the man who will do it."[96]

* Lane gave this file to Bob, who kept it in the top drawer of his desk for many years.

Before he concluded his sentence, Robinson "leaped to his feet and stamped down the aisle on the Democratic side, shouting his demands that his point of order be sustained, and that La Follette be forced to his seat."[97] The Senate was in an uproar. The two men argued the point hotly within arm's length of each other, while the Presiding Officer banged his gavel, vainly trying to restore order. As their voices rose, Senators rushed into the Chamber from the cloakroom. "Democrats, many of them warned of the coup to be sprung, hurried in with confident smiles to enjoy the spectacle of seeing a filibuster pitted against a filibuster."[98]

Saulsbury sustained Robinson's point of order that La Follette was not stating a parliamentary inquiry. Bob promptly appealed and, when Robinson moved to lay the appeal on the table, demanded the yeas and nays, shouting, "We shall see whether Senators are to be deprived of their constitutional rights on this floor." His appeal was tabled by a vote of 52 to 12, 29 Senators not voting.[99] He sat down, and Hitchcock went on with his speech. But his son remembers "that at the time" he was not satisfied "the trouble was over. Judging from the expression on Dad's face, I knew he had not yet given up the issue of recognition."[100]

Hitchcock then went on to denounce the "shabby treatment" given the bill; he severely arraigned Bob, who had "managed this campaign of delay," and the Senators who had objected "to a vote at this session." Others joined in disapproval, Williams describing it as "humiliating."[101] Bob sat silent throughout this attack.

Later, however, he sought through a question to point out the inconsistency of Hitchcock's position. When Hitchcock replied that the case had not been "correctly stated," Bob retorted with a biting irony of inflection, "It can scarcely be expected that the Senator from Wisconsin can, in one brief sentence comprising one interrogatory, state his position upon this bill, . . . or define it properly."[102]

But at 10:15, when Hitchcock again impatiently asked if he would consent to a vote, Bob, quickly availing himself of this chance to record his position even briefly, said he would be "delighted" to answer the Senator. An angry roar of jeering from the Senate greeted his statement that he could "not conscientiously,"* in the

* The *Boston Herald*, March 5, 1917, in a special Washington dispatch records that there was an outburst of jeering at this phrase. The author, who was present, also recalls it.

discharge of his duties under the Constitution, consent to a vote until all Senators who wished to be heard had been given the opportunity. Raising his powerful voice above the howl of derision, he insisted there was no reason to limit debate to the remaining hour and forty-five minutes of this session, since the President had the power to convene Congress the following Monday, when, as provided by the Constitution, it could "pass upon whether we shall have war or peace."[103]

Hitchcock interrupted, declining to yield further. In a tone of mocking solicitude he expressed regret that the Senator from Wisconsin, whom he had been "very anxious to hear," had allotted to those he "apparently engineered" and "put forward to speak" so much time and "reserved so little for himself, at such risk of losing the opportunity to speak." Bob rose quickly and addressed the Chair. But again Hitchcock said, "I can not yield." Bob shot back, "No; I should think the Senator could not after that statement. It would not be safe." Shortly after eleven, Hitchcock again sought unanimous consent to a vote at 11:30 o'clock. Bob then made the point of order that the request had not been presented under the rule. When the President pro tempore ignored this and asked if there was objection, Bob's voice rang out clearly, "Yes: I object now; and I will object again—. . . And as often as the request is made until I have the opportunity to be heard." Williams called him to order with the biting remark, "He is habitually and constantly violating the rules of the Senate." Not observing Senate custom, Bob dropped the third-person form, retorting tartly: "So are you. You have not been recognized yet."[104]

An exchange of angry charges followed. Two correspondents in the press gallery noted that when Bob, after repeating his objection, added, "I still desire to be heard," another Senator charged: "That is not true. The Senator has been heard." Bob, rising from his seat, demanded, "Did the Senator from Georgia say that that was not true?" "Yes," Smith answered. "The Senator from Georgia states a falsehood when he says that," Bob indignantly retorted.[105]

After meeting another determined refusal from Bob to consent to a vote before noon, Hitchcock continued speaking, thus carrying through the strategy planned "quietly in the cloakrooms" during "the early morning hours" to show Bob had blocked the bill and, at the same time, to deny him an opportunity to get his argument to the country.[106] Bob sat watching Hitchcock grimly. His tone of voice and expression had revealed the indignation he felt during what he described as "the sparring back and forth in which Williams[,] Hokus Pokus Smith" and he had "mixed the fighting."[107]

His son, Bob, Jr., standing over near the door on the left of the Vice President, observed the tense scene with growing anxiety and sent his father a penciled note: "Please, Please, be calm—you know what the press will do—remember Mother."[108] His father replied, "Bobbie what do you expect when I am making a statement and a Senator in a tone heard over the the [sic] chamber [says] that 'it is not so.' " On the same sheet of paper his son answered: "Daddy, I expect you to make your protest but there must be a limit to the lengths which you go. Robinson has taken the chair for no idle purpose.* You can not afford to get into a physical argument or be arrested by the Serg[ean]t at Arms for misconduct. You are noticeably & extremely excited. For God's sake make your protest & prevent passage of bill if you like but if previous question is made & sustained do not try to fight Senate physically. I am almost crazy with strain B."[109]

Bob, Jr., recalls that after sending his father "many notes urging him to be calm I rushed up to the Senate family gallery where Gilbert Roe was sitting and asked him for a suggestion on how to handle the situation. He said, 'Tell Bob the way to meet those fellows is to smile at them.' I went back to the Senate floor and sent him a note which conveyed this advice to Dad. He immediately smiled at me and from then on he followed Gilbert's advice."[110] Those who noticed Bob's sudden and complete change from angry defiance to an ironic but smiling composure probably attributed it to the now evident victory of the filibuster.

As the hour of automatic adjournment drew near, Hitchcock interrupted his own speech. Forced at last, by Bob's insistence, to follow the Senate rule, he submitted his request for unanimous consent in writing, at 11:43.[111] Robinson, then the Presiding Officer, directed the Secretary to read the agreement calling for a vote at 11:45. Bob promptly objected. Hitchcock asked for a roll call to show the presence of a quorum, after which Robinson again put the unanimous-consent request.

* During Hitchcock's speech Robinson had replaced Saulsbury as Presiding Officer.

Bob objected and further delayed proceedings by raising the point of order for which he had long been preparing: Formal submission of the unanimous-consent request and a roll call constituted the transaction of business. Hitchcock, having spoken twice on the same subject in the same legislative day, and having yielded the floor, was, therefore, not entitled to be recognized again. Time was consumed while the point was sharply debated. Finally a parliamentary detour was found and, on another Senator's motion, Hitchcock was permitted to proceed by order of the Senate. Bob, "smiling satirically, with one eye on the clock," demanded a division, which took time, although the motion was adopted 64 to 2. When Hitchcock resumed, Bob folded his arms, and, still smiling, appeared to be giving him the closest attention.[112]

During part of this turbulent debate, the President had been at the Capitol in his room off the corridor some twenty feet back of the Senate Chamber. While he was signing bills and waiting for the adjournment hour when he was to take the oath of office for his second term, Senate leaders reported what was happening on the floor and sought his advice.[113]

Only a few moments of the session remained. The time-honored subterfuge of turning back the clock would not be invoked this noon.

In a final angry blast, expressing the outraged and unreasoning temper of many Senators, Hitchcock was saying in conclusion: "Twelve men in this Senate have defeated the will of 70 or 75 or possibly 80 men, and have defeated that will by resorting to one of the most reprehensible filibusters ever recorded in the history of any civilized country. Mr. President, I am using rather strong language and possibly I ought to apologize—".[114]

"Oh, no: not at all. It is perfectly safe when no one has a right to reply," Bob interrupted in a tone of ironic courtesy which could be heard distinctly throughout the Chamber.[115]

A few moments later the Senate adjourned sine die.

Bob left the Senate with his son and Hannan, going directly to his office in the Capitol. There he found Gilbert and Netha Roe, his daughter Fola, and his close friend Andrew Furuseth, president of the Seamen's Union. That morning before Bob had gone to the floor, expecting to speak until adjournment, Furuseth had been in the office, pacing silently up and down. Suddenly he had turned and said in a tense, almost angry, voice, "Bob, if you defeat that bill, they'll crucify you." "I know it," Bob replied curtly, as he left. When he returned to his office, he said: "That bill meant war. I had only two choices, to resign or defeat it." Furuseth went over and put his arm around him. "Bob," he said, "they'll crucify you. But God bless you."[116]

That evening Bob wired a night letter to Belle at Madison: "Fought it through to the finish. Feeling here intense. I must take the gaff for a time. But believe it will postpone aggressive action which would have resulted in our getting into war immediately until as I hope the cricis [*sic*] passes and we may in the providence of God be spared the awful catastrophy [*sic*] of entering this world war on the issue presented. If it does work out that way it will be the greatest service which could be rendered our country and humanity. If war comes in the end despite what we have done or may yet do it can not be helped."[117]

At their home in Wisconsin, Belle, that very evening, before receiving his telegram, was writing him with the complete understanding of his purpose which characterized their relationship: "It is my heartfelt conviction that you have rendered the world the greatest service it has ever come to you to render and that you have used the power and opportunity that was yours for humanity and democracy. I could not and I cannot see how you could take any other course and I am filled with a deep sense of thanksgiving beyond all words to express.

"You are sure to be terribly maligned and misunderstood and probably the general public will never get on to the absurdity and dangerous trend of Wilson[']s usurpation of power, but oh, what a deep satisfaction wells up from within that all these long years of discipline and hardening have made you ready to meet this crisis and stem the awful tide of destruction without fear of its consequences to yourself."[118]

CHAPTER XLIV

One of Wilson's Willful Men

After the adjournment of Congress at noon on March 4, Wilson had returned from the Capitol to the White House in an angry mood. That afternoon he typed out a statement which was given to the press that night with the approval of House, McAdoo, Burleson, and Tumulty.[1] The following morning the newspapers throughout the country carried the President's statement. It contained the famous phrase which unleashed an organized campaign of denunciation, to continue throughout the war, against the eleven Senators who had dared openly to oppose the bill and force an extra session. He declared: "A little group of willful men, representing no opinion but their own, have rendered the great Government of the United States helpless and contemptible."[2]

Bob had fought the Armed Ship bill because he thought that it meant war and that it violated an essential provision of the Constitution by indirectly giving the war-making power to the President. He believed in democracy and he was convinced that a majority of the American people did not want war. It was his profound conviction that "representative government depends upon the direct responsibility of the representative, not to the President, but to the people" and that any "abject surrender of the legislative to the executive will" would, in the long run, result in the loss of fundamental democracy.[3] Although expressed in jesting terms, his family understood the deep conviction which had made his action inevitable, when he wrote a few days after the filibuster: "I couldn't have done anything else unless I went down & slipped into the Potomac & the water's too cold for that now. Lots of people on the street-cars & round the Capitol want to eat me—but conclude I'd be too tough I guess."[4]

The belief that his action had been in the best service of democracy and his country was shared by the woman he had long ago described as his "wisest and best counsellor."[5] To an intimate friend Belle wrote, the day after the President's denunciation appeared in the press: "Immediate war has been averted. . . . it is a great thing to have this respite. . . . Of all the service Bob has been able to render this is the biggest, but of course all the work that he had done was preparation and it needed a life time of experience and seasoning to meet this crisis. It looks as though the flood-gates of bitterness and hate were going to be opened on him nationally much as they were in this state the first term he was governor. But the issue is clearer and the stake is worth whatever sacrifice it may cost."[6]

Two days later several Senators boldly charged that Wilson's denunciation had deliberately misrepresented the legislative situation at the close of the Sixty-fourth Congress. These charges were made during the customary special session which had been called to confirm the Executive appointments. Norris expressed the opinion, held by Bob and others, that those who had refused to be coerced by the Executive had been denounced by the President "wrongfully, without cause, without reason, and contrary to the real facts. What they said and what they did in defense of their convictions on the floor of the Senate never reached the people of the United States. What the President said and what those said who favored the legislation was carried by the newspapers and spread broadcast, but the real issue . . . was never told." Norris predicted that after they were dead some student of history would discover that "the President of the United States did a great wrong to men who were conscientiously trying to do their duty as they saw it."[7] Years later Secretary Lansing admitted that the President overstated it when he asserted that the Government had been made "helpless" by "a little group of wilful men."[8]

Even the supporters of the Armed Ship bill were indignant. Sherman of Illinois, who had voted for it, read the President's statement into the *Record*, charging that a portion of the truth was deliberately omitted to make a stronger case, and thereby arouse greater resentment against the few Senators who opposed the bill.[9] Townsend, who had signed the round robin denouncing the opposition, also arraigned Wilson for heaping unjust criticism on Congress. The

President knew, he declared, as every Senator knew, "that all he had to do was to call Congress together on the 5th of March to get consideration for the measure."[10]

Some of the Old Guard openly expressed resentment at "the presumption of the President to dictate the rules of the legislative branch."[11] No one was more amused than Bob at the strange irony of senatorial solidarity which led Smoot, who had signed the round robin, to defend the "willful men." Smoot carefully estimated from the *Congressional Record* the apportionment of time during the debate, and no one questioned the facts when he declared that the friends of the measure occupied more time than those who were opposed. "I have not the least doubt," he said, "but that the bill could have been passed if its opponents had been the only Senators who desired to discuss it."[12]

Although Bob made no comment at the time, he believed that the President, in his determination to punish those who had dared question his wisdom, had willfully distorted the facts to incite press attacks which would intimidate Congress and remove all effective opposition to his program. Whatever Wilson's conscious purpose, and although his biographer records that he subsequently regretted his angry statement,[13] nevertheless his denunciation unleashed a fury of war hysteria which robbed men of reason. Intolerance became confused with patriotism, subverting democratic procedure in numerous legislative halls, and suspending academic freedom in many schools, colleges, and universities. News and feature services, cartoonists, special correspondents, and editorial writers united in a flaming barrage against the Senate group that was striving to prevent our entry into the European War.

A resolution, criticizing Bob and demanding he support the President, was introduced in the Wisconsin State Senate. When a majority vote prevented immediate consideration, sixteen of the thirty-three members signed a round robin and forwarded it with the resolution to the President. The text was typical of the nation-wide misrepresentation of both the purpose and effect of the minority group's opposition: "Wisconsin," it said, "is still loyal to the President and to the government of the United States. Its citizens deeply regret the conduct of certain Senators of the United States, and particularly Robert M. La Follette, . . . which denied the right of a majority to rule, and which prevented the passage of many vitally important measures to prevent war and which gave the impression abroad that we are not only helpless against attack from foreign countries but divided and disloyal at home."[14]

In the same issue which carried the President's statement, the *New York Times* published thirty-three editorials from different newspapers. Three-fourths supported the President in condemning the "willful men."[15] Of these, twenty-one were from Eastern, seven from Southern, three from Midwestern, and two from Western papers. The *Times'* own editorial predicted that if war should come, "the odium of treasonable purpose and achievement" would "rest upon their names forevermore."[16] Two days later it singled out Bob as leader of the filibuster, noting the fact that even German-language newspapers condemned him, and predicting that his last term had begun.[17] The New York *World,* under title of "Delinquents and Dastards," charged "those wretches in the Senate" with having "denied their consciences and courage in order to make a Prussian holiday," crying, "Shame on them, now and forever!"[18] The *Literary Digest* printed several pages of editorial quotations ranging from the *Boston Evening Transcript*'s comparatively mild comment that the filibustering Senators had "flirted with treason" to the *New York Herald*'s prediction that they would be fortunate if their names did "not go down into history bracketed with that of Benedict Arnold."[19] Other metropolitan newspaper editorials characterized the "willful" Senators as "unsocialized creatures,"[20] "Knaves who betrayed the nation in the interest of Germany,"[21] and even as "La Follette and his little group of perverts."[22]

The United Press distributed a dispatch from Amsterdam purporting to summarize German editorial opinion on the defeat of the Armed Ship bill. On the strength of this the *Cincinnati Post* printed a smiling photograph of Bob at the telephone, with the caption, "His Master's Voice," and an imaginary conversation between "von La Follette and the Kaiser."[23] A series of powerful cartoons by the famous artist, Rollin Kirby, began on March 5 in the New York *World*. On successive days Bob was pictured fleeing under the scourging sword of an indignant Columbia; as a pirate aboard the Ship of State spiking the guns of "the Nation's Honor"; and as the leader of the "willful twelve," standing in front of the group, while a mailed fist pinned an iron cross upon his breast.[24] Many years later Kirby wrote expressing his desire to correct as far as possible

The Only Adequate Reward
By Rollin Kirby in the New York *World*,
March 7, 1917

The Russell
45 Park Avenue
New York

My object in writing This is to
try to correct as far as is possible
at this late date the damage such
cartoons as I made for the N. Y. World
during Senator Robert La Follette's
fight against this country's participation
in the World War.

Time has brought a better sense of
values to me and I have come to see
that what seemed to me at the time as
the action of a wicked, unpatriotic
man was, on the contrary, a brave
fight against an overwhelming tide
of chauvinism and war hysteria.
Few men have been asked to pay
as Senator La Follette
such a high price for their convictions.
It is with a profound sense of
regret and humiliation that I
remember that I added my tiny bit
to his burden.

Rollin Kirby

April-6-1940

"at this late date the damage [done by] such cartoons as I made for the N.Y. World during Senator Robert La Follette's fight against this country's participation in the World War. Time has brought a better sense of values to me and I have come to see that what seemed to me at the time as the action of a wilful, unpatriotic man was, on the contrary, a brave fight against an overwhelming tide of chauvinism and war hysteria. Few men have been asked to pay such a high price as Senator La Follette for their convictions. It is with a profound sense of regret and humiliation that I remember that I added my tiny bit to his burden."[25]

The Kirby cartoons and many others were sent to Bob anonymously through the mails with vile, unprintable comments scrawled across them. Many were carefully filed with his papers; on some he wrote "Libelous." One cartoon from the New York *Telegram* showed Bob and four other Senators,* all named, with the ghost of Benedict Arnold gazing at them, saying, "And They Called Me Traitor." Gilbert Roe, Bob's most intimate friend, enclosed this cartoon in a letter, describing it as the most atrocious libel he had ever seen. Bob replied, by telegraph, that this was mild in comparison to some he had.[26]

Following the publication of Wilson's denunciation, great publicity had been given to meetings held in many large cities pledging support to the President and condemning the Senators he had charged with rendering the Government "helpless and contemptible." A mass meeting of three thousand in Carnegie Hall, New York, on March 5 under the auspices of the American Rights League, where each mention of the Senators who had opposed the Armed Ship bill brought cries of "Traitor!" and "Hang Them!" was widely reported.[27]

Four days later the Emergency Peace Federation held another large meeting in Carnegie Hall, which was given less publicity. A man Bob did not know personally, who was present on both occasions, wrote him, "I heard the War mass-meeting at Carnegie Hall pillory you and the rest of the twelve as 'traitors' but I also heard the Peace mass-meeting of last night in the same place give you one of the two greatest ovations of the evening."[28]

It is hard to exaggerate the effect of these denunciations at the national Capital. War advocates who had hitherto worked under

* Cummins, La Follette, O'Gorman, Stone, and Vardaman.

cover now came boldly into the open. Bitter resentment was expressed in menacing terms. Commenting on the Republican Senators, who had actually helped the filibuster by their deliberately dilatory tactics on the Revenue bill, David Lawrence wrote that the persons who had secretly encouraged Bob were now the loudest in their denunciation. There was, he said, a stoical courage in the way some of these men were "acting in the face of nation-wide criticism. . . . Many of them realize they can never be reelected. . . . Norris and La Follette . . . would have acted as they did irrespective of the effect on their political fortunes."[29]

A few friends who disagreed with Bob understood his motives and continued to believe in his integrity. Four days after the defeat of the Armed Ship bill, when the newspaper condemnation was intense, Justice Brandeis, while sitting in Court, wrote a note saying, "Dear Bob: I think you are wrong, but I love you all the same. Won't you come and dine with me this evening?"[30] In a letter that same day Bob wrote his family that he had to decline because of work but had promised to drop in to see him as soon as the immediate pressure was off. He also told them of a beautiful letter he had received from Elizabeth Evans.[31]

Although a speaking date was canceled in West Virginia, and he was denounced as a traitor at certain other widely publicized meetings, Bob was convinced that the inflammatory newspaper headlines and editorials did not represent the sober judgment of men and women throughout the country. Individual opinions coming to him directly from the sources he had always trusted convinced him the majority did not want war. Newspaper criticism was no novelty to him; he had been schooled in it for years; he had learned that the press did not always reflect the wish of the people. In spite of the hostility of the newspapers, the people of Wisconsin had understood his fundamental purposes and had repeatedly returned him to office to carry on his program.

Four days after the filibuster he wrote to his family: "My letters came in yesterday and today at the rate of about 500 per day [.] At least 4 to 1 are strong and beautiful in their support [.] They come from all over the country [.] I dont know how long it will keep up but we are swamped at present. First the telegrams came for about 3 days and yesterday the 7th the letters began to arrive."[32] Three weeks later, when he had heard from approximately ten thousand people, he wrote to his son Phil that about one out of ten condemned him, "some in vile words," but that the other nine wrote "words of strong commendation and encouragement."[33] Bob, Jr., who was taking charge of filing the letters, wrote to his brother and sister at Madison, "Gee there are sure a lot of people among 'the silent masses' that know how to talk when they want to. It would do your heart good just to read them."[34]

With a letter to the family on March 8 Bob enclosed a part of the carbon copy of a letter Captain Walter K. Wilson had written to a fellow officer in New York. In replying to this officer's criticism, Captain Wilson, who was seeing Bob every day, had written: "Why in the name of conscience can't you look beyond the New York newspapers, and see that Senator La Follette is the real hero of the hour? A man who, believing that Congress cannot shift its Constitutional responsibility for declaring war by granting the President power to commit certain acts which in themselves are virtually acts of war, and believing that a brief delay for more deliberation might keep his country out of a bloody war, yet knowing full well that his actions would be misinterpreted by the press, did, nevertheless, for the sake of his country, pursue his course unflinchingly and forced the delay."[35]

At the national Capital bitterness and resentment prevailed. Glared at, and even spat upon in a street car, reminded at every turn of the rancor seething against the group he had led twenty-four hours before, Bob returned to the Senate shortly before noon on March 5 to take the oath of office for his third term. That morning, as he rode to the Capitol, the street scene was ominous for one who hoped his country might remain at peace. Regular Army troops, detectives, secret service men, and policemen guarded the route, making a lane of steel from the White House to the Capitol, where the President was to deliver his inaugural address. Not since the inauguration of Lincoln had such precautions been taken to guard a President.

The inauguration ceremonies began at 11:45, when the members of the House entered the Senate Chamber. As the Senate Chaplain finished his prayer, Bob came in alone and walked down the center aisle towards his seat in the first row, "the observed of the galleries, the Senate, the House, the Supreme Court, the Diplomatic Corps, the Cabinet, and the President, who sat directly facing him." Finding his own seat occupied, he stood for a moment, looking about, and then walked slowly back until he saw an empty seat and started to occupy it. But as he made the move, "Senator Tillman came forward and with a stony face put his own hand on the chair saying 'pardon me.'" Bob started to reply, but Tillman "did not seem to hear him and simply sat down." Bob then "walked around the hall until he found a chair between two desks, and sat there with no companion on either side of him."[36]

As the names of the Senators were called by the Secretary, Bob, escorted by Husting of Wisconsin, walked from the rear of the Chamber to the Vice President's desk and, with King, Knox, and Lodge, took the oath of office.

Immediately after the newly elected Senators had been sworn in, the procession formed according to custom, and Bob, with the other Senators, proceeded to the East front of the Capitol to hear Wilson's inaugural address. The President did not indicate any purpose to lead the country into war. In fact, many who still believed him the wisest guardian of this country's neutrality might have found hope in his declaration that if America was but true to herself, the "shadows that now lie dark upon our path will soon be dispelled and we shall walk with the light all about us."[37] But Bob had lost confidence, and the address made him even more apprehensive. The following day he wrote Belle predicting that the President would "make conditions force war upon us."[38]

Apparently an early victim of that intolerance which he himself had foreseen would result from our entry into the war,[39] Wilson now attributed only petty motives to those who dared question his policy. In his room at the Capitol, while awaiting the inaugural ceremony, he commented on the "vanity of La Follette" and the "slipperiness of Stone,"[40] and the next day, at a luncheon for members of the Democratic National Committee, the newspapers reported that Wilson "threw aside all reserve" in expressing his anger at the defeat of his bill.[41] Opposition to his plans had evidently obliterated all the love he had expressed only a few years before for "lonely figures" when he had doffed his cap to "that indomitable little figure," Bob La Follette, who had "never taken his eye for a single moment from the goal he set out to reach" and had "walked a straight line to it in spite of every temptation."[42]

The afternoon of the day Bob took the oath of office, the *Mil-*

waukee Journal, which then had the largest circulation of any Wisconsin newspaper, printed an editorial declaring that La Follette stood "repudiated by the whole press of America" and that the voice of the nation proclaimed "him unfaithful to his trust."[43]* That night he was hanged in effigy by students at the University of Illinois, and Lane, called by some "Oregon's Traitor," was threatened with recall.[44]†

When the Senate met, the day after the inauguration, it was evident that the defeat of the Armed Ship bill, Wilson's denunciation of the "willful men," and the bombardment of the press had all combined to crystallize a strong sentiment in the Senate for a change in the rules to prevent unlimited debate.[45] A cloture rule was agreed upon in caucuses by both parties. Convinced that there was an "understanding between the Democrats and the standpatters to agree on Cloture," neither Bob nor Gronna had attended the Republican caucus on the afternoon of March 6. Both were determined to vote against it.[46] The cloture rule provided that upon a petition signed by sixteen Senators the Senate might at any time by a two-thirds vote limit debate to one hour by each Senator upon any measure.[47] Responding to the President's demand to alter Senate procedure at once, the rule was introduced on March 8, and unanimous consent was obtained for immediate consideration. Bob came upon the floor a minute or two later and announced he would have objected, had he been present, to disposing of so important a measure in one day.[48] All the speakers but three favored its adoption, although some admitted the rule went too far.

Bob, in closing the debate on an issue he believed vital to democracy, again opposed the President. There had been no opportunity to prepare a speech, but while listening to the discussion he remembered another debate on cloture in 1891 when he was a member of the House. Sending for the *Congressional Record* he read historic arguments on the subject, reminding his colleagues that from early days there had been free discussion in the Senate and that

---

* Since early in February the *Milwaukee Journal* had been publishing editorials from leading Wisconsin newspapers demanding that La Follette support the President. It now carried excerpts from editorials condemning him and others who had prevented passage of the Armed Ship bill.

† The recall threat was not tested by a vote. Lane died in San Francisco on May 23, 1917.

the ablest statesmanship had overwhelmingly defeated the kind
of rule they were about to vote on.

He maintained that the minority right of unlimited debate,
derived from the Constitution and the Senate rules, was a necessary
instrument in preserving the democratic process. For, he said, a
minority in Congress might at times represent a majority of the
electorate. During the long intervals between elections, this minority right to defeat legislation by unlimited debate then becomes
the only defense against the autocratic bipartisan committee control of legislation so little understood by the public. Speaking out
of his own legislative experience, he described to new Senators this
aspect of behind-the-scenes government he had dramatized to audiences throughout the country ever since he came to the Senate.
He warned them they would soon discover that when it suits the
will of the combined organizations, legislation is held back until the
closing hours of the session. Pressure then becomes irresistible. The
Senators, one after the other, "break down and yield, and the program goes through, no matter what it may contain."[49]

As a recent example of this bipartisan control, he recalled the
way the huge appropriation bills had been deliberately held back
until the closing hours of the previous Congress. Then the Armed
Ship bill, an infringement on the constitutional authority of Congress, had been brought in only five days before adjournment. "I
realize," he said, "how the hysteria of the moment may be driving
Senators to acquiesce here in a procedure which at another time
they would resist with all their force. But so far as I am concerned
I will never by my voice or vote consent to a rule which will put an
end to freedom of debate in the Senate."[50] During his entire speech
Bob made no comment on the President's censure of the little group
of "willful men." The cloture rule was adopted 76 to 3, only Gronna,
Bob, and Sherman of Illinois voting against it.[51] Bob believed the
Senate's hasty capitulation to the President's demand for a change
in the rules set a precedent dangerous to democratic institutions.

The great metropolitan newspapers had been almost unanimous
in demanding Congress support the President. Many were already
clamoring for a declaration of war. Dissent was condemned as "disloyal," "pro-German," or "pacifist."[52] There were a few newspapers
and a number of able editors who did not join the popular chorus
of condemnation. Bob's files show that editors and publishers of

many small papers in different parts of the country understood his purpose in opposing the Armed Ship bill and wrote asking for copies of his undelivered speech. A letter from La Grande, Oregon, is typical. The editor of the *Evening Observer*, published in the rich wheat-growing country, with 1,704 subscribers, wrote that although members of the Senate had refused to give him a hearing during the closing minutes of the Congress, the *Observer*, in a much smaller way, would give him the opportunity of placing before its readers his "convictions in the matter which has stirred the country."[53]

Indicative of the great discrepancy between the metropolitan press reports and Bob's correspondence from many States at this time, was a message from H. M. Esterly, the Democratic National Committeeman of Oregon, who telegraphed that the attempt "to arouse enthusiasm for war not successful notwithstanding newspaper reports [;] people in favor of keeping out of war [;] want you to know how people of Oregon stand."[54]

There was no Gallup poll then to sample and record public opinion, but time has slowly revealed that Bob and the men who tried to maintain neutrality were not alone in their conviction that the American people did not want war. The contemporary *American Press Résumés,* sent out by Sir Gilbert Parker's Ministry of Information, show that after our entry into the war the British continued through April, May, and part of June, to find the lack of American enthusiasm disappointing. Memoirs and letters published long after also indicate that even members of the Administration had privately conceded that the people were not with them wholeheartedly.[55] On March 9, four days after the President's denunciation was published, the British Ambassador reported to Balfour, "All I can record for certain is that the vast majority of the country desire peace and would do a great deal to secure peace."[56]

This desire for peace found little space in the great newspapers, and therefore left almost no printed record. But the thousands of letters received by Bob, Gronna,[57] Lane,[58] Works,[59] and other Senators who opposed the bill, echo from the past a testimony which supports the opinion of the historian who, twenty-two years later, said, "these wilful men did represent opinion other than their own— primarily those of people who voted for Wilson in 1916 on the slogan, 'He kept us out of war.' "[60]

As the newspaper reports of the attacks upon Bob accumulated and grew more virulent, intimate friends became deeply concerned that he should find some way to clarify his position to the public. Friends in Madison thought it was a calamity that he had been prevented from making his speech on the Armed Ship bill during the debate in the Senate. Belle wrote suggesting that he might get his point of view over to many people by devoting the entire March issue of *La Follette's Magazine* to a calm and dispassionate editorial setting forth his position so specifically and simply that the man on the street would be convinced by just looking at it. She thought the first thing to do was to show that it meant war if the President ordered the ships armed. Then the point should be pressed home that the President was asking for just the kind of "unlimited autocratic power that the Kaiser and Czar and all the other crowned heads of Europe and Lord Grey asked for. 'Believe in me, Go it blind, I have the divine insight, and am going to do everything for your good[.]' The people who say stand by the President, right or wrong are doing exactly what the people of Germany and England and all the European nations did."[61] Bob at once started writing a statement along these lines. But he was delayed in completing it by unavoidable interruptions. Although he worked late nights, Senate sessions and important conferences with Norris, Lane, Gronna, Stone, and others made it difficult to find consecutive time during the day.

A few days after the filibuster, Bob had said in a letter to Belle: "I have been on the verge of sending for you a dozen times. . . . I have needed your counsel and help these days. It has been an awful trial."[62] When the President issued a proclamation on March 10 declaring that an extraordinary occasion required Congress to convene on April 16, Bob, Jr., immediately wrote his mother that it was vitally important she should be in Washington when the extra session met.[63]

Two days later Belle took the train for Washington. It was hard to leave Phil and Mary alone at the farm. The denunciations of Bob which appeared almost daily in the newspapers were beginning to be reflected among people who, although politically hostile, had always been their close personal friends. From Chicago she wrote: "My heart aches more and more at the thought of leaving you. But I hope it is not for long. What joy it has been to be together in the quiet and protection of the Farm. We can always look back upon it with thanksgiving And whatever we can do to make the lives of the many happier and freer from pain and stress, we should gladly do—shouldn't we?"[64] From Washington she wrote the children that although Bob was tired, he looked well and was "just as *strong* and determined as ever." Later that same day she joined him and Bob, Jr., at the Senate Office Building to discuss the question of giving out a statement on the Armed Ship bill requested by a press syndicate, and whether Bob should accept the urgent invitations he was receiving every day to speak in the large cities. Senator Stone was anxious to have him speak in the Senate, and had suggested that he might steer the way.[65]

A few days later, when Bob had his statement ready, the syndicate said "it was too late for them to take any extended statement" he might make.[66] It was published as a three-and-a-half-page editorial in the March issue of *La Follette's Magazine* under the title "The Armed Ship Bill Meant War," and excerpts were carried in some newspapers. Later, at the request of Congressman John M. Nelson of Wisconsin, it was printed in the *Congressional Record*.[67] Bob also cast the editorial into the form of a letter which went out to the thousands of people who had written him. In a two-thousand-word article ordered by *Pearson's Magazine* Bob wrote another clear statement of his reasons for opposing the Armed Ship bill. Although sent off by telegraph at the same time as his editorial, it was not published until May.[68]

While Bob was still working on his statements about the Armed Ship bill filibuster, the newspapers reported that revolution had overthrown the Imperial Government in Russia. On March 15 Czar Nicholas abdicated, and a Provisional Government was formed. Bob hoped that this meant the end of autocratic rule in that country and that it would contribute toward the democratization of Europe. An editorial in *La Follette's Magazine* entitled "Breaking Cruel Shackles" expressed a feeling which was shared by many people in this country at that time when it said, "What is happening in Russia to-day brings joy to every lover of democracy and freedom."[69] With President Wilson's approval, the American Ambassador to Russia, David R. Francis, was instructed to recognize the new Provisional Government, and did so formally on March 22.[70] The next day Great Britain, France, and Italy took similar action. The Sunday after the czar's abdication Bob and Belle walked over to the nearest newsstand to get all the New York papers, and spent the morning reading them. A letter she wrote that same day reflects their immediate reaction to the reports that were then coming through from Russia: "The Russian revolution is a world event of such tremendous meaning and possibilities that I can hardly think of anything else. Of course, there will be reaction and a long struggle, but what has happened must stir the world to new ideals and give the oppressed new courage and the believers in ultimate democracy a new faith. It is a blow to all monarchical forms of government. The words Kaiser and King and Czar and hereditary power in government have suddenly been revealed as the insignia of a past order."[71]

The following morning Steffens, who was planning a trip to Mexico, arrived in Washington and spent the day seeing Secretary of War Baker, Secretary Daniels, Counselor Frank L. Polk of the State Department, and others. He found Baker rejoicing in the Russian Revolution, and confidentially saying to his old friend, "Well I guess this king business is pretty near over." After these visits Steffens felt it was plain that all the men he talked with at the State, War, and Navy Departments thought the United States would soon enter the European War aggressively with both Navy and Army.[72] However, the State Department advised him to go to Mexico in any event, and he invited Bob, Jr., to go with him.

Two days later, when Steffens saw Bob, he undoubtedly told him of his talks with these men. He also explained that his own plans had been suddenly changed by a chance meeting on the Washington streets with their mutual friend Charles R. Crane. Crane had been on his way to the State Department and had invited Steffens to go to Russia with him. Steffens felt this opportunity was too great to let slip. Crane had long been interested in Russia, had been there frequently, and knew everyone in power in the new Provisional Government. Bob's two friends sailed from New York on the same ship which carried Leon Trotsky as a steerage passenger. Trotsky was taken off the ship at Halifax and detained there for weeks. But Crane and Steffens arrived safely in Petrograd.[73]

Bob had thought the President would not dare to arm merchant ships without authority from Congress. But he was mistaken, for on March 12, a week after the defeat of his bill, Wilson had notified foreign governments that American ships clearing for European ports through the German zone would sail with guns and gunners furnished by the Navy Department.[74] Fortified by the opinions of Attorney General Gregory and Secretary Lansing, Wilson thus exercised the authority he had asserted was his when he asked Congress to pass the Armed Ship bill. From this time on the President "knew that war was all but inevitable."[75]

When the Cabinet met on March 20, Wilson found the members unanimous in their desire for a declaration of war, but he indicated no positive decision to them. After the meeting he privately asked Lansing and Burleson how long it would take to prepare the necessary legislation if war should be declared.[76] The next day he summoned Congress to meet two weeks earlier than the date he had previously set.

From the Senate Office Building where she was working that day, Belle wrote Phil that there was "tension and strain in the very air you breathe in Washington."[77] Bob thought the date for the extra session was advanced because the President feared delay might permit the opposition to war which existed throughout the country to register on Congress. A cable to the British Government from its Washington Embassy informing them of a conversation with Colonel House the night before Wilson issued the call indicates that Bob's interpretation may have been correct. House was reported to have said that while the Cabinet was for war and was trying to force the issue, Wilson was rather hesitating about the attitude the new Congress might adopt; that they were uncertain about Congress and were anxious about the danger of the public's feeling cooling down.[78]

The President's position became more difficult every day. His diplomacy had led where retreat seemed to him impossible. The insistence that Congress stand behind the President had imposed on him practically the entire responsibility of deciding for peace or war. Pressure was brought to bear on him from many quarters and for varied motives. The members of his Cabinet were unanimous in their desire for a declaration of war. At the Union League Club in New York, on the same day that the Cabinet met, six hundred leaders of the Republican Party, headed by Theodore Roosevelt, Charles Evans Hughes, Elihu Root, and Joseph H. Choate, supported resolutions recognizing that "war now exists by the act of Germany."[79] Two days later J. P. Morgan and Company announced a bond issue of $1,000,000,000 for a war loan to France. The clamor of the press for a declaration of war grew more insistent day by day.

On March 23, although Congress had taken no action, the British Ambassador was confident of the outcome. Just fourteen days after he had written that the vast majority of the country desired peace, he was able to tell Balfour that enough had been said and hinted in official circles and in the press to justify the assertion that the die had been cast and that the country had drifted into war.[80]

Nine days after the British Ambassador had sent this confidential message to England, Belle wrote in a family letter that the telegrams Bob was receiving from all over the country seemed to indicate plainly that sentiment was shaping to resist war, although she feared it might be too late because Congress had been "too thoroughly and completely intimidated."[81] Throughout the weeks of denunciation which had followed the Armed Ship bill filibuster Bob's determination had never wavered. He was convinced that strict neutrality was the only wise and realistic policy. Unaware that the President had already made his great decision, and had been working on his message to Congress for several days,[82] Bob wrote late in March that it would be a service to prolong debate on every phase of the war issue, "thus giving time for more rational and well considered action."[83] Within his own family Bob found complete understanding of his purpose. His youngest daughter, Mary, who had been jeered at on the streets of Madison and pointed out as "the traitor's daughter" by young schoolmates, wrote calmly asking for all the facts about the Armed Ship bill filibuster.

Phil, then nineteen and a student at the university, wrote frequently informing his father of the shifting cross currents of sentiment and the strange political realignments taking place under the tension of impending war. In his detailed record of facts and opinions, as well as reports on the correspondence pouring into the office of *La Follette's Magazine*, there were some words meant only for father and son. In a long letter, marked "strictly personally," written after what Phil described as "the 'willful twelve' event," he said: "Oh dear Daddy, I love you so much for your courage . . . but most for fortitude which gives you the courage and strength to do as you see without making you bitter. Oh I pray God that I may in some small way be worthy of you. I do so want to make my life worth-while, but you have set an almost unattainable ideal for us. *But I'll do the best I can* . . .

"Dad, I haven't said what I wanted to—but this is sure, I was for you through all this . . . , am for you now, and you can count on me, until hell freezes over, till the crack of doom and then a hell of a while after that ! ! ! ! "[84]

A few days before the new Congress met, Bob wrote to Phil: "*Whatever the cost* of my course [on the Armed Ship bill]—never have I been in a better position to render so great a service—though I should be better satisfied if I could have gotten on record and to the country the reasons which prompted me to take that course. It may not prevent war. It did stop its coming for the time being but more important if possible than that it prevented the surrender to the President of the war-making power. That was a real service to democracy—to constitutional liberty."[85]

During the last week in March, Gilbert Roe came down to Washington to help Bob, Belle, and Bob, Jr., who were working under intense pressure preparing material for the debate on the war issue which was expected to begin immediately after Wilson delivered his message to the special session of Congress on April 2. Although the press was predicting Congress would declare war, they continued to hope that something might happen to avert the catastrophe. After dinner on the night of April 1, they were all sitting on the large porch of the Sixteenth Street house when Mrs. Florence Kelley, Julia Lathrop, David Thompson, and Lady Barlow's son, Jack, called. At midnight, after the guests had gone, Belle wrote Phil and Mary that as the time drew near for the President's message they all felt oppressed.[86]

CHAPTER XLV

The Last Stand Against War

On Monday, April 2, 1917, special trains brought thousands of citizens to Washington; some to hear the President, others to appeal to him and Congress to keep the United States out of war. The President refused to receive at the White House a delegation from the Emergency Peace Federation; all parades were prohibited; and the authorities forbade the use of any Government building for a peace meeting. Bob had tried to get a permit for the delegates to hold a meeting at the Capitol to present their resolutions and petitions, but it was denied. One reporter noted that as Congress went into session thousands of these bannered delegates assembled in an impressive, silent mass around the steps of the Capitol.[1] Hostile press dispatches described them as "the white rabbits of pacifism" and Bob as "their chief apostle."[2] He and many others believed that one reason for prohibiting the two parades which had been planned was the fear that the peace demonstration might outnumber the war advocates.[3]

Peace efforts were in ill repute. Those who were asking Congress to avoid war were denounced as "pacifists" or labeled "pro-German" and excoriated as agents of German propaganda.

Bob was present when the Senate met for the first session of the Sixty-fourth Congress, at noon, April 2, and heard the reading of the President's proclamation declaring that an extraordinary occasion required the Congress of the United States to convene in extra session. Shortly after 8:15 that evening Bob went with other Senators to the House to receive the President's message. Preceded by the Sergeant at Arms and headed by Vice President Marshall and the Secretary of the Senate, they marched into the Chamber two by two, most of them carrying or wearing tucked in their breast pockets small American flags. The press caustically noted that Bob was not the author of the innovation, since he and one or two others did not display this "badge of patriotism."[4] Sitting well toward the front, beside Senator Lane of Oregon and not far from Stone and Norris, he was described as "one of the centers of conversation . . . watched by hundreds, eager to see how he, acknowledged leader of the pacifists of both houses, took the President's message."[5]

Never before had such a scene taken place at the Capitol. In the galleries and on the floor every seat was occupied, and people were standing in every available space. Since 3:30 the Capitol had been closed to visitors, and only those having cards were admitted. Two troops of cavalry guarded the approach; the building swarmed with police and secret service men. As an additional precaution they had also "been stationed at intervals above the glass ceiling." Outside, it was raining intermittently. "Now and then a flash of lightning illuminated the scene followed by . . . the grumble of distant thunder. . . . The measured tread of infantry, the rumble of artillery, the clang of sword and sabre and the stamping of cavalry hoofs upon the hard surface of the streets . . . were audible in the great building, and lent dramatic effect to an occasion already surcharged with acutely nervous tension."[6]

Directly in front of the Speaker, and facing him, sat the Supreme Court Justices without their customary official robes. At the side, near the front, was a group which would have astonished George Washington and Thomas Jefferson. For the first time that anyone could remember, the diplomatic representatives of foreign countries sat together officially on the floor of the House, a symbol of a new era in American history.[7] Behind them were the American Cabinet officials.

The President, escorted by a troop of cavalry, arrived at the Capitol at 8:30. As he entered the House Chamber everyone rose; cheers swept the vast room. Bob stood with arms crossed and head bowed; he did not join in the applause. Throughout the message and the cheering which greeted it he listened silently. "Once, when the president urged that Germany's warlike acts be met with war, and again, when the president recommended the raising of an army under the principle of general service," he "seemed to smile a little cynically. That was the only display of what he was feeling that his features disclosed."[8]

To Bob this hour was an ordeal. It cut to the very roots of his life work and made him fear for the future of his country. If the United States entered the war, he knew that constructive solutions of vital domestic problems necessary to the preservation of democracy would be devastated by preparation for distant battles. He also believed that the expressed wish of the country was being frustrated by the demand the President was making. Convinced that the people had reelected Wilson in the faith that he would continue to keep the country at peace, Bob, with deep resentment and sorrow, heard him demand a declaration of war within one month of his second inauguration.

After reciting the grievances we had against Germany, the President referred briefly to the submarine issue upon which he had broken off diplomatic relations with Germany on February 3. The silence became "so painfully intense that it was almost audible"[9] as he explained his decision to abandon the arming of merchant ships: ". . . armed neutrality, it now appears, is impracticable. Because submarines are in effect outlaws when used as the German submarines have been used against merchant shipping, it is impossible to defend ships against their attacks. . . . Armed neutrality is ineffectual enough at best; in such circumstances . . . it is worse than ineffectual: . . . it is practically certain to draw us into the war without either the rights or the effectiveness of belligerents."[10]

With astonishment Bob heard the President make this statement. It was an argument he himself had intended to make against the Armed Ship bill. In fact, a portion of his editorial published in *La Follette's Magazine,* and quoted that very morning in the *New York Times,* criticized the bill in similar terms.[11] In advocating a declaration of war, the President had condemned and repudiated his own "armed neutrality" policy in an argument similar to that made only a few weeks before by the very Senators he had characterized as a "little group of willful men, representing no opinion but their own."[12]

As the President announced, "we will not choose the path of submission," and advised Congress to declare a state of war,[13] ecstatic demonstrations of approval swept the Chamber. Chief Justice White of the Supreme Court "sprang to his feet and raising his hands high above his head, led the applause. . . . though the cheering really needed no leader, he was its leader."[14] Those on the floor and in the galleries "followed him with a roar like a storm."[15] Throughout this demonstration two Senators, Stone and La Follette, less than fifty feet from Wilson, were silent. "Stone, sitting in the second row, rested his head on his hands and listened with a grim face."[16] Bob felt that an outburst of cheering was a strange response to a request for a declaration of war.

Finally, when the cheering ceased, the President went on to outline his program. His statement foreshadowing his support of conscription evoked "by far the greatest outburst" of applause.[17] But to Bob there was only bitter irony in advocating compulsory military service on foreign soil in a war for democracy. To the end of his life he believed this was a violation of the constitutional rights of American citizens.[18]

Once during the reading of the message the audience was startled by a crash on the glass skylight above the Chamber. So vivid was the impression that the country was already at war, that, as the President looked up, the thought flashed to some of those present that a bomb had exploded.[19] It was later discovered that one of the soldiers stationed above had dropped his gun.

The President closed his address with an eloquent peroration containing those brilliant phrases which were to become the idealistic battle cries of the war: "The world must be made safe for democracy . . . ," he said. "We are but one of the champions of the rights of mankind. . . . To such a task we can dedicate our lives and our fortunes, . . . with the pride of those who know that the day has come when America is privileged to spend her blood and her might for the principles that gave her birth and happiness and the peace which she has treasured. God helping her, she can do no other."[20]

Thus the message ended. The President had spoken for thirty-six minutes. "The act he had dreaded to do was done. For seconds the stillness remained unbroken. Then, as with a single impulse, the audience broke into tumultuous, roaring, deafening applause. . . . The approval was indeed all but unanimous. But La Follette, opposition etched in every grim look, was silent, arms folded high on his chest, contemptuous of the defeat that the moment held for him."[21] The majority had responded to Wilson's dramatic appeal with unbounded enthusiasm. But Lane, Stone, and La Follette "did not join in the storms of applause."[22] Wilson is reported to have said on his return to the White House, "My message to-day was a message of death for our young men. How strange it seems to applaud that."[23]

Although neither knew it, the President and Bob had been momentarily in accord.

Silently, his head bowed in sorrow, Bob left the Chamber. Convinced that a majority of the people wanted peace, the demonstration he had just witnessed made him fear the combined power of President and press would, in a barrage of idealistic rhetoric, soon sweep the country into a disastrous foreign war. American youth would then, he believed, be futilely sacrificed to diplomatic blunders and unrealistic thinking. He was opposed to declaring war on either England or Germany for their "ruthless" and "relentless" violation of our neutral rights. He looked "upon Europe as cursed with a contagious, . . . deadly plague, whose spread threatens to devastate the civilized world." Regardless of "material loss, or commercial inconvenience," he thought we should "keep our people at home" and "quarantine against it" as we would if it were actually "the Black Death."[24] He could not forget the deep economic causes, the old national hatreds, the clashing imperialistic aims, existing in all the belligerent countries. He was convinced there were secret commitments based on the very conflicts which had caused the European holocaust. Above all, he feared what war and involvement in these ancient European conflicts would do to our own struggle to solve the problems we confronted at home in perfecting and preserving our own democratic form of government.

When the Senate met at noon the next day, Bob was in his seat. Although Congress had not yet acted on the President's message, war measures were rushed through, out of the regular order, by unanimous consent. That morning the Committee on Foreign Relations had quickly reported out the war resolution[25] prepared by Lansing with the President's approval[26] and introduced the previous evening. The only negative vote was cast by the chairman, Stone, who then "took up his hat and left the Committee room alone."[27] Without waiting for the customary printing, Hitchcock rushed to the floor,[28] introduced the resolution, and asked unanimous consent for immediate consideration. Under the rule, designed to permit study of legislation, objection by a single Senator could compel the resolution to go over for a day. Bob objected. Evidently thinking objection was because it had not yet been printed, Hitchcock assured him a printed copy would be on every Senator's desk within five minutes. Bob, making no explanation, quietly but firmly insisted on the rule which requires it to go over for a day.

As the Vice President started to sustain the objection, Martin, the Democratic floor leader, interrupted, reproving Bob and repeatedly reminding him of "the momentous consequences involved in this joint resolution." Bob cut the reproof short by tartly remarking, "it is quite unnecessary for the Senator to call my attention to the momentous consequences of this joint resolution. I think I realize them quite as fully as he does." He then demanded the "regular order"—a quick parliamentary way to shut off debate.[29]

The Vice President ruled the resolution must go over for the day. Martin moved to adjourn, and when another Senator sought recognition, "cut him short with a roar like a wounded bull,"[30] objecting to the presentation of business of any sort until the joint resolution declaring war was disposed of. Contrary to the Senate rules, this was greeted by "a thunder of applause" from the galleries and on the Senate floor. "John Sharp Williams was standing by Martin in the front row applauding with all his might."[31]

Immediately after adjournment the Foreign Relations Committee held an impromptu meeting in its room at the Capitol. One newspaper reported that while they were conferring "to meet the President's call to arms, Senator La Follette, far underground below their feet, in a little cubbyhole of a room in the subbasement reached by a labyrinth, was busily whispering with a dozen pacifists."[32] The fact was that on returning to his office Bob found cards with encouraging messages from Mary McDowell, Mrs. Samuel Untermyer, and several others who had called while he was on the Senate floor. One of these messages read: "God bless you. The people do." He placed the cards in an envelope on which he wrote, "called on April 3." It was found in his desk after his death.[33]

Newspaper men and Senators knew that a day or two earlier, Stone and Bob had held a long conference in the latter's office in the Capitol.[34] This was interpreted as threatening a filibuster. A signed Washington dispatch disclosed that both Republicans and Democrats were planning on "taking drastic action against La Follette and

Stone if they attempted any filibustering tactics."[35] Describing Bob as "the only man the supporters of the President's American policy are afraid of," Angus McSween reported to the Philadelphia *North American* on April 3 that Senators Martin and Gallinger, leaders of the Democratic and Republican sides, "sent out letters tonight asking every Senator to be in his seat at 10 o'clock tomorrow morning and informing them that the Senate will be kept in continuous session until the resolution has been adopted. . . . The Senate leaders are getting ready for Mr. La Follette."[36]

That same evening a distinguished professor of sociology and the history of civilization, Franklin H. Giddings of Columbia University, speaking before the Institute of Arts and Sciences at the Horace Mann Auditorium, was reported as saying: "We read tonight that a declaration of war that might have been made today was delayed by one Robert La Follette. Men have often made up lists of 'immortals.' Among the 'immortals' whose 'immortality' is sure are Robert La Follette, William Jennings Bryan, James Buchanan, Benedict Arnold, and Judas Iscariot. Their claim is safe." The same report noted, "Hisses burst forth at every mention of the name of La Follette."[37]

Near the boundaries of another historic temple of learning, an incident occurred that same night which was reported to several Western papers: "Students at Massachusetts Institute of Technology made a dummy La Follette, tagged it that all might know it was La Follette, and then on the edge of the Charles river basin, where it could be seen for miles, set it on fire. Long lines of students executed an Indian war dance about the burning La Follette, meantime singing and jeering."[38]

The next day the *Wisconsin State Journal* reported this burning in effigy,[39] and the *Madison Democrat* printed an editorial which his son Phil read before going to his classes at the university:[40] "Wisconsin is disappointed, chagrined, indignant. Exasperation must soon ensue—then disgust. 'Is La Follette mad?' is being freely asked; and answered in saddened tone by those who gladly would excuse. It is a charitable view at least but does not satisfy."[41]

The stock market, always sensitive, had gone up following the President's address. It slumped after the Senate's enforced postponement of the war resolution.[42] "La Follette caused a complete change in market sentiment," the *Washington Herald* reported the following morning, and, driving the point home, added, "Wall Street was angered at the attitude taken by Senator La Follette."[43] Among Bob's papers is a clipping of this *Herald* story mounted on a sheet of Senate stationery. Written on the margin is the following notation, which he probably made the day he spoke against the declaration of war: "Wall St.'s anger is a matter of utter indifference to me. It may not be so with others. Be that as it may, I have never experimented with the dubious business of trying to serve two masters—the people of the country and the interests of Wall Street."[44]

The war clamor and denunciation of the press were as a whisper in his ears compared to the voices which were calling to him through letters, telegrams, petitions, and referendums throughout the country. This Lincoln Steffens had understood when he wrote that La Follette trusted the people "as no other leader has ever trusted them."[45]

To a degree understood only by his family and intimate friends, Bob valued these direct communications as the most authentic record of the thought of the hard-working folk of America. These were the men and women he meant when he referred to "the people." Whatever service he had been able to render had been due, he believed, to their understanding and support. Years later he wrote: "I should have been a traitor to the people, in my opinion, had I not voiced and voted my opposition to a declaration of war. Despite the vast war propaganda with which the country had been flooded, . . . the American people were in their hearts at that time opposed to war, and I believe the instinct of the people was sound."[46]

When the Senate met on April 4, a newspaper correspondent noted that Bob was present.[47] In a single session, beginning at ten and continuing until eleven fifteen that night, the war resolution was taken up for the first time, debated, and voted on. The letters sent out the previous night by Gallinger and Martin had been effective. Almost every Senator was present when Hitchcock asked unanimous consent to proceed to consideration of the war resolution. There was no objection. Correspondents in the press gallery looked for La Follette. But he had left the Chamber and was absent during much of Hitchcock's address, conferring with Gronna and others who expected to oppose the resolution.[48] That afternoon the front page of the *Wisconsin State Journal,* in the same issue that carried the report of the burning in effigy, spread the story, "Senator La Follette, one of the 'willful twelve,' was not present when the Senate began its patriotic program," and erroneously reported that "he entered the upper chamber for the first time today shortly before 4 o'clock."[49]

Only five Senators spoke against a declaration of war: Bob, Norris, and Gronna, progressive Republicans, joined Vardaman and Stone, Democrats, in opposition. Seventeen spoke for it. Several explained why they had shifted from advocating neutrality to supporting the President. The debate was opened by Hitchcock, who obviously found it difficult to reconcile his present position with his former insistence on strict neutrality. Disclosing that he was not in complete accord with the President's message, he asserted Germany had violated no pledge in resuming unrestricted submarine warfare, but had exercised a right she had reserved.[50] In the principal address for the resolution, Swanson of Virginia declared: "The issue is not peace or war. War has already been wantonly and lawlessly prosecuted against us."[51] He thus voiced the feeling which had led those who had long advocated war to denounce as treason Bob's brief twenty-four-hour postponement of Senate action. Lodge, formerly a severe critic of the Administration, followed with a fervent appeal to join the united front in support of the President.

It was Vardaman, Senator from the same State that John Sharp Williams was from, who first voiced the opposition. Although often oratorical, his brief speech was delivered on this occasion in a quiet voice. It was singularly moving to those who, like Bob, were sympathetic to his point of view. Motivated by sincere feeling, which doubtless grew out of his own experience in the Spanish-American War, he expressed the conviction which was to take him out of public life at the election of 1918 when patriotic fervor was at its peak. Expressing the opinion subsequently voiced by Bob and Gronna, Vardaman declared: "I will say, . . . that if the people of the United States—I mean the plain, honest people, the masses who are to bear the burden of taxation and fight the nation's battles, were consulted—the United States would not make a declaration of war against Germany today."[52]

Stone, who followed, also had faith in the verdict of time, though he did not live to see his course vindicated by public opinion. He knew that for its effect on the country a unanimous vote for the war declaration was desired by the Administration. A prominent Democrat, Senator James A. Reed, had been asked to see Stone. Reed had warned him opposition would ruin him politically. Stone had answered that this did not weigh with him on an issue like war. His refusal to vote for it "was not," he said, "because this war will cost billions, which these fools think will cost only millions; it's not even because of the loss of American lives although I would not sacrifice one American boy for all the European belligerents. I won't vote for this war because if we go into it, we will never again have this same old Republic."[53]

Stone's profound conviction was now making him an outcast among his life-long associates. He had listened to most of the debate for the resolution. Rising slowly to address the Senate, this Democrat, who had cast the only negative vote in the Foreign Relations Committee, spoke less than five minutes: "Mr. President, I fear that the Congress is about to involve the United States in this European war, and when you do that my belief is that you will commit the greatest national blunder in history." He then uttered the words which were to be engraved on his tomb a year later: "I shall vote against this mistake, to prevent which, God helping me, I would gladly lay down my life."[54]

In a speech which brought bitter denunciation, Norris declared that if we had maintained strictest neutrality from the beginning he did not believe we would now be "on the verge of war."[55] The great combination of wealth that had a direct financial interest in our participation in the war had, he said, misled many honest and patriotic citizens regarding the true facts. As evidence of "the Wall Street view," he read into the *Record* an excerpt from a letter written by a member of the New York Stock Exchange to its customers. This had come to Norris from a Senator who wanted it put in the *Record* but did not "have the courage to read it himself." Though opposed to our entry into the war, he had decided to vote for it.[56] A portion of this letter said: "The popular view is that stocks would have a quick, clear, sharp reaction immediately upon the outbreak of hostilities and that then they would enjoy an old-fashioned bull market such as followed the outbreak of war with Spain in 1898. . . . If the United States does not go to war, it is nevertheless good opinion that the preparedness program will compensate in good measure for the loss of the stimulus of actual war."[57]

"We are going into war upon the command of gold," Norris warned. "I feel we are about to put the dollar sign upon the American flag." His bold words set off angry debate. Reed challenged as "near to treason" the charge that "we are about to put the dollar sign upon the American flag." Williams broke in to say, "If it be not treason it grazes the edge of treason."[58]

The bitter attacks by Reed and Williams, joined later by Pomerene and Ollie James, upon men like Norris, whose integrity had hitherto been unquestioned, reveal the feeling in the Senate that day. It was also voiced by Kenyon of Iowa when he spoke for the resolution: "It is no time to talk about mistakes," he warned, "no time for criticism of the President, of the Cabinet, of Congress. . . . It is no time for divided allegiance. It is time for 100% Americanism."[59] This phrase became the popular slogan to silence minority criticism of administration policies in the conduct of a war to make the world safe for democracy.

Gronna of North Dakota, "a man of great intellectual integrity,"[60] had received petitions from thousands of American citizens asking him "to oppose a declaration of war with any of the nations of Europe." Speaking with intense conviction, he said: "We criticize European monarchies for forcing their subjects into war against their will, but we refuse to ascertain by a referendum vote of the American people whether they desire peace or war. . . . I shall vote against war because I believe it would have been possible to maintain an honorable peace."[61] This conviction grew naturally out of Gronna's own experience and the democratic tradition of his Norwegian ancestors. He occupied the seat next to Bob, and there was a bond of understanding between them which went back to the 1912 campaign. The two men came from similar pioneer backgrounds. Both sincerely believed that the letters and petitions they had received were more authentic evidence of what the American citizens were thinking than the "boiler plate" propaganda which the National Security League was sending out to 1,700 or 1,800 newspapers throughout the country.[62]

Following the Senate adjournment at 1:03 P.M. on April 3, Bob had stayed on at the Capitol until after midnight, working into final form the material Roe, Belle, Hannan, and Bob, Jr., had been helping him to gather. He had directed the office force to stay on all night if necessary. Although for many months he had been studying the questions involved in our conflicts with the belligerents, he had had little consecutive time to prepare a speech during the day and two nights following the President's request for a declaration of war.

Ever since the debate on the Armed Ship bill, Roe had been spending as much time in Washington as his law practice permitted, working with Bob and Belle on questions of international law. These two men, former law partners and intimate friends, had entered upon one of the most important of their many collaborations. United in an undertaking they believed of vital import to the future of their country, it is often difficult in this period to distinguish where the work of one leaves off and the other's contribution begins. Their thought functioned in extraordinary harmony; a similar background had determined their measure of values and objectives. It never occurred to either to weigh the cost of differing with a powerful President on the eve of war.

Bob's stand on the war caused many friends to turn from him. But it also renewed relationships which had been strained or broken by his refusal to withdraw in Roosevelt's favor in 1912. While he was at work that evening, a friend, for whom he had great affection but had not seen since 1912, called at his office. Uncertain as to his reception after his bitter speeches during that campaign, Henry Cochems had first asked Hannan if he "thought La Follette would see him." The two men saw each other alone. No one knows what was said; but when Cochems came out it was obvious both had been profoundly stirred.[63]

The next afternoon, during Bob's speech, Gilson Gardner and Amos Pinchot sat together in the press gallery. Both were deeply moved, and sent notes to Bob on the floor.[64] This also was the first communication between Bob and Gardner since the pre-convention campaign of 1912. A day or two later, when Bob saw Gardner in the gallery, he sent him a note: "Gilson—I beg your pardon for not having acknowledged receipt of your card. Let's close the old books and open a new set. It's a time when friends of democracy should work together to save as much of the wreckage as possible. Bob."[65] Gardner called in response to this note. From that day until Bob's death their relationship was one of mutual affection and confidence.

In so far as anyone knew, they never discussed or referred to the incidents which had led to their estrangement.

When Bob began speaking on Wednesday afternoon, April 4, shortly before four o'clock, Senators who had been in the smoking room hurried to their seats; men and women in the crowded galleries leaned forward expectantly.[66] The stir of interest was followed by unusual quiet in the galleries and on the floor. Throughout his entire three-hour speech he had the "solem[n] attention of almost every Senator."[67] Only three times was he interrupted. He read from manuscript and seldom moved from his desk in the first row of the center aisle, directly in front of the Presiding Officer.

There was no conflict within himself. He had, during this period, the strength and serenity which come only from inner unity. His steady course was guided by the pattern of the past. He was sustained against outward attack by the faith that was in him. It was a simple faith, but a faith deeply rooted in the experience of his own life. Its origin must be sought in the little town of Primrose and the State of Wisconsin, where he grew up among hard-working pioneer folk from many different lands. To them or their ancestors, as to his own, America had meant escape from the very burdens he was convinced war would bring to the United States.

Just as he was going on the floor, he received a telegram from Congressman Helgesen, "who was sick unto death"[68] in a Washington hospital.* Helgesen had sent it with the request that Bob read to the Senate this plea from a "North Dakota Farm Woman," typical of the thousands of messages which brought to him "one uniform protest against war."[69]

After reading the telegram, Bob turned to his manuscript and at once began his answer to the doctrine of "standing back of the President." Those on the floor and in the galleries listened intently as he said in a clear, distinct tone, "I had supposed until recently that it was the duty of Senators and Representatives in Congress to vote and act according to their convictions.

"Quite another doctrine has recently been promulgated . . . and that is the doctrine of 'standing back of the President,' without inquiring whether the President is right or wrong. For myself I have never subscribed to that doctrine and never shall. I shall support

* Helgesen died on April 10, 1917.

the President in the measures he proposes when I believe them to be right. I shall oppose measures proposed by the President when I believe them to be wrong. . . . If it is important for us to speak and vote our convictions in matters of internal policy, though we may unfortunately be in disagreement with the President, it is infinitely more important for us to speak and vote our convictions when the question is one of peace or war, certain to involve the lives and fortunes of many of our people and, it may be, the destiny of all of them and of the civilized world as well. If . . . the most patient research and conscientious consideration leave us in disagreement with the President, I know of no course to take except to oppose, regretfully but not less firmly, the demands of the Executive."

Then, for the first time in the Senate, he commented on Wilson's denunciation of a month before: "I regret to say that the President . . . saw fit to characterize as 'willful' the conduct of the Senators who, in obedience to their consciences and their oaths of office, opposed the armed-ship bill, and to charge that in so doing they were not representing the people by whose suffrages they are here. I know of no graver charge that could be made against the official conduct of any Member of this body . . ." He then offered testimony which he believed directly refuted the President's charge. An analysis of 15,000 letters and telegrams sent him from 44 States revealed that 9 out of 10 were an "unqualified indorsement" of his course "in opposing war with Germany on the issue presented." Reading a few typical messages hastily selected just before he came on the floor, he included individual opinions and reports on various types of referendums from different parts of the country. He read a telegram from Monroe, Wisconsin, announcing the result of an election conducted by the legal election board of the city in conjunction with the city election. The telegram reported what was perhaps the first official war referendum ever held in this country: "For peace, 954; for war, 95."[70] Fathered by Judge John M. Becker of Monroe, then Judge of Green County, an office to which he had been elected nine times, it had aroused heated controversy in the State, and was widely cited in Eastern papers as proof that Wisconsin was pro-German.[71]

The result of a referendum taken by sending out 20,000 postal cards to representative citizens of Massachusetts had been brought to Bob by Elizabeth Glendower Evans, who had been active in making the survey, and was now in the gallery listening to his speech.

These showed, he told the Senate, that 66 per cent were against war and 63 per cent against conscription. He cited five other polls—all against war, and also submitted a significant telegram received that very afternoon from Grace Abbott at Hull House.[72]

As further evidence refuting the President's estimate of public opinion, he cited a vote taken in Minneapolis. A few days after Wilson's denunciation, Congressman Lundeen had called and given Bob "the results on the war ballot which he had sent out to the poll lists of voters in his district."[73] The returns showed, Bob told the Senate, that nearly 8,000 voters were against declaring war to less than 800 who favored it. "Do not these messages indicate on the part of the people," he asked earnestly, "a deep seated conviction that the United States should not enter the European war?"[74]

After a brief extemporaneous warning predicting that the people of this country would some day register the protest he was convinced they now felt against entry into the European War, he returned to his manuscript, relentlessly analyzing the danger of immediate, unquestioning acceptance of the Chief Executive's judgment: "If the President was wrong when he proposed arming the ships; if that policy was, as he now says, 'certain to draw us into the war without either the rights or the effectiveness of belligerents,' is it so certain he is right now when he demands an unqualified declaration of war against Germany?" Directly addressing his colleagues he asked, "If the armed-ship bill involved a course of action that was hasty and ill-advised, may it not well be that this proposed declaration of war, which is being so hotly pressed, is also ill-advised?"[75]

Then, as a lawyer might analyze his opponent's brief, he took up one passage after another from the President's speech, arguing and answering each point as if the Senators, who followed him with close attention, were a Supreme Court. Quoting the President's statement that this was a war "for democracy, for the right of those who submit to authority to have a voice in their own government," Bob challenged the President and supporters of the resolution to "submit it to a vote of the people before the declaration of war goes into effect." Turning directly to the Senators on the floor, he said, "You who support it dare not do it, for you know that by a vote of more than ten to one the American people as a body would register their declaration against it." He boldly charged, "The espionage bills, the conscription bills, and other forcible military measures . . . being ground out by the war machine in this country" were the complete proof that those responsible for this war "fear that it has no popular support."[76]

On the eve of our declaration of war, he arraigned European secret diplomacy, including that of our future allies. For the first time on the Senate floor he now voiced his suspicion as to the secret agreements among the Allies which he had anxiously discussed in private ever since he thought this country was being led into war.[77] "We do not know what they are," he said. "We do not know what is in the minds of those who have made the compact, but we are to subscribe to it. We are irrevocably, by our votes here," he warned the Senators, "to marry ourselves to a nondivorceable proposition veiled from us now. Once enlisted, once in the copartnership, we will be carried through with the purposes, whatever they may be, of which we now know nothing." The European War, he maintained, had "originated from causes beyond the sphere of our influence and outside the realm of our responsibility. . . . the Government of each country engaged in it is at fault for it." He predicted history would find the real cause for this was in the fact that "England would tolerate no commercial rivalry. Germany would not submit to isolation."[78]

As he uttered these words he could not know that one of the first historians to fulfill his prophecy would be President Wilson himself when he said in a public speech at St. Louis on September 5, 1919: "The real reason that the war we have just finished took place was that Germany was afraid her commercial rivals were going to get the better of her, and the reason why some nations went into the war against Germany was that they thought that Germany would get the commercial advantage of them."[79] *

Step by step Bob traced what he believed had been the diplomatic blunders of President and State Department. These had brought us to the brink of war. Earnestly but calmly he presented and argued for the strictly neutral action he was convinced could have kept us out of war. He spoke as if he believed, even now, Presi-

---

* This quotation was reprinted on the editorial page of the Washington *Times-Herald*, Jan. 22, 1940, in connection with two cartoons, under the heading, "There would be much less war if statesmen were as frank while getting us into war as they are when the war is over." One cartoon depicts Wilson speaking in the Senate April 2, 1917, and quotes from this speech. The other cartoon depicts him speaking on Sept. 5, 1919, and quotes from the speech in St. Louis on that date.

dent, Senators, and Congressmen might listen to logic and choose a wiser, reasoned course.

He first contrasted the replies of both countries toward our inquiry as to their willingness to adhere to the Declaration of London. This he described as "the best and most humane statement of the rules of naval warfare which could be prepared" by the accredited representatives of the leading nations meeting at London in 1909.[80] Germany and Austria had promptly answered they would be bound by it, but England had demanded so many modifications and additions that the essential principles were destroyed and her reply was practically a refusal. Great Britain, because it suited her naval policy,[81] thus "made waste paper of this declaration."[82] Analyzing the most important provisions of the London declaration, Bob concluded that had they been applied by both belligerents the present conflict between the United States and Germany would never have developed.[83]

Following Great Britain's refusal to adhere to the Declaration of London, he recalled that we made many protests "against Germany and some against Great Britain and her allies," claiming "international law had been violated."[84] Germany had again and again yielded to our protests, but, Bob said, he could not remember "a single instance in which a protest we have made to Great Britain has won for us the slightest consideration, except for a short time in the case of cotton."[85]

Bob suspected, but could not then prove, that the lack of real neutrality among the United States' representatives in the State Department and abroad was an important factor in preventing Great Britain from taking our protests seriously. Letters and memoirs published long after the war have supplied the testimony he could not subpoena into the Senate that day.[86] Lansing himself admitted in 1935 that the notes sent to Great Britain "were long and exhaustive treatises which opened up new subjects of discussion rather than closing those in controversy. Short and emphatic notes were dangerous. Everything was submerged in verbosity. It was done with deliberate purpose. It insured continuance of the controversies and left the questions unsettled, which was necessary in order to leave this country free to act and even to act illegally when it entered the war."[87]

Bob believed, and stated in his speech, as Norris had earlier that same day, that England had been the first of the belligerents to mine the high seas.[88] His statement was based upon a proclamation issued by the secretary of the British Admiralty, November 2, 1914, giving "notice that the whole of the North Sea must be considered a military area."[89] Neither this proclamation nor any United States protest against it had been included in the published volumes of diplomatic correspondence made available to him by our State Department up to the time he spoke. He had known of the proclamation ever since November 3, 1914, when it had been published in the press of this country.[90] The importance of this document in shaping his opinion can scarcely be overestimated. For reasons of its own the State Department had withheld from publication any United States protest to Great Britain. At Bob's direction repeated telephone inquiries had been made to the State Department regarding further publication of diplomatic correspondence, but he did not know that another volume was to be "printed and distributed April 4, 1917," the very day he spoke.* He had carefully studied all the information he was able to secure up to that time. Therefore he believed and stated on the Senate floor that the British Admiralty's proclamation of November 2, 1914, had been the first declaration to mine the high seas and that the United States had never "uttered a word of protest" against this "act of piracy." He declared this order was "the most ruthless and sweeping in its violation of neutral rights that up to that time had ever emanated from a civilized government." In thus agreeing to this lawless act, the Administration had bound us, he said, as completely as if "we had entered into a contract with Great Britain, signed and sealed under the great seals of the respective countries." Pointing out that England based this action upon her own assertion that mines had been scattered in the open sea around the British Isles by Germany, he declared, "no proof of it has ever been furnished, so far as I am aware."[91]

Germany waited three months, he said, until February 4, and "then did as a matter of retaliation and defense what Great Britain had done months previously purely as an offensive measure—established a war zone" including "in it portions of the sea about the

---

* This volume contained the notice of the British Admiralty of Nov. 2, 1914, and protests of the United States, hitherto withheld from publication; also, Germany's notice of Aug. 7, 1914, regarding mining of the high seas.

British islands. . . . It is Germany's insistence upon her right to blindly destroy with mines and submarines in the area she has declared a war zone all ships that enter there, that causes the whole trouble existing between us and Germany to-day. It is for this, and this only, that we are urged to make war. Yet in asserting this right or in sinking the ships in the prescribed area without warning, Germany is doing only that which England is doing in her prescribed area, with our consent. . . .

"The English mines are intended to destroy without warning every ship that enters the war zone she has prescribed, killing or drowning every passenger that can not find some means of escape. It is neither more nor less than that which Germany tries to do with her submarines in her war zone. We acquiesced in England's action without protest. It is proposed that we now go to war with Germany for identically the same action upon her part." He called the Senators' attention to the "singular" fact that the State Department had omitted from the published volumes of diplomatic correspondence "the British order in council (of November 2, 1914) mining the North Sea" but had included "all the correspondence about the submarines of Germany."[92]

During the debate that same evening, and again two days later, memoranda from the State Department and a letter from Lansing to Senator King were introduced to refute statements made by Bob and Norris that England had been the first to mine the high seas and Bob's other statement that the Administration had not protested the British proclamation of November 2.[93] Bob, Jr., recalls that his father was not disturbed about the material furnished to King and Husting by the State Department because he "felt it had been sent up for the purpose of refuting his statement and that the State Department had not been frank and open in relation to the publication of correspondence. He felt that all was not known about its attitude and that it would all come out in the wash later."[94]

Correspondence and memoirs published long after the war indicate Bob's intuition as to the really unneutral intent of the Administration's procedure was more accurate than appeared evident in the memoranda submitted by Lansing and the State Department soon after he spoke.

Bob charged the President with a misstatement of the law when he had said that Germany's responsibility for her note was not contingent upon the action of England. The President's phrase, "Responsibility in such matters is single, not joint; absolute, not relative," Bob declared, "misstates the law; it asserts a principle that can not be maintained for one moment with a decent regard for equal rights between nations [at war] with whom we are dealing on a basis of neutrality. . . . when we are dealing with Germany and Great Britain, warring against each other, so evenly balanced in strength that a little help to one or a little hindrance to the other turns the scale and spells victory for one and defeat for the other, in that situation I say the principle of international law steps in which declares that any failure on our part to enforce our rights equally against both is a gross act of unneutrality."[95]

After citing various historical precedents, he concluded: "Had the plain principle of international law announced by Jefferson been followed by us, we would not be called on today to declare war upon any of the belligerents. The failure to treat the belligerent nations of Europe alike, the failure to reject the unlawful 'war zones' of both Germany and Great Britain, is wholly accountable for our present dilemma. We should not seek to hide our blunder behind the smoke of battle, to inflame the mind of our people by half truths into the frenzy of war, in order that they may never appreciate the real cause of it until it is too late. I do not believe that our national honor is served by such a course. The right way is the honorable way."

He ended his speech by offering two alternatives: One was to admit our initial blunder and demand that both England and Germany respect our neutral rights upon the high seas; the other was to "withdraw our commerce from both." He thought, "The mere suggestion that food supplies would be withheld from both sides impartially would compel belligerents to observe the principle of freedom of the seas for neutral commerce."[96]

Only once did Bob digress from his prepared argument. Laying down his manuscript, he had spoken with intensity of his belief that a minority in Congress might in fact represent the majority opinion of the country. The exercise of this minority right was, he maintained, a duty. It had been conferred by the Constitution "to perpetuate not the semblance of democracy but real democracy." Back of Congresses, statutes and Presidents was "the sovereign power of the people" to "correct our errors and mistakes and our wrong doing. They can take us out of our places and if we abuse any power which the Constitution puts in the hands of a minority, it lies with them to call us to account; . . . We need not disturb ourselves because of what a minority may do." Listening from the galleries, Belle and his intimate friends knew he expressed the burning conviction behind his determined opposition to a declaration of war when he said: "There is always lodged, and always will be, thank the God above us, power in the people supreme. Sometimes it sleeps, sometimes it seems the sleep of death; but, sir, the sovereign power of the people never dies. It may be suppressed for a time, it may be misled, be fooled, silenced. I think, Mr. President, that it is being denied expression now. I think there will come a day when it will have expression.

"The poor, sir, who are the ones called upon to rot in the trenches, have no organized power, have no press to voice their will upon this question of peace or war; but, oh, Mr. President, at some time they will be heard. I hope and I believe they will be heard in an orderly and a peaceful way. I think they may be heard from before long. . . . there will come an awakening; they will have their day and they will be heard. It will be as certain and as inevitable as the return of the tides, and as resistless, too."[97]

This faith, in the midst of almost overwhelming condemnation, enabled him to carry on his work and bide the judgment of time.

He finished speaking at 6:45.[98] Earlier in the day it had been expected his address would close the debate. But Williams of Mississippi now rose. It may be that Bob had some intimation of what was to follow. For two days earlier, in advance of the President's address, Williams had made a fiery declaration urging an aggressive war and the sending of a million men abroad, where he hoped "for the sake of the South" that the bands would play "Dixie" as our troops "deploy into position."[99] Under the tension of his own feeling about the war, Williams now directed his exceptional power of personal vituperation against Bob.

"Mr. President," he began, in a voice quivering with emotion, "if immortality could be attained by a verbal eternity, the Senator from Wisconsin would have approximated immortality. We have waited and have heard a speech from him which would have better become Herr Bethmann-Hollweg, of the German Parliament, than an American Senator. In fact, he has gone much further than Herr Bethmann-Hollweg ever dared to go." Pausing for a moment to search out Bob, who was then standing in the rear of the chamber, "Williams cried in a loud tone:"[100] "I fully expected before he took his seat to hear him defend the invasion of Belgium—the most absolutely barbarous act that ever took place in the history of any nation anywhere. I heard from him a speech which was pro-German, pretty nearly pro-Goth, and pro-Vandal, which was anti-American President and anti-American Congress and anti-American people. . . . I have loved the Senator from Wisconsin, in a way, until recently. . . . Tell me that the American Congress is 'about to involve the American people in war!' The man who says that is a knave or a fool."[101]

Throughout this speech, which fills a little over seven columns of the *Record*, no one called him to order, although his attack had repeatedly violated the accepted Senate rule. Immediately after Bob had concluded his argument, he had gathered up his manuscript and walked to the rear of the Chamber. There he stopped a moment to give instructions to his Secretary as to when he wished to be called back.[102] While he was talking to Hannan, "Williams raised his voice in an effort" to attract his attention "and goad him to reply."[103] Bob, without even turning to look at Williams, "walked into the cloakroom and out of the sound of the speaker's voice."[104] Six Senators followed Williams, all speaking for the resolution. Husting of Wisconsin, in a speech almost as long as Bob's, defended the President's position.[105]

When the resolution finally came to a vote, people were standing in the aisles and sitting on the steps of the crowded galleries. On the Senate floor, back of the Senators' seats, almost half the membership of the House had gathered to hear the result. The Senators were unusually grave and quiet. The silence was tense as the clerk called the roll; many answered to their names in voices that quivered with emotion. But Bob said his "No" to the war in a clear, firm voice which was heard distinctly in the hushed Chamber. Only Gronna, Lane, Norris, Stone, and Vardaman voted with Bob against the declaration.[106] When the clerk announced the vote of 82 to 6 there was no applause. Only a grave silence greeted the Senate's decision.

As Senators left the Chamber, Bob's colleagues avoided him. With his son and Hannan he walked to his office through corridors filled with the hostile crowds who had listened to the debate from the gallery. A stranger came forward and handed him a rope.

The next evening the *Boston Evening Transcript* described his

speech as "the disloyal culmination of a career of selfish Ishmaelit-
ism. . . . It will naturally be the end of him. . . . Hereafter any cause
or purpose that he advocates will be damned. . . . He is an example
of the self-destructive effect of the basest form of egotism. Standing
against his own country and for his country's enemies, he is gone
and fallen. . . . Henceforth he is the Man without a Country."[107]

During the Senate debate the House had marked time. Thursday
morning, April 5, it met at ten to open the debate on the war resolution which was to last until dawn Friday morning—over sixteen
hours. Again, as a month before during the Armed Ship controversy,
it was chiefly the West and Midwest that opposed the President's
policy. The twenty who spoke against the resolution were not "pacifists." Some had seen war, had been a part of it. Many had voted
for a generous preparedness. Nearly all voiced the same conviction
Bob had expressed—that the American people did not want war.

Thursday afternoon Bob was on the floor of the House listening
to the debate when, at about three o'clock, Claude Kitchin, the
Democratic majority leader, began his speech against the war declaration.[108] Aware that trial by fire must have preceded this decision
to break with President and party, Bob was deeply stirred by the
high courage and clear thought revealed in every word Kitchin read
with deliberate emphasis from his manuscript.

Finally, after listening, with few signs of impatience, to nearly
one hundred speeches, the House voted for war at 3:12 on the morning of Good Friday, April 6, by an overwhelming majority of 373
to 50. Bob always felt the record of the Wisconsin Congressmen was
a courageous page in the State's history. Nine of the eleven Members
voted "No" to our entry into the war.

That night, while the House debated, a "patriotic demonstration"
at Cleburn, Texas, reverted to ancient ritual and was climaxed "by
the burning of Senator La Follette in·effigy on the public square.
The destruction of the figure was attended by cries of derision from
the crowd."[109] Toward morning at the nation's Capital, a Washington policeman, responding to a call from the center of the business
district at 14th and H Streets, found hanging in front of a shop a
small figure of a man. "It was made of white cloth, five feet high,
with eyes, nose and mouth crudely marked with black paint and

stuffed with newspapers. On one side the name 'Stone' appeared; on the other 'La Follette.' Down the back was a broad streak of yellow and dangling from the feet was a streamer bearing the inscription 'Traitors.' "[110] No arrests were made.

The United States was at war.

Notes

Chapter I
(Pages 1–12)

[1] In the courthouse at Greencastle, Putnam County, Ind., there is a bronze tablet, erected by the Sons of the American Revolution, on which the name of Joseph La Follette is inscribed with those of thirty-two other Revolutionary soldiers buried in Putnam County.

[2] The court records show that Thomas Lincoln, Joseph La Follette, and others were appointed to appraise the estate of a deceased neighbor in 1814.

[3] Robert W. Lincoln, *Lives of the Presidents of the United States* (New York, Edward Kearny, 1844); J. Olney, *A Practical System of Modern Geography; or A Veiw of the Present Status of the World. Simplified and Adapted to the Capacity of Youth* (New York, Robinson Pratt & Co., 1844).

Chapter II
(Pages 13–20)

[1] Carrie Baker to Josephine La Follette, April 4, 1870, La Follette Papers, Library of Congress (hereafter cited as LFP).

Chapter III
(Pages 21–33)

[1] *Record*, 59th Cong., 1st Sess., Vol. 40, June 25, 1906, p. 9091.

[2] *La Follette's Autobiography: A Personal Narrative of Political Experiences* (Madison, Wis., Robert M. La Follette Co., 1913), p. 18.

[3] *Ibid.*, pp. 23-24.

[4] *University Press*, April 5, 1876.

[5] Lucy Daniels Thompson, *Twentieth Century Magazine*, Vol. V, No. 3, p. 209.

[6] *Madison Democrat,* March 23, 1878.
[7] *University Press,* April 3, 1878.

Chapter IV

(Pages 34–41)

[1] *Palimpsest,* Vol. XII, No. 5, pp. 187-188, May, 1931, Iowa City, Iowa, State Historical Society.
[2] *Beloit Free Press,* May 10, 1879.
[3] *La Follette's Autobiography,* p. 27.
[4] Edward A. Birge, president emeritus, University of Wisconsin, *Progressive,* Nov. 7, 1931, p. 6.
[5] John Bascom, *Things Learned by Living* (New York, G. P. Putnam's Sons, 1913), p. 211.

Chapter V

(Pages 42–57)

[1] W. A. Housel to B. C. L.
[2] Manuscript note, LFP.
[3] "Private Journal and Night Thoughts R. M. L.," LFP.
[4] *Ibid.*
[5] *Ibid.*
[6] *Madison Democrat,* Nov. 18, 1879.
[7] Republican campaign document, fall of 1880.
[8] Unpublished notes for *La Follette's Autobiography,* LFP.
[9] *La Follette's Autobiography,* p. 11.
[10] *Wisconsin State Journal,* Oct. 7, 1880.
[11] Unpublished notes for *La Follette's Autobiography,* LFP.
[12] *Ibid.*
[13] *Address to Class of 1885-86, Law Department, Howard University* (Washington, D.C., May 31, 1886), p. 8 (published by the Law Department by permission), LFP.
[14] To Isabel Bacon La Follette, April 30, 1925.

Chapter VI

(Pages 58–73)

[1] *Madison Democrat,* Sept. 10, 1884.
[2] *La Follette's Autobiography,* p. 54.
[3] *Ibid.,* pp. 55-56.

[4] *Record,* 49th Cong., 1st Sess., Vol. 17, pp. 3747-3748, April 22, 1886.
[5] *Dodgeville Chronicle,* Sept. 17, 1886.

Chapter VII
(Pages 74–89)

[1] *Record,* 49th Cong., 2nd Sess., Vol. 18, App., p. 188, speech of Jan. 20, 1887.
[2] *Ibid.,* p. 185, speech of Jan. 20, 1887.
[3] *La Follette's Autobiography,* p. 119.
[4] *Record,* 49th Cong., 2nd Sess., Vol. 18, App., p. 147, speech of Feb. 25, 1887.
[5] *La Follette's Autobiography,* p. 97.
[6] *Record,* 51st Cong., 1st Sess., Vol. 21, pp. 4474-4475, May 10, 1890.
[7] *Daily Inter-Ocean,* May 11, 1890.
[8] *La Follette's Autobiography,* p. 72.
[9] *Ibid.,* p. 80.
[10] *Ibid.,* pp. 80-84.
[11] *Milwaukee Sentinel,* Oct. 30, 1890

Chapter VIII
(Pages 90–100)

[1] *Wisconsin State Journal,* Feb. 9, 1900.
[2] Gilbert E. Roe, *In Memoriam Robert M. La Follette,* address delivered before Dane County Bar Association, March 30, 1929 (Madison, Wis., Democrat Printing Co.), pp. 5, 7, LFP. See also Gilbert E. Roe, "Practicing Law With La Follette," *La Follette's Magazine,* August, 1926, pp. 121-122, 124.
[3] Gilbert E. Roe, *In Memoriam Robert M. La Follette,* pp. 7-8.
[4] Gilbert E. Roe, "Practicing Law With La Follette," *La Follette's Magazine,* August, 1926, p. 124.
[5] *La Follette's Autobiography,* p. 146.
[6] *Ibid.,* p. 143.
[7] *Ibid.,* pp. 145-148.
[8] *Ibid.,* p. 150.
[9] *Chicago Times,* Oct. 25, 1891.
[10] *La Follette's Autobiography,* p. 155.
[11] *Madison Democrat,* Nov. 20, 1891.
[12] *Wisconsin State Journal,* Nov. 20, 1891.

Chapter IX

(Pages 101–115)

[1] *La Follette's Autobiography*, p. 203.

[2] *Ibid.*, p. 212.

[3] *Ibid.*, p. 172.

[4] *Milwaukee Journal*, July 24, 1894.

[5] R. M. L. to B. C. L., [July] 25, 1894, LFP.

[6] *Madison Democrat*, July 27, 1894.

[7] Assemblyman James O. Davidson, subsequently governor, who assisted in the clerical work on the referendum, is authority for this statement.

[8] *Whitewater Register*, Whitewater, Wis., July 2, 1896.

Chapter X

(Pages 116–128)

[1] *Milwaukee Sentinel*, Aug. 7, 1896.

[2] *Ibid.*, Nov. 3, 1896.

[3] Unpublished notes for *La Follette's Autobiography*, LFP.

[4] *La Follette's Autobiography*, pp. 129-131. On this trip to Washington R. M. L. had two talks with McKinley at the White House; one on the afternoon of July 16, the other on the morning of July 17, 1897. R. M. L. to B. C. L. July 18, 1897, LFP.

[5] R. M. L. to B. C. L., July 18, 1897, LFP.

[6] *Chippewa Falls Independent*, quoted in the *Milwaukee Sentinel*, Oct. 1, 1897, "The State Press" column.

[7] Albert O. Barton, *La Follette's Winning of Wisconsin*, pp. 91-92.

[8] R. M. L. to B. C. L., Sept. 16, 1897, LFP.

[9] *Idem*, Sept. 22, 1897.

[10] *Milwaukee Journal*, Oct. 2, 1897.

[11] *Milwaukee Sentinel*, July 25, 1898.

[12] *La Follette's Autobiography*, p. 220.

[13] The final ballot was: Scofield, 620½; La Follette, 436½; Estabrook, 6; Baensch, 2.

Chapter XI

(Pages 129–135)

[1] *La Follette's Autobiography*, p. 229.

[2] *Ibid.*, pp. 231-237.

[3] *Milwaukee Daily News*, May 16, 1900; *Milwaukee Sentinel*, May 18, 19, 1900.

[4] *Milwaukee Sentinel,* May 31, 1900.

[5] *Ibid.,* July 6, 1900.

[6] Albert O. Barton, *La Follette's Winning of Wisconsin,* p. 156.

[7] *Ibid.,* p. 157.

[8] *Milwaukee Sentinel,* Aug. 9, 1900.

[9] *Milwaukee Journal,* Aug. 8, 1900. See also the *Milwaukee Sentinel,* Aug. 9, 1900.

[10] *Milwaukee Sentinel,* Sept. 11, 1900.

[11] *Ibid.,* Sept. 20, 1900.

[12] *Ibid.,* Nov. 4, 1900. "La Follette's Remarkable Campaign."

Chapter XII

(Pages 136–144)

[1] *La Follette's Autobiography,* pp. 241-242; *Wisconsin State Journal,* Jan. 9, 1901.

[2] On Feb. 19, 1901, an editorial in the *Sentinel* announced, "The Sentinel is issued today under the auspices of a new ownership and management."

[3] *La Follette's Autobiography,* pp. 251-253.

[4] Irvine L. Lenroot to the editor of the *Milwaukee Free Press,* 1902, published in *Voters' Hand-Book,* p. 46, LFP.

[5] *La Follette's Autobiography,* pp. 248-249.

[6] *1902 Voters' Hand-Book,* p. 86.

[7] Ernst C. Meyer, *Nominating Systems* (Madison, Wis., Ernst C. Meyer, 1902), p. 252 footnote.

[8] *Journal of the Assembly,* State of Wisconsin, 1901, pp. 1080-1084.

[9] *Milwaukee Sentinel,* Nov. 2, 1904, interview with Henry Allen Cooper, Wisconsin Congressman.

[10] E. Ray Stevens, "La Follette-Spooner Campaign," *World's Work,* Vol. 4, No. 6, p. 2679, Oct., 1902.

[11] *Journal of the Senate,* State of Wisconsin, 1901, pp. 1026-1035.

[12] *La Follette's Autobiography,* pp. 268-270.

[13] *Journal of the Senate,* State of Wisconsin, 1901, p. 1032.

[14] *Ibid.* The La Follette veto message was on May 10, 1901. See also the *Milwaukee Sentinel,* May 12, 1901, "Criticism Is Resented."

[15] *Outlook,* May 25, 1901, Vol. 68, No. 44, pp. 199-200; *Portland Oregonian,* May 22, 1901.

Chapter XIII

(Pages 145–152)

[1] *La Follette's Autobiography,* p. 28.

[2] *1902 Voters' Hand-Book,* p. 96, LFP.

[3] R. M. La Follette address, June 7, 1901, *1902 Voters' Hand-Book*, pp. 109-110.

[4] *La Follette's Autobiography*, p. 734.

[5] The *Milwaukee Sentinel* cooperated in keeping this meeting secret by not reporting it; but the *Milwaukee Free Press* printed a big story about it.

[6] *Jefferson County Union*, March 7, 1902.

[7] *Milwaukee Journal*, Feb. 10, 1902.

[8] *Milwaukee Sentinel*, March 20, 1902.

[9] *Ibid.*, March 21, 1902.

[10] *Wisconsin State Journal*, April 24, 1902, report of statement made by Roosevelt on April 19, in New York City, to L. D. Harvey, Wisconsin Superintendent of Public Instruction from 1899 to 1903. An editorial on April 24 in the *Journal* also said: "It is not news that President Roosevelt highly appreciates Senator Spooner, to the extent of imperatively needing him as an adviser and 'a right hand man,' but the conspicuous and fresh assertion of the fact through the *Germania*, the Great Republican daily, will make a profound impression on Wisconsin. Colonel Brumder, of the *Germania*, on his recent visit to Washington was assured of the president's insistent appeal to the voters of this state to demand of Senator Spooner that he consent to re-election, and to accord that re-election."

[11] The *Milwaukee Journal*, April 26, 1902, reprints excerpts from various newspapers.

[12] *Milwaukee Sentinel*, July 12, 1902.

[13] Eight-page pamphlet entitled *The Battle Only Half Over*, LFP.

[14] *Milwaukee Free Press*, July 5, 1902.

[15] *Milwaukee Sentinel*, July 16, 1902.

[16] *The Blue Book of the State of Wisconsin* (1903), pp. 1032-1034.

[17] Pamphlet, *Republican Platform and Gov. La Follette's Acceptance Speech*, LFP.

Chapter XIV

(Pages 153-164)

[1] *Jefferson County Union*, Oct. 3, 1902.

[2] *Commoner*, Vol. 2, No. 34, p. 2, Sept. 12, 1902.

[3] *Milwaukee Free Press*, Nov. 8, 1902.

[4] *Ibid.*, Oct. 14, 1902.

[5] *Ibid.*, Oct. 26, 1902.

[6] *Ibid.*, Oct. 26, 1902.

[7] *Ibid.*, Nov. 2, 1902.

[8] *Milwaukee Sentinel*, Dec. 10, 1902.

[9] Editorial in *Oshkosh Northwestern* a year later. Date not found.

[10] *Journal of the Senate*, State of Wisconsin, April 23, 1903, pp. 848-850.

[11] *Milwaukee Sentinel*, April 30, 1903.

[12] *Ibid.*
[13] *Wisconsin State Journal,* May 1, 1903.
[14] *Ibid.,* April 30, 1903.
[15] Emanuel L. Philipp and Edgar T. Wheelock, *Political Reform in Wisconsin* (Milwaukee, Wis., E. L. Philipp), p. 70.
[16] Henry Casson, "Recollections of His Father," *Madison Democrat,* Dec. 7, 1919.
[17] *Milwaukee Journal,* March 26, 1903.
[18] *Ibid.*
[19] *La Follette's Autobiography,* p. 293.
[20] *Ibid.,* p. 29.
[21] *Ibid.,* p. 31.

Chapter XV

(Pages 165–173)

[1] John Barrymore to R. M. L., LFP.
[2] *Milwaukee Free Press,* July 20, 1903.
[3] *Colorado Springs Gazette,* Aug. 8, 1903.
[4] *La Follette's Autobiography,* p. 305.
[5] R. M. L. to B. C. L., 1903, LFP.
[6] *Milwaukee Journal,* Oct. 1, 1903.
[7] *Milwaukee Free Press,* April 11, 1904.
[8] *Madison Democrat,* April 14, 1904.

Chapter XVI

(Pages 174–186)

[1] *Record Evidence Proceedings and Precedents,* to the Republican National Committee, filed by Herbert W. Chynoweth and Gilbert E. Roe, p. 15, LFP.
[2] A. O. Barton, *La Follette's Winning of Wisconsin,* p. 347.
[3] *Ibid.,* p. 359.
[4] *Ibid.,* p. 365.
[5] Albert O. Barton to B. C. L.
[6] *Chicago Record-Herald,* Oct. 18, 1904.
[7] *Milwaukee Journal,* June 17, 1904.
[8] *Milwaukee Daily News,* June 17, 1904.
[9] *La Follette's Autobiography,* pp. 328-329.
[10] Walter Wellman, *Sunday Record-Herald,* Chicago, June 19, 1904.
[11] Barton, *op. cit.,* p. 390.
[12] *Chicago Record-Herald,* June 22, 1904.
[13] *La Follette's Magazine,* March 30, 1912, p. 6.

[14] For Steffens' recollection of this incident, see his *Autobiography*, p. 457.

[15] *Milwaukee Sentinel*, June 28, 1904.

[16] Barton, *op. cit.*, p. 432.

[17] *Milwaukee Sentinel*, Sept. 23, 1904.

[18] J. Lincoln Steffens, "Enemies of the Republic. Wisconsin: A State Where the People Have Restored Representative Government—The Story of Governor La Follette," *McClure's Magazine*, Vol. XXIII, pp. 563-579, October, 1904.

[19] *Milwaukee Sentinel*, Nov. 6, 1904.

[20] *Ibid.*, Nov. 1, 1904.

[21] *Ibid.*, Nov. 7, 1904.

Chapter XVII

(Pages 187–198)

[1] *Chicago Record-Herald*, Oct. 15, 1904.

[2] *Journal of the Senate*, State of Wisconsin, Jan. 12, 1905, pp. 19-126.

[3] John R. Commons, *Myself* (New York, The Macmillan Company, 1934), pp. 101-102.

[4] *Journal of the Senate*, State of Wisconsin, Jan. 25, 1905, Vol. I, p. 173.

[5] *Wisconsin State Journal*, March 14, 1905.

[6] *Milwaukee Free Press*, March 11, 1905.

[7] *La Follette's Autobiography*, p. 341.

[8] *Journal of the Senate*, State of Wisconsin, April 12, 1905, Vol. I, pp. 732-734.

[9] *La Follette's Autobiography*, p. 369.

[10] B. C. L. to R. M. L., June 24, 1905, LFP.

[11] R. M. L. to B. C. L., June 28, 1905, LFP.

[12] *Idem*, July 9 and 10, 1905, LFP.

[13] *Idem*, Sept. 29, 1905.

[14] *Idem*, June 28, 1905.

[15] For a description of the school, see Mary Ellen Chase, *A Goodly Fellowship* (New York, The Macmillan Company, 1939), pp. 87-121.

Chapter XVIII

(Pages 199–216)

[1] *Washington Post*, Jan. 4, 1906.

[2] R. M. L. to Alfred T. Rogers, Jan. 7, 1906, LFP.

[3] *La Follette's Autobiography*, p. 405.

[4] *Ibid.*, p. 407.

[5] *Ibid.*, pp. 409-410.

[6] R. M. L.'s unpublished dictation for *La Follette's Autobiography*, type-written, p. 583.

[7] Speech of April 19, 1906, *Record*, 59th Cong., 1st Sess., Vol. 40, p. 5688, April 23, 1906; *La Follette's Autobiography*, p. 412.

[8] Lucy Daniels Thompson, *Twentieth Century Magazine*, January, 1912, Vol. 5, p. 212.

[9] Speech of April 20, *Record*, 59th Cong., 1st Sess., Vol. 40, p. 5702, April 23, 1906.

[10] *Ibid.*, p. 5706.

[11] B. C. L. to Fola, April 24, 1906, LFP.

[12] *La Follette's Autobiography*, pp. 417-418.

[13] *Record*, 59th Cong., 1st Sess., Vol. 40, p. 6821, May 14, 1906.

[14] House Bill 239, *Record*, 59th Cong., 1st Sess., Vol. 40, p. 7662, May 31, 1906; p. 7696, June 1, 1906.

[15] John J. Hannan to Fola La Follette, memorandum of April 16, 1933, pp. 4-5.

[16] *Record*, 59th Cong., 1st Sess., Vol. 40, p. 9789, June 30, 1906; the *Milwaukee Journal*, Jan. 18, 1907.

[17] R. M. L. to B. C. L., June 29, 1906, LFP.

[18] *Record*, 59th Cong., 1st Sess., Vol. 40, p. 9683, June 29, 1906.

[19] *Ibid.*, pp. 7832-7833, June 5, 1906.

[20] R. M. L. to B. C. L., June 22, 1906, LFP.

[21] *La Follette's Autobiography*, p. 379.

[22] *Record*, 59th Cong., 1st Sess., Vol. 40, pp. 3207-3214, March 1, 1906; *ibid.*, pp. 3254-3272, March 2, 1906.

[23] *Ibid.*, p. 8763, June 20, 1906.

[24] *La Follette's Autobiography*, p. 383.

[25] R. M. L. to B. C. L., June 21, 1906, LFP.

[26] *Idem* to Gilbert E. Roe, June 21, 1906, LFP.

[27] *Idem* to B. C. L., July 4, 1906, LFP.

[28] *Idem*, Aug. 7, 1906, LFP.

[29] B. C. L. to R. M. L. [November, 1907], LFP.

[30] *Kansas City Journal*, Sept. 9, 1906.

[31] R. M. L. to B. C. L., Nov. 17, 1906, LFP.

[32] *Idem*, Nov. 23, 1906.

Chapter XIX

(Pages 217–227)

[1] R. M. L. to B. C. L., Dec. 4, 1906, LFP.

[2] *Idem*, Dec. 5, 1906, LFP.

[3] R. M. L. to R. M. L., Jr., Dec. 9, 1906, LFP.

[4] *Idem* to B. C. L., Dec. 14, 1906, LFP.

[5] *Idem* to Mary, Dec. 11, 1906, LFP.

[6] *Idem* to B. C. L., Jan. 11, 1907, LFP.

[7] *Washington Times,* Jan. 11, 1907.

[8] R. M. L. to B. C. L., Jan. 11, 1907, LFP.

[9] B. C. L. to R. M. L., Jan. 27, 1907, LFP.

[10] R. M. L. to B. C. L., Jan. 16, 1907, LFP.

[11] Theodore Roosevelt to Joseph G. Cannon, Feb. 6, 1907, LFP.

[12] R. M. L. to B. C. L., Dec. 6, 1906, LFP.

[13] *Idem,* Dec. 16, 1906, LFP.

[14] *Idem.*

[15] *Idem,* Dec. 19, 1906, LFP.

[16] Theodore Roosevelt to Charles D. Walcott, Dec. 17, 1906, LFP.

[17] *La Follette's Autobiography,* pp. 384-385.

[18] R. M. L. to B. C. L., Jan. 20, 1907, LFP.

[19] *La Follette's Autobiography,* p. 385.

[20] R. M. L. to B. C. L., Jan. 23, 1907, LFP.

[21] *Idem,* Jan. 28, 30, 1907, LFP.

[22] *Idem,* Jan. 28, 1907, LFP.

[23] *Idem,* Jan. 30, 1907, LFP.

[24] Theodore Roosevelt to R. M. L., Feb. 5, 1907, LFP.

[25] R. M. L. to Theodore Roosevelt, Feb. 19, 1907, LFP.

[26] *Idem* to B. C. L., undated but written soon after Feb. 5, 1907, LFP.

[27] *Record,* 59th Cong., 2d Sess., Vol. 41, p. 567, Dec. 20, 1906.

[28] R. M. L. to B. C. L., Jan. 30, 1907, LFP.

[29] *Idem,* Feb. 19, 1907, LFP. See also the *Washington Times,* Feb. 20, 1907.

[30] R. M. L. to B. C. L., Feb. 13, 1907, LFP.

[31] *Idem,* Feb. 23, 1907, LFP.

[32] B. C. L. to R. M. L., Dec. 13, 1906, LFP.

[33] R. M. L. to R. M. L., Jr., Feb. 5, 1907, LFP.

[34] *Idem* to Phil, Feb. 14, 1907, LFP.

[35] B. C. L. to R. M. L., Dec. 13, 1906, LFP.

[36] *Idem,* 1907.

[37] *Idem,* Feb. 2, 1907, LFP.

[38] *Idem,* Jan. 2, 1907, LFP.

[39] *Idem,* Feb. 21, 1907, LFP.

[40] R. M. L. to B. C. L., Jan. 20, 1907, LFP.

[41] *Munsey's Magazine,* February, 1907, XXXVI, 655-659.

[42] *New York Times,* Feb. 11, 1907.

Chapter XX

(Pages 228–237)

[1] R. M. L. to B. C. L., March 4, 1907, LFP.

[2] *Idem.*

[3] *Milwaukee Free Press,* March 4, 1907.

[4] B. C. L. to Josephine La Follette Siebecker, March 10, 1907, LFP.
[5] *Milwaukee Free Press*, May 31, 1907.
[6] *Milwaukee Journal*, Jan. 18, 1907.
[7] R. M. L. to B. C. L., March 27, 1907, LFP.
[8] *Idem*, April 9, 1907, LFP.
[9] *Idem*, April 14, 1907, LFP.
[10] *Idem.*
[11] *Idem*, April 26, 1907, LFP.
[12] *Idem*, April 28, 1907, LFP.
[13] *Idem*, April 28, 1907, LFP.
[14] *Idem*, May 12, 1907, LFP.
[15] *Idem*, July 24, 1907, LFP.
[16] *Pittsburgh Post*, Aug. 30, 1907.
[17] *Ibid.*

Chapter XXI

(Pages 238–256)

[1] *Chicago Daily Tribune*, Jan. 2, 1908.
[2] *La Follette's Autobiography*, p. 461.
[3] *Record*, 60th Cong., 1st Sess., Vol. 42, p. 3434, March 17, 1908.
[4] *Ibid.*, p. 3570, March 19, 1908.
[5] *Ibid.*, p. 3447, March 17, 1908.
[6] *Ibid.*, p. 3450, March 17, 1908.
[7] *Ibid.*, pp. 3452-3453, March 17, 1908.
[8] *Ibid.*, pp. 3793-3795, March 24, 1908.
[9] *Ibid.*, p. 3569, March 19, 1908.
[10] *Ibid.*, pp. 4018-4020, March 27, 1908.
[11] *Ibid.*, Vol. 48, p. 7076, May 27, 1908.
[12] *Ibid.*, p. 7069, May 27, 1908.
[13] *Ibid.*, p. 7179, May 29, 1908.
[14] John C. Crockett to Fola La Follette, Jan. 19, 1940, LFP.
[15] *World*, New York, May 30, 1908.
[16] *La Follette's Autobiography*, p. 478, prints a facsimile page of the official Senate stenographer's transcript.
[17] *Record*, 60th Cong., 1st Sess., Vol. 48, p. 7168, May 29, 1908.
[18] *New York Times*, May 31, 1908.
[19] *Record*, 60th Cong., 1st Sess., Vol. 48, p. 7168, May 29, 1908.
[20] *Chicago Record-Herald*, May 30, 1908.
[21] *Record*, 60th Cong., 1st Sess., Vol. 48, pp. 7168-7169, May 30, 1908.
[22] *Ibid.*, p. 7172, May 29, 1908. See also *Kansas City Star*, May 29, 1908.
[23] *Record*, 60th Cong., 1st Sess., Vol. 48, p. 7190, May 29, 1908.
[24] *Sun*, Baltimore, May 31, 1908
[25] *Washington Times*, May 29, 1908.

[26] *North American,* Philadelphia, May 31, 1908, signed dispatch by Angus McSween; also, recollection of Fola La Follette.

[27] *New York Times,* May 30, 1908.

[28] *Washington Times,* May 30, 1908.

[29] Recollection of Fola La Follette; letter from Fola to B. C. L., Friday night [May 29, 1908], LFP.

[30] *New York Times,* May 30, 1908.

[31] R. M. L. to B. C. L., June 1, 1908, LFP.

[32] *Record,* 60th Cong., 1st Sess., Vol. 48, p. 7195, May 29, 1908.

[33] *Ibid.,* p. 7196, May 29, 1908.

[34] *Ibid.,* p. 7220, May 30, 1908.

[35] *Ibid.,* p. 7226, May 30, 1908.

[36] *Ibid.,* p. 7246, May 30, 1908.

[37] *New York Times,* May 31, 1908.

[38] *Ibid.*

[39] Thomas P. Gore to Fola La Follette, June 22, 1943, LFP.

[40] Nathaniel Wright Stephenson, *Nelson W. Aldrich: A Leader in American Politics* (New York, Charles Scribner's Sons, 1930), p. 331.

[41] *Record,* 60th Cong., 1st Sess., Vol. 48, p. 7259, May 30, 1908.

[42] *Sunday Record-Herald,* Chicago, May 31, 1908, signed dispatch by Walter Wellman. See also, *Record,* 60th Cong., 1st Sess., Vol. 48, pp. 7261-7262, May 30, 1908.

[43] *New York Times,* May 31, 1908.

Chapter XXII

(Pages 257–265)

[1] *Everybody's Magazine,* June, 1908, XVIII, 723-726.

[2] Lincoln Steffens to R. M. L., May 28, 1908, LFP.

[3] Henry Cabot Lodge, *Selections from the Correspondence of Theodore Roosevelt and Henry Cabot Lodge* (New York, Charles Scribner's Sons, 1925), II, 297.

[4] Alfred T. Rogers to Gilbert E. Roe, June 23, 1908, LFP.

[5] *Milwaukee Journal,* June 19, 1908.

[6] Albert J. Beveridge to R. M. L., June 29, 1908, in Claude G. Bowers, *Beveridge and the Progressive Era* (Cambridge, Mass., Houghton Mifflin Company, 1932), pp. 287-288.

[7] *Chicago Record-Herald,* June 19, 1908.

[8] Alfred T. Rogers to Gilbert E. Roe, June 23, 1908, LFP.

[9] R. M. L. to William Howard Taft, June 18, 1908. See also the *Milwaukee Journal,* June 19, 1908.

[10] *Chicago Record-Herald,* June 20, 1908.

[11] *Milwaukee Free Press,* July 16, 1908.

[12] Theodore Roosevelt to Elmer J. Burkett, Aug. 18, 1908. See also *Nebraska State Journal,* Aug. 22, 1908.

[13] *Milwaukee Journal,* Aug. 29 and 31, 1908; *Wisconsin State Journal,* Aug. 31, 1908.

[14] William Allen White to R. M. L., Aug. 5, 1908. See also *Nebraska State Journal,* Aug. 6, 1908.

[15] *National Tribune,* Aug. 13, 1908.

[16] *Wisconsin State Journal,* Sept. 24, 1908.

[17] *Milwaukee Journal,* Sept. 24, 1908; March 4, 1909.

[18] Edward Lowry, in *World's Work,* Vol. 48, p. 515.

[19] *Wisconsin State Journal,* Oct. 19, 1908.

[20] *New York Times,* Nov. 8, 1908.

Chapter XXIII

(Pages 266–271)

[1] *La Follette's Autobiography,* p. 395.

[2] *La Follette's Magazine,* Nov. 20, 1909, p. 6.

[3] *Record,* 60th Cong., 2nd Sess., Vol. 43, p. 2200, Feb. 11, 1909.

[4] *Ibid.,* p. 2201, Feb. 11, 1909.

[5] *La Follette's Autobiography,* p. 394.

[6] *Ibid.,* p. 434.

[7] *La Follette's Magazine,* March 20, 1909, p. 6.

[8] *Ibid.,* March 13, 1909, p. 10.

[9] *Ibid.,* Jan. 16, 1909, p. 8.

[10] Herbert Smith Duffy, *William Howard Taft* (New York, Minton, Balch & Company, 1930), pp. 226-227.

Chapter XXIV

(Pages 272–278)

[1] *La Follette's Autobiography,* p. 436.

[2] *Ibid.,* p. 438.

[3] *Ibid.*

[4] *Ibid.,* p. 440.

[5] *Ibid.,* p. 428.

[6] *Ibid.,* p. 446.

[7] *La Follette's Magazine,* Oct. 9, 1909, p. 6.

[8] Joseph L. Bristow to Harold Chase, May 22, 1909, Bristow Papers.

[9] *Record,* 61st Cong., 1st Sess., Vol. 44, p. 3022, June 9, 1909.

[10] Joseph L. Bristow to Harold Chase, May 22, 1909, Bristow Papers.

[11] *Record,* 61st Cong., 1st Sess., Vol. 44, p. 3013, June 9, 1909.

[12] B. C. L. to Fola [June 12, 1909], LFP.

[13] *Idem.*

[14] *Record,* 61st Cong., 1st Sess., Vol. 44, p. 3127, June 11, 1909.

[15] B. C. L. to Fola [June 12, 1909], LFP.

[16] *Record*, 61st Cong., 1st Sess., Vol. 44, p. 4316, July 8, 1909.

[17] Lincoln Steffens to R. M. L., May 5, 1909, LFP.

[18] Albert J. Beveridge to Mrs. Beveridge, June 12, 1909, in Claude G. Bowers, *Beveridge and the Progressive Era* (Cambridge, Houghton Mifflin Company, 1932), p. 349.

[19] *La Follette's Autobiography*, pp. 448-449.

[20] *Washington Times*, July 12, 1909.

[21] R. M. L. to William Howard Taft, July 13, 1909, LFP.

[22] *Idem* to B. C. L., July 23, 1909, LFP.

[23] *La Follette's Autobiography*, p. 451.

[24] *Ibid.*, p. 452.

[25] *Record*, 61st Cong., 1st Sess., Vol. 44, p. 4954, Aug. 5, 1909.

Chapter XXV

(Pages 279–285)

[1] *Brooklyn Daily Eagle*, Aug. 6, 1909.

[2] R. M. L. to B. C. L., R. M. L., Jr., Phil, and Mary, Aug. 20, 1909, LFP.

[3] *Idem.*, Aug. 30, 1909, LFP.

[4] B. C. L. to R. M. L., Oct. 23, 1909, LFP.

[5] R. M. L. to B. C. L., R. M. L., Jr., Phil, and Mary, Oct. 31, 1909, LFP.

[6] Elizabeth Glendower Evans, in the *Springfield Republican*, April 15, 1931.

[7] Henry F. Pringle, *The Life and Times of William Howard Taft* (New York, Farrar and Rinehart, 1939), I, 454-456.

[8] Jonathan P. Dolliver to R. M. L., Oct. 13, 1909, LFP.

[9] R. M. L. to B. C. L., Oct. 31, 1909, LFP.

[10] *Idem*, Oct. 25, 1909, LFP.

[11] *Spokesman-Review*, Spokane, Oct. 20, 1909.

[12] R. M. L. to B. C. L., Nov. 4, 1909, LFP.

[13] B. C. L. to R. M. L., Nov. 11, 1909, LFP.

[14] R. M. L. to B. C. L., Nov. 15, 1909, LFP.

[15] *Capitol News*, Washington, D.C., Dec. 17, 1909, interview by John E. Lathrop.

Chapter XXVI

(Pages 286–294)

[1] *La Follette's Magazine*, Aug. 21, 1909.

[2] *Collier's Weekly*, Nov. 13, 1909.

[3] *La Follette's Magazine*, Nov. 20, 1909, pp. 8-9.

[4] *Record*, 61st Cong., 2nd Sess., Vol. 45, pp. 367-368, Jan. 6, 1910.

[5] *La Follette's Magazine,* Jan. 15, 1910, pp. 3-4.

[6] *La Follette's Autobiography,* pp. 484-485.

[7] *Ibid.,* pp. 705-706.

Chapter XXVII

(Pages 295-312)

[1] Louis D. Brandeis to author, Aug. 31, 1937, LFP.

[2] *Ibid.*

[3] *La Follette's Autobiography,* p. 424.

[4] *Record,* 61st Cong., 2nd Sess., Vol. 45, pp. 4549-4561, April 12, 1910; pp. 5563-5566, April 29, 1910; pp. 6882-6909, May 25, 26, 1910; pp. 7139-7144, May 31, 1910; pp. 7372-7374, June 3, 1910.

[5] *Sun,* New York, April 13, 1910.

[6] *Ibid.*

[7] *Washington Times,* April 10, 1910, editorial. For comment on the Associated Press report of Bob's speech, see: John J. Hannan to author, 1939, LFP; *La Follette's Magazine,* April 30, 1910, p. 1.

[8] *Record,* 61st Cong., 2nd Sess., Vol. 45, p. 7373, June 3, 1910.

[9] *Ibid.,* p. 2780, March 5, 1910.

[10] *Ibid.,* p. 8741, June 22, 1910.

[11] *La Follette's Magazine,* Sept. 24, 1910, p. 4.

[12] R. M. L. to Louis D. Brandeis, June 20, 1910, LFP.

[13] *La Follette's Magazine,* June 18, 1910, p. 13.

[14] R. M. L. to Gilbert E. Roe, April 4, 1910, LFP.

[15] *Idem* to B. C. L., June 19, 1910, LFP.

[16] Theodore Roosevelt to Henry Cabot Lodge, June 8, 1908, *Selections from the Correspondence of Theodore Roosevelt and Henry Cabot Lodge,* II, 297.

[17] Henry Cabot Lodge to Theodore Roosevelt, Oct. 20, 1909, *ibid.,* II, 350.

[18] *La Follette's Magazine,* June 18, 1910, pp. 9-12.

[19] Theodore Roosevelt to Henry Cabot Lodge, July 19, 1910, *op. cit.,* II, 385-386; Theodore Roosevelt to Henry Cabot Lodge, Sept. 12, 1910, *ibid.,* II, 391-392.

[20] The New York *World,* on June 28, 1910, in an Oyster Bay dispatch dated June 27, the same day Bob had called there, stated Roosevelt had said, "In this morning's mail were letters from Senator La Follette and Representatives Madison and Burkett asking for appointments, but La Follette was the only one he was able to reach."

[21] R. M. L. to Fremont Older, July 11, 1910, LFP. See also Phil to B. C. L., June 26, 1910, LFP.

[22] *La Follette's Autobiography,* pp. 487-488.

[23] R. M. L. to Fremont Older, July 11, 1910, LFP.

[24] *Idem.*

[25] *La Follette's Autobiography,* p. 489.

[26] R. M. L. to Jonathan Bourne, July 11, 1910.

[27] *New York Times* and *World*, June 28, 1910.

[28] Netha Roe (Mrs. Gilbert E. Roe) to author.

[29] *La Follette's Magazine*, July 23, 1910, p. 10.

[30] Fremont Older to R. M. L., July 2, 1910, LFP.

[31] R. M. L. to Fremont Older, July 11, 1910, LFP.

[32] *La Follette's Magazine*, Oct. 8, 1910, pp. 5-6.

[33] *Ibid.*, Sept. 17, 1910, p. 1.

[34] *Ibid.*, Sept. 24, 1910, pp. 10-11.

[35] B. C. L. to R. M. L., Sept. 5, 1910, LFP.

[36] *La Follette's Magazine*, Sept. 24, 1910, p. 13.

[37] *Milwaukee Journal*, Sept. 7, 1910. See also *La Follette's Magazine*, Sept. 17, 1910, p. 4.

[38] *La Follette's Magazine*, Oct. 8, 1910, pp. 7-9.

[39] Gilbert E. Roe to Governor Francis E. McGovern, Oct. 10, 1910, LFP.

[40] Ray Stannard Baker to R. M. L., Oct. 22, 1910, LFP.

[41] *Kansas City Star*, editorial, Sept. 29, 1910. See also *La Follette's Magazine*, Oct. 15, 1910, p. 1.

[42] *La Follette's Magazine*, Oct. 8, 1910, p. 8.

[43] *Ibid.*, July 2, 1910, pp. 3-4.

[44] *Ibid.*, Oct. 8, 1910, p. 12.

[45] B. C. L. to her children, Oct. 7, 1910, LFP.

[46] Lincoln Steffens to Fola, Oct. 6, 1910, LFP.

[47] B. C. L. to her children, Oct. 12, 1910, LFP.

[48] *Idem* to R. M. L., Jr., Phil, and Mary, Oct. 11, 1910, LFP.

[49] *La Follette's Magazine*, Oct. 22, 1910.

[50] B. C. L. to Ray Stannard Baker, Oct. 28, 1910, original MS letter with Ray Stannard Baker Papers (hereafter cited as Baker Papers), copy with LFP.

[51] *La Follette's Magazine*, Nov. 12, 1910, pp. 3-4.

[52] Theodore Roosevelt to Henry Cabot Lodge, Sept. 12, 1910, *op. cit.*, II, 391-392.

[53] R. M. L. to Fremont Older, July 11, 1910, LFP; R. M. L. to Jonathan Bourne, July 11, 1910, LFP.

[54] Ray Stannard Baker to R. M. L., Oct. 22, 1910, LFP.

[55] B. C. L. to Ray Stannard Baker, Oct. 28, 1910, copy with LFP. Original MS letter with Baker Papers.

[56] *Chicago Record-Herald*, Nov. 10, 1910.

[57] R. M. L. to Henry F. Cochems, Nov. 13, 1910, LFP.

[58] Archibald W. Butt, *Taft and Roosevelt* (New York, Doubleday, Doran & Company, 1930), II, 555.

[59] *Outlook*, Sept. 24, 1910.

[60] Louis D. Brandeis to R. M. L., November 9, 1910, LFP.

[61] Butt, *op. cit.*, II, 556.

[62] Theodore Roosevelt to Henry Cabot Lodge, Nov. 11, 1910, *op. cit.*, II, 394.

[63] *Idem* to Joseph Bucklin Bishop, Nov. 21, 1910, in Joseph B. Bishop,

Theodore Roosevelt and His Times (New York, Charles Scribner's Sons, 1920), II, 308.

[64] *La Follette's Magazine*, Nov. 19, 1910, p. 3.

[65] William Kent to R. M. L., Nov. 24, 1910, LFP.

[66] *La Follette's Magazine*, Nov. 19, 1910, p. 3.

[67] R. M. L. to Jonathan Bourne, Jr., Nov. 1910, LFP.

[68] Ray Stannard Baker to R. M. L., Nov. 29, 1910, LFP.

Chapter XXVIII

(Pages 313–321)

[1] R. M. L. to George Loftus, Dec. 30, 1910, LFP.

[2] *Idem* to B. C. L., Dec. 5, 1910, LFP.

[3] *Idem to* William H. Taft, Dec. 5, 1910, LFP.

[4] *Idem* to B. C. L., Dec. 5, 1910, LFP.

[5] *Idem* to Robert G. Siebecker, Dec. 11, 1910, LFP.

[6] *Seattle Daily Times*, Oct. 21, 1909. See also *Spokesman Review*, Oct. 21, 1909.

[7] *La Follette's Magazine*, Oct. 30, 1909, p. 12. See also *Milwaukee Journal*, Oct. 21, 1909.

[8] George L. Record to R. M. L., Jan. 5, 1911, LFP.

[9] Theodore Roosevelt to R. M. L., Dec. 19, 1910, LFP.

[10] R. M. L. to Theodore Roosevelt, Dec. 23, 1910, LFP.

[11] Theodore Roosevelt to R. M. L., Dec. 27 [1910], LFP.

[12] R. M. L. to Theodore Roosevelt, Dec. 28, 1910, LFP.

[13] *Idem* to Louis D. Brandeis, Dec. 30, 1910, LFP.

[14] *La Follette's Magazine*, Feb. 4, 1911, pp. 7–9.

[15] Theodore Roosevelt to Jonathan Bourne, Jan. 2, 1911, copy with LFP.

[16] *Idem* to R. M. L., Jan. 3, 1911, LFP.

[17] George L. Record to R. M. L., Jan. 5, 1911, LFP.

[18] Theodore Roosevelt to R. M. L., Jan. 17, 1911, LFP.

[19] R. M. L. to Theodore Roosevelt, Jan. 19, 1911, LFP.

[20] *La Follette's Magazine*, Feb. 4, 1911, pp. 7–9.

[21] *Ibid.*, Feb. 4, 1911, pp. 7, 8, 9, 12.

[22] Theodore Roosevelt to R. M. L., Jan. 24, 1911, LFP.

[23] E. W. Scripps to William Kent, Dec. 24, 1910, Kent Papers, Yale Library; and to Judge Ben B. Lindsey, Nov. 24, 1910; copy with LFP.

[24] This statement is based upon the author's recollection, the correspondence in the La Follette papers, and in other papers consulted by the author.

[25] E. W. Scripps to Judge Ben B. Lindsey, Jan. 2, 1911; copy with LFP.

[26] *La Follette's Autobiography,* pp. 508-509.

[27] *Ibid.*, p. 502.

[28] Theodore Roosevelt to R. M. L., Feb. 20, 1911, LFP; Gifford Pinchot

to Theodore Roosevelt, Feb. 23, 1911, Theodore Roosevelt Papers (hereafter cited as TR Papers).

[29] Gifford Pinchot to Theodore Roosevelt, Feb. 28, 1911, TR Papers; *idem,* March 5, 1911, TR Papers.

[30] R. M. L. to Gifford Pinchot, March 6, 1911, LFP; R. M. L. to Theodore Roosevelt, March 7, 1911, LFP.

Chapter XXIX

(Pages 322–335)

[1] Speech of April 19, 1906, *Record,* 59th Cong., 1st Sess., Vol. 40, p. 5688, April 23, 1906. See also *La Follette's Autobiography,* p. 412.

[2] Ray Stannard Baker, "The Meaning of Insurgency," *American Magazine,* May, 1911, LXXII, 63.

[3] *North American,* Philadelphia, April 14, 1911.

[4] "Storming the Citadel," *American Magazine,* September, 1911, LXXII, 571. Typewritten pages of this article were enclosed in a letter from John S. Phillips to R. M. L., May 24, 1911, LFP.

[5] *Register and Leader,* Des Moines, April 5, 1911; *Globe and Commercial Advertiser,* New York, April 4, 1911.

[6] *Chicago Record-Herald,* April 6, 1911, signed dispatch by Sumner [M. Curtis].

[7] R. M. L. to Rudolph Spreckles, April 7, 1911, LFP.

[8] *Record,* 62nd Cong., 1st Sess., Vol. 47, pp. 1183-1189, May 11, 1911.

[9] *Ibid.,* p. 1184, May 11, 1911.

[10] *New York Times,* May 12, 1911.

[11] *Ibid.*

[12] *La Follette's Magazine,* April 29, 1911, p. 1.

[13] *Ibid.*

[14] *Record,* 62nd Cong., 1st Sess., Vol. 47, p. 714, April 28, 1911.

[15] *Ibid.,* p. 105, April 6, 1911.

[16] *Ibid.,* p. 121, April 10, 1911.

[17] *Ibid.,* p. 439, April 20, 1911.

[18] *Ibid.,* p. 713, April 28, 1911.

[19] *Ibid.,* p. 1072, May 8, 1911.

[20] *Ibid.,* p. 926, May 4, 1911.

[21] Charles E. Merriam to author, Feb. 27, March 11, 1938.

[22] *Globe and Commercial Advertiser,* New York, April 6, 1911. See also *New York Times,* April 7, 1911; *Chicago Record-Herald,* April 7, 1911; *San Francisco Call,* April 7, 1911.

[23] *Record,* 62nd Cong., 1st Sess., Vol. 47, pp. 1434-1437, May 22, 1911; *ibid.,* pp. 1490-1495, May 23, 1911; *ibid.,* pp. 1547-1557, May 24, 1911; *ibid.,* pp. 1600-1605, May 25, 1911.

[24] *Ibid.,* pp. 1609-1610, May 20, 1911.

[25] *Ibid.*, p. 1682, June 1, 1911.

[26] *Ibid.*, pp. 1732-1734, June 7, 1911.

[27] *Chicago Record-Herald*, July 14, 1912.

[28] *Record*, 62nd Cong., 2nd Sess., Vol. 48, p. 8987, July 13, 1912.

[29] *La Follette's Magazine*, July 20, 1912, p. 9; July 27, 1912, pp. 5, 6, 12, 13.

[30] William Kittle to R. M. L., April 16, 1911, LFP. Kittle was a guest at the Executive Residence breakfast and was also present at Roosevelt's speeches (William Kittle to author, LFP). The report to Kittle came from a reliable informant who rode in the carriage with Roosevelt.

[31] William Kittle to R. M. L., April 16, 1911, LFP.

[32] Rudolph Spreckels to R. M. L., April 10, 1911, LFP.

[33] Fremont Older to R. M. L., April 6, 1911, LFP.

[34] R. M. L. to Fremont Older, April 18, 1911, LFP.

[35] Gardner had an engagement to lunch with Roosevelt on April 22, 1911, TR Papers.

[36] *La Follette's Autobiography*, pp. 512-513. See also Irvine L. Lenroot to author, April 2, 1938, LFP.

[37] *Ibid.*, pp. 517-518. See also Irvine L. Lenroot to author, April 2, 1938, LFP.

[38] *Ibid.*, pp. 518-521. See also Irvine L. Lenroot to author, April 2, 1938, LFP.

[39] R. M. L. to Gilbert E. Roe, April 7, 1911, LFP; *idem* to Rudolph Spreckels, April 25, 1911, LFP.

[40] William Kent to Alfred L. Baker, May 10, 1911, Kent Papers, Yale Library (hereafter cited as Kent Papers); William Kent pledge of $10,000 to La Follette Presidential campaign, LFP.

[41] *La Follette's Autobiography*, p. 521.

[42] Archibald W. Butt, *Taft and Roosevelt*, II, 618-620.

[43] Elizabeth G. Evans to Mrs. Louis D. Brandeis, May 6, 1911, LFP.

[44] *La Follette's Autobiography*, p. 525.

[45] Elizabeth G. Evans to Mrs. Louis D. Brandeis, May 7, 1911, LFP.

[46] William Kent to Alfred L. Baker, May 10, 1911, Kent Papers. See also William Kent to Rudolph Spreckels, May 10, 1911, Kent Papers.

[47] William Kent to Theodore Roosevelt, May 11, 1911, Kent Papers. Mrs. William Kent recalls that Kent did not go to Oyster Bay at this time (Mrs. William Kent to author, Feb. 12, 1943, LFP).

[48] Theodore Roosevelt to William Kent, May 16, 1911, Kent Papers.

[49] William Kent to Theodore Roosevelt, May 11, 1911, Kent Papers.

[50] Irvine L. Lenroot to William Kent, May 17, 1911, Kent Papers.

[51] B. C. L. to Elizabeth G. Evans, May 18, 1911, LFP.

[52] R. M. L. to Frank A. Harrison, June 12, 1911, LFP.

[53] *La Follette's Autobiography*, p. 526.

[54] *Outlook*, May 27, 1911.

[55] *La Follette's Magazine*, June 3, 1911.

Chapter XXX
(Pages 336–348)

[1] *Standard Oil Co.* v. *United States,* 221 U.S. Reports 1.

[2] *New York Times,* May 16, 1911.

[3] *La Follette's Magazine,* May 27, 1911, p. 3.

[4] B. C. L. to Elizabeth G. Evans, May 18, 1911, LFP.

[5] R. M. L. to Louis D. Brandeis, May 16, 1911, LFP.

[6] Louis D. Brandeis to R. M. L., May 23, 1911. copy with LFP; R. M. L. to Louis D. Brandeis, May 24, 1911, copy with LFP; Louis D. Brandeis to R. M. L., May 26, 1911, copy with LFP; *idem* to R. M. L., June 13, 1911, copy with LFP.

[7] At Chicago, Jan. 3, 1912; printed in *La Follette's Magazine,* Jan. 13, 1912, p. 9.

[8] *United States* v. *American Tobacco Co.,* 221 U.S. Reports, 106.

[9] *La Follette's Magazine,* June 17, 1911; Sept. 16, 1911; and Gilbert E. Roe, *Our Judicial Oligarchy* (New York, B. W. Huebsch, 1912).

[10] R. M. L. to Theodore Roosevelt, June 8, 1911, LFP.

[11] Theodore Roosevelt to R. M. L., June 13, 1911, LFP.

[12] *Sun,* Baltimore, June 7, 1911; *Evening Star,* Washington, D.C., June 7, 1911.

[13] *Evening Star,* Washington, D.C., June 15, 1911.

[14] *Saint Paul Pioneer Press,* June 16, 1911.

[15] John J. Hannan to Frank A. Harrison, July 20, 1911, LFP.

[16] *Nebraska State Journal,* July 6, 1911.

[17] John J. Hannan to Gifford Pinchot, June 18, 1911, LFP.

[18] *Washington Times,* June 17, 1911.

[19] John J. Hannan to Gifford Pinchot, June 18, 1911, LFP.

[20] *Record,* 62nd Cong., 1st Sess., Vol. 47, pp. 1963-1964, June 13, 1911.

[21] *Ibid.,* pp. 2396-2398, June 21, 1911.

[22] Fola to George Middleton, June 22, 1911, LFP.

[23] Louis D. Brandeis to R. M. L., June 22, 1911; carbon with Brandeis Papers, copy with LFP. Brandeis had conferred with R. M. L. at the latter's home on the evening of May 18, 1911.

[24] Archibald W. Butt, *Taft and Roosevelt,* II, 684.

[25] *New York Times,* June 28, 1911; *Record,* 62nd Cong., 1st Sess., Vol. 47, pp. 2518-2525, June 26, 1911.

[26] *Record,* 62nd Cong., 1st Sess., Vol. 47, p. 3140, July 21, 1911. The Herman Ridder letter to newspaper editors was dated Feb. 17, 1911.

[27] Archibald W. Butt, II, 700-701.

[28] B. C. L. to Elizabeth G. Evans, July 8, 1911, copy with LFP.

[29] *Op. cit.,* II, 701-702 (letter to his sister, July 20, 1911).

[30] *Record,* 61st Cong., 1st Sess., Vol. 47, pp. 3264-3265, 3279-3280, July 27, 1911 (legislative day, July 26).

[31] B. C. L. to Elizabeth G. Evans, July 28, 1911, LFP.

[32] *Record,* 62nd Cong., 1st Sess., Vol. 47, p. 3963, Aug. 15, 1911.

[33] *Ibid.,* p. 3953, Aug. 15, 1911.

[34] *Ibid.,* pp. 4002-4003, Aug. 16, 1911.

[35] Frank Harrison to Walter L. Houser, Aug. 11, 1911, LFP.

[36] Herbert Williams to R. M. L., Aug. 9, 1911, LFP.

[37] *Idem* to editor of Ashtabula *Beacon Record,* Aug. 9, 1911, LFP.

[38] Elizabeth G. Evans to B. C. L., Aug. 1, 1911, LFP. See also *Boston Evening Transcript,* July 29, 1911.

[39] Charles Johnston, in *Harper's Weekly,* June 24, 1911, p. 9.

[40] Chase S. Osborn to R. M. L., June 14, 1911, LFP.

[41] *World's Work,* XXII, 14591-14600.

[42] B. C. L. to Phil, July 8, 1911, LFP.

[43] John R. Commons to R. M. L., Friday [Aug. 18, 1911], LFP.

[44] *Record,* 62nd Cong., 1st Sess., Vol. 47, pp. 4183-4184, Aug. 19, 1911.

[45] *Ibid.,* pp. 4184-4193, Aug. 19, 1911.

[46] In a speech Taft made at New Haven on June 21, 1911, *New Haven Evening Register,* June 22, 1911.

[47] *Record,* 61st Cong., 2nd Sess., Vol. 45, p. 382, Jan. 7, 1910. See also *Record,* 62nd Cong., 1st Sess., Vol. 47, pp. 4187-4188, Aug. 19, 1911.

[48] *Ibid.,* 62nd Cong., 1st Sess., Vol. 47, p. 2550, June 27, 1911.

[49] *Ibid.,* pp. 3204-3209, July 26, 1911.

[50] Louis D. Brandeis to R. M. L., Aug. 1, 1911, with enclosure dated July 29, 1911, copy of letter with LFP; *idem* to Gifford Pinchot, July 29, 1911, copy with LFP.

[51] *Idem* to R. M. L., July 31, 1911, LFP.

[52] *Record,* 62nd Cong., 1st Sess., Vol. 47, p. 4197, Aug. 19, 1911.

[53] *Ibid.,* pp. 4262-4304, Aug. 21, 1911.

[54] R. M. L. to Louis D. Brandeis, undated MS letter stamped as received June 26, 1911; original with Brandeis Papers, copy with LFP.

[55] *Idem* to Robert G. Siebecker, Aug. 27, 1911, LFP.

[56] Theodore Roosevelt to R. M. L., Sept. 29, 1911, LFP.

[57] R. M. L. to Theodore Roosevelt, Oct. 4, 1911, LFP.

Chapter XXXI

(Pages 349–369)

[1] George Middleton, *These Things Are Mine* (New York, The Macmillan Company, 1947), pp. 92-93.

[2] Moses E. Clapp to John J. Hannan, Sept. 15, 1911, LFP.

[3] *Nebraska State Journal,* Sept. 5, 1911.

[4] George W. Norris to Walter L. Houser, Sept. 24, 1911, LFP.

[5] *Wisconsin State Journal,* Sept. 1, 1911.

[6] James M. Pierce to R. M. L., May 11, 1911, LFP; N. W. Ayer & Son's *American Newspaper Annual and Directory.*

[7] *Minneapolis Journal,* Sept. 8, 1911.

[8] *Wisconsin State Journal,* Sept. 13, 1911.

[9] *Bulletin,* San Francisco, Sept. 13, 1911.

[10] *Daily Argus Leader,* Sioux Falls, S.D., Sept. 13, 1911.

[11] Moses E. Clapp to John J. Hannan, Sept. 15, 1911, LFP.

[12] William Allen White to Medill McCormick, Sept. 8, 1911, LFP.

[13] Rudolph Spreckels to Medill McCormick, Monday, Sept. 25, 1911, LFP.

[14] *North American,* Philadelphia, Oct. 16, 1911.

[15] *New York Times,* Oct. 17, 1911.

[16] *World,* New York, Oct. 17, 1911.

[17] *New York Times,* Oct. 17, 1911.

[18] Medill McCormick to Gifford Pinchot, Oct. 11, 1911, LFP.

[19] *New York Tribune,* Oct. 16, 1911; *North American,* Philadelphia, Oct. 13, 1911.

[20] James R. Garfield to R. M. L., Oct. 17, 1911, LFP.

[21] *Idem* to Theodore Roosevelt, Oct. 17, 1911, with enclosure of letter to La Follette, TR Papers.

[22] Herbert Williams to Walter L. Houser, Oct. 19, 1911, LFP.

[23] John D. Fackler to Walter L. Houser, Oct. 19, 1911, LFP.

[24] Unsigned carbon copy of letter to James R. Garfield, Oct. 23, 1911, LFP. This letter has penciled initials W. L. H. and M. M. It is the opinion of John J. Hannan, to whom it was submitted by the author, that this letter was never sent.

[25] John D. Fackler to Walter L. Houser, Sept. 25, 1911, LFP.

[26] *Idem* to Walter L. Houser, Oct. 10, 1911, LFP; *idem* to James R. Garfield, Oct. 10, 1911, LFP.

[27] *New York Tribune,* Oct. 10, 16, 1911; *North American,* Philadelphia, Oct. 13, 1911; *World,* New York, Oct. 16, 1911; *New York Times,* Oct. 17, 1911; *Minneapolis Journal,* Oct. 16, 1911.

[28] John D. Fackler to Walter L. Houser, Oct. 12, 1911, LFP.

[29] *Outlook,* Oct. 28, 1911, Vol. 99, p. 439.

[30] *La Follette's Magazine,* Nov. 4, 1911, p. 3.

[31] R. M. L. to John Hicks, April 10, 1911, LFP. Although written in April, this letter accurately represents the relationship throughout October and November, 1911.

[32] Gilson Gardner to Walter L. Houser, Oct. 8, 1911, LFP.

[33] *Idem* to Theodore Roosevelt, Oct. 8, 1911, TR Papers.

[34] Statement by George S. Loftus, *Sunday Journal,* Minneapolis, March 17, 1912.

[35] *La Follette's Autobiography,* pp. 534-535.

[36] Gilson Gardner to Theodore Roosevelt, Oct. 19, 1911, TR Papers. Undated carbon copy of telegram attached to foregoing from Theodore Roosevelt to Gilson Gardner states T.R. will be glad to see Gardner tomorrow at eleven. Nat Wright, editor of the Cleveland *Leader,* had an appointment to see Roosevelt that same day.

[37] *La Follette's Autobiography,* pp. 535-536.

[38] *Ibid.,* p. 537.

[39] *Ibid.,* p. 538. Although La Follette did not know it, the *Leader*'s edi-

torial met with Roosevelt's confidential approval. Dan Hanna had an appointment to see Roosevelt on November 24; the editorial appeared in the Cleveland *Leader* on November 28.

[40] John D. Fackler to Walter L. Houser, Oct. 19, 1911, LFP; *Rocky Mountain News*, Denver, Colo., Oct. 17, 29, 1911.

[41] *Cleveland Plain Dealer*, Nov. 4, 1911.

[42] *Ibid.*

[43] *Ibid.*, Nov. 8, 1911; John D. Fackler to Walter J. Fahy, Nov. 8, 1911, LFP.

[44] *Cleveland Plain Dealer*, Nov. 9, 1911.

[45] *Cincinnati Enquirer*, Nov. 11, 1911.

[46] *Outlook*, Nov. 18, 1911, Vol. 99, pp. 649-656.

[47] *Cleveland Plain Dealer*, Nov. 18, 1911.

[48] James R. Garfield to Theodore Roosevelt, Nov. 13, 1911, TR Papers. This refers to the letter from James R. Garfield to R. M. L., Oct. 17, 1911.

[49] *La Follette's Autobiography*, p. 539.

[50] *World*, New York, Jan. 24, 1912, in an editorial entitled "A Decoy Duck" offers a later example of the interpretation newspapers were making earlier in November and January.

[51] *La Follette's Autobiography*, p. 540.

[52] Walter S. Rogers to Walter L. Houser, Nov. 20, 1911, LFP.

[53] Medill McCormick to Walter L. Houser, Nov. 20, 1911, LFP.

[54] Walter L. Houser to Medill McCormick, Nov. 21, 1911, LFP.

[55] These two speeches were given to the press, although one newspaper report indicates they were not delivered at the banquet because so much time was consumed by another speaker.

[56] Walter W. Pollock to author, November, 1937.

[57] Garfield had an appointment to see Roosevelt at the *Outlook* office on Friday morning, Nov. 17, 1911: Frank Harper to James R. Garfield, Nov. 14, 1911; James R. Garfield to Frank Harper, Nov. 15, 1911, TR Papers.

[58] Gilson Gardner to Theodore Roosevelt, Nov. 21, 1911, TR Papers.

[59] Theodore Roosevelt to Gilson Gardner, Nov. 23, 1911, TR Papers.

[60] Ray Stannard Baker to author, Aug. 16, 1937, LFP.

[61] Entry in Ray Stannard Baker's diary, Nov. 26, 1911, read to author Aug. 16, 1937, LFP.

[62] *North American*, Philadelphia, Nov. 27, 1911.

[63] *Wisconsin State Journal*, Nov. 27, 1911.

[64] *New York Times*, Nov. 28, 1911. See also the *Press*, New York, Nov. 28, 1911.

[65] *Chicago Daily Tribune*, Dec. 8, 1911.

[66] Ray Stannard Baker to R. M. L., Dec. 8, 1911, LFP.

[67] R. M. L. to Ray Stannard Baker, Dec. 9, 1911, LFP.

[68] William Allen White to Theodore Roosevelt, Dec. 5, 1911, TR Papers.

[69] Theodore Roosevelt to William Allen White, Dec. 9, 1911, TR Papers.

[70] *Cleveland Plain Dealer*, Dec. 10, 1911.

[71] *La Follette's Autobiography*, p. 542.

[72] Irvine L. Lenroot to author, April 30, 1938.

[73] *Idem.*

[74] Louis D. Brandeis to Alfred Brandeis, Dec. 19, 1911, Brandeis Papers.

[75] *Idem* to author, Aug. 31, 1937, LFP.

[76] *La Follette's Autobiography*, p. 545.

[77] *Ibid.*, p. 546.

[78] *Ibid.*, pp. 547-548.

[79] *Sunday Herald*, Boston, Dec. 17, 1911.

[80] *Boston Transcript*, Dec. 13, 1911; *North American*, Philadelphia, Dec. 14, 1911; *Boston Journal*, Dec. 14, 1911.

[81] *Boston Sunday Globe*, Dec. 17, 1911.

[82] Elizabeth G. Evans to B. C. L., Dec. 17, 1911, LFP.

[83] Matthew Hale to Theodore Roosevelt, Dec. 10, 1911, TR Papers.

[84] *La Follette's Autobiography*, p. 550.

[85] The *New York Times*, Dec. 16, 1911, p. 2, c. 6 reported:
"Col. Roosevelt was at the office of *The Outlook* for several hours yesterday. There were lots of visitors. The most important of these was ex-Chief Forester Gifford Pinchot, who has been traveling around making more or less trouble for Mr. Taft. Mr. Pinchot spent an hour with the Colonel. Neither he nor the Colonel was willing to say anything regarding the political situation."

[86] *La Follette's Autobiography*, pp. 550-551.

[87] John J. Hannan to Walter L. Houser, Dec. 16, 1911, LFP.

[88] MS by Amos Pinchot, *Progressive Party*, original loaned to author by Amos Pinchot; copy of paragraphs dealing with this episode are with LFP; interview with author May 9, 1938, annotation by Amos Pinchot and letter to author, Sept. 5, 1939, LFP.

[89] Irvine L. Lenroot to author, April 2, 1938, LFP.

[90] In the files of TR Papers the author found a letter to Theodore Roosevelt signed by Walter L. Houser, dated Dec. 18, 1911, which appears to be the same form letter that was being sent out from La Follette Washington headquarters urging the formation of La Follette clubs.

[91] *La Follette's Autobiography*, pp. 551-553. See also R. M. L. to G. E. Roe, Jan. 29, 1913, LFP, for R. M. L.'s direct quotation of Kent's emphatic phrasing regarding Roosevelt.

[92] *Cleveland Plain Dealer*, Dec. 19, 1911.

[93] R. M. L. to Gilbert E. Roe, Dec. 14, 1911, LFP.

[94] R. M. L. to C. A. Deadman, Dec. 15, 1911, LFP.

Chapter XXXII

(Pages 370–393)

[1] *North American*, Philadelphia, Dec. 22, 1911.

[2] *Cleveland Plain Dealer*, Dec. 9, 1911.

[3] *La Follette's Autobiography*, p. 560.

[4] *Cleveland Plain Dealer*, Dec. 28, 1911.

[5] *North American*, Philadelphia, Dec. 28, 1911.

[6] *Cleveland Plain Dealer*, Dec. 28, 1911.

[7] *Ibid.*

[8] *Ibid.*, Dec. 29, 1911.

[9] John J. Hannan to author, June 7, 1937, LFP.

[10] R. M. L. to B. C. L., Dec. 31, 1911, LFP.

[11] Walter W. Pollock to author, November, 1937, interview and letters, LFP; John J. Hannan to author, March 16, 1938, LFP.

[12] *Enquirer*, Cincinnati, Dec. 31, 1911.

[13] *Cleveland Plain Dealer*, Jan. 1, 1912.

[14] *Ohio State Journal*, Jan. 1, 1912.

[15] *North American*, Philadelphia, Jan. 2, 1912.

[16] *New York Times*, Jan. 2, 1912.

[17] Walter W. Pollock to author, letters, October and November, 1937, and interview, November, 1937, LFP.

[18] *Cleveland Plain Dealer*, Jan. 2, 1912, Columbus dispatch signed by A. A. McKee.

[19] *New York Times*, Jan. 2, 1912.

[20] Confidential letter of delegate to secretary of Louis D. Brandeis, Sept. 29, 1934, Brandeis Papers.

[21] *Cleveland Plain Dealer*, Jan. 2, 1912.

[22] *New York Times*, Jan. 2, 1912.

[23] *North American*, Philadelphia, Jan. 2, 1912.

[24] *New York Times*, Jan. 2, 1912.

[25] *Ibid.*

[26] Walter W. Pollock to author, October and November, 1937, letters and interview, LFP; Delo E. Mook to author, Aug. 3, 1938, LFP.

[27] Walter W. Pollock to John M. Nelson, April 19, 1912, LFP.

[28] *Washington Times*, Jan. 2, 1912.

[29] Judson Welliver to author, October, 1938.

[30] *Detroit Journal*, Jan. 1, 1912.

[31] *Detroit News*, Jan. 1, 1912.

[32] *North American*, Philadelphia, Jan. 3, 1912, dispatch from Lansing signed by Angus McSween.

[33] *Grand Rapids Herald*, Jan. 2, 1912.

[34] *Ibid.*

[35] Claude G. Bowers, *Beveridge and the Progressive Era*, p. 416.

[36] Osborn sent a copy of this speech to Roosevelt with a letter dated Jan. 4, 1912, TR Papers.

[37] *Detroit Journal*, Jan. 2, 1912, dispatch from Lansing.

[38] *Grand Rapids Herald*, Jan. 2, 1912, dispatch from Lansing.

[39] *Detroit Journal*, Jan. 3, 1912, dispatch from Lansing.

[40] *Ibid.*, Jan. 2, 1912.

[41] *Ibid.*, Jan. 3, 1912.

[42] *Grand Rapids Herald*, Jan. 3, 1912.

[43] Chase S. Osborn to R. M. L., June 14, 1911, LFP.

[44] *Detroit Free Press*, Jan. 3, 1912.

[45] *Grand Rapids Herald*, Jan. 3, 1912.

[46] *Cleveland Plain Dealer*, Jan. 3, 1912. See also the *Call*, San Francisco, Jan. 3, 1912.

[47] *Chicago Record-Herald*, Jan. 3, 1912.

[48] *Wisconsin State Journal*, Jan. 3, 1912.

[49] *Detroit News*, Jan. 4, 1912; *Cleveland Plain Dealer*, Jan. 4, 1912.

[50] *Day Book*, Chicago, Jan. 5, 1912. See also *Wisconsin State Journal*, Jan. 6, 1912.

[51] *Chicago Record-Herald*, Jan. 4, 1912.

[52] *Inter-Ocean*, Chicago, Jan. 4, 1912.

[53] *Ibid.*

[54] *Wisconsin State Journal*, Jan. 5, 1912; Gilbert E. Roe to B. C. L., Jan. 6, 1912, LFP.

[55] Fred MacKenzie to Gilbert E. Roe, Jan. 26, 1912, LFP.

[56] *Ohio State Journal*, Jan. 2, 1912, dispatch from Canton, Ohio.

[57] *La Follette's Magazine*, Feb. 3, 1912, p. 5, printed from the stenographic report of Brandeis' speech at Chicago, Jan. 3, 1912.

[58] B. C. L. to George Boyd, Jan. 13, 1912, LFP.

[59] Gilbert E. Roe to Walter L. Houser, Dec. 21, 1911, LFP.

[60] *La Follette's Autobiography*, p. 556.

[61] *Ibid.*

[62] Medill McCormick to John M. Nelson, Jan. 4, 1912, LFP.

[63] The account of this campaign-pamphlet episode is based upon the following sources: author's interview with John M. Nelson, Feb. 14, 1938; *La Follette's Autobiography*, pp. 554-558; correspondence in La Follette papers, LFP.

[64] R. M. L. to S. H. Clark, Jan. 15, 1912, refers to telegram sent Jan. 13, 1912, LFP.

[65] R. M. L. to S. H. Clark, Jan. 15, 1912, LFP.

[66] Edward P. Costigan to R. M. L., Jan. 14, 1912, refers to the receiving of this telegram, LFP.

[67] John O. Yeiser to "Dear Sir" [Alfred T. Rogers], Dec. 8, 1911, LFP; *idem*, Dec. 30, 1911, LFP; Frank Knox to Theodore Roosevelt, Dec. 6, 1911; Jan. 3, 9, 1912, TR Papers.

[68] *La Follette's Autobiography*, p. 579; *New York Times*, Jan. 11, 1912.

[69] *Emporia Daily Gazette*, Jan. 10, 1912, photostat of editorial with LFP.

[70] *Washington Times*, Jan. 11, 1912.

[71] John J. Hannan to author, June 7, 1937, LFP.

[72] Merle D. Vincent to Walter L. Houser, Dec. 28, 1911, LFP.

[73] Gifford Pinchot to J. S. Temple, Jan. 12, 1912; published in *Papers of Edward P. Costigan Relating to the Progressive Movement in Colorado 1902-1917* (Boulder, Colo., University of Colorado, 1941), pp. 181-182.

[74] J. S. Temple to Gifford Pinchot, Jan. 19, 1912; digest published in *op. cit.*, p. 181. See also Edward P. Costigan to Walter L. Houser, Feb. 1, 1912, LFP.

[75] *La Follette's Autobiography*, pp. 583-584.

[76] *Cleveland Plain Dealer*, Jan. 22, 1912; *Chicago Record-Herald*, Jan. 23, 1912.

[77] *La Follette's Autobiography*, pp. 584-585.

[78] *Ibid.*, p. 590.

[79] *Ibid.*, p. 593. The account of this conference is based on *La Follette's Autobiography*, pp. 590-593. La Follette gives the date of the conference as "about January 18." It certainly took place between Jan. 15 and 22. Heney was in Mobile, Ala., Jan. 14, en route to Washington, according to the *New York Times* of Jan. 15, 1912. La Follette left Washington for New York on the morning of Jan. 22. The *Cleveland Plain Dealer*, Jan. 26, 1912, prints a Washington dispatch, dated Jan. 25, by Ben F. Allen, about a conference which had previously taken place. The story does not give the date, but the content indicates that reference is to this conference.

[80] Henry Howland, *Theodore Roosevelt and His Times* (New Haven, Yale University Press, 1921), pp. 209 ff.

[81] Mark Sullivan, *Our Times* (New York, Charles Scribner's Sons, 1932), IV, 471, footnote 2.

[82] John D. Fackler to Moses E. Clapp, Sept. 11, 1924, LFP.

[83] *Idem* to Walter L. Houser, two telegrams sent at different hours, each dated Jan. 20, 1912, LFP.

[84] Carbon copy of letter from Moses E. Clapp to John D. Fackler, Oct. 1, 1924, LFP.

[85] John J. Hannan to author, June 7, 1937, LFP.

[86] *North American*, Philadelphia, Jan. 21, 1912; *Morning Oregonian*, Portland, Jan. 21, 1912.

[87] *San Francisco Examiner*, Jan. 21, 1912.

[88] *North American*, Philadelphia, Jan. 24, 1912.

[89] John R. Commons to R. M. L., Friday [Aug. 18, 1911], LFP.

[90] *Kansas City Star*, Jan. 21, 1912.

[91] *World*, New York, Jan. 22, 1912.

[92] *La Follette's Autobiography*, p. 587.

[93] R. M. L. to Kenesaw M. Landis, Jan. 29, 1912, LFP.

[94] *La Follette's Autobiography*, p. 588.

[95] *Globe and Commercial Advertiser*, New York, Feb. 3, 1912.

[96] MS by Amos Pinchot, entitled "Progressive Party," lent to author by Amos Pinchot. Copy of parts of this manuscript is with LFP, original with Amos Pinchot Papers, Library of Congress.

[97] *Sun*, New York, Jan. 23, 1912.

[98] *Press*, New York, Jan. 23, 1912.

[99] *New York Times*, Jan. 23, 1912.

[100] *Ibid.*

[101] *Ibid.*

[102] *Ibid.*

[103] *World*, New York, Jan. 23, 1912.

[104] Entry in diary of Ray Stannard Baker, Jan. 23, 1912, read to author Aug. 17, 1937.

[105] Amos Pinchot MS, "Progressive Party."

[106] The source for the above account and for the quotations is an entry in the diary of Ray Stannard Baker, Jan. 23, 1912, read to author Aug. 17, 1937, notes with LFP.

[107] Lincoln Steffens to Allen H. Suggett, Jan. 24, 1912, in *The Letters of Lincoln Steffens* (New York, Harcourt, Brace & Company, 1938), I, 287.

[108] *La Follette's Autobiography*, p. 595.

[109] Walter L. Houser to Charles R. Crane, Jan. 24, 1912, LFP; Charles R. Crane to Walter L. Houser, Jan. 23, 1912, LFP; Walter L. Houser to Gifford Pinchot, Jan. 24, 1912, LFP; *idem* to Amos R. E. Pinchot, Jan. 24, 1912, LFP.

[110] *North American*, Philadelphia, Jan. 24, 1912.

[111] *Globe and Commercial Advertiser*, Jan. 24, 1912.

[112] *Washington Times*, Jan. 24, 1912; *Morning Oregonian*, Portland, Jan. 24, 1912; *San Francisco Examiner*, Jan. 23, 1912.

[113] *World*, New York, Jan. 24, 1912.

[114] R. M. L. to Ray Stannard Baker, Dec. 9, 1911, LFP.

[115] *Idem* to S. H. Clark, Jan. 27, 1912, copy with LFP, original in possession of Barrett Clark.

[116] *Idem* to Fred L. Holmes, Jan. 27, 1912, LFP.

[117] *Idem* to Charles McCarthy, Jan. 27, 1912, LFP.

[118] *Idem* to Amos Pinchot, Jan. 27, 1912, LFP.

Chapter XXXIII
(Pages 394–414)

[1] In his *Autobiography* Bob attributed the calling of this conference solely to Gifford Pinchot. But letters which he undoubtedly neither saw nor knew of were found in 1936 by the author which show that Gifford and Amos Pinchot, Walter L. Houser, Medill McCormick, Walter S. Rogers, Charles R. Crane, and possibly others cooperated in the calling of this conference. Telegram from Charles R. Crane to Walter L. Houser, Jan. 23, 1912; letter from Walter L. Houser to Gifford Pinchot, Jan. 24, 1912, LFP.

[2] *La Follette's Autobiography*, pp. 597-598.

[3] *Ibid.*, p. 598.

[4] *Chicago Daily News*, Jan. 29, 1912.

[5] *La Follette's Autobiography*, p. 599.

[6] Irvine L. Lenroot to author, April 2, 1938, LFP; Louis D. Brandeis to author.

[7] *La Follette's Autobiography*, pp. 599-602. In an interview on April 2, 1938, Irvine L. Lenroot stated that the account given in these pages of *La Follette's Autobiography* was in accord with his recollection (LFP).

[8] Walter L. Houser to Frank P. Robards, Jan. 30, 1912, LFP.

[9] *Idem*, Jan. 31, 1912, LFP.

[10] John M. Nelson to author, Feb. 14, 1938, LFP.

[11] Francis J. Heney to R. M. L., Jan. 29, 1912, LFP.

[12] R. M. L. to Hiram Johnson, Jan. 30, 1912, LFP.

[13] Amos Pinchot to R. M. L., Feb. 1, 1912, LFP.

[14] B. C. L. to George Middleton, Jan. 29, 1912, LFP.

[15] John J. Hannan to author, May 12, 1938, LFP.

[16] Recollection of George Middleton, LFP; John J. Hannan to author, May 12, 1938, LFP.

[17] *Public Ledger*, Philadelphia, Feb. 4, 1912.

[18] *North American*, Philadelphia, Feb. 4, 1912.

[19] *Public Ledger*, Philadelphia, Feb. 4, 1912.

[20] Recollection of George Middleton, LFP.

[21] Contemporary accounts and recollections differ as to the exact length of his speech.

[22] Recollection of George Middleton, LFP.

[23] *Public Ledger*, Philadelphia, Feb. 4, 1912.

[24] Three articles by William Kittle, entitled "The Making of Public Opinion," published in *La Follette's Magazine*, July 3, 10, and 17, 1909, are good examples.

[25] *La Follette's Autobiography*, p. 603.

[26] Author's interview with a newspaper publisher, Dec. 30, 1937, LFP.

[27] John S. Phillips to author, May 11, 1937, LFP.

[28] *La Follette's Autobiography*, pp. 762-797; *La Follette's Magazine*, March 23, 30, 1912.

[29] John S. Phillips to author, May 11, 1937, LFP.

[30] *Public Ledger*, Philadelphia, Feb. 4, 1912.

[31] Recollection of George Middleton, LFP.

[32] R. M. L. to John S. Phillips, Feb. 4, 1911, LFP.

[33] Recollection of George Middleton, LFP.

[34] *North American*, Philadelphia, Feb. 5, 1912.

[35] *Public Ledger*, Philadelphia, Feb. 3, 1912.

[36] *Ibid.*, Feb. 4, 1912.

[37] *Ibid.*

[38] Bessie Beatty to author, July, 1937, LFP.

[39] John J. Hannan to Gilbert E. Roe, July 21, 1916; Gilbert E. Roe to John J. Hannan, July 22, 1916, re the *Philadelphia Inquirer* editorial, July 21, 1916, LFP.

[40] *Harper's Magazine*, Vol. 160, pp. 669-670, May 30, 1930.

[41] John Spencer Bassett, *A Short History of the United States* (New York, The Macmillan Company, 1939), p. 833.

[42] This statement is based upon the La Follette Papers and other collections; also upon newspapers and upon the author's own recollection of contemporary reports made by reliable individuals.

[43] Louis D. Brandeis to B. C. L., Feb. 7, 1912, LFP.

[44] C. R. Williams, of the Progressive County Executive Committee, and Delo E. Mook, secretary, Cuyahoga County Progressive League, to R. M. L., February 5, 1912, LFP.

[45] Fola to B. C. L., Feb. 8, 1912, LFP.

[46] R. M. L. to John S. Phillips, Feb. 4, 1912, LFP.

[47] Dr. Albert Ochsner to B. C. L., Feb. 10, 1912, LFP.

[48] B. C. L. to Mrs. Charles Mayo, Feb. 20, 1912, LFP.

[49] *Idem* to Frances Squire Potter, Feb. 15, 1912, LFP.

[50] Dr. John B. Darling to Dr. George Keenan, March 1, 1912, LFP.

[51] Dr. George Keenan to Dr. John B. Darling, March 4, 1912, LFP.

[52] John M. Nelson to author, Feb. 14, 1938, LFP.

[53] *Idem.*

[54] John D. Fackler to Moses E. Clapp, Sept. 11, 1924, LFP. The author sought an interview with Senator Bourne, but the Senator was one of the few men who refused to grant one.

[55] Joseph L. Bristow to author, July 16, 1937, LFP.

[56] John J. Hannan to author, June 7, 1937, LFP; Irvine L. Lenroot to author, June 12, 1937, April 5, 1938, LFP.

[57] John D. Fackler to Moses E. Clapp, Sept. 11, 1924, LFP; *idem* to Walter L. Houser, Feb. 8, 1912, LFP; R. M. Buck to John J. Hannan, Feb. 20, and 21, 1912, LFP.

[58] Amos Pinchot MS, "Progressive Party"; copy of portion quoted is with LFP.

[59] Irvine L. Lenroot to author, April 5, 1938, LFP; John J. Hannan to author, Aug. 8, 1938, LFP.

[60] John J. Hannan to author, Aug. 8, 1938, LFP; Irvine L. Lenroot to author, June 12, 1937; April 5, 1938, LFP.

[61] B. C. L. to Gilbert E. Roe, Feb. 6, 1912, LFP.

[62] Pinchot MS, "Progressive Party"; copy of portion quoted is with LFP.

[63] *Chicago Daily Tribune*, Feb. 6, 1912.

[64] Mrs. Lynn Haines to author, Aug. 8, 1937, LFP.

[65] R. M. L. to Josephine La Follette Siebecker, Feb. 5, 1912, LFP.

[66] *New York Times*, Feb. 6, 1912.

[67] R. M. L. to Gilbert E. Roe, Feb. 6, 1912, LFP.

[68] *Idem* to Will B. Colver, night letter in response to telegram from Will B. Colver, Feb. 5, 1912, LFP.

Chapter XXXIV

(Pages 415–443)

[1] Mrs. Asle J. Gronna to author. See also Walter D. Corrigan to author, interview; recollection of Walter D. Corrigan, "The 1912 North Dakota Primary," p. 3, LFP.

[2] Frank A. Harrison to John J. Hannan, Feb. 26, 1912, LFP.

[3] Carbon copies of letters in TR Papers.

[4] *Papers of Edward P. Costigan Relating to the Progressive Movement in Colorado, 1902-1917*, E. P. Costigan to J. S. Temple, Feb. 6, 1912; *idem* to ———, Feb. 6, 1912, pp. 194-195; *idem* to J. C. Harper, Feb. 22, 1912, pp. 185-187. See also *Rocky Mountain News*, Feb. 17, 1912, "Colorado

Progressive Republican Leader Home After Conference with Roosevelt in Office of Outlook."

[5] *North American,* Philadelphia, Feb. 6, 1912.

[6] *New York Times,* Feb. 6, 1912.

[7] George L. Record to Walter L. Houser, telegram, 8:16 A.M., Feb. 5, 1912, LFP.

[8] Irvine L. Lenroot to author, April 5, 1938, LFP.

[9] *Newark Evening News,* Feb. 5, 1912; John J. Hannan to author, March 14, Aug. 8, 1938, LFP.

[10] R. M. L. to Josephine La Follette Siebecker, Monday night, Feb. 5, 1912, LFP.

[11] James E. Pope to author, June 14, 1937, and July 7, 1937, LFP; also, confidential source to author, June 15, 1937, LFP; Gilbert E. Roe to Rudolph Spreckels, April 13, 1912, LFP.

[12] *Newark Evening News,* Feb. 6, 1912.

[13] *Globe and Commercial Advertiser,* New York, Feb. 6, 1912. The New York *World* and other newspapers carried similar reports of Record's speech. The *Globe* account is substantially as the speech was reported to James E. Pope by friends who had attended the dinner. James E. Pope to author, July 7, 1937, LFP.

[14] Irvine L. Lenroot to author, April 2, 1938, LFP.

[15] *Globe and Commercial Advertiser,* New York, Feb. 6, 1912; George L. Record to Hiram Johnson, telegram, March 27-28, 1912, published in San Francisco *Bulletin,* April 5, 1912; *idem* to William M. Barr, July 20, 1933, pp. 66-67, essay by William M. Barr, submitted for degree of Master of Arts, Columbia University, 1936, photostat with LFP.

[16] *Chicago Daily Tribune,* Feb. 12, 1912.

[17] B. C. L. to Jean Bascom, Feb. 21, 1912, LFP.

[18] *Idem* to Emily M. Bishop, Feb. 20, 1912, LFP.

[19] George Loftus to R. M. L., Feb. 6, 1912, LFP; *Minneapolis Journal,* Feb. 7, 1912; *Public Ledger,* Philadelphia, Feb. 7, 1912.

[20] Charles A. Lindbergh to George Loftus, Feb. 10, 1912, LFP.

[21] *Minneapolis Journal,* Feb. 11, 1912.

[22] Walter L. Houser to John J. Hannan, Feb. 10, 1912, LFP.

[23] Gilbert E. Roe to R. M. L., Feb. 8, 1912, LFP.

[24] Netha Roe to author.

[25] R. M. L. to Rudolph Spreckels, April 7, 1912, LFP.

[26] *Idem* to Dr. George Keenan, Feb. 12, 1912, LFP.

[27] William Kent to Amos Pinchot, Feb. 14, 1912, copy with LFP.

[28] *Idem* to R. M. L., Feb. 12, 1912. Copy sent to author by Amos Pinchot is with LFP.

[29] R. M. L. to William Kent, Feb. 15, 1912, LFP.

[30] Typescript of telegram from Chester H. Rowell to W. L. Houser [February] 19 [1912], LFP.

[31] Typescript copy of telegram from Fremont Older to Walter L. Houser, Feb. 20, 1912, LFP.

[32] R. M. L. to Gilbert E. Roe, March 26, 1912, LFP.

[33] *Washington Post*, Feb. 19, 1912.

[34] Amos Pinchot MS, "Progressive Party."

[35] Theodore Roosevelt, *The Works of Theodore Roosevelt*, National Edition (New York, Charles Scribner's Sons, 1926), XVII, 149.

[36] R. M. L. to Dr. George Keenan, Feb. 12, 1912, LFP.

[37] *Idem* to Irvine L. Lenroot, March 1, 1912, LFP; Irvine L. Lenroot to R. M. L., Feb. 26, 27, 1912, referred to in R. M. L.'s letter of March 1 to Irvine L. Lenroot.

[38] B. C. L. to Elizabeth G. Evans, March 5, 1912, LFP.

[39] R. M. L. to Dr. George Keenan, Feb. 12, 1912, LFP.

[40] B. C. L. to Ben B. Lindsey, Feb. 20, 1912, LFP.

[41] *Idem* to Mrs. Charles R. Crane, Feb. 20, 1912, LFP.

[42] *Idem* to Ben B. Lindsey, Feb. 20, 1912, LFP.

[43] *Idem* to Prof. S. H. Clark, March 2, 1912, copy with LFP, original in possession of Barrett Clark.

[44] *Idem* to George Middleton, March 6, 1912, LFP.

[45] Walter D. Corrigan to author, interview, and letter, March 22, 1938, with enclosure of his recollections of "The 1912 North Dakota Primary," p. 1, LFP.

[46] *Fargo Forum*, Fargo, N.D., March 8, 1912.

[47] *Ibid.*, March 7, 1912.

[48] *Minneapolis Journal*, March 7, 1912.

[49] B. C. L. to Fola and Mid, March 11, 1912, LFP.

[50] *Minneapolis Morning Tribune*, March 15, 1912.

[51] *Fargo Forum*, March 15, 1912.

[52] *Ibid.*, March 16, 1912.

[53] *Minneapolis Sunday Tribune*, March 17, 1912.

[54] *Minneapolis Morning Tribune*, March 15, 1912.

[55] *Minneapolis Sunday Tribune*, March 17, 1912.

[56] *Ibid.*, dispatch signed by George F. Authier.

[57] *Minneapolis Morning Tribune*, March 23, 1912.

[58] Frank A. Harrison to R. M. L., with enclosures of cards and envelope, March 5, 1912, LFP.

[59] *Idem* to John J. Hannan, March 20, 1912, LFP.

[60] *World-Herald*, Omaha, April 5, 1912.

[61] B. C. L. to R. M. L., Jr., Phil, and Mary, April 8, 1912, LFP.

[62] *Nebraska State Journal*, April 6, 1912.

[63] *Sunday World-Herald*, Omaha, April 7, 1912.

[64] *World-Herald*, Omaha, April 12, 1912.

[65] *Sunday Oregonian*, April 14, 1912.

[66] *Morning Oregonian*, April 16, 1912.

[67] Oswald West to R. M. L., Jr., Nov. 18, 1928, LFP.

[68] Original carbon copy of typewritten manuscript of Governor Oswald West's introduction of R. M. La Follette, at Salem, Ore., April 15, 1912, sent to R. M. L., Jr., as enclosure with letter Nov. 18, 1928, LFP.

[69] *Morning Oregonian*, April 17, 1912.

[70] B. C. L. to Elizabeth G. Evans, April 20, 1912, LFP.

71 *Bulletin*, San Francisco, April 17, 1912.

72 *Ibid.*, April 5, 1912. The *Morning Oregonian*, April 5, 1912, prints John-son's statement and also Thomas McCusker's recollection of a talk with Francis J. Heney which refuted in substance Johnson's assertion that Roose-velt had not encouraged La Follette to become a candidate.

73 *Omaha Daily News*, to R. M. L., April 6, 1912, LFP.

74 R. M. L. to Robert F. Paine [April 6, 1912], LFP.

75 *Idem* to Rudolph Spreckels, April 7, 1912, LFP [telegram dated April 8 in newspapers]. See also *San Francisco Call*, April 9, 1912; *Washington Times*, April 8, 1912; *Morning Oregonian*, April 8, 1912.

76 *San Francisco Examiner*, April 21, 1912.

77 *San Francisco Call*, April 21, 1912.

78 *San Francisco Examiner*, April 21, 1912.

79 *San Francisco Call*, May 14, 1912.

80 B. C. L. to Netha Roe, May 18, 1912, LFP.

81 James E. Pope to author, June 14, July 7, 1937, LFP. See also John J. Hannan to author, Feb. 23, 1940, LFP; Netha Roe to author.

82 *Washington Times*, June 9, 1912, signed dispatch by Judson C. Welliver.

83 Gilbert E. Roe to R. M. L., June 8, 1912, LFP.

84 Mrs. Gilbert E. Roe to author; John M. Scoble to Mrs. Gilbert E. Roe, June 11, 1937, LFP.

85 *La Follette's Autobiography*, pp. 647-648.

86 John J. Hannan to author, June 7, 1937, LFP.

87 *La Follette's Autobiography*, p. 669.

88 R. M. L. to Gilbert E. Roe, June 10, 1912, LFP.

89 Recollection of author.

90 *Record of Meetings of Wisconsin Delegation To The National Con-vention of the Republican Party To Be Held At Chicago June 18, 1912*, LFP.

91 *Wisconsin State Journal*, June 20, 1912.

92 *Nebraska State Journal*, June 19, 1912.

93 Fola to R. M. L., June 18, 1912; Fola to B. C. L., June 19, 1912, LFP.

94 *Public Ledger*, Philadelphia, June 19, 1912; *Chicago Record-Herald*, June 19, 1912.

95 B. C. L. to R. M. L., telegram, June 20, 1912; letter of Friday morning [June 21, 1912], LFP.

96 *New York Times*, June 20, 1912.

97 Senator William E. Borah to author, March 18, 1938, LFP.

98 Claudius O. Johnson, *Borah of Idaho* (New York, Longmans, Green and Company, 1936), pp. 139-140.

99 Frank Harrison to R. M. L., June 24, 1912, LFP.

100 R. M. L. to Frank A. Harrison, June 24 [June 25], 1912, LFP.

101 *Idem* to Joseph E. Davies, June 24 [June 25], 1912, LFP.

102 *Idem* to Gilbert E. Roe, July 8, 1912, LFP; *idem* to John R. Com-mons, July 24, 1912, LFP.

103 *Sun*, Baltimore, June 28, 1912.

104 R. M. L. to Gilbert E. Roe, July 8, 1912, LFP.

Chapter XXXV
(Pages 444–457)

[1] R. M. L. to Gilbert E. Roe, July 8, 1912, LFP.

[2] *Idem* to Rudolph Spreckels, July 12, 1912, LFP.

[3] Luke Lea to Woodrow Wilson, July 13, 1913, Woodrow Wilson Papers, Library of Congress (hereafter cited as Wilson Papers).

[4] R. M. L. to Rudolph Spreckels, July 12, 1912, LFP.

[5] *Idem* to Charles A. Crane, Aug. 21, 1912, LFP.

[6] *Idem; La Follette's Magazine,* July 27, 1912, p. 4.

[7] R. M. L. to Rudolph Spreckels, Aug. 20, 1912, LFP.

[8] *Record,* 62nd Cong., 2nd Sess., Vol. 48, p. 9634, July 25, 1912.

[9] R. M. L. to Rudolph Spreckels, Aug. 20, 1912, LFP.

[10] B. C. L. to Lucy Daniels Thompson, July 27, 1912, LFP.

[11] R. M. L. to Rudolph Spreckels, Aug. 20, 1912, LFP.

[12] *Record,* 62nd Cong., 2nd Sess., Vol. 48, pp. 10603-10604, Aug. 9, 1912.

[13] R. M. L. to Charles A. Crane, Aug. 21, 1912, LFP.

[14] *Record,* 62nd Cong., 2nd Sess., Vol. 48, p. 10177, Aug. 5, 1912. See J. David Thompson, "The Amendment of the Federal Constitution," read at the meeting of the Academy of Political Science in the city of New York, Oct. 26, 1912, *Proceedings of the Academy of Political Science,* Vol. III, No. 2, Jan., 1913, pp. 65-77.

[15] *Record,* 62nd Cong., 2nd Sess., Vol. 48, pp. 10728-10733, Aug. 12, 1912. See also *World,* New York, Aug. 13, 14, 1912; *Milwaukee Journal,* Aug. 13, 1912.

[16] *Record,* 62nd Cong., 2nd Sess., Vol. 48, pp. 11792-11793, Aug. 24, 1912. See also *World,* Aug. 26, 1912; *Newark Evening News,* Aug. 26, 1912; *Milwaukee Journal,* Aug. 26, 1912.

[17] R. M. L. to Gilbert E. Roe, Aug. 30, 1912, LFP.

[18] *Washington Times,* Sept. 7, 1912. See also *Wisconsin State Journal,* Sept. 7, 1912.

[19] *Milwaukee Journal,* Oct. 23, 1912.

[20] *La Follette's Magazine,* Oct. 12, 1912, pp. 6-8, 19-22.

[21] R. M. L. to Rudolph Spreckels, Aug. 20, 1912, LFP.

[22] Elizabeth G. Evans to R. M. L., July 17, 1912, LFP.

[23] Ray Stannard Baker to R. M. L., Aug. 2, 1912, LFP.

[24] R. M. L. to Ray Stannard Baker, Aug. 10, 1912, LFP.

[25] Woodrow Wilson speech at Wilmington, Del., Oct. 17, 1912, stenographic notes of Charles L. Swem, Wilson Papers.

[26] *Minneapolis Journal,* Oct. 12, 1912.

[27] *Ibid.*

[28] R. M. L. to Louis D. Brandeis, Nov. 8, 1912, LFP.

[29] *Record,* 59th Cong., 1st Sess., Vol. 40, p. 5688, April 23, 1906.

[30] *Chicago Record-Herald,* Feb. 16, 1913.

[31] Elizabeth G. Evans to Mrs. Louis D. Brandeis, Feb. 16, 1913, LFP.

[32] *Sunday Record-Herald,* Chicago, Feb. 16, 1913.

[33] .(S. 8202) *Record,* 62nd Cong., 3rd Sess., Vol. 49, p. 1762, Jan. 20, 1913; the same bill with amendment (S. 8337) introduced Feb. 3, 1913, p. 2468; reported favorably from Committee on the Library, Feb. 4, 1913, p. 3472.

[34] (H.R. 18720) *Record,* 62nd Cong., 2nd Sess., Vol. 48, p. 1324, Jan. 25, 1912.

[35] (S. 7723) *Record,* 62nd Cong., 3rd Sess., Vol. 49, pp. 4208-4209, Feb. 27, 1913.

[36] *Ibid.,* 1st Sess., Vol. 47, p. 105, April 6, 1911.

[37] *Ibid.,* 2nd Sess., Vol. 48, p. 4068, March 29, 1912.

[38] *Ibid.,* 3rd Sess., Vol. 49, p. 4256, Feb. 27, 1913.

[39] *Ibid.,* p. 177, Dec. 5, 1912.

[40] *La Follette's Magazine,* March 8, 1913, p. 5, article by John R. Commons.

[41] Elizabeth G. Evans to Mrs. Louis D. Brandeis, Feb. 16, 1913, LFP.

[42] *Record,* 62nd Cong., 3rd Sess., Vol. 49, p. 3568, Feb. 21, 1913.

[43] Elizabeth G. Evans to Mrs. Louis D. Brandeis, Feb. 25, 1913, LFP. See also *Record,* 62nd Cong., 3rd Sess., Vol. 49, p. 3779, Feb. 24, 1913; *Chicago Record-Herald,* Feb. 25, 1913.

[44] *Record,* 62nd Cong., 3rd Sess., Vol. 49, p. 3806, Feb. 24, 1913.

[45] *Ibid.,* pp. 3795-3801, Feb. 24, 1913.

[46] Elizabeth G. Evans to Mrs. Louis D. Brandeis, Feb. 25, 1913, LFP.

[47] *Wisconsin State Journal,* March 3, 1913.

[48] *La Follette's Magazine,* March 8, 1913, p. 5.

[49] *Chicago Record-Herald,* Feb. 25, 1913, Washington dispatch by Sumner Curtis, dated Feb. 24.

[50] *La Follette's Magazine,* March 15, 1913, p. 4.

Chapter XXXVI
(Pages 458-483)

[1] *Milwaukee Journal,* Jan. 18, 1913.

[2] *Wisconsin State Journal,* Jan. 29, 1913. See also *Newark Evening News,* Jan. 29, 1913.

[3] *Milwaukee Journal,* Jan. 30, 1913. The *Newark Star,* Jan. 29, 1913, reported that Governor Wilson was accompanied by his stenographer "as a precaution against being misquoted," but the Charles L. Swem stenographic notes in the Wilson Papers contain no report of this speech.

[4] *Milwaukee Journal,* Jan. 30, 1913.

[5] Charles A. Crane to Woodrow Wilson, Feb. 10, 1913, Wilson Papers.

[6] Edward M. House to Woodrow Wilson, Jan. 9, 1913, Wilson Papers.

[7] Elizabeth G. Evans to Mrs. Louis D. Brandeis, Feb. 16, 1913, LFP.

[8] B. C. L. to Mrs. Louis D. Brandeis, Feb. 18, 1913, LFP.

[9] Elizabeth G. Evans to Mrs. Louis D. Brandeis, Feb. 25, 1913, LFP.

[10] *North American*, Philadelphia, March 1, 2, 3, 1913; also, recollection of Netha Roe.

[11] *New York Times*, March 2, 1913.

[12] *Springfield Daily Republican*, April 16, 1931.

[13] *North American*, Philadelphia, March 4, 1913, dispatch signed by Angus McSween.

[14] *New York Times*, March 5, 1913.

[15] *World*, New York, March 4, 1913.

[16] *North American*, Philadelphia, March 4, 1913.

[17] R. M. L. to Louis D. Brandeis, March 4, 1913, LFP.

[18] *Idem* to Josephine La Follette Siebecker, March 6, 1913, LFP.

[19] Louis D. Brandeis to R. M. L., March 5, 1913, LFP.

[20] Elizabeth G. Evans to B. C. L., Oct. 4, 1912, LFP; also, Ray Stannard Baker, *Woodrow Wilson—Life and Letters* (New York, Doubleday, Doran & Company, Vols. I-VIII, 1927-1937), IV, 358 (hereafter cited as *Woodrow Wilson*).

[21] *La Follette's Magazine*, Dec. 13, 1913, p. 1.

[22] Rudolph Spreckels to R. M. L., March 8, 1913, LFP.

[23] White House Diary entry, March 7, 1913, Wilson Papers.

[24] Louis D. Brandeis to George Middleton, March 12, 1913, LFP.

[25] *New York Times*, March 14, 1913.

[26] *Chicago Record-Herald*, March 14, 1913.

[27] *Milwaukee Journal*, March 14, 1913.

[28] *Springfield Daily Republican*, March 15, 1913. See also *Public Ledger*, Philadelphia, March 15, 1913; *Globe and Commercial Advertiser*, New York, March 15, 1913; *North American*, Philadelphia, March 15, 1913.

[29] *New York Times*, March 15, 1913.

[30] Woodrow Wilson to Rudolph Spreckels, March 15, 1913, Wilson Papers.

[31] Charles R. Crane to Woodrow Wilson, March 24, 1913, Wilson Papers.

[32] *La Follette's Magazine*, April 5, 1913, p. 1.

[33] *Ibid.*, July 19, 1913, p. 6, article by B. C. L. See also *Wisconsin State Journal*, May 6, 1913, article by Emily Chynoweth.

[34] *Record*, 63rd Cong., 1st Sess., Vol. 50, p. 51, April 7, 1913.

[35] Letters from publishers to Ray Stannard Baker, Baker Papers; *idem* to R. M. L., LFP.

[36] Walter H. Page to Ray Stannard Baker, Oct. 13, 1911, Baker Papers.

[37] *Idem*, Oct. 11, 1911, LFP. See also entry of Oct. 19, 1911, Ray Stannard Baker Pocket Diary, Baker Papers; Walter H. Page to R M. L., Oct. 24, 1911, LFP.

[38] R. M. L. to Walter H. Page, Nov. 21, 1911, LFP.

[39] Gilbert E. Roe to R. M. L., Feb. 21, 1912, LFP; Walter H. Page to R. M. L., Feb. 23, 1912, LFP; Gilbert E. Roe to Walter H. Page, Dec. 28, 1912, LFP.

[40] R. M. L. to Doubleday, Page & Co., April 5, 1912, LFP. *Idem* to Ray Stannard Baker, April 7, 19, 1912, LFP; *idem* to John S. Phillips, April 21, 1912, LFP; *idem* to Walter H. Page, Jan. 5, 1912, LFP.

[41] Doubleday, Page & Co. to Gilbert E. Roe, Nov. 14, 1912, LFP.

[42] Gilson Gardner to Walter H. Page, Nov. 18, 1912, copy with LFP.

[43] R. M. L. to Gilbert E. Roe, Nov. 20, 1912, LFP.

[44] Francis E. McGovern to Doubleday, Page & Co., Dec. 12, 1912, copy with LFP.

[45] Walter H. Page to Gilbert E. Roe, Dec. 17, 1912, LFP. See also Gilbert E. Roe to Walter H. Page, Dec. 18, 1912, LFP.

[46] Walter H. Page to Gilbert E. Roe, Dec. 24, 1912, LFP.

[47] This account is based upon many letters written during November and December, 1912, and January, 1913, by Walter H. Page, Arthur W. Page, Doubleday, Page & Co., Gilbert E. Roe, and R. M. L., LFP; also, recollection of Mrs. Gilbert E. Roe and of author.

[48] Doubleday, Page & Co. to R. M. L., Jan. 13, 1913, LFP.

[49] B. C. L. to Gilbert E. Roe, Jan. 22, 1913, LFP. See also Doubleday, Page & Co., to Mrs. R. M. La Follette, Jan. 24, 25, 1913, LFP; *idem* to R. M. L., Jan. 24, 1913, LFP; Gilbert E. Roe to Walter H. Page, Jan. 24, 1913, LFP; Walter H. Page to Gilbert E. Roe, Jan. 27, 1913, LFP; Gilbert E. Roe to Doubleday, Page & Co., Jan. 28, 1913, LFP.

[50] R. M. L. to Alfred T. Rogers, April 10, May 28, June 11, 1913, LFP.

[51] Medill McCormick to Theodore Roosevelt, May 30, 1913, TR Papers.

[52] R. M. L. to Alfred T. Rogers, April 10, May 28, 1913, LFP; *idem* to "Dear Sir," April 10, 1913, LFP.

[53] Fred L. Holmes to author, Sept. 19, 1935.

[54] *New York Times*, May 25, 1913.

[55] *Globe and Commercial Advertiser*, May 10, 1913.

[56] *Evening Mail*, New York, July 5, 1913.

[57] *St. Louis Post-Dispatch*, June 2, 1913.

[58] *Literary Digest*, July 5, 1913.

[59] *Springfield Daily Republican*, May 26, 1913.

[60] *Political Science Quarterly*, XXIX, 160-161.

[61] *Telegram*, Winnipeg, Can., May 24, 1913, review by W. T. Allison; *Witness and Canadian Homestead*, Montreal, Can., May 31, 1913; *Mail And Empire*, Toronto, Can., June 2, 1913; *Globe*, Toronto, Can., June 21, 1913.

[62] May 10, 1913.

[63] Clyde H. Tavenner to R. M. L., May 1, 1913, LFP. See also *Evening Crescent*, Appleton, Wis., April 25, 1913; *Johnstown Democrat*, Johnstown, Pa., April 25, 1913; *Argus*, Rock Island, Ill., April 25, 1913; *Quincy Journal*, Quincy, Ill., April 26, 1913, editorial signed by Tavenner; *Dispatch*, Moline, Ill., April 28, 1913; *Daily Union*, Salina, Kan., April 25, 1913; *Gazette*, Hutchinson, Kan., May 6, 1913; *Hawk-Eye*, Burlington, Iowa, June 3, 1913; *Globe-Gazette*, Mason City, Iowa, June 6, 1913.

[64] R. M. L. to Charles A. Beard, May 10, 1913, LFP. See also undated draft of circular, LFP.

[65] Charles A. Beard to R. M. L., May 14, 1913, LFP.

[66] Ray Stannard Baker to R. M. L., May 22, 1913, LFP.

[67] *Record*, 63rd Cong., 1st Sess., Vol. 50, p. 1393, May 9, 1913.

[68] *Ibid.*, pp. 1596-1597, May 16, 1913.

[69] *Ibid.*, p. 1502, May 13, 1913; pp. 1597-1599, 1608, May 16, 1913; *New York Times*, May 17, 1913.

[70] *La Follette's Magazine,* July 5, 1913, pp. 1, 3.

[71] *Record,* 63rd Cong., 1st Sess., Vol. 50, p. 1812, May 29, 1913.

[72] *Ibid.,* pp. 1815-1817, May 29, 1913.

[73] *La Follette's Magazine,* July 12, 1913, p. 1.

[74] *Maintenance of a Lobby to Influence Legislation,* Hearings before Sub-committee of Senate Committee on the Judiciary, I, 193-200, June 3, 1913; *New York Times,* June 4, 1913.

[75] *New York Times,* June 4, 1913.

[76] Alpheus T. Mason, *Brandeis: A Free Man's Life* (New York, Viking Press, 1946), p. 398. See also Ray Stannard Baker, *Woodrow Wilson,* IV, 163.

[77] Louis D. Brandeis to Alice G. Brandeis, June, 1913, copy of excerpt with LFP; Phil to Fola, June 13, 1913, LFP; Louis D. Brandeis to Woodrow Wilson, June 14, 1913, Wilson Papers.

[78] S. 2552, *Record,* 63rd Cong., 1st Sess., Vol. 50, pp. 1992, 2019, 2073, June 13, 17, 18, 1913; S. 3276, *Record,* 62nd Cong., 1st Sess., Vol. 47, pp. 4183-4193, Aug. 19, 1911; *ibid.,* 2nd Sess., Vol. 48, p. 295, Dec. 13, 1913; S. 4931, *ibid.,* p. 1518, Jan. 30, 1912.

[79] House Hearings of the Judiciary Committee on Trust Legislation, 1912, Serial No. 1, pp. 104-105, 129-130, typescript copy of material Louis D. Brandeis lent to author, LFP.

[80] R. M. L. to Louis D. Brandeis, May 21, 1913, LFP; Louis D. Brandeis to R. M. L., May 27, 1913, LFP.

[81] *New York Times,* June 14, 1913.

[82] *La Follette's Magazine,* July 19, 1913, p. 4. For discussion of principles underlying this proposed legislation, see *ibid.,* Oct. 28, 1911, "Relief for Business Uncertainty"; *ibid.,* Jan. 13, 1912, "How to Solve the Trust Problem"; *ibid.,* Jan. 27 and Feb. 3, 1912, "Protect Law-Abiding Business," by Louis D. Brandeis.

[83] Printed copy of S. 2552, Wilson Papers.

[84] *North American,* Philadelphia, July 29, 1913; *New York Times,* July 29, 1913.

[85] *La Follette's Autobiography,* p. 452. Six Republicans voted against the bill, but Senator Knute Nelson was not classed as "progressive."

[86] *La Follette's Magazine,* Aug. 9, 1913, p. 10.

[87] George Middleton, *These Things Are Mine,* p. 124.

[88] *Woman's Journal,* XLIV, March 8, 15, 1913; *Evening Post,* New York, May 30, 1913.

[89] *Evening Star,* Washington, D.C., April 26, 1913; *Woman's Journal,* XLIV, 137, 142, May 3, 1913.

[90] B. C. L. to Joe Mitchell Chapple, June 3, 1913, LFP; Joe Mitchell Chapple to B. C. L., May 27, June 19, 1913, LFP.

[91] Galley proof enclosed with letter from Joe Mitchell Chapple to B. C. L., May 27, 1913, LFP. See also *National Magazine,* XXXVIII, 562-563. As published, a few lines were cut from galley proof.

[92] *Record,* 63rd Cong., 1st Sess., Vol. 50, p. 2951, July 31, 1913.

[93] R. M. La Follette, "My Own Story," *Washington Daily News*, Sept. 20, 1924. See also *La Follette's Autobiography*, pp. 104-107.

[94] *Record*, 63rd Cong., 1st Sess., Vol. 50, pp. 4044-4047, 4138, 4244-4245, 4294-4295, 4445, 4449, 4567-4616, Sept. 1-9, 1913. See also Henry C. Emery to R. M. L., June 5, 1913, LFP.

[95] *New York Times*, May 26, 1913.

[96] For his advocacy of this method, see: *State of Wisconsin Senate Journal*, 47th Sess., p. 38, Jan. 12, 1905; *La Follette's Magazine*, Oct. 5, 1912, pp. 7, 8, 22, 23; *ibid.*, Sept. 6, 1913, pp. 1, 3; Kenneth Hechler, *Insurgency* (New York, Columbia University Press, 1940), p. 491; and letter from Joseph L. Bristow to E. C. Manning, April 23, 1909, copy of excerpt with LFP.

[97] *Record*, 63rd Cong., 1st Sess., Vol. 50, pp. 3805, 3819-3821, Aug. 27, 1913; *Chicago Record-Herald*, Aug. 28, 1913; *Public Ledger*, Philadelphia, Aug. 28, 1913.

[98] *North American*, Philadelphia, Aug. 29, Sept. 1, 1913; *Public Ledger*, Philadelphia, Aug. 29, 1913; *Chicago Record-Herald*, Aug. 29, 30, 1913; *Springfield Daily Republican*, Aug. 29, 30, Sept. 1, 2, 7, 1913; *World*, New York, Sept. 5, 1913.

[99] *Record*, 63rd Cong., 1st Sess., Vol. 50, p. 3830, Aug. 28, 1913.

[100] *Public Ledger*, Philadelphia, Aug. 30, 1913.

[101] *La Follette's Magazine*, Sept. 20, 1913, p. 4; Nov. 22, 1913, pp. 1-2; *Record*, 63rd Cong., 1st Sess., Vol. 50, pp. 1597-1599, May 16, 1913.

[102] R. M. L. to Gilbert E. Roe, Aug. 28, 1913, LFP.

[103] *World*, New York, Sept. 4, 1913.

[104] *Springfield Daily Republican*, Sept. 4, 5, 1913.

[105] *World*, New York, Sept. 5, 1913.

[106] B. C. L. to Fola, Sept. 10, 1913, LFP.

[107] *Springfield Daily Republican*, Sept. 10, 1913.

[108] *World*, New York, Sept. 10, 1913.

[109] *Record*, 63rd Cong., 1st Sess., Vol. 50, p. 4617, Sept. 9, 1913.

[110] *New York Times*, Sept. 10, 1913.

[111] *Albany Evening Journal*, Sept. 10, 1913. See also *La Follette's Magazine*, Sept. 20, 1913, pp. 9-10; Oct. 4, 1913, p. 14.

[112] *North American*, Philadelphia, Sept. 10, 1913.

[113] *Springfield Daily Republican*, Sept. 11, 1913.

[114] *Harper's Weekly*, LVIII, 3-4, Oct. 4, 1913.

Chapter XXXVII
(Pages 484–520)

[1] R. M. L. to R. M. L., Jr., Sept. 19, 1913, LFP.

[2] *Milwaukee Journal*, Oct. 24, 1913.

[3] R. M. L. to R. M. L., Jr., Oct. 24, 1913, LFP.

[4] *Idem*, Nov. 8, 1913, LFP.

[5] R. M. L. to B. C. L., Oct. 24, 1913, LFP.

[6] John J. Hannan to R. M. L., Nov. 1, 1913, LFP.

[7] *News and Observer,* Raleigh, N.C., Oct. 29, 1913; *Charlotte Daily Observer,* Nov. 1, 1913; *Atlanta Constitution,* Nov. 6, 1913; *Atlanta Journal,* Nov. 6, 1913; *Age-Herald,* Birmingham, Ala., Nov. 8, 1913.

[8] *Record,* 63rd Cong., 2nd Sess., Vol. 51, pp. 43-45, Dec. 2, 1913.

[9] *Ibid.,* 60th Cong., 1st Sess., Vol. 42, p. 3569, March 19, 1908.

[10] *La Follette's Magazine,* Dec. 13, 1913, p. 1.

[11] *Ibid.,* Sept. 27, 1913, p. 1; Dec. 13, 1913, p. 1.

[12] *Ibid.*

[13] John J. Hannan to R. M. L., Oct. 29, 1913, LFP.

[14] R. M. L. to C. H. Thompson, Feb. 9, 1914, LFP.

[15] *Record,* 63rd Cong., 2nd Sess., Vol. 51, pp. 1228-1229, Dec. 19, 1913; United States Code, Title 12, Sec. 303.

[16] *Record,* 63rd Cong., 2nd Sess., Vol. 51, pp. 1229-1230, Dec. 19, 1913.

[17] Transcript of stenographic notes of speech by R. M. L. at Des Moines, Iowa, Oct. 15, 1924, pp. 10-12, LFP.

[18] *La Follette's Magazine,* Jan. 31, 1914, p. 1.

[19] *Record,* 63rd Cong., 2nd Sess., Vol. 51, pp. 1962-1964, Jan. 20, 1914.

[20] *Milwaukee Journal,* Jan. 2, 1914.

[21] *North American,* Philadelphia, Jan. 15, 1914.

[22] R. M. L. to Rudolph Spreckels, Feb. 16, 1914, LFP.

[23] B. C. L. to R. M. L., Jr., Feb. 20, 1914, LFP.

[24] *New York Times,* Feb. 19, 1914.

[25] *Newark Evening News,* Feb. 3, 1914.

[26] Winthrop M. Daniels to Woodrow Wilson, Feb. 3, 1914, Wilson Papers.

[27] Woodrow Wilson to Winthrop M. Daniels, Feb. 6, 1914, Wilson Papers.

[28] Edward W. Bemis to R. M. L., March 5, 1914, LFP.

[29] R. M. L. to Rudolph Spreckels, Feb. 16, 1914, LFP.

[30] *Newark Evening News,* April 3, 4, 1914.

[31] *La Follette's Magazine,* April 18, 1914, p. 1.

[32] *Record,* 63rd Cong., 2nd Sess., Vol. 51, p. 6180, April 3, 1914.

[33] *Newark Evening News,* April 4, 1914.

[34] *New York Times,* April 4, 1914.

[35] Joseph L. Bristow to author, 1938, LFP.

[36] *La Follette's Magazine,* April 18, 1914, p. 1.

[37] *Ray Stannard Baker,* Notebook I, entry, Jan. 6, 1914, pp. 81-85, Baker Papers; *La Follette's Magazine,* Aug. 23, pp. 6-7; Aug. 30, p. 6; Sept. 13, p. 6; Dec. 13, p. 6, 1913; Jan. 24, pp. 6-7; Feb. 14, p. 6, 1914.

[38] *La Follette's Magazine,* May 9, 23, 30, June 6, 1914.

[39] R. M. L. to B. C. L., April 9, 1914, LFP.

[40] Fola to R. M. L., April 13, 1914, LFP.

[41] B. C. L. to R. M. L., April 10, 1914, LFP.

[42] R. M. L. to B. C. L., April 9, 1914, LFP.

[43] *Idem,* April 16, 1914, LFP.

[44] *Idem.*

[45] R. M. L. to B. C. L., April 9, 1914, LFP.

[46] *Idem,* April 24, 1914, LFP.

[47] Edward W. Bemis to R. M. L., March 6, 1914, LFP.

[48] *La Follette's Magazine*, April 4, 1914, p. 2.

[49] *Record*, 63rd Cong., 2nd Sess., Vol. 51, p. 5275, March 23, 1914.

[50] *Ibid.*, pp. 7305, 7356, April 27, 28, 1914.

[51] *Ibid.*, pp. 7727-8093, May 5, 1914; *La Follette's Magazine*, May 16, 1914, pp. 1-2; *North American*, Philadelphia, May 6, 1914.

[52] *North American*, Philadelphia, May 7, 1914.

[53] Charles F. Amidon to R. M. L., April 11, 1914, LFP.

[54] *La Follette's Magazine*, March 29, 1913, p. 1.

[55] *Ibid.*, Aug. 16, 1913, p. 1.

[56] Ray Stannard Baker, *Woodrow Wilson*, IV, 274.

[57] *La Follette's Magazine*, Sept. 6, 1913, p. 6.

[58] *Record*, 63rd Cong., 2nd Sess., Vol. 51, p. 6925, April 20, 1914.

[59] Phil to B. C. L., April 24, 1914, LFP.

[60] *Record*, 63rd Cong., 2nd Sess., Vol. 51, pp. 7007-7008, April 21, 1914.

[61] *La Follette's Magazine*, May 2, 1914, p. 1.

[62] R. M. L. to B. C. L., April 24, 1914, LFP.

[63] Elizabeth G. Evans to B. C. L., May 18, 1914, LFP.

[64] B. C. L. to Elizabeth G. Evans, May 22, 1914, LFP.

[65] *Idem* to R. M. L., Jr., May 16, 1914, LFP.

[66] R. M. L. to Fola, July, 1914, LFP.

[67] *Idem* to B. C. L., Aug. 22, 1914, LFP.

[68] *La Follette's Magazine*, Sept. 19, 1914, p. 6.

[69] R. M. L. to B. C. L., Aug. 26, 1914, LFP.

[70] Letters in LFP; Fola La Follette, "Suffragetting on the Chautauqua Circuit," *Ladies' Home Journal*, Jan., 1916.

[71] R. M. L. to Fola, July 31, 1914, LFP.

[72] *Idem* to B. C. L., Aug. 2, 1914, LFP.

[73] *Idem*, July 31, 1914, LFP.

[74] *Idem*.

[75] R. M. L. to Seth Richardson, July 22, 1914, LFP.

[76] *La Follette's Magazine*, Oct. 24, 1914, p. 4.

[77] *Ibid.*, July 4, 1914, p. 1.

[78] R. M. L., Jr., to B. C. L., July 31, 1914, LFP.

[79] R. M. L. to B. C. L., Aug. 2, 1914, LFP.

[80] *Idem* to Phil, Aug. 4, 1914, LFP.

[81] B. C. L. to R. M. L., Aug. 8, 1914, LFP.

[82] Ray Stannard Baker, *Woodrow Wilson*, V, 18. See also *New York Times*, Aug. 19, 1914.

[83] *La Follette's Magazine*, Aug. 29, 1914, p. 2.

[84] Ray Stannard Baker, *Woodrow Wilson*, VII, 77.

[85] *La Follette's Magazine*, June 20, 27, July 4, Aug. 8, 1914.

[86] *Ibid.*, Oct. 3, 1914, pp. 1-2.

[87] *Ibid.*, June 20, July 18, Sept. 26, Oct. 3, 24, 31, 1914.

[88] R. M. L. to Francis J. Heney, Sept. 28, 1914, LFP.

[89] *La Follette's Magazine*, Oct. 24, 1914, p. 6.

[90] R. M. L. to Jerre C. Murphy, May 11, 1914, LFP.

[91] *La Follette's Magazine*, Nov., 1914, p. 2; Jan. 18, June 21, 1913.

[92] *Ibid.*, Aug. 29, 1914, p. 1.

[93] *Ibid.*, Sept. 19, Oct. 10, 17, 24, 1914.

[94] B. C. L. to Elizabeth G. Evans, Sept. 5, 1914, LFP.

[95] R. M. L. to Alfred T. Rogers, Sept. 10, 1914, LFP. See also Gilbert E. Roe to Rudolph Spreckels, Sept. 16, 1914, LFP.

[96] R. M. L. to Alfred T. Rogers, Sept. 4, 1914, LFP.

[97] *Idem*, Sept. 10, 1914, LFP. See also B. C. L. to Elizabeth G. Evans, Sept. 23, 1914, LFP.

[98] B. C. L. to R. M. L., Jr., Sept. 22, 1914, LFP.

[99] Gilbert E. Roe to R. M. L., Sept. 16, 1914, LFP.

[100] R. M. L. to Gilbert E. Roe, Sept. 17, 1914, LFP.

[101] B. C. L. to Elizabeth G. Evans, Sept. 23, 1914, LFP.

[102] R. M. L. to Richard Lloyd Jones, Oct. 3, 1914, in *La Follette's Magazine*, Oct. 10, 1914, p. 3.

[103] *Idem* to Elizabeth G. Evans, June 5, 1914, LFP; *idem* to Gilbert E. Roe, Feb. 19, 28, 1914, LFP.

[104] Louis D. Brandeis to Gilbert E. Roe, Sept. 18, 1914, LFP; Rudolph Spreckels to Gilbert E. Roe, Aug. 10, Sept. 23, 1914, LFP; B. C. L. to Elizabeth G. Evans, Sept. 23, 1914, LFP.

[105] Gilbert E. Roe to Rudolph Spreckels, Aug. 6, 1914, LFP.

[106] B. C. L. to Elizabeth G. Evans, Sept. 23, 24, 1914, LFP.

[107] *New York Times*, Nov. 2, 1914.

[108] R. M. L. to B. C. L., Nov. 1, 1914, LFP.

[109] *La Follette's Magazine*, December, 1914, p. 2; February, 1915, p. 28.

[110] Gilbert E. Roe to R. M. L., Nov. 9, 10, 1914, LFP.

[111] *Milwaukee Journal*, Nov. 4, 1914.

[112] *New York Times*, Nov. 25, 1914.

[113] Francis E. McGovern to Theodore Roosevelt, Nov. 19, 1914, TR Papers.

[114] B. C. L. to R. M. L., Jr., Nov. 5, 1914, LFP.

[115] *Idem* to Elizabeth G. Evans, Nov. 5, 1914, LFP.

[116] R. M. L. to R. M. L., Jr., Nov. 7, 1914, LFP.

[117] *Idem*, Nov. 18, 1914, LFP.

[118] R. M. L., Jr., to R. M. L. and B. C. L., undated, LFP.

[119] *Record*, 63rd Cong., 3rd Sess., Vol. 52, pp. 20-21, Dec. 8, 1914.

[120] *La Follette's Magazine*, Jan., 1915, p. 10.

[121] B. C. L. to R. M. L., Jr., Dec. 9, 1914, LFP.

[122] *La Follette's Magazine*, Oct. 31, 1914, p. 1-2.

[123] R. M. L. to Guy and Fred La Follette and Maude La Follette, Jan. 13, 1915, LFP.

[124] Edward M. House to Woodrow Wilson, Jan. 5, 1915, Wilson Papers.

[125] R. M. L. to Gilbert E. Roe, Jan. 12, 1915, LFP.

[126] Charles Seymour, *The Intimate Papers of Colonel House* (Boston, Houghton Mifflin Company, 1926-1930), I, 350.

[127] B. C. L. to R. M. L., Jr., Feb. 23, 1915, LFP.

[128] *New York Times*, Feb. 27, 1915.

[129] R. M. L. to Rudolph Spreckels, Jan. 7, 1915, LFP.

[130] *Idem* to R. M. L., Jr., Jan. 26, 1915, LFP.

[131] *La Follette's Magazine*, Feb. 1915, pp. 1-2.

[132] *Record*, 63rd Cong., 3rd Sess., Vol. 52, p. 2851, Feb. 2, 1915.

[133] *New York Times*, Feb. 3, 1915.

[134] B. C. L. to R. M. L., Jr., Feb. 3, 1915, LFP.

[135] *Record*, 63rd Cong., 3rd Sess., Vol. 52, p. 3254, Feb. 8, 1915.

[136] *Ibid.*, p. 3230, Feb. 8, 1915.

[137] Gilbert E. Roe to R. M. L., Feb. 9, 1915, LFP.

[138] *Sun*, New York, Feb. 9, 1915.

[139] *Sun*, Baltimore, Feb. 10, 1915.

[140] Feb. 9, 1915.

[141] *Record*, 63rd Cong., 3rd Sess., Vol. 52, pp. 3631-3634, Feb. 12, 1915.

[142] Belle Case La Follette, article in *La Follette's Magazine*, October, 1920, pp. 154-155, 157.

[143] Robert M. La Follette, "My Own Story," *Washington Daily News*, Sept. 18, 1924.

Chapter XXXVIII

(Pages 521–536)

[1] *La Follette's Magazine*, April, 1915, p. 2. See also Survey, May 1, 1915, pp. 116-117, 125-128; and *A Symposium on Andrew Furuseth*, collected by Silas Blake Axtell (New Bedford, Mass., The Darwin Press, 1949).

[2] *A Short History of the International Seaman's Union* (Law Department, I.S.U., 1934); *La Follette's Magazine*, April, 1915, p. 2.

[3] *La Follette's Magazine*, April, 1915, p. 2.

[4] *Ibid.*

[5] Paul S. Taylor, *The Sailors' Union on the Pacific* (New York, The Roland Press, 1923), p. 110.

[6] *Record*, 61st Cong., 2nd Sess., Vol. 45, p. 1479, Feb. 4, 1910; *ibid.*, 62nd Cong., 1st Sess., Vol. 47, p. 121, April 10, 1911.

[7] *La Follette's Magazine*, March, 1915, p. 1.

[8] *Record*, 62nd Cong., 2nd Sess., Vol. 48, p. 10172, Aug. 3, 1912.

[9] *Ibid.*, 63rd Cong., 3rd Sess., Vol. 49, pp. 4409-4410, March 1, 1913.

[10] *Ibid.*, pp. 4581-4588, March 2, 1913; *La Follette's Magazine*, March 29, 1913, pp. 4, 14-15.

[11] *La Follette's Magazine*, Oct. 18, 1913, p. 3.

[12] *Record*, 63rd Cong., 1st Sess., Vol. 50, p. 51, April 7, 1913.

[13] Andrew Furuseth to Woodrow Wilson, June 26, 1913, Wilson Papers; *La Follette's Magazine*, Oct. 25, 1913, p. 4.

[14] Woodrow Wilson to Andrew Furuseth, June 30, 1913, Wilson Papers.

[15] *Record*, 63rd Cong., 1st Sess., Vol. 50, p. 5298, Oct. 2, 1913.

[16] *La Follette's Magazine*, Oct. 18, 1913, p. 3.

[17] Woodrow Wilson to William C. Redfield, Oct. 20, 1913, Wilson Papers; William C. Redfield to Woodrow Wilson, Oct. 17, 1913, Wilson Papers.

[18] R. M. L. to Rudolph Spreckels, Oct. 12, 1913, LFP.

[19] *Record*, 63rd Cong., 1st Sess., Vol. 50, p. 5495, Oct. 7, 1913.

[20] R. M. L. to R. M. L., Jr., Oct. 7, 1913, LFP.

[21] *Idem* to Rudolph Spreckels, Oct. 12, 1913, LFP. See also *Record*, 63rd Cong., 1st Sess., Vol. 50, pp. 5516-5518, Oct. 9, 1913.

[22] B. C. L. to R. M. L., Jr., Oct. 14, 1913, LFP.

[23] *Record*, 63rd Cong., 1st Sess., Vol. 50, p. 5720, Oct. 21, 1913. See also *American Federationist*, Vol. 20, pp. 1036-1039, October, 1913.

[24] *Record*, 63rd Cong., 1st Sess., Vol. 50, p. 5667, Oct. 16, 1913.

[25] *Ibid.*, p. 5675, Oct. 16, 1913.

[26] Andrew Furuseth to Woodrow Wilson, June 26, 1913, Wilson Papers.

[27] *Record*, 63rd Cong., 1st Sess., Vol. 50, pp. 5712-5714, Oct. 21, 1913. See also *La Follette's Magazine*, Nov. 1, 1913, pp. 1, 3.

[28] *Record*, 63rd Cong., 1st Sess., Vol. 50, p. 5712, Oct. 21, 1913. See also *New York Times*, Oct. 22, 1913; *La Follette's Magazine*, Nov. 1, 1913, pp. 4, 11; R. M. L. to B. C. L., Oct. 22, 1913, LFP.

[29] *Record*, 63rd Cong., 1st Sess., Vol. 50, pp. 5715-5720, Oct. 21, 1913.

[30] R. M. L. to B. C. L. [Oct. 24, 1913], LFP.

[31] *Record*, 63rd Cong., 1st Sess., Vol. 50, pp. 5764, 5770-5772, Oct. 23, 1913.

[32] *Cleveland Plain Dealer*, Oct. 24, 1913.

[33] *Record*, 63rd Cong., 1st Sess., Vol. 50, pp. 5777, 5781, Oct. 23, 1913.

[34] R. M. L. to B. C. L. [Oct. 24, 1913], LFP; *idem* to R. M. L., Jr., Oct. 24, 1913, LFP.

[35] *Record*, 63rd Cong., 1st Sess., Vol. 50, pp. 5777-5792, Oct. 23, 1913.

[36] R. M. L. to B. C. L. [Oct. 24, 1913], LFP.

[37] Andrew Furuseth to R. M. L., Oct. 25, 1913, LFP.

[38] R. M. L. to R. M. L., Jr., Oct. 24, 1913, LFP.

[39] *Idem.*

[40] *La Follette's Magazine*, Nov. 1, 1913, March 28, 1914.

[41] *Ibid.*, Jan. 3, 10, 31, Feb. 7, 14, 21, 28, March 7, 1914.

[42] *Record*, 63rd Cong., 2nd Sess., Vol. 51, pp. 43-45, Dec. 2, 1913.

[43] *La Follette's Magazine*, March 28, 1914, p. 3.

[44] Andrew Furuseth to Woodrow Wilson, Dec. 22, 1913, Wilson Papers; *idem*, Jan. 12, 1914, Wilson Papers.

[45] Senate Document (6594), Vol. 27, Nos. 463, 476.

[46] *La Follette's Magazine*, March 28, 1914, p. 3.

[47] R. M. L. to B. C. L., July 31, Aug. 26, 1914, LFP.

[48] *Record*, 63rd Cong., 2nd Sess., Vol. 50, pp. 14341-14362, Aug. 27, 1914.

[49] *La Follette's Magazine*, January, 1915, pp. 2-3.

[50] *New York Times*, Dec. 16, 17, 1914; *Document Catalogue*, 12, 63rd Congress, 1913-1915, p. 1718; *American Journal of International Law*, 1919, Vol. 13, pp. 3-5.

[51] *Record*, 63rd Cong., 3rd Sess., Vol. 52, pp. 4560-4568, Feb. 25, 1915.

[52] B. C. L. to R. M. L., Jr., Feb. 23, 1915, LFP.

[53] *Record*, 63rd Cong., 3rd Sess., Vol. 52, p. 4654, Feb. 25, 1915.

[54] *Ibid.*, p. 4808, Feb. 27, 1915.

⁵⁵ *Ibid.*, p. 4817, Feb. 27, 1915; *New York Times*, Feb. 28, 1915; *La Follette's Magazine*, April, 1915, p. 24.

⁵⁶ Woodrow Wilson to Newton D. Baker, March 5, 1915, Wilson Papers.

⁵⁷ White House memorandum for the President, Feb. 27, 1915, with notation in manuscript of Woodrow Wilson, Wilson Papers.

⁵⁸ Andrew Furuseth to Woodrow Wilson, March 1, 1915, Wilson Papers; Woodrow Wilson to Andrew Furuseth, March 2, 1915, Wilson Papers.

⁵⁹ Robert M. La Follette, "My Own Story," *Washington Daily News*, Sept. 18, 1924.

⁶⁰ William J. Bryan to Woodrow Wilson, March 2, 1915, with enclosure from Robert Lansing to William J. Bryan, March 2, 1915, Wilson Papers.

⁶¹ Typescript of stenographic record of conversation between Gilbert E. Roe and Andrew Furuseth, Oct. 2, 1929, LFP.

⁶² R. M. L. to Woodrow Wilson, March 3, 1915, LFP.

⁶³ Robert M. La Follette, *loc. cit.*; also Joseph P. Tumulty to author and George Middleton.

⁶⁴ Robert M. La Follette, *loc. cit.*

⁶⁵ B. C. L. to R. M. L., Jr., March 4, 1915, LFP.

Chapter XXXIX

(Pages 539–552)

¹ William J. Bryan to R. M. L., April 17, 1915, LFP.

² *Idem* to Woodrow Wilson, Feb. 15, 1915, William J. Bryan Papers, Library of Congress (hereafter cited as Bryan Papers).

³ *Foreign Relations*, Supplement, 1915, pp. 96-97.

⁴ Charles Seymour, *The Intimate Papers of Colonel House*, I, 361.

⁵ *Foreign Relations*, Supplement, 1915, pp. 100-101.

⁶ *Ibid.*, pp. 98-100.

⁷ *Record*, 63rd Cong., 3rd Sess., Vol. 52, p. 3632, Feb. 12, 1915.

⁸ *Foreign Relations*, Supplement, 1915, pp. 119-120.

⁹ *Ibid.*, pp. 129-130.

¹⁰ *Ibid.*, pp. 140-143.

¹¹ Woodrow Wilson to William J. Bryan, April 22, 1915, *Foreign Relations, The Lansing Papers* (Washington, D.C., United States Government Printing Office, Vols. I-II, 1939-1940), I, 377-378 (hereafter cited as *The Lansing Papers*).

¹² William J. Bryan to Woodrow Wilson, April 23, 1915, *ibid.*, I, 378-380.

¹³ Mary Baird Bryan, *The Memoirs of William Jennings Bryan* (Chicago, The John C. Winston Company, 1925), p. 420.

¹⁴ Woodrow Wilson to William J. Bryan, April 28, 1915, *The Lansing Papers*, I, 380; William J. Bryan to Woodrow Wilson, May 5, 1915, Wilson Papers; *idem*, May 12, 1915, *The Lansing Papers*, I, 392-394; Mary Baird Bryan, *op. cit.*, pp. 398-428.

¹⁵ *Sun*, New York, May 1, 1915. A clipping containing this advertisement

in the New York *Sun* was enclosed with a Lansing memorandum sent to the President by Bryan with his own letter of May 1 to the President.

[16] *Foreign Relations*, Supplement, 1915, pp. 378, 381, 397, 419, *et seq.*

[17] Ray Stannard Baker, *Woodrow Wilson*, V, 324-325.

[18] Report of Secretary of State Hughes, March 31, 1922, Senate Document 176, 67th Cong., 2nd Sess., p. 2.

[19] *New York Times*, May 9, 1915.

[20] *Ibid.*, May 12, 1915.

[21] *Milwaukee Journal*, May 10, 1915.

[22] *New York Times*, May 8, 1915.

[23] Burton J. Hendrick, *The Life and Letters of Walter H. Page* (Garden City, N.Y., Doubleday, Page and Company, Vols. I-III, 1922-1926), II, 2.

[24] Seymour, *op. cit.*, I, 434.

[25] Hendrick, *op. cit.*, II, 5.

[26] *Foreign Relations*, Supplement, 1915, p. 385.

[27] *The Public Papers of Woodrow Wilson*, ed. Ray Stannard Baker and W. E. Dodd (New York, Harper & Brothers, 1926), III, 321.

[28] *New York Times*, May 12, 1915; *Evening Star*, Washington, D.C., May 11, 1915; *Chicago Herald*, May 12, 1915.

[29] *Nashville Tennessean* and *Nashville American*, May 30, 1915.

[30] *Foreign Relations*, Supplement, 1915, pp. 393-396.

[31] William J. Bryan to Woodrow Wilson [May 12, 1915], *The Lansing Papers*, I, 392-393.

[32] *Foreign Relations*, Supplement, 1915, pp. 419-421 (note of May 28-29, received in Washington May 31, 1:30 A.M.)

[33] Ray Stannard Baker, *Woodrow Wilson*, V, 350-352.

[34] William J. Bryan to Woodrow Wilson, June 3, 1915, Wilson Papers.

[35] *Idem*, June 5, 1915, Wilson Papers.

[36] Ray Stannard Baker, *Woodrow Wilson*, V, 357-358.

[37] *Nashville Tennessean* and *Nashville American*, June 11, 1915.

[38] B. C. L. to R. M. L., June 10, 11, 1915, LFP.

[39] R. M. L. to B. C. L., June 4, 1915, LFP.

[40] *Idem* to R. M. L., Jr., June 29, 1915, LFP.

[41] *Idem* to B. C. L., June 18, 1915, LFP.

[42] *Idem*, June 13 and June 18, 1915, LFP.

[43] B. C. L. to R. M. L., July 8, 1915, LFP.

[44] *Atlanta Journal*, July 1, 1915. See also the *Constitution*, Atlanta, July 2, 1915.

[45] B. C. L. to "Dear Ones," July 12, 1915, LFP.

[46] R. M. L. to B. C. L., R. M. L., Jr., and Phil, July 25, 1915, LFP.

[47] *Idem*, Aug. 20, 1915, LFP.

[48] *La Follette's Magazine*, August, 1915, p. 1. See also *ibid.*, October, 1915, pp. 6-7, for article by V. A. Olander, secretary, the Lake Seamen's Union.

[49] *New York Times Magazine*, July 15, 1934, p. 15, article by Zona Gale.

[50] R. M. L. to B. C. L. and R. M. L., Jr., Nov. 12, 1915, LFP.

[51] *Idem*, Oct. 15, 1915, LFP.

[52] *Idem*, Oct. 24, 1915, LFP.

[53] Susan Miller Quackenbush to B. C. L., Jan. 8 [9], 1916, LFP.

[54] *Foreign Relations*, Supplement, 1914, p. 580. See also Ray Stannard Baker, *Woodrow Wilson*, V, 175-176.

[55] *The Public Papers of Woodrow Wilson*, III, 157-159.

[56] *La Follette's Magazine*, September, 1915, p. 1.

[57] *Foreign Relations*, Supplement, 1915, pp. 530-531.

[58] *New York Times*, Dec. 3, 4, 1915.

[59] *Record*, 64th Cong., 1st Sess., Vol. 53, pp. 95-100, Dec. 7, 1915.

[60] William J. Stone to Woodrow Wilson, Dec. 13, 1915, Wilson Papers.

[61] *St. Paul Pioneer Press*, Dec. 10, 1915; *Minneapolis Journal*, Dec. 10, 1915.

[62] *La Follette's Magazine*, January, 1916, p. 1.

[63] R. M. L. to B. C. L., Jan. 13, 1916; B. C. L. to Fola, Jan. 15, 1916, LFP.

[64] Joseph P. Tumulty, *Woodrow Wilson As I Know Him* (New York, Doubleday, Page & Company, 1921), p. 242.

[65] *The Lansing Papers*, I, 523-525.

[66] *The Public Papers of Woodrow Wilson*, IV, 42, 44.

[67] In his actual address Wilson used this phrase. As printed in *The Public Papers of Woodrow Wilson*, IV, 114, the phrasing is, "incomparably the most adequate navy in the world." See explanatory footnote in Ray Stannard Baker, *Woodrow Wilson*, VI, 29.

[68] *Record*, 64th Cong., 1st Sess., Vol. 53, p. 1612, Jan. 27, 1916.

[69] *Ibid.*, p. 1619, Jan. 27, 1916.

Chapter XL

(Pages 553–569)

[1] R. M. L. to William Ellery Leonard, April 24, 1916, LFP.

[2] *Record*, 64th Cong., 1st Sess., Vol. 53, p. 495, Jan. 5, 1916; Ray Stannard Baker, *Woodrow Wilson*, VI, 157.

[3] *Foreign Relations*, Supplement, 1916, pp. 163-166.

[4] *Wisconsin State Journal*, Feb. 11, 1916. See also *Washington Post*, Feb. 14, 1916.

[5] *Foreign Relations*, Supplement, 1916, p. 170, circular telegram sent to diplomatic officers in European countries on February 16.

[6] William Allen White, *Woodrow Wilson* (Boston, Houghton Mifflin Company, 1924), p. 290, memorandum prepared by Ida M. Tarbell.

[7] *Record*, 64th Cong., 1st Sess., Vol. 53, p. 2756, Feb. 17, 1916.

[8] *Ibid.*, p. 2958, Feb. 22, 1916; *New York Times*, Feb. 26, 1916.

[9] Joseph P. Tumulty, *Woodrow Wilson As I Know Him*, pp. 203-206.

[10] William J. Stone to Woodrow Wilson, Feb. 24, 1916, Wilson Papers.

[11] *New York Times*, Feb. 24, 1916; *Evening Post*, New York, Feb. 24, 1916.

[12] *New York Times*, Feb. 26, 1916.

[13] Alex Mathews Arnett, *Claude Kitchin and the Wilson War Policies* (Boston, Little, Brown and Company, 1937), p. 160.

[14] *New York Times,* Feb. 25, 1916.

[15] Irvine L. Lenroot to author, March 27, 1939, LFP.

[16] *New York Times,* March 1, 1916.

[17] *The Public Papers of Woodrow Wilson,* IV, 129.

[18] *New York Times,* March 1, 1916.

[19] *Wisconsin State Journal,* March 1, 1916.

[20] *Chicago Herald,* March 1, 1916, Washington dispatch by John Callan O'Laughlin.

[21] *Record,* 64th Cong., 1st Sess., Vol. 53, pp. 3458-3459, March 3, 1916.

[22] *Ibid.,* pp. 3463-3465, March 3, 1916.

[23] *Ibid.,* pp. 3485-3486, March 3, 1916; George W. Norris to Charles Skalla, May 4, 1916; George W. Norris to A. F. Buechler, May 1, 1916, Norris Papers.

[24] *New York Times,* March 7, 1916.

[25] *La Follette's Magazine,* March, 1916, p. 1.

[26] *Record,* 64th Cong., 1st Sess., Vol. 53, p. 3760, March 8, 1916.

[27] B. C. L. to "Dear Ones," March 13, 1916, LFP.

[28] *Record,* 64th Cong., 1st Sess., Vol. 53, p. 3886, March 10, 1916.

[29] Woodrow Wilson, *Constitutional Government in the United States* (New York, The Columbia University Press, 1911), pp. 77-78.

[30] *Record,* 64th Cong., 1st Sess., Vol. 53, pp. 3887-3889, March 10, 1914.

[31] *Ibid.,* p. 3890, March 10, 1916. See also *La Follette's Magazine,* March, 1916, p. 1.

[32] B. C. L. to "Dear Ones," March 13, 1916, LFP.

[33] *Wisconsin State Journal,* March 10, 1916.

[34] Public statement by President Wilson, March 13, 1916, in *Foreign Relations,* 1916, p. 489.

[35] *For. Rel.,* 1916, pp. 684-685, 689.

[36] R. M. L. to Gilbert E. Roe, March 13, 1916, LFP.

[37] *Idem,* March 16, 1916, LFP.

[38] Ray Stannard Baker Collection C, Wilson Papers.

[39] *Foreign Relations,* 1916, pp. 480-490.

[40] *Record,* 64th Cong., 1st Sess., Vol. 53, p. 4274, March 17, 1916.

[41] *Wisconsin State Journal,* Feb. 23, 1916.

[42] R. M. L. to B. C. L., R. M. L., Jr., and Mary, March 28, 1916, LFP.

[43] *Idem* to B. C. L., April 4 and 5, 1916, LFP.

[44] *New York Times, Washington Times, Washington Post,* April 5, 1916; *Chicago Daily Tribune,* April 6, 1916.

[45] April 6, 1916.

[46] B. C. L. to Elizabeth Evans, April 7, 1916, LFP.

[47] *Wisconsin State Journal,* April 11, 1916; *La Follette's Magazine,* April, 1916, p. 10.

[48] April 16, 1916, part 5, p. 1. See also *Literary Digest,* Vol. 52, p. 1332, May 6, 1916.

[49] Ray Stannard Baker, *Woodrow Wilson,* VI, 178, footnote, states that

"the President believed during the crisis, and indeed until February 1917, that American lives had been lost."

[50] *Foreign Relations,* Supplement, 1916, pp. 227-229.

[51] Ray Stannard Baker, *Woodrow Wilson,* VI, 185.

[52] Baker, diary entry for April 15, 1916.

[53] *Foreign Relations,* Supplement, 1916, pp. 232-234.

[54] *Record,* 64th Cong., 1st Sess., Vol. 53, pp. 6421-6422, April 19, 1916.

[55] *New York Times, Washington Post, World,* New York, April 20, 1916.

[56] *Washington Post,* April 20, 1916.

[57] *La Follette's Magazine,* May, 1916, p. 1.

[58] *Record,* 64th Cong., 1st Sess., Vol. 53, p. 7018, April 29, 1916, S. 5796 introduced; Stone's motion entered p. 7311, May 3, 1916; Stone's motion debated pp. 7451-7456, May 5, 1916.

[59] *Foreign Relations,* Supplement, 1916, pp. 257-260.

[60] *Ibid.,* p. 263.

[61] *For. Rel.,* 1916, pp. 689-690.

[62] *The Autobiography of Lincoln Steffens* (New York, Harcourt, Brace & Company, 1931), II, 736.

[63] *Letters of Lincoln Steffens* (New York, Harcourt, Brace & Company, 1938), I, 371-372.

[64] *La Follette's Magazine,* May, 1916, p. 6.

[65] Phil to author; John J. Hannan to author, LFP.

[66] R. M. L. to Phil, Jan. 30, 1916, LFP.

[67] Louis D. Brandeis to author.

[68] *La Follette's Magazine,* February, 1916, pp. 1-2; April, 1916, pp. 1-2.

[69] *Ibid.,* June, 1916, p. 3.

[70] Mrs. Louis D. Brandeis to B. C. L., March 14, 1916, LFP.

[71] R. M. L. to Gilbert E. Roe, March 16, 1916, LFP.

[72] B. C. L. to Elizabeth G. Evans, April 7, 1916, LFP.

[73] *Idem* to Mrs. Louis D. Brandeis, May 31, 1916, photostat with LFP, original MS letter with Brandeis Papers.

[74] Mrs. Louis D. Brandeis to author.

Chapter XLI

(Pages 570–585)

[1] Lincoln Steffens to Allen H. Suggett, April 30, 1916, *Letters of Lincoln Steffens,* I, 371.

[2] Phil to R. M. L., June 14, 1916, LFP.

[3] *La Follette's Magazine,* June, 1916, p. 3.

[4] *Chicago Herald,* June 10, 1916.

[5] Herman Hagedorn, *That Human Being, Leonard Wood* (New York, Harcourt, Brace & Company, 1920), II, 189-190. See also *Selections from the Correspondence of Theodore Roosevelt and Henry Cabot Lodge,* II,

486-489, for Roosevelt's letter, June 10, 1916, to conferees of the Progressive Party.

[6] B. C. L. to Phil, June 12, 1916, LFP.

[7] *Idem* to Elizabeth G. Evans, July 4, 1916, LFP.

[8] *The Democratic Text Book, 1916,* pp. 376-377. See also *New York Times,* June 15, 1916.

[9] *Foreign Relations,* 1916, p. 581 *et seq.*

[10] Ray Stannard Baker, *Woodrow Wilson,* VI, 76.

[11] *Record,* 64th Cong., 1st Sess., Vol. 53, p. 10193, June 29, 1916.

[12] *Ibid.,* pp. 9996-9997, June 26, 1916.

[13] B. C. L. to Phil and Mary, June 26, 1916, LFP.

[14] *The Autobiography of Lincoln Steffens,* II, 736.

[15] *Ibid.,* 736-740; B. C. L. to Phil and Mary, July 7, 1916, LFP; R. M. L., Jr., to author.

[16] B. C. L. to Phil and Mary, July 7, 1916, LFP.

[17] R. M. L. to Charles H. Crownhart, July 8, 1916, LFP.

[18] *Foreign Relations,* 1916, p. 604.

[19] Lincoln Steffens to Gilbert E. Roe, July 22, 1916, copy with LFP.

[20] Joseph P. Tumulty, *Woodrow Wilson As I Know Him,* p. 247.

[21] *Record,* 64th Cong., 1st Sess., Vol. 53, pp. 11313-11318, July 19; pp. 11323-11329, July 20, 1916.

[22] *Ibid.,* p. 11330, July 20, 1916.

[23] July 20, 1916.

[24] *Record,* 64th Cong., 1st Sess., Vol. 53, p. 11330, July 20, 1916.

[25] *Ibid.,* pp. 11334-11336, July 20, 1916.

[26] *Ibid.,* p. 11344, July 20, 1916.

[27] *Evening Post,* New York, July 20, 1916.

[28] *Record,* 64th Cong., 1st Sess., Vol. 53, pp. 11344-11345, July 20, 1916.

[29] *Ibid.,* p. 11347, July 20, 1916.

[30] *Ibid.,* p. 11350, July 20, 1916.

[31] Lincoln Steffens to Gilbert E. Roe, July 22, 1916, copy with LFP.

[32] B. C. L. to Mary, Friday, July 26 [July 28], 1916, LFP.

[33] Charles H. Crownhart to John J. Hannan, May 8, 1916, LFP.

[34] R. M. L. to Charles H. Crownhart, May 2, May 12, 1916, LFP; *idem* to Alfred T. Rogers, May 13, 1916, LFP; Alfred T. Rogers to R. M. L., June 26, 1916, LFP; *Wisconsin State Journal,* June 23, 1916.

[35] *Milwaukee Sentinel,* July 13, 1916.

[36] *Wisconsin State Journal,* Aug. 17, Oct. 22, 1916.

[37] *La Follette's Magazine,* August, 1916, p. 2.

[38] July 19, 1916. See also *La Follette's Magazine,* August, 1916, p. 4.

[39] Charles H. Crownhart to John J. Hannan, Aug. 21, 1916, LFP. See also *Wisconsin State Journal,* Aug. 20, 1916, Bristow letter; Aug. 23, Borah letter; Nov. 6, Heney letter.

[40] *La Follette's Magazine,* July 19, 1913, p. 3.

[41] *Record,* 64th Cong., 1st Sess., Vol. 53, p. 13655, Sept. 2, 1916.

[42] *La Follette's Magazine,* September, 1916, p. 3.

[43] *Milwaukee Journal,* Aug. 19, 1916.

[44] *Wisconsin State Journal,* Oct. 7, 1916.

[45] *Ibid.,* Nov. 5, 1916.

[46] *Milwaukee Journal,* Oct. 4, 1916.

[47] *Ibid.,* Oct. 12, 1916.

[48] R. M. L., Jr., to author.

[49] *Milwaukee Journal,* Oct. 25, 1916.

[50] *Ibid.,* Oct. 31, 1916.

[51] *Sunday Journal,* Nov. 5, 1916.

[52] John J. Hannan to Elizabeth G. Evans, Charles R. Crane, Louis D. Brandeis, William Kent, Rudolph Spreckels, Nov. 10, 1916, LFP.

[53] Nov. 13, 1916.

[54] Stephen Gwyn, ed., *The Letters and Friendships of Sir Cecil Spring-Rice* (London, Constable & Company, 1929), II, 354.

[55] *La Follette's Magazine,* November, 1916, p. 1.

Chapter XLII

(Pages 586–602)

[1] R. M. L. to B. C. L., R. M. L., Jr., Phil, and Mary, Dec. 5, 1916, LFP.

[2] *Idem,* Dec. 10, 1916, LFP.

[3] *Idem,* Dec. 12, 1916, LFP.

[4] *Record,* 64th Cong., 2nd Sess., Vol. 54, p. 257, Dec. 13, 1916.

[5] R. M. L. to B. C. L., R. M. L., Jr., Phil, and Mary, Dec. 15, 1916, LFP.

[6] *Foreign Relations,* Supplement, 1916, pp. 94-95.

[7] *Ibid.,* pp. 97-99.

[8] *Record,* 63rd Cong., 3rd Sess., Vol. 52, pp. 3230, 3621-3633, Feb. 8, 1915.

[9] *Ibid.,* 64th Cong., 2nd Sess., Vol. 54, p. 897, Jan. 5, 1917.

[10] *Foreign Relations,* Supplement, 1916, pp. 117-118.

[11] *Ibid.,* 1917, pp. 5-9.

[12] R. M. L. to B. C. L., Phil, and Mary, Jan. 21, 1917, LFP.

[13] *Idem* to B. C. L., R. M. L., Jr., Phil, and Mary, Jan. 22, 1917, LFP. See also *Record,* 64th Cong., 2nd Sess., Vol. 54, pp. 1755-1756, Jan. 22, 1917.

[14] Julia Lathrop to B. C. L., Nov. 6, 1930, LFP.

[15] *Record,* 64th Cong., 2nd Sess., Vol. 54, pp. 1741-1743, Jan. 22, 1917.

[16] Jan. 23, 1917.

[17] *Record,* 64th Cong., 2nd Sess., Vol. 54, p. 1743, Jan. 22, 1917.

[18] Jan. 23, 1917.

[19] Grey of Fallodon, *Twenty-Five Years* (Boston, Houghton Mifflin Company, 1926), II, 126-127.

[20] Charles Seymour, *The Intimate Papers of Colonel House,* II, 200-201; Ray Stannard Baker, *Woodrow Wilson,* VI, 152-153.

[21] *Foreign Relations,* Supplement I, 1917, pp. 33-34; Ambassador Sharp to the Secretary of State, Jan. 27, 1917.

[22] *New York Times,* Jan. 27, 1917.

[23] R. M. L. to B. C. L., R. M. L., Jr., Phil, and Mary, Jan. 31, 1917, LFP.

[24] *Foreign Relations,* 1917, Supp. I, Part II, pp. 97-102.

[25] R. M. L. to B. C. L., R. M. L., Jr., Phil, and Mary, Feb. 2, 1917, LFP.

[26] *Idem,* Feb. 3, 1917, LFP.

[27] Ray Stannard Baker, *Woodrow Wilson,* VI, 458, 452.

[28] *Ibid.,* VI, 458.

[29] R. M. L. to B. C. L., R. M. L., Jr., Phil, and Mary, Feb. 3, 1917, LFP.

[30] William J. Bryan to Mary B. Bryan, Saturday night 3 [Feb. 3, 1917], Bryan Papers.

[31] R. M. L. to B. C. L., R. M. L., Jr., Phil, and Mary, Feb. 3, 1917, LFP.

[32] *Idem,* Feb. 4, 1917, LFP.

[33] William J. Bryan to Mary B. Bryan, Saturday night 3 [Feb. 3, 1917], Bryan Papers.

[34] R. M. L. to B. C. L., R. M. L., Jr., Phil, and Mary, Feb. 6, 1917, LFP.

[35] *Idem.*

[36] *Record,* 64th Cong., 2nd Sess., Vol. 54, pp. 2731-2750, Feb. 7, 1917.

[37] *Ibid.,* pp. 2809-2810, Feb. 8, 1917.

[38] R. M. L. to B. C. L., R. M. L., Jr., Phil, and Mary, Feb. 7, 1917, LFP.

[39] Henry Cabot Lodge to Theodore Roosevelt, Feb. 7, 1917, *Selections from the Correspondence of Theodore Roosevelt and Henry Cabot Lodge,* II, 493-494.

[40] Theodore Roosevelt to Henry Cabot Lodge, Feb. 12, 1917, *op. cit.,* II, 494-495.

[41] *New York Times,* Feb. 2, 3, 1917.

[42] *Ibid.,* Feb. 4, 1917.

[43] Ray Stannard Baker, *Woodrow Wilson,* VI, 461.

[44] *New York Times,* Feb. 6, 8, 1917.

[45] Feb. 9, 1917.

[46] R. M. L. to B. C. L., R. M. L., Jr., Phil, and Mary, Feb. 8, 1917, LFP.

[47] *Foreign Relations,* 1917, Supplement I, p. 108.

[48] *Ibid.,* pp. 116-144; Seymour, *op. cit.,* II, 445.

[49] *Pearson's Magazine,* May, 1917, Vol. 37, No. 5, p. 455, article by R. M. La Follette, "America's War Madness," pp. 453-455.

[50] *Record,* 64th Cong., 2nd Sess., Vol. 54, p. 3064, Feb. 12, 1917; R. M. L. to B. C. L., R. M. L., Jr., Phil, and Mary, Feb. 13, 1917, LFP.

[51] R. M. L. to B. C. L., R. M. L., Jr., Phil, and Mary, Feb. 4, 1917, LFP.

[52] *Evening Post,* New York, Feb. 13, 1917, special dispatch by D. L. See also *Washington Times,* Feb. 12, 13, 1917.

[53] R. M. L. to B. C. L., R. M. L., Jr., Phil, and Mary, Feb. 15, 1917, LFP.

[54] Feb. 13, 1917.

[55] R. M. L. to B. C. L., R. M. L., Jr., Phil, and Mary, Feb. 18, 1917, LFP.

[56] *Idem,* Feb. 4, 1917, LFP.

[57] *Idem,* Feb. 15, 1917, LFP.

[58] *Idem,* Feb. 11, 1917, LFP. See also copy of letter from R. M. L. to John Bassett Moore, enclosed with letter from R. M. L. to B. C. L., R. M. L., Jr., Phil, and Mary, Feb. 13, 1917, LFP.

[59] *Washington Herald,* Feb. 14, 1917; *Washington Times,* Feb. 15, 1917.

[60] R. M. L. to B. C. L., R. M. L., Jr., Phil, and Mary, Feb. 16, 1917, LFP.

[61] Ray Stannard Baker, *Woodrow Wilson,* VI, 470-471; David F. Houston, *Eight Years with Wilson's Cabinet* (New York, Doubleday, Page & Company, 1926), I, 233-234; Franklin K. Lane, *Letters,* ed. Anne W. Lane and Louise H. Wall (Boston, Houghton Mifflin Company, 1922), pp. 234-235.

[62] Houston, *op. cit.,* I, 235-237; Lane, *op. cit.,* pp. 239-240.

[63] R. M. L. to B. C. L., R. M. L., Jr., Phil, and Mary, Feb. 17, 1917, LFP.

[64] *Washington Post,* Feb. 18, 1917; *Evening Star,* Washington, D.C., Feb. 18, 1917.

[65] R. M. L. to B. C. L., R. M. L., Jr., Phil, and Mary, Feb. 18, 1917, LFP.

[66] R. M. L., Jr., to B. C. L., Phil, and Mary, Feb. 22, 1917, LFP.

[67] *Washington Post,* Feb. 24, 1917.

[68] *Ibid.*

[69] *Record,* 64th Cong., 2nd Sess., Vol. 54, p. 4087, Feb. 24, 1917.

[70] March 1, 1917.

[71] R. M. L., Jr., to B. C. L., Phil, and Mary, Feb. 26, 1917, LFP.

[72] *Idem.*

[73] *Record,* 64th Cong., 2nd Sess., Vol. 54, p. 4273, Feb. 26, 1917.

[74] Baker, *Woodrow Wilson,* VI, 476, author's memorandum.

Chapter XLIII

(Pages 603–625)

[1] R. M. L., Jr., to B. C. L., Feb. 26, 1917, LFP.

[2] *Record,* 64th Cong., 2nd Sess., Vol. 54, p. 4400, Feb. 27, 1917.

[3] *Evening Star,* Washington, D.C., Feb. 28, 1917.

[4] *La Follette's Magazine,* March, 1917, p. 2.

[5] *Pearson's Magazine,* Vol. 37, No. 5, pp. 453-455, May, 1917.

[6] R. M. L. to B. C. L., R. M. L., Jr., Phil, and Mary, Feb. 16, 1917, LFP.

[7] Suzanne La Follette Diary entry, LFP.

[8] Suzanne La Follette to Fola, March 22, 1939, LFP.

[9] *Oregon Daily Journal,* March 3, 1917.

[10] *Record,* 64th Cong., 2nd Sess., Vol. 54, p. 4593, March 1, 1917.

[11] *Detroit News,* March 1, 1917; *Evening Post,* New York, March 2, 1917.

[12] *Record,* 64th Cong., 2nd Sess., Vol. 54, p. 4594, March 1, 1917.

[13] *Foreign Relations,* 1917, Supplement I, p. 147; *New York Times,* March 1, 1917.

[14] *Brooklyn Daily Eagle,* March 1, 1917.

[15] *Chicago Record Herald,* March 1, 1917.

[16] *Record,* 64th Cong., 2nd Sess., Vol. 54, p. 4569, March 1, 1917.

[17] *Ibid.,* p. 4598, March 1, 1917.

[18] Undated penciled note in manuscript of R. M. L., LFP.

[19] Burton J. Hendrick, *Life and Letters of Walter H. Page,* III, 336-337;

Official German Documents Relating to the World War (New York, Oxford University Press, American Branch, 1923), II, 1337, footnote.

[20] *Foreign Relations,* 1917, Supplement I, p. 147. The message was received at 8:30 p.m.

[21] Robert Lansing, *War Memoirs* (Indianapolis, Bobbs-Merrill Company, 1935), p. 228.

[22] Charles Seymour, *The Intimate Papers of Colonel House,* II, 452.

[23] Lansing, *op. cit.,* pp. 228-229.

[24] *Ibid.,* pp. 228-229.

[25] *Record,* 64th Cong., 2nd Sess., Vol. 54, p. 4692, March 1, 1917.

[26] *Selections from the Correspondence of Theodore Roosevelt and Henry Cabot Lodge,* II, 499-500; *New York Times,* March 5, 1917.

[27] *New York Times,* March 2, 3, 1917; *Milwaukee Journal,* March 1, 1917.

[28] March 3, 1917.

[29] *Record,* 64th Cong., 2nd Sess., Vol. 54, pp. 4719-4720, March 2, 1917.

[30] *Ibid.,* pp. 4632-4633, March 1, 1917.

[31] *Ibid.,* 63rd Cong., 3rd Sess., Vol. 52, p. 4016, Feb. 18, 1915.

[32] *New York Times,* March 5, 1917.

[33] *Record,* 64th Cong., 2nd Sess., Vol. 54, p. 4747, March 2, 1917.

[34] *Selections from the Correspondence of Theodore Roosevelt and Henry Cabot Lodge,* II, 499-500.

[35] *Record,* 64th Cong., 2nd Sess., Vol. 54, p. 4753, March 2, 1917.

[36] *Ibid.,* p. 4774, March 2, 1917.

[37] *Ibid.,* p. 4777, March 2, 1917.

[38] *Ibid.,* p. 4780, March 2, 1917.

[39] R. M. L., Jr., to author, July 10, 1939, LFP; John J. Hannan to author, Aug. 2, 1939, LFP.

[40] *Record,* 64th Cong., 2nd Sess., Vol. 54, p. 4781, March 2, 1917.

[41] *Commercial Tribune,* Cincinnati, March 3, 1917. Representative Louis Ludlow was Washington correspondent at this time.

[42] Ray Stannard Baker, *Woodrow Wilson,* VI, 480.

[43] George W. Norris to author, Feb. 15, 1939, LFP.

[44] B. C. L. to R. M. L., March 3, 1917, LFP.

[45] *Oregon Daily Journal,* March 3, 1917.

[46] *Record,* 64th Cong., 2nd Sess., Vol. 54, p. 4870, March 3, 1917.

[47] *La Follette's Magazine,* March, 1917, p. 2.

[48] *La Follette's Autobiography,* p. 473.

[49] *Philadelphia Public Ledger,* March 4, 1917.

[50] *Record,* 64th Cong., 2nd Sess., Vol. 54, pp. 4877-4878, March 3, 1917.

[51] *Ibid.,* p. 4890, March 3, 1917.

[52] *Ibid.,* p. 4883, March 3, 1917.

[53] *Ibid.,* p. 1743, Jan. 22, 1917.

[54] *Ibid.,* pp. 4892-4893, March 3, 1917.

[55] *Sun,* New York, March 4, 1917.

[56] *Milwaukee Journal,* March 4, 1917; *Evening Star,* Washington, D.C., March 4, 1917.

[57] *Record,* 64th Cong., 2nd Sess., Vol. 54, p. 4895, March 3, 1917.

[58] *Ibid.*, p. 4895, March 3, 1917.

[59] *Detroit News Tribune,* March 4, 1917.

[60] *Ibid.*

[61] *New York Times*, March 4, 1917.

[62] *Record*, 64th Cong., 2nd Sess., Vol. 54, p. 4988, March 4, 1917. Among the Senators reported to have prepared this bipartisan manifesto "were Simmons, Hardwick, Hughes and Pomerene for the democrats and Lodge, Fall, Sutherland and Nelson for the republicans" (*Evening Star*, March 4, 1917). The *New York American,* March 4, 1917, refers to Senator Borah as having prepared the manifesto presented to the Senate on the morning of March 4, 1917.

[63] *Record*, 64th Cong., 2nd Sess., Vol. 54, p. 4988, March 4, 1917.

[64] Undated penciled note in manuscript of R. M. L., LFP.

[65] *Record*, 64th Cong., 2nd Sess., Vol. 54, pp. 4988-4990, March 4, 1917.

[66] *Ibid.*, p. 4990, March 4, 1917.

[67] *Ibid.*

[68] *Ibid.*, p. 4992, March 4, 1917.

[69] *Ibid.*, p. 4995, March 4, 1917.

[70] *Ibid.*, p. 4997, March 4, 1917.

[71] *Ibid.*

[72] *Ibid.*, pp. 5000-5001, March 4, 1917.

[73] *Ibid.*, pp. 5002-5004, March 4, 1917.

[74] *Ibid.*, p. 5005, March 4, 1917.

[75] *Ibid.*, 65th Cong., Spec. Sess. of Senate, Vol. 55, March 8, 1917, p. 34, for Cummins statement; pp. 37-38, for Smoot statement.

[76] *New York Times*, March 4, 1917.

[77] *Ibid.*

[78] R. M. L. to B. C. L., Phil, and Mary, March 6, 1917, LFP.

[79] Letter, George W. Norris to author, March 13, 1939, and interview, Feb. 15, 1939, LFP.

[80] R. M. L. to B. C. L., Phil, and Mary, March 6, 1917, LFP.

[81] *Ibid.*

[82] *Ibid.*

[83] *Ibid.*

[84] R. M. L., Jr., Statement, Dec. 27, 1930. See also MS of John J. Hannan, LFP.

[85] R. M. L., Jr., Statement, Dec. 27, 1930, LFP.

[86] MS of John J. Hannan, LFP.

[87] *Record*, 64th Cong., 2nd Sess., Vol. 54, pp. 5009-5010, March 4, 1917.

[88] R. M. L. to B. C. L., Phil, and Mary, March 6, 1917, LFP.

[89] Statement of R. M. L., Jr., Dec. 27, 1930, LFP.

[90] *Record*, 64th Cong., 2nd Sess., Vol. 54, p. 5012, March 4, 1917.

[91] R. M. L. to B. C. L., Phil, and Mary, March 6, 1917, LFP. The *Record*, p. 5012, records Owen as saying only, "I yield the floor."

[92] *Record*, 64th Cong., 2nd Sess., Vol. 54, p. 5012, March 4, 1917.

[93] R. M. L., Jr., Statement, Dec. 27, 1930, LFP. See also MS of John J. Hannan, LFP.

[94] George W. Norris to author, Feb. 15, 1939, LFP.

[95] Statement of R. M. L., Jr., Dec. 27, 1930, LFP.

[96] *Record*, 64th Cong., 2nd Sess., Vol. 54, p. 5012, March 4, 1917.

[97] *New York Times*, March 5, 1917. The *Des Moines Register*, March 5, 1917, has a similar description. The *Commercial Tribune*, Cincinnati, March 5, 1917, also prints a similar story.

[98] *Commercial Tribune*, Cincinnati, March 5, 1917. Representative Louis Ludlow was Washington correspondent at this time.

[99] *Record*, 64th Cong., 2nd Sess., Vol. 54, p. 5013, March 4, 1917.

[100] R. M. L., Jr., Statement, Dec. 27, 1930, LFP.

[101] *Record*, 64th Cong., 2nd Sess., Vol. 54, pp. 5013-5014, March 4, 1917.

[102] *Ibid.*, p. 5015, March 4, 1917.

[103] *Ibid.*

[104] *Ibid.*, pp. 5015-5016, March 4, 1917. See also *New York Times*, March 4, 1917.

[105] *New York Times*, March 5, 1917. See also *Commercial Tribune*, Cincinnati, March 5, 1917.

[106] *New York Times*, March 5, 1917.

[107] R. M. L. to B. C. L., Phil, and Mary, March 6, 1917, LFP.

[108] R. M. L., Jr., to R. M. L., undated [March 4, 1917], LFP.

[109] *Idem.*

[110] R. M. L., Jr., to author, July 10, 1939, LFP.

[111] *Record*, 64th Cong., 2nd Sess., Vol. 54, p. 5018, March 4, 1917.

[112] *New York Times*, March 5, 1917. See also *Record*, 64th Cong., 2nd Sess., Vol. 54, p. 5019, March 4, 1917.

[113] *Boston Herald*, March 5, 1917.

[114] *Record*, 64th Cong., 2nd Sess., Vol. 54, p. 5019, March 4, 1917.

[115] *Ibid.*

[116] Recollection of Netha Roe, John J. Hannan, R. M. L., Jr., and author.

[117] R. M. L. to B. C. L., March 5, 1917, LFP.

[118] B. C. L. to R. M. L., March 5, 1917, LFP.

Chapter XLIV

(Pages 626–644)

[1] Charles Seymour, *The Intimate Papers of Colonel House*, II, 457.

[2] *New York Times*, March 5, 1917.

[3] *La Follette's Magazine*, Jan., 1915, p. 3.

[4] R. M. L. to B. C. L., Phil, and Mary, March 8, 1917, LFP.

[5] *La Follette's Autobiography*, p. 314.

[6] B. C. L. to Netha Roe, March 6, 1917, LFP.

[7] *Record*, 65th Cong., Special Sess., Vol. 55, p. 28, March 8, 1917.

[8] Robert Lansing, *War Memoirs*, p. 225.

[9] *Record,* 65th Cong., Special Sess., Vol. 55, p. 20, March 8, 1917.

[10] *Ibid.,* p. 36, March 8, 1917.

[11] R. M. L., Jr., to B. C. L., March 6, 1917, LFP.

[12] *Record,* 65th Cong., Special Sess., Vol. 55, pp. 37-38, March 8, 1917.

[13] Ray Stannard Baker, *Woodrow Wilson,* VI, 481.

[14] *Milwaukee Journal,* March 8, 1917. The Wisconsin Senate later passed a pledge of loyalty to President Wilson, but omitted any rebuke to La Follette (*Milwaukee Journal,* March 22, 1917).

[15] March 5, 1917.

[16] *Ibid.*

[17] *Ibid.,* March 7, 1917.

[18] March 5, 1917.

[19] Vol. 54, No. 11, p. 691, March 17, 1917.

[20] *Globe and Commercial Advertiser,* New York, March 5, 1917.

[21] *Toledo Blade,* March 8, 1917.

[22] *Cincinnati Times-Star,* March 5, 1917.

[23] Clippings with LFP.

[24] March 5, 6, 7, 1917.

[25] Statement of Rollin Kirby, April 6, 1940, LFP.

[26] R. M. L. to Gilbert E. Roe, March 7, 1917, LFP.

[27] *New York Times,* March 6, 1917.

[28] Ralph M. Pearson to R. M. L., March 10, 1917, LFP.

[29] *Evening Post,* New York, March 6, 1917.

[30] Louis D. Brandeis, conversation with author, Aug. 31, 1937; author to Louis D. Brandeis, March 10, 1939; Louis D. Brandeis to author, March 12, 1939, LFP.

[31] R. M. L. to B. C. L., Phil, and Mary, March 8, 1917, LFP.

[32] *Idem.*

[33] R. M. L. to Phil, March 27, 1917, LFP.

[34] R. M. L., Jr., to Phil and Mary, March 15, 1917, LFP.

[35] Captain [Major General] Walter K. Wilson to a fellow officer [March, 1917], enclosure with letter from R. M. L. to B. C. L., Phil, and Mary, March 8, 1917.

[36] *New York Times,* March 6, 1917.

[37] *The Public Papers of Woodrow Wilson,* V, 1-5; *Record,* 65th Cong., Special Sess., Vol. 55, p. 3, March 5, 1917.

[38] R. M. L. to B. C. L., March 6, 1917, LFP.

[39] Ray Stannard Baker, *Woodrow Wilson,* VI, 505-507, quotes from and cites Cobb of *"The World."*

[40] David F. Houston, *Eight Years with Wilson's Cabinet,* I, 240.

[41] *New York Times,* March 7, 1917.

[42] Woodrow Wilson speech at Wilmington, Del., Oct. 17, 1912, stenographic notes of Charles L. Swem, Wilson Papers.

[43] *Milwaukee Journal,* March 5, 1917.

[44] *New York Times,* March 6, 1917.

[45] R. M. L. to B. C. L., March 6, 1917, LFP.

[46] *Idem* to B. C. L., Phil, and Mary, March 6, 1917, LFP.

⁴⁷ *Record,* 65th Cong., Special Sess., Vol. 55, pp. 19-20, March 8, 1917.
⁴⁸ *Ibid.,* p. 41, March 8, 1917.
⁴⁹ *Ibid.,* p. 42, March 8, 1917. See also *La Follette's Autobiography,* p. 302, pp. 375-376.
⁵⁰ *Record,* 65th Cong., Special Sess., Vol. 55, pp. 44-45, March 8, 1917.
⁵¹ In re subsequent adoption of cloture, see Franklin L. Burdette, *Filibustering in the Senate* (Princeton, Princeton University Press, 1940), p. 222.
⁵² *World,* New York, March 9, 1917, editorial, typical of metropolitan newspaper comment on Senators voting against cloture.
⁵³ Clark Leiter to R. M. L., March 5, 1917, LFP.
⁵⁴ H. M. Esterly to R. M. L., March 31, 1917, LFP. This telegram was in accord with letters Bob was receiving at this time from Oregon.
⁵⁵ H. C. Peterson, *Propaganda for War* (University of Oklahoma Press, 1939), pp. 323-324.
⁵⁶ Stephen L. Gwynn, *The Letters and Friendships of Sir Cecil Spring-Rice,* II, 387.
⁵⁷ *Record,* 65th Cong., 1st Sess., Vol. 55, p. 220, April 4, 1917.
⁵⁸ *Oregon Daily Journal,* April 5, 1917.
⁵⁹ *Record,* 64th Cong., 2nd Sess., Vol. 54, p. 4997, March 4, 1917.
⁶⁰ Peterson, *op. cit.,* p. 316.
⁶¹ B. C. L. to R. M. L., March 6, 1917, LFP.
⁶² R. M. L. to B. C. L., Phil, and Mary, March 8, 1917, LFP.
⁶³ R. M. L., Jr., to B. C. L., March 10, 1917, LFP.
⁶⁴ B. C. L. to Phil and Mary, March 12, 1917, LFP.
⁶⁵ *Idem,* March 13, 14, 15, 1917, LFP.
⁶⁶ *Idem,* March 18, 1917, LFP.
⁶⁷ *Record,* 65th Cong., 1st Sess., Vol. 55, App., p. 39.
⁶⁸ *Pearson's Magazine,* Vol. 37, No. 5, May, 1917, pp. 453-455, article by Robert M. La Follette, "America's War Madness."
⁶⁹ *La Follette's Magazine,* March, 1917, p. 5.
⁷⁰ *Foreign Relations,* 1917, p. 1211.
⁷¹ B. C. L. to Phil and Mary, March 18, 1917, LFP.
⁷² *The Letters of Lincoln Steffens,* I, 393-394.
⁷³ *The Autobiography of Lincoln Steffens,* II, 743-746.
⁷⁴ *Foreign Relations,* Supplement I, 1917, p. 171.
⁷⁵ Ray Stannard Baker, *Woodrow Wilson,* VI, 485.
⁷⁶ *Ibid.,* VI, 503.
⁷⁷ B. C. L. to Phil, March 21, 1917, LFP.
⁷⁸ David Lloyd George, *War Memoirs* (London, Ivor Nicholson & Watson, 1933), III, 1669. Cable received by the British Government from its Washington Embassy, March 21, 1917.
⁷⁹ *New York Times,* March 21, 1917.
⁸⁰ Gwynn, *op. cit.,* II, 387.
⁸¹ B. C. L. to Phil and Mary, April 1, 1917, LFP.
⁸² Ray Stannard Baker, *Woodrow Wilson,* VI, 505.
⁸³ R. M. L. to Phil, March 27, 1917, LFP.
⁸⁴ Phil to R. M. L., March 10, 1917, LFP.

85 R. M. L. to Phil, March 27, 1917, LFP.
86 B. C. L. to Phil and Mary, April 1, 1917, LFP.

Chapter XLV

(Pages 645–668)

1 *Evening Post*, New York, April 2, 1917.
2 *Des Moines Register*, April 3, 1917.
3 *Detroit News*, March 31, 1917.
4 *Chicago Herald*, April 3, 1917. See also *New York Times*, April 3, 1917.
5 *Milwaukee Journal*, April 3, 1917.
6 William Tyler Page, Pair Clerk to the House Minority, unpublished MS.
7 *Boston Herald*, April 3, 1917; *Current History* (a monthly magazine of the *New York Times*), May, 1917, Vol. VI, No. 2, p. 208.
8 *Milwaukee Journal*, April 3, 1917.
9 *Boston Herald*, April 3, 1917.
10 *Record*, 65th Cong., 1st Sess., Vol. 55, p. 103, April 2, 1917. Even while the President was addressing Congress, word was speeding to Washington of the sinking of the steamer *Aztec*, the first American ship to be attacked (*New York Times*, April 3, 1917; *Foreign Relations*, 1917, Supplement I, pp. 203-205). On April 3, 1917, the New York *World* stated editorially that this must serve as a reminder that "guns are no protection against torpedo attack."
11 R. M. L.'s editorial on the Armed Ship bill was printed in *La Follette's Magazine*, March, 1917, p. 3. It was summarized and quoted in part in the *New York Times*, April 2, 1917. It was also quoted in the New York *Evening Post*, March 27, 1917.
12 *New York Times*, March 5, 1917.
13 *Record*, 65th Cong., 1st Sess., Vol. 55, p. 103, April 2, 1917.
14 *New York Times*, April 3, 1917.
15 *Boston Herald*, April 3, 1917..
16 *North American*, April 3, 1917.
17 *Ibid*.
18 Julius A. Truesdell to author, July 18, 1937, LFP.
19 Page, unpublished MS; also, author's interviews with other individuals present on this occasion.
20 *Record*, 65th Cong., 1st Sess., Vol. 55, p. 104, April 2, 1917.
21 Ray Stannard Baker, *Woodrow Wilson*, VI, 514-515.
22 *World*, New York, April 3, 1917.
23 Joseph P. Tumulty, *Woodrow Wilson As I Know Him*, p. 256.
24 *La Follette's Magazine*, March, 1917, pp. 3-4.
25 *Proceedings of the Foreign Relations Committee*, April 3, 1917, pp. 107-108.
26 Robert Lansing, *War Memoirs*, p. 238.

[27] *Boston Herald*, April 4, 1917.

[28] *Ibid.*

[29] *Record*, 65th Cong., 1st Sess., Vol. 55, p. 155, April 3, 1917.

[30] *Boston Herald*, April 4, 1917.

[31] *Public Ledger*, April 4, 1917.

[32] *Ibid.*

[33] LFP.

[34] Grace Lynch to author, March 1, 1939; John J. Hannan to author, March 22, 1940, LFP.

[35] *Oregon Daily Journal*, April 4, 1917.

[36] April 4, 1917, Washington dispatch signed by Angus McSween, dated April 3.

[37] *New York American*, April 4, 1917.

[38] *Detroit News*, April 4, 1917; *Boston Herald*, April 4, 1917.

[39] *Wisconsin State Journal*, April 4, 1917.

[40] Phil to author, Feb. 7, 1940, LFP.

[41] *Madison Democrat*, April 4, 1917.

[42] *World*, New York, April 4, 1917.

[43] April 4, 1917.

[44] LFP.

[45] Lincoln Steffens to B. C. L., June 20, 1925, LFP.

[46] Robert M. La Follette, "My Own Story," *Washington Daily News*, Sept. 22, 1924, p. 12.

[47] *Brooklyn Eagle*, April 4, 1917.

[48] *Milwaukee Journal*, April 4, 1917.

[49] *Wisconsin State Journal*, April 4, 1917.

[50] *Record*, 65th Cong., 1st Sess., Vol. 55, p. 201, April 4, 1917.

[51] *Ibid.*, pp. 201-202, April 4, 1917.

[52] *Ibid.*, p. 209, April 4, 1917.

[53] Senator James Reed to author, April 28, 1938, LFP.

[54] *Record*, 65th Cong., 1st Sess., Vol. 55, p. 210, April 4, 1917.

[55] *Ibid.*, p. 213, April 4, 1917.

[56] George W. Norris to author, Feb. 15, 1939, LFP.

[57] *Record*, 65th Cong., 1st Sess., Vol. 55, p. 213, April 4, 1917.

[58] *Ibid.*, pp. 214-215, April 4, 1917.

[59] *Ibid.*, p. 219, April 4, 1917.

[60] Senator William E. Borah to author, Nov. 21, 1939, LFP.

[61] *Record*, 65th Cong., 1st Sess., Vol. 55, p. 220, April 4, 1917.

[62] *Investigation of National Security League*, Special House Committee, 65th Cong., 3rd Sess., Report No. 1173.

[63] John J. Hannan to author, March 1, 1939, LFP.

[64] Amos Pinchot to author, March 23, 1939, LFP.

[65] Undated note, LFP.

[66] *World*, New York, April 5, 1917.

[67] R. M. L., Jr., to Phil and Mary, April 4, 1917, LFP. See also *Christian Science Monitor*, April 5, 1917.

[68] Gilbert E. Roe to Rudolph Spreckels, May 3, 1917, LFP.

[69] *Record,* 65th Cong., 1st Sess., Vol. 55, p. 223, April 4, 1917.

[70] *Record,* 65th Cong., 1st Sess., Vol. 55, pp. 223-224, April 4, 1917. See also Emma Becker to R. M. L., Jr., Jan. 28, 1939, with photostat of ballot, LFP.

[71] Becker later became a candidate for governor and endorsed La Follette's war record. Subsequently, in a Federal prosecution under the Espionage Law, the Monroe referendum was held to be proof of Becker's "intent to stop war operations" (*Wisconsin State Journal,* Aug. 8, 1918).

[72] *Record,* 65th Cong., 1st Sess., Vol. 55, p. 224, April 4, 1917.

[73] Senator Ernest Lundeen to author, Feb. 25, 1939, LFP.

[74] *Record,* 65th Cong., 1st Sess., Vol. 55, p. 225, April 4, 1917.

[75] *Ibid.,* p. 226, April 4, 1917.

[76] *Ibid.,* p. 228, April 4, 1917.

[77] Recollection of Mrs. Gilbert E. Roe; also, recollection of author.

[78] *Record,* 65th Cong., 1st Sess., Vol. 55, pp. 227-229, April 4, 1917.

[79] *St. Louis Post Dispatch,* Sept. 6, 1919.

[80] *Record,* 65th Cong., 1st Sess., Vol. 55, p. 230, April 4, 1917.

[81] It was later freely admitted by the British that the rules of the Declaration of London would have hampered them in their naval warfare (Grey of Fallodon, *Twenty-Five Years,* II, 105-106). The United States made suggestions as to how Great Britain might accept the declaration and yet continue to do as she pleased (letters of Robert Lansing and the President to Ambassador Page, Oct. 16, 1914, *Foreign Relations,* 1914, Supplement, pp. 249-250; 252-253).

[82] *Record,* 65th Cong., 1st Sess., Vol. 55, p. 230, April 4, 1917.

[83] For a discussion of the Declaration of London and the significance to the United States of its repudiation by the Allied Powers, see Edwin Borchard and W. P. Lage, *Neutrality for the United States* (New Haven, Yale University Press, 1937), pp. 59-78. For the views of the United States Ambassador to Great Britain, see Burton J. Hendrick, *Life and Letters of Walter H. Page,* I, 373, *et seq.*; III, 176-188.

[84] *Record,* 65th Cong., 1st Sess., Vol. 55, p. 232, April 4, 1917.

[85] *Ibid.,* p. 231, April 4, 1917.

[86] Grey, *op. cit.,* II, 101, states, "From the first he [Ambassador Page] considered that the United States could be brought into the war early on the side of the Allies if the issue were rightly presented to it and a great appeal made to the President." Robert Lansing, in *War Memoirs,* p. 166, commented on Ambassador Page's attitude after his visit to the United States in 1916: "I gained the impression from our conversations, and I think that Mr. Wilson held the same opinion, that Mr. Page had come to the United States to explain the attitude of the British people toward the United States and to plead their cause with the American Government. He certainly sought to have us surrender many of the legal rights of American citizens on the high seas instead of trying to persuade the British to cease their illegal interference with those rights." Copyright, 1935, used by permission of the publishers, The Bobbs-Merrill Company, Inc.

[87] Lansing, *War Memoirs,* p. 128, copyright, 1935, used by special permission of the publishers, The Bobbs-Merrill Company, Inc.

[88] *Record*, 65th Cong., 1st Sess., Vol. 55, pp. 232-233, April 4, 1917, for La Follette statement; *Record*, 65th Cong., 1st Sess., Vol. 55, p. 212-213, April 4, 1917, for Norris statement.

[89] *The Times Documentary History of the War* (London), IV, Naval, Part 2, pp. 14-15.

[90] *New York Times*, Nov. 3, 1914.

[91] *Record*, 65th Cong., 1st Sess., Vol. 55, p. 232, April 4, 1917.

[92] *Ibid.*, p. 233, April 4, 1917.

[93] Lansing, in his letter of April 5, 1917, to Senator King in support of his contention that Germany first mined the high seas, referred to "the notice issued by Germany on August 7, 1914, that the trade routes to English ports would be closed by German mines." This was not an entirely accurate description of the telegram reporting the German verbal note sent by Ambassador Gerard from Berlin on Aug. 7, 1914, saying: "Foreign Office informs me German ports strewn with mines and requests that shippers be warned in time against navigating in ports which might serve as bases for foreign forces" (File No. 763, 72/257; *Foreign Relations*, 1914, Supplement, p. 454). The exact text of this verbal note was, for some reason, not received in the State Department until 1920. It shows that the Gerard telegram also "inaccurately summarized" the verbal note. See Carlton Savage, *Policy of the United States Toward Maritime Commerce in War* (Washington, D.C., U.S. Government Printing Office, 1936), II, 185.

[94] R. M. L., Jr., to author, March 12, 1940. The independent recollections of John J. Hannan and Grace Lynch were in substance the same.

[95] *Record*, 65th Cong., 1st Sess., Vol. 55, pp. 233-234, April 4, 1917.

[96] *Ibid.*, p. 234, April 4, 1917.

[97] *Ibid.*, p. 226, April 4, 1917.

[98] *Des Moines Register*, April 5, 1917.

[99] *New York Times*, April 3, 1917.

[100] *World*, New York, April 5, 1917.

[101] *Record*, 65th Cong., 1st Sess., Vol. 55, pp. 234-235, April 4, 1917.

[102] Letter, John J. Hannan, June 29, 1939, LFP.

[103] *New York American*, April 5, 1917. The *World*, New York, April 5, 1917, prints a similar report.

[104] *Ibid.*

[105] *Record*, 65th Cong., 1st Sess., Vol. 55, pp. 238-249, April 4, 1917. Husting's speech fills 21 columns of the *Record*, and had no interruptions, as compared with La Follette's of 22 2/3 columns, including interruptions.

[106] Of the eight absentee Senators, all had been recorded as in favor of the resolution except Gore, who had been ill for some time. How he would have voted was not announced (*Record*, 65th Cong., 1st Sess., Vol. 55, p. 261, April 4, 1917).

[107] April 5, 1917.

[108] *Boston Herald*, April 6, 1917.

[109] *New York Times*, April 6, 1917.

[110] *Washington Post*, April 6, 1917.